D1308559

The Author

Dr. J. Ronnie Davis is a native of Shreveport, Louisiana, but grew up in Pascagoula, Mississippi. He was graduated from the University of Southern Mississippi with a bachelor's degree and a master's degree in economics. His doctorate in economics was earned from the University of Virginia, where he was a student of James McGill Buchanan, who won the Nobel Prize in Economics in 1986. His doctoral dissertation, *Pre-Keynesian Economic Policy Proposals in the United States During the Great Depression*, won the prestigious Tipton R. Snavely Award, judged by Ronald H. Coase who won the Nobel Prize in Economics in 1991.

Dr. Davis held a faculty position in economics at Iowa State University and at the University of Florida. Now a professor of economics at the University of New Orleans, he previously served three universities as their business school dean, including the University of New Orleans from 1989 to 1994. Previously, he was Dean of the College of Business and Management Studies at the University of South Alabama from 1983 to 1989 and Dean of the College of Business and Economics at Western Washington University from 1981 to 1983.

Dr. Davis has been recognized as an exceptional teacher, winning numerous awards for teaching and mentoring students. He teaches Managerial Economics in the MBA program. Dr. Davis has been Teacher of the Year in the College of Business Administration at the University of New Orleans. EMBA students in New Orleans and Puerto Rico have recognized him numerous years as Teacher of the Year and as Mentor of the Year.

Dr. Davis has been published widely in economics and political science. He is the author of more than thirty articles in scholarly journals, including *American Economic Review*, *American Political Science Review*, and *Economic Journal*. For more than twenty years, Dr. Davis was Editor of the scholarly journal, *Public Finance Quarterly*, renamed *Public Finance Review* in 1997, an international journal for the study of the public sector of the economy published by Sage Publications in California. He is the author of ten books, ancillaries, and monographs dealing with the history of economic thought, public finance, and managerial economics. His most recent book is *Organizational Misbehavior: The Case for Personal Integrity*.

Dr. Davis has worked around the country and world as a management consultant. His extensive consulting has involved engagements in strategic planning, management auditing, and improving cost and productivity. He learned quality methods under the tutelage of Dr. W. Edwards Deming. Dr. Davis is regarded as an authority on Six Sigma. Most of his consulting experience has been in the chemical and automobile industries. His clients have included *Fortune* 500 companies as well as small businesses, law firms, public school systems, cities, and federal government agencies. Because of his academic and consulting experience in the United States and around the world, Dr. Davis has earned a wide and deep platform of followers who know his reputation, who respect his character, and who seek his advice.

Foreword

When I began my academic career at Iowa State University, I was a faculty member in the College of Sciences and Humanities. At the time, ISU did not have a business school. I was an academic economist with no business experience whatsoever. After four years at ISU, I relocated to the University of Florida. There, I was on the faculty in the business school, still without any business experience. Almost immediately, I was engaged as an expert witness in a case argued in a south Florida courtroom. Another expert witness was associated with the consulting practice of a major national accounting firm. He and I liked and respected each other. As the case wound down in court, he asked if I would be interested in occasional work with his firm. I said I would be delighted to work with him and his firm. However, I never expected to hear from him again. He called two weeks later.

I was told that the firm was preparing to submit a response to an RFP. I was clueless. I had no idea that RFP was a reference to a request for a proposal. I just listened. The proposal was a management audit of one of the largest public school systems in the country. Again, I was clueless. I had no idea what a management audit was. He said I could play a role if I was interested. I was interested. As it turned out, he merely wanted to use my credentials to improve on the chances of having his proposal chosen. When the proposal was presented, I attended but only as an ornament. I did not have a speaking role. I was merely dangled before the clients as someone who would be working with the management audit team. We won the engagement. Through this fluke occurrence, my consulting life was launched.

In the mid-1970s, I was continually engaged as a consultant with two consulting firms. I also partnered with an industrial psychologist to form a consulting practice. He and I focused on the chemical industry in southeastern states from Florida to South Carolina and over to Mississippi. At an exit meeting in South Carolina, a plant manager pulled me aside. He said the kind of work I did reminded him of Deming. I had no idea who Deming was. After returning to Gainesville, I asked around the business school if anyone knew who Deming was. Finally, someone directed me to Industrial and Systems Engineering. I was told ISE taught Deming. One of the ISE faculty members gave me two hours of information regarding W. Edwards Deming, the spokesman and leader of the quality movement that culminated in Six Sigma.

At the time, I was traveling back and forth from Gainesville to Washington. I was doing agency work. I learned that Deming was offering a workshop. The workshop was before his famed four-day seminars of the 1980s. I signed up. At the time, I was somewhat cynical. All I expected from the workshop was one new idea, one new friend, and one new joke. Instead, my life was transformed. Deming led me to realize that I was not the man that I could be and that I ought to be. I was not the man I was meant to be. I was drifting through life without any sense of purpose. I began the transformation journey that weekend. Afterwards, Deming vouched for me. My consulting focus was improving cost, productivity, and profit. After learning strategic planning from a professional, I also undertook a number of strategic planning engagements.

When the business school dean learned of my consulting experience, he asked me to teach the managerial economics course in the MBA program at the University of Florida. I did not use a textbook. Textbooks for managerial economics were written by economists who had no business experience whatsoever, and thus were chock-full of topics that managers would never use and would never need to know in business practice. I based my lectures on business experience, emphasizing what managers would use in business practice and thus what managers would need to know. Years later, I wrote a textbook, *Principles of Managerial Economics*, with Semoon Chang. We wrote the textbook for the market, meaning we included topics of no use in business practice that instructors nonetheless wanted in the textbook. I never have used my own textbook because it was cram full of theories and other constructs that are irrelevant to decisions and strategies that are commonplace in business practice. As a matter of personal integrity, I could not bring myself to ask students to read material that would never be used in a business career, whether line, staff, or entrepreneurial.

In the early 1990s, I was the business school dean at the University of New Orleans. As a dean at three different universities, I taught a course every semester. I believe in leading by example. When I asked faculty members to do a good job of teaching, I believed I should teach a course and do a good job. I taught the managerial economics course. When I asked faculty members to be published, I believed I should be published. Indeed, I was the editor of a scholarly journal, *Public Finance Review*. I also continued with consulting engagements that took fifty to a hundred hours monthly. After resigning as dean in 1994 to teach, write, and consult more, I had an interest in writing a book that articulates the economics that students and management practitioners need to know in business practice. Once completed, I used the manuscript in my managerial economics course and in my consulting practice. I kept revising and updating the manuscript over several years. Finally, I believed that the manuscript was ready for publication as *Economics for Executives*.

Economics for Executives is based on my business experience. I have a good grasp on the economics that business students and business practitioners need to know and that they will use in business practice. The nexus between economics and business practice actuates the topics covered in the pursuant chapters. As a textbook for courses in managerial economics, the entire book can be covered in a semester. For the manager, the book is a compendium of basic knowledge required for informed practice or a reminder of concepts and principles once learned but forgotten in the fog of narrowly circumscribed tasks. My gratification and fulfillment will come from students and managers who read *Economics for Executives* and feel that they have learned something useful.

Let me conclude with acknowledgement of many who have helped me throughout the course of developing *Economics for Executives*. I want to thank my students in New Orleans, San Juan, and Kingston. In particular, I want to thank my EMBA students on campus of the University of New Orleans. Their suggestions, often arising from their own business experiences, were thoughtful and meaningful, thus greatly improving the manuscript that led to publication of *Economics for Executives*. Finally, I want to thank Bora Ozkan and Francisco Rubio for their work on the figures that appear throughout *Economics for Executives*.

IN MEMORIAM

James M. Buchanan

Marion Fuller Davis

W. Edwards Deming

O. Dean Martin

[The men who have had a great impact on my life and career]

DEDICATED TO

Arthurine Payton Davis

[Wifey]

Amanda Lee Davis Hughes

Dakota Payton Joseph

[Our daughters]

Table of Contents

1. Management and Economics

ECONOMICS FOR EXECUTIVES

Often, economics is regarded as a collection of notional theories distanced far from the real world. Yet, economists maintain that theories are the foundation for predictions about what to expect in the real world. The disconnection seems particularly strong among undergraduate students immediately after taking principles of microeconomics and principles of macroeconomics. As freshman and sophomore students with no experience with the real world, they simply do not comprehend how economics can possibly be used. Later as seniors who major in business, they might have rare glimpses of economics as useful in making business decisions and crafting business strategies. After graduation and amidst their experience with business practice, they might finally see that economic principles underlie business analysis, business decisions, and business strategies.

Frequently, business analysis is reductionism of complex matters into simple constituents that are studied through the lens of economic principles. In the same way, business decisions are practical applications of economic principles, and business strategies are informed by economic principles. Accordingly, managerial economics is essentially economics applied by managers, directors, and executives in their roles as decision makers and strategists. Accordingly, the focus of managerial economics should be on what managers, directors, and executives need to know and will use in business practice. Circumscribing managerial economics in this way, a lot of economics is not applied in business practice and can be left outside the limits of need to know. However, a lot of economics lies within the boundaries of use in business practice and need to know. Economics for managers, directors, and executives is centered on bringing economic principles to bear on business practices and business strategies.

Of course, decisions are made and strategies are crafted within an organization, perhaps a business firm, nonprofit organization, or government agency. Regardless, organizations face countless problems requiring decisions or strategies to accomplish some mission or to achieve some objective subject to constraints, competitive or otherwise. Certain economic principles guide and lead to decisions and strategies that minimize exposure to adverse effects on organizational performance or that maximize favorable effects on organizational performance. Principles, practices, and strategies have purpose in their application to solving problems, minimizing threats, and realizing opportunities.

Economics for Executives has purposeful intent. It is meant to develop comprehension of and comfort in application of economics actually used in business practice. Moreover, it is meant to address the economics that managers, directors, and executives really need to know for meaningful careers in business. Of course, this intent leaves out theories, abstractions, concepts, and constructs that might have significance and importance in other contexts such as public policy but not for business practice.

THE MANAGERIAL REVOLUTION IN AMERICA

The founder of philosophical Taoism, Lau Tzu, told us, "The longest journey begins beneath one's feet." In the United States, the Chinese aphorism is usually mistranslated to fit a different culture and time. Americans say, "The journey of a thousand miles begins with a single step." In the sixth century BCE, however, Lau-tzu had no knowledge of miles and did not consider the first step at all. He regarded action as a departure from stillness in the same way that emotion is a departure from calm. Thus, we understand Lau Tzu better if we translate that even the longest journey begins from where a person stands. In this sense, where business practice stands now began with where business practice stood in the late 1880s when the rise of the modern enterprise spurred the professionalization of management as well as business schools to meet the rising need for managers.

In the mid-1800s, the typical American business firm was an enterprise owned by an individual or a small number of individuals such as a family. With few exceptions, manufactured goods were produced by small, personally owned or family owned businesses. Usually, manufacturing firms dealt in one product line, operated in one geographic area, and thus sold one product in one market. Owners directed operations. In some instances, an owner hired salaried employees to oversee day-to-day operations. Essentially, these salaried workers were first-line supervisors. In such cases, therefore, owners of manufacturing firms employed supervisors equivalent to lowest management in modern business enterprises. As late as 1850 or so, however, there were no middle managers who supervised the work of other managers and who reported to top managers.

Continuous Process Machines

In the late 1870s and early 1880s, mass production was introduced in several industries. The underlying impetus for large volume production was continuous process machinery. Workers did little more than feed raw materials into a machine and oversee machine operations. These machines made large volume production feasible. When large volume production was realized, output per worker was increased greatly, and unit costs of production were reduced sharply. Enterprises that first adopted such machinery also acquired vast and immediate market power difficult to overtake by latecomers to the industry.

An example of continuous process machinery is found in the tobacco products industry. In 1880, James Albert Bonsack applied for a patent on a cigarette-making machine capable of producing over 70,000 cigarettes in a 10-hour day. It was registered as the Bonsack Cigarette Machine. The patent was granted in 1881. In 1883, James Buchanan "Buck" Duke leased two Bonsack machines. Duke's engineers improved the Bonsack machine to turn out 120,000 cigarettes in a ten-hour day. At that time, the most highly skilled hand workers, known as cigarette girls, were capable of making 2,400 to 3,000 cigarettes a day. Remarkably, therefore, one Bonsack machine could do the work of forty or fifty of the most highly skilled hand workers! Duke himself invented a "crush-proof" package as well as machinery for packaging cigarettes.

The first two firms to adopt the Bonsack machine were Duke's American Tobacco Company in the United States and the Imperial Tobacco Company in England. Cost reduction was spectacular. At the American Tobacco Company, cost per thousand cigarettes was quickly reduced from eighty cents to twenty-four cents, which was less than one-third of the cost of cigarettes made by cigarette girls. At the Imperial Tobacco Company in England, Bonsack machines reduced cost per thousand cigarettes from sixty pence to ten pence, an astonishing cost reduction of more than eighty percent! American Tobacco and Imperial Tobacco consequently dominated the cigarette industry in its own country.

Continuous Process Factories

Creation of a continuous process factory was more complicated than a continuous process machine since such factories involved a number of inventions that had to be synchronized in operation. An important example was the gradual reduction mill that processed wheat into flour. Before such mills, flour was milled from one grinding by stones set close together. These new mills utilized three to five grindings by stones progressively closer together, thus making them gradual reduction mills. The result was finer flour with fewer impurities. Moreover, these mills produced more flour per bushel of wheat. Independently, Cadwallander Colden Washburn and Charles Alfred Pillsbury developed such mills.

Washburn partnered with John Crosby to form Washburn, Crosby & Company in 1877. Washburn and Pillsbury perfected gradual reduction mills, which produced high quality wheat flour in large volume and at low unit cost. As Duke did in tobacco, Pillsbury and Washburn began to package and brand their products. After Washburn won the gold medal for flour at the 1880 Millers International Exhibition in Cincinnati, he thereafter used the brand name Gold Medal for his flour, a brand that has endured. After acquiring a number of other mills, General Mills was formed under Washburn, Crosby leadership in 1928. General Mills acquired the Pillsbury Company in 2001.

Comparable developments occurred in milling oats, barley, rye, and other grains. What Washburn, Crosby and Pillsbury did for processing wheat, Henry P. Crowell did for oats in 1882. His company, which became Quaker Oats, created a nationwide marketing network, and he became a first mover in the breakfast cereal industry. Indeed, the volume of oats was so large that the modern breakfast cereal industry had to be invented as demand for oats and thus to dispose of the large volumes the company produced!

A comparable continuous process factory for processing agricultural crops came in 1883. Edwin Norton built the first automatic-line canning factory. His can line consisted of special-purpose machines and a conveyor system. The can line brought work to the worker. Norton's can line machines were capable of soldering cans at the rate of 3,000 per hour along with other machines that added tops and bottoms. In 1901, Norton purchased and consolidated sixty tin container companies and organized the American Can Company, which soon accounted for more than ninety percent of all cans produced in the United States. After retiring in 1902, he backed his son to form the Continental Can Company in 1904.

Firms that first used the new canning system on a year-round basis were Borden, Campbell Soup, and Heinz. These first movers became some of the largest canners in the United States. Each is an example of first mover advantage, which is an insurmountable advantage gained by the first significant company to enter a market or to adopt an innovative technology. In this case, first movers included Gail Borden, who expanded facilities for canning milk and extended his capacity for marketing milk. John Dorrance did the same for Campbell Soup products. Henry John Heinz did the same with his 57 varieties of pickles, sauces, and other products. Libby, McNeill & Libby did the same with canned meat.

In the same way but apart from canning operations, other companies turned to mass production, branding, and multi-market distribution made necessary to sell large volumes. Procter & Gamble became a first mover in consumer chemicals. Sherwin-Williams in paints and Parke-Davis in pharmaceuticals also expanded their production facilities and built international marketing networks. Producers of fresh meat and other perishable products made their initial investment in distribution. Gustavus V. Swift, a Chicago meatpacker, financed the development of the refrigerator car and built a nationwide distribution organization. At the same time, Milwaukee and St. Louis beer brewers expanded by creating comparable networks. Their expansion was facilitated by development of railroad cars specialized for transporting beer. The Fleischmann Company developed a refrigerated network for distribution of yeast to large bakeries. United Fruit Company built a network of refrigerated cars, ships, and depots comparable to the networks of meatpackers and brewers.[1]

Professionalization of Management

In the mid-1800s, much of business was conducted through orchestration of factors, agents, and brokers. A factor was a merchant who bought goods from producers and brought these goods to major markets to drum up business. Hence, they were called drummers. For example, farmers in South Carolina would assign cotton to a factor that would transport the cotton to a major market such as New Orleans or Mobile in search of buyers. Some buyers might be local. Other buyers might not be local. An agent was a buyer who represented out-of-town merchants, domestic or perhaps foreign. Factors and agents rarely dealt directly with each other. Instead, they dealt with a broker, who served as a kind of matchmaker between factors and agents, sellers and buyers. A broker would buy cotton from the factor and then sell cotton to the agent. Cotton factors, agents, and brokers conducted their business in the New Orleans Cotton Exchange or the Mobile Cotton Exchange. In addition to cotton were factors, agents, and brokers who dealt in other commodities such as sugar and molasses.

In the late 1800s, increased volume of output and sales, branding of products, and far-reaching distribution networks became commonplace. These circumstances triangulated and contributed mightily to the demise of the factor-agent-broker way of doing business. Developments such as continuous process machinery and factories elevated an owner-operator's responsibilities in functional areas of business such as purchasing, sales, distribution, and finance. In turn, these developments led to establishment of a central office to ensure that everything from acquisition of raw materials to production runs and deliveries of finished products was accomplished smoothly and seamlessly. Manufacturing firms increasingly

---

1   See Alfred D. Chandler, Jr., *The Visible Hand: The Managerial Revolution in American Business* (Cambridge, MA: Harvard University Press, 1977), pp. 250-253. In this book, Chandler traces the ascendency of management in America. In 1978, Chandler was awarded the Pulitzer Prize in History. Chandler wrote a three-book sequence regarded as a trilogy. The first was *Strategy and Structure*. Chandler examined the organizations of DuPont, Standard Oil of New Jersey, General Motors, and Sears, Roebuck. He concluded that their organizations were developed in response to their business strategies. He stated a business principle that should be heeded at all times: structure follows strategy [p. 14]. He emphasized the importance of a cadre of managers to a large organization. This emphasis led to *The Visible Hand*. The final book in the trilogy was *Scale and Scope*. Chandler explicated the success of large American businesses compared to Germany and British counterparts that were slow to develop professional management. Chandler, who died in 2007, was a professor of business history in the Harvard Business School. He taught at M.I.T. and John Hopkins before joining the faculty at Harvard in 1970.

chose to acquire raw materials and distribute finished products themselves rather than rely on factors, agents, and brokers. To administer their extensive investments in large-scale production facilities and far-flung distribution networks, manufacturers required lower-level managers to administer operations as well as to take charge of marketing, purchasing, and so forth. Next, they needed middle and top managers to coordinate and monitor the activities of operating units and to allocate financial wherewithal for the growth of the enterprise. The nonpareil business historian, Alfred D. Chandler, Jr., contended that these new forms of organization were enabled by the development of management as a profession.

wBusiness Schools

Professionalization of management began in America's colleges. In the mid-nineteenth century, business schools in colleges had not been established to accommodate the rapidly rising need for managers. Furthermore, no programs for advanced study in business had been instituted. Medicine and law had been professionalized and medical schools and law schools provided the curriculum and training for practice in these traditional professions. The need to professionalize management was growing, however, and a corresponding need to provide programs for preparing young people for the profession of management was evident. In this way, young gentlemen would have an alternative to practice in the professions of medicine and law. Responding to this emerging need in 1881, the Wharton School of Finance and Economy was formed at the University of Pennsylvania, making it America's first business school. In 1900, the Tuck School of Business of Dartmouth College offered the first postgraduate program in commercial sciences, the forebear of the MBA. With the onset of such programs of study, fulfilling the rising need for managers had begun, and a new profession was birthed as the equal of medicine and law. To date, the MBA is regarded as a professional degree.

RISE OF THE MODERN ENTERPRISE

Before the rise of mass production by continuous process, industrial enterprises engaged in essentially one business function, operations. They manufactured goods. Middlemen handled other business functions normally associated with the modern enterprise. Purchase of inputs and sale of outputs, for example, were functions performed by middlemen such as factors, agents, and brokers. Production technologies as well as related purchasing, storage, and distribution requirements introduced in the 1870s and 1880s generally compelled the owner-operator to increase volume of output and sales substantially to recover the costs of investment in plant and equipment. Functions previously performed by factors, agents, and brokers were internalized. As enterprises grew in scale and scope, they required more elaborate organizational structures.

The first organizational structures to accommodate large volume production and sales were functional in nature. People engaged in the purchasing or procurement function were placed in one department, those in research and development in a second, production or operations in a third, marketing in a fourth, sales in a fifth, and so on. Direction and coordination of the various functional units were the job of senior managers. The finance function might be held in the central office. Figure 1.1 depicts this kind of functional organization that was typical at the turn of the century. This functional form met needs well as long as the firm produced one product or a few closely related products. As the firm expanded the scope of products, however, the functional form was less useful. People in purchasing, for example, were less related in what they were procuring. The same was true for people in other functions.

FIGURE 1.1
FUNCTIONAL FORM

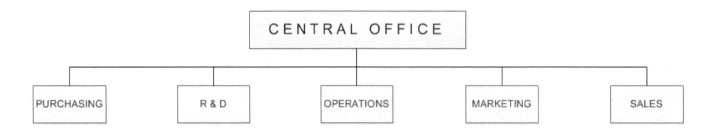

THE M-FORM

New production technologies opened the door for firms to produce a wider scope of products at lower unit cost. Functional structure conflicted with a wide scope of product lines, raising a perplexing question regarding organizational structure. Mainly, the question concerned whether function or product line was more important. By the 1920s, product line expansion had created unbearable strains on organizational structures built around business functions. From this hodgepodge of product lines came a new organizational form. It was the multidivisional organization, still known as the M-form. Pioneers of the M-form were DuPont, General Motors, Standard Oil of New Jersey, and Sears, Roebuck. Many give seminal credit to DuPont.

Firms such as DuPont and General Motors learned that increased size and corresponding complexity of multiproduct operations required reorganization into semiautonomous divisions. Each division made operating decisions, and a separate corporate office made decisions such as capital budgeting that affected the entire corporation. Divisions were formed to represent product categories, and then each division was subdivided by functional category. In this way, the organizational structure was built first on product line and then on function within product line. The result was the M-form of organization structured around divisions for different product lines. The M in M-form means a multidivisional form of organization. A typical M-form of organization is portrayed in Figure 1.2. Each division has its own functional departments such as purchasing, research and development, operations, marketing, and sales.

FIGURE 1.2
M - FORM

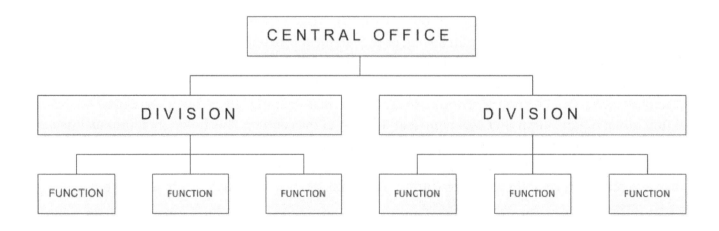

By 1920, DuPont was struggling with organizational difficulties associated with diversifying into paints, chemicals, and dyestuffs. DuPont's centralized structure did not accommodate a diverse product line. In 1921, the Board of Directors approved a restructuring plan that created ten autonomous divisions organized. The ten divisions were explosives, plastics, finishes, dyestuffs and organic chemicals, pigments, rayon and cellophane, heavy chemicals, ammonia, electro chemicals, and photographic film. These divisions produced and sold goods along their respective product lines. A general manager directed each division. The general manager was responsible and accountable for performance of the division. Moreover, each division had its own sales, research, and support functions. The M-form of organization pioneered by DuPont is rendered in Figure 1.3. Each autonomous division had its own functional departments.

FIGURE 1.3
DUPONT M-FORM

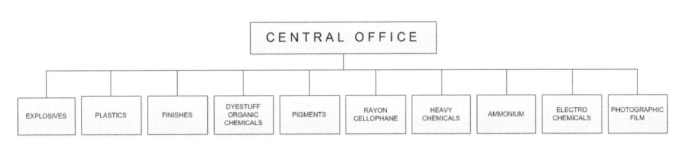

Under the leadership of Alfred Sloan, General Motors was also highly successful at implementing the new multidivisional form of organization. In the case of GM, the objective was to bring loosely federated entities under stronger centralized control. In December 1920, GM's Board of Directors approved Sloan's plan to organize autonomous divisions under a central office with coordinating control. From economy line to luxury line, the divisions were Chevrolet, Oakland, Buick, Oldsmobile, and Cadillac. The belief behind this plan was that consumers would find the stratified choices offered by GM more compelling than the iconic Model T that Ford chose for them. Inspired by alliteration, Sloan said he wanted a car for every purse and purpose. The M-form of organization established by General Motors is shown in Figure 1.4. As in the case of DuPont, each division had its own functional departments.

FIGURE 1.4
GENERAL MOTORS M-FORM

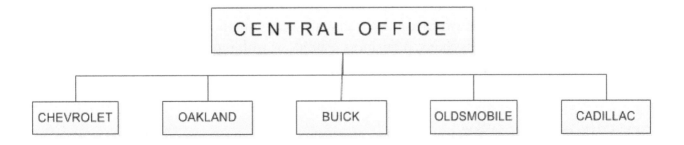

The Transformation

The M-form of organization was highly suited to accommodate and manage expansion in both scale (size) and scope (breadth of product line). Growth of highly integrated firms, each producing products in high volume and at low unit cost, typically reduced the number of firms in an industry. Mergers, acquisitions, and trusts were widespread in industries such as oil, tobacco, steel, and aluminum. Price competition was curbed, and enterprises grew to unprecedented size. These large enterprises began to operate in different locations, engage in different activities, and deal in different lines of goods and services. Activities of these units and transactions between them were monitored and coordinated by salaried employees who were top and middle managers. The multi-unit enterprise administered by a hierarchy of managers who monitored and coordinated the work of units under their control can be termed modern.

This remarkable transformation led business historian Alfred D. Chandler, Jr., to comment, "Rarely in the history of the world has an institution grown to be so important and so pervasive in so short a period of time."[2] Chandler pointed out that "the multidivisional type of administrative structure, which hardly existed in 1920, had by 1960 become the accepted form of management for the most complex and diverse of American industrial enterprises."[3] From 1920 to 1960, most companies in the United States adopted the M-form. Indeed, the M-form played a leading role in the rapid growth of American businesses through this period. The M-form was a fitting response to increasing size and diversity of product line. By the 1960s, the M-form was prevalent in the United States. In the United Kingdom, on the other hand, widespread diffusion of the M-form did not begin until the 1960s. By the 1970s, perhaps two-thirds of major British companies used the M-form, and perhaps half of major German and Japanese companies used the M-form. Since the 1970s, the M-form has become more prevalent in all three countries.

The M-Form in the 2010s

In the last fifty years, ways of doing business in America have changed profoundly. Global competition alone has overtaken many strategies once effective when American firms competed mostly against each other. Firms that relied on cost advantages became vulnerable to niche firms relying on differentiation advantages. The scope of product lines grew. Some of the diversification was the result of antitrust concerns that prevented large firms from growing even larger by acquiring rivals in the same industry. In addition, new opportunities were recognized in related markets and distribution channels. Consumer product companies realized they could distribute a much wider scope of products through their existing distribution channels. These transforming tendencies are a sample of the larger set of ineluctable trends.

Rigid, exacting adherence to the M-form of organization has worn thin. Strict organizational structures based on the M-form can be afflicted with deep hierarchies of management characterized by inflexibility and sluggishness in recognizing and reacting to competitive changes in markets as well as changes in customer needs, requirements, and tastes. Nowadays, the pace of business is fast, faster than ever. Products, markets, and even customers are dynamic rather than static. Information requirements are immediate and urgent. The competitive context is global. Consequently, many firms have adapted their version of the M-form to address changed business conditions with rapid responses. Other companies have turned from the M-form to different forms of organization.

2　Chandler, *The Visible Hand*, p. 4.

3　Chandler, *Strategy and Structure*, pp. 48-49.

Some firms have organized or reorganized around matrix structures in which two or more overlapping hierarchies are used to coordinate complicated production processes across different customer groups and market areas. Some companies increasingly utilize flat hierarchies and small corporate staffs. Firms such as Nike have organized around simple internal hierarchies. These firms control product design and brand image, but they leave most other functions such as manufacturing, distribution, and retailing to independent market specialists. These firms thrive on outsourcing business functions. Aggressive market specialists such as EDS (systems development, integration, and management), ServiceMaster (janitorial services), and Aramark (coffee and vending services and food management) are widely engaged under contract to handle functions previously undertaken in-house in large hierarchal firms.

GLOBAL CORPORATIONS

One of the most significant business trends of the late twentieth century was the rise of stateless corporations. These transnational companies build production facilities and sell their products outside the home country where they are headquartered. These companies also have shareholders who are scattered around the world. The trend toward transnational corporations is irreversible, and going global has become an essential competitive strategy. Companies that were entirely domestic and merely exported some of their output found that to be competitive and to win in world competition, they had to become global players. U.S. companies found that they could no longer produce goods here and sell goods there. They had to have a presence there. The necessity to be insiders in major world markets rather than mere exporters is clear. Multinational players have far-flung operations, facilities, and personnel spanning the globe. To expand abroad and remain competitive at home, even smaller companies often form joint ventures or strategic alliances with foreign companies.

In some cases, most sales of transnational companies are outside the home country. Many corporations with headquarters in the United States, Europe, or Japan sell more of their products and make more of their profits in countries outside the one in which corporate headquarters are located. This observation is evident in the following table, Table 1.1. Bear in mind that Table 1.1 is out of date by more than twenty years, but salient points are more evident and more pronounced today. As long ago as 1989, all twenty-one of these corporations had more than half of sales outside their home country. With globalization and transnational operations, this case is more pronounced than ever.

Table 1.1 Global Corporations, 1989			
Company	Home Country	1989 Sales ($Billions)	Sales Outside Home Country (%)
Nestlé	Switzerland	39.9	98
Philips	Netherlands	30.0	94
Electrolux	Sweden	13.8	83
Volvo	Sweden	14.8	80
ICI	United Kingdom	22.1	78
Michelin	France	9.4	78
Canon	Japan	9.4	69
Sony	Japan	16.3	66
Bayer	Germany	25.8	65
Gillette	United States	3.8	65
Colgate	United States	5.0	64
Honda	Japan	26.4	63
Daimler Benz	Germany	45.5	61
IBM	United States	62.7	59
Coca-Cola	United States	9.0	54
Digital	United States	12.7	54
Dow Chemical	United States	17.6	54
Saint-Gobain	France	11.6	54
Xerox	United States	12.4	54
Catepillar	United States	11.1	53
Hewlett-Packard	United States	11.9	53

Source: William J. Holstein, "The Stateless Corporation," Business Week (May 14, 1990), pp. 98-105.

Years later in 2007, not much had changed. Many well known companies rely on foreign sales for more than half of their business receipts. An extreme case is ArcelorMittal, which relies totally on foreign sales! Consider Table 1.2, which shows percentage of foreign sales for sixteen global companies.

Table 1.2 Global Corporations, 2007			
Company	Home Country	2007 Sales ($Billion)	Foreign Sales (%)
ArcelorMittal	Luxembourg	105.2	100.0
Honda	Japan	105.3	82.9
British Petroleum	United Kingdom	284.4	78.5
Daimler	Germany	146.3	77.3
Total	France	233.7	76.1
Volkswagen	Germany	160.3	75.3
Siemens	Germany	106.7	71.2
Exxon Mobil	United States	390.3	69.0
Hewlett-Packard	United States	104.3	66.6
Toyota	Japan	230.6	63.2
Royal Dutch/Shell	United Kingdom/Netherlands	355.8	58.3
Eni Group	Italy	128.5	57.2
Chevron	United States	214.1	56.1
Carrefour	France	120.9	54.2
Ford	United States	172.5	53.1
General Electric	United States	172.7	50.1

Source: United Nations, World Investment Report 2009 (New York: United Nations, 2009), Table A.I.9, pp. 225-227.

Borders Are So 20th Century

Nowadays, one point rises above others. To coin a phrase, borders are so 20th century. For example, Trend Micro has spread its executives, engineers, and support staff around the world. The company is based in Japan. Its main virus response center is in the Philippines with labs scattered from Munich to Tokyo. Indeed, executives and core corporate functions are dispersed in different countries. In the case of Trend Micro, financial headquarters are in Tokyo, product development in Taiwan, and sales in the Silicon Valley.

Management guru C.K. Prahalad calls this dispersal of executives and business functions the fourth stage of globalization. In the first stage, companies have operations in one country and sell their products in other countries. In the second stage, companies establish foreign subsidiaries to facilitate sales. In the third stage, companies establish operations in other countries. In the fourth stage, companies go beyond worldwide operations to disperse business functions advantageously in far-flung locations that transcend nationality. This fourth stage is a new kind of business model based on a strategy of globalizing core corporate functions.[4]

---

4   See Steve Hamm, "Borders Are So 20th Century," *Business Week* (September 22, 2003), pp. 68ff.

GLOBAL BRANDS

In a global economy, corporations develop strategies to reach customers in markets ever farther from their home base. Whether domestically or internationally, a strong brand is invaluable when companies enter new markets or offer new products. A powerful brand can fit new products under the brand umbrella. Moreover, a robust brand has the might to fetch a premium price from customers. Companies now realize that a highly recognized brand is an asset as surely as tangibles such as factories, inventories, and cash.

Interbrand is a global branding consultancy. Each year, Interbrand ranks global brands by dollar value. Many brand names are also the name of the parent company, *e.g.*, General Electric, but the assigned value is based strictly on the brand itself. On the other hand, Gillette is a brand name, but Gillette is a product line of Procter & Gamble. Interbrand does not rank parent companies such as Procter & Gamble, only brands of P&G. A number of criteria are used to qualify a brand as global. One or more of these criteria exclude brands such as Visa, Wal-Mart, and CNN.

Procedurally, Interbrand first figures out the revenues and earnings attributable to a brand. Next, five-year sales and earnings are projected for the brand. Interbrand then deducts operating costs, taxes, and a charge for the cost of capital employed. Income generated beyond such costs and charges presumably is attributable to intangible factors such as patents, customer lists, and brands. The next step is to strip out intangibles other than brand to winnow earnings generated by the brand itself. The last step is to determine the riskiness of future earnings. The risk analysis results in a discount rate applied to brand earnings to calculate the net present value of a brand, which is the dollar worth of the brand. Table 1.3 shows the top twelve global brands for 2013 as well as selected brands of companies headquartered in countries other than those represented in the top twelve.

Table 1.3 Best Global Brands, 2013					
Rank 2013	Brand	Region/Country	Sector	Brand Value 2013 ($Billion)	Percent Change From 2012
1	Apple	USA	Technology	98.316	+28%
2	Google	USA	Technology	93.291	+34%
3	Coca-Cola	USA	Beverages	79.213	+2%
4	IBM	USA	Business Services	78.808	+4%
5	Microsoft	USA	Technology	59.546	+3%
6	General Electric	USA	Diversified	46.947	+7%
7	McDonald's	USA	Restaurants	41.992	+5%
8	Samsung	Korea, South	Technology	39.610	+20%
9	Intel	USA	Technology	37.257	−5%
10	Toyota	Japan	Automotive	35.346	+17%
11	Mercedes-Benz	Germany	Automotive	31.904	+6%
12	BMW	Germany	Automotive	31.839	+10%
17	Louis Vuitton	France	Luxury	24.893	+6%
21	H&M	Sweden	Apparel	18.168	+10%
32	HSBC	United Kingdom	Financial Services	12.183	+7%
36	Zara	Spain	Apparel	10.821	+14%
37	Nescafé	Switzerland	Beverages	10.651	−4%
38	Gucci	Italy	Luxury	10.151	+7%
40	Phillips	Netherlands	Electronics	9,813	+8%
41	Accenture	USA	Business Services	9.471	+8%
42	Ford	USA	Automotive	9.181	+15%
47	Thomson Reuters	Canada	Media	8.103	−4%
52	Facebook	USA	Technology	7.732	+43%
57	Nokia	Finland	Electronics	7.444	−65%
78	MTV	USA	Media	4.980	−12%
82	Johnnie Walker	United Kingdom	Alcohol	4.745	+10%
86	Jack Daniel's	USA	Alcohol	4.642	+7%
92	Heineken	Netherlands	Alcohol	4.331	+10%
96	Harley-Davidson	USA	Automotive	4.230	+10%
98	Moet & Chandon	France	Alcohol	3.943	+3%
100	Gap	USA	Apparel	3.920	+5%

Source: "Best Global Brands 2012," Interbrand

Moving Overseas, Moving Upmarket

Pizza Hut is a declining fast-food chain in the United States. The number of Pizza Hut stores in the United States has fallen. In China and other overseas markets, however, Pizza Hut is thriving. Stores are being added rapidly. Indeed, the master of overseas reinvention is Yum! Brands, the company that owns Pizza Hut as well as KFC, Taco Bell, and Long John Silver's, an odd choice of names since Long John Silver was the villain in *Treasure Island*. All of its brands are surging overseas. KFC is closing stores in the United States but KFC stores are opening in China at the rate of almost one per day!

Brands can acquire a heightened character when they cross borders. Marketing professionals call it the country of origin effect, which refers to an elevated status when products traverse borders. When products travel, they must move upscale to justify the higher costs of exporting. Heineken was merely a mainstream beer in the Netherlands. Nevertheless, Heineken became a premium beer commanding a premium price when the Dutch company began exporting it to the United States in the 1950s. Some brands fail in repositioning themselves upmarket. Gap failed as a premium brand in Germany. Stella Artois is a run-of-the-mill working class beer in Belgium, but it has failed so far to achieve the same premium image in the United States as Heineken.[5]

STRATEGY AND PRINCIPLES

In business, the term strategy has been borrowed directly from military usage. In the military context, strategy means positioning forces advantageously in advance of actual contact with the enemy. In business usage, strategy has the same essential meaning. Strategy deals with positioning your own business or your own product advantageously in advance of actual competitive contact with rival businesses. The analogy with military usage has its limits, however. Modern warfare is based on destruction of opposing forces and their capabilities. Business is not like that. In business, success comes from adding value to your own business, not diminishing the value of your competitors. Put differently, strategy in business is focused on developing your own distinctive capabilities more fully rather than centered on destroying the capabilities of your competitors.

Vision, Mission, and Core Values

As an extension of the military concept, strategic planning in business once was adapted and refined into what seemed at its best to be a precise science. At its worst, strategic planning was similar to central planning in the old Soviet Union. Since the 1980s, however, strategic planning in this sense has been discredited as a failed methodology. Strategic planning has been regenerated with a focus on vision, mission, and core values. The new leader is one who articulates the organizational vision and mission, and then inspires, motivates, and aligns people to realize the vision and accomplish the mission. Recast in this way, strategies become means of realizing the vision and accomplishing the mission. Strategies are what must be done to realize the vision and accomplish the mission while respecting core values of the business at all times without compromise. Core values are the attitudes, conduct, and beliefs that make up an organization's culture.

---

5   See Jack Ewing, "Brands: Moving Overseas to Move Upmarket," *Business Week* (September 18, 2008).

Strategies are based on business principles. Principles are different from recipes, which are mere directions or procedures. Recipes tell people what to do, but not why. Unlike recipes, principles provide the why. Principles are economic and behavioral relationships that are general enough to be applicable to a wide range of business circumstances or market conditions. Because these relationships are robust, principles allow us to understand why certain business strategies, business practices, and organizational forms are appropriate for one set of conditions but not for others. Fortunately for students of business and practitioners of business, these principles are discoverable and learnable. Strategies based on these principles are understandable.

The enormous differences in business practices and business structures illustrate that successful strategies ensue from application of consistent business principles to constantly changing business conditions. Strategies are responsive to conditions, adaptive to changing conditions. Moreover, strategies are disciplined responses based on sound business principles. No known recipes will assure success for all firms under all circumstances and all conditions. Formulaic recipes purported to work for any firm under any market conditions are more likely blueprints for failure sooner or later.

Principles versus Behaviors

The need to learn business principles is undermined by people who claim the key to success in business is imitating certain behaviors of successful firms. This kind of thinking was diffused throughout the famous book, *In Search of Excellence*, written by Thomas Peters and Robert Waterman and published in 1982.[6] The authors studied forty-three firms they characterized as superior performers in terms of growth and profit. The authors concluded that these successful firms shared certain distinguishing behaviors. They identified eight such behaviors, *viz.*, bias for action; close to the customer; autonomy and entrepreneurship; productivity through people; hands-on, value-driven; stick to the knitting, simple form, lean staff; and simultaneous loose-tight properties. The implication was that mere imitation of such behaviors would lead low-performing firms to high performance.

In business, however, strategies are based on sound business principles, not on imitated behaviors. In other words, strategy is based on what the firm must do to achieve its vision and accomplish its mission while respecting core values. In any case, within only two years of publication, *In Search of Excellence* began to fall into disfavor if not ridicule. Business analysts recognized that the choice of companies was poor. Within five years of the surveys conducted by Peters and Waterman, one-third of the forty-three firms were in serious financial difficulty! The financial failures were particularly evident in the technology sector. Companies such as Atari, Data General, DEC, IBM, Lanier, NCR, Wang, and Xerox did not produce excellent results in the 1980s. Indeed, Atari, Data General, DEC, and Wang fell into such financial disarray that the companies had to seek acquisition angels and vanished. In the same way, the search for excellence through behavior imitation also should have vanished. Nevertheless, this failed theory was resurrected twenty years later.

The resurrection was *Good to Great*, written by Jim Collins.[7] He studied firms that elevated above-average performance to what he called great performance. Only eleven firms met his criteria, *viz.*, Abbott, Circuit City, Fannie Mae, Gillette, Kimberly-Clark, Kroger, Nucor, Philip Morris, Pitney Bowes, Walgreens, and

---

6   Thomas J. Peters and Robert H. Waterman, *In Search of Excellence* (New York: Harper and Row, 1982).

7   James C. Collins, *Good to Great* (New York: Harper Business, 2001).

Wells Fargo. He found several common behavioral traits within these eleven firms, including leaders who shun the spotlight and confront the brutal facts of their situation. The implication was that all a firm must do to make the journey from good to great is insist on leaders who have personal humility and professional will and who do not ignore reality. He asserted that any business could improve its performance from good to great if it conscientiously applies the framework of behaviors characterizing his chosen eleven firms. The implication is that imitating these behavioral factors inexorably leads to equivalent successful results. Observing unsuccessful firms might reveal that they behaved in the same way as successful firms. Using the experiences of any one firm or any eleven firms to understand what would make any firm successful is extremely doubtful. By the way, Circuit City went into bankruptcy and was liquidated in 2009. Fannie Mae was forced into conservatorship under auspices of the Federal Housing Finance Agency in late 2008. In 2005, Procter & Gamble acquired Gillette.

Despite the semantics of *Good to Great*, imitation of behavior and application of any framework of behaviors do not address any fundamental aspect of the business. If leaders shun the spotlight while the business bases its strategies on wrong-headed business principles if based on any business principles whatsoever, the business will fail nevertheless. *Good to Great* claims that great companies became great by keeping focus centered on their products, their customers, and their businesses; by avoiding complacency; by acting on genuine passion about their products; by fostering leadership that is not driven by ego; and by developing organizational structures that are responsive to change. Managers already knew as much. Managers also knew good companies make good decisions based on solid business principles, and great companies make great decisions based on the sound business principles.

The value of studying behavior lies in helping to discern general principles that underpin and thus explain why firms behave the way they do rather than trying to stipulate lists of characteristics that lead somehow to automatic success. Success does not come at random to those who follow current fashions. Instead, success can be understood by recognizing the basic principles of strategic action that were applied. Knowing the reasons for success is important. Reasons provide the why and separate principles from recipes. What is important is learning the principles that lie behind the way firms behave, not trying to develop a list of behaviors that lead to automatic success. There is no such list. General principles underlie strategic decisions. Successful managers recognize sound business principles that fit a firm's business conditions and then take strategic action.

The sequence, therefore, is first to learn the principles and then to understand the strategies based on the principles. Complex business strategies often are based on fairly simple business principles and concepts. These principles and concepts are the essential keys to decrypt strategies. Without learning the principles and concepts, business strategies remain inaccessible and amount to mere storytelling like parables without any sense of underlying truth. In other words, there would be no answers to the question: "Why?"

Knowing Answers Versus Making Up Answers

Conventional wisdom is a term that originated with the Harvard economist, John Kenneth Galbraith. Conventional wisdom is something everyone knows but isn't true.[8] For example, everyone knows St. Patrick was Irish, but it isn't true. Patricius was Romano British, a citizen of Roman Britain. When Patricius

---

8   See John Kenneth Galbraith, *The Affluent Society* (Boston, MA: Houghton Mifflin, 1958).

was a teenager, he was captured by Irish raiders and taken as a slave to Ireland where he herded sheep for six years before escaping and returning to his family and home in Britain. He later returned to Ireland as a missionary to save the souls of people who had kidnaped and enslaved him. Often, conventional wisdom is an obstacle to knowing what is true, mainly through discouraging or even discrediting genuine inquiry. In the spirit of disdaining conventional wisdom, a final comment should be made about the need to learn principles deals with the difference between making up answers to questions and knowing the answers to questions. Presumably, students and practitioners of business want to know answers rather than to make up answers to questions.

For example, suppose someone takes a sheet of printer paper, folds it in half, folds it in half again, and keeps folding it in half a total of twenty-four times. How thick would the final folded sheet be? A foot? Two feet? Any such answers are made up. Knowing the answer is different from making up an answer. Information is needed to know the answer. With information that a ream of 500 sheets of paper is two inches thick, the answer can be determined and known. Since a ream of 500 sheets of paper is two inches thick, each sheet is 2/500=0.004 of an inch thick. After one fold, a sheet of paper has the thickness of two sheets; after two folds, the thickness of four sheets; after three folds, the thickness of eight sheets; and so forth. Two, four, and eight also could be expressed as two to the power of one (2^1), two to the power of two (2^2), two to the power of three (2^3), and so forth. After twenty-four folds, therefore, the sheet has the thickness of two to the power of twenty-four (2^{24}), which is the thickness of 16,777,216 sheets. That number multiplied times 0.004, which is the thickness of one sheet, equals approximately 67,108 inches. Divided by twelve, which is the number of inches in a foot, the result is approximately 5,592 feet, which is a little over a mile thick! Making up the answer will not succeed in getting anywhere close to the right answer. A little bit of information, a little bit of thinking about the problem, and a few calculations obtain the right answer.

Another example is a question that corporate recruiters have asked in interview settings. How many golf balls are required to fill up an Olympic-sized swimming pool? Recruiters do not expect an answer or even know the answer. They expect job candidates to ask the right questions to determine information required to know the answer to the question. What are the dimensions of an Olympic-sized swimming pool? What is the diameter of a golf ball? With this little bit of information, a reasonable answer can be calculated.

MANAGERIAL PROBLEM SOLVING

To analyze anything is to separate it into parts to determine the nature of the whole. In business practice, analysis underlies decisions. Business decisions often ensue from problem solving. Decision making and problem solving are integral cognitive roles of managing an enterprise, thus involving awareness, perception, intuition, reasoning, knowledge, and judgment. Students of business and practitioners of business, therefore, must have a fundamental understanding of and appreciation for decision making and problem solving. In a sense, managerial economics is a study of the economic context for decision making and problem solving. Decisions often come at the end of problem solving, which normally is undertaken step-by-step in a formal process for problem-solving teams.

For the most complex and far-reaching problems and even for some simple problems, the problem solving process can be separated into phases, although the phases often overlap. In general, the problem-solving process begins with establishing objectives if objectives have not been established already. The objectives should be expressed in concrete operational terms. In that way, managers can determine whether an action advances achievement of objectives. The second phase is defining the problem that makes a decision necessary. After all, the process is meant to find solutions for problems. The third phase is identifying factors that have potential impact on the problem and its solutions. In effect, this phase deals with determining possible causes of the problem. The fourth phase is identifying courses of action that represent possible solutions and decisions. In other words, this phase deals with actions that could remove altogether or at least mitigate the known cause(s) of the problem. Focus is centered on fundamental changes aimed at removing what are believed to be the most significant causes. In business, this focus is called elephant hunting, the notion of getting the largest results from your efforts. The opposite of elephant hunting is mouse milking, getting the least results from your efforts. The fifth phase is evaluating courses of action. Experiments are conducted, pilot projects are undertaken, or other small-scale tests are involved. Pertinent data and information are used to evaluate results expected from each possible decision. The best alternative course of action is the one that achieves established objectives or that comes closest to achievement. The final phase of the decision process is implementing the decision. The implemented decision also must be evaluated and monitored, however.

Fishbone Diagrams

Many businesses use a fishbone diagram as an aid in problem solving. Dr. Kaoru Ishikawa, Tokyo University, developed the fishbone diagram in 1943. He pioneered this device for Kawasaki shipyards. In Japan, the fishbone diagram is known as an Ishikawa diagram. When applied to processes, a fishbone diagram is used as a device to establish the objective, articulate the problem, organize ideas about the possible root cause(s) of the problem, and to evaluate potential solutions. A fishbone diagram classifies the possible causes of a problem into categories of materials, methods, machinery, and people, which are the common, intrinsic elements of a process or system. When applied to administration or service, a fishbone diagram often categorizes possible causes into equipment, policies, procedures, and people. In effect, the fishbone diagram ensures a systematic, step-by-step application of the decision-making process.

For example, consider a chemical company that produces a crystalline fertilizer product, diammonium phosphate. Usually, the product is shipped domestically by barge and offloaded to trucks or railroad cars. Customers complain that the fertilizer is breaking down into dustlike "fines" when offloaded. One customer made a video while offloading the fertilizer and noted a white cloud arising from the barge. His voiceover said, "You see that cloud? That's product we paid for. That's our money blowing away in the wind." The chemical company formed a problem-solving team. The team agreed that the objective was to meet or exceed the needs, requirements, and expectations of customers so that they would continue to buy fertilizer from the company. They also agreed that the problem was fines, which compromised the integrity of diammonium phosphate.

To organize their thinking about possible causes of the problem, they constructed a fishbone diagram. When discussion of possible causes of the problem began, someone said, "Maybe there are solids in the phosphoric acid we're using." This possible cause was written under Materials. Someone else said, "Maybe the frontend loaders used in our warehouse are crushing the product." This possible cause was written under Machinery. Someone else said, "The conveyors we use to move product from the warehouse down to barges have several drops. Maybe each drop breaks down the product." This possible cause was written under Methods. Finally, someone said, "Maybe workers throughout all of our processes are not properly trained." This possible cause was written under People. Of course, other possible causes were suggested in each category and written accordingly in the fishbone diagram. Figure 1.5 depicts the fishbone diagram.

FIGURE 1.5
FISHBONE DIAGRAM

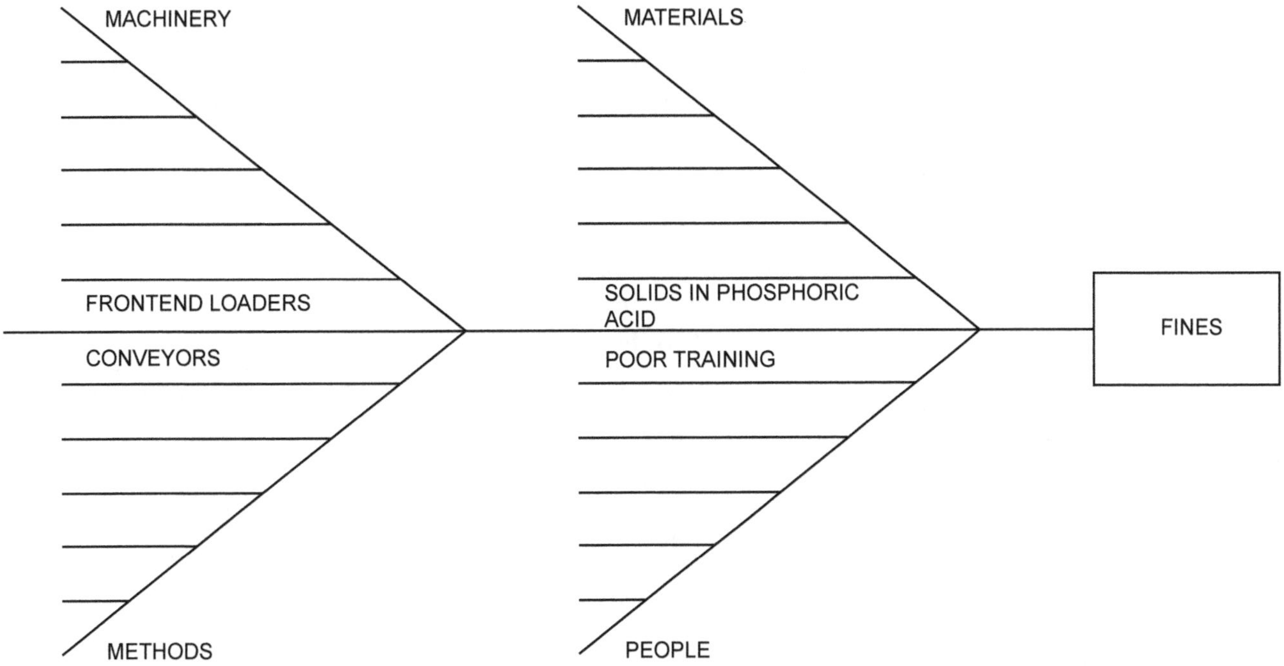

Next, the team identified the most likely and most significant causes of the problem as well as potential solutions to the problem. Afterwards, the team tried out these solutions on a small scale. Based on analysis of results from these experiments, the solution(s) that passed the smell test were implemented.

Whether fishbone diagrams are utilized or not, many businesses have institutionalized their own steps required for decision making. Top management expects these steps to be followed in each instance, even no-brainers. For example, an executive of Enviro-Chem once said, "Even when you hit a home run, you have to touch every base."

CHARACTERISTICS OF BEST MANAGEMENT

Sound managerial decisions are based on a solid foundation of adherence to certain basic principles. Capable managers must be competent to make sound decisions. At a minimum, best managers have skills to set and pursue accomplishment of goals; recognize the nature and importance of profits; understand incentives and motivations; and know their customers, products, and markets. This overview suggests that best management is not merely being a boss. Anyone can be bossy and issue uncontested orders, but being effective in managing work and leading people requires knowledge in addition to power. After all, when a leader says, "Follow me," the leader presumably has knowledge about where he or she is going and how to get there.

Setting and Pursuing Goals

Presumably, the basic and ultimate goal of any business is to maximize the value of the firm, although this presumption is far from settled. One measure of the value of a firm is market capitalization, sometimes called market cap. Market capitalization for a corporation is price of a share of its common stock multiplied by number of its outstanding shares of common stock. In this sense, market capitalization is simply the market value of a company measured by the total value of its common stock. From week to week in mid-2011, Exxon Mobil and Apple battled for the top spot, but Apple's common stock price soared. Consequently, Apple distanced itself well beyond Exxon Mobil. Indeed, the market cap of Apple exceeded six hundred billion dollars in April 2012, making the company the largest in history measured by market cap. Table 1.4 shows the twenty largest U.S. companies by market cap at the close of 18 October 2013.

Table 1.4 Twenty Largest U.S. Companies by Market Capitalization 18 October 2013 ($Billion)		
Company	**Symbol**	**Market Capitalization**
Apple	AAP_L	439.39
Exxon Mobil	XON	403.32
Google	GOOG	257.40
Berkshire Hathaway	BRK.A	243.60
Wal-Mart	WMT	238.85
General Electric	GE	236.78
Microsoft	MSFT	233.53
Chevron	CVX	228.01
IBM	IBM	226.03
Johnson & Johnson	JNJ	210.06
Procter & Gamble	P_G	207.55
AT&T	T	202.21
Pfizer	PFE	198.72
Wells Fargo	WFC	186.93
JP_Morgan Chase	JP_M	186.80
Coca-Cola	KO	168.46
Oracle	ORCL	166.22
Philip Morris	P_M	150.58
Bank of America	BAC	131.98
Citigroup	C	130.06

Source: The Online Investor

Market cap ignores the encumbrance of debt, which can be substantial enough to distort the sense of value. For example, suppose two companies have the same market cap, but one company is debt-free, whereas the other company is debt-heavy. Investors interested in acquisition would not be likely to pay as much for the company that is debt-heavy. Moreover, suppose two companies have the same market cap, and neither company has any debt. However, one company has negligible cash and cash equivalents on hand, whereas the other company has a large amount of cash and cash equivalents on hand. Investors interested in acquisition would be willing to pay more for the company with a lot of cash and cash equivalents. Market cap alone, therefore, is not the sole measure of what investors would be willing to pay for a firm.

Market cap should not be confused with another measure of the value of a firm known as enterprise value. In effect, enterprise value is an estimate of takeover cost, *i.e.*, how much would be required of investors to buy and own a company outright. Enterprise value is the market value of common stock, plus the book value of preferred stock, plus the market value of outstanding debt, minus cash and cash equivalents. Thus, enterprise value is a sum of claims of all holders of stock and debt minus cash and cash equivalents. Cash and cash equivalents are subtracted because once the company has been acquired the cash and cash equivalents go to the acquiring investors, thus replacing some of the cash expended to acquire the company.

Recognizing the Nature and Importance of Profits

If the ultimate goal of a firm is to maximize the firm's value, the principal means is to maximize profits. Recognizing the nature and importance of profits is critical. The general public and the business community typically think of profit in terms of an accounting concept. In the simplest sense, profit is generally understood as the difference between revenue from sales and cost of doing business. Often, this definition of profit is called accounting profit. However, the invested capital of owners is the equivalent of non-purchased inputs used in production, and these owners expect a return on their invested capital. Economic cost includes all out-of-pocket costs and the opportunity cost of invested capital, which is the return on equity capital forgone when invested by owners in their own business. In other words, economic cost includes forgone return on invested equity capital.

Economic profit is the difference between revenue from sales and economic cost, which includes both out-of-pocket costs and the imputed opportunity costs of non-purchased inputs such as invested capital. This simple concept has been elevated into a major managerial model called Economic Value Added (EVA). In the EVA framework, net operating profit after taxes (NOPAT) is made using debt and equity capital, and a charge for this capital is subtracted from NOPAT. If the cost of capital is less than NOPAT, value is added to the firm. If the cost of capital is more than NOPAT, value is reduced.

Understanding Incentives and Motivation

Capable managers have a firm grasp on the role of incentives, and they know how to shape incentives to induce proper effort from those under supervision. Indeed, incentives are shaped and implemented to energize and animate people to reflect the organization's personality, which is its organizational culture. Like human personality, organizational culture tends to be unique to a particular organization, and this organizational culture is concerned with custom, tradition, and shared beliefs about organizational life. In this light, culture in an organization can be seen as the pattern of assumptions found to be useful in coping with the internal and external environment and taught to new members as the correct way to perceive, think, and feel about their work. Organizational culture is a powerful determinant of individual and team behavior. It affects virtually all aspects of organizational life, ranging from the ways people interact with each other to how they perform their work.

Incentives deal with motivation, which literally means a reason to move to action. In other words, an incentive is something that induces action or motivates effort. This meaning is so well known that we sometimes speak of incentives as inducements. In addition to a narrow financial approach to incentives and motivation, several other points need to be made briefly.

First, a number of people have observed that most organizations are overmanaged and underled. Grace Hopper was one of these people. Making a career of the U.S. Navy, Grace Murray Hopper (1906-1992) was a remarkable woman. In 1934, she was the first woman to be awarded a Ph.D. in mathematics at Yale University. Hopper was the third programmer on the famed Mark I at Harvard, which was an electro/mechanical computer built by IBM and delivered in summer 1944 for use by the U.S. Navy. In 1952, she developed FLOW-MATIC, the immediate forerunner of COBOL (Common Business-Oriented Language). One might say that FLOW-MATIC was the mother of COBOL, the first commercial high-level programming language. In November 1985, at the age of 79, the nomenclature of Hopper's rank of Commodore was changed to Rear Admiral. She thus became one of the few women admirals in the history of the U.S. Navy. She retired on 14 August 1986 in a ceremony aboard the U.S.S. Constitution in Boston. After retirement, "Amazing Grace" worked as Senior Consultant for DEC (Digital Equipment Corporation) until eighteen months before her death on 1 January 1992. She was buried with full Naval honors at Arlington National Cemetery on 7 January 1992.[9]

Rear Admiral Hopper once said, "You manage things, and you lead people." The general idea is to manage work and lead people. Management is directive when dealing with workers, whereas leadership relies on inspiring and motivating workers. Leadership depends on vision, which must be detailed, communicated, shared, and supported. Leaders articulate a vision, develop strategies to accomplish the vision, and then inspire, motivate, and align others to accomplish the vision. All of these leadership roles deal with people, whereas management deals with work. Incidentally, Rear Admiral Hopper also is remembered for a comment she made on television in 1983: "It is much easier to apologize than to get permission." Nowadays, this comment usually is stated as, "It is easier to ask forgiveness than to get permission." She should have added, "Unless you are a married man."

Another giant of the twentieth century also concentrated on incentives and motivation, also emphasizing the central role of leadership rather than management. Dr. W. Edwards Deming (1900-1993) was an exceptional man, truly one of the most influential people of the twentieth century. In 1928, he earned his doctorate in mathematical physics from Yale. Along with Dr. Walter Shewhart (1891-1967), Deming is regarded as the founder of the quality movement worldwide and certainly was its spokesman throughout his life. Dr. Deming emphasized transformation. He developed fourteen principles for transformation of an organization from what it is to what it can be and ought to be. What an organization is, what it can be, and what it ought to be can be described in terms of physical and behavioral aspects. He argued that transformation required leadership. Throughout his lifetime, Dr. Deming said that the aim of leadership is not to find and record the failures of people but to remove the causes of failure so that people can do a better job.

---

9   For an excellent readable biography, see Kathleen Broome Williams, *Grace Hopper: Admiral of the Cyber Sea* (Annapolis, MD: Naval Institute Press, 2004).

Second, emphasis in the 2010s is on team rather than individual incentives. An example from mining illustrates the hazards of emphasizing individual performance. When a phosphate mining manager was asked if he had told other mining managers in the same company about a breakthrough idea he had implemented, he said, "Hell, no! Let them figure it out the hard way just like we did." In fairness to the manager, it must be said that he was acting in response to company incentives that motivated people to behave in this way. Historically, the way to get ahead in the company was to elevate one's own job performance above that of rivals. In this case, the longer the mining manager could keep his breakthrough idea from other mining managers, the longer his mining results would look better by comparison to the performance of other mining managers. Of course, keeping the breakthrough idea from being implemented in other company mines harmed the overall performance of the company and harmed the interests of owners. The company moved to change its culture so that incentives motivated managers to act in concert as a team for the advancement of company goals and objectives.

Knowing the Customer, Product, and Market

Best managers understand their products and their product markets. They analyze and understand competitive conditions in their product markets. They develop a deep sense of the internal rivalry among incumbent firms as well as forces that would intensify competition and thus threaten profitability. In addition, capable managers know their customers. Businesses are driven to meet if not exceed the needs, requirements, and expectations of customers. Best managers also know the factors that affect sales of their products and know something about the sensitivity of sales to each of these factors. For example, they know how sensitive sales of a particular product are to the price of the product itself, to the prices of competing products, to per capita income in the market area, and to advertising outlays. Understanding a company's customers, products, and markets is integral to competitive analysis, and competitive analysis is critical in formulation of business strategies.

PRACTICE QUESTIONS

1. How did continuous production technologies lead to the rise of modern enterprise?

2. What is the M-form of organization?

3. What is a first mover advantage?

4. As a middle manager for a manufacturer, suppose you are asked to head up a team of eight people asked to focus on a perplexing problem involved in the production and distribution of a household lawn water sprinkler product. The problem is that, when customers buy the product at retail stores such as Home Depot, some of them find the product malfunctions because of a missing screw that governs a pulsating mechanism. The result is that unhappy customers return the defective sprinklers to retailers. As team leader, top management has tasked you and the team to follow the step-by-step decision-making process. Describe the step-by-step process through which you would lead the team in making ultimate decisions in this particular case.

5. Describe a fishbone diagram and briefly describe how it is related to the steps or phases of problem solving and decision making

6. What is the market capitalized value of a firm?

PRACTICE QUESTIONS (*AND ANSWERS*)

1. How did continuous-production technologies lead to the rise of modern enterprise?

Continuous-production machines and factories required owners to increase volume of output substantially to recover the costs of investment in such technologies. This requirement alone led to substantially larger firms. The increased volume and size of operations correspondingly increased the owner's responsibilities in functional areas such as purchasing, sales, distribution, and finance, which in turn required a central office to ensure that production runs and deliveries of finished products went smoothly. Manufacturing firms increasingly chose to acquire raw materials and distribute final products themselves. In addition to increased scale, these continuous production technologies led to increased scope. In other words, these technologies allowed firms to produce a wider scope of products at lower cost. As a result, firms expanded their product lines. Increased size and corresponding complexity of multiproduct operations required further reorganization into semiautomomous divisions. The organizational form known as the multidivisional or M-form became widespread and was typical of the largest industrial firms.

2. What is the M-form of organization?

The M-form originated as an organizational structure built around product line rather than business function. Semiautonomous divisions were formed to accommodate the functional needs of products. Each product division has its own operating decisions and is subdivided into business functions. A corporate office makes decisions representing the entire organization, essentially capital decisions.

3. What is a first mover advantage?

First mover advantage is an insurmountable advantage gained by the first significant company to enter a market or to adopt a new technology.

4. As a middle manager for a manufacturer, suppose you are asked to head up a team of eight people asked to focus on a perplexing problem involved in the production and distribution of a household lawn water sprinkler product. The problem is that, when customers buy the product at retail stores such as Home Depot, some of them find the product malfunctions because of a missing screw that governs a pulsating mechanism. The result is that unhappy customers return the defective sprinklers to retailers. As team leader, top management has tasked you and the team to follow the step-by-step decision-making process. Describe the step-by-step process through which you would lead the team in making ultimate decisions in this particular case.

First, you want to establish agreement among team members about objectives to be accomplished. Next, you would want to see if they agree on the problem to be solved. Then, you might use a fishbone diagram to identify possible causes of the problem and identify courses of action to remove such causes. These courses of action represent possible decisions, and each one must be evaluated. Pertinent data and information are used to evaluate results expected from each possible decision. The best alternative course of action is the one that achieves established objectives or that comes closest to achievement. If the team agrees on a course of action, the recommendation would be presented to top management for authority to act. The final phase of the decision process is implementing the decision.

5. Describe a fishbone diagram and briefly describe how it is related to the steps or phases of problem solving and decision making.

For complex and simple problems, the decision process can be separated into steps or phases. The process begins with establishing objectives expressed in concrete, operational terms. The second phase is defining the problem that makes a decision necessary. The third phase is identifying factors related to the problem. The fourth phase is identifying alternative courses of action. These alternatives represent possible decisions. The fifth phase is evaluating the alternative courses of action. Collection and analysis of data in the process of evaluating alternatives are central to this phase. Pertinent data and information are used to evaluate results expected from each possible decision. The best alternative course of action is the one that achieves established objectives or that comes closest to achievement. The final phase of the decision process is implementing the decision. Many businesses use a process improvement tool called a fishbone diagram as an aid in problem solving. A fishbone diagram is used as a device to articulate the problem, organize ideas about the possible root cause(s) of the problem into categories such as materials, methods, machinery, and people, and finally to evaluate potential solutions that remove such root causes or mitigate their effects. In effect, the fishbone diagram is a tool that ensures a systematic, step-by-step application of the decision making process.

6. What is the market capitalized value of a firm?

For a corporation, the market capitalized value of a firm, usually called market cap, is the price of a share of common stock times the number of shares of common stock outstanding.

2. Supply and Demand in Business Practice

UNIVERSUM ANNUAL SURVEY OF MBA STUDENTS

Universum is a company founded by Lars-Hendrik Friis-Molin in 1988 when he was an MBA student at the Stockholm School of Economics. Each year, Universum surveys MBA candidates to determine for whom they would like to work after graduation. From December 2012 through March 2013, the company surveyed MBA students at 135 business schools nationwide. There were 3,739 respondents, 1,622 women and 2,097 men. From a list of 175 companies, MBA students were asked to select the five companies for which they would most like to work. Respondents also were given the opportunity to write in the name of any company for which they would like to work but did not appear on the list. Results are reported as the percentage of MBA students who listed a company in their top five.

For many years, consulting and financial services dominated the top ten companies, often claiming eight of the top ten spots. McKinsey & Co., regarded as the best consulting firm on the planet Earth, usually topped the list. In 2007, however, McKinsey was displaced at the top by Google, which ended McKinsey's reign of twelve years at the top. Google was not on the list in the 2005 survey, but Google still received enough write-in entries to finish 129th among 179 companies. Google now has a skein of seven years at the top. Table 2.1 shows the top twenty-five companies in the 2013 survey and their rankings for 2009 through 2013. NA indicates not among the top 100.

					Table 2.1 Universum Survey of MBA Students, 2009-2013	
2009	**2010**	**2011**	**2012**	**2013**	**Company**	**Percentage**
1	1	1	1	1	Google (55)	28.38
2	2	2	2	2	McKinsey & Company	16.58
5	5	3	3	3	Apple (6)	14.82
18	11	8	6	4	Amazon (49)	14.41
6	4	5	5	5	Boston Consulting Group	12.19
3	6	6	4	6	Bain & Company	11.63
8	9	10	9	7	Nike (126)	10.72
7	8	11	12	8	Walt Disney (66)	10.54
16	12	12	11	9	Deloitte	9.78
4	3	4	7	10	Goldman Sachs (68)	8.50
NA	NA	7	8	11	Facebook (482)	7.89
9	7	9	10	12	J.P. Morgan (18)	7.46
15	18	16	13	13	IDEO	7.45
12	15	18	17	14	Microsoft (35)	7.39
27	24	23	20	15	Starbucks (208)	6.07
10	10	14	15	16	Johnson & Johnson (41)	6.04
11	13	13	14	17	Blackstone Group	5.91
17	17	19	18	18	Procter & Gamble (28)	5.06
31	30	24	22	19	IBM (20)	5.04
13	16	17	16	20	General Electric (8)	4.88
19	19	21	21	21	Coca-Cola (57)	4.49
30	28	22	24	22	LVMH	4.44
22	27	20	23	23	BMW Group	4.18
46	33	32	37	24	3M (101)	3.93
25	42	37	30	25	U.S. Department of State	3.83

DEMAND AND SUPPLY: THE INTERVIEW FROM HELL

At Stanford, first year MBA students interview in the spring for summer jobs between their first and second years in the program. More often than not, these summer jobs lead to first jobs after graduation. One of these MBA students was Peter Robinson, who was graduated in 1990. For six years before entering the Stanford MBA program, Robinson was a speechwriter for President Ronald Reagan. He wrote the speech that President Reagan delivered at the Brandenburg Gate of the Berlin Wall on 12 June 1987. The speech that Robinson wrote is still recalled for the famous words spoken by President Reagan on that day, "Mr. Gorbachev, tear down this wall!"

Robinson kept a journal during his two years at Stanford. Based on his journal, he wrote a popular book about his first year in the program, *Snapshots from Hell: The Making of an MBA.*[10] Robinson wanted a summer job with McKinsey and afterwards a career with the consulting company. Access to an interview with McKinsey was highly competitive because so many Stanford MBA students sought one. Because of his impressive résumé, Robinson earned a first-round interview, which went well enough to earn a second-round interview with a McKinsey partner. The following excerpt is Peter Robinson's account of the interview with the partner.

In the second-round interviews, consulting firms would often spring a case on a candidate, asking him to solve it out loud....

"I'll just give you a case out of my own experience, if that's all right," the partner said. He wore a starched white shirt and trousers with creases that could have sliced cake. He assured me dryly that he had worked on this case when he was my age and just starting at McKinsey.

"The case involved a freight forwarding company. Any idea what a freight forwarder does?"

This sounded ominous. I certainly had no idea....

"A freight forwarder," he said, "picks up freight, packages it–usually they'll build a standard-sized wooden frame or crate around each shipment–takes it to a ship or airplane for transport, picks it up at the dock or airport at the other end, stores it, then uncrates it and delivers it to its final destination on the appropriate date. So the business is basically trucking, storage, and handling."

The partner explained that his client had been in the freight forwarding business for several decades, always profitably. Then over a period of just a few months, the client suddenly found itself losing money. As often happened in a business that hadn't changed much in many years, the managers had grown lax in their bookkeeping.

"Cost accounting?" the partner said. "Non-existent. So they couldn't figure out what had happened, and they turned to us."

For McKinsey, the partner said, straightening out the cost accounting proved elementary–"not that it didn't take a lot of time and brains." McKinsey concluded that the freight forwarder had begun to lose money because of a single expense, air charges.

"The airlines," he said, concluding his presentation, "were suddenly charging our client more–a lot more–to carry its freight. My question to you is, Why would that happen?"

I froze.

After a tense moment of silence, the partner repeated the question. He looked at me grimly.

"You understand the question, right? Why would the airlines start charging more?" He wasn't trying to make this easy.

"Fuel costs?" I finally said. "Was this by any chance taking place during the Arab oil embargoes of the early seventies?"

---

10   Peter Robinson, *Snapshots from Hell: The Making of an MBA* (New York: Warner Books, 1995).

"No," he said flatly. "It was after that. The higher price of oil had already been absorbed into the airlines' price structures."

Another tense silence.

The partner said, "Let's look at it another way." During the same period, he stated, airfares for passengers were holding steady or actually dropping. Yet here the airlines were, imposing sharp increases on freight forwarders. "To recommend what our client should do about it, we had to figure out what was going on. So what would you guess?"

"There was no other airline that would have charged less?" I asked. Even I recognized this as a stupid question–before spending tens of thousands of dollars to hire McKinsey, the client would obviously have spent a few quarters to telephone other airlines. And yet I was desperate. "All the airlines were raising their fares?"

The partner confirmed that all the airlines were raising their fares. "But you're getting someplace," he said. That surprised me. "If all the airlines were raising their fares at the same time, what could be the reason?" I had no idea, which did not surprise me.

Once again, I froze.... [T]he McKinsey partner simply gazed at me. Then he gave up.

"What about supply and demand?" he said.

If all the airlines were charging higher fares, the partner said, the demand for cargo space must have risen to a new level. Yet despite this increase in demand, the supply of cargo space was more or less fixed; it took many months for airlines to order new planes, get them delivered, and finally put them into service. "So the airlines were charging our client higher rates because they didn't really need his business. Other freight forwarders were out there, bidding up the price of a relatively fixed supply of cargo space. Makes sense, right?"

Of course, it made sense.[11]

Because he could not recognize a simple case of supply and demand, Peter Robinson was not offered the summer job. After graduation, he did not go to work for McKinsey. The partner simply wanted him to demonstrate awareness of the most basic market forces, *i.e.*, supply and demand. "I'd blown it," Robinson said. The interview from Hell was a microcosm of *Snapshots From Hell*.

The principles of demand and supply are relevant for business practitioners. The principles of demand and supply also are relevant for management consultants, even McKinsey partners. Moreover, knowledge of these principles and recognition of these principles are essential to managers. Ask Peter Robinson. He would tell you that the MBA degree will get a person an interview, but what the person learns in the MBA program will get him or her the job. What the person did not learn and understand in the MBA program will cost him or her the job. In his case, what Robinson had not learned cost him his dream job.

UNDERSTANDING THE MARKET

Best managers understand their market. They know their customers, and they are driven to meet customer needs, requirements, and expectations. They also know who their competitors are, and they understand competitive forces that affect their business. They know and understand the factors that

---

11   *Ibid.*, pp.164-167.

affect unit sales of their products. To reiterate, best managers know their market and understand their market. Otherwise, informed decisions could not be made in the best interests of the firm producing and offering a product for sale.

The customer side and competitor side of the market are, respectively, the buyer side and the seller side of the market. These two sides are called the demand side and the supply side of the market. In a narrow sense, demand and supply refer to the amount that buyers want to purchase and the amount sellers want to produce and offer for sale. In a broader context, however, demand is consideration of factors affecting the units of something buyers want to purchase. In the same sense, supply represents a somewhat different set of factors determining the units of something sellers want to produce and offer for sale. Together, demand and supply influence if not determine amounts of an item that are bought and sold. In addition, demand and supply influence if not determine the market price of a product.

Some terminology in economics is derived from science, particularly physics. The use of forces is a good example. Independently, Gottfried Leibniz (1646-1716) and Sir Isaac Newton (1642-1727) developed infinitesimal calculus. Leibniz is believed to have priority. He gave us the name of calculus instead of fluxions, the name Newton gave to differential calculus. Leibniz's mathematical notation is still used. Newton is better known for formulating the basic theories of universal gravitation and terrestrial mechanics. In effect, Newton discovered the laws that govern the physical universe. Followers were known as Newtonians. They believed that if the laws that govern the physical universe created by God were discoverable by humankind, so could the laws that govern history or economics.

Adam Smith (1723-1790), a Scottish moral philosopher and political economist, was a Newtonian. When he wrote his seminal work, *An Inquiry into the Nature and Causes of the Wealth of Nations* (1776), he used some of the scientific language of Newton, including words such as forces, laws, and equilibrium. Afterwards, the forces of supply and demand, the law of supply, the law of demand, and market equilibrium entered the language. Once introduced, the terms that originated in physics are coined regularly as part of the language of economics and business.

Understanding markets and analyzing competitive conditions in markets are obverse and reverse of the same coin. Michael E. Porter, a Harvard economist, found ways to break through the communications barrier that once separated economists from MBAs and also separated economists from managers. He developed a framework known as five forces analysis to organize thinking about competitive analysis of markets and industries.[12] This use of forces is related to forces used heretofore only in the sense that both refer to causal factors. At the core of these five forces is internal rivalry among firms in an industry, each jockeying for positions of advantage among incumbent competitors. Apart from internal rivalry but nonetheless affecting competitive conditions and shaping the nature and intensity of internal rivalry are the threat of new entry, the bargaining power of suppliers, the bargaining power of buyers, and the threat of substitute products or services. Underlying the nature and intensity of rivalry, threats of entry and substitutes, and bargaining powers of suppliers and buyers lurk the forces of demand and supply.

---

12   Michael E. Porter, *Competitive Strategy: Techniques for Analyzing Industries and Competitors* (New York: Free Press, 1980).

PRICE TAKERS AND PRICE SETTERS

In highly competitive markets, the price of a product is determined in the overall market as the outcome of countless transactions between buyers and sellers. Buyers are on the demand side of the market, and sellers are on the supply side of the market. Demand for and supply of a product in such markets interacts to determine the price of the product. Once this market price is determined, firms producing and selling in the market take this price as the price of their product. This situation is common for a wide range of commodities, including food such as wheat and corn, fibers such as cotton and wool, metals such as copper and aluminum, and many other homogeneous, undifferentiated goods. Firms in these highly competitive markets are price takers since these firms take the market price as the price of their product. They are not in a position to set their own prices for their own products. Indeed, if they insisted on a price even slightly higher than the market price, they would lose all of their sales.

On the other hand, most firms have some control over the price of their product(s). Whereas price takers generally deal in undifferentiated products and have no control over price, firms that have control over price generally deal in differentiated products. In this sense, these firms are not price takers but rather are price setters. For such firms, demand for their product is every bit as relevant as in the case of price takers, but supply is a little different. For price takers, supply is an aggregation of how much all sellers want to produce and offer for sale. For price setters, supply is how much a particular firm chooses to produce and offer for sale.

QUANTITY DEMANDED AND DEMAND

The amount of a product that customers want to purchase at a particular price, given all other factors that influence their willingness and ability to make these purchases, is called the quantity demanded. For example, the amount of ground sirloin that households buy per month at $3.59 per pound is the quantity of such ground sirloin demanded at that particular price. Quantity demanded can be understood as unit sales at a particular price, in this case, $3.59 per pound.

On the other hand, amounts demanded or unit sales expected at various prices establish a relationship between quantities demanded and prices. Functions, tables, or graphs used to show amounts expected to be purchased at numerous and various different prices, other factors remaining the same, are called the demand for a product. "Other things being equal" is the literal translation of a Latin phrase, *ceteris paribus*, which is pronounced KAY-ter-is P_AIR-ah-bus. What *ceteris paribus* means is other factors involved in the determination of something are held constant at fixed values. In the case of demand, for example, many factors are involved in determining the amounts expected to be purchased at various prices. Factors other than price of the product include prices of related products, income, and advertising outlays on the product. These factors other than price of the product are held constant at fixed values so that a function, table, or graph can isolate the relationship between various prices of the product and amounts of the product that would be purchased at those prices.

To summarize, the demand for a product is amounts that would be purchased at various prices of the product with other factors held constant at fixed values. Therefore, demand is amounts (plural) that would be purchased at various prices (plural), other factors held constant. In this way, demand, which is amounts expected to be purchased at various prices, is seen to be different from quantity demanded, which is an amount (singular) expected to purchased at a particular price (singular). In this light, demand is seen as a pattern that shows the relationship between price of a product and amount of the product that buyers would purchase. A pattern cannot be shown if only one price and one amount are observed. In business or otherwise, a pattern cannot be discerned from only one observation. Demand is a pattern based on several observations, several prices and amounts that would be purchased at those prices. Quantity demanded is a single observation, the amount purchased at a particular price. When used properly, demand is descriptive of a relationship, not an amount, whereas quantity demanded is descriptive of an amount, not a relationship.

HOW MUCH DO BUYERS WANT TO PURCHASE?

The relationship between unit sales of a product and determinants of such unit sales is based on factors that significantly affect the amount of the product that buyers want to purchase. For example, the most important factors might be the number of people in the market area, income per person in the market area, price of the product, prices of other products, and advertising outlays on the product. Of course, other factors undoubtedly influence unit sales, but they are less important and generally insignificant.

Consider a food product, Brand X. In general, factors can be expressed functionally with unit sales of Brand X as the dependent variable and factors that influence unit sales of Brand X as independent variables, which is

$$Q_X = f(P_X, P_S, P_C, Y, A_X, U)$$

The variables are

Q_X = unit sales of Brand X, measured in thousands of units per week;

P_X = price of Brand X;

P_S = price of Brand S, a substitute for Brand X;

P_C = price of Product C, a complement for Brand X;

Y = per capita income in the market area for Brand X;

A_X = advertising outlays on Brand X; and

U = unspecified factors (*e.g.*, population, ethnicity, tastes, advertising outlays on Product S, advertising outlays on Product C, wealth, and so forth).

Unit sales should not be confused with sales revenue, which are business receipts from sale of a product. Unit sales is a reference to the number of a product sold, *e.g.*, number of automobile tires, tons of wheat, cases of peanut butter, hundredweights of potatoes, pounds of beef, cubic yards of cement, and so forth.

A dependent variable is a quantitative value that is determined by the quantitative values for independent variables. An independent variable is a quantitative value that determines the quantitative value of a dependent variable. In this case, unit sales of Brand X depend on the quantitative values for each factor within the parentheses, which are the independent variables.

Some factors may have a direct relationship and other factors an inverse relationship. A direct relationship between two variables means the two variables increase and decrease in conjunction. For example, consider two variables, A and B. If A is increased, then B also increases. If A is decreased, then B also decreases. An inverse relationship between two variables means one variable increases when the other decreases. If A is increased, then B decreases. If A is decreased, then B increases.

The Law of Demand

The relationship between unit sales of a product and price of a product is an inverse association. Unit sales are negatively affected by an increase in price and positively affected by a decrease in price. The inverse relationship is known as the law of demand. Recall *ceteris paribus*, other things being equal. Given the price of Brand S, the price of Product C, per capita income, and advertising outlays on Brand X, unit sales of Brand X are negatively affected by an increase in the price of Brand X and positively affected by a decrease in the price of Brand X.

Substitutes and Complements

Substitutes are products that satisfy to some degree the same want, need, requirement, taste, or other characteristic. For people who enjoy seafood, grouper is a substitute for mahi-mahi. For people who buy jarred marinara sauce, Prego and Bertolli are substitutes. Substitutes can be considered to be competitive products. When two products are substitutes and the price of one product is raised, the effect of this price rise is to increase unit sales of the other product. When the price of one product is reduced, the effect is to decrease unit sales of the other product. This cause-and-effect relationship is direct since changes in the price of one product and unit sales of the other product both move in the same direction. For example, suppose Tropicana raises the price of its orange juice while the price of Simply Orange is unchanged. Some buyers will switch from Tropicana to Simply Orange. The price of Tropicana has increased, and unit sales of Simply Orange also have increased. Thus, the relationship between the price of Tropicana and unit sales of Simply Orange is direct, indicating that they are substitutes.

Complements are products used together. For example, peanut butter and jelly are used together as are red beans and rice, bagels and cream cheese, breakfast cereal and milk, hot dogs and hot dog buns, gin and tonic. Fusion razors and Fusion razor blades are used together as are Hewlett-Packard desktop printers and Hewlett-Packard toner cartridges. As a word, "complement" is almost the nonexistent word "completement," suggesting that products are used together and thus complete a set. Compliment is another matter. Compliments are statements of praise or admiration ("My dear, you look lovely this evening") or actions of respect or courtesy ("The *crème brûlée* is compliments of the chef").

In a sense, therefore, complements are products that complete a set. When two products are complements and the price of one product is increased, the increased price has a negative effect on unit sales of that product and unit sales of the other complementary product. When the price of one product is lowered, the decreased price has a positive effect on unit sales of that product and unit sales of the other complementary product. This cause-and-effect relationship is an inverse association since changes in the price of one product and unit sales of the other product move in opposite directions. For example, suppose a peanut crop failure in Georgia causes the price of peanuts to rise. Consequently, the price of peanut butter also will rise, and people will buy less peanut butter. Since jelly is used with peanut butter, people also will buy less jelly. The higher price of peanut butter has a negative effect on unit sales of jelly. Thus, the relationship between the price of peanut butter and unit sales of jelly is inverse, indicating that they are complements.

Normal and Inferior Goods

Almost always, an increase in per capita income in a market will increase the amount of a product sold, *ceteris paribus*, which implies a direct relationship between unit sales and income. Products for which this generalization is true are called normal goods because the direct relationship is normally the case. Products for which this generalization is not true are called inferior goods. In the case of inferior goods, the relationship between income and unit sales is an inverse association. Unit sales of an inferior good increase with a decline in income and decrease with a rise in income. When a product is inferior in this sense, a preferred but more expensive substitute is available. As income rises, unit sales of the inferior product decline as people turn to the preferred but more expensive product, which is now more affordable.

Nonfat dry milk is believed to be an inferior good. In a household with low income, nonfat dry milk might be purchased and reconstituted with water as the household source of milk for drinking or cooking. The only attraction is low cost. A gallon of reconstituted dry milk costs a trifling fraction of the price of whole milk from the dairy case. As household income increases, whole milk is more affordable and thus purchased rather than nonfat dry milk. Cheap cuts of beef also are known to be inferior. Low income families might purchase USDA standard or USDA commercial cuts of beef, but as income rises, more expensive USDA select, USDA choice, or USDA prime cuts of beef are purchased rather than more and more of the cheap cuts.

Informative and Persuasive Advertising

Advertising often provides information about the availability or quality of a product, which in turn induces purchases of the product. This type of advertising is known as informative advertising. Advertising also can try to influence unit sales by changing preferences or tastes. This type of advertising is called persuasive advertising. Whether informative or persuasive, the relationship between unit sales of a product and advertising outlays is always meant to be direct. Otherwise, advertising is not merely ineffective but perverse, meaning it has an effect opposite from the intended outcome.

For example, Taco Bell commercials featuring the Chihuahua dog were highly popular, but the television ads did nothing for sales. The ads were aired first in 1998. Taco Bell sales were flat in 1999 and then down in 2000. For many viewers, perhaps the message was that Taco Bell offered food that dogs like. Dog food was a sobriquet for its food that Taco Bell sought to overcome. In mid-2000, the Chihuahua dog was dumped like an abandoned pet. The advertising agency that produced the ads lost the Taco Bell account. However, the ads did wonders for the popularity of Chihuahua dogs. Unlike Taco Bell products, the demand for Chihuahua dogs soared to unprecedented heights. One is tempted to say the increase in demand for Chihuahua dogs was eye bulging, but that would be as cheesy as a quesadilla.

Summary of Relationships

Table 2.2 summarizes the expected relationships between unit sales of Brand X and each of the independent variables, price of Brand X, price of Brand S, price of Product C, per capita income, and advertising outlays on Brand X. Assumptions are that Brand X is a normal good and that advertising outlays on Brand X have a positive effect on unit sales of Brand X.

Table 2.2 Relationships Between Unit Sales of Brand X, Prices, Income, and Advertising	
Unit Sales of Brand X With Respect to:	**Relationship**
Price of Brand X	Inverse If P_X is increased, negative effect on Q_X If P_X is decreased, positive effect on Q_X
Price of Brand S	Direct If P_S is increased, positive effect on Q_X If P_S is decreased, negative effect on Q_X
Price of Product C	Inverse If P_C is increased, negative effect on Q_X If P_C is decreased, positive effect on Q_X
Income	Direct If Y increases, positive effect on Q_X If Y decreases, negative effect on Q_X
Advertising	Direct If A_X is increased, positive effect on Q_X If A_X is decreased, negative effect on Q_X

THE SALES FUNCTION FOR BRAND X

Using statistics, a sales function can be estimated to determine the relationship between unit sales of a product and independent factors. Product managers, sometimes called brand managers, want to know these relationships. He or she would want to know the extent to which unit sales of a product are affected by changes in the price of the product itself, changes in the prices of competitive products, changes in the prices of complementary products, changes in per capita income, advertising outlays on the product, and changes in other factors that affect sales.

Usually, consultants sign a nondisclosure agreement, meaning they cannot disclose private information about a company or its products. The following case cannot disclose product names. The case involves Brand X, a food item commonly sold nationally in grocery stores. Weekly, monthly, and quarterly data on various factors were collected over the previous five years for a large urban market. In other words, as many as 260 observations were collected for variables, including some variables that were found to be statistically significant and others that were found to be statistically insignificant. Data were entered into statistical software to obtain a multiple linear regression function. The purpose of a multiple regression is to determine and analyze the relationship between a dependent variable and each of a set of independent variables.

Based on data for a large urban market, a multiple linear regression function was estimated for Brand X. This function was unique to Brand X. Data on other products would result in a different function. The function for Brand X was

$$Q_X = 1.3 - 2.1P_X + 1.2P_S - 0.5P_C + 0.0002Y + 0.001A_X$$

Variables in the function are

Q_X=unit sales of Brand X, measured in thousands of units per week;

P_X=price of Brand X;

P_S=price of Brand S, a substitute for Brand X;

P_C=price of Product C, a complement for Brand X;

Y=per capita income; and

A_X=monthly advertising outlays on Brand X.

This algebraic expression is the sales function for Brand X. It establishes a relationship between unit sales of Brand X and the price of Brand X, unit sales of Brand X and the price of Brand S, unit sales of Brand X and the price of Product C, unit sales of Brand X and per capita income, as well as unit sales of Brand X and monthly outlays on Brand X advertising.

Often, a sales function is used to forecast unit sales. Substituting current values for the price of Brand X, the price of Brand S, the price of Product C, per capita income, and advertising outlays on Brand X, unit sales of Brand X can be forecast. The standalone number, 1.3, accounts for the cumulative effect of unspecified factors. Think of 1.3 as a kind of correction factor. After accounting for the effects on unit sales of Brand X due to the price of Brand X, the price of Brand S, the price of Product C, per capita income, and advertising outlays on Brand X, there is a remaining effect of unspecified factors on unit sales of Brand X. Unspecified factors might include population in the market for Brand X, number of grocery stores in the market for Brand X, advertising outlays on Brand S, and advertising outlays on Product C. The standalone number, 1.3, reflects the remaining effect of such unspecified factors. The positive 1.3 means that using current values for all of the specified variables in the sales function would result in underestimation of unit sales by that amount. Adding 1.3 corrects for the underestimation and thus makes forecasted unit sales closer to actual unit sales.

Interpretation of Coefficients

A negative coefficient indicates an inverse relationship, whereas a positive coefficient infers a direct relationship. Consider the coefficients in the sales function for Brand X. The coefficient for an independent variable indicates the amount by which unit sales of Brand X are expected to change as the result of a change in the independent variable. In mathematical notation, for example, the coefficient for P_X is $\Delta Q_X / \Delta P_X$, which is interpreted as the change in unit sales of Brand X when the price of Brand X changes. The coefficient for P_X is –2.1, which means that if the price of Brand X were increased by \$1, unit sales would decline by 2.1 thousand units (2,100) per week as the result of that change alone. If the price of Brand X were decreased by \$0.50, unit sales would increase by 1.05 thousand units (1,050) per week.

This interpretation can be generalized for each of the other coefficients. The numerator is always ΔQ_X, and the denominator is a change in one of the independent variables, P_X, P_S, P_C, Y, or A_X. Therefore, the coefficients are $\Delta Q_X / \Delta P_X$, $\Delta Q_X / \Delta P_S$, $\Delta Q_X / \Delta P_C$, $\Delta Q_X / \Delta Y$, and $\Delta Q_X / \Delta A_X$. Moreover, both the numerator and the denominator are always units, never percentages. The numerator is always unit change in sales, never percentage change in sales. The denominator is always the change in dollar units, never percentage change in dollar units. Now, other coefficients can be considered.

The coefficient for P_S is $\Delta Q_X / \Delta P_S$, which is +1.2. Since the coefficient is positive, a direct relationship is indicated. If the price of Brand S were increased by $1, unit sales of Brand X would increase by 1.2 thousand units (1,200) per week as a result of that change alone. If the price of Brand S were decreased by $0.25, unit sales of Brand X would decrease by 0.3 thousand units (300) per week.

The coefficient for P_C is $\Delta Q_X / \Delta P_C$, which is −0.5. Since the coefficient is negative, an inverse relationship is indicated. If the price of Product C were increased by $1, unit sales of Brand X would decrease by 0.5 thousand units (500) per week as a result of that change alone. If the price of Product C were decreased by $0.50, unit sales of Brand X would increase by 0.25 thousand units (250) per week.

The coefficient for Y is $\Delta Q_X / \Delta_Y$, which is +0.0002. Since positive, a direct relationship is indicated. If per capita income were to rise by $100, unit sales of Brand X would increase by 0.02 thousand units (20) per week as a result of that change alone. If per capita income were to fall by $200, unit sales of Brand X would decrease by 0.04 thousand units (40) per week.

The coefficient for A_X is $\Delta Q_X / \Delta A_X$, which is 0.001. Since positive, a direct relationship is indicated. If monthly advertising outlays on Brand X were increased by $1,000, unit sales of Brand X would increase by 1.0 thousand units (1,000) per week as a result of that change alone. If monthly advertising outlays on Brand X were reduced by $250, unit sales of Brand X would decrease by 0.25 thousand units (250) per week.

THE DEMAND FUNCTION FOR BRAND X

Unit sales of a product can be expressed as a function of the price of the product alone, holding the values of all other independent variables constant. In the same way, unit sales of a product can be graphed as a function of the price of the product alone, holding the values of all other independent variables constant. The result is called the demand function.

Suppose the price of Brand S, a substitute for Brand X, is $2; the price of Product C, a complement for Brand X, is $1; per capita income in the market is $15,000; and monthly advertising outlays on Brand X in the market are $500. By substitution, expected sales of Brand X can be stated as a relationship to the price of Brand X alone, which is

$Q_X = 1.3 - 2.1 P_X + 1.2(2) - 0.5(1) + 0.0002(15,000) + 0.001(500)$

$Q_X = 1.3 - 2.1 P_X + 2.4 - 0.5 + 3.0 + 0.5$

$Q_X = 6.7 - 2.1 P_X$

This demand function expresses the relationship between unit sales of Brand X and the price of Brand X alone. The dependent variable is unit sales of Brand X, and the independent variable is the price of Brand X. When graphed, the intercept on the vertical axis is 6.7, and the slope is −2.1. The inverse relationship between unit sales of Brand X and the price of Brand X is indicated by the minus sign of the coefficient and the negative slope when graphed. The demand function for Brand X is graphed in Figure 2.1. Unit sales of Brand X (Q_X) are graphed as the dependent variable on the vertical axis, and the price of Brand X (P_X) is graphed on the horizontal axis. In other words, unit sales of Brand X depend on the price of Brand X. The vertical intercept is 6.7, and the slope is −2.1.

FIGURE 2.1
DEMAND FUNCTION FOR BRAND X

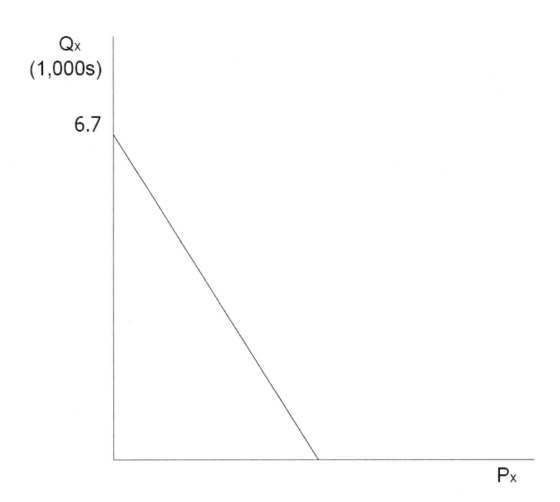

THE DEMAND CURVE FOR BRAND X

In business practice, graphs of demand ordinarily are depicted with price as the dependent variable and unit sales as the independent variable. In other words, price is measured on the vertical axis and unit sales on the horizontal axis. Therefore, the demand function must be restated with price on the left of the equation so that price appears as the dependent variable and with unit sales on the right of the equation so that unit sales appear as the independent variable. The result is the demand curve for Brand X.

With a little algebraic manipulation, an equation for the demand curve for Brand X can be obtained and graphed. Recall the relationship between unit sales of Brand X and the price of Brand X alone, which is the demand function for Brand X:

$Q_X = 6.7 - 2.1P_X$

Solving for P_X,

$2.1P_X = 6.7 - Q_X$

$P_X = (6.7/2.1) - (1/2.1)Q_X$

$P_X = 3.19 - 0.48Q_X$

When graphed, this function is the demand curve for Brand X. The demand curve for Brand X implies that the price of Brand X depends on unit sales of Brand X, which is backwards. Unit sales of Brand X depend on the price of Brand X.

When the demand curve is graphed, the intercept on the vertical axis is 3.19, and the slope is −0.48. The vertical intercept of the demand curve (3.19) is the price at which expected sales would be zero. In the same way, the intercept on the horizontal axis of the demand curve (6.7) is expected sales if the price is zero. Of course, unit sales of 0.00 and price of $0.00 are a kind of statistical fiction that is the nature of linear functions. All sales and price data come from prices and unit sales over a particular range distinctly apart from the intercepts. The graph of the demand curve for Brand X is shown in Figure 2.2.

FIGURE 2.2
DEMAND CURVE FOR BRAND X

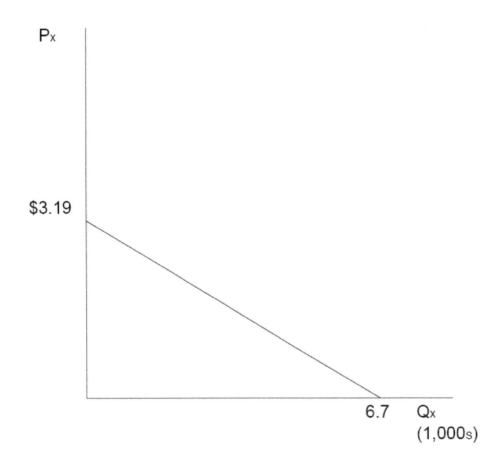

THE DEMAND SCHEDULE FOR BRAND X

In economics, tables showing amounts of a product that would be purchased at various prices, *ceteris paribus,* are called demand schedules. Consider the sales function for Brand X, bearing in mind that the price of Brand S is held constant at $2, the price of Product C is held constant at $1, the level of income is held constant at $15,000 per capita and monthly advertising outlays on Brand X are held constant at $500. By substituting various prices for Brand X into the sales function, demand function, or demand curve for Brand X, a demand schedule or table can be developed to show the relationship between unit sales of Brand X and the price of Brand X. Consider the following table, Table 2.3, which is a demand schedule for Brand X. Table 2.3 shows expected unit sales of Brand X at various selected prices of Brand X.

Table 2.3 Demand Schedule for Brand X	
Price of Brand X	**Unit Sales of Brand X (1,000s)**
$3.19	0.00
$3.00	0.40
$2.50	1.45
$2.00	2.50
$1.50	3.55
$1.00	4.60
$0.50	5.65
$0.00	6.70

INCREASE IN DEMAND FOR BRAND X

Clearly, unit sales of Brand X could be increased if the price of Brand X is lowered. For example, if the price of Brand X were reduced from $2 to $1.50, unit sales would be increased from 2,500 units to 3,550 units per week. Demand for Brand X has not increased. Given the demand for Brand X, unit sales increased because the price of Brand X has been reduced. Figure 2.3 illustrates this point that with given demand for Brand X represented by the demand curve, unit sales increase from 2,500 to 3,550 per week.

On the other hand, suppose the price of Brand X is $2. Yet, unit sales nonetheless increase from 2,500 units to 3,100 units per week. This increase in unit sales of Brand X at a price of $2 is not attributable to a reduction in the price of Brand X. The demand for Brand X must have increased. In other words, the demand curve for Brand X must have shifted to the right. Indeed, at any price of Brand X, unit sales presumably would be greater than before, which means that a new relationship or pattern of unit sales with respect to price is established.

FIGURE 2.3
INCREASE IN UNIT SALES OF BRAND X

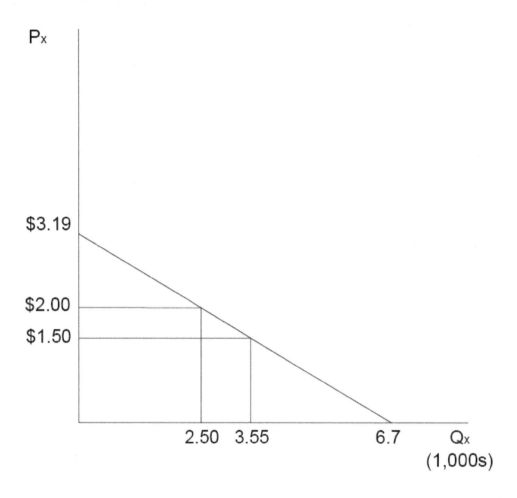

On the other hand, suppose the price of Brand X is $2. Yet, unit sales nonetheless increase from 2,500 units to 3,100 units per week. This increase in unit sales of Brand X at a price of $2 is not attributable to a reduction in the price of Brand X. The demand for Brand X must have increased. In other words, the demand curve for Brand X must have shifted to the right. Indeed, at any price of Brand X, unit sales presumably would be greater than before, which means that a new relationship or pattern of unit sales with respect to price is established.

Increases in demand are cases in which one or more of the independent variables other than price changes, and the result is an increase in the intercept term and a rightward shift in the linear demand curve. With no change in the price of Brand X, an increase in the price of Brand S, a decrease in the price of Product C, an increase in per capita income, or an increase in monthly advertising outlays on Brand X would increase unit sales of Brand X at the given price of Brand X. For example, suppose the price of Brand S, which is a substitute for Brand X, is increased from $2 to $2.50. By substitution into the sales function, the demand function is

$$Q_X = 1.3 - 2.1P_X + 1.2(2.50) - 0.5(1) + 0.0002(15,000) + 0.001(500)$$

$$Q_X = 1.3 - 2.1P_X + 3 - 0.5 + 3 + 0.5$$

$$Q_X = 7.3 - 2.1P_X$$

Notice that the coefficient for P_X, which is –2.1, has not changed. The effect of a change in one of the independent variables, which in this case is an increase in the price of a substitute product, is to change the vertical intercept term from 6.7 to 7.3. Since the intercept term now is greater than before the change in P_S, the entire demand function evidently has shifted to the right, meaning that the demand for Brand X has increased. Figure 2.4 is a graph that shows the new demand function to the right of the old demand function. The shift of the demand function to the right is a result of the increased price of Brand S.

To see this point in a step-by-step way, consider an example of two competing breakfast cereals, Brand X and Brand S. If the price of Brand S cereal is increased at a time when the price of Brand X cereal is unchanged, unit sales of Brand S cereal would be expected to decline as some buyers of breakfast cereal switch their purchases from Brand S cereal to Brand X cereal. Therefore, unit sales of Brand X increase when the price of Brand S cereal is increased even though the price of Brand X cereal has not changed. This kind of relationship between unit sales of Brand X and the price of Brand S can be seen in the sales function for Brand X. The coefficient for P_S is positive, meaning that unit sales of Brand X are expected to move in the same direction as the price of Brand S, unit sales of Brand X increasing when P_S is increased and unit sales of Brand X decreasing when P_S is decreased.

FIGURE 2.4
SHIFT OF DEMAND FUNCTION TO THE RIGHT

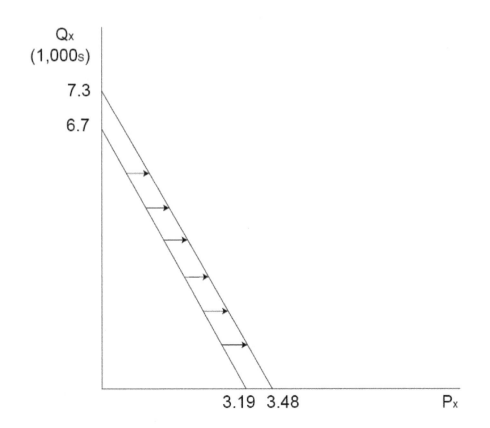

Shift of the Demand Curve for Brand X to the Right

This new relationship between sales of Brand X and the price of Brand X can be expressed with P_X as the dependent variable. With respect to P_X, the demand curve is

$Q_X = 7.3 - 2.1P_X$

$2.1P_X = 7.3 - Q_X$

$P_X = 3.48 - 0.48Q_X$

When graphed, the demand curve is now located to the right of the previous demand curve. This rightward shift in the demand curve for Brand X is what is meant by an increase in demand. A mere movement down and along the given demand curve for a product due to a decrease in the price of the product itself is not an increase in demand. An increase in demand means an increase in expected unit sales even with no change in price. For example, at the price of $2, unit sales increase from 2.5 thousand to 3.10 thousand. This increase in unit sales with no change in price represents an increase in demand. On the other hand, reducing the price from $2 to $1.50 would increase unit sales from 2.5 thousand to 3.55 thousand, which is a movement down and along unchanged demand rather than an increase in demand. Figure 2.5 shows the rightward shift of the demand curve, which indicates an increase in demand for Brand X.

FIGURE 2.5
SHIFT OF DEMAND CURVE TO THE RIGHT

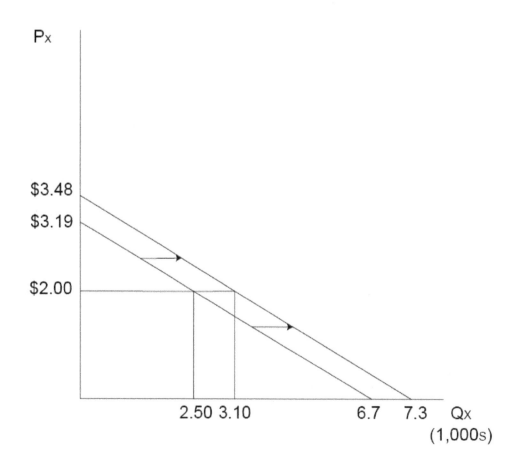

In the fewest and simplest words, a demand curve establishes the relationship between the price of a product and unit sales of the product. Any change in price, say a decrease in price, results in movement along the demand curve, down the demand curve in the case of a decrease in price. Any change in factors other than price results in a shift rightward or a shift leftward in the demand curve. An increase in the price of a substitute product, a decrease in the price of a complementary product, an increase in per capita income if the product is a normal good, or an increase in monthly advertising outlays will result in a rightward shift in the demand curve.

Reconsider the demand schedule illustrated above in Table 2.3. The amounts of Brand X that would be purchased at various prices when P_s is $2 can be compared to amounts that would be purchased when P_s is $2.50. This comparison is shown in the following table, Table 2.4. Notice that unit sales of Brand X when P_s is $2.50 are greater at any price of Brand X by comparison to unit sales of Brand X when P_s is $2. This observation is the meaning of an increase in demand.

Table 2.4 Comparative Demand Schedules for Brand X With Respect to an Increase in P_s		
Price of Brand X	**Unit Sales of Brand X** $P_s=\$2.00$ $Q_x=6.7-2.1P_x$ **(1,000s)**	**Unit Sales of Brand X** $P_s=\$2.50$ $Q_x=7.3-2.1P_x$ **(1,000s)**
$3.48	NA	0.00
$3.19	0.00	0.60
$3.00	0.40	1.00
$2.50	1.45	2.05
$2.00	2.50	3.10
$1.50	3.55	4.15
$1.00	4.60	5.20
$0.50	5.65	6.25
$0.00	6.70	7.30

NA: Not applicable since sales would be negative

DECREASE IN DEMAND FOR BRAND X

If the price of Brand X were increased, unit sales of Brand X would decline. For example, if the price of Brand X were increased from $2 to $2.50, unit sales would decline from 2,500 units to 1,450 units per week. Demand for Brand X has not decreased. Given the demand for Brand X, unit sales have decreased because the price of Brand X has been increased. On the other hand, suppose that the price of Brand X is $2, and unit sales nonetheless decrease from 2,500 units to 2,400 units per week. This reduction in unit sales of Brand X at the price of $2 is not attributable to an increase in the price of Brand X. The demand for Brand X must have decreased.

Decreases in demand are cases in which one of the independent variables other than price changes. The result is a decrease in the intercept term and a leftward shift in the linear demand curve. With no change in the price of Brand X, a decrease in the price of Brand S, an increase in the price of Product C, a decrease in per capita income, or a decrease in monthly advertising outlays on Brand X would decrease unit sales of Brand X. For example, suppose per capita income falls from \$15,000 to \$14,500. By substitution, the demand function is

$Q_X=1.3-2.1P_X+1.2(2)-0.5(1)+0.0002(14,500)+0.001(500)$

$Q_X=1.3-2.1P_X+2.4-0.5+2.9+0.5$

$Q_X=6.6-2.1P_X$

Notice that the coefficient for P_X, which is –2.1, has not changed. The effect of a change in one of the independent variables, which in this case is a decrease in per capita income, is to change the intercept term from 6.7 to 6.6. Since the intercept term now is less than before the decline in income, the demand for Brand X is less than before, meaning that the entire demand function has shifted to the left. This relationship can be seen in the sales function itself. The coefficient for income is positive, which means that unit sales of Brand X are expected to move in the same direction as changes in per capita income, unit sales increasing when per capita income increases and decreasing when per capita income decreases. Figure 2.6 is a graph of the new demand function, which shows the leftward shift and thus a decrease in the demand for Brand X.

FIGURE 2.6
SHIFT OF DEMAND FUNCTION TO THE LEFT

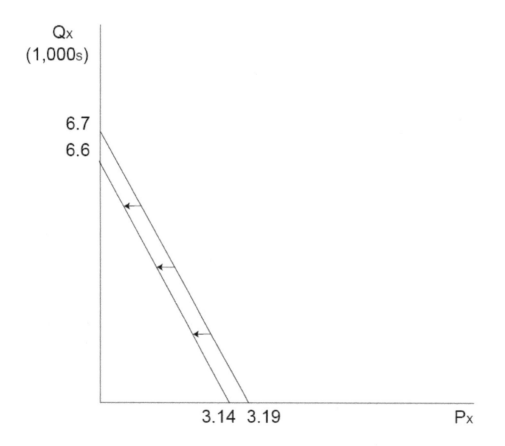

Shift of the Demand Curve for Brand X to the Left

This new relationship between sales of Brand X and the price of Brand X can be expressed with P_X as the dependent variable. With respect to P_X, the demand curve is

$Q_X = 6.6 - 2.1P_X$

$2.1P_X = 6.6 - Q_X$

$P_X = 3.14 - 0.48Q_X$

When graphed, the demand curve is now located to the left and parallel to the previous demand curve. This leftward shift in the demand curve for Brand X is what is meant by a decrease in demand. A mere movement up and along the given demand curve for a product due to an increase in the price of the product itself is not a decrease in demand. Demand refers to a relationship, whereas quantity demanded is an amount. A decrease in demand means a decrease in expected unit sales even with no change in price. For example, at the price of $2, unit sales decrease from 2.5 thousand to 2.4 thousand. This decrease in unit sales with no change in price represents a decrease in demand. On the other hand, increasing the price from $2 to $2.50 would decrease unit sales from 2.5 thousand to 1.45 thousand, which is a movement up and along unchanged demand rather than an increase in demand. Figure 2.7 shows the leftward shift of the demand curve for Brand X.

FIGURE 2.7
SHIFT OF DEMAND CURVE TO THE LEFT

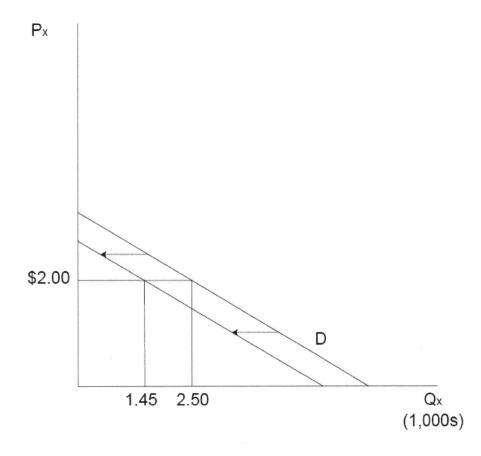

Once again, in the fewest and simplest words, a demand curve establishes a relationship between the price of a product and unit sales of the product. Any change in price, say an increase in price, results in movement along the demand curve, up and along the demand curve in the case of an increase in price. Any change in factors other than price results in a shift rightward or leftward in the demand curve. A decrease in the price of a substitute product, an increase in the price of a complementary product, a decrease in per capita income if the product is a normal good, or a decrease in monthly advertising outlays will result in a leftward shift in the demand curve.

Reconsider the demand schedule originally illustrated above in Table 2.3. The amounts of Brand X that would be purchased at various selected prices of Brand X when per capita income is $15,000 can be compared to amounts that would be purchased when per capita income is $14,500. This comparison is shown below in Table 2.5. Notice that unit sales of Brand X at any price of Brand X when income is $14,500 is less than at any price when income is $15,000. This observation is the meaning of a decrease in demand.

Table 2.5 Comparative Demand Schedules for Brand X With Respect to a Decrease in Per Capita Income		
Price of Brand X	Unit Sales of Brand X $Y=\$15,000$ $Q_x=6.7-2.1P_x$ (1,000s)	Unit Sales of Brand X $Y=\$14,500$ $Q_x=6.6-2.1P_x$ (1,000s)
$3.19	0.00	NA
$3.00	0.40	0.30
$2.50	1.45	1.35
$2.00	2.50	2.40
$1.50	3.55	3.45
$1.00	4.60	4.50
$0.50	5.65	5.55
$0.00	6.70	6.60

NA: Not applicable since sales would be negative

A SUMMARY STATEMENT ABOUT CHANGES IN DEMAND

Consider that demand is a relationship between price and unit sales. Given the demand curve for a product, a change in price of the product is a movement up or down the given demand curve. After all, the demand curve establishes the relationship between price and unit sales with other factors held constant at fixed values. On the other hand, a change in some factor other than price will shift the demand curve to the right or to the left. Increases in demand are rightward shifts in the demand curve as the result of (1) an increase in the price of a substitute product, (2) a decrease in the price of a complementary product, (3) an increase in per capita income if the product is a normal good, (4) an increase in monthly advertising outlays on the product, or (5) changes in other unspecified factors that favorably influence the amounts of a product buyers want to purchase at various prices of the product itself. Decreases in demand are leftward shifts in the demand curve as the result of (1) a decrease in the price of a substitute product, (2) an increase in the price of a complementary product, (3) a decrease in per capita income if the product is a normal good, (4) a decrease in monthly advertising outlays on the product, or (5) changes in other unspecified factors that unfavorably influence the amounts of a product buyers want to purchase at various prices of the product itself. These changes in demand for Brand X are summarized in Table 2.6.

Table 2.6 Changes in Demand for Brand X	
Increase in Demand for Brand X	**Decrease in Demand for Brand X**
Increase in the Price of Brand S	Decrease in the Price of Brand S
Decrease in the Price of Product C	Increase in the Price of Product C
Increase in Per Capita Income	Decrease in Per Capita Income
Increase in Advertising Outlays on Brand X	Decrease in Advertising Outlays on Brand X
Favorable Changes in Unspecified Factors	Unfavorable Changes in Unspecified Factors

The point is that a change in the price of the product itself does not cause either an increase or a decrease in the demand for the product, and a change in the price of the product itself does not shift the demand curve for the product to the right or to the left. Since the demand curve for a product is a relationship between price and unit sales, a change in the price of the product results in movement up or down the demand curve. Changes in any other relevant factor result in a shift in the demand curve to the right or to the left, meaning an increase or decrease in demand.

Therefore, changes in the price of Brand X cause an increase or decrease in unit sales with unchanged demand for Brand X, depicted as movement up or down the demand curve. Changes in the price of Brand S, the price of Product C, per capita income, or weekly advertising outlays on Brand X will shift the demand curve for Brand X to the right or to the left, depicting an increase or decrease in the demand for Brand X.

DIFFERENT FORMS OF ESTIMATED DEMAND

Sales functions, demand functions, and demand curves for many different kinds of products and services are estimated for business and public policy purposes. However, access to estimated functions for business purposes is virtually denied to the general public. These estimated functions are proprietary and thus private information, and access to them is strictly limited to internal uses.

A trade association is an organization formed to promote the common interests of companies in an industry. Trade associations provide services for their members, including analysis, statistics, and other information. Trade associations also lobby local, state, and federal government officials on behalf of legislation that favors the industry and opposition to legislation that harms the industry. Examples of trade associations are the American Bakers Association, National Milk Producers Federation, National Beer Wholesalers Association, and Dairy Farmers of America. Results of any analysis of data, including estimated sales functions, demand functions, or demand curves would be subject to nondisclosure and "eyes only" access to its membership. On the other hand, a product manager might engage consultants or direct internal staff members to estimate the sales and demand functions for the product under his or her supervision. Again, the results would be considered private information. Such information is vital for purposes of strategy, whether aggressive or defensive in nature. The product manager would not want such information to fall into the hands of the enemy, which is the competition.

In some cases, however, sales functions and related demand functions are published in popular, practitioner, academic, or government periodicals. Some of these estimated functions take the conventional form like those expressed for Brand X. However, estimated sales functions often depart from the standard form, but the departure is more apparent than real. In other words, estimated functions might look different, but they are nonetheless sales and demand functions.

Demand for Sweet Potatoes

Demand for various agricultural commodities has been estimated routinely for many years. In many cases, the estimated functions take the conventional form. In other cases, estimated functions include unusual variables. For example, one study estimated the demand for sweet potatoes and accounted for a time trend.[13] The equivalent of a sales function was

$$Q = 7{,}609 - 1{,}606 P_S + 59 POP + 947Y + 479 P_S - 271T$$

The variables were

Q=quantity of sweet potatoes sold per year in the United States per 1,000 hundredweight (cwt);

P_S=real dollar price of sweet potatoes per hundredweight received by farmers;

POP=two-year moving average of total U.S. population, in millions;

Y=real per capita personal disposable income, in thousands of dollars;

P_S=real dollar price of white potatoes per hundredweight received by farmers; and

T=a time trend (T=1 for 1949, T=2 for 1950,…, T=24 for 1972).

This estimated demand for sweet potatoes indicates that the quantity of sweet potatoes demanded per year in 1,000 hundred weight (100,000) units declines by 1,606 for each \$1 increase in the price of sweet potatoes, increases by 59 for each one million increase in population, increases by 947 for each \$1,000 increase in real per capita income, increases by 497 for each \$1 increase in the price of white potatoes, and declines 271 for each year since 1949.

The study indicated standard results: an inverse relationship between sales of sweet potatoes and the price of sweet potatoes; a direct relationship between unit sales and population; a direct relationship between unit sales and income, indicating that sweet potatoes are a normal good; and a direct relationship between unit sales of sweet potatoes and the price of white potatoes, indicating that white potatoes are a substitute for sweet potatoes. In addition to these standard results, the negative sign for the trend coefficient clearly indicates that passage of time alone has a negative effect on sales of sweet potatoes. Other factors may have a positive effect on unit sales of sweet potatoes, but the time trend has a negative effect. Consequently, unit sales of sweet potatoes can increase despite the negative effect of the time trend.

---

13   Ronald A. Schrimper and Gene A. Mathia, "Reservation and Market Demands for Sweet Potatoes at the Farm Level," *American Journal of Agricultural Economics*, 57 (February 1975).

QUANTITY SUPPLIED AND SUPPLY

The amount of a product that producers want to sell at a particular price, given all other factors that influence their willingness and ability to produce, is called the quantity supplied. For example, the amount of South Louisiana sweet crude oil that producers offer for sale at $100 per barrel is the quantity of such petroleum supplied. On the other hand, amounts that would be supplied at various prices establish a relationship between quantities supplied and price. Functions, tables, and graphs used to indicate amounts that would be produced and offered for sale at various prices, other things being equal, are called the supply of the product. Recall the Latin phrase, *ceteris paribus*. In the case of supply, many factors are involved in determining the amounts expected to be produced and offered for sale at various prices. The supply of a product is amounts that would be produced and offered for sale at various prices of a product with each of the other factors held constant at fixed values.

To summarize, supply is amounts (plural) that would be produced and offered for sale at various prices (plural). In this way, supply, which is amounts expected to be produced and offered for sale at various prices, is seen to be different from quantity supplied, which is an amount expected to be produced and offered for sale at a particular price. Supply establishes a pattern, a relationship between prices and amounts produced and offered for sale. Supply is descriptive of a relationship, not an amount. Quantity supplied is descriptive of an amount, not a relationship.

HOW MUCH DO SELLERS WANT TO OFFER FOR SALE?

The relationship between amounts produced and offered for sale can be expressed as a simple list of everything that might influence the amount of the product produced and offered for sale. For example, the most important factors on the list might be the number of sellers in the market and factors dealing with profitability such as the cost of materials, price of the product, and prices of other products that could be produced with the same workers, equipment, and materials. Other factors also might be involved in the determination of amounts offered for purchase, but these factors are less important. In general, therefore, this list can be stated functionally with amounts produced and offered for sale as the dependent variable and factors that influence such amounts as independent variables. When done, the functional form might be

$$Q_1 = f(N, P_{IN}, T, P_1, P_2, U)$$

The variables are

Q_1=quantity of Product 1 supplied;

N=number of firms producing Product 1;

P_{IN}=prices of inputs used in producing Product 1;

T=technology used in producing Product 1;

P_1=price of Product 1;

P_2=price of another product that could be produced with the same inputs used in producing Product 1; and

U=unspecified factors.

The number of firms in an industry influences the amount of a product produced and offered for sale. The relationship is direct, meaning the more firms in the industry, the greater the amount produced and offered for sale. Business firms are motivated by profit, and businesses develop strategies to make the most profit while producing and selling products. Anything that happens to increase profitability in an industry will motivate entry into the industry and a greater amount of the product produced and offered for sale by incumbent firms. On the other hand, anything that diminishes profitability in an industry motivates exit and a smaller amount of the product produced and offered for sale by incumbent firms. For example, an increase in the cost per unit of an input used in producing a product adversely affects profitability unless price increases correspondingly. Adverse effects on profitability would be expected to decrease the amount of the product produced and offered for sale at a particular price. This inverse relationship means that the amount of a product produced and offered for sale varies inversely with respect to the costs per unit of inputs used in producing the product. A change in technology favoring production costs of a product also favors profitability and would increase the amount of the product produced and offered for sale. This relationship is direct.

The Law of Supply

The price of the product itself affects profitability. *Ceteris paribus*, a higher price favors profitability and increases the amount of the product produced and offered for sale, and a lower price disfavors profitability and decreases the amount of the product produced and offered for sale. The relationship between price of a product and amount of the product produced and offered for sale is direct. An increase in price has a positive effect on amount produced and offered for sale, and a decrease in price has a negative effect on amount produced and offered for sale. This relationship is known as the law of supply.

Relative Profitability

Consider two products, say, corn and soybeans. Take for granted that corn and soybeans can be produced with the same inputs. The same land, same fertilizer, same machinery, and same workers can be used to produce either corn or soybeans. Suppose the price of soybeans falls significantly while the price of corn is unchanged. The fall in price reduces the profitability of soybeans, and some of the inputs used to produce soybeans will be redeployed to production of corn even though the price of corn was unchanged. On the other hand, an increase in the price of soybeans will increase the profitability of producing soybeans. Consequently, some inputs used to produce corn will be redeployed to soybeans. This inverse relationship indicates that the higher the price of soybeans, the lower the amount of corn produced and offered for sale. The lower the price of soybeans, the greater amount of corn produced and offered for sale. When the profitability of producing soybeans increases relative to the profitability of producing corn, the effect is an increase in the supply of soybeans and a decrease in the supply of corn. When the profitability of producing soybeans decreases relative to the profitability of producing corn, the effect is a decrease in the supply of soybeans and an increase in the supply of corn.

THE SUPPLY FUNCTION FOR WHEAT

Using statistics, linear supply functions have been estimated. These functions estimate the relationship between amounts produced and offered for sale and factors such as those identified above. For example, the relationship for U.S. wheat was estimated using data from 1975 to 1979 with focus on wheat and coarse grain.[14] Coarse grain includes corn, barley, oats, and soybeans. With respect to the price of wheat and the price of coarse grain, the functional relationship was estimated as

$$Q_{SW}=74.3893+0.1504P_S-0.1445P_G$$

The variables are

Q_{SW}=amount of wheat produced and offered for sale, measured in millions of tons;

P_S=price per ton of wheat; and

P_G=price per ton of coarse grain.

The coefficient for each variable indicates how much the amount of wheat produced and offered for sale is expected to change as the result of a change in the variable. The coefficient for P_S is $\Delta Q_{SW}/\Delta P_S$, which is interpreted as the change in amount of wheat produced and offered for sale when the price of wheat changes. The coefficient for P_S is +0.1504, which means that if the price of wheat were to increase by $1 per ton, the amount of wheat produced and offered for sale would increase by 0.1504 million tons (150,400 tons). The coefficient for P_G is $\Delta Q_{SW}/\Delta P_G$, which is interpreted as the change in amount of wheat produced and offered for sale when the price of coarse grain changes. The coefficient for P_G is −0.1445, which means that if the price of coarse grain were to increase by $1 per ton, the amount of wheat produced and offered for sales would decrease by 0.1445 million tons (144,500 tons). The main reason for this decrease is that some wheat producers switch from producing wheat to producing other coarse grains such as corn or soybeans.

Suppose the price of coarse grain (P_G) is $80 per ton. By substitution, the amount of wheat that would be produced and sold can be expressed as a relationship to the price of wheat alone, which is

$$Q_{SW}=74.3893+0.1504P_S-0.1445(80)$$

$$Q_{SW}=74.3893+0.1504P_S-11.56$$

$$Q_{SW}=62.8293+0.1504P_S$$

This function is the supply function for wheat. When this supply function for wheat is graphed, quantity of wheat supplied is the dependent variable measured on the vertical axis, and the price of wheat is the independent variable measured on the horizontal axis. The intercept on the ordinate is 62.83 when rounded, and the slope is +0.1504. Clearly, the relationship between amounts of wheat produced and offered for sale and the price of wheat is direct, which is indicated by the plus sign in the price coefficient and the positive slope when graphed. The supply function for wheat is graphed in Figure 2.8.

---

14   The following supply function is adapted from Philip L. Paarlberg and Robert L. Thompson, "Interrelated Production and the Effects of an Import Tariff," *Agricultural Economics Research*, 32 (October 1980), pp. 21-32.

FIGURE 2.8
SUPPLY FUNCTION FOR WHEAT

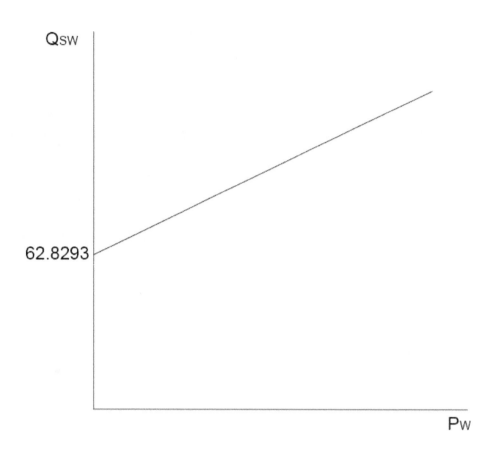

THE SUPPLY CURVE FOR WHEAT

The supply function for wheat also can be expressed as though the price of wheat is the dependent variable and quantity of wheat supplied the independent variable. To do so, the supply function is solved for price. In the present case of wheat, the result is

$$Q_{sw}=62.8293+0.1504P_s$$

$$-0.1504\,P_s=62.8293-Q_{sw}$$

$$P_s=-417.7480+6.6489Q_{sw}$$

When graphed, this function is the supply curve for wheat. The price of wheat is measured on the vertical axis and the amount of wheat produced and offered for sale on the horizontal axis. The intercept on the ordinate is -417.7480, and the slope is $+6.6489$. Actually, however, the intercept on the vertical axis is of no interest because it indicates a negative price. Perhaps in a parallel universe where production of wheat is governed by anti-prices rather than prices, this negative price would have some meaning. In actual experience, negative prices have no interpretation. Therefore, interest is limited to amounts that would be produced at prices ranging from zero up. Even a price of zero is of little interest. All of the price data probably fell within a narrow range of no more than $110 per ton and no less than $90 per ton.

To solve for this intercept on the horizontal axis, the equation is solved for a price of zero, which is

$$0 = -417.7480 + 6.6489Q_{SW}$$

$$-6.6489Q_{SW} = -417.7480$$

$$Q_{SW} = 62.83$$

The supply curve intersects the horizontal axis at 62.83 million tons, and the slope remains +6.6489 as calculated above. The supply curve for wheat is graphed in Figure 2.9.

FIGURE 2.9
SUPPLY CURVE FOR WHEAT

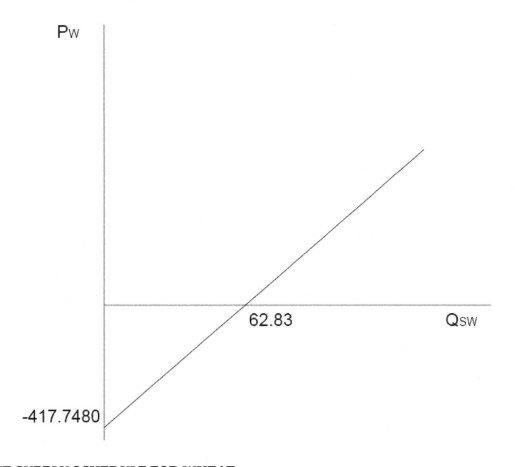

THE SUPPLY SCHEDULE FOR WHEAT

In economics, a table showing the amounts that would be produced and offered for sale at various prices is called a supply schedule. By substituting various prices into the supply function, a table can be developed to show the relationship between amounts of wheat produced and offered for sale and the price of wheat. The supply schedule shown below in Table 2.7 depicts amounts of wheat supplied at selected prices.

Table 2.7 Supply Schedule for Wheat	
Price of Wheat Per Ton	**Amount of Wheat (Millions of Tons)**
$200	92.91
$175	89.15
$150	85.39
$125	81.63
$100	77.87
$75	74.11
$50	70.35
$25	66.59
$0	62.83

INCREASES IN THE SUPPLY OF WHEAT

Changes in supply are cases in which one of the factors other than the price of the product changes so that the result is a change in the intercept and a rightward or leftward shift in the supply curve. For example, recall the supply function for wheat when the price of coarse grain (P_G) is $80 per ton:

$Q_{SW}=62.8293+0.1504P_S$

When expressed with the price of wheat as though it is the dependent variable, the equation for the supply curve for wheat is

$P_S=-417.7480+6.6489Q_{SW}$

Now, suppose the price of coarse grain falls to half its previous level. When P_G is $40, the supply function for wheat would be

$Q_{SW}=74.3893+0.1504P_S-0.1445(40)$

$Q_{SW}=74.3893+0.1504P_S-5.7800$

$Q_{SW}=68.6093+0.1504P_S$

The new supply function for wheat is graphed in Figure 2.10. When rounded, the intercept is 68.53.

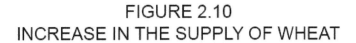

FIGURE 2.10
INCREASE IN THE SUPPLY OF WHEAT

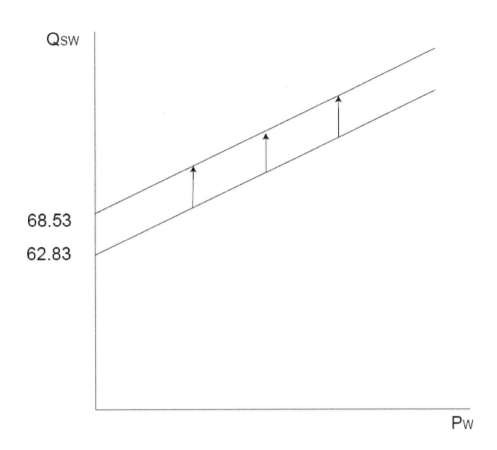

Shift of the Supply Curve for Wheat to the Right

This new relationship between the amounts of wheat produced and the price of wheat can be expressed with the price of wheat as the dependent variable. With respect to P_S,

$$Q_{SW}=68.5284+0.1504P_S$$

$$-0.1504P_S=68.6093-Q_{SW}$$

$$P_S=-456.1789+6.6489Q_{SW}$$

When graphed, this function is the new supply curve for wheat. When graphed, the supply curve is now located to the right of the previous supply curve. This rightward shift in the supply curve is what is meant by an increase in the supply. A mere movement up and along the existing supply curve for a product due to a higher price of the product itself is not an increase in supply. An increase in supply means an increase in expected amount of product produced and offered for sale even with no change in price of the product itself. Figure 2.11 shows the rightward shift of the supply curve for wheat, which represents an increase in supply.

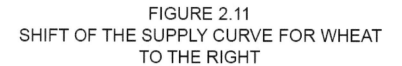

FIGURE 2.11
SHIFT OF THE SUPPLY CURVE FOR WHEAT
TO THE RIGHT

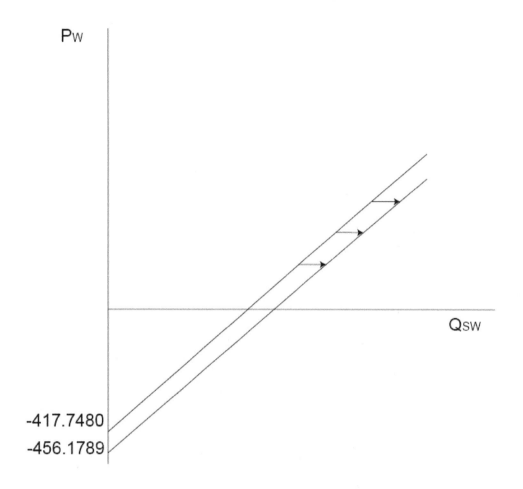

For example, at the price of $100 per ton of wheat and the price of coarse grain is $80 per ton, the amount of wheat produced and offered for sale is 77.87 million tons, but when the price of coarse grain falls from $80 to $40, the amount of wheat produced and offered for sale at the price of $100 per ton of wheat increases to 83.65 million tons. This increase in tons of wheat produced and offered for sale at the price of $100 per ton of wheat is an increase in supply. On the other hand, if the price of wheat rises from $100 per ton to $125 per ton while the price of coarse grain is $80 per ton, the amount of wheat produced and offered for sale increases from 77.87 million tons to 81.63 million tons. This increase in the amount of wheat produced and offered for sale is not the result of an increase in supply. Given the supply of wheat, more wheat is produced and offered for sale when the price rises, depicted as a movement up and along the given supply curve for wheat.

In the fewest and simplest words, a supply curve establishes a relationship between the price of a product and amount of the product produced and offered for sale. An increase in price results in movement up and along the supply curve. Any change in factors other than price results in a shift rightward or leftward in the supply curve. A decrease in the price of another product that can be produced with the same inputs, for example, will result in a rightward shift in the supply curve.

Reconsider the supply schedule illustrated above in Table 2.7. The amounts of wheat that would be produced and offered for sale at various prices when the price of coarse grain is $80 can be compared to amounts of wheat that would be supplied when the price of coarse grain is $40. This comparison is shown in Table 2.8. Notice that the amount of wheat produced and offered for sale when P_G is $40 is greater at any price of wheat by comparison to the amount of wheat produced and offered for sale when P_G is $80. This observation is the meaning of an increase in supply.

	Table 2.8 Comparative Supply Schedules for Wheat With Respect to a Decrease in P_G		
Price of Wheat Per Ton	**Amount of Wheat (Millions of Tons) P_G=$80 Q_{SW}=62.8293+0.1504P_S**	**Amount of Wheat (Millions of Tons) P_G=$40 Q_{SW}=68.6093+0.1504P_S**
$200	92.91	98.69
$175	89.15	94.93
$150	85.39	91.17
$125	81.63	87.41
$100	77.87	83.65
$75	74.11	79.89
$50	70.35	76.13
$25	66.59	72.37
$0	62.83	68.61

DECREASES IN THE SUPPLY OF WHEAT

To restate a point made previously in regard to increases in supply, changes in supply are cases in which one of the factors other than the price of the product changes so that the result is a change in the intercept and a rightward or leftward shift in the supply curve. For example, recall that the supply function for wheat when the price of coarse grain (P_G) is $80, is

Q_{SW}=62.8293+0.1504P_S

Expressed with the price of wheat as though it is the dependent variable, the equation for the supply curve for wheat is

P_S=−417.7480+6.6489Q_{SW}

Now, suppose the price of coarse grain rises to twice its present level. When P_G is $160, the supply function for wheat would be

Q_{SW}=74.3893+0.1504P_S−0.1445(160)

Q_{SW}=74.3893+0.1504P_S−23.1200

Q_{SW}=51.2693+0.1504P_S

The new supply function for wheat when the price of coarse grain is $160 lies to the left of and parallel to the supply function for wheat when the price of coarse grain is $80. The leftward shift of the supply function, which indicates a decrease in the supply of wheat, is shown in Figure 2.12.

FIGURE 2.12
DECREASE IN THE SUPPLY OF WHEAT

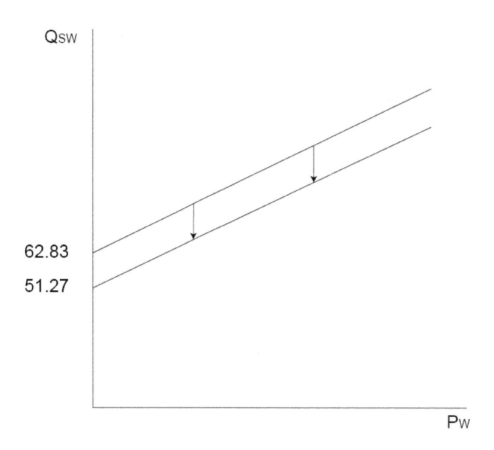

Shift of the Supply Curve for Wheat to the Left

This new relationship between the amounts of wheat produced and the price of wheat can be expressed with the price of wheat as the dependent variable. With respect to P_S,

$Q_{SW} = 51.2693 + 0.1504 P_S$

$-0.1504 P_S = 51.2693 - Q_{SW}$

$P_S = -340.8863 + 6.6489 Q_{SW}$

When graphed, this function is the new supply curve for wheat. The supply curve is now located to the left and parallel to the previous supply curve. This leftward shift in the supply curve is what is meant by a decrease in the supply. A mere movement down and along the existing supply curve for a product due to a lower price of the product is not a decrease in supply. A decrease in supply means a decrease in expected amount of product produced and offered for sale even with no change in price of the product itself. Figure 2.13 shows the leftward shift of the supply curve for wheat, indicating a decrease in the supply of wheat.

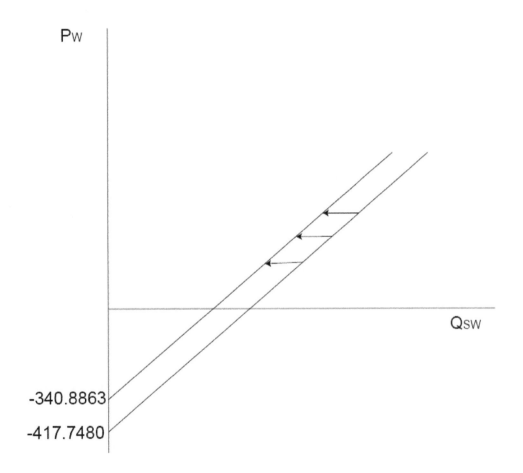

FIGURE 2.13
SHIFT OF THE SUPPLY CURVE FOR WHEAT
TO THE LEFT

For example, when the price of wheat is $100 per ton and the price of coarse grain is $80 per ton, the amount of wheat produced and offered for sale is 77.87 million tons, but when the price of coarse grain rises from $80 to $160 per ton, the amount of wheat produced and offered for sale at the price of $100 per ton of wheat decreases to 66.31 million tons. This decrease in tons of wheat produced and offered for sale at the price of $100 per ton of wheat is a decrease in supply. On the other hand, if the price of wheat falls from $100 per ton to $75 per ton while the price of coarse grain is $80 per ton, the amount of wheat produced and offered for sale decreases from 77.87 million tons to 74.11 million tons. This decrease in the amount of wheat produced and offered for sale is not the result of a decrease in supply. Given the supply of wheat, less wheat is produced and offered for sale when the price falls, depicted as a movement down and along the given supply curve for wheat.

Once again, in the fewest and simplest words, a supply curve establishes a relationship between the price of a product and amount of the product produced and offered for sale. A decrease in price results in movement down along the supply curve, down the supply curve in the case of a decrease in price. Any change in factors other than price results in a shift rightward or leftward in the supply curve. An increase in the price of another product that can be produced with the same inputs, for example, will result in a leftward shift in the supply curve.

Reconsider the supply schedule illustrated above in Table 2.7. The amounts of wheat that would be produced and offered for sale at various prices when the price of coarse grain is $80 per ton can be compared to amounts of wheat that would be supplied when the price of coarse grain is $160 per ton. This comparison is shown in Table 2.9. Notice that the amount of wheat produced and offered for sale when P_G is $160 per ton is less at any price of wheat by comparison to the amount of wheat produced and offered for sale when P_G is $80. This observation is the meaning of a decrease in supply.

Table 2.9
Comparative Supply Schedules for Wheat
With Respect to an Increase in P_G

Price of Wheat Per Ton	Amount of Wheat (Millions of Tons) $P_G=\$80$ $Q_{sw}=62.8293+0.1504P_s$	Amount of Wheat (Millions of Tons) $P_G=\$160$ $Q_{sw}=51.2693+0.1504P_s$
$200	92.91	81.35
$175	89.15	77.59
$150	85.39	73.83
$125	81.63	70.07
$100	77.87	66.31
$75	74.11	62.55
$50	70.35	58.79
$25	66.59	55.03
$0	62.83	51.27

THE DEMAND FOR WHEAT

The supply function and the supply curve for wheat presented above are based on data from 1975 to 1979. The demand function for wheat also was estimated for the same period.[15] First, consider expected purchases of wheat with respect to the price of wheat and the price of coarse grain. The functional relationship for U.S. wheat, which is the equivalent of a sales function, was estimated as

$$Q_{DW}=83.1018-0.0924P_s+0.0592P_G$$

The variables are

Q_{DW}=amount of wheat buyers want to purchase, measured in millions of tons;

15   The following functions are adapted from Paarlberg and Thompson, *loc. cit.*

P_S=price per ton of wheat; and

P_G=price per ton of coarse grain.

When the price of coarse grain is $80 per ton,

Q_{DW}=83.1018−0.0924P_S+0.0592(80)

Q_{DW}=83.1018−0.0924P_S+4.7360

Q_{DW}=87.8378−0.0924P_S

This expression is the demand function for wheat, which establishes the relationship between expected purchases of wheat and the price of wheat alone. The demand function for wheat is graphed in Figure 2.14.

FIGURE 2.14
DEMAND FUNCTION FOR WHEAT

The Demand Curve for Wheat

The demand curve for wheat can be derived from the demand function for wheat by solving for price. The demand function for wheat was

$Q_{DW}=87.8378-0.0924P_S$

Solving for price,

$0.0924P_S=87.8378-Q_{DW}$

$P_S=950.6255-10.8225Q_{DW}$

When graphed, this function is the demand curve for wheat. The demand curve for wheat is shown in Figure 2.15.

FIGURE 2.15
DEMAND CURVE FOR WHEAT

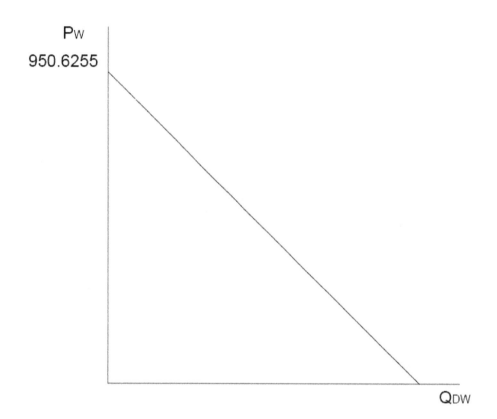

Amounts of wheat that would be purchased at selected prices can be shown in a demand schedule. Consider Table 2.10, which shows expected sales of wheat at various prices.

Table 2.10 Demand Schedule for Wheat	
Price of Wheat Per Ton	Sales of Wheat (Millions of Tons) $Q_{DW}=87.8378-0.0924P_S$
$200	69.36
$175	71.67
$150	73.98
$125	76.29
$100	78.60
$75	80.91
$50	83.22
$25	85.53
$0	87.84

MARKET EQUILIBRIUM FOR WHEAT

The demand for and supply of a product determine the price of the product and the amount of the product sold and bought at that price. Market equilibrium refers to a market price at which the amount that sellers produce and offer for sale is equal to the amount buyers want to purchase. In such cases, the market is cleared. Recall that the supply function for U.S. wheat, given P_G is $80 per ton, was

$Q_{SW}=62.8293+0.1504P_S$

This supply function can be restated as the equation for the supply curve for wheat,

$P_S=-417.7480+6.6489Q_{SW}$

In addition, recall that the demand function for U.S. wheat, given P_G is $80, was

$Q_{DW}=87.8378-0.0924P_S$

This demand function can be restated as the equation for the demand curve for wheat,

$P_S=950.6255-10.8225Q_{DW}$

Consider Table 2.11. Selected prices of wheat are shown along with amounts that would be demanded and supplied at those various prices. Product produced and offered for sale but not bought at a particular price is called a surplus. Surplus is a case in which the amount sellers offer for sale at a particular price is greater than the amount buyers want to purchase at that same price. For example, at a price of $150 per ton, a surplus of 11.41 million tons of wheat would be expected. The surplus of wheat at the price of $150 would put downward pressure on the price of wheat. Product that buyers want to purchase but that is not produced and offered for sale at a particular price is called a shortage. Shortage is a case in which the amount buyers want to purchase at a particular price is greater than the amount that sellers offer for sale at that same price. For example, at a price of $50 per ton, a shortage of 12.87 million tons would be expected. The shortage of wheat at the price of $50 would put upward pressure on the price of wheat.

Table 2.11 Demand and Supply Schedules for Wheat With Corresponding Surpluses or Shortages				
Price of Wheat Per Ton	Amount of Wheat Demanded (Millions of Tons)	Amount of Wheat Supplied (Millions of Tons)	Surplus of Wheat (Millions of Tons)	Shortage of Wheat (Millions of Tons)
$200	69.36	92.91	23.55	
$175	71.67	89.15	17.48	
$150	73.98	85.39	11.41	
$125	76.29	81.63	5.34	
$100	78.60	77.87		0.73
$75	80.91	74.11		6.80
$50	83.22	70.35		12.87
$25	85.53	66.59		18.94
$0	87.84	62.83		25.01

Clearing the Market

When a market is cleared, neither a surplus nor a shortage is evident. In Table 2.11, notice that at each selected price of wheat, either a surplus or a shortage would be expected. None of these prices clears the market, and thus none of these selected prices is a market equilibrium price. Since the market equilibrium price is the price of wheat at which the amount of wheat buyers want to purchase is equal to the amount sellers produce and offer for sale, the demand and supply functions for wheat can be used to solve for the market equilibrium price, or the equations for the demand and supply curves can be used to solve for the market equilibrium price. Figure 2.16 depicts the demand curve for wheat and the supply curve for wheat. The intersection of the demand curve and the supply curve clears the market, which means neither a surplus nor a shortage materializes, and thus infers the market equilibrium price and amount bought and sold at that unique price.

FIGURE 2.16
MARKET EQUILIBRIUM FOR WHEAT

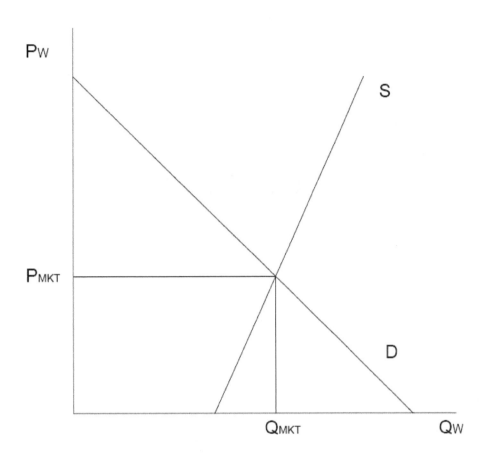

Market equilibrium can be determined by setting the equation for the demand curve equal to the equation for the supply curve,

$950.6255-10.8225QW=-417.7480+6.6489QW$

$-17.4714QW=-1,368.3735$

$QW=78.3208$

When the wheat market is in equilibrium, the amount of wheat bought and sold is 78.3208 million tons. Substituting 78.3208 into the equation for the supply curve and solving for price,

$P_S=-417.7480+6.6489(78.3208)$

$P_S=-417.7480+520.7472$

$P_S=103$

The market equilibrium price for wheat, therefore, is $103 per ton. Alternatively, substituting 78.3208 into the equation for the demand curve and solving for price,

$P_S = 950.6255 - 10.8225(78.3208)$

$P_S = 950.6255 - 847.6269$

$P_S = 103$

Again, the market equilibrium price of wheat is $103 per ton. At this price per ton, $103, wheat that farmers would produce and offer for sale is 78.3208 million tons of wheat, and wheat that buyers would purchase is 78.3208 million tons of wheat. At this price per ton of wheat, $103, there is neither a surplus nor a shortage. At this price per ton of wheat, $103, the market is cleared. No upward pressure or downward pressure on price causes price to change, which is the nature of equilibrium. Figure 2.17 shows the market equilibrium of $103 and 78.3208 million tons.

FIGURE 2.17
MARKET EQUILIBRIUM PRICE AND QUANTITY
FOR WHEAT

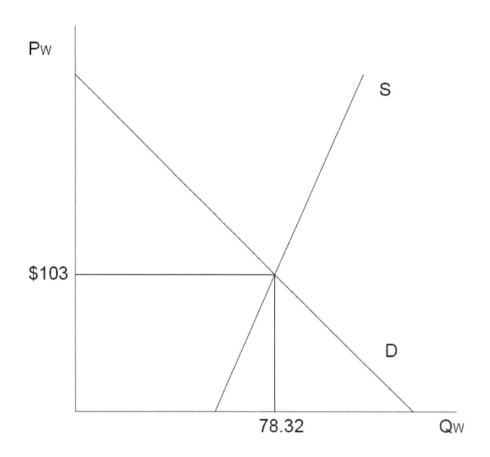

MARKET EQUILIBRIUM PRICE

A market equilibrium price is the price from which there is no tendency to change, given demand and supply conditions. If there is a shortage at some price, sellers who customarily carry inventories find themselves stocking out. Buyers who cope with less than the amount they want to purchase begin to bid up the price. A higher price will cause some buyers to cut back their purchases. A higher price also will induce some sellers to produce and offer more of the product for sale. These behaviors will occur and reoccur until the price rises to its market equilibrium level. At that price, these behaviors are dissipated, thus relieving upward pressure on price. If there is a surplus, sellers find their inventories are excessive and try to reduce them by cutting price. The lower price leads to greater purchases by buyers. At the lower price, sellers reduce the amounts they produce and offer for sale. The price will fall until the market equilibrium price is realized, these behaviors will be dissipated, and there are no forces to cause price to change. Market disequilibrium of either a surplus or a shortage originates correcting forces and triggers behaviors among buyers and sellers that onset movement toward market equilibrium. Once reached, this market equilibrium price and amount bought and sold will persist as long as demand and supply do not change. Changes in demand and supply cause surpluses or shortages that are corrected by changes in price and amounts bought and sold.

Equilibrium in Physics and Economics

Emanuel Derman earned a Ph.D. in theoretical physics from Columbia University in 1973. From 1985 to 2002, Derman worked for Goldman Sachs and Salomon Brothers. Quantitative refugees from alien disciplines often find permanent residence in the financial world. They were and are called quants. Derman was best known as head of the quantitative strategies group at Goldman Sachs where he led a group of thirty quants. He is credited with being one of the originators of a model for valuing bond options and pricing interest rate options. Derman now is a professor at Columbia University, focusing on financial engineering in the Department of Industrial Engineering and Operations Research.

In 2004, Derman had a book published about his experiences in the financial world. He expressed the nature of equilibrium market prices as parallel to equilibrium in physics.

Equilibrium is a common and very powerful concept in physics. Numerical values for quantities in a stable system are values that cause two opposing forces to cancel exactly. The temperature of a body stops rising at the equilibrium temperature at which the heat flowing into the body is canceled by the heat flowing out. Market prices are determined by similar cancellations.[16]

Where Derman uses the language "determined by similar cancellations," he is referencing supply and demand.

Disequilibrium

An exact market equilibrium price is not always observed. At times, a market can be in disequilibrium. Characteristics of disequilibrium are used to determine what is expected to happen to prices and quantities bought and sold. For example, suppose a construction company routinely buys copper wire and copper pipes and learns of spot shortages of copper. The company can expect to receive notification of an increase in the prices of copper wire and copper pipes. If a fertilizer company finds that its inventories are high and hears about similar situations experienced by competitors in the same business, the company must brace itself for a drop in price. Indeed, the company might call a big customer and offer to unload some inventory by shading the price a bit or perhaps a lot. The only problem is that the company

---

16   Emanuel Derman, *My Life as a Quant: Reflections on Physics and Finance* (New York: John Wiley & Sons, 2004), p. 145.

must make this important telephone call before its competitors make such telephone calls. The general point is that market prices and amounts bought and sold move toward equilibrium.

CHANGES IN DEMAND AND SUPPLY

Market conditions can be analyzed to understand and anticipate the effects of economic changes. Demand and supply change, and markets are momentarily in disequilibrium. The consequences of a change or changes can be anticipated by taking step-by-step procedures: (1) start with equilibrium; (2) specify a change, holding other factors unchanged; (3) determine the effect on demand or supply; and (4) state the outcome as the difference between the old equilibrium and the new equilibrium. Usually, this comparative method can be implemented by shifting demand and supply curves on a graph. Decision makers must be able to focus on a particular factor, consider a change in the factor, and then analyze the change to determine the effects and anticipate the outcome. The following eight cases encompass the range of basic changes. In the first four, demand or supply increases or decreases. In the remaining four cases, simultaneous changes in both demand and supply are considered.

Increase in Demand with Constant Supply

Suppose something occurs, *e.g.*, an increase in the price of a competitive product, which causes an increase in the demand for the product. This occurrence would cause a rightward shift in the demand curve. Consequently, a shortage would develop at the present price. The amount buyers are trying to buy is now greater than the amount sellers are offering for sale at the present price. This shortage at the present price results in upward pressure on price until a new market equilibrium price is established where the increased demand curve intersects the unchanged supply curve. Given the supply curve, the higher price induces sellers to produce and offer for sale more of the product. Therefore, an increase in demand with constant supply results in a higher price and a greater amount of the product bought and sold. Figure 2.18 shows the rightward shift in the demand curve as well as the new market equilibrium at a higher price and greater amount of the product bought and sold.

FIGURE 2.18
INCREASE IN DEMAND, CONSTANT SUPPLY

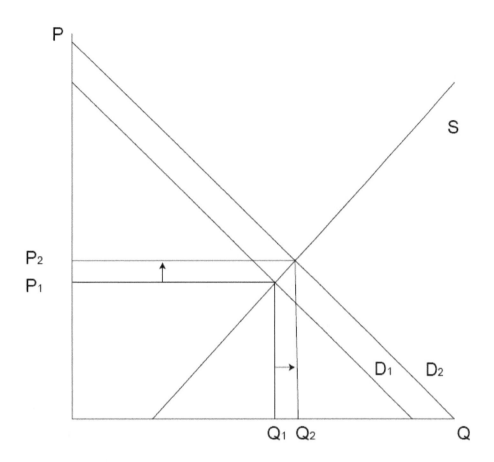

Decrease in Demand with Constant Supply

Suppose something occurs, *e.g.*, an increase in the price of a complementary product, which causes a decrease in the demand for the product. This occurrence would cause a leftward shift in the demand curve with no change in the supply curve. Consequently, a surplus would develop at the present price. The amount buyers are willing to buy is now less than the amount sellers are offering for sale at the present price. This surplus at the present price results in downward pressure on price until a new market equilibrium price is established where the decreased demand curve intersects the unchanged supply curve. Given the supply curve, the lower price induces sellers to produce and offer for sale less of the product. Therefore, a decrease in demand with constant supply results in a lower price and a smaller amount of the product bought and sold. Figure 2.19 shows the leftward shift in the demand curve as well as the new market equilibrium at a lower price and smaller amount of the product bought and sold.

FIGURE 2.19
DECREASE IN DEMAND, CONSTANT SUPPLY

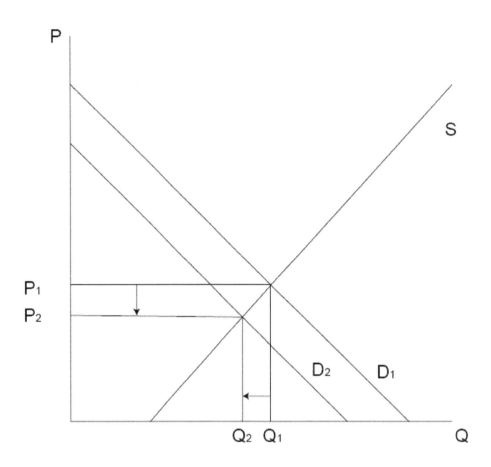

Increase in Supply with Constant Demand

Suppose something occurs, *e.g.*, a decrease in prices of inputs required in production, which causes an increase in the supply of a product. This occurrence would cause a rightward shift in the supply curve with no change in the demand curve. Consequently, a surplus would develop at the present price. The amount sellers are willing to offer for sale is now greater than the amount buyers are willing to buy at the present price. This surplus at the present price results in downward pressure on price until a new market equilibrium price is established where the increased supply curve intersects the unchanged demand curve. Given the demand curve, the lower price induces buyers to purchase more of the product. Therefore, an increase in supply with constant demand results in a lower price and a greater amount of the product bought and sold. Figure 2.20 shows the rightward shift in the supply curve as well as the new market equilibrium at a lower price and greater amount of the product bought and sold.

FIGURE 2.20
INCREASE IN SUPPLY, CONSTANT DEMAND

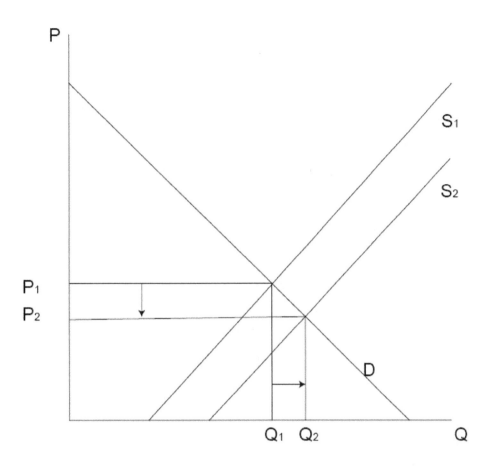

Decrease in Supply with Constant Demand

Suppose something occurs, *e.g.*, an increase in the price of another product that could be produced with the same inputs, which causes a decrease in the supply of a product. This occurrence would cause a leftward shift in the supply curve with no change in the demand curve. Consequently, a shortage would develop at the present price. The amount sellers are willing to offer for sale is now less than the amount buyers are trying to buy at the present price. This shortage at the present price results in upward pressure on price until a new market equilibrium price is established where the decreased supply curve intersects the unchanged demand curve. Given the demand curve, the higher price induces buyers to purchase less of the product. Therefore, a decrease in supply with constant demand results in a higher price and a smaller amount of the product bought and sold. Figure 2.21 shows the leftward shift in the supply curve as well as the new market equilibrium at a higher price and smaller amount of the product bought and sold.

FIGURE 2.21
DECREASE IN SUPPLY, CONSTANT DEMAND

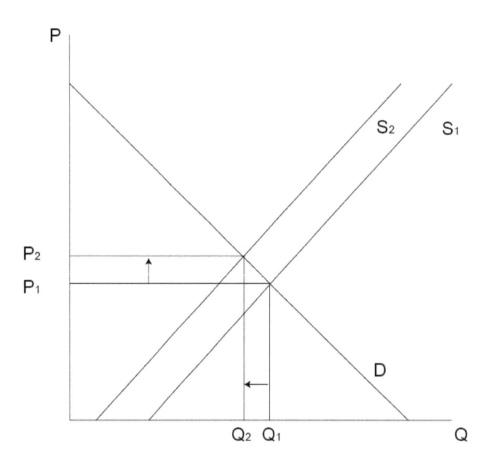

Simultaneous Increases in Both Demand and Supply

Suppose an increase in the price of a competitive product and a decrease in prices of inputs required in production cause simultaneous increases in both the demand for and supply of a product. The effect of the increase in demand is to put upward pressure on price as well as upward pressure on amount of the product bought and sold. The effect of the increase in supply is to put downward pressure on price but upward pressure on amount of the product bought and sold. The influences on amount bought and sold are reinforcing. Since the effects of both the increase in demand and the increase in supply on the amount of the product bought and sold are in the same direction, the amount bought and sold clearly will rise.

However, the effects on price are opposing. The increases in demand and supply pressure price in different directions. The net outcome on price depends on the comparative magnitudes of increase. If the increase in demand is proportionately greater than the increase in supply, the effect of the increase in demand would be greater and price will rise. If the increase in supply is proportionately greater than the increase in demand, the effect of the increase in supply would be greater and price will fall. If the increase in demand and the increase in supply were proportionate, price would neither rise nor fall because the two opposing effects are balanced and offset each other. Therefore, without information regarding proportions, simultaneous increases in both demand and supply result in a greater amount of the product bought and sold, but price can rise, fall, or remain unchanged.

Figure 2.22 depicts three panels, each showing different proportions of change in demand and supply. Figure 2.22(a) shows an increase in demand that is proportionately more than an increase in supply. Price rises, and quantity also increases. Figure 2.22(b) shows an increase in supply that is proportionately more than an increase in demand. Price falls, but quantity increases. Figure 2.22(c) shows proportionate increases in both demand and supply. Price is unchanged, but quantity increases.

FIGURE 2.22
INCREASE IN BOTH DEMAND AND SUPPLY

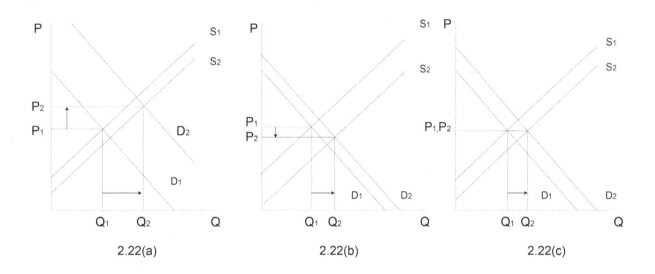

2.22(a)   2.22(b)   2.22(c)

Simultaneous Decreases in both Demand and Supply

Suppose an increase in the price of a complementary product and an increase in the price of another product that could be produced with the same inputs cause simultaneous decreases in both the demand for and supply of a product. The effect of the decrease in demand is to put downward pressure on price as well as downward pressure on amount of the product bought and sold. The effect of the decrease in supply is to put upward pressure on price but downward pressure on amount of the product bought and sold. The effects on amount bought and sold are reinforcing. Since the effects of both the decrease in demand and the decrease in supply on the amount of the product bought and sold are in the same direction, the amount bought and sold clearly will fall.

However, the effects on price are opposing. Decreases in demand and supply pressure price in different directions. The net outcome on price depends on the comparative magnitudes of decrease. If the decrease in demand is proportionately greater than the decrease in supply, the effect of the decrease in demand would be greater and price will fall. If the decrease in supply is proportionately greater than the decrease in demand, the effect of the decrease in supply would be greater and price will rise. If the increase in demand and the increase in supply were proportionate, price will neither rise nor fall because the two opposing effects are balanced and offset each other. Therefore, without information regarding proportions, simultaneous decreases in both demand and supply result in a smaller amount of the product bought and sold, but price can rise, fall, or remain unchanged.

Figure 2.23 depicts three panels, each showing different proportions of change in demand and supply. Figure 2.23(a) shows a decrease in demand that is proportionately less than a decrease in supply. Price rises, but quantity decreases. Figure 2.23(b) shows a decrease in demand that is proportionately more than a decrease in demand. Price falls, but quantity decreases. Figure 2.23(c) shows proportionate decreases in both demand and supply. Price is unchanged, but quantity decreases.

FIGURE 2.23
DECREASE IN BOTH DEMAND AND SUPPLY

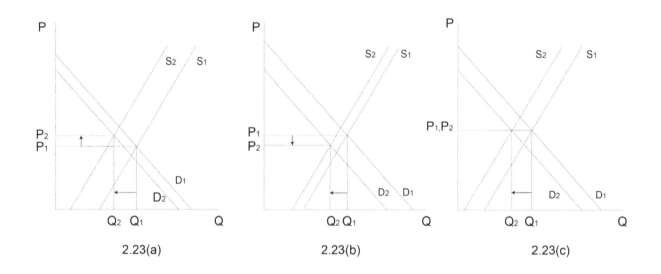

2.23(a)   2.23(b)   2.23(c)

Simultaneous Increase in Demand and Decrease in Supply

Suppose an increase in the price of a competitive product and an increase in the price of another product that could be produced with the same inputs cause a simultaneous increase in the demand for a product and decrease in the supply of the product. The effect of the increase in demand is to put upward pressure on price as well as upward pressure on amount of the product bought and sold. The effect of the decrease in supply is to put upward pressure on price but downward pressure on amount of the product bought and sold. The effects on price are reinforcing. Since the effects of both the increase in demand and the decrease in supply on the price of the product are in the same direction, the price of the product clearly will rise.

However, the effects on the amount bought and sold are opposing. The increase in demand and decrease in supply pressure amount bought and sold in different directions. The net outcome on amount bought and sold depends on the comparative magnitudes of change. If the increase in demand is proportionately greater than the decrease in supply, the influence of the increase in demand would be greater and the amount bought and sold will rise. If the increase in supply is proportionately greater than the decrease in demand, the influence of the decrease in supply would be greater and the amount bought and sold will fall. If the increase in demand and the decrease in supply were proportionate, the amount bought and sold would neither rise nor fall because the two opposing influences are balanced and offset each other. Therefore, without information regarding proportions, a simultaneous increase in demand and decrease in supply result in a higher price, but the amount of the product bought and sold can rise, fall, or remain unchanged.

Figure 2.24 depicts three panels, each showing different proportions of change in demand and supply. Figure 2.24(a) shows an increase in demand that is proportionately more than a decrease in supply. Price rises, and quantity also increases. Figure 2.24(b) shows an increase in demand that is proportionately less than a decrease in supply. Price rises, but quantity decreases. Figure 2.24(c) shows a proportionate increase in demand and decrease in supply. Price rises, but quantity is unchanged.

FIGURE 2.24
INCREASE IN DEMAND, DECREASE IN SUPPLY

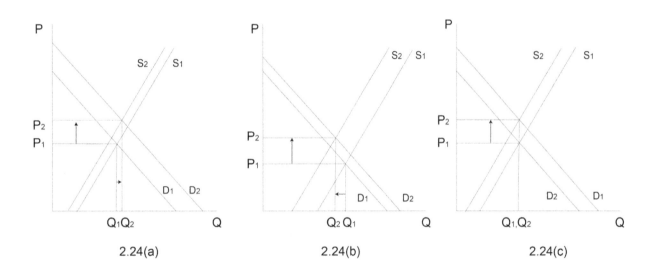

2.24(a)   2.24(b)   2.24(c)

Simultaneous Decrease in Demand and Increase in Supply

Suppose an increase in the price of a complementary product and a decrease in prices of inputs required in production cause a simultaneous decrease in the demand for a product and increase in the supply of the product. The effect of the decrease in demand is to put downward pressure on price as well as downward pressure on amount of the product bought and sold. The effect of the increase in supply is to put downward pressure on price but upward pressure on amount of the product bought and sold. The effects on price are reinforcing. Since the effects of both the decrease in demand and the increase in supply on the price of the product are in the same direction, the price of the product clearly will fall.

However, the effects on the amount bought and sold are opposing, with the decrease in demand and increase in supply pressuring amount bought and sold in different directions. The net outcome on amount bought and sold depends on the comparative magnitudes of change. If the decrease in demand is proportionately greater than the increase in supply, the influence of the decrease in demand would be greater and the amount bought and sold will fall. If the decrease in supply is proportionately greater than the increase in demand, the effect of the increase in supply would be greater and the amount bought and sold will rise. If the decrease in demand and the increase in supply were proportionate, the amount bought and sold would neither rise nor fall because the two opposing influences are balanced and offset each other. Therefore, without information regarding proportions, a simultaneous decrease in demand and increase in supply result in a lower price, but the amount of the product bought and sold can rise, fall, or remain unchanged.

Figure 2.25 depicts three panels, each showing different proportions of change in demand and supply. Figure 2.25(a) shows a decrease in demand that is proportionately less than an increase in supply. Price falls, but quantity increases. Figure 2.25(b) shows an increase in demand that is proportionately more than an increase in supply. Price falls, and quantity also decreases. Figure 2.25(c) shows a proportionate increase in demand and decrease in supply. Price falls, but quantity is unchanged.

FIGURE 2.25
DECREASE IN DEMAND, INCREASE IN SUPPLY

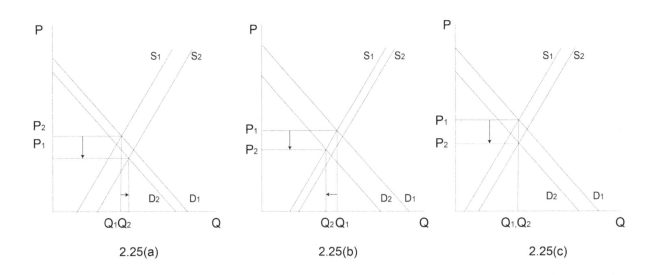

2.25(a)   2.25(b)   2.25(c)

A Summary

Table 2.12 summarizes the eight cases. The first column shows the change of each case, and the pressure on price and amount bought and sold is shown in the next two columns. The expected outcome is shown in the final column. Notice that when pressures are reinforcing, the outcome is definitive, and when pressures are opposing, the outcome depends on relative proportions of change.

Change(s)	Pressure on Price	Pressure on Amount Bought and Sold	Effect on Price and Amount Bought and Sold
Table 2.12 **Summary of Effects on Price and Amount Bought and Sold** **With Respect to Changes in Demand and Supply**			
Increase in Demand Constant Supply	Higher	More	Higher Price More Bought and Sold
Decrease in Demand Constant Supply	Lower	Less	Lower Price Less Bought and Sold
Constant Demand Increase in Supply	Lower	More	Lower Price More Bought and Sold
Constant Demand Decrease in Supply	Higher	Less	Higher Price Less Bought and Sold
Increase in Demand Increase in Supply	Higher, Lower,or Unchanged	More	Higher, Lower, or Unchanged Price, Depending on Relative Proportion of Change More Bought and Sold
Decrease in Demand Decrease in Supply	Higher, Lower, or Unchanged	Less	Higher, Lower, or Unchanged Price, Depending on Relative Proportion of Change Less Bought and Sold
Increase in Demand Decrease in Supply	Higher	More, Less, or Unchanged	Higher Price More, Less, or Unchanged Amount Bought and Sold, Depending on Relative Proportion of Change
Decrease in Demand Increase in Supply	Lower	More, Less, or Unchanged	Lower Price More, Less, or Unchanged Amount Bought and Sold, Depending on Relative Proportion of Change

BRIEF CASE STUDIES

Scholarly journals and periodicals such as *The Wall Street Journal*, *Business Week*, *Fortune*, and *The Economist* sometimes publish articles that essentially are case studies in demand and supply. Many of these cases are interesting and worthy of thought and consideration since changes in demand or supply can be observed, and the outcomes also can be observed.

Meatless Fridays and the Roman Catholic Church

For more than a thousand years, the Roman Catholic Church required its faithful to abstain from eating meat on Fridays as penance. In November 1966, American Catholic bishops ended obligatory meatless Fridays except Fridays falling within Lent. Thus, except during Lent, American Catholics can now eat meat on Fridays only if they substitute some other act of penance such as works of charity or exercises of piety. Roman Catholics conveniently forget or blithely ignore the latter.

Frederick W. Bell studied the impact of this decision on the price of fish in New England, where almost half of the population is Roman Catholic. The decision caused a significant decrease in the demand for fish. A decrease in the demand for fish with no change in the supply of fish should result in a lower price of fish. Bell compared a 10-year period (January 1957 to November 1966) prior to the decision with the 9-month period (December 1966 to August 1967) immediately after the decision. Bell found a 12.5% average decline in fish prices attributable to the Church decision. His findings clearly showed that the decrease in demand for fish resulted in a corresponding decline in fish prices, evidently caused by the Church decision.[17]

Fluctuations in the Demand for Copper

The primary use of copper is in the construction industry. In the early 1980s, two recessions occurred, the first from January 1980 to July 1980 and the second from July 1981 to November 1982. These back-to-back recessions reduced overall economic activity and slowed construction activity. The result was a substantial drop in the demand for copper. The price per pound of copper fell by forty percent. Starting in November 1982 and continuing through July 1990, there was a historically unprecedented expansion in the economy. The demand for copper increased correspondingly. The price per pound of copper more than doubled.

Aluminum and the Breakup of the USSR

Before the dissolution of the USSR in December 1991, the Soviet aluminum industry primarily served materiel needs of the military sector. Afterwards, Russia began selling aluminum on the world market. In four years, Russian exports of aluminum caused an increase in supply that pushed the supply curve for aluminum to the right. Within two years, the price per pound of aluminum fell by more than forty percent. In 1994, Russia agreed to cut its output. Western producers also cut output. Price almost doubled.

Fluctuations in the Supply of Coffee

Coffee is grown on a plant that actually is a tropical evergreen shrub rather than a tree. The fruit of the coffee plant is called a cherry. Each cherry-sized fruit contains two coffee beans. Six or seven pounds of coffee cherries will produce approximately one pound of coffee beans, which are like the pit of an olive. Coffee beans ordinarily are sold by the hundredweight, one hundred pounds, or by the quintal, a unit of weight in the British Imperial System equal to 112 pounds.

In mid-1993, the price of green, unroasted coffee beans was about 50¢ per pound. In early 1994, Brazil's coffee crop was damaged by severe freezes. In Colombia, the coffee crop was harmed by a worm infestation. On the island of Java, Indonesia, heavy rains hampered the coffee harvest. These natural misfortunes had severe adverse effects on the supply of coffee beans. Price spiraled to about $1.60 per pound. Still another killing frost in key coffee-growing regions of Brazil sent coffee bean prices soaring still higher. In hectic trading, the price of coffee beans rose to more than $2.30 per pound.

---

17   Frederick W. Bell, "The Pope and the Price of Fish," *American Economic Review*, 58 (December 1968), pp. 1346-1350.

More recently, the supply of coffee beans has increased. Countries such as Vietnam started to produce and export coffee beans. Indeed, Vietnam is now the second largest exporter of coffee beans. More established growers in Brazil, the largest exporter, Colombia, Indonesia, and Honduras have sharply increased their exports.

Civet Coffee: Good to the Last Plop

In Indonesia, the civet is a common animal regarded as a kind of wildcat. One of the civet's favorite foods is the coffee cherry. The fruit is like an olive with a fleshy outside and two beans inside rather than a pit. At night, the civet pulls the fruit from the coffee plant and eats the whole thing, including the intact beans. As the coffee beans work their way through the civet, the beans are undigested and fermented by digestive enzymes. Sooner or later, civets carry out the final act in this drama, and the undigested, fermented coffee beans are plopped on the ground along with everything else that is excreted. Plantation workers harvest the undigested, fermented coffee beans. With apologies to Maxwell House and its slogan "good to the last drop," civet coffee is regarded as good to the last plop.

Civet coffee is called kopi luwak. Kopi is Indonesian for coffee. Luwak is the local word for the civet. The coffee itself is reported to have a unique flavor, described as a strong flavor and a strong aroma. Well, duh! Kopi luwak is widely available on the Internet at various prices and undoubtedly in various degrees of authenticity, if any. Genuine civet beans are rare by comparison to ordinary coffee beans. Supply is thus severely limited, and civet beans are regarded as a great delicacy, leading to rather high demand. After civet beans are cleaned, roasted, and eventually sold in markets such as New York, the price can be $200 or more per pound. In such places, people usually buy, say, a quarter pound costing about $50, and then invite friends over for a coffee party at which everyone gets a small cup of the exotic coffee. Why $200 per pound? It's simple. Supply and demand!

Increased Supply: Potatoes and Alligators

In 1996, potatoes and alligators had a lot in common. Supplies were up and prices were down. Farmers produced the most potatoes in history, sending the price per 100 pounds down to $2 to $3 in Maine compared with $8 to $9 in 1995. The cost to grow 100 pounds of potatoes was $6, well above the price of $2 to $3 per hundredweight. "The farmers right now are literally giving them away," said Mike Corey, executive director of the Maine Potato Board. Several farmers and processors filed for bankruptcy.[18]

At the same time, biologists with the Louisiana Department of Wildlife and Fisheries reported a harvest of 26,000 alligators during the season that began 7 September 1996 and ended 6 October 1996. It was the third largest harvest since 1972. The bad news was that prices dropped. The average price was $41 per foot in 1995 but plunged to $25 per foot in 1996.[19]

Supply in the Headlines: Summer 2012

The spring and summer of 2012 were uncommonly hot and dry. Drought settled over several agricultural states. By July 2012, newspapers and other media reported case after case of adverse effects on the supply

---

18   "Potato Farms In Maine May Get Sacked," New Orleans, LA, *Times-Picayune* (December 24, 1996), p. C1ff.

19   "Alligator Take Is Up, But Prices Are Down," New Orleans, LA, *Times-Picayune* (December 28,1996), p. B5.

of agricultural commodities. In particular, tart cherries stood out. Supply of tart cherries was decimated. On the other hand, the supply of lobsters swelled.

Seventy percent of America's tart cherries are grown and harvested in Michigan. March 2012 was freakishly warm, which caused cherry trees to bud. In April, a hard freeze killed the blossoms. This freakish weather destroyed Michigan's cherry crop. New York and Wisconsin have smaller but significant tart cherry harvests, but these states suffered the same calamitous weather damage. Cherry processors scrambled to obtain tart cherries from sources as far away as Poland and Turkey, but they were still left wanting for the most part. The end result was a substantial decrease in the supply of tart cherries with no corresponding change in demand. The price of tart cherries at the farm level more than doubled.

In Maine, early July is when lobster catches surge as lobsters begin to shed their hard shells in favor of their soft shells. In 2012, however, soft shell lobsters began to flood traps weeks earlier than normal. Most of these lobsters are sold in local markets or sold to Canadian processors. However, Canadian processors were not able to handle the Maine catch because Canadian lobstermen had abundant catches during their own spring. Consequently, the supply greatly exceeded the demand at prevailing prices. The price of soft shell lobsters received by lobstermen plummeted.

Ford's Write-Off

In 2002, newspapers and other publications reported that Ford was writing off one billion dollars as an inventory adjustment related to its holdings of palladium. Palladium is a precious metal used in making catalytic converters. Between 1992 and 2000, palladium prices increased almost tenfold, rising to about $750 per ounce. Ford engineers were urged to find ways to reduce the palladium required to produce catalytic converters. At the same time, commodity managers at Ford decided to stockpile palladium to guard against future price increases. The supply of palladium is rather inflexible. When Ford started to build up its inventory of palladium, the increase in demand sent the price of palladium soaring. By 2001, Ford was stockpiling palladium at prices well over $1,000 per ounce.

Shortly after this manic run-up of palladium inventory, Ford engineers devised a method that required less palladium to make catalytic converters. Beginning with its 2003 models, Ford reduced its use of palladium by half. This breakthrough was copied by other automobile makers and thus reduced the industry demand for palladium. The price fell from over $1,000 per ounce to under $300 per ounce. Ford's inventory of palladium was worth only a fraction of its acquisition cost. Ford wrote off one billion dollars of inventory valuation. Palladium has rebounded somewhat. In late 2012, the price of palladium was in the range of $680 to $690 per ounce.

Steel Prices: One Month Up, Next Month Down

In the summer of 2009, rising demand for steel led to higher prices. Hot-rolled steel is processed into automobile vehicles, building structures, and household appliances. In August, the price of hot-rolled steel was in the range of $600 to $620 per metric ton. A month later in September, the price fell to the range of $550 to $570, a decline of eight percent. With rising demand, why did steel prices drop? When stimulus packages were announced, steelmakers thought they saw an opportunity to bring production back online after steep cutbacks earlier in the recession that began in December 2007. ArcelorMittal, the world's largest steelmaker, fired up its mills in the United States, Europe, and elsewhere. Baosteel

Group, the largest steelmaker in China, also increased production. The increased demand for steel put upward pressure on the price of steel, but the supply response put even greater downward pressure on the price of steel.[20]

LEGAL MAXIMUM AND LEGAL MINIMUM PRICES

Disequilibrium prices are usually temporary and transitory. Market forces correct the disequilibrium, resulting in higher or lower prices that reestablish market equilibrium. In some cases, however, prices are prevented from adjusting to market equilibrium and the resulting surplus or shortage must be tolerated. When prices are prevented from falling to the market equilibrium or rising to the market equilibrium, people must live with and endure the consequences of surplus or shortage. In other words, just deal with it.

From time to time, some level of government intervenes directly in markets. This direct intervention is manifested as maximum prices or minimum prices. Maximum prices are called price ceilings, and minimum prices are called price floors or price supports. This language adopts a room as metaphor. The upper limit of a room is its ceiling. Hence, a legal maximum price places an upper limit on price and is called a price ceiling. The lower limit of a room is its floor. Therefore, a legal minimum price places a lower limit on price and is called a price floor. Both have economic consequences.

Figure 2.26 depicts a price ceiling below the market equilibrium price. Without government intervention, the legal maximum price would result in shortage that would put upward pressure on price. The price would rise to the market equilibrium. However, price cannot rise above the legal maximum price. Consequences would include a persistent shortage. If a price ceiling were above the market equilibrium price, the price ceiling would be ineffective, meaning that the price ceiling would have no effect. Presumably, the market equilibrium price would be reached since a price ceiling places a legal maximum price and the market equilibrium price is below the legal maximum price. The intent of a price ceiling is to keep price below what otherwise would be the market equilibrium price.

---

20   Robert Guy Matthews, "Steel Prices Drop, Reversing Course in Sign Mills Ramped Up Too Quickly," *Wall Street Journal* (September 14, 2009), pp. B1, B3.

FIGURE 2.26
PRICE CEILING

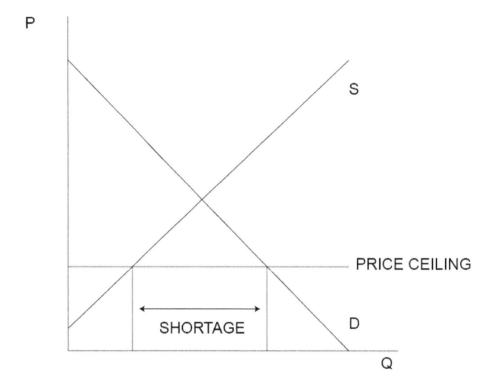

Figure 2.27 illustrates a price floor above the market equilibrium price. Without government intrusion, the legal minimum price would result in surplus that would exert downward pressure on price. The price would fall to the market equilibrium. However, price cannot fall below the legal minimum price. Consequences would include a persistent surplus. If the price floor were below the market equilibrium price, the price floor would be ineffective, meaning that the price floor would have no effect. Presumably, the market equilibrium price would prevail since a price floor imposes a legal minimum price and the market equilibrium price is above the legal minimum price. The intent of a price floor is to keep price above what otherwise would be the market equilibrium price.

FIGURE 2.27
PRICE FLOOR

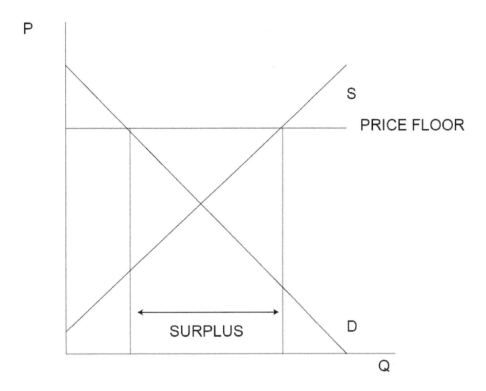

PRICE CEILINGS

One example of a price ceiling is rent control in large cities. More than two hundred cities have rent control of some form. These cities include Washington, D.C., Boston, Los Angeles, New York, and San Francisco. As much as ten percent of rental housing in the United States is rent controlled. Rent control in New York began in 1943. New York still has elaborate systems of rent control and rent stabilization. Over the years, this rent regulation resulted in a serious shortage of rental units. Rent control contributed to the loss of countless housing units. Landlords could avoid rent control by converting rental housing to industrial and commercial property for which rents were not controlled. Landlords also could convert an apartment building to a condominium. However, tenants in rent-regulated apartments were protected from eviction. Tenants could renew their lease at a modest increase in rent, buy their apartments at discounted prices, or accept payments from the landlord in return for giving up their tenant rights. The overall consequence of rent control was a shortage of privately owned rental property and laxity in maintaining rental property.

In 1997, rent control was not fully reauthorized by the New York legislature. As one observer commented, "The end of rent regulation couldn't come a moment too soon. Perennially justified as protecting tenants from...landlords, rent regulations have in fact hastened the decay and abandonment of old buildings and discouraged construction of new buildings–perpetuating the housing shortage...and keeping rents high for those who aren't established in regulated apartments."[21]

In addition to rent controls, other examples of price ceilings had similar consequences. In the late 1970s, for example, a serious shortage of natural gas developed in many states because the price of natural gas shipped interstate was regulated below the market equilibrium price. The price of natural gas shipped intrastate was not regulated. At the same time, a serious shortage of natural gas occurred in northeastern states attributable to interstate regulation, but no such shortage of natural gas was experienced in Texas and Louisiana where natural gas was produced. In these states, natural gas sold at the higher market price rather than the regulated price.

PRICE FLOORS: AGRICULTURAL PRICE SUPPORTS

Examples of price floors include the system of price supports for many agricultural commodities such as sugar, peanuts, tobacco, and dairy products. In agriculture, a price floor is called a price support, suggesting that the price paid to producers can fall no lower that the price supported by law. Excess supplies or surpluses of these commodities develop as a direct consequence of the price supports. For example, the federal government once supported the price of milk by guaranteeing to purchase milk that could not be sold at the federally established support price. The 2008 Farm Bill made reforms. A government owned and government operated entity known as the Commodity Credit Corporation (CCC) now purchases manufactured dairy products such as butter, cheddar cheese, and nonfat dry milk from dairy processors, not milk.

Price floors are one form of protectionism, which is a system of protecting domestic producers of particular products by taxing, impeding, or limiting the importation of foreign products of the same type. The result is higher domestic prices of protected products such as sugar. The domestic sugar price is inflated by import restrictions designed to protect U.S. sugar growers. Recently, the difference between the world price of sugar and the U.S. domestic price of sugar widened to an unprecedented gap. In late March 2010, the domestic price of sugar was 35.02 cents per pound, whereas the world price was 19.67 cents per pound, a price gap of 15.35 cents per pound. The difference was due to a sugar quota of 1.3 million metric tons. As a result, U.S. companies that produce products with sugar as a major raw material are encouraged to move their production to other countries such as Canada or Mexico where sugar can be purchased at the much lower world price.

In 2003, for example, Kraft closed its LifeSavers plant in Holland, Michigan, where it had been operated for seventy-five years. Operations were moved to Quebec, Canada. More than six hundred jobs were lost. By moving to Canada where sugar could be purchased at the world price, the company could save about fifteen million dollars annually on the cost of sugar. Also in 2003, Brach's Convections ended production in Chicago's West Side. Operations were moved to Mexico. Only a decade earlier, Brach's had employed more than 2,300 people at the large manufacturing plant. Ironically, protectionism is touted on grounds that it saves jobs, when the opposite is clearly the case.

Protection of sugar results in higher prices for consumers. Consumers pay higher prices for all products that use sugar as an ingredient, everything from catsup to soft drinks. In addition, millions of dollars

---

21   Roger Starr, "Rent Control Loses Its New York Lease," *Wall Street Journal* (May 1, 1997), p. A₁8. In addition, see John Tierney, "At the Intersection of Supply and Demand," *New York Times Magazine* (May 4, 1997), p. 38ff.

in benefits are paid to sugar producers. Moreover, sugar protectionism is godsend economics for companies such as Archer Daniels Midland (ADM) that produce high fructose corn sweetener (HFCS). High domestic sugar prices have created a boom in the production and sale of corn sweeteners. Manufacturers of HFCS have made extraordinary profits merely by selling their corn sweetener a few cents below the domestic price of sugar.

The high domestic price of sugar has encouraged smuggling and other schemes to circumvent quotas and tariffs on sugar. In the 1980s, for example, Canadian entrepreneurs cleverly created super high octane sugared ice tea. The tea was not meant for consumption as a beverage. The idea was to ship the product into the United States where the sugar could be refined from the tea and then sold or used. To combat this circumvention, the U.S. government created high tariffs on such sugar-saturated products as iced tea, cake mixes, and cocoa.

The 2002 Annual Report of the Federal Reserve Bank of Dallas focused on the advantages of free trade. The FRB of Dallas estimated that an average of $231,289 was the annual cost per job saved across twenty protected industries. Protectionism costs U.S. consumers nearly a hundred billion dollars annually. According to the FRB of Dallas, the annual cost per job saved in the sugar industry is $826,104! Protectionism increases not just the cost of the protected items. Protectionism also increases the cost of downstream products that use the protected items as materials. For example, protecting sugar raises candy and soft drink prices. In addition, there are job losses in downstream industries because of higher costs and prices.

PRICE FLOORS: THE MINIMUM WAGE

Another example of a price floor is the minimum wage. Labor markets for unskilled workers are essentially local markets. In some local markets, the prevailing wage for unskilled workers is well above the minimum wage. Thus, the minimum wage is ineffective, meaning that it has no effect in such markets. In other local markets, however, the wage that would be paid absent a minimum wage is well below the minimum wage. Thus, the minimum wage is effective, meaning that it has an effect in such markets.

The Fair Labor Standards Act of 1938 and subsequent amendments have mandated minimum hourly wage rates applicable to nonsupervisory employment categories. The minimum wage was 25 cents in 1938. In more recent times, the minimum wage was $5.15 from 1 September 1997 to 24 July 2007 when it was raised to $5.85. Legislation provided increases to $6.55 in 2008 and $7.25 in 2009. Increases in the minimum wage cause increases in unemployment, which is acknowledged even by supporters of such increases. In 1988, for example, the Congressional Budget Office (CBO) analyzed a proposed increase in the minimum wage. The initial estimate by CBO showed the legislation would reduce employment by as much as 500,000 jobs. When Democrats complained, CBO issued a revised report that deleted any reference to lost jobs.[22]

Empirical studies have found that the minimum wage is highly significant in explaining unemployment among teenagers. Evidence from such studies has linked minimum wage laws with teenage unemployment. Each ten percent increase in the minimum wage is associated with about a three percent reduction in teenage employment. Minimum wages also reduce employment of young adults aged 20 to 24 and of

---

22   Bruce Bartlett, "Keynes Is Still King at the CBO," *Wall Street Journal* (November 18, 1988), p. A22.

elderly people.[23] A more recent study estimated that each ten percent increase in the minimum wage produces job losses of about one percent of all minimum-wage workers or about 60,000 workers in total.[24] A recent survey of empirical studies showed a negative two percent effect for every ten percent increase in the minimum wage.[25] The minimum wage has the most adverse effect on employment in low-wage industries such as retail sales. Employers often react to increases in minimum wages by decreasing the quality of working conditions and reducing fringe benefits. As the minimum wage rises, the pace of work is increased and the number of vacation days tends to decline.[26]

Who works at the minimum wage? Of all hourly-paid workers age sixteen and over, 4.7 percent worked at or below the federal minimum wage in 2012. Twelve percent of the cohort of workers age sixteen to twenty-four, which includes high school dropouts through wet behind the ears college graduates, worked at or below the minimum wage. For full-time workers, only 2.3 percent of hourly-paid workers worked at the minimum wage, whereas 11.2 percent of part-time workers worked at the federal minimum wage. The most common occupations for those who work at the minimum wage are found in the service sector, including healthcare support, protective service, food preparation and food service, building and grounds cleaning and maintenance, and personal care and personal service.[27]

In local markets where the minimum wage is effective, the minimum wage mainly hurts the poor. In a noteworthy article, Gary Becker and Richard Posner pointed out that raising the minimum wage makes the poor even poorer.[28] Becker won the Nobel Prize for Economics in 1992, and Posner is a federal judge of the U.S. Court of Appeals for the Seventh Circuit. At the time the article was published, Congress was considering an increase in the minimum wage from $5.15 to $7.25, a forty percent increase. In their article, Nobel Laureate Becker and Judge Posner say,

> An increase in the minimum wage raises the costs of fast foods and other goods produced with large inputs of unskilled labor. Producers adjust both by substituting capital inputs and/or high-skilled labor for minimum-wage workers and, because substitutes are more costly (otherwise the substitutions would have been made already), by raising prices....

> Although some workers benefit–those who were paid the old minimum wage but are worth the new, higher one to the employers–others are pushed into unemployment, the underground economy or crime. The losers are therefore likely to lose more than the gainers gain; they are also likely to be poorer people. And poor families are disproportionately hurt by the rise in the price of fast foods

---

23   For a summary of these studies, see Charles Brown, Curtis Gilroy, and Andrew Kohen, "The Effect of the Minimum Wage on Employment and Unemployment," *Journal of Economic Literature*, 20 (June 1982), pp. 487-528.

24   Donald Deere and Finis Welch, "Minimum Wages and Employment," unpublished paper presented at the Annual Meeting of the American Economic Association, Washington, D.C., January 8, 1995. Cf. David Card and Alan Krueger, "Estimating the Impact of Minimum Wages on Employment," unpublished paper presented at the Annual Meeting of the American Economic Association, Washington, D.C., January 8, 1995.

25   David A. Macphearson, "Living Wage Laws and the Case for a Targeted Wage Subsidy," *Living Wage Movements: Global Perspectives*, ed. Deborah M. Figart (London and New York: Routledge, 2004), pp. 46-47.

26   Walter J. Wessels, *Minimum Wages: Fringe Benefits and Working Conditions* (Washington, D.C.: American Enterprise Institute for Public Policy Research, 1980).

27   Bureau of Labor Statistics, Household Data Annual Averages, Table 44 and Table 45.

28   Gary A. Becker and Richard A. Posner, "How to Make the Poor Poorer," *Wall Street Journal* (January 26, 2007), p. A₁1.

and other goods produced with low-skilled labor because these families spend a relatively large fraction of their incomes on such goods....

Moreover, poor people tend not to vote; and the number of non-poor, who'd be directly benefitted by an increase in the minimum wage, when combined with the number of non-poor workers whose incomes would rise because of reduced competition from minimum-wage workers, probably exceeds the number of non-poor who would lose jobs. Teenagers would be among the hardest hit–and few of them are voters (if under 18, they're ineligible). While workers who receive a wage increase when the minimum wage is hiked realize they've benefitted from the hike, many hurt by the hike don't realize it; teenagers and retirees who have trouble finding a job are unlikely to realize that it's because there are fewer jobs in the economy for minimum-wage workers.

The Living Wage Movement

Recently, some have called for legislation to require employers to pay so-called living wages. A living wage is the earnings a family would need to support itself at the poverty level. A wage of ten dollars or more per hour would be required to bring a family of four above the poverty level. Like the minimum wage, a living wage would reduce employment for unskilled and low-skilled workers. A recent study estimated that a fifty percent increase in the living wage would increase the wages of workers in the bottom ten percent of the wage distribution by about three percent but also would reduce employment of those workers by about six percent.[29]

Why?

Why do congressmen and congresswomen who represent poor districts support increases in the minimum wage while knowing that increasing the minimum wage would increase unemployment? Although it is home to Yankee Stadium, Fordham University, and the Bronx Zoo, the poorest congressional district in the United States is the 16th Congressional District of New York, located in the South Bronx. Almost half of residents live below the poverty line. The unemployment rate hovers at twenty-five percent. The high unemployment rate was undoubtedly caused partly if not largely by the minimum wage. Yet, a congressman representing the district once said privately, "I know the minimum wage causes unemployment in my district. That's what welfare is for." He also said, "When people lose their job because of a higher minimum wage, they blame their employers. When people keep their jobs at a higher minimum wage, they give me the credit. My objective is to be reelected. Supporting a higher minimum wage might be bad economics, but it's good politics." The general point is that constituents who lose their jobs because of a higher minimum wage become eligible for public welfare programs and may not be worsened. The lucky ones who do not lose their jobs earn the higher wage rate and may earn higher earnings if hours worked are not reduced. This offset is diminished in the wake of welfare reform.

Why do labor unions support increases in the minimum wage? After all, not a single member of an organized labor union works at the minimum wage. An increase in the minimum wage raises the cost of unskilled labor. To some extent, unskilled and skilled workers are substitutes. The increased cost of unskilled workers increases demand for skilled workers to the extent that employers substitute skilled

---

29   Scott Adams and David Neumark, "A Decade of Living Wages: What Have We Learned?" *California Economic Policy*, vol. 1, no. 3 (San Francisco: Public Policy Institute of California, 2005).

workers for unskilled workers.[30] For example, crops can be harvested with stoop labor or with costly machinery made with skilled workers who belong to the AFL-CIO. As a result, unskilled labor often competes directly or indirectly with semiskilled and skilled labor. This observation explains why the AFL-CIO regards an increase in the minimum wage so important even though AFL-CIO workers earn far more than the minimum wage. Increasing the minimum wage is organized labor's attempt to price unskilled workers out of the market.

PRACTICE QUESTIONS

Answer each of the next FIVE questions based on the estimated sales function expressed immediately below and any additional information given in a particular question. Suppose that the demand function for a product A has been estimated as:

$$Q_A = 10.5 - 0.8P_A - 0.2P_B + 0.1P_C + 0.0005Y$$

The variables are

Q_A is the quantity of product A demanded, in thousands per month;

P_A is the price of product A;

P_B is the price of a product B, which is currently $10;

P_C is the price of a product C, which is currently $5; and

Y is the level of per capita income, which is currently $10,000.

1. Of the following changes, which one would cause an increase in the demand for product A: a decrease in the price of product A, an increase in the price of product A, an increase in the price of product B, an increase in the price of product C, or a decrease in the level of per capita income?

2. Is product A normal or inferior? Are product A and product B substitutes or complements? Are product A and product C substitutes or complements?

3. Express the relationship between expected sales of product A and the price of product A alone, which is the demand function for product A.

4. When the price of product A is $5, what is the amount of expected sales of product A?

5. If a demand curve were graphed for product A, what would be the equation for the graphed demand curve?

Answer each of the next FIVE questions based on the following sales function for a woolen commodity, Lambda:

$$Q_L = 7.0 - 1.6P_L - 0.2P_C + 0.8P_S + 0.0005Y + 0.0004A$$

The variables are

Q_L = amount of sales of Lambda, in thousands per month;

P_L = price per each of Lambda, which is currently $15;

P_C = price per each of Chi, which is currently $25;

---

30   See Keith B. Leffler, "Minimum Wages, Welfare, and Wealth Transfer to the Poor," *Journal of Law and Economics*, 21 (October 1978), pp. 345-358.

P_S=price per each of Sigma, which is currently $20;

Y=income in the market area for Lambda, which is currently $20,000; and

A=monthly advertising on Lambda, which is currently $15,000.

6. Express the functional relationship between the amount of sales of Lambda (Q_L) and the price of Lambda (P_L) alone, which is the demand function for Lambda.

7. Express the equation for the demand curve for Lambda.

8. Identify all changes in the sales function for Lambda that would cause an increase in the demand for Lambda.

9. Calculate expected sales of Lambda at current values for all variables in the sales function for Lambda.

10. Interpret the coefficient (+0.0004) for advertising (A).

Answer each of the next THREE questions based on the demand and supply functions expressed below for a product X and any other information provided in the questions:

$Q_{XD}=100-0.5P_X$

$Q_{XS}=20+0.3P_X$

The variables are

Q_{XD} is the quantity of product X demanded, in thousands per month,

Q_{XS} is the quantity of product supplied, in thousands per month, and

P_X is the price of product X.

11. 11. What is the equilibrium market price for product X and quantity of product X demanded and supplied at the equilibrium price?

12. 12. Suppose that the U.S. Congress passed legislation authorizing a federal agency to establish, maintain, and enforce a price floor for product X and that officials of the agency set a price floor of $80. How much of product X would be bought and sold? Would a shortage or surplus be observed in the market for product X?

13. 13. Suppose that the U.S. Congress passed legislation authorizing a federal agency to establish, maintain, and enforce a price ceiling for product X and that officials of the agency set a price ceiling of $80. How much of product X would be bought and sold? Would a shortage or surplus be observed in the market for product X?

14. 14. Suppose the demand for a product increases at a time that the supply for the product is unchanged. What are the expected effects on market equilibrium price and the equilibrium amount bought and sold?

15. 15. Suppose the supply for a product increases at a time that the demand for the product is unchanged. What are the expected effects on market equilibrium price and the equilibrium amount bought and sold?

16. Suppose that both the demand and the supply for a product increase. What are the expected effects on market equilibrium price and the equilibrium amount bought and sold?

17. Suppose the demand for a product increases at a time when the supply for the product decreases. What are the expected effects on market equilibrium price and the equilibrium amount of the product bought and sold?

18. Suppose the market for a product, Omega, is in equilibrium. Then, something happens to increase the supply of Omega while the demand for it is unchanged. What effect would this disturbance of market equilibrium have on the market equilibrium price of Omega and the market equilibrium amount of it bought and sold?

19. Suppose the market for a product, Theta, is in equilibrium. Then, market factors change to increase both the demand for and supply of Theta. What effect would this disturbance of market equilibrium have on the market equilibrium price of Theta and the market equilibrium amount of it bought and sold?

20. Suppose the market for a consumer product, Delta, is in equilibrium. Delta is a normal good. Then, a recession results in a significant fall in household incomes at a time that the cost of a raw material used in producing Delta rises significantly. What effect would this disturbance of market equilibrium have on the market equilibrium price of Delta and the market equilibrium amount of it bought and sold?

21. Suppose the market for an agricultural product, Iota, is in equilibrium. Iota is a normal good. Then, the price of a substitute, competing product, Pi, rises substantially. At the same time, the price of a product, Upsilon, this is a product that producers of Iota could produce with inputs of the same resources required to produce Iota, also rises substantially. What effect would this disturbance of market equilibrium have on the market equilibrium price of Iota and the market equilibrium amount of it bought and sold?

22. In the 1990s, personal computer prices were falling. Using demand and supply analysis, offer an explanation for this observation.

23. In the late 1990s, copper and gold prices were falling. Using demand and supply analysis, offer an explanation for this observation.

24. Suppose demand for an agricultural product increases during a time in which supply of the agricultural product is unchanged. Would the market equilibrium price be expected to rise or fall? Would revenue from sales of the agricultural product be expected to rise or fall?

25. Suppose the demand for and supply of an agricultural product increase during a particular time period. Would the market equilibrium price be expected to rise or fall?

26. Suppose the supply of an agricultural product decreases during a time in which demand for the agricultural product increased. Would the market equilibrium price be expected to rise or fall?

27. In Spring 1997, print and broadcast media reported that coffee prices were going up. Folgers, for example, announced a forthcoming price increase of 7%. Using basic supply and demand analysis, what are possible causes of this price increase? Which one of the possibilities is the most likely cause of this price increase?

28. In an article published in the 12 February 1997 *Times-Picayune*, Texaco's CEO, Peter Bijur, was reported as saying about the demand and supply of fossil fuels (oil, gas, and coal), "...[S]uccesses generated

by 3-D seismic imaging and horizontal drilling have opened up deep-water exploration, which has added several billion barrels to world reserves. In the refining segment, there have been advances such as coolants and oil that do not need to be changed frequently." He added that fossil fuels "will be increasingly in demand. Not only is the supply growing, but world demand is expected to grow by 21 million barrels a day by the year 2010." What can we expect to happen to the prices of oil, gas, and coal over this horizon?

29. A brand manager for Procter & Gamble monitors unit sales of his product carefully and routinely uses a sales function to develop sales expectations as a metric to judge sales performance. For months, unit sales have been within the range of expectations. In the following months, the brand manager once reduced the price of the product and unit sales increased as forecast. At another time, unit sales increased beyond forecast at a time when price of the product was unchanged. Comment on each of these sales events in terms of demand for the product, *i.e.*, whether either event is or both events are an increase in demand for the product.

30. The brand manager for a consumer product (Product 1) has an estimated sales function for the product, which is

$Q_1 = 93 - 10P_1 - 5P_2 + 4P_3 + 0.006Y + 0.0005A_1$

The variables are

Q_1 = unit sales of Product 1;

P_1 = price of Product 1, which currently is $15;

P_2 = price of a second consumer product, Product 2, which currently is $5;

P_3 = price of a third consumer product, Product 3, which currently is $10;

Y = per capita income in the market, which currently is $12,000; and

A_1 = advertising outlay on Product 1, which currently is $100,000.

    a. Write a narrative interpretation of the coefficient for P_3.

    b. Calculate expected unit sales.

    c. Based on the sales function, solve for and write out the demand function.

    d. Based on the demand function, solve for and write out the equation for the demand curve.

31. A commodities market analyst has estimated the sales and supply functions for an agricultural commodity, A, as follows:

$Q_D = 150 - 8P_A + 4P_B + 0.005Y$

$Q_S = 100 + 2P_A$

The variables are

Q_D = amount of agricultural commodity A demanded;

Q_S = amount of agricultural commodity A supplied;

P_A = price of agricultural commodity A;

P_B=price of another agricultural commodity, B, which currently is $100; and

Y=per capita income, which currently is $10,000.

   a. Calculate the market equilibrium price for agricultural commodity A.

   b. Calculate the amount of agricultural commodity A bought and sold at the market equilibrium price.

   c. Suppose a price floor of $60 is established for agricultural commodity A. Would the price floor be effective or ineffective? Calculate the amount of surplus or shortage if any that would be expected at the price floor.

   d. Suppose a price ceiling of $40 is established for agricultural commodity A. Would the price ceiling be effective or ineffective? Calculate the amount of surplus or shortage if any that would be expected at the price ceiling.

32. Suppose you are the market analyst for an agricultural commodity. Changes are expected in the market for this commodity. Based on the changes identified below, what would you expect in this market with respect to price and amount bought and sold?

   a. You expect the demand for the commodity to increase but the supply of the commodity to remain unchanged.

   b. You expect the demand for the commodity to increase but the supply of the commodity to decrease.

   c. You expect the demand for the commodity to increase significantly but the supply of the commodity to increase only slightly by comparison.

PRACTICE QUESTIONS *(AND ANSWERS)*

Answer each of the next FIVE questions based on the estimated sales function expressed immediately below and any additional information given in a particular question. Suppose that the demand function for a product A has been estimated as:

   $Q_A = 10.5 - 0.8P_A - 0.2P_B + 0.1P_C + 0.0005Y$

The variables are

   Q_A is the quantity of product A demanded, in thousands per month;

   P_A is the price of product A;

   P_B is the price of a product B, which is currently $10;

   P_C is the price of a product C, which is currently $5; and

   Y is the level of per capita income, which is currently $10,000.

1. Of the following changes, which one would cause an increase in the demand for product A: a decrease in the price of product A, an increase in the price of product A, an increase in the price of product B, an increase in the price of product C, or a decrease in the level of per capita income?

   An increase in the price of product C would increase the demand for product A, interpreted as a rightward shift in the demand curve for the product. A decrease in the price of product A would cause an increase in the quantity of product A demanded, i.e., movement down and along the demand curve, rather than an increase in the demand for product A, i.e., a rightward shift in the demand curve.

2. Is product A normal or inferior? Are product A and product B substitutes or complements? Are product A and product C substitutes or complements?

Since the coefficient for Y is positive (+0.0005), product A is a normal good. Since the coefficient for P_B is negative (−0.2), products A and B are complements. Since the coefficient for P_C is positive (+0.1), products A and C are substitutes.

3. Express the relationship between expected sales of product A and the price of product A alone, which is the demand function for product A.

By substitution,

$Q_A=10.5-0.8P_A-0.2(10)+0.1(5)+0.0005(10,000)$

$Q_A=14-0.8P_A$

The demand function states the relationship between sales of A and the price of A alone and thus is the demand function for A.

4. When the price of product A is $5, what is the amount of expected sales of product A?

By substitution,

$Q_A=14-0.8(5)=14-4=10$

The amount of sales expected is 10 thousand units per month.

5. If a demand curve were graphed for product A, what would be the equation for the graphed demand curve?

The demand function for A is

$Q_A=14-0.8P_A$

$0.8P_A=14-Q_A$

$P_A=(14/0.8)-(1/0.8)$

$P_A=17.5-1.25Q_A$

This function is the demand curve for A.

Answer each of the next FIVE questions based on the following sales function for a woolen commodity, Lambda:

$Q_L=7.0-1.6P_L-0.2P_C+0.8P_S+0.0005Y+0.0004A$

The variables are

Q_L=amount of sales of Lambda, in thousands per month;

P_L=price per each of Lambda, which is currently $15;

P_C=price per each of Chi, which is currently $25;

P_S=price per each of Sigma, which is currently $20;

Y=income in the market area for Lambda, which is currently $20,000; and

A=monthly advertising on Lambda, which is currently $15,000.

6. Express the functional relationship between the amount of sales of Lambda (Q_L) and the price of Lambda (P_L) alone, which is the demand function for Lambda.

By substitution,

$Q_L=7-1.6P_L-0.2(25)+0.8(20)+0.0005(20,000)+0.0004(15,000)$

$Q_L=7-1.6P_L-5+16+10+6$

$Q_L=34-1.6P_L$

7. Express the equation for the demand curve for Lambda.

The demand function for Lambda is

$Q_L=34-1.6P_L$

$1.6P_L=34-Q_L$

$P_L=21.25-0.625Q_L$

This function is the demand curve for Lambda.

8. Identify all changes in the sales function for Lambda that would cause an increase in the demand for Lambda.

Since an increase in demand for Lambda is interpreted as a rightward shift in the demand curve for the product, the only known causes of such a shift would be a fall in P_C, a rise in P_S, a rise in Y, a rise in A.

9. Calculate expected sales of Lambda at current values for all variables in the sales function for Lambda.

By substitution,

$Q_L=7-1.6(15)-0.2(25)+0.8(20)+0.0005(20,000)+0.0004(15,000)$

$Q_L=7-24-5+16+10+6$

$Q_L=10$

Expected sales are 10 thousand units.

10. Interpret the coefficient (+0.0004) for advertising (A).

For every $1 increase in the monthly advertising budget, there is an increase in monthly sales of Lambda of 0.0004 thousand units. In other words, for every $1 increase, there is a 0.4 unit increase in sales. For example, an increase of $1,000 in the monthly budget will result in a sales increase of 400 units.

Answer each of the next THREE questions based on the demand and supply functions expressed below for a product X and any other information provided in the questions:

$Q_{XD}=100-0.5P_X$

$Q_{XS}=20+0.3P_X$

The variables are

Q_{XD} is the quantity of product X demanded, in thousands per month,

Q_{XS} is the quantity of product supplied, in thousands per month, and

P_X is the price of product X.

11. What is the equilibrium market price for product X and quantity of product X demanded and supplied at the equilibrium price?

Setting the demand function equal to the supply function,

$100-0.5P_X=20+0.3P_X$

$-0.8P_X=-80$

$P_X=100$

The equilibrium market price is $100. By substitution in the demand function,

$Q_{XD}=100-0.5(100)$

$Q_{XD}=100-50$

$Q_{XD}=50$

The quantity of product X demanded at the equilibrium price is 50 thousand units per month. By substitution in the supply function,

$Q_{XS}=20+0.3(100)$

$Q_{XS}=20+30$

$Q_{XS}=50$

The quantity of product X supplied at the equilibrium price is 50 thousand units per month.

12. Suppose that the U.S. Congress passed legislation authorizing a federal agency to establish, maintain, and enforce a price floor for product X and that officials of the agency set a price floor of $80. How much of product X would be bought and sold? Would a shortage or surplus be observed in the market for product X?

Since the price floor is below the market equilibrium price of $100, it is ineffective, and 50 thousand units of product X would be bought and sold per month. Neither a shortage nor a surplus would be observed.

13. Suppose that the U.S. Congress passed legislation authorizing a federal agency to establish, maintain, and enforce a price ceiling for product X and those officials of the agency set a price ceiling of $80. How much of product X would be bought and sold? Would a shortage or surplus be observed in the market for product X?

The price ceiling is below the market price of $100 and thus is effective. The amount of product X buyers want to purchase at the price ceiling of $80 is

$Q_{XD}=100-0.5(80)$

$Q_{XD}=100-40=60$

The amount of product X that buyers want to purchase at the price ceiling is 60 thousand units per month. The amount of product X that sellers want to offer for sale at the price ceiling of $80 is

$Q_{XS}=20+0.3(80)$

$Q_{XS}=20+24=44$

The amount of product X that sellers want to offer for sale is 44 thousand units per month. Therefore, at the price ceiling of $80, people would want to buy 60 thousand units per month, but firms would want to provide only 44 thousand units per month. A shortage of 16 thousand units per month would be observed. The quantity of product X bought and sold at the price ceiling of $80 would be 44 thousand units per month.

14. Suppose the demand for a product increases at a time that the supply for the product is unchanged. What are the expected effects on market equilibrium price and the equilibrium amount bought and sold?

Price is expected to rise. Amount bought and sold also is expected to rise.

15. Suppose the supply for a product increases at a time that the demand for the product is unchanged. What are the expected effects on market equilibrium price and the equilibrium amount bought and sold?

Price is expected to fall. Amount bought and sold is expected to rise.

16. Suppose that both the demand and the supply for a product increase. What are the expected effects on market equilibrium price and the equilibrium amount bought and sold?

Depending on the relative increases in demand and supply, price might rise, fall, or remain constant. Regardless of the relative increases in demand and supply, the amount bought and sold is expected to rise.

17. Suppose the demand for a product increases at a time when the supply for the product decreases. What are the expected effects on market equilibrium price and the equilibrium amount of the product bought and sold?

Depending on the relative changes in demand and supply, the amount bought and sold might rise, fall, or remain constant. Regardless of the relative changes in demand and supply, price is expected to rise.

18. Suppose the market for a product, Omega, is in equilibrium. Then, something happens to increase the supply of Omega while the demand for it is unchanged. What effect would this disturbance of market equilibrium have on the market equilibrium price of Omega and the market equilibrium amount of it bought and sold?

The market equilibrium price of Omega would fall, and the market equilibrium amount of Omega bought and sold would rise.

19. Suppose the market for a product, Theta, is in equilibrium. Then, market factors change to increase both the demand for and supply of Theta. What effect would this disturbance of market equilibrium have on the market equilibrium price of Theta and the market equilibrium amount of it bought and sold?

The market equilibrium amount of Theta would rise, but the market equilibrium price of Theta would rise, fall, or remain unchanged depending on the comparative increases in the demand for and supply of Theta.

20. Suppose the market for a consumer product, Delta, is in equilibrium. Delta is a normal good. Then, a recession results in a significant fall in household incomes at a time that the cost of a raw material used in producing Delta rises significantly. What effect would this disturbance of market equilibrium have on the market equilibrium price of Delta and the market equilibrium amount of it bought and sold?

These simultaneous changes constitute decreases in both the demand for and supply of Delta. The market equilibrium amount of Delta bought and sold would fall, but the market equilibrium price of Delta would rise, fall, or remain unchanged depending on the comparative decreases in the demand for and supply of Delta.

21. Suppose the market for an agricultural product, Iota, is in equilibrium. Iota is a normal good. Then, the price of a substitute, competing product, Pi, rises substantially. At the same time, the price of a product, Upsilon, this is a product that producers of Iota could produce with inputs of the same resources required to produce Iota, also rises substantially. What effect would this disturbance of market equilibrium have on the market equilibrium price of Iota and the market equilibrium amount of it bought and sold?

These simultaneous changes constitute an increase in the demand for Iota and a decrease in the supply of Iota. The market equilibrium price of Iota would rise, but the market equilibrium amount of Iota bought and sold would rise, fall, or remain unchanged depending on the comparative changes in the demand for and supply of Iota.

22. In the 1990s, personal computer prices were falling. Using demand and supply analysis, offer an explanation for this observation.

Of possible explanations, the most likely is that both demand for and supply of computers was increasing, with supply increasing to a greater degree than demand. Increased demand gives rise to upward pressure on price, but increased supply originates downward pressure on price. By degree, the downward pressure was dominant and computer prices fell.

23. In the late 1990s, copper and gold prices were falling. Using demand and supply analysis, offer an explanation for this observation.

Of possible explanations, the most likely is that demand for copper and demand for gold were decreasing without any significant change in supply.

24. Suppose demand for an agricultural product increases during a time in which supply of the agricultural product is unchanged. Would the market equilibrium price be expected to rise or fall? Would revenue from sales of the agricultural product be expected to rise or fall?

The increase in demand initiates upward pressure on price. The market equilibrium price would be expected to rise. In addition, the amount bought and sold would be expected to rise. Since both price and amount sold are expected to rise, revenue from sales of the product would be expected to rise.

25. Suppose the demand for and supply of an agricultural product increase during a particular time period. Would the market equilibrium price be expected to rise or fall?

These two changes involve offsetting pressures on price, the increase in demand involving upward pressure on price and the increase in supply involving downward pressure on price. Based on this information alone, no expectations about the ultimate effect on market equilibrium price can be expressed unequivocally. If demand increases to a greater degree than supply, price will rise. If supply increases to a greater degree than demand, price will fall. If demand and supply increase by the same degree, price will remain unchanged.

26. Suppose the supply of an agricultural product decreases during a time in which demand for the agricultural product increased. Would the market equilibrium price be expected to rise or fall?

These two changes involve reinforcing pressures on price, the decrease in supply involving upward pressure on price and the increase in demand also involving upward pressure on price. The market equilibrium price would be expected to rise.

27. In Spring 1997, print and broadcast media reported that coffee prices were going up. Folgers, for example, announced a forthcoming price increase of 7%. Using basic supply and demand analysis, what are possible causes of this price increase? Which one of the possibilities is the most likely cause of this price increase?

Using basic supply and demand analysis, the possible causes of this price increase are (1) an increase in demand with constant supply; (2) a decrease in supply with constant demand; (3) an increase in demand with a decrease in supply; (4) an increase in both demand and supply, with the increase in demand greater than the increase in supply; (5) a decrease in both demand and supply, with the decrease in supply greater than the decrease in demand. The most likely cause of a sudden price increase is a simple decrease in supply with constant demand.

28. In an article published in the 12 February 1997 *Times-Picayune*, Texaco's CEO, Peter Bijur, was reported as saying about the demand and supply of fossil fuels (oil, gas, and coal), "...[S]uccesses generated by 3-D seismic imaging and horizontal drilling have opened up deep-water exploration, which has added several billion barrels to world reserves. In the refining segment, there have been advances such as coolants and oil that do not need to be changed frequently." He added that fossil fuels "will be increasingly in demand. Not only is the supply growing, but world demand is expected to grow by 21 million barrels a day by the year 2010." What can we expect to happen to the prices of oil, gas, and coal over this horizon?

Bijur is stating that he expects both demand and supply of fossil fuels to increase. Using basic supply and demand analysis, the amounts of fossil fuels supplied and demanded and thus bought and sold are expected to increase, but, depending on the comparative magnitudes of increase, price can rise, fall, or even remain constant.

29. A brand manager for Procter & Gamble monitors unit sales of his product carefully and routinely uses a sales function to develop sales expectations as a metric to judge sales performance. For months, unit sales have been within the range of expectations. In the following months, the brand manager once reduced the price of the product and unit sales increased as forecast. At another time, unit sales increased beyond forecast at a time when price of the product was unchanged. Comment on each of these sales events in terms of demand for the product, *i.e.*, whether either event is or both events are an increase in demand for the product.

In events of the first kind, the brand manager reduces the price of the product and, given demand, sales of the product are increased. The demand for the product has not changed. In terms of the demand curve, this event involves movement down and along a given demand curve. In events of the second kind, the demand for the product has increased as a result of factors other than the price of the product–e.g., price of a substitute has been increased, price of a complement has been reduced, income has increased (assuming the product is a normal good), or advertising on the product has been increased. In terms of the demand curve, this event involves a shift to the right of the entire demand curve.

30. The brand manager for a consumer product (Product 1) has an estimated sales function for the product, which is

$Q_1=93-10P_1-5P_2+4P_3+0.006Y+0.0005A_1$

The variables are

Q_1=unit sales of Product 1;

P_1=price of Product 1, which currently is \$15;

P_2=price of a second consumer product, Product 2, which currently is \$5;

P_3=price of a third consumer product, Product 3, which currently is \$10;

Y=per capita income in the market, which currently is \$12,000; and

A_1=advertising outlay on Product 1, which currently is \$100,000.

a. Write a narrative interpretation of the coefficient for P_3.

The coefficient for P_3 is 4, which is $\Delta Q_1/\Delta P_3$ or change in sales of Q_1/change in P_3. In other words, the coefficient for P_3 is a measure of the change in unit sales of Product 1 expected with respect to a change in the price of Product 3. If P_3 is increased by \$1, then Q_1 is expected to increase by 4 units.

b. Calculate expected unit sales.

The sales function is

$Q_1=93-10P_1-5P_2+4P_3+0.006Y+0.0005A_1$

By substitution,

$Q_1=93-10(15)-5(5)+4(10)+0.006(12,000)+0.0005(100,000)$

$Q_1=93-150-25+40+72+50$

$Q_1=80$

Expected sales are 80 units.

c. Based on the sales function, solve for and write out the demand function.

The demand function states the relationship between unit sales and price of the product alone, which is

$Q_1=93-10P_1-5(5)+4(10)+0.006(12,000)+0.0005(100,000)$

$Q_1=93-10P_1-25+40+72+50$

$Q_1=230-10P_1$

d. Based on the demand function, solve for and write out the equation for the demand curve.

The equation for the demand curve solves the demand function for price, which is

$Q_1=230-10P_1$

$10P_1=230-Q_1$

$P_1=23-0.1Q_1$

31. A commodities market analyst has estimated the sales and supply functions for an agricultural commodity, A, as follows:

$Q_D = 150 - 8P_A + 4P_B + 0.005Y$

$Q_S = 100 + 2P_A$

The variables are

Q_D = amount of agricultural commodity A demanded;

Q_S = amount of agricultural commodity A supplied;

P_A = price of agricultural commodity A;

P_B = price of another agricultural commodity, B, which currently is $100; and

Y = per capita income, which currently is $10,000.

a. Calculate the market equilibrium price for agricultural commodity A.

First, to obtain the demand function, by substitution,

$Q_A = 150 - 8P_A + 4(100) + 0.005(10,000)$

$Q_A = 150 - 8P_A + 400 + 50$

$Q_A = 600 - 8P_A$

Setting the demand function equal to the supply function,

$600 - 8P_A = 100 + 2P_A$

Solving for P_A,

$-10P_A = -500$

$P_A = 50$

The market equilibrium price is $50.

b. Calculate the amount of agricultural commodity A bought and sold at the market equilibrium price.

By substitution in the demand function,

$Q_{AD} = 600 - 8(50) = 600 - 400 = 200$

By substitution in the supply function,

$Q_{AS} = 100 + 2(50) = 100 + 100 = 200$

The amount of commodity A bought and sold at the market equilibrium price is 200 units.

c. Suppose a price floor of $60 is established for agricultural commodity A. Would the price floor be effective or ineffective? Calculate the amount of surplus or shortage if any that would be expected at the price floor.

The price floor is effective since it is established above the market equilibrium price. The amount demanded at the price floor of $60 is, by substitution,

$Q_{AD}=600-8(60)=600-480=120$

The amount supplied at the price floor of $60 is, by substitution,

$Q_{AS}=100+2(60)=100+120=220$

The amount supplied at $60 is greater than the amount demanded at $60, which is a surplus of 220–120=100 units.

d. Suppose a price ceiling of $40 is established for agricultural commodity A. Would the price ceiling be effective or ineffective? Calculate the amount of surplus or shortage if any that would be expected at the price ceiling.

The price ceiling is effective since it is established below the market equilibrium price. The amount demanded at the price ceiling of $40 is, by substitution,

$Q_{AD}=600-8(40)=600-320=280$

The amount supplied at the price ceiling of $40 is, by substitution,

$Q_{AS}=100+2(40)=100+80=180$

The amount demanded at $40 is greater than the amount supplied at $40, which is a shortage of 280–80=100 units.

32. Suppose you are the market analyst for an agricultural commodity. Changes are expected in the market for this commodity. Based on the changes identified below, what would you expect in this market with respect to price and amount bought and sold?

a. You expect the demand for the commodity to increase but the supply of the commodity to remain unchanged.

The price should rise, and the amount bought and sold also should rise.

b. You expect the demand for the commodity to increase but the supply of the commodity to decrease.

The price should rise, but without further information regarding the degree of increase in demand and the degree of decrease in supply, the effect on amount bought and sold is indeterminate, meaning the amount could rise, fall, or remain unchanged.

c. You expect the demand for the commodity to increase significantly but the supply of the commodity to increase only slightly by comparison.

The upward pressure on price as the result of the significant increase in demand is greater than the downward pressure on price as the result of the comparatively slight increase in supply. Consequently, the price should rise. The amount bought and sold should rise.

3. Demand Elasticity in Business Practice

ELASTICITY

In economics and business, elasticity generally means sensitivity or responsiveness, particularly a measure of how sensitive or responsive one thing is to changes in another thing. As a noun, elasticity is preceded by an adjective that indicates the context for the particular sensitivity. For example, price elasticity refers to the sensitivity of demand for a product with respect to changes in its price. Income elasticity deals with the sensitivity of demand for a product with respect to changes in income. Unit sales of a product might be tracked against the amount spent on advertising the product to determine sensitivity of unit sales to changes in advertising outlays, which implies advertising elasticity of demand, sometimes called promotional elasticity of demand. Even with respect to demand, elasticity is not confined to conventional independent variables such as price of a product, income, prices of substitutes or complements, and advertising outlays. For example, natural gas companies often use daily temperature to forecast unit sales of natural gas. The idea implicit in this practice is the temperature elasticity of demand for natural gas.

In general, any variable that causally affects something else might be the basis for a calculated elasticity. In an article published by the Federal Reserve Bank of Dallas, the author used elasticity to describe how rig count affects oil jobs. Rig count is the number of drilling rigs actively exploring for or developing oil. In the article, the author concluded, "As a summary statistic of how the rig count affects oil jobs, we can compute an implied elasticity of 0.376, defined as the percent change in Houston oil jobs for a one percent change in domestic rig count."[31] Therefore, if the rig count increases by ten percent, then oil jobs would increase by ten times 0.376, which is 3.76 percent.

Any elasticity is interpreted in terms of percentages. Therefore, any calculated elasticity of demand is interpreted as the percentage change in unit sales with respect to a percentage change in an independent

---

31   Bill Gilmer, "Oil and the Houston Economy Today," *Houston Business* (January 2000), p. 7.

variable. On the other hand, recall that coefficients are always interpreted in terms of units, not percentages. The wise student or manager will keep this distinction in mind.

DEMAND ELASTICITY

From a decision-making perspective, management of a business needs to know the effect of changes in any of the independent variables affecting unit sales of its product(s). Some of these independent variables are under the control of management and thus are a matter of managerial practice and strategy. For example, the price of a product, advertising outlays on a product, product quality, and customer service are under the control of management. For these variables, management would like to know the effects of these factors and the effects of changes in these factors on unit sales of a product. If for no other reason, the need to know is based on the need to assess the advisability of initiating changes. On the other hand, per capita income and prices charged by other firms for competitive products are beyond and outside the control of management. Even when dealing with factors outside the control of management, forecasting unit sales as well as formulating strategies to maintain or grow unit sales are based on the ability of management to measure the impact of changes in variables on unit sales. This ability is a kind of demand sensitivity analysis, knowing the sensitivity or responsiveness of unit sales to changes in factors that make up the underlying demand.

When any one of the independent demand variables changes, the amount of a product sold changes. Unit sales of a product may be relatively sensitive or relatively insensitive to changes in the price of the product itself, prices of other products, income, or advertising on the product. Knowledge of the sensitivity of unit sales is facilitated by the concept and calculation of demand elasticity, which measures the responsiveness of unit sales to changes in the factors that influence the demand for a product. In this sense, demand elasticity can be regarded as sales elasticity. To measure this sensitivity of unit sales, demand elasticity is expressed narratively as

Elasticity=Percentage Change in Unit Sales÷Percentage Change in an Independent Variable

This general narrative form can be restated in a more conventional form as

Elasticity=%ΔUnit Sales/%ΔIndependent Variable

In business and economics, the Greek letter Δ (delta) is used to indicate change. When Δ appears in an expression, it is translated as change in whatever follows the expression. Thus, %Δ means percentage change in whatever follows the expression.

In the case of demand elasticity, percentage change in unit sales is always in the numerator, and percentage change in one of the independent variables is always in the denominator. Price elasticity of demand measures the sensitivity of unit sales of a product to changes in the price of the product itself. Cross elasticity of demand measures the sensitivity of unit sales of a product to changes in the price of another product, either a substitute or a complement. Income elasticity of demand measures the sensitivity of unit sales of a product to changes in income. Advertising elasticity of demand measures the sensitivity of unit sales of a product to changes in advertising outlays on the product.

PRICE ELASTICITY OF DEMAND

Consider the position of management of a firm considering an increase in the price of the firm's product. Management understands that the increase in price is likely to result in a negative effect on unit sales.

This loss of unit sales may be acceptable to management if the loss is not significant. If unit sales do not decline much, the firm might increase its sales revenue when the price of the firm's product is raised. If unit sales decline significantly, however, sales revenue may decline after the price increase, and the firm could be worsened as a result. After all, sales revenue is one of two components comprising profit, cost of production being the other component. Underlying this matter is the price elasticity of demand.

If all independent variables affecting the demand for a product except the price of the product are constant at given values, the sensitivity of unit sales to the price of the product itself can be measured by the price elasticity of demand. Essentially, the price elasticity of demand measures the percentage change in unit sales of a product due to a percentage change in the price of the product itself.

Letting Q represent unit sales of the product and P the price of the product, price elasticity of demand can be expressed generally as

$$E_{PRICE} = \%\Delta Q / \%\Delta P$$

This expression can be restated as

$$E_{PRICE} = (\Delta Q/Q)/(\Delta P/P)$$

Inverting the denominator and multiplying,

$$E_{PRICE} = (\Delta Q/Q)(P/\Delta P)$$

Rearranging terms,

$$E_{PRICE} = (\Delta Q/\Delta P)(P/Q)$$

This final expression of price elasticity of demand is convenient for calculation.

Calculating the Price Elasticity of Demand for Brand X

Recall the sales function for Brand X, which established the relationship between unit sales of Brand X (Q_X) and a number of independent variables, including the price of Brand X (P_X), price of Brand S (P_S), price of Product C (P_C), per capita income (Y), and advertising outlays on Brand X (A_X). The sales function for Brand X was

$$Q_X = 1.3 - 2.1P_X + 1.2P_S - 0.5P_C + 0.0002Y + 0.001A_X$$

In this sales function for Brand X, the coefficient for each independent variable indicates the expected change in unit sales of Brand X sold due to a change in the respective independent variable. For example, the coefficient for the price of Brand X (P_X) is –2.1, which means that

$$\Delta Q_X / \Delta P_X = -2.1$$

The coefficient for P_X, which is $\Delta Q_X / \Delta P_X$, is highly useful in calculating the price elasticity of demand for Brand X. The coefficient for P_X is the first term in calculating the price elasticity of demand for

Brand X and may be substituted directly, which is

$$E_{PRICE} = -2.1(P_X/Q_X)$$

To complete the calculation of price elasticity, the second term in parentheses must be determined from information on price and unit sales.

Suppose the price of Brand X is \$2, the price of Brand S is \$2; the price of Product C is \$1; per capita income is \$15,000; and monthly advertising outlays on Brand X are \$500. By substitution into the sales function, expected sales of Brand X are

$Q_X = 1.3 - 2.1(2) + 1.2(2) - 0.5(1) + 0.0002(15,000) + 0.001(500)$

$Q_X = 1.3 - 4.2 + 2.4 - 0.5 + 3.0 + 0.5$

$Q_X = 2.5$

Unit sales of 2.5 thousand (2,500) units per week are expected. The price and sales information can be used for the second term in the price elasticity of demand. Substituting \$2 for the price of Brand X and 2.5 for unit sales of Brand X,

$E_{PRICE} = -2.1(2/2.5)$

$E_{PRICE} = -2.1(0.80)$

$E_{PRICE} = -1.68$

The price elasticity of demand for Brand X is –1.68 when the price of Brand X is \$2 and the other independent variables are fixed and constant at given values. The price elasticity of –1.68 is a pure number. No percentage sign follows –1.68. However, the interpretation of the pure number is in terms of percentage.

The interpretation of –1.68 is that for every one percent change in the price of Brand X, there is a corresponding inverse 1.68 percent change in unit sales of Brand X. If there were a 1% increase in the price of Brand X (from \$2 to \$2.02), there would be an estimated 1.68% decrease in unit sales of Brand X (from 2,500 to 2,458 units). Nothing is magic, special, or necessary about one percent. One percent is used here to facilitate understanding and interpretation. If price were increased by 2% (from \$2 to \$2.04), for example, a corresponding decline in unit sales of 2(–1.68)=–3.36% is expected. If there were a 10% decrease in the price of Brand X (from \$2 to \$1.80), there would be an estimated 16.8% increase in unit sales of Brand X (from 2,500 to 2,920 units).

Price elasticity of demand for Brand X is not the same for all prices. For example, price elasticity when price is \$2, which is –1.68, is different from price elasticity when price is \$2.50, which is –3.62, or when price is \$1, which is –0.46. In calculation of price elasticity, the first term (–2.1) does not change from one calculation to another because it is obtained from the price coefficient in the sales function, but the second term changes from one price to another. The second term changes from one point on the demand curve for Brand X to another. Figure 3.1 shows the demand curve for Brand X with associated price elasticity of demand for selected prices for Brand X.

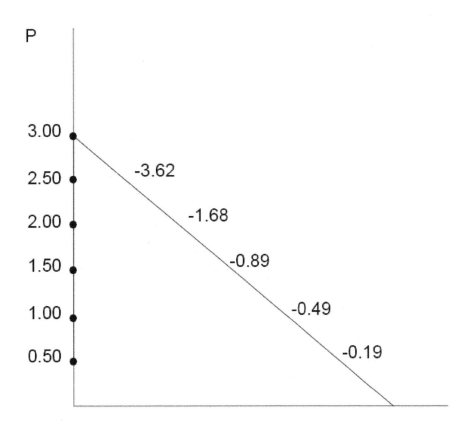

FIGURE 3.1
PRICE ELASTICITY FOR BRAND X AT
SELECTED PRICES

Arc Price Elasticity of Demand

The preceding approach to price elasticity is called the point price elasticity of demand because the price elasticity of demand is being calculated at a specific price, which can be interpreted as a specific point on the demand curve for a product. When using point price elasticity, care must be taken when using the calculation to estimate the expected effect on unit sales of a rather large change in price. The point price elasticity at one price might be significantly different from point price elasticity at another.

Another approach is called the arc price elasticity of demand, which essentially calculates the average price elasticity of demand for the segment of a demand curve between two prices. Thus, arc price elasticity is average price elasticity between two prices, which is

E_{PRICE}=(Change in Q/Average Q)÷(Change in P/Average P)

Arc price elasticity of demand can be restated as

E_{PRICE}=%ΔAverage Sales/%ΔAverage Price

Arc price elasticity of demand can be rewritten as

$E_{PRICE}=[(Q_2-Q_1)\div(Q_2+Q_1)/2]/[(P_2-P_1)\div(P_2+P_1)/2]$

The variables are

Q_1=amount sold at P_1,

Q_2=amount sold at P_2,

P_1=price at which Q_1 was sold, and

P_2=price at which Q_2 was sold.

The term Q_2-Q_1 represents ΔQ, and the term P_2-P_1 represents ΔP. The term $(Q_2+Q_1)/2$ represents average amount sold in the range over which the price elasticity is being calculated, and the term $(P_2+P_1)/2$ represents average price over this range. The numerator gives percentage change in average sales, and the denominator gives percentage change in average price. The designations Q_1, Q_2, P_1, and P_2 are interchangeable. What is important is linking unit sales at one price and unit sales at the other price, i.e., Q_1 with P_1 and Q_2 with P_2. Whether designating one price and corresponding quantity as P_1 and Q_1 or P_2 and Q_2 does not matter. The result will be identical.

As a rule, arc price elasticity of demand is calculated as an approximation when data on price and amount sold consist of only two observations. When knowledge is limited to amount sold at one price and amount sold at another price, arc approximation can be used to calculate price elasticity of demand. If robust data are available, of course, a sales or demand function can be estimated, and a point price elasticity of demand can be calculated.

To illustrate arc price elasticity of demand, suppose management of the business producing Brand X knows from experience that sales were 400 units when a price of $3.00 was charged and 2,500 when a price of $2.00 was charged. The arc price elasticity of demand can be calculated from this information. By substitution,

$E_{PRICE}=[(2,500-400)\div(2,500+400)/2]/[(2-3)\div(2+3)/2]$

$E_{PRICE}=[2,100\div1,450]/[-1\div2.5]$

$E_{PRICE}=1.4483/-0.4$

$E_{PRICE}=-3.62$

This calculation suggests that, over the range of experience and the two observations, there is a corresponding and inverse 3.62% change in unit sales for every one percent change in the price of this product. In effect, –3.62 is the arc price elasticity of demand for $2.50, which lies midway between $3.00 and $2.00.

By comparison, consider point elasticity of demand when the price of Brand X is $2.50. Sales expected at $2.50 would be, by substitution,

$Q_X=6.7-2.1\ (2.50)$

$Q_X=6.7-5.25$

$Q_X=1.45$

Unit sales of 1.45 (1,450) are expected when the price of Brand X is $2.50. By substitution as the second term in price elasticity,

$E_{PRICE} = -2.1(2.50/1.45)$

$E_{PRICE} = -2.1(1.72)$

$E_{PRICE} = -3.62$

The arc approximation of price elasticity over the range of $3 to $2 was –3.62, matching the point price elasticity for $2.50. Accordingly, arc approximation is a splendid means of estimating price elasticity when sales and demand functions are not available.

Arc Price Elasticity for Housing

Sometimes, data are not available for a refined point estimate of price elasticity. This lack of data is the case when a sales function has not been estimated. In such cases, limited data often are used to estimate a quick and dirty estimate or a back of the envelope calculation. For example, consider the following information. According to the National Association of Realtors, the median sales price of existing single-family homes in the United States was $183,900 in September 2012, and completed transactions were at a seasonally adjusted annual rate of 4.75 million homes. In October 2012, the median price was $178,600, and completed transactions were at a seasonally adjusted annual rate of 4.79 million homes. From this information, an arc price elasticity of demand for single-family housing can be estimated, which is

$E_{PRICE} = [(4.79-4.75) \div (4.79+4.75)/2] / [(178,600-183,900) \div (178,600+183,900)/2]$

$E_{PRICE} = [0.04/4.77] / [-5,300/181,250]$

$E_{PRICE} = [0.0084/-0.0292]$

$E_{PRICE} = -0.29$

From this rough estimate of price elasticity, sales of single-family houses would decline by 0.29 percent for every one percent increase in the median price of such housing and would be expected to increase by 0.29 percent for every one percent decrease in median price. If the estimation seems too quick and too dirty, remember that even the most refined point estimates are still only an estimate of the true but unknown price elasticity. A cautionary note is appropriate, particularly with respect to housing. The demand for single-family housing depends significantly on factors other than price. For example, demand for housing depends significantly on income and mortgage interest rates. At a time when mortgage interest rates are low, existing home sales might increase even while the median sales price also increases. This observation is not an exception or violation of the law of demand. It is simply a matter of a factor other than price increasing demand and thus increasing price. In such cases, both the amount purchased and the price both increase.

Arc Price Elasticity for Vanity License Plates

Instead of regular license plates for automobiles, personalized or vanity license plates can be purchased. Instead of a standard plate such as RPT209, a Chicago Cubs fan might want something personal such as CUBSWIN1, or a deep-sea fisherman might want something like NACLH2O. States will sell a license plate expressing almost anything as long as it uses no more than a certain number of alphanumeric symbols and is not obviously vulgar, profane, or otherwise offensive.

In 1986, Texas increased the price of vanity plates from \$25 to \$75. State newspapers reported that 150,000 vanity plates were sold at the old price, but only 60,000 people ordered such plates at the new price.[32] From this information, the arc price elasticity of demand for vanity can be measured, which is

$$E_{PRICE}=[(150,000-60,000) \div (150,000+60,000)/2]/[(25-75) \div (25+75)/2]$$

$$E_{PRICE}=[90,000/105,000]/[-50/50]$$

$$E_{PRICE}=0.8571/-1$$

$$E_{PRICE}=-0.86$$

Again, this estimate is quick and dirty, the kind of estimate that might be scribbled on the back of an envelope or on a paper napkin. It also is ephemeral in the sense that the estimate might not be a good predictor of what to expect if the price of vanity plates were raised from \$75 to \$225.

Price Elastic and Price Inelastic Demand

Price elasticity of demand is always negative because of the inverse relationship between price and quantity of the product demanded, which is the law of demand. Theoretically, the price elasticity can be zero, which is nonnegative. Perhaps a more technically correct statement is that the calculated price elasticity of demand is never positive. Because the price elasticity of demand is negative, it is important to remember that, for example, the number −0.29 is larger than −1.68. Therefore, the larger the price elasticity, the less sensitive unit sales are to a change of price, and the smaller the price elasticity, the more sensitive unit sales are to a change of price. This kind of upside down thinking is awkward. The need to remember what appears to be a smaller negative number is really a larger negative number is a nuisance.

When calculated price elasticity is interpreted, it is convenient to ignore the minus sign and use absolute value, denoted by two vertical lines, as in

$$E_{PRICE}=|-1.68|=1.68$$

$$E_{PRICE}=|-0.86|=0.86$$

$$E_{PRICE}=|-0.29|=0.29$$

Using absolute value is the equivalent of ignoring the minus sign. When the minus sign is ignored, the price elasticity of demand is unsigned, which means the elasticity is negative but the negative sign is implied. Unsigned price elasticity can be seen clearly in terms immediately understandable. The larger the unsigned price elasticity, the more sensitive sales of a product are to changes in its own price. The smaller the unsigned price elasticity, the less sensitive sales of a product are to changes in its own price.

When the unsigned price elasticity of demand is greater than one, unit sales of a product are relatively sensitive to changes in the price of the product. For any given percentage change in the price of a product, an even greater percentage change in unit sales of the product is expected. In this case, demand for the product is said to be price elastic. When the unsigned price elasticity is less than one, unit sales of a product are relatively insensitive to changes in the price of the product. For any given percentage change

---

32   Barbara Boughton, "A License for Vanity," *Houston Post* (October 19, 1986), pp. 1G, 10G.

in the price of a product, a smaller percentage change in unit sales of the product is expected. In this case, demand is said to be price inelastic. When the unsigned price elasticity is equal to one, demand has unitary price elasticity. Unitary price elasticity means simply that price elasticity is equal to one. For any given percentage change in price, an equivalent percentage change in unit sales is expected.

Price Elasticity of Demand for Newsprint

According to a 1984 study, the demand for newsprint in the northeastern United States was estimated as

   $Q=2,672-0.51P$

Q is the amount of newsprint sold in thousands of metric tons and P is the price per metric ton of newsprint.[33] Suppose the price of newsprint was $400 per metric ton. By substitution,

   $Q=2,672-0.51(400)$

   $Q=2,672-204$

   $Q=2,468$

The quantity of newsprint that buyers would purchase at the price of $400 per metric ton is 2.468 million metric tons. By substitution,

   $E_{PRICE}=-0.51(400/2,468)$

   $E_{PRICE}=-0.51(0.1621)$

   $E_{PRICE}=-0.08$

Since the unsigned price elasticity of demand for newsprint is 0.08, which is less than one, the demand for newsprint is price inelastic. Indeed, unit sales of newsprint are remarkably unresponsive to changes in the price of newsprint. For example, if the price of newsprint were to rise by ten percent, unit sales of newsprint would be expected to fall by less than one percent.

General Determinants of Price Elasticity of Demand

People are rarely if ever completely insensitive to the price of a product. Price is more important as an influence on unit sales and purchases of some products than it is for others. Three main factors generally influence price elasticity of demand: percentage of income spent on the product, time people have to adjust to changes in price, and availability and closeness of substitutes. For specific products, factors in addition to these general influences might be involved.

First, the proportion of income spent on a product is a factor. Some products do not cost enough for people to change their purchases significantly when prices of those products rise or fall. When expenditure on certain products is small as a proportion of income, unit sales of these products tend to be relatively insensitive to even whopping percentage increases in price. For example, Diamond Large Kitchen Matches sell for about twenty-five cents per box of 250 matches. If the price doubled, the price would be only fifty cents per box, hardly a significant proportion of income. Shopping around for a lower price is not worthwhile. If buyer expenditure on a product is a large fraction of income or budget, however, savings from finding a comparable item at a lower price can be large. A GE Profile Refrigerator is priced at about

33   F. Guder and J. Buongiorno, "An Interregional Analysis of the North American Newsprint Industry," *Interfaces* (September-October 1984), pp. 85-95.

two thousand dollars. Consequently, buyers tend to shop more for such pricey items or even postpone purchase. Refrigerators, washing machines, dryers, furniture, and other consumer durables are good examples of products with price sensitive demand because buyers are motivated to shop around before making final decisions about purchases. Moreover, purchase of consumer durables can be postponed.

Second, time is an important factor in the price elasticity of demand. The effect of a price change takes time to have its full impact on unit sales. Consider a sharp price increase. Supplies in inventory are used up before they are replenished through purchase at the higher price. Converting from one product to another takes time, a lot of time in some cases. For example, if the price of home heating oil rises sharply relative to the price of natural gas and the disparity is expected to continue, people with oil furnaces might adjust their thermostats in the short term but consider eventual conversion from an oil furnace to a natural gas furnace. Acting on such consideration takes time. In a similar way, consider the sharp rise in gasoline prices. When the price of regular gasoline rises from about three dollars per gallon to about four dollars per gallon, people at first keep driving their gasoline guzzlers while cutting back their mileage driven. Later, however, they plan to trade their guzzlers for vehicles that have significantly better gas mileage. Indeed, the short run price elasticity of demand for gasoline has been estimated as −0.5, meaning the demand for gasoline is price inelastic in the short run. The long run price elasticity of demand for gasoline has been estimated as –1.5, meaning the demand for gasoline is price elastic in the long run. The point is that, when the price of a product changes, the effect of the price change on unit sales is greater with the length of time people have to adjust to the changed price.

Third, the principal reason that the demand for some products is more sensitive to price than that for others is the availability and closeness of substitutes. Most products have substitutes. The more available are substitutes for a product, the more sensitive unit sales are to changes in the price of the product. For example, Braswell's Vidalia Onion Poppyseed Salad Dressing and Rouses Supermarket Vidalia Onion Poppyseed Salad Dressing are close substitutes, actually perfect substitutes since Braswell makes the Rouses house brand. If the price of the Rouses brand is raised from $3.25 per twelve ounce bottle to $3.38, a modest four percent increase, while the price of the Braswell brand remains at $3.25, then informed customers would buy the Braswell brand rather than the Rouses brand.

Estimated Price Elasticity of Demand

In many cases, price elasticity of demand has been estimated. Some estimates are based on U.S. Department of Agriculture estimates for basic foodstuffs. Other estimates are traced to trade associations or perhaps economists who focus their research on industrial organization. Demand is price inelastic for butter, chicken, pork, milk, eggs, coffee, beer, wine, cigarettes, shoes, tires, household appliances, and movies. Demand is price elastic for steak, fresh fruit, fresh peas, canned peas, fresh tomatoes, canned tomatoes, restaurant meals, wool, furniture, and airline travel. Notice that most basic foodstuffs are price inelastic. However, even though fresh peas and canned peas as well as fresh tomatoes and canned tomatoes are not perfect substitutes, they are close enough to make them price elastic. Demand for gasoline is price inelastic in the short run and price elastic in the long run.

It would be wrong to suppose that, because industry demand for a product is price inelastic, demand for the product of each firm in that industry is price inelastic. Industry price elasticity deals with the sensitivity of industry sales with respect to industry wide price changes, whereas firm price elasticity deals with the sensitivity of a firm's sales with respect to a change in that firm's own price, with no change in prices charged by other firms in the industry. Consider cigarettes, for example. Numerous studies have shown that the demand for cigarettes is price inelastic. The calculated unsigned price elasticity is well below one, which is typical of addictive products. This finding implies that a general increase in the price of all brands of cigarettes would affect overall cigarette sales only modestly. However, if the price of only one brand of cigarettes were increased, the demand for that brand would decline more substantially because some smokers would switch to other lower-priced brands. While demand can be price inelastic at the industry level, demand can be price elastic at the firm level.

Unsigned price elasticity for a firm are higher than industry price elasticity because customers have greater substitution possibilities when the price of only one brand is raised. When the prices of cigarettes are raised across the industry, the options are to smoke less or give up smoking altogether. If the price of one brand of cigarette is raised at a time when the prices of all other brands are left unchanged, an option is to switch brands. Unsigned price elasticity for a firm also increases as more firms enter the market and more brands are offered. In other words, sales of a particular brand are likely to become more sensitive to changes in the price of that brand as other brands are offered in the market.

Firm price elasticity and industry price elasticity have been estimated in a number of studies. These studies indicate sensitivity of a firm's sales to a change in its own price when no other firm in the industry changes price and sensitivity of a firm's sales to a change in every firm's price, including the firm in question. Table 3.1 presents comparative estimates for selected industries and for selected sectors of the economy along with estimates for a typical firm in these selected industries and sectors.

Table 3.1 Price Elasticity of Demand, Industry and Firm, By Selected Industry and Sector		
Group	**Price Elasticity of Market Demand (Industry Price Elasticity)**	**Price Elasticity of Demand for a Typical Firm (Firm Price Elasticity)**
Industry		
Food	−1.0	−3.8
Tobacco	−1.3	−1.3
Textiles	−1.5	−4.7
Apparel	−1.1	−4.1
Paper	−1.5	−1.7
Printing and publishing	−1.8	−3.2
Chemicals	−1.5	−1.5
Petroleum	−1.5	−1.7
Rubber	−1.8	−2.3
Leather	−1.2	−2.3
Sector		
Agriculture	−1.8	−96.2
Construction	−1.0	−5.2
Durable manufacturing	−1.4	−3.5
Nondurable manufacturing	−1.3	−3.4
Transportation	−1.0	−1.9
Communication and utilities	−1.2	−1.8
Wholesale trade	−1.5	−1.6
Retail trade	−1.2	−1.8
Finance	−0.1	−5.5
Services	−1.2	−26.4

Source: Matthew D. Shapiro, "Measuring Market Power in U.S. Industry," National Bureau of Economic Research, Working Paper No. 2212 (1987).

Consider the textiles industry. Unit sales of a firm are more than three times as sensitive to a change in its own price when no other firm in the textiles industry changes price than unit sales of this firm are to a change in price by every firm in the textiles industry. Notice the astounding price elasticity of demand for a typical firm in the agricultural sector. For example, if a wheat farmer raised the price of his or her U.S. no. 2 soft red winter wheat by one percent over the market price of such wheat at a time when all other wheat farmers continued to sell the same grade of wheat at the market price, the one wheat farmer would lose 96.2 percent of his or her wheat sales! In the agricultural sector, products are undifferentiated, homogeneous commodities. Unit sales of a typical firm are more than fifty times more sensitive to a change in its own price when no other firm in the agricultural sector changes price than sales of this firm are to a change in price by every firm in the agricultural sector.

Whether industry or firm price elasticity should be used to assess the impact of a price change on unit sales depends on what managers expect rivals to do in response. If management of a firm expects rival firms to match a price change quickly, then the industry price elasticity is appropriate. By contrast, if management of the firm expects that rival firms will not match its price change or will match the price change only after a long time lag, then the firm price elasticity is appropriate.

Price Elasticity of Demand and Sales Revenue

The price elasticity of demand for a product is highly important in product pricing policies, decisions, and strategies. If a firm is interested in realizing the most profit from sale of its product(s), management must know something about the behavior of revenues and costs as more or less of the product is produced and offered for sale. Profit depends on costs of production and revenues from sales. Just as a firm is interested in the impact of a change in volume on its costs, the firm also is interested in how a change in volume will affect its revenues.

A firm's total revenue function or sales revenue function indicates how the firm's sales revenue varies as a function of how much product it sells. Sales revenue is simply the price of a product multiplied by the quantity of the product sold at that price, which can be stated as

TR=PQ

The variables are

TR=total revenue from sales of a product,

P=price of the product, and

Q=amount of the product sold

Consider a contrived example. Suppose 100 units of a product are sold at a price of $10. Therefore, total revenue from sales of the product is $1,000. In addition, suppose the price elasticity of demand for the product is −0.5. If the price of the product were increased by ten percent (from $10 to $11), unit sales would decline by five percent (from 100 to 95). Sales revenue would increase from $1,000 to $1,045. If price of the product were decreased by ten percent (from $10 to $9), unit sales would increase by five percent (from 100 to 105). Sales revenue would decrease from $1,000 to $945. When demand for a product is price inelastic, therefore, sales revenue is expected to increase with an increase in price and decrease with a decrease in price. Table 3.2 shows this relationship when the price elasticity of demand for the product is −0.5.

Table 3.2 Sales Revenue With Price Inelastic Demand, −0.5		
Price	**Quantity**	**Sales Revenue**
$11	95	$1,045
$10	100	$1,000
$9	105	$945

On the other hand, suppose the price elasticity of demand for the product is –2. If price of the product were increased by ten percent (from $10 to $11), unit sales would decline by twenty percent (from 100 to 80). Sales revenue would decrease from $1,000 to $880. If price of the product were decreased by ten percent (from $10 to $9), unit sales would increase by twenty percent (from 100 to 120). Sales revenue would increase from $1,000 to $1,080. When demand for a product is price elastic, therefore, sales revenue is expected to decrease with an increase in price and increase with a decrease in price. Table 3.3 shows this relationship when the price elasticity of demand for the product is –2.0.

Table 3.3 Sales Revenue With Price Elastic Demand, −2.0		
Price	**Quantity**	**Sales Revenue**
$11	80	$880
$10	100	$1,000
$9	120	$1,080

This well-known relationship between price elasticity of demand and sales revenue has significance in price strategy. For example, the relationship might have particular importance in decisions regarding items to put on sale. A cautionary note is in order, however. The relationship deals with price elasticity of demand and sales revenue, not profit. For example, consider a manufactured product. If demand for the product is price elastic and its price is reduced, sales revenue is expected to increase as more is sold. However, cost of producing a greater quantity of the product also will increase. The question is whether sales revenue increases by more than cost of production increases. If so, profit is increased. If not, profit is decreased.

These important principles are stated in terms of the given demand curve for a product. As price is reduced over any segment of a given demand curve that is price elastic, total revenue from sales rises, and as price is reduced over any segment of a demand curve that is price inelastic, total revenue from sales falls. On the other hand, as price is increased over any segment that is price inelastic, total revenue from sales also rises, and as price is increased over any segment that is price elastic, total revenue from sales falls. Finally, total revenue from sales is maximized at the precise point on a given demand curve at which price elasticity of demand is unitary. To see this point, consider Figure 3.2, which shows sales revenue for selected prices of Brand X from $0.50 to $3.00. Sales revenue is maximized at a price of $1.60 at which price elasticity of demand is –1. At the price of $1.60, unit sales would be 3,340, and sales revenue would be $5,344. To restate an earlier caveat, sales revenue, not profit, is maximized where price elasticity of demand is –1.

FIGURE 3.2
SALES REVENUE FOR SELECTED PRICES OF
BRAND X

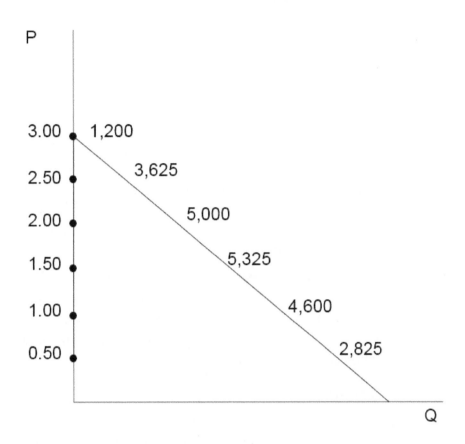

How to Price a Video

Video cassette players were mass marketed in the late 1970s and early 1980s. Original marketing plans for videos were based on rentals only. Video stores such as Blockbuster would buy videos, and households would rent them from video stores. No one in the movie business expected households to buy videos. Only a few people ever saw a movie more than once in a theater. Only these few people were expected to watch a video more than once at home. The market was believed to be limited to video stores. Videos were sold to video stores, not rented as movie prints were to theaters. Revenue that the film producer derived from sale of a video copy of *E.T.* was received in one sum from the video store. The marketing implication was that videos should be priced high and they were, usually about $80.

In 1984, Paramount sensed another sales market for selected videos. Paramount imagined that a whole new market of household customers was untapped. Before Christmas of that year, Paramount slashed prices of several popular titles to $25. The results were spectacular. More than a million videos were sold over the Christmas holidays. The number that would have been sold at higher prices is unknown, of course, but one Paramount executive said, "Every time you drop the price of a title $10, you double the willingness to buy a title." If willingness to buy meant number of units sold, demand was price elastic.

Pricing videos for sale clearly turned on the price elasticity of demand. According to one Paramount executive, the customer's buy-or-rent decision is rational. For the producer, films with a reduced sales price "should be highly repeatable family fare that has comedy, music, or action-adventure. Heavy drama like *Fatal Attraction* isn't the kind of program you put on TV every Saturday night for family entertainment." In short, if the customer expects only one-time or infrequent viewing, he or she would not buy the video. Even at a low sale price, renting was more economical, and the demand would not be particularly price elastic.[34]

Cigarette Taxes

From time to time, President Bill Clinton pushed for a large increase in federal taxes on cigarettes. After all, he didn't inhale when he experimented with funny cigarettes in England. Critics pointed out that President Clinton's proposals were designed to accomplish two mutually exclusive goals, raise revenue and discourage smoking. If demand for cigarettes were price inelastic, tax revenues would rise if cigarette taxation was increased, but purchases of cigarettes would not decline significantly. On the other hand, if demand for cigarettes were price elastic, tax revenues would fall if the tax rate was increased, but purchases of cigarettes would decline significantly.

Empirical evidence indicates that the demand for cigarettes is relatively price inelastic.[35] Price elasticity varies by age group: −1.20 for young people aged 12-17, −0.74 for young people aged 20-25, −0.44 for smokers between 26 and 35 years old, −0.15 for smokers over 35 years old. Studies of federal cigarette tax revenues take for granted that demand for cigarettes is price inelastic and thus predict higher tax revenues from tax hikes without much effect on sales of cigarettes.

CROSS PRICE ELASTICITY OF DEMAND

A few years ago, an interesting "fast fact" appeared in an airline magazine. "A one percent rise in gas prices causes a 1.74 percent drop in hotel room demand, according to recent findings by the Cornell University School of Hotel Administration. The findings came as a surprise to Cornell, and were based on analysis of monthly data from major hotel brands from 1988 through 2000...."[36] This "fast fact" thus involved the effect of the price of one product (gasoline) on unit sales of another product (hotel stays).

Unit sales of a product depend on the prices of other related products that satisfy the same buyer wants (competitive products) or complete a set in use (complementary products). Substitutes more or less satisfy the same buyer needs or requirements, and unit sales of such products are competitive with sales of other products. Complements are products that more or less complete a set in use, and unit sales of such products rise or fall in tandem as though they are one product. Managers need to know how unit sales of their product are affected by prices charged for other related products that are either substitutes or complements. In addition, people engaged in public policy aimed at monopoly and business practices meant to foster monopoly power need to know about economically related products. Indeed,

---

34   See R. Alsop, "Making Video Buyers out of Renters," and "Sales Can Soar, If the Price is Right," *Wall Street Journal* (September 23, 1988), p. B2.

35   See Michael Grossman, Jody Sindelar, John Mullahy, and Richard Andersen, "Alcohol and Cigarette Taxes," *Journal of Economic Perspectives*, 7 (Fall 1993), pp. 211-222.

36   For the article on which this "fast fact" was based, see Bruce Adams, "Effect of Gas Prices on Occupancy Debated," *Hotel and Motel Management* (September 2, 2002), pp. 3-4.

decisions in certain court cases have turned on measures of such relatedness as a means of determining the degree to which products are competitive.

Cross elasticity of demand measures the sensitivity of unit sales of a product to the price of another product. Technically, the term "cross price elasticity of demand" is preferred over merely "cross elasticity of demand" because other measures of cross elasticity are used. For example, unit sales of one product may depend in part on advertising expenditures on still another product. In that case, the cross advertising elasticity of demand might be measured.

Consider two products, Product 1 and Product 2, and prices of these two products, P_1 and P_2, respectively. If all independent variables affecting unit sales of Product 1 except the price of Product 2 are fixed at given levels, then the sensitivity of unit sales of Product 1 with respect to the price of Product 2 can be measured by the cross price elasticity of demand for Product 1 with respect to changes in P_2. Essentially, cross price elasticity of demand is the percentage change in unit sales of Product 1, which can be expressed as Q_1, due to a percentage change in P_2, given that all other independent variables are held constant, including the price of Product 1.

Thus, cross elasticity of demand for Product 1 with respect to the price of Product 2 can be expressed generally as

$$E_{CROSS} = \%\Delta Q_1 / \%\Delta P_2$$

This expression can be restated as

$$E_{CROSS} = (\Delta Q_1 / Q_1) \div (\Delta P_2 / P_2)$$

As in the case of the price elasticity of demand, the denominator can be inverted and multiplied times the numerator, so that

$$E_{CROSS} = (\Delta Q_1 / Q_1)(P_2 / \Delta P_2)$$

After rearranging terms,

$$E_{CROSS} = (\Delta Q_1 / \Delta P_2)(P_2 / Q_1)$$

This expression of cross price elasticity of demand parallels the previously stated price elasticity of demand except the price of another product is in play. As in the case of price elasticity, the cross elasticity of demand can be used to measure percentage change in unit sales of one product as the result of a percentage change in the price of another product. Cross elasticity of demand also can be used to determine if another product is economically related as either a substitute or a complement.

Substitutes

Think about two products that satisfy the same buyer wants, needs, or requirements. In other words, these products are substitutes. For example, grouper, cod, mahi-mahi, and flounder are fish with large, flaky fillets that are mild in flavor. Although not perfect substitutes, these fish are substitutes when used in recipes. If the price of grouper rose, unit sales of grouper would be expected to decline as some fish lovers switch to cod, mahi-mahi, or flounder if their prices have not risen. When the price of grouper increases, the amount of cod, mahi-mahi, or flounder sold also increases. This observation suggests a direct relationship between unit sales of grouper and the prices of cod, mahi-mahi, or flounder.

In a mathematical expression, this direct relationship would be represented as a plus sign, meaning that the dependent variable increases with increases in the independent variable, and the dependent variable decreases with decreases in the independent variable. In the case of grouper and cod, mahi-mahi, or flounder, the amount of grouper sold is the dependent variable and the prices of cod, mahi-mahi, and flounder are the independent variables. A plus sign before the coefficient for the price of cod, mahi-mahi, or flounder would be expected, indicating that unit sales of grouper increase with an increase in the price of cod, mahi-mahi, or flounder and decrease with a decrease in the prices of cod, mahi-mahi, or flounder.

Calculating the Cross Elasticity of Demand for Brand X With Respect to the Price of Brand S

When two products are substitutes, the cross price elasticity of demand is positive. Indeed, the test to determine if two products are substitutes is whether the cross price elasticity of demand is positive. The more highly positive is the cross elasticity between two products, the closer the substitutability or interchangeability of the two products.

Recall the sales function for Brand X. Suppose the price of Brand X is $2, the price of Brand S is $2, the price of Product C is $1, per capita income is $15,000, and monthly advertising outlays on Brand X are $500. By substitution into the sales function,

$$Q_X = 1.3 - 2.1(2) + 1.2(2) - 0.5(1) + 0.0002(15,000) + 0.001(500)$$

$$Q_X = 1.3 - 4.2 + 2.4 - 0.5 + 3.0 + 0.5$$

$$Q_X = 2.5$$

Unit sales of 2.5 thousand (2,500) units per week are expected.

To calculate the cross elasticity of demand for Brand X with respect to the price of Brand S, the two terms in cross price elasticity of demand must be determined. The first term, $\Delta Q_X / \Delta P_S$, is the coefficient for P_S, which is +1.2. The second term, P_S / Q_X, is 2/2.85. Now, the cross elasticity can be calculated. The cross elasticity of demand for Brand X with respect to the price of Brand S when P_S is $2 is, by substitution,

$$E_{CROSS} = 1.2(2/2.5)$$

$$E_{CROSS} = 1.2(0.8)$$

$$E_{CROSS} = 0.96$$

The cross elasticity of demand for Brand X with respect to the price of Brand S is 0.96.

The meaning of this calculated cross elasticity of demand parallels that of price elasticity of demand. For every one percent change in the price of Brand S, there is a corresponding direct 0.96 percent change in unit sales of Brand X. If the price of Brand S were increased by 10% (from $2 to $2.20), unit sales of Brand X would increase by 9.6% (from 2,500 to 2,740 units). If the price of Brand S were reduced by 5% (from $2 to $1.90), then unit sales of Brand X would decrease by 4.8% (from 2,500 to 2,380 units).

A Quirk in the Futures Market

In 1992, rumors spread that the Bush administration was close to a deal that would send large quantities of meat to the newly independent republics of the former Soviet Union. According to these rumors, the meat to be exported was pork. Although the rumor involved pork, speculation had a stronger impact on beef futures. Commodity traders recognized that pork and beef are substitutes. After the large shipment, the reduction in domestic supply of pork was expected to increase the domestic price of pork. In turn, the higher price of pork would increase the demand for beef and raise its price. Therefore, cattle futures rose on the rumor regarding pork, a substitute. On 2 August 1992, the rumors were confirmed. President Bush announced U.S. government subsidized sales under the Export Enhancement Program. Up to thirty thousand metric tons of pork was offered to the Commonwealth of Independent States.

Complements

Think about two products commonly used together. For examples, consider peanut butter and jelly, razors and razor blades, beans and rice, bagels and cream cheese, breakfast cereal and milk, gin and tonic water. Such products are used jointly and, in a sense, complete a set. For this reason, each pair of products is regarded as complements or complementary products.

Suppose a peanut crop failure in Georgia results in a sharp rise in the price of peanuts and thus in the price of peanut butter. As a result, buyers will purchase less peanut butter and eat fewer peanut butter and jelly sandwiches. Consequently, buyers also will purchase less jelly. Unit sales of jelly fall when the price of peanut butter rises, and unit sales of jelly rise when the price of peanut butter falls. This observation indicates an inverse relationship between unit sales of jelly and the price of peanut butter.

In a mathematical expression, a negative sign would indicate an inverse relationship. The dependent variable increases with decreases in the independent variable and decreases with increases in the independent variable. In the case of jelly and peanut butter, the amount of jelly sold is the dependent variable and the price of peanut butter is one of the independent variables. A negative sign before the coefficient for the price of peanut butter would be expected, indicating that unit sales of jelly increase with a decrease in the price of peanut butter and decrease with an increase in the price of peanut butter.

Calculating the Cross Elasticity of Demand for Brand X With Respect to the Price of Product C

When two products are complements, the cross elasticity of demand is negative. Indeed, the test to determine if two products are complements is whether the cross price elasticity of demand is negative or not. Once more, recall the sales function for Brand X. Suppose the price of Brand X is $2, the price of Brand S is $2, the price of Product C is $1, per capita income is $15,000, and monthly advertising outlays on Brand X are $500. By substitution into the sales function, expected sales of Brand X are

$Q_X=1.3-2.1(2)+1.2(2)-0.5(1)+0.0002(15,000)+0.001(500)$

$Q_X=1.3-4.2+2.4-0.5+3.0+0.5$

$Q_X=2.5$

Unit sales of 2.5 thousand (2,500) units per week are expected.

Now, the cross elasticity can be calculated. The cross elasticity of demand for Brand X with respect to the price of Product C when P_C is $1 is, by substitution,

$E_{CROSS}=-0.5(1/2.5)$

$E_{CROSS}=-0.5(0.4)$

$E_{CROSS}=-0.2$

The cross elasticity of demand for Brand X with respect to the price of product C is −0.2.

The meaning of this calculated cross elasticity of demand parallels that of price elasticity of demand. For every one percent change in the price of Product C, there is a corresponding but inverse 0.2 percent change in unit sales of Brand X. If the price of Product C were increased by 10% (from $1.00 to $1.10), unit sales of Brand X would fall by 2% (from 2,500 to 2,450 units). If the price of Product C were reduced by 5% (from $1 to $0.95), then unit sales of Brand X would increase by 1% (from 2,500 to 2,525 units).

Producing and Selling Complementary Products

The concept and measurement of cross elasticity of demand are important in managerial decision making. Management needs to know how sensitive unit sales of its own product are to the pricing policies of other firms. Such knowledge is critical for formulation of a firm's own pricing strategy. It is also an important concept for internal use by management of a multiproduct firm. Significant substitution or complementary interrelationships may be revealed by measuring cross elasticity among the product line of a multiproduct firm. For example, a firm producing and selling two products that are strongly complementary might realize more profit by a price strategy of setting a low price on one product to stimulate sales of the other product. The objective is to realize the most profit from sales of both products. Before digital technology overtook film in photography, Polaroid might sell its cameras at low prices, even at a loss, to stimulate sales of its film. Gillette might sell its Fusion ProGlide razors at low prices, even at a loss, to stimulate sales of its Fusion ProGlide blades at a high profit margin.

Estimated Cross Elasticity of Demand

Cross price elasticity of demand has been estimated for a number of products, including services. For example, the cross elasticity of demand for chicken with respect to the price of pork is positive, which indicates that chicken and pork are substitutes. The cross elasticity of demand for electricity with respect to the price of natural gas also is positive, also indicating they are substitutes. On the other hand, the cross elasticity of demand for rice with respect to the price of fish has been found to be negative, which indicates that fish and rice are complements.

The cross elasticity of demand for butter with respect to the price of margarine is not the same as the cross elasticity of demand for margarine with respect to the price of butter. The cross elasticity of demand for butter with respect to the price of margarine has been estimated to be about 0.7. However, the cross elasticity of demand for margarine with respect to the price of butter has been estimated to be about 1.5. Therefore, if the price of margarine were to increase by ten percent, unit sales of butter would increase by seven percent. If the price of butter were to increase by ten percent, unit sales of margarine would increase by fifteen percent. Evidently, margarine is a substitute for butter more than butter is a substitute for margarine. This curious observation might be explained by health concerns dealing with cholesterol or saturated fats in butter.

In a classic study, the cross elasticity of demand for beef with respect to the price of pork was found to be 0.28, which indicated that beef is a substitute for pork. If the price of pork were to rise by 10%, then sales of beef would be expected to increase by 2.8%. On the other hand, the cross elasticity of demand for pork with respect to the price of beef was only 0.14. If the price of beef were to rise by 10%, then sales of pork would be expected to rise by only 1.4%. People who eat pork also eat beef, but many people who eat beef do not eat pork. Therefore, when the price of pork rises, many people might substitute beef. However, when the price of beef rises, many people do not substitute pork. Religious and cultural factors undoubtedly accounted for the sizable difference in cross elasticity for the two products. Beef is a substitute for pork more than pork is a substitute for beef.[37]

Cross Elasticity in Antitrust Cases

Antitrust is another word for antimonopoly. In the United States, the basic antitrust law is the Sherman Antitrust Act of 1890. At the time, a trust was the form of monopoly that gave rise to passage of America's first antimonopoly law. Hence, the term antitrust entered the language and remains. An important issue in antitrust cases sometimes involves definition of the relevant product market used in computing measures of market share. When determining the relevant market for a product, both product and geographic markets are defined. In competition law, a relevant product market includes all products regarded as interchangeable or substitutable because of their characteristics, their prices, and their intended use. Determining the relevant market turns on determining whether products are interchangeable or substitutable, which often is based on the cross elasticity of demand.

An interesting antitrust case dealt with DuPont's production and sales of cellophane, the familiar thin, transparent cellulose material made from wood pulp. DuPont began making cellophane at its Buffalo, N.Y., plant in 1924. By the 1950s, DuPont produced seventy-five percent of cellophane, and Sylvania, a licensee, produced the remaining twenty-five percent. The Antitrust Division of the U.S. Department of Justice sued DuPont for monopolizing the cellophane industry and thus violating the Sherman Antitrust Act. The Department of Justice considered the relevant market to be cellophane. DuPont argued that the relevant market was not cellophane but rather flexible packaging materials. According to DuPont, the relevant market included cellophane as well as glassine, greaseproof and vegetable parchment papers, waxing papers, sulphite bag and wrapping papers, aluminum foil, cellulose acetate, pliofilm, polyethylene, saran, and cry-o-rap. DuPont presented evidence of a high and positive cross elasticity of demand for cellophane with respect to prices of other flexible packaging materials. When other flexible packaging materials were included in the relevant market definition, DuPont's market share dropped to a modest eighteen percent. Therefore, DuPont argued, its apparent domination of the cellophane industry was not evidence of monopoly because the cross elasticity showed substantial competition. In 1956, the U.S. Supreme Court agreed and decided in favor of DuPont.[38]

A few years later in 1964, the Department of Justice (DOJ) won a case heard before the U.S. Supreme Court by showing a high and positive cross elasticity of demand for metal cans and glass jars. Continental Can was the second largest metal can producer, and Hazel-Atlas Glass was the third largest producer of glass containers. The two companies merged in 1956, but the DOJ went to federal court seeking an order forcing Continental Can to divest assets acquired in the merger. The DOJ used cross elasticity to show that the two firms were in competition with each other and that a merger would lessen competition substantially. One of the Supreme Court findings was, "Interchangeability in use and cross-elasticity of demand are...to be used to...identify competition where, in fact, competition exists." The merger was disallowed, and Continental Can was ordered to divest assets acquired in the merger.[39]

---

37   See Herman Wold and Lars Jureen, *Demand Analysis: A Study in Econometrics* (New York: Wiley, 1953), p. 285.

38   *United States v. E.I. DuPont de Nemours and Company*, 351 U.S. 377 (1956).

39   *United States v. Continental Can Company et al.*, 378 U.S. 441 (1964).

INCOME ELASTICITY OF DEMAND

Unit sales of a product depend not only on the price of the product and perhaps the prices of certain other products but also on the level of income in the market for the product. Suppose a firm is selling its product(s) into the New England market. When average incomes or per capita incomes are rising rapidly in New England, the firm probably will sell more of its product(s) in that market. For almost all products, unit sales increase with increases in income. If a recession in economic activity resulted in falling incomes in New England, the firm probably would sell less of its product(s) in that market. For almost all products, unit sales decrease with decreases in income. Since these relationships between unit sales and incomes are found for almost all goods and services, such products are called normal goods. After all, they are the normal case.

On the other hand, some products have preferred but more expensive substitutes. When incomes rise, the preferred substitute becomes more affordable, and some switching to the preferred substitute would be expected. For such products, unit sales decline when incomes rise, and unit sales of these products rise when incomes fall. Examples are few in number because they are not the normal case, but these rare cases include certain basic foodstuffs and generic products as well as certain services such as mass transit bus rides. Cheap cuts of beef are known to be inferior goods because these cuts have preferred but more expensive substitutes, *viz.*, cuts of select, choice, or prime grades of beef. For example, non-fed beef was found to be an inferior good. Non-fed beef comes from cattle that have not been fed a special diet just before being taken to market. Most cattle are fed corn for 90 to 120 days before going to market and thus produce more tender beef and more tasty beef than non-fed cattle. The income elasticity of demand for non-fed beef was estimated at –1.94, which indicates that non-fed beef is an inferior good. For every one percent increase in income, sales of non-fed beef are expected to decline by 1.94 percent.[40]

The income elasticity of demand measures the sensitivity of unit sales of a product to income. If all independent variables except income are fixed and constant at given levels, then the sensitivity of unit sales of a product can be measured by the income elasticity of demand for the product. Essentially, income elasticity of demand is the percentage change in unit sales of a product due to a percentage change in income, given that all other independent variables are held constant, which can be expressed generally as

$$E_{INCOME}=\%\Delta Q/\%\Delta Y$$

This expression can be restated as

$$E_{INCOME}=(\Delta Q/Q)\div(\Delta Y/Y)$$

As in the case of the price elasticity of demand, the denominator is inverted and multiplied times the numerator,

$$E_{INCOME}=(\Delta Q/Q)(Y/\Delta Y)$$

After rearranging terms,

$$E_{INCOME}=(\Delta Q/\Delta Y)(Y/Q)$$

This expression of income elasticity of demand parallels the previously stated price elasticity of demand and cross elasticity of demand. As in the case of price elasticity, the income elasticity of demand can be

---

40   See G.W. Brester and M.K. Wohlsenant, "Estimating Interrelated Demands for Meats Using New Measures for Ground and Table Cut Beef," *American Journal of Agricultural Economics*, 73 (November 1991), p. 21.

used to measure percentage change in unit sales expected as the result of a percentage change in income. Income elasticity of demand also can be used to determine if a product is a normal good or an inferior good. When calculated, the income elasticity of demand for normal goods is positive. The income elasticity for inferior goods is negative.

Calculating the Income Elasticity of Demand for Brand X

Recall the sales function for Brand X, and suppose the price of Brand X is $2, the price of Brand S is $2, the price of Product C is $1, per capita income is $15,000, and monthly advertising outlays on Brand X are $500. By substitution into the sales function, expected sales of Brand X are

$Q_X=1.3-2.1(2)+1.2(2)-0.5(1)+0.0002(15,000)+0.001(500)$

$Q_X=1.3-4.2+2.4-0.5+3.0+0.5$

$Q_X=2.5$

Unit sales of 2.5 thousand (2,500) units per week are expected.

Now, income elasticity can be calculated. The income elasticity of demand for Brand X when Y is $15,000 is, by substitution,

$E_{INCOME}=0.0002(15,000/2.5)$

$E_{INCOME}=0.0002(6,000)$

$E_{INCOME}=1.2$

The income elasticity of demand for Brand X is 1.2.

The meaning of this calculated income elasticity of demand parallels that of price elasticity of demand and cross elasticity of demand. For every one percent change in income, there is a corresponding direct 1.2 percent change in unit sales of Brand X. If per income were to rise by 2% (from $15,000 to $15,300), sales of Brand X would increase by 2.4% (from 2,500 units to 2,560 units). If per capita income were to fall by 5% (from $15,000 to $14,250), then unit sales of Brand X would decrease by 6% (from 2,500 units to 2,350 units). Since the income elasticity of demand for Brand X is positive, Brand X is a normal good.

Cyclical and Noncyclical Normal Goods

Brand X is a normal good, indicated by positive income elasticity. At times, a dividing line is used to distinguish between cyclical and noncyclical normal goods. The dividing line is +1. Noncyclical normal goods have income elasticity below +1, and cyclical normal goods have income elasticity above +1. Therefore, Brand X is normal and cyclical.

Normal goods with an income elasticity of demand that is positive but less than +1 are products with unit sales that are directly related but relatively insensitive to changes in income. Demand for such products is relatively unaffected by changes in economic conditions and thus by changes in income. Unit sales of most convenience products such as toothpaste and other basic toiletries as well as candy, soda, liquor, cigarettes, and movie tickets are examples of noncyclical normal goods. Noncyclical normal products often are called necessities, although such products rarely are necessities in the sense of life's true requisites.

Normal goods with an income elasticity of demand that is positive but more than +1 are products with unit sales that are relatively sensitive to changes in income. In other words, demand for these products is greatly affected by economic conditions and thus by income. Purchases of big-ticket items such as houses, automobiles, furniture, high-end lady's clothing, jewelry, boats, and recreational vehicles can be postponed or cancelled during economic downturns. As a result, demand for these products can collapse like a sinkhole during recessions and take off like a skyrocket during economic expansions. Such products often are called luxuries or luxury goods.

Management of firms that produce and sell products that are highly cyclical normal goods can anticipate robust growth of unit sales as the economy and income grow in its market region. Firms that produce and sell goods that are noncyclical normal goods are somewhat recession-proof in the sense that their unit sales are relatively stable in an economic downturn.

Income elasticity has been estimated for a range of products. Most products are indeed normal. Moreover, some products are cyclical. Examples of normal cyclical goods are steak, gasoline, books, furniture, private education, and wine. Other products are noncyclical. Examples of normal noncyclical goods are chicken, fresh tomatoes, milk, oranges, and beer. An oddity is coffee, which has an income elasticity of 0.0. For someone who drinks two cups of coffee at breakfast every morning, he or she is not likely to drink four cups of coffee if income were doubled. Unit consumption of coffee is not particularly dependent on income. On the other hand, if income doubled, the person who drinks two cups of coffee every morning might choose a better grade of coffee. In that case, unit consumption of coffee would not change, but expenditures on coffee would increase. Income elasticity deals with percentage change in unit sales, not expenditures. Although rare, some products have been found to be inferior. Examples are ground beef and potatoes. With an increase in income, unit sales of these products decline.

ADVERTISING ELASTICITY OF DEMAND

Unit sales of a product depend not only on the price of the product, prices of other related products such as substitutes or complements, and income, but also on advertising outlays on the product. The relationship between sales of the product and advertising outlays on the product is expected to be direct. An increase in advertising outlays on a product should result in an increase in unit sales of the product. As in the case of the price of a product, advertising outlays on the product are under the control of management. In some cases, management decides between a reduction in price and an increase in advertising outlays as means of increasing unit sales of a product or maintaining unit sales of a product in the face of a price cut initiated by a competitive firm.

If all independent variables except advertising outlays on the product are fixed and constant at given levels, then the sensitivity of unit sales of a product to changes in advertising outlays on the product can be measured by the advertising elasticity of demand, which is essentially the percentage change in unit sales due to a percentage change in advertising outlays, given that all other independent variables are held constant. The advertising elasticity of demand can be expressed generally as

$$E_{ADVERTISING} = \%\Delta Q / \%\Delta A$$

This expression can be restated as

$$E_{ADVERTISING} = (\Delta Q/Q) \div (\Delta A/A)$$

As in the case of price elasticity of demand, the denominator is inverted and multiplied times the numerator,

$$E_{ADVERTISING}=(\Delta Q/Q)(A/\Delta A)$$

After rearranging terms,

$$E_{ADVERTISING}=(\Delta Q/\Delta A)(A/Q)$$

Advertising elasticity of demand is similar to price, cross, and income elasticity of demand. The advertising elasticity of demand can be used to measure percentage change in unit sales expected as the result of a percentage change in advertising outlays.

Calculating the Advertising Elasticity of Demand for Brand X

Recall the sales function for Brand X. Suppose the price of Brand X is $2, the price of Brand S is $2, the price of Product C is $1, per capita income is $15,000, and monthly advertising outlays on Brand X are $500. By substitution into the sales function,

$$Q_X=1.3–2.1(2)+1.2(2)–0.5(1)+0.0002(15,000)+0.001(500)$$

$$Q_X=1.3–4.2+2.4–0.5+3.0+0.5$$

$$Q_X=2.5$$

Unit sales of 2.5 thousand (2,500) units per week are expected.

Now, the advertising elasticity can be calculated. The advertising elasticity of demand for Brand X when A_X is $500 is, by substitution,

$$E_{ADVERTISING}=0.001(500/2.5)$$

$$E_{ADVERTISING}=0.001(200)$$

$$E_{ADVERTISING}=0.2$$

The advertising elasticity of demand for Brand X is 0.2.

The meaning of this calculated advertising elasticity of demand parallels those of price elasticity of demand, cross elasticity of demand, and income elasticity of demand. For every one percent change in monthly advertising outlays, there is a corresponding and direct 0.2 percent change in unit sales of Brand X. If monthly advertising outlays were increased by 10% (from $500 to $550), unit sales of Brand X would increase by 2% (from 2,500 units to 2,550 units). If monthly advertising outlays were reduced by 5% (from $500 to $475), then unit sales of Brand X would decrease by 1% (from 2,500 units to 2,475 units).

Money is the Message

In a classic paper published in 1974, Phillip Nelson argued that a great deal of seemingly wasteful advertising is in fact intended to send a subliminal signal to consumers.[41] From this perspective, what the advertisement says is not important and thus does not matter. What is important is that consumers can see the firm is spending big outlays on advertising. The firm believes in its product. Otherwise, the

---

41   Phillip L. Nelson, "Advertising as Information," *Journal of Political Economy*, 28 (July/August 1974), pp. 729-754.

firm would not spend so much on advertising the product. These clever ads work because consumers understand the implicit signal.

On the whole, the argument advanced by Nelson remains convincing. The argument suggests that products with quality that can be verified only through experience should have more signal advertising. More recent studies based on experiments suggest that people associate more ads with higher quality. However, the reason is not because people have a sophisticated understanding of the signal. Instead, they simply see lots of ads for a product. If seeing leads to believing, then firms may be able to create the impression of high quality by advertising.[42]

INCREASE ADVERTISING OR CUT PRICE TO MAINTAIN SALES

Buyers make choices among differentiated products along a number of dimensions such as price, taste, service, quality, reliability, durability, appearance, and other factors. Each of the non-price factors can desensitize buyers to price differences, whether these price differences are of long standing or new. When a competitor cuts price, management of a firm needs to consider a number of issues related to understanding why the competitor reduced its price. Perhaps the rival cut price to grab increased market share. Maybe the rival cut price to utilize excess production capacity or to respond to changing cost conditions. The competitor might be planning only a temporary price reduction.

Often, market leaders face aggressive price reductions by its competitors. To maintain sales, management can either cut its own price or increase advertising outlays. A company might maintain its own price while believing that too much profit would be lost if its price is reduced. Perhaps the company believes it is better to increase advertising outlays to improve its quality image than to cut its price and operate at a lower profit margin. To address issues and evaluate options, management wants to make informed decisions. Informed decisions are based on knowledge and analysis. Clearly, knowing something about the sensitivity of unit sales to advertising outlays is important to management in framing an informed response. In the same way, knowing something about the sensitivity of unit sales to product price is also important.

A classic management problem is how to respond to a price cut announced by a firm producing and selling a competitive product. If management wants to maintain unit sales, it can cut the firm's own price or increase the firm's advertising outlays. To maintain unit sales, how deep a cut in the firm's own price would be required? To maintain unit sales, how much would advertising outlays need to be increased? Answers to these questions are the starting point for deciding how to respond to a price cut initiated by a competitor.

Elasticity as Information

Suppose that the price elasticity for Brand X, cross elasticity of demand for Brand X with respect to the price of Brand S, and advertising elasticity of demand for Brand X have been estimated. The price elasticity for Brand X is –1.68, cross elasticity with respect to the price of Brand S is 0.96, and advertising elasticity for Brand X is 0.2. Now, suppose the firm that produces Brand S reduces its price by 10%. The effect on sales of Brand X would be determined by the cross elasticity of demand for Brand X with respect to the price of Brand S, which is

---

42   See "The Money in the Message," *The Economist* (February 12, 1998), p. 78.

$\%\Delta Q_X / \%\Delta P_S = 0.96$

By substitution,

$\%\Delta Q_X / -10\% = 0.96$

By cross multiplying,

$\%\Delta Q_X = -9.6\%$

A 9.6% loss of unit sales of Brand X is expected if nothing is done. Using previous values for all independent variables in the sales function for Brand X, a 10% reduction of the price of Brand S would have a negative 9.6% effect on unit sales of Brand X.

To maintain unit sales by reducing the price of Brand X, something under the control of management must be changed to have a positive 9.6% effect on unit sales of Brand X to offset the negative 9.6% effect resulting from the reduction in price of Brand S. To maintain unit sales, the price of Brand X could be reduced enough to have a positive 9.6% effect. Recall that the price elasticity of demand is

$\%\Delta Q_X / \%\Delta P_X = -1.68$

To have a positive 9.6% effect to offset the 9.6% negative effect on sales, by substitution,

$9.6\% / \%\Delta P_X = -1.68$

Cross multiplying and solving,

$-1.68\% \Delta P_X = 9.6\%$

$\%\Delta P_X = -5.714\%$

The price of Brand X must be reduced by 5.714% to offset the 10% cut in the price of Brand S. Using stipulated values for independent variables, the required price reduction would be approximately $0.11, from $2.00 to $1.89.

Instead of reducing the price of Brand X, management could increase monthly advertising outlays to have a positive 9.6% effect on unit sales of Brand X. Recall that the advertising elasticity of demand is

$\%\Delta Q_X / \%\Delta A_X = 0.2$

To offset the 9.6% negative effect on unit sales, by substitution,

$9.6 / \%\Delta A_X = 0.2$

Cross multiplying and solving,

$0.2\% \Delta A_X = 9.6$

$\%\Delta A_X = 48$

Monthly advertising outlays on Brand X must be increased by 48% to offset the 10% cut in the price of Brand S. Using previous values for independent variables, monthly advertising outlays on Brand X must be increased by $240, from $500 to $740.

Management now knows that the price of Brand X must be reduced by 5.714% (from $2.00 to $1.89) or monthly advertising outlays must be increased by 48% (from $500 to $740) to have a positive 9.6% effect on unit sales of Brand X and thus offset the negative 9.6% effect resulting from the 10% reduction in the price of Brand S. This information is used to decide the best response to the lowered price of Brand S. This information does not make the decision for management. This information forms the basis for an informed decision.

DEMAND ELASTICITY SUMMARY

Elasticity of demand deals with different issues. In the case of price elasticity of demand, the issue is whether the unsigned price elasticity is greater than one or less than one. If the unsigned price elasticity is greater than one, demand for the product is price elastic. If the unsigned price elasticity is less than one, demand for the product is price inelastic. In the case of cross elasticity of demand, the issue is whether the calculated cross elasticity is positive or negative. If the cross elasticity is positive, the two products are substitutes. If the cross elasticity is negative, the two products are complements. If the case of income elasticity of demand, the issue is whether the income elasticity is positive or negative. If the income elasticity is positive, the product is a normal good. If the income elasticity is negative, the product is an inferior good. If the product is a normal good, the issue turns to whether it is cyclical or noncyclical. If the income elasticity is positive and greater than one, the product is cyclical. If the income elasticity is positive and less than one, the product is noncyclical.

Now, much is known about Brand X. Since the price elasticity of demand for Brand X is –1.68, demand for Brand X is known to be price elastic. Since the cross elasticity of demand for Brand X with respect to the price of Brand S is 0.96, Brand X and Brand S are known to be substitutes. Since the cross elasticity of demand for Brand X with respect to Product C is negative, –0.2, Brand X and Product C are known to be complements. Since the income elasticity of demand for Brand X is 1.2, Brand X is known to be a normal cyclical good. Since the advertising elasticity of demand for Brand X is 0.2, advertising outlays on Brand X are known to have a direct effect on sales of Brand X.

THE ADDITIVE PROPERTY OF DEMAND ELASTICITIES

So far, demand elasticity has been isolated and calculated independently. Suppose two or more factors that affect demand change simultaneously. The net effect on unit sales can be calculated. Recall the price elasticity of demand for Brand X. When the price of Brand X was $2, price elasticity was –1.68. In addition, recall the cross elasticity of demand for Brand X with respect to the price of Brand S was 0.96. Now, suppose management of the firm producing and selling Brand X plans to increase its price by ten percent and expects the firm producing and selling Brand S to increase its price by ten percent. The effect of the price increases is additive. The effect of the price increase on unit sales of Brand X is 10 times –1.68, which indicates a negative effect of 16.8% on unit sales as the result of the increased price of Brand X alone. The effect of the ten percent increase in the price of Brand S is 10 times 0.96, which indicates a positive effect of 9.6% on unit sales of Brand X as the result of the increased price of Brand S alone. The combined effect is additive, which is to say –16.8% plus 9.6%, for a net effect of –7.2%. The net effect of the price increases is a 7.2% loss of unit sales of Brand X.

Suppose many changes occur at once. For example, suppose per capita income declines by 5% in a recession, and the firm producing Brand X attempts to temper the negative effect on unit sales by cutting the price of Brand X by 5% and increasing advertising expenditures by 5%. At the same time, however, the firm providing Brand S cuts the price of Brand S by 5%. Recall that the price elasticity of demand for Brand X was –1.68, the cross elasticity of demand for Brand X with respect to the price of Brand S was 0.96, the income elasticity of demand for Brand X was 1.2, and the advertising elasticity of demand was 0.2. Therefore, the effect on unit sales of Brand X is –5(1.2)=–6%, which accounts for the effect of a 5% decline in income; plus –5(–1.68)=8.4%, which accounts for the effect of a 5% cut in the price of Brand X; plus 5(0.2)=1.0%, which accounts for the 5% increase in advertising expenditures; plus –5(0.96)=–4.8%, which accounts for the 10% reduction in the price of Brand S. The expected net effect, therefore, is –6.0%+8.4% +1.0%–4.8%=–1.4%. The net effect of all changes on unit sales of Brand X is a 1.4% loss of unit sales.

PRACTICE QUESTIONS

Answer each of the next FOUR questions based on the following sales function for an agricultural product, Product 1:

$$Q_1 = 4.0 - 0.8P_1 - 0.4P_2 + 2.0P_3 + 0.0004Y + 0.000001A$$

The variables are

Q_1=sales of Product 1, measured in millions of tons;

P_1=price per bushel of Product 1, which currently is $5;

P_2=price per bushel of Product 2, which currently is $2.50;

P_3=price per bushel of Product 3, which currently is $4;

Y=per capita income in the market, which currently is $10,000; and

A=annual advertising outlays on Product 1 by a trade association, which currently are $5,000,000.

1. At current observations for all variables, what is the price elasticity of demand for Product 1? Interpret this calculation.

2. At current observations for all variables, what is the cross elasticity of demand for Product 1 with respect to the price of Product 3? Suppose P_3 were to rise by 25%. What percentage effect on sales of Product 1 would be expected?

3. At current observations for all variables, what is the income elasticity of demand for Product 1? Suppose a recession is expected to reduce per capita income by 4%. What percentage effect on sales of Product 1 would be expected?

4. At current observations for all variables, what is the advertising elasticity of demand for Product 1? Interpret this calculation.

Answer each of the next TWO questions based on the demand and supply functions expressed below for a Product X and any other information provided in the questions:

$$Q_{XD} = 100 - 0.5P_X$$

$$Q_{XS} = 20 + 0.3P_X$$

The variables are

Q_{XD}=amount of Product X demanded, in thousands per month,

Q_{XS}=amount of Product X supplied, in thousands per month, and

P_X=price of product X.

5. What is the equilibrium market price for Product X and amount of Product X bought and sold at the equilibrium price?

6. At the market equilibrium, is demand for Product X price elastic or price inelastic?

Answer each of the next FOUR questions based on the following demand and supply functions for an agricultural product:

$Q_D = 200 - 2.0P$

$Q_S = 40 + 6.0P$

The variables are

Q_D = amount of the product demanded,

Q_S = amount of the product supplied, and

P = price of the product.

7. What is the market equilibrium price of the agricultural product?

8. What is the amount of the agricultural product sold and bought at the market equilibrium price?

9. At the market equilibrium price, is demand for the agricultural product price elastic or price inelastic? What is the basis for your answer?

10. Suppose demand for the agricultural product increases during a time in which supply of the agricultural product is unchanged. Would the market equilibrium price be expected to rise or fall?

Answer each of the next FIVE questions based on the following sales function estimated for a chemical product:

$Q_M = 150.0 - 4.0P_M + 5.0P_{CG} + 0.02Y_{USA} + 0.05Y_{OS}$

The variables are

Q_M = annual sales of a chemical product produced by Firm M, measured in thousands of tons;

P_M = price of the chemical product produced by Firm M, which is currently $200;

P_{CG} = price of an undifferentiated competing product produced by Firm CG, which is currently $200;

Y_{USA} = per capita income in the U.S. market, which is currently $10,000; and

Y_{OS} = per capita income in an overseas market, which is currently $5,000.

11. Based on this sales function, what is the amount of expected sales for the current year?

12. Based on this sales function, what is the price elasticity of demand? Is demand for the product price elastic or price inelastic?

13. Based on this demand function, what is the cross elasticity of demand for the chemical product produced by Firm M with respect to the price charged by Firm CG?

14. Based on the cross elasticity, what percentage change in annual sales would be expected if Firm CG raised its price by 4%?

15. Based on this demand function, is demand for the chemical product cyclical or noncyclical? What is the basis for your answer?

Answer each of the next EIGHT questions based on the following sales function for a woolen commodity, Lambda:

$$Q_L = 7.0 - 1.6P_L - 0.2P_C + 0.8P_S + 0.0005Y + 0.0004A$$

The variables are

Q_L = amount of sales of Lambda, in 1,000s per month;

P_L = price per each of Lambda, which is currently \$15;

P_C = price per each of Chi, which is currently \$25;

P_S = price per each of Sigma, which is currently \$20;

Y = income in the market area for Lambda, which is currently \$20,000; and

A = monthly advertising outlays on Lambda, which is currently \$15,000.

16. Express the functional relationship between the amount of sales of Lambda (Q_L) and the price of Lambda (P_L) alone.

17. Calculate expected sales of Lambda at current values for all variables in the sales function for Lambda.

18. At current values for all variables, calculate the price elasticity of demand for Lambda. Is the demand for Lambda price elastic or price inelastic? How do you know?

19. Using the price elasticity of demand for Lambda, what percentage change in sales would be expected if management of the business producing Lambda increases its price by \$5 to match the price charged for Sigma?

20. At current values for all variables, calculate the cross elasticity of demand between Lambda and the price of Sigma? Interpret this calculation.

21. Using the cross elasticity of demand for Lambda with respect to the price of Sigma, what percentage change in sales of Lambda would be expected if management of the business producing Sigma decreased its price by \$5 so that the prices of Lambda and Sigma are the same?

22. Based on current values for all variables, calculate the income elasticity of demand for Lambda. Using this calculation, what percentage change in sales of Lambda would be expected if a recession in the market area caused a 10 percent decline in income?

23. Interpret the coefficient (+0.0004) for advertising (A).

24. Consider a product with a price elasticity of demand estimated to be –1.25. In the current quarter, sales of this product are at an annualized rate of 120,000 units. A member of middle management recommends lowering the price of the product as a means of increasing sales revenue. Would you agree that a lower price is expected to increase revenue from sales of the product? Why?

Answer each of the next THREE questions based on the following information. Annual unit sales of a product are 5 million. The price elasticity of demand for the product is –1.5, the income elasticity of demand for the product is 1.2, and the cross elasticity of demand between this product and the price of still another product is 0.25.

25. Is the product a normal good? What is a normal good?

26. What percentage effect on unit sales of the product would be expected if the price of the product were cut by 5% and management of the other firm responded by cutting the price of the other product by 10%?

27. Suppose the price of the product is cut by 5% and the other firm does not match the price cut. What would be expected to happen to sales revenues from the product?

Consider the following information about a consumer product, Omega. The price elasticity of demand for Omega is –2.5; the cross elasticity of demand for Omega with respect to the price of another product, Alpha, is 0.75; the cross elasticity of demand for Omega with respect to the price of another product, Beta, is –0.50; the income elasticity of demand for Omega is 3.0; and the advertising elasticity of demand for Omega is 1.0. Answer each of the next SIX questions based on this information.

28. If the price of Omega were increased by 5%, by what percentage would sales of Omega change?

29. If the price of Alpha were increased by 5%, by what percentage would sales of Omega change?

30. If income in the geographical market area for Omega increased by 5%, by what percentage would sales of Omega change?

31. Suppose the firm that produces Alpha reduced the price of its product by 20%. If the firm that produces Omega wants to maintain its sales, by what percentage must it reduce the price of its product?

32. Suppose the firm that produces Alpha reduced the price of its product by 20%. If the firm that produces Omega wants to maintain its sales, by what percentage must it increase advertising?

33. Suppose the price of Beta rises sharply, by 25%, at the same time that the price of Alpha falls sharply, by 20%. However, income in the market area has risen modestly, by 2%, but as part of a cost-cutting initiative, advertising on Omega has been reduced by 10%. What combined effect of these changes is expected with respect to sales of Omega?

34. Suppose the demand for product Alpha has been estimated as

$$Q_A = 8,000 - 5P_A + 10P_B + 0.01A$$

The variables are

Q_A=monthly unit sales of product Alpha;

P_A=price per unit of product Alpha, which is currently $200;

P_B=price per unit of product Beta, which is currently $200; and

A=annual budget for advertising on product Alpha, which is currently $100,000.

Now, suppose the business firm that produces Beta reduces its price from $200 to $180. Management of the business firm that produces Alpha wants to maintain the same level of unit sales of its product for the upcoming year. To maintain sales of Alpha, how much would management need to reduce price or increase advertising outlays?

35. Suppose the demand for Product A has been estimated as

$Q_A = 1,000 - 2P_A + 5P_B + 0.005A$

The variables are

  Q_A=monthly unit sales of Product A;

  P_A=price of Product A, which is currently $200;

  P_B=price of Product B, which is currently $120; and

  A=annual budget for advertising on Product A, which is currently $100,000.

Now, suppose the business firm that produces Product B reduces the price of Product B from $120 to $100. Management of the business firm that produces Product A wants to maintain the same level of unit sales of Product A. To maintain sales of Product A, how much should management reduce the price of Product A or increase the annual budget for advertising on Product A?

36. The brand manager for a consumer product (Product 1) has an estimated sales function for the product, which is

$Q_1 = 93 - 10P_1 - 5P_2 + 4P_3 + 0.006Y + 0.0005A_1$

The variables are

  Q_1=unit sales of Product 1;

  P_1=price of Product 1, which currently is $15;

  P_2=price of a second consumer product, Product 2, which currently is $5;

  P_3=price of a third consumer product, Product 3, which currently is $10;

  Y=per capita income in the market, which currently is $12,000; and

  A_1=advertising outlay on Product 1, which currently is $100,000.

a. Calculate the price elasticity of demand for Product 1. Write a narrative interpretation of the calculation. Is the demand for Product 1 price elastic or price inelastic?

b. Calculate the cross elasticity of demand for Product 1 with respect to the price of Product 3. Write a narrative interpretation of the calculation. Are Product 1 and Product 3 substitutes or complements?

c. Calculate the income elasticity of demand for Product 1. Write a narrative interpretation of the calculation. Is Product 1 a normal good or an inferior good? If normal, is Product 1 cyclical or noncyclical?

37. Suppose you are a retailer and do not have a sales function for any of your product line. However, you do have some limited information about weekly sales and prices for all of your product line. You want to estimate the price elasticity of demand for one of your products with use of the "arc" technique. You determine that two particular weekly periods are not unduly influenced by seasonal or other factors and thus are comparable for this one product. You record weekly sales and prices charged during the two periods, which are sales of 500 at $9, and 300 at $11. Calculate the arc price elasticity of demand for the product. Is demand price elastic or price inelastic? How do you know? With given demand for the product, would you expect revenues from sales of the product to increase or decrease with a reduction in price? How do you know?

38. Suppose you are the brand manager for Magnum, a product manufactured and sold directly to ultimate customers. Staff members have calculated estimates of demand elasticity as

    Price elasticity of demand for Magnum: –2.0;

    Cross elasticity of demand for Magnum with respect to the price of Packard, another

        manufactured product: 0.8;

    Cross elasticity of demand for Magnum with respect to the price of Arrow, still another

        manufactured product: –0.6;

    Income elasticity of demand for Magnum: 1.4; and

        Advertising elasticity of demand for Magnum: 0.5.

    a. Calculate the expectation of what will happen to sales of Magnum if the producer of Packard cuts price by ten percent.

    b. Calculate the expectation of what will happen to sales of Magnum if the producer of Arrow cuts price by ten percent.

    c. Calculate the expectation of what will happen to sales of Magnum if a recession results in a five percent decline in per capita income.

    d. Calculate the expectation of what will happen to sales of Magnum if, concurrently, the producer of Packard cuts price by ten percent, the producer of Arrow cuts price by ten percent, and a recession results in a five percent decline in per capita income.

    e. Suppose changes in the prices of Packard and Arrow result in a ten percent negative effect on sales of Magnum. By what percentage must the price of Magnum be reduced to maintain sales? By what percentage must advertising on Magnum be increased to maintain sales?

39. Consider the following information regarding a manufactured product, Uno:

Price of Uno=$100;

Price of Dos=$100;

Price of Tres=$200;

Per capita income=$30,000;

    Advertising outlay on Uno=$120,000;

    Price elasticity of demand for Uno=–1.5;

    Cross elasticity of demand for Uno with respect to the price of Dos=0.8;

    Cross elasticity of demand for Uno with respect to the price of Tres=–0.6

    Income elasticity of demand for Uno=2.0

    Advertising elasticity of demand for Uno=0.5

a. Suppose the maker of Dos reduces its price from $100 to $85. To maintain sales, how much would the maker of Uno need to reduce its price?

b. Suppose the maker of Dos reduces its price from $100 to $85. To maintain sales, how much would the maker of Uno need to increase advertising outlay?

Consider the following sales function for Brand Z, and answer the following FOUR questions based on the sales function:

$$Q_Z = 10.0 - 2.0P_Z + 1.5P_A - P_B + 0.002Y + 0.001A_Z$$

The variables are

Q_Z = unit sales of Brand Z;

P_Z = price of Brand Z, which is $50;

P_A = price of Brand A, which is $80;

P_B = price of Brand B, which is $20;

Y = per capita income, which is $10,000; and

A_Z = advertising outlays on Brand Z, which is $50,000.

40. Answer the following questions.

a. Calculate the price elasticity of demand for Brand Z. Is the demand for Brand Z price elastic or price inelastic?

b. Write a narrative interpretation of the calculation.

c. Given the demand for Brand Z, would sales revenues increase or decrease if the price of Brand Z is reduced from $50 to $40? Why?

41. Answer the following questions.

a. Calculate the cross elasticity of demand for Brand Z with respect to the price of Brand B. Are Brand Z and Brand B complements or substitutes? Why?

b. Write a narrative interpretation of the calculation.

c. If the price of Brand B were increased by forty (40) percent, what is expected regarding unit sales of Brand Z?

42. Answer the following questions.

a. Calculate the income elasticity of demand for Brand Z. Is Brand Z normal or inferior? Why? Is Brand Z cyclical or noncyclical? Why?

b. Write a narrative interpretation of the calculation.

c. If a recession lowers per capita income by eight (8) percent, what is expected regarding unit sales of Brand Z.

43. Answer the following questions.

a. Suppose the maker of Brand A reduces its price from $80 to $60. To maintain sales, how much would the maker of Brand Z have to reduce its price?

b. Suppose the maker of Brand A reduces its price from $80 to $60. To maintain sales, how much would the maker of Brand Z have to increase advertising outlays?

44. Consider the following information regarding a manufactured product, Uno:

Price of Uno=$100;

Price of Dos=$100;

Price of Tres=$50;

Per capita income=$20,000;

Advertising outlay on Uno=$100,000;

Price elasticity of demand for Uno=−2.0;

Cross elasticity of demand for Uno with respect to the price of Dos=0.5;

Cross elasticity of demand for Uno with respect to the price of Tres=−0.4

Income elasticity of demand for Uno=2.0

Advertising elasticity of demand for Uno=0.5

a. Suppose the maker of Dos reduces its price from $100 to $90. To maintain sales, how much would the maker of Uno need to reduce its price?

b. Suppose the maker of Dos reduces its price from $100 to $90. To maintain sales, how much would the maker of Uno need to increase advertising outlay?

PRACTICE QUESTIONS (*AND ANSWERS*)

Answer each of the next FOUR questions based on the following sales function for an agricultural product, Product 1:

$$Q_1=4.0-0.8P_1-0.4P_2+2.0P_3+0.0004Y+0.000001A$$

The variables are

Q_1=sales of Product 1, measured in millions of tons;

P_1=price per bushel of Product 1, which currently is $5;

P_2=price per bushel of Product 2, which currently is $2.50;

P_3=price per bushel of Product 3, which currently is $4;

Y=per capita income in the market, which currently is $10,000; and

A=annual advertising outlays on Product 1 by a trade association, which currently are

$5,000,000.

1. At current observations for all variables, what is the price elasticity of demand for Product 1? Interpret this calculation.

By substitution,

$Q_1=4.0-0.8P_1-0.4(2.50)+2.0(4)+0.0004(10,000)+0.000001(5,000,000)$

$Q_1=4.0-0.8P_1-1.0+8.0+4.0+5.0=20-0.8P_1$

$Q_1=20-0.8(5)=20-4=16$

Therefore, price elasticity of demand is

$E_{PRICE}=-0.8(5/16)=-0.8(0.3125)=-0.25$

The interpretation of −0.25 is that, for every 1% change in P_1, there is a corresponding but inverse 0.25% change in Q_1. For example, for a 1% increase in P_1, there is a 0.25% decrease in Q_1.

2. At current observations for all variables, what is the cross elasticity of demand for Product 1 with respect to the price of Product 3? Suppose P_3 were to rise by 25%. What percentage effect on sales of Product 1 would be expected?

Cross elasticity of demand for Product 1 with respect to the price of Product 3 is

$E_{CROSS}=2.0(4/16)=2.0(0.25)=0.5$

The interpretation of 0.5 is that, for every 1% change in P_3, there is a corresponding and direct 0.5% change in Q_1. If P_3 were to rise by 25%, then Q_1 would rise by 0.5(25)=12.5, which is 12.5%.

3. At current observations for all variables, what is the income elasticity of demand for Product 1? Suppose a recession is expected to reduce per capita income by 4%. What percentage effect on sales of Product 1 would be expected?

The income elasticity of demand for Product 1 is

$E_{INCOME}=0.0004(10,000/16)=0.0004(625)=0.25$

The interpretation of 0.25 is that, for every 1% change in Y, there is a corresponding and direct 0.25% change in Q_1. If Y were to fall by 4%, then Q_1 would fall by 0.25(4)=1, which is 1%.

4. At current observations for all variables, what is the advertising elasticity of demand for Product 1? Interpret this calculation.

The advertising elasticity of demand for Product 1 is

$E_{ADVERTISING}=0.000001(5,000,000/16)=0.000001(312500)=0.3125$

The interpretation of 0.3125 is that, for every 1% change in A, there is a corresponding and direct 0.3125% change in Q_1. If A were increased by 10%, then Q_1 would increase by 0.3125(10)=3.125, which is 3.125%.

Answer each of the next TWO questions based on the demand and supply functions expressed below for a Product X and any other information provided in the questions:

$$Q_{XD}=100-0.5P_X$$

$$Q_{XS}=20+0.3P_X$$

The variables are

Q_{XD}=amount of Product X demanded, in thousands per month,

Q_{XS}=amount of Product X supplied, in thousands per month, and

P_X=price of product X.

5. What is the equilibrium market price for Product X and amount of Product X bought and sold at the equilibrium price?

Setting the demand function equal to the supply function,

$$100-0.5P_X=20+0.3P_X$$

$$-0.8P_X=-80$$

$$P_X=100$$

Substituting the price of $100 in the demand function,

$$Q_{XD}=100-0.5(100)$$

$$Q_{XD}=100-50$$

$$Q_{XD}=50$$

Substituting the price of $100 in the supply function,

$$Q_{XS}=20+0.3(100)$$

$$Q_{XS}=20+30$$

$$Q_{XS}=50$$

The market equilibrium price is $100, and the amount of Product X bought and sold at $100 is 50,000 per month.

6. At the market equilibrium price, is demand for Product X price elastic or price inelastic?

Substituting the equilibrium price and amount of Product X bought and sold at the equilibrium price,

$$E_{PRICE}=-0.5(100/50)=-0.5(2)=-1$$

Demand is neither price elastic nor price inelastic. Demand evidences unitary price elasticity.

Answer each of the next FOUR questions based on the following demand and supply functions for an agricultural product:

$Q_D=200-2.0P$

$Q_S=40+6.0P$

The variables are

Q_D=amount of the product demanded,

Q_S=amount of the product supplied, and

P=price of the product.

7. What is the market equilibrium price of the agricultural product?

Setting the demand function equal to the supply function,

200−2.0P=40+6.0P

−8P=−160

P=20

The market equilibrium price is $20.

8. What is the amount of the agricultural product sold and bought at the market equilibrium price?

Substituting in the demand function,

$Q_D=200-2.0(20)=200-40=160$

Substituting in the supply function,

$Q_S=40+6.0(20)=40+120=160$

The amount bought and sold at $20 is 160 units.

9. At the market equilibrium, is demand for the agricultural product price elastic or price inelastic? What is the basis for your answer?

The price elasticity of demand is

$E_{PRICE}=-2(20/160)=-2(0.125)=-0.25$

Since the unsigned price elasticity of demand is less than one, demand for the agricultural product is price inelastic.

10. Suppose demand for the agricultural product increases during a time in which supply of the agricultural product is unchanged. Would the market equilibrium price be expected to rise or fall? Would revenue from sales of the agricultural product be expected to rise or fall?

The increase in demand initiates upward pressure on price. The market equilibrium price would be expected to rise. In addition, the amount of the product bought and sold would be expected to rise. Since both price and quantity are expected to rise, revenue from sales would be expected to rise.

Answer each of the next FIVE questions based on the following sales function estimated for a chemical product:

$$Q_M = 150.0 - 4.0 P_M + 5.0 P_{CG} + 0.02 Y_{USA} + 0.05 Y_{OS}$$

The variables are

Q_M=annual sales of a chemical product produced by Firm M, measured in thousands of tons;

P_M=price of the chemical product produced by Firm M, which is currently \$200;

P_{CG}=price of an undifferentiated competing product produced by Firm CG, which is currently \$200;

Y_{USA}=per capita income in the U.S. market, which is currently \$10,000; and

Y_{OS}=per capita income in an overseas market, which is currently \$5,000.

11. Based on this sales function, what is the amount of expected sales for the current year?

Expected sales are

$Q_M=150-4.0(200)+5.0(200)+0.02(10,000)+0.05(5,000)$

$Q_M=150-800+1,000+200+250$

$Q_M=800$

Unit sales of 800 thousand tons are expected.

12. Based on this demand function, what is the price elasticity of demand? Is demand for the product price elastic or price inelastic?

Price elasticity of demand is

$E_{PRICE}=-4(200/800)=-4(0.25)=-1$

Demand is neither price elastic nor price inelastic. Demand evidences unitary price elasticity.

13. Based on this demand function, what is the cross elasticity of demand for the chemical product produced by Firm M with respect to the price charged by Firm CG?

Cross elasticity of demand is

$E_{CROSS}=5(200/800)=5(0.25)=1.25$

14. Based on the cross elasticity, what percentage change in annual sales would be expected if Firm CG raised its price by 4%?

By substitution,

1.25=%ΔSales of M/4%

%ΔSales of M=4%(1.25)=5%

15. Based on this demand function, is demand for the chemical product cyclical or noncyclical? What is the basis for your answer?

Normal goods are disaggregated into cyclical and noncyclical categories, depending on their respective income elasticity of demand. If the income elasticity of demand for a product is greater than one, it is cyclical, meaning that fluctuations in sales of the product will be greater than fluctuations in production, employment, and incomes. If the income elasticity of demand for a product is less than one, it is noncyclical, meaning that fluctuation in sales of the product will be less than fluctuations in production, employment, and incomes. In this case, the U.S. income elasticity of demand for Product M is

$E_{INCOME}=0.02(10,000/800)=0.02(12.5)=0.25$

The overseas income elasticity of demand for Product M is

$E_{INCOME}=0.05(5,000/800)=0.05(6.25)=0.3125$

Demand for Product M is noncyclical in the U.S. market, noncyclical in the overseas market, and noncyclical overall in the two markets.

Answer each of the next EIGHT questions based on the following sales function for a woolen commodity, Lambda:

$Q_L=7.0-1.6P_L-0.2P_C+0.8P_S+0.0005Y+0.0004A$

The variables are

Q_L=amount of sales of Lambda, in 1,000s per month;

P_L=price per each of Lambda, which is currently $15;

P_C=price per each of Chi, which is currently $25;

P_S=price per each of Sigma, which is currently $20;

Y=income in the market area for Lambda, which is currently $20,000; and

A=monthly advertising outlays on Lambda, which is currently $15,000.

16. Express the functional relationship between the amount of sales of Lambda (Q_L) and the price of Lambda (P_L) alone.

By substitution,

$Q_L=7-1.6P_L-0.2(25)+0.8(20)+0.0005(20,000)+0.0004(15,000)$

$Q_L=7-1.6P_L-5+16+10+6$

$Q_L=34-1.6P_L$

This function is the demand function for Lambda.

17. Calculate expected sales of Lambda at current values for all variables in the sales function for Lambda.

By substitution, sales of Lambda are

$Q_L=7-1.6(15)-0.2(25)+0.8(20)+0.0005(20,000)+0.0004(15,000)$

$Q_L=7-24-5+16+10+6=10$

Unit sales are 10 thousand per month.

18. At current values for all variables, calculate the price elasticity of demand for Lambda. Is the demand for Lambda price elastic or price inelastic? How do you know?

By substitution, the price elasticity of demand for Lambda is

$E_{PRICE}=-1.6(15/10)=-2.4$

Demand is price elastic because the unsigned price elasticity of demand is greater than 1.

19. Using the price elasticity of demand for Lambda, what percentage change in sales would be expected if management of the business producing Lambda increases its price by $5 to match the price charged for Sigma?

The percentage increase in the price of Lambda is 5/15=33.3, which is 33.3%. Therefore, the percentage effect on sales of Lambda is 33.3(−2.4)=−79.8, which is a decline of 79.8%.

20. At current values for all variables, calculate the cross elasticity of demand between Lambda and the price of Sigma? Interpret this calculation.

The cross elasticity of demand for Lambda with respect to the price of Sigma is

$E_{CROSS}=0.8(20/10)=1.6$

For every 1% change in P_S, there is a direct 1.6% change in Q_L.

21. Using the cross elasticity of demand for Lambda with respect to the price of Sigma, what percentage change in sales of Lambda would be expected if management of the business producing Sigma decreased its price by $5 so that the prices of Lambda and Sigma are the same?

The percentage decrease in the price of Sigma is −5/20=−25, which is 25%. Therefore, the percentage effect on sales of Lambda is −25(1.6)=−40, which is a decline of 40%.

22. Based on current values for all variables, calculate the income elasticity of demand for Lambda. Using this calculation, what percentage change in sales of Lambda would be expected if a recession in the market area caused a 10 percent decline in income?

The income elasticity of demand for Lambda is

$E_{INCOME}=0.0005(20,000/10)=1$

The result of a 10% decline in income would be −10(1)=−10, which is a 10% decline in sales of Lambda.

23. Interpret the coefficient (+0.0004) for advertising (A).

For every $1 increase in the monthly advertising budget, there is an increase in monthly sales of Lambda of 0.0004 thousand units. In other words, for every $1 increase, there is a 0.4 unit increase in sales. For example, an increase of $1,000 in the monthly budget will result in a sales increase of 400 units.

24. Consider a product with a price elasticity of demand estimated to be −1.25. In the current quarter, sales of this product are at an annualized rate of 120,000 units. A member of middle management recommends lowering the price of the product as a means of increasing sales revenue. Would you agree that a lower price is expected to increase revenue from sales of the product? Why?

Yes. When the demand for a product is price elastic (as indicated by −1.25, since the absolute value is greater than one), lowering price will increase sales revenue.

Answer each of the next THREE questions based on the following information. Annual unit sales of a product are 5 million. The price elasticity of demand for the product is −1.5, the income elasticity of demand for the product is 1.2, and the cross elasticity of demand between this product and the price of still another product is 0.25.

25. Is the product a normal good? What is a normal good?

The product is a normal good, which is known from the income elasticity of demand (+1.2). When the income elasticity of demand for a product is positive, the product is normal. A normal good is one for which the relationship between sales and income is direct, meaning that sales increase with an increase in income, and sales decrease with a decrease in income.

26. What percentage effect on unit sales of the product would be expected if the price of the product were cut by 5% and management of the other firm responded by cutting the price of the other product by 10%?

The effect on sales of cutting the price of the product itself by 5% is –5(–1.5)=+7.5%. The effect of the other firm cutting the price of its product by 10% is –10(0.25)=–2.5%. The net effect on sales is 7.5%–2.5%=5%. Unit sales of the product are expected to increase by 5%.

27. Suppose the price of the product is cut by 5% and the other firm does not match the price cut. What would be expected to happen to sales revenues from the product?

Since demand for the product is price elastic (–1.5), reducing the price of the product will increase revenues from sales of the product, but the dollar magnitude of the increase cannot be calculated from the information given.

Consider the following information about a consumer product, Omega. The price elasticity of demand for Omega is –2.5; the cross elasticity of demand for Omega with respect to the price of another product, Alpha, is 0.75; the cross elasticity of demand for Omega with respect to the price of another product, Beta, is –0.50; the income elasticity of demand for Omega is 3.0; and the advertising elasticity of demand for Omega is 1.0. Answer each of the next SIX questions based on this information.

28. If the price of Omega were increased by 5%, by what percentage would sales of Omega change?

By substitution,

–2.5=%ΔSales of Omega/5%

%ΔSales of Omega=–2.5(5%)=–12.5%

Sales of Omega would decline by 12.5%.

29. If the price of Alpha were increased by 5%, by what percentage would sales of Omega change?

By substitution,

0.75=%ΔSales of Omega/5%

%ΔSales of Omega=0.75(5%)=3.75%

Sales of Omega would increase by 3.75%.

30. If income in the geographical market area for Omega increased by 5%, by what percentage would sales of Omega change?

By substitution,

3.0=%ΔSales of Omega/5%

%ΔSales of Omega=3.0(5%)=15%

Sales of Omega would increase by 15%.

31. Suppose the firm that produces Alpha reduced the price of its product by 20%. If the firm that produces Omega wants to maintain its sales, by what percentage must it reduce the price of its product?

The effect of the 20% reduction in the price of Alpha on sales of Omega would be

0.75=%ΔSales of Omega/–20%

%ΔSales of Omega=0.75(–20%)=–15%

If the firm that produces Omega does nothing, sales will decline by 15%. To neutralize this negative effect on sales and thus to maintain sales of Omega, the price of Omega would need to be reduced enough to have a positive 15% effect on sales. Therefore,

–2.5=15%/%ΔPrice of Omega

–2.5(%ΔPrice of Omega)=15%

%ΔPrice of Omega=–6%

To maintain sales, the price of Omega must be reduced by 6%.

32. Suppose the firm that produces Alpha reduced the price of its product by 20%. If the firm that produces Omega wants to maintain its sales, by what percentage must it increase advertising?

The effect of the 20% reduction in the price of Alpha on sales of Omega would be

0.75=%ΔSales of Omega/–20%

%ΔSales of Omega=0.75(–20%)=–15%

If the firm that produces Omega does nothing, sales will decline by 15%. To neutralize this negative effect on sales and thus to maintain sales of Omega, advertising on Omega would need to be increased enough to have a positive 15% effect on sales. Therefore,

1.0=15%/%ΔAdvertising on Omega

1.0(%ΔAdvertising on Omega)=15%

%ΔAdvertising on Omega=15%

To maintain sales, advertising on Omega would need to be increased by 15%.

33. Suppose the price of Beta rises sharply, by 25%, at the same time that the price of Alpha falls sharply, by 20%. However, income in the market area has risen modestly, by 2%, but as part of a cost-cutting initiative, advertising on Omega has been reduced by 10%. What combined effect of these changes is expected with respect to sales of Omega?

The effect of the 25% increase in the price of Beta is

–0.50=%ΔSales of Omega/25%

%ΔSales of Omega=–0.50(25%)=–12.5%

Unit sales are expected to decline by 12.5%. The effect of the 20% decrease in the price of Alpha is

0.75=%ΔSales of Omega/–20%

%ΔSales of Omega=0.75(–20%)=–15%

Unit sales are expected to decline by 15%. The effect of the 2% rise in income is

$3.0=\%\Delta Sales\ of\ Omega/2\%$

$\%\Delta Sales\ of\ Omega=3.0(2\%)=6\%$

Unit sales are expected to increase by 6%. The effect of the 10% reduction in advertising on Omega is

$1.0=\%\Delta Sales\ of\ Omega/-10\%$

$\%\Delta Sales\ of\ Omega=1.0(-10\%)=-10\%$

Unit sales are expected to decline by 10%. The overall effect of these changes is

$-12.5\%+(-15\%)+6\%+(-10\%)=-31.5\%$

The overall effect is a 31.5% decline in sales of Omega.

34. Suppose the demand for product Alpha has been estimated as

$Q_A=8,000-5P_A+10P_B+0.01A$

The variables are

Q_A=monthly unit sales of product Alpha;

P_A=price per unit of product Alpha, which is currently $200;

P_B=price per unit of product Beta, which is currently $200; and

A=annual budget for advertising on product Alpha, which is currently $100,000.

Now, suppose the business firm that produces Beta reduces its price from $200 to $180. Management of the business firm that produces Alpha wants to maintain the same level of unit sales of its product for the upcoming year. To maintain sales of Alpha, how much would management need to reduce price or increase advertising outlays?

If management does nothing, sales of Alpha will decline by $\Delta Q_A/-20=10$, and $\Delta Q_A=-200$, which is a monthly loss of sales of 200 units. If management reduces the price of Alpha, the reduction required to maintain sales after P_B is reduced to $180 is $200/\Delta P_A=-5$, $-5\Delta P_A=200$, and $\Delta P_A=-40$, which means that the price of Alpha must be reduced by $40 per unit to $160. If management increases advertising, the increase necessary is $200/\Delta A=0.01$, $0.01\Delta A=200$, and $\Delta A=20,000$, which is $20,000.

35. Suppose the demand for Product A has been estimated as

$Q_A=1,000-2P_A+5P_B+0.005A$

The variables are

Q_A=monthly unit sales of Product A;

P_A=price of Product A, which is currently $200;

P_B=price of Product B, which is currently $120; and

A=annual budget for advertising on Product A, which is currently $100,000.

Now, suppose the business firm that produces Product B reduces the price of Product B from $120 to $100. Management of the business firm that produces Product A wants to maintain the same level of unit sales of Product A. To maintain sales of Product A, how much should management reduce the price of Product A or increase the annual budget for advertising on Product A?

Initially, sales of Product A are

$Q_A=1,000-2(200)+5(120)+0.005(100,000)=1,000-400+600+500=1,700$

If management does nothing when the competing business reduces the price of its product, sales of Product A will be

$Q_A=1,000-400+5(100)+500=1,600$

To maintain sales at 1,700, management must choose between reducing the price of Product A enough to increase sales by 100 and increasing advertising enough to increase sales by 100. Since $\Delta Q_A/\Delta P_A=-2$, $100/\Delta P_A=-2$, and therefore, $\Delta P_A=50$. Management must reduce price by \$50 to maintain sales. Since $\Delta Q_A/\Delta A=0.005$, $100/\Delta A=0.005$, and therefore, $\Delta A=\$20,000$. Advertising outlays must be increased by \$20,000 to maintain sales.

36. The brand manager for a consumer product (Product 1) has an estimated sales function for the product, which is

$Q_1=93-10P_1-5P_2+4P_3+0.006Y+0.0005A_1$

The variables are

Q_1=unit sales of Product 1;

P_1=price of Product 1, which currently is \$15;

P_2=price of a second consumer product, Product 2, which currently is \$5;

P_3=price of a third consumer product, Product 3, which currently is \$10;

Y=per capita income in the market, which currently is \$12,000; and

A_1=advertising outlay on Product 1, which currently is \$100,000.

a. Calculate the price elasticity of demand for Product 1. Write a narrative interpretation of the calculation. Is the demand for Product 1 price elastic or price inelastic?

The sales function is

$Q_1=93-10P_1-5P_2+4P_3+0.006Y+0.0005A_1$

By substitution,

$Q_1=93-10(15)-5(5)+4(10)+0.006(12,000)+0.0005(100,000)$

$Q_1=93-150-25+40+72+50$

$Q_1=80$

Unit sales are 80 units. Therefore, by substitution,

$E_{PRICE}=-10(15/80)=-10(0.1875)=-1.875$

For every 1% change in the price of Product 1, there is an expected inverse 1.875% change in unit sales of Product 1. Since the unsigned price elasticity of demand is greater than 1, demand is price elastic.

b. the cross elasticity of demand for Product 1 with respect to the price of Product 3. Write a narrative interpretation of the calculation. Are Product 1 and Product 3 substitutes or complements?

By substitution,

$E_{CROSS}=4(10/80)=4(0.125)=0.5$

For every 1% change in the price of Product 3, there is an expected direct 0.5% change in unit sales of Product 1. Since the cross elasticity of demand is positive, Product 1 and Product 3 are substitutes.

c. Calculate the income elasticity of demand for Product 1. Write a narrative interpretation of the calculation. Is Product 1 a normal good or an inferior good? If normal, is Product 1 cyclical or noncyclical?

By substitution,

$E_{INCOME}=0.006(12,000/80)=0.006(150)=0.9$

For every 1% change in per capita income, there is an expected direct 0.9% change in unit sales of Product 1. Since the income elasticity of demand is positive, Product 1 is a normal good. Since Product 1 is a normal good and the income elasticity is less than one, it is a noncyclical good.

37. Suppose you are a retailer and do not have a sales function for any of your product line. However, you do have some limited information about weekly sales and prices for all of your product line. You want to estimate the price elasticity of demand for one of your products with use of the "arc" technique. You determine that two particular weekly periods are not unduly influenced by seasonal or other factors and thus are comparable for this one product. You record weekly sales and prices charged during the two periods, which are sales of 500 at $9, and 300 at $11. Calculate the arc price elasticity of demand for the product. Is demand price elastic or price inelastic? How do you know? With given demand for the product, would you expect revenues from sales of the product to increase or decrease with a reduction in price? How do you know?

The arc price elasticity of demand is

$E_{PRICE}=\{(500-300)/[(500+300)/2]\}\div\{(9-11)/[(9+11)/2]\}$

$E_{PRICE}=\{200/400\}\div\{-2)/10\}$

$E_{PRICE}=\{0.5/-0.2\}$

$E_{PRICE}=-2.5$

Demand is price elastic since the unsigned price elasticity is greater than one. With given demand, sales revenue would increase with a reduction in price since demand is price elastic.

38. Suppose you are the brand manager for Magnum, a product manufactured and sold directly to ultimate customers. Staff members have calculated estimates of demand elasticity as

Price elasticity of demand for Magnum: –2.0;

Cross elasticity of demand for Magnum with respect to the price of Packard, another

manufactured product: 0.8;

Cross elasticity of demand for Magnum with respect to the price of Arrow, still another

manufactured product: –0.6;

Income elasticity of demand for Magnum: 1.4; and

Advertising elasticity of demand for Magnum: 0.5.

a. Calculate the expectation of what will happen to sales of Magnum if the producer of Packard cuts price by ten percent.

The expected effect on sales of Magnum is

%ΔQ/–10%=0.8

%ΔQ=–8%

Unit sales would decline by 8%.

b. Calculate the expectation of what will happen to sales of Magnum if the producer of Arrow cuts price by ten percent.

The expected effect on sales of Magnum is

%ΔQ/–10%=–0.6

%ΔQ=6%

Unit sales would increase by 6%.

c. Calculate the expectation of what will happen to sales of Magnum if a recession results in a five percent decline in per capita income.

The expected effect on sales of Magnum is

%ΔQ/–5%=1.4

%ΔQ=–7%

Unit sales would decrease by 7%.

d. Calculate the expectation of what will happen to sales of Magnum if, concurrently, the producer of Packard cuts price by ten percent, the producer of Arrow cuts price by ten percent, and a recession results in a five percent decline in per capita income.

The expected effect on sales of Magnum is additive, and cumulating the effects would be –8+6–7=–9, which indicates a decrease of 9%.

e. Suppose changes in the prices of Packard and Arrow result in a ten percent negative effect on sales of Magnum. By what percentage must the price of Magnum be reduced to maintain sales? By what percentage must advertising on Magnum be increased to maintain sales?

To reduce the price of Magnum enough to have a positive 10% effect on sales and offset the negative 10% effect,

10%/%ΔP$_M$AGNUM=–2

–2%ΔP$_M$AGNUM=10%

%ΔP$_M$AGNUM=–5%

The price of Magnum must be reduced by 5% to maintain sales. To increase advertising enough to have a positive 10% effect on sales and offset the negative 10% effect,

10%/%ΔA=0.5

0.5%ΔA=10%

%ΔA=20%

Advertising on Magnum must be increased by 20% to maintain sales.

39. Consider the following information regarding a manufactured product, Uno:

   Price of Uno=$100;

   Price of Dos=$100;

   Price of Tres=$200;

   Per capita income=$30,000;

   Advertising outlay on Uno=$120,000;

   Price elasticity of demand for Uno=−1.5;

   Cross elasticity of demand for Uno with respect to the price of Dos=0.8;

   Cross elasticity of demand for Uno with respect to the price of Tres=−0.6

   Income elasticity of demand for Uno=2.0

   Advertising elasticity of demand for Uno=0.5

a. Suppose the maker of Dos reduces its price from $100 to $85. To maintain sales, how much would the maker of Uno need to reduce its price?

   The price of Dos has been reduced by 15%. The cross elasticity of demand for Uno with respect to the price of Dos is 0.8. Therefore, the effect of the 15% reduction in price is, by substitution,

   %ΔQ$_{UNO}$/−15%=0.8

   Cross multiplying,

   %ΔQ$_{UNO}$=−12%

   To offset this negative 12% effect on sales, the price of Uno must be reduced to have a positive 12% effect on sales. Therefore, by substitution,

   12%/%ΔP$_{UNO}$=−1.5

   Cross multiplying and solving,

   −1.5%ΔP$_{UNO}$=12%

   %ΔP$_{UNO}$=−8

   The price of Uno must be reduced by 8% to maintain sales. Therefore, the price of Uno must be reduced from $100 to $92 to maintain sales.

b. Suppose the maker of Dos reduces its price from $100 to $85. To maintain sales, how much would the maker of Uno need to increase advertising outlay?

The price of Dos has been reduced by 15%. The cross elasticity of demand for Uno with respect to the price of Dos is 0.8. Therefore, the effect of the 15% reduction in price is, by substitution,

$\%\Delta Q_{UNO}/-15\%=0.8$

Cross multiplying,

$\%\Delta Q_{UNO}=-12\%$

To offset this negative 12% effect on sales, advertising outlay on Uno must be increased to have a positive 12% effect on sales. Therefore, by substitution,

$12\%/\%\Delta A_{UNO}=0.5$

Cross multiplying and solving,

$0.5\%\Delta A_{UNO}=12\%$

$\%\Delta A_{UNO}=24$

Advertising outlay on Uno must be increased by 24% to maintain sales. Therefore, advertising outlay on Uno must be from $120,000 to $148,800.

Consider the following sales function for Brand Z, and answer the following FOUR questions based on the sales function:

$Q_Z=10.0-2.0P_Z+1.5P_A-P_B+0.002Y+0.001A_Z$

The variables are

   Q_Z=unit sales of Brand Z;

   P_Z=price of Brand Z, which is $50;

   P_A=price of Brand A, which is $80;

   P_B=price of Brand B, which is $20;

   Y=per capita income, which is $10,000; and

   A_Z=advertising outlays on Brand Z, which is $50,000.

40. Answer the following questions.

a. Calculate the price elasticity of demand for Brand Z. Is the demand for Brand Z price elastic or price inelastic?

   By substitution, price elasticity is

   $E_{PRICE}=-2(50/80)=-2(0.625)=-1.25$

   Demand is price elastic.

b. Write a narrative interpretation of the calculation.

   For every 1% change in the price of Brand Z, there is a corresponding inverse 1.25% change in unit sales of Brand Z.

c. Given the demand for Brand Z, would sales revenues increase or decrease if the price of Brand Z is reduced from $50 to $40? Why?

Given the demand for Brand Z, sales revenues would increase because demand for Brand Z is price elastic.

41. Answer the following questions.

a. Calculate the cross elasticity of demand for Brand Z with respect to the price of Brand B. Are Brand Z and Brand B complements or substitutes? Why?

The cross elasticity is

$E_{CROSS}=-1(20/80)=-1(0.25)=-0.25$

Brand Z and Brand B are complements because the cross elasticity of demand is negative.

b. Write a narrative interpretation of the calculation.

For every 1% change in the price of Brand B, there is a corresponding inverse 0.25% change in unit sales of Brand Z.

c. If the price of Brand B were increased by forty (40) percent, what is expected regarding unit sales of Brand Z?

By substitution,

$\%\Delta Q_z/40\%=-0.25$

Cross multiplying,

$\%\Delta Q_z=-10\%$

Unit sales of Brand Z would be expected to decrease by 10%.

42. Answer the following questions.

a. Calculate the income elasticity of demand for Brand Z. Is Brand Z normal or inferior? Why? Is Brand Z cyclical or noncyclical? Why?

The income elasticity is

$E_{INCOME}=0.002(10,000/80)=0.002(125)=0.25$

Brand Z is a normal good since the income elasticity of demand is positive. Brand Z is noncyclical because income elasticity is positive but less than one.

b. Write a narrative interpretation of the calculation.

For every 1% change in per capita income, there is a corresponding direct 0.25% change in unit sales of Brand Z.

c. If a recession lowers per capita income by eight (8) percent, what is expected regarding unit sales of Brand Z?

By substitution,

$\%\Delta Q_z/-8\%=0.25$

Cross multiplying,

$\%\Delta Q_z=-2\%$

Unit sales of Brand Z would be expected to decrease by 2%.

43. Answer the following questions.

a. Suppose the maker of Brand A reduces its price from \$80 to \$60. To maintain sales, how much would the maker of Brand Z have to reduce its price?

The coefficient for the price of Brand A is 1.5, meaning $\Delta Q_A/\Delta P_A = 1.5$. Therefore, the effect of the reduction in price is, by substitution,

$\Delta Q_Z/-20 = 1.5$

Cross multiplying,

$\Delta Q_Z = -30$

The effect on sales of Brand Z is negative 30. To offset this negative effect and maintain sales, the price of Brand Z must be reduced. The coefficient for the price of Brand Z is $\Delta Q_Z/\Delta P_Z = 2.0$. Therefore, to offset the negative effect on sales of Brand Z, by substitution,

$30/\Delta P_Z = -2.0$

Cross multiplying and solving,

$-2\Delta P_Z = 30$

$\Delta P_Z = -15$

Therefore, the price of Brand Z must be reduced by \$15, from \$50 to \$35. The same answer could be calculated from use of demand elasticity estimates. The cross elasticity of demand for Brand Z with respect to the price of Brand A is

$E_{CROSS} = 1.5(80/80) = 1.5(1) = 1.5$

Therefore, the effect of the reduction in price is, by substitution,

$\%\Delta Q_Z/-25\% = 1.5$

Cross multiplying,

$\%\Delta Q_Z = -37.5\%$

To offset this negative 37.5% effect on sales, the price of Brand Z must be reduced to have a positive 37.5% effect on sales. Therefore, by substitution,

$37.5\%/\%\Delta P_Z = -1.25$

Cross multiplying,

$\%\Delta P_Z = -30\%$

The price of Brand Z must be reduced by 30% to maintain sales. Therefore, the price of Brand Z must be reduced from \$50 to \$35 to maintain sales.

b. Suppose the maker of Brand A reduces its price by 25 percent. To maintain sales, how much would the maker of Brand Z have to increase advertising outlays?

The coefficient for advertising on Brand Z is $\Delta Q_z/\Delta A_z=0.001$. Therefore, to offset the negative effect on sales of Brand Z, by substitution,

$30/\Delta A_z=0.001$

Cross multiplying and solving,

$0.001\Delta A_z=30$

$\Delta A_z=30,000$

Therefore, advertising outlays on Brand Z must be increased by $30,000, from $50,000 to $80,000. The same answer could be calculated from use of demand elasticity estimates. The advertising elasticity of demand for Brand Z is

$E_{ADVERTISING}=0.001(50,000/80)=0.001(625)=0.625$

To offset the negative 37.5% effect on sales, advertising outlays must be increased to have a positive 37.5% effect on sales. Therefore, by substitution,

$37.5\%/\Delta A_z=0.625$

Cross multiplying,

$\%\Delta P_z=60\%$

Advertising outlays on Brand Z must be increased by 60% to maintain sales. Therefore, advertising outlays on Brand Z must be increased from $50,000 to $80,000.

44. Consider the following information regarding a manufactured product, Uno:

Price of Uno=$100;

Price of Dos=$100;

Price of Tres=$50;

Per capita income=$20,000;

Advertising outlay on Uno=$100,000;

Price elasticity of demand for Uno=−2.0;

Cross elasticity of demand for Uno with respect to the price of Dos=0.5;

Cross elasticity of demand for Uno with respect to the price of Tres=−0.4

Income elasticity of demand for Uno=2.0

Advertising elasticity of demand for Uno=0.5

a. Suppose the maker of Dos reduces its price from $100 to $90. To maintain sales, how much would the maker of Uno need to reduce its price?

The price of Dos has been reduced by 10%. The cross elasticity of demand for Uno with respect to the price of Dos is 0.5. Therefore, the effect of the 10% reduction in price is, by substitution,

%ΔQUNO/−10%=0.5

Cross multiplying,

%ΔQUNO=−5%

To offset this negative 5% effect on sales, the price of Uno must be reduced to have a positive 5% effect on sales. Therefore, by substitution,

5%/%ΔPUNO=−2

Cross multiplying and solving,

−2%ΔPUNO=5%

%ΔPUNO=−2.5

The price of Uno must be reduced by 2.5% to maintain sales. Therefore, the price of Uno must be reduced from $100 to $97.50 to maintain sales.

b. Suppose the maker of Dos reduces its price from $100 to $90. To maintain sales, how much would the maker of Uno need to increase advertising outlay?

The price of Dos has been reduced by 10%. The cross elasticity of demand for Uno with respect to the price of Dos is 0.5. Therefore, the effect of the 10% reduction in price is, by substitution,

%ΔQUNO/−10%=0.5

Cross multiplying,

%ΔQUNO=−5%

To offset this negative 5% effect on sales, advertising outlay on Uno must be increased to have a positive 5% effect on sales. Therefore, by substitution,

5%/%ΔA$_{UNO}$=0.5

Cross multiplying and solving,

0.5%ΔA$_{UNO}$=5%

%ΔA$_{UNO}$=10

Advertising outlay on Uno must be increased by 10% to maintain sales. Therefore, advertising outlay on Uno must be increased from $100,000 to $110,000.

4. Productivity And Cost

Operations Management

Firms are in the business of producing products, whether goods or services, and offering them for sale. Managers are placed in positions to provide and coordinate everything required and used in the production process and to govern the overall costs incurred. Productivity is generally a reference to output per worker or value of output per worker. Increased output per worker or increased value of output per worker lowers unit cost. Seen in this way, productivity and cost are obverse and reverse of the same coin, which is to say two ways to look at the same thing. Managers usually speak about productivity and cost jointly. For example, a plant manager who engages a consultant might ask for help in improving productivity and cost at the plant, meaning that actions that improve productivity also improve unit cost.

At the plant level, activities involved in managing production processes clearly constitute the domain of production management. Within any organization such as a manufacturing plant or chemical processing plant, operations management is a term often used to refer to production management. Operations management thus deals with all aspects of the production process. The production process in turn deals with transforming inputs of natural, human, and capital resources into output of goods and services. Production decisions have corresponding cost implications.

PRODUCTION

In a general sense, production is any activity that creates something that has economic value. In particular, production is the creation of any good or service that has economic value to either consumers or other producers. In the private sector, economic value is evidenced by a price people are willing to pay. In addition to material goods, production also includes services such as legal advice, medical care, tax preparation, gardening, day care, and massages. In the public sector, economic value is substantiated by taxes, which are a kind of coercive price paid to provide goods or services such as public education, fire protection, crime protection, national defense, and judicial systems. The list of goods and services produced by business firms, not-for-profit organizations, and governments is practically endless.

Modern production requires coordination among many different kinds of workers, several types of capital, and various kinds of natural resources. Usually, there is a place where machinery and equipment are installed, where materials are used, and where workers perform their labor services. The place may be called different names such as factory, farm, store, shop, stadium, auditorium, arena, office, laboratory, hospital, school, studio, salon, spa, restaurant, diner, brewery, courthouse, tavern, hotel, casino, or bakery. All such places are locations or facilities where production can be accommodated. Each such place is a physical venue known generically as a plant. In some cases, the term plant is used explicitly as in manufacturing plant, assembly plant, and chemical plant. However, as Shakespeare's Juliet says, "What's in a name? That which we call a rose by any other name would smell as sweet." By any other name such as store, stadium, office, school, restaurant, courthouse, or whatever, each is a plant as surely as a manufacturing plant, assembly plant, or chemical plant.

In business, the plant is owned or operated by a firm, which is legal in nature and refers to organization. In short, business firms are organizations established for the purpose of making profit for its owner(s) by making one or more goods or services available for sale. Plants are physical structures or locations at which a firm's owners or employees conduct their business. Some firms have only one plant, whereas other firms operate many plants, and still other firms operate different plants for various stages of production. An industry is a group of firms that make and sell similar, competitive products in a market.

More than thirty million business enterprises are operating in the United States. Some of these businesses are individually owned proprietorships, some are partnerships of two or more people, and some are corporations. Number of firms, business receipts, and net income by type of business are shown in Table 4.1. Data are based on number of tax returns filed by type of business. Proprietorships include only individually owned nonfarm businesses. Business receipts and sales revenues are equivalent terms.

Table 4.1 Number of Firms, Business Receipts, and Net Income by Type of Business, 2008				
Type of Business	Number of Firms (1,000s)	Percent of Total Firms	Percent of Business Receipts	Percent of Net Income
Proprietorships	22,614	72.5	3.9	15.5
Partnerships	3,146	10.0	14.8	26.8
Corporations	5,847	18.5	81.3	57.7
Total	31,607	100.0	100.0	100.0

Source: U.S. Census Bureau, 2012 Statistical Abstract of the United States (Washington, D.C.: U.S. Government Printing Office, 2011), Table 744, Number of Tax Returns, Receipts, and Net Income by Type of Business: 1990 to 2008

Proprietorships

Proprietary is a word rooted in ancientry. In Middle English and Old French, it meant ownership of property. Proprietorship has the same roots. In the simplest language, proprietorship is a business structure in which an individual and his or her company are considered a single entity for tax and liability purposes. The owner does not pay income taxes apart from the company. Instead, business income or loss is reported on his or her individual income tax return. In this way, the owner is inseparable from the company, and he or she is personally liable for any debts of the company. Proprietorship is the most basic type of business firm. Indeed, most businesses that morph into other types of business structure were started as proprietorships. By far, proprietorship is the most common form of business organization in the United States, accounting for more than seventy-two percent of all business firms. However, these twenty-two million or so proprietorships account for only about four percent of all business receipts. Moreover, proprietorships account for only a little more than fifteen percent of net income. In these lights, proprietorships are seen as relatively numerous but relatively small, thus accounting for little in overall business receipts and profits.

Partnerships

A partnership is a business owned by two or more persons, each having an ownership interest and receiving a portion of any profits. Sometimes, one of the "persons" is an organization such as a corporation or an estate. General partners manage the business and are equally liable for any business debts. Limited partners invest in the business, but they are not involved in management directly and are liable for any business debts only to the extent of their investments. A partnership itself does not pay taxes. Each partner reports his or her share of business profit or loss on an individual income tax return. Partnerships are common in the professions, *viz.*, accounting, law, and medicine, in which entrants begin as associates and hope to make partner. A little more than three million firms are formed as partnerships. Partnerships are the least common type of business organization in the United States, accounting for ten percent of all firms and for almost fifteen percent of business receipts. Partnerships account for almost twenty-seven percent of net income.

Corporations

In both partnerships and proprietorships, owners are personally liable for a firm's debts and for any judgments imposed by a court of law. The alternative to proprietorships and partnerships is the corporation, which is a business legally established under state laws that grant it an identity separate from that of its owners. Often, a corporation is dubbed a legal fiction, which is a preposterous term used by lawyers and others. From a legal standpoint, however, a corporation is perceived as the equivalent of a fictitious person with legal standing. By incorporating, owners create an organization that can own property, incur debts, and assume many other legal rights and legal obligations of a citizen, including the right to engage in litigation. Any person or group of people can form a corporation by obtaining a corporate charter from one of the fifty states, a process so easy that it requires only paying a fee and filing appropriate forms. Almost six million corporations conduct business in the United States. Although these corporations represent a little more than eighteen percent of all firms, they account for more than eighty-one percent of business receipts. Moreover, corporations account for almost fifty-eight percent of net income. Thus, corporations are relatively large, however measured by business receipts or profits.

THE PRODUCTION PROCESS

Productive activity is conducted in various ways. The most basic type is production of a unique product. Each product is distinct and perhaps made to specific order. For example, in any city such as Boston, Chicago, Los Angeles, or New Orleans, furniture makers can be found. These furniture makers produce pieces that are handcrafted and thus unique. This type of productive activity ordinarily is operated at small volumes of output. On the other hand, rigid mass production involves output of a standardized product in large volume. Parts and components are usually the output of rigid mass production. Even some final products are made from rigid mass production. Flexible mass production involves assembly from standardized and mass-produced components, but final assembled products are different and distinct to meet diverse customer needs, requirements, tastes, or preferences.

Flexible mass production has led to an extreme known as mass customization, which is changing the way products are made and marketed.[43] In effect, choice has become a value more important than brand. In recent years, for example, Levi's offered 750 versions of jeans combining different colors, cuts, leg openings, and types of fly. Custom Foot in Westport, Connecticut, is a shoe store without racks and shelves filled with shoes. Customers have their feet scanned to detect even the slightest differences in size, width, and contour that typically distinguish right foot from left foot. Data are transmitted to fabricators where the shoes are made to order and delivered within two weeks. In this way, Custom Foot has shoes fabricated that meet individual tastes and size requirements, yet has these customized shoes mass produced in large volume and then sold at prices comparable to many premium brands off the shelf. Another company, Footmaxx, uses computerized gait and pressure technologies to analyze an individual's unique walk and build custom orthotics. A patient walks across a force plate that contains 960 pressure points, scans 150 times per second, and tracks eight key points along the plantar surface of the foot. Data are used to produce diagnostics from which custom orthotics are built to correct each patient's biomechanics. Thus, shoes and sandals are virtually unmatched for comfort, construction, and design.

Mass customization has led to outrageous proliferation of product lines that add unique features to meet different customer needs and tastes. For example, households once had a choice between Colgate and Crest toothpaste. Now, households who prefer Colgate have a choice of Colgate Total Advanced (three versions), Colgate Total (three versions), Colgate Max Fresh (three versions), Colgate ProClinical White (two versions), Colgate 2 in1 (three versions), Colgate Cavity Protection, Colgate Tartar Protection with Whitening (two versions), Ultra Brite (two versions), Colgate Optic White, Colgate Sensitive Pro-Relief (three versions), Colgate Luminous, Colgate Sensitive (three versions), Colgate Sparkling White (two versions), Colgate Baking Soda and Peroxide Whitening Bubbles (two versions), Colgate Triple Action, and Kids' Toothpastes (three versions). So, a person once faced a grocery store shelf with only Colgate and Crest. Do the math. The same person faces a shelf with thirty-two different adult Colgate toothpastes, thirty-five Colgate toothpastes when including Colgate Dora the Explorer, Colgate SpongeBob SquarePants, and Colgate 2 in1 for kids! Colgate epitomizes the proliferation of mass customization.

Fixed and Variable Factors of Production

Whatever the type of productive activity, production is a process. Transforming inputs of natural, human, and capital resources into outputs of product is called the production process. Each resource actively contributes to the production process. For this reason, resources used in production often are called factors of production or simply inputs. These factors or inputs can be classified as either fixed or variable depending on whether their usage can be changed during a production run, which is a continuous period of operation or production. Usage of a fixed factor of production cannot be changed with volume of output during a production run, whereas utilization of a variable factor of production can be changed with volume of output during a production run. For example, in a short production run, worker-hours of labor and amounts of raw materials can be varied in most cases and thus are variable factors

---

43   For a readable article on mass customization, see "The Right Stuff: America's Move to Mass Customization," Federal Reserve Bank of Dallas, 1998 Annual Report.

of production, whereas plant and certain equipment cannot be varied in most cases and thus are fixed factors of production.

THE PRODUCTION FUNCTION

With a given technology determined by technical knowledge and capability, volume of output depends on amounts of various inputs used in production. A firm's production function is an estimation of the volume of output that can be produced from various combinations of input amounts, given the production technology. To illustrate a production function, consider experiments conducted for corn production in Iowa. Land, labor, and machinery were held constant while two types of fertilizer were varied. Nitrogen and phosphate fertilizers were varied in increments of forty pounds from zero to 320 pounds per acre on eighty-one different parcels of land. Based on yields of corn per acre, a production function was statistically estimated on the independent variables, nitrogen and phosphate. The estimated production function was

$$Q = -7.51 + 0.584N + 0.664P - 0.0016N^2 - 0.0018P^2 + 0.00081NP$$

The variables are

Q=bushels of corn per acre,

N=pounds of nitrogen per acre, and

P=pounds of phosphate per acre.

Based on the production function, bushels of corn per acre as a function of nitrogen and phosphate are shown as entries in Table 4.2. This table shows the relationship between production of corn, measured in bushels per acre, and inputs of nitrogen and phosphate, both measured in pounds per acre. Notice that the maximum yield is 144.1 bushels per acre when 240 pounds of both nitrogen and phosphate are applied. Any more or any less nitrogen or phosphate results in a smaller number of bushels per acre.

Table 4.2 Bushels of Corn per Acre as a Funciton of Nittogen and Phosphate Fertilizers									
Pounds of Phosphate Per Acre	Pounds of Nitrogen Per Acre								
	0	40	80	120	160	200	240	280	320
0	−7.5	13.3	29.2	39.8	45.5	46.1	41.7	32.2	17.6
40	16.2	38.3	55.4	67.4	74.4	76.3	73.1	64.9	51.6
80	34.1	57.5	75.9	89.2	97.5	100.7	98.8	91.9	79.9
120	46.3	71.0	90.7	105.3	114.9	119.4	118.8	113.2	102.5
160	53.0	78.7	99.8	115.6	126.6	132.3	133.0	128.7	119.3
200	53.4	80.7	103.0	120.2	132.3	139.4	141.5	138.4	130.4
240	48.3	76.9	100.5	119.0	132.5	140.8	144.1	142.4	135.7
280	37.5	67.4	92.3	112.0	126.8	136.5	141.1	140.7	132.2
320	20.9	52.1	78.3	99.4	115.4	126.4	132.3	133.2	129.0

Source: Earl O. Heady and John L. Dillion, Agricultural Production Functions (Ames, IA: Iowa State University Press, 1961), p. 478.

THE LAW OF DIMINISHING RETURNS

From at least the early 19th Century, a law has been expressed as an empirical generalization about the way output responds to successive increases in the amount of a variable factor of production used with given amounts of fixed factors of production. The law of diminishing returns states that, if technology and inputs of all factors of production except one are held constant, then successive equal increments of the variable factor of production yield increments in output of product that eventually will diminish. In less technical words, the law of diminishing returns states that increasing the use of one variable factor of production while holding the use of all other factors of production constant eventually causes output to increase at a diminishing rate. In informal, conversational usage, diminishing returns has a looser meaning. In ordinary conversation, diminishing returns simply is a reference to the tendency for continuing application of effort or exertion toward accomplishment of a particular project, objective, or goal to decline in effectiveness after certain results have been achieved.

The basis for the law of diminishing returns is straightforward, more a physical than an economic law. A world in which it would not hold is unimaginable. Consider a simple farming example with fertilizer as the variable factor. With a fixed amount of all other factors used on a given parcel of land of any given size, wheat yield could be increased if the soil is enriched with an application of fertilizer. If successive, equal applications of fertilizer were added to the soil, however, the additional wheat yield eventually would diminish. The tenth or hundredth application of fertilizer would not be expected to add as much to wheat yield as the first, second, or third application.

To paraphrase John Stuart Mill (1806-1873), if it weren't for the law of diminishing returns, we could grow the world's food supply in a flowerpot! In fact, Mill expressed the law of diminishing returns as the law of diminishing returns in agriculture. In a somewhat convoluted way, Mill pointed out, "...in any given state of agricultural skill and knowledge, by increasing the labor, the produce is not increased in equal degree;...or to express the same thing in other words, every increase of produce is obtained by a more than proportional increase in the application of labor to the land."[44] Eventually, diminishing returns were known to be applicable not only to agriculture but to manufacturing, processing, assembly, and other kinds of production.

As an aside, *Ask Marilyn* is a column published weekly in *Parade*. She often gives readers an answer and invites them to suggest a question. In her 8 December 2002 column, questions were published to the answer, "The Law of Diminishing Returns." The questions published were (1) "What term do retailers use to describe the two-week period after Christmas?" (2) "What phenomenon is observed when a restaurant hires a mediocre chef?" (3) "What principle applies to my investment choices?" and (4) "What lets you know when it's time to quit playing fetch with your dog?"

Diminishing Returns in Corn Yield

Diminishing returns are seen clearly in Table 4.2, which shows production of corn per acre and pounds of nitrogen and phosphate per acre. Look down any column, which shows bushels of corn per acre as pounds of phosphate per acre are varied with fixed pounds of phosphate per acre. For example, consider the column with 240 pounds of nitrogen fertilizer. With no phosphate fertilizer whatsoever applied, corn yield is 41.7 bushels per acre. With 40 pounds of phosphate, yield is 73.1 bushels. The increment to yield

---

44   John Stuart Mill, *Principles of Political Economy*, 5th ed. (London: Parker, Son, and Bourn, West Stand, 1862), p. 217.

is 31.4 bushels per acre. With still another 40 pounds of phosphate, yield is 98.8 bushels per acre, and the increment to yield thus is only 25.7 bushels per acre. Diminishing returns already are experienced since the increment is smaller, and increments continue to diminish through 240 pounds of phosphate. With still another 40 pounds of phosphate, yield is 118.8 bushels per acre, and the increment to yield is only 20.0 bushels per acre. With still another 40 pounds of phosphate, yield is 133.0 bushels per acre, and the increment to yield is 14.2 bushels per acre. With still another 40 pounds of phosphate, yield is 141.5 bushels per acre, and the increment to yield is 7.5 bushels per acre. With still another 40 pounds of phosphate, yield is 144.1 bushels per acre, and the increment to yield is 2.6 bushels per acre. Diminishing returns are observed and experienced over the range of 0 to 240 pounds of phosphate. Further use of phosphate results in negative, not diminishing returns.

Diminishing Returns in Manufacturing

A manufacturing example with labor as the variable factor illustrates the same basis for the law of diminishing returns. With fixed plant and equipment, adding a certain number of workers at first might result in larger and larger increments to output. Eventually, however, adding this certain number of workers to fixed facilities results in smaller and smaller increments to output. As soon as the increments to output are smaller, the point of diminishing returns has been reached. At an extreme, the number of workers could become so large that adding this certain number of workers to the fixed facilities involves so many workers relative to the confines of available space and equipment that they hinder the production process and thus cause negative increments in output.

Consider Table 4.3, which is a contrived example of production workers added in ten worker increments with fixed and given plant and equipment. The point of diminishing returns is 150 workers. At this point, the increment to output first begins to decline. Diminishing returns are observed from 150 workers to 180 workers. Diminishing returns does not mean no further hiring of workers. Managers would make hiring decisions based on the cost of adding ten more workers and the revenue that could be realized when the increment to output is sold. Even though the point of diminishing returns has been reached, additional workers could be hired and used if revenue from selling increments to output exceeds the cost of additional workers.

Table 4.3 The Point of Diminishing Returns in Manufacturing		
Number of Production Workers	**Volume of Output**	**Increment to Output**
100	10,000	
110	10,100	100
120	10,250	150
130	10,450	200
140	10,700	250
150	10,900	200
160	11,050	150
170	11,150	100
180	11,200	50
190	11,150	−50
200	11,050	−100

For a more concrete example, consider a factory with an assembly line for production of household appliances. If only one worker staffs the assembly line, that one person must perform every activity necessary to assemble the final product. Output is likely to be relatively low. As additional workers are added to the assembly line, each specialized to perform a particular operation, output of refrigerators is likely to rise significantly. Eventually, any further additions to output attributable to additional workers used on the given assembly line will not be as large as earlier additional use of workers. The increase in output now is diminishing. The point of diminishing returns has been reached. Total output is still rising with each additional assembly worker. However, the number added to total product is declining, observed as a declining rate at which total product is rising.

RETURNS TO SCALE

In the long run, all factors of production are variable, which simply means that use of all factors of production can be varied with respect to output of product. Plant and equipment, for example, can be expanded. In fact, the insightful aspect of the long run is that additional output of product can be produced with increased inputs of all factors of production, whereas in the short run, additional output of product can be produced with increased inputs of some but not all factors of production. Ordinarily, managers do not talk about the long run. They use equivalent language, however, when they speak of a planning decision. What they mean is that such decisions are not merely operating decisions dealing with given facilities but rather decisions dealing with size of operations. Another term for size of operations is scale. In an industry in which a certain commodity is produced, a business operating a plant of 2,000,000 square feet equipped with 1,000 standard machines operated by 1,500 production workers is a larger scale of production than a plant of 1,000,000 square feet plant equipped with 500 standard machines operated by 750 production workers.

Increased utilization of fixed and given facilities is an operating decision, not a planning decision. For example, a plant in which volume of production is 500,000 per month but with capacity of 1,000,000 is operating at capacity utilization of fifty percent. With these fixed and given facilities, volume could be increased to 750,000 per month, which would be operating at capacity utilization of seventy-five percent. This increased utilization of plant capacity is an operating decision. On the other hand, consider a plant in which volume of production is 500,000 per month, which is its capacity. To increase production to a volume of 750,000, additional plant and equipment would be required. Any decision to expand plant and equipment, to add to fixed and given facilities, is a planning decision. Returns to scale do not refer to operating decisions affecting capacity utilization of fixed and given facilities. Returns to scale refer to planning decisions to expand capacity.

Returns to scale is a term referring to the relationship between output and scale of production, meaning size of operations such as plant size. When the scale of production is increased, only three general effects on output are possible. If size of operations increases by some proportion, output of product could (1) increase by a greater proportion, (2) increase by the same proportion, or (3) increase by a lesser proportion. For example, when inputs of all factors of production are doubled, the scale of production is doubled. When scale is doubled, output of product can more than double, double, or less than double. Each of these cases has a name.

Increasing, Decreasing, and Constant Returns to Scale

When inputs of all factors of production are increased by some proportion and output of product increases by an even greater proportion, there are increasing returns to scale. For example, if inputs were doubled and output would more than double, this case evidences increasing returns to scale. When inputs of all factors of production are increased by some proportion and output of product increases by the same proportion, there are constant returns to scale. For example, if inputs were doubled and output would also double, this case evidences constant returns to scale. When inputs of all factors of production are increased by some proportion and output of product increases by a lesser proportion, there are decreasing returns to scale. For example, if inputs were doubled and output would less than double, this case evidences decreasing returns to scale. Nothing is magic about doubling, however. The same point can be made with respect to increasing scale by ten percent. Then, the question is whether output increases by more than ten percent, ten percent, or less than ten percent.

Increasing returns to scale arise mainly because, as size of operations increases, greater division and specialization of labor and more specialized and productive machinery can be used. Some techniques cannot be used at small scales but can at larger scale. Some inputs are not available in small units. For example, half a robot cannot be installed. Because of indivisibility of this sort, increasing returns to scale may occur. Although a firm operating a small factory could double its capacity by building another small factory of identical capacity, this doubling by building another small plant may be inefficient. One large factory may be far more efficient because it is large enough to use certain techniques and inputs that smaller factories cannot employ efficiently. On the other hand, decreasing returns to scale arise mainly because managing a firm and coordinating various operations and divisions become increasingly more difficult with scale. In fact, forces that drive increasing or decreasing returns to scale operate side by side. The forces that drive increasing returns usually overwhelm the forces that drive decreasing returns at small volumes of output, and thus increasing returns prevail. The forces that drive decreasing returns can overcome the forces that drive increasing returns at very large volumes of output, and thus decreasing returns prevail.

COST CONCEPTS

In the simplest formulation, a firm's profit is its revenues minus its costs. Essentially, however, managers make production decisions, not cost decisions. Cost is simply the consequence of production decisions. In other words, when managers make production decisions regarding what to produce, how much to produce, where to produce, and how to produce, cost consequences ensue from these decisions. For this reason alone, production and cost are seen as two sides of the same coin. They go hand in hand, hand in glove. They are two views into the same room, each view seen through a different window. Improving one is improving the other, which is why managers often speak of improving a firm's cost and productivity.

The centrality of cost is obfuscated by the profusion of cost concepts. This profusion is more apparent than real. The term "cost" can be and is defined in numerous ways. Cost is even confounded with other terms. Conversationally, for example, cost often refers to the price that must be paid for an item. The appropriate definition of cost is situational. Various situations require different notions of cost. Few problems arise if a business buys inputs with cash and uses these inputs immediately. Complications arise if a business buys inputs, stores them for a time, and then uses them. Complications are exacerbated if the input is a long-lived asset such as structures, machinery, or equipment used over an indeterminate time horizon. Such problems alone originate the need for different aspects of cost.

The situational nature of cost should not suggest that cost is a fuzzy, indistinct concept in which any person's usage is as good as another's in a kind of linguistic free-for-all where, in contrast to a *lingua franca*, everyone speaks a different language. To the contrary, each concept of cost is distinct, and each concept has its accounting or economic correctness. In this light, different concepts of cost are seen merely as different aspects of the same object.

Opportunity Cost

Periodically, firms make reports that support and accommodate analysis of their financial condition. A firm's balance sheet is a statement of its financial position at a certain time showing all its assets and liabilities. The balance sheet has three main components: assets, liabilities, and capital. The statement can be seen as the net worth of owners, which essentially is the value of assets minus liabilities. The firm's profit and loss account, also called its income statement, is a report of profit or loss based on the books of the business. Costs entered into these statements reflect the accounting concept of costs. This accounting concept of cost is grounded in the principles of accrual accounting, which emphasizes cash outlays on items such as raw materials, capital equipment, and the services of labor. Accounting statements, particularly balance sheets and income statements, are designed to serve the needs of owners as well as certain people external to the firm such as lenders and equity advisors. In this way, accounting numbers must be objective and verifiable, principles well served by historical costs. However, historical costs that appear as entries in accounting statements are not necessarily appropriate for decision making.

The true cost of something is what a person or a business gives up to obtain it. Choosing wisely from options requires persons or businesses to ask what is given up and whether it is worth more or less than what is obtained. For a person choosing to attend a university full-time for four years, the cost of the undergraduate degree certainly includes out-of-pocket expenses such as tuition, books, housing, and food. The cost also includes what is given up, which would include four years of income that could have been earned from a full-time job. Presumably, undergraduate students believe that a university degree will be worth more over time than the out-of-pocket expenses and forgone income.

Business decisions often require the measurement of economic costs, which are based on the concept of opportunity cost. This concept suggests that the economic cost of deploying resources to a particular activity is the value of the best forgone alternative use of these resources, which is the value assigned to what is given up or forgone. Capital investment decisions particularly stress opportunity cost. Opportunity costs of a resource used in an investment decision are the net benefits the resource could generate if it were employed in a forgone alternative use. Every investment decision involves the sacrifice of an alternative use for that resource.

Traditionally, accounting systems do not identify opportunity costs explicitly. Nonetheless, it is the responsibility of a manager to identify and consider investment decision opportunity costs. Many have documented management's tendency to ignore or underweight opportunity costs in investment decisions, focusing instead on outlay costs in making such decisions. Others have pointed out that managers consider opportunity costs when they are provided explicitly. Indeed, some have shown that making opportunity costs explicit alters the framing of investment decisions and leads to better investment decisions.[45]

COST FUNCTIONS

Cost consequences that ensue from production decisions are brought together in various financial statements. The reports that are most helpful are the balance sheet and the income statement. A balance sheet presents the financial picture of a business in terms of its assets, liabilities, and ownership on a given date. On the other hand, an income statement measures costs and expenses against sales revenues over a period of time such as a month, quarter, or year to show the net profit or loss of the business. In business, therefore, managers are most familiar with cost when presented in an income statement.

All of the information entered into financial statements is essentially retrospective. It tells managers what happened in the past. Suppose management is interested in determining whether a price reduction will increase profits. The price cut presumably will stimulate additional sales. Management needs to know how costs would change if production were increased. A cost function represents the relationship between a firm's total costs and the volume of output it produces. In this way, a cost function provides management with information regarding costs for each volume of output a firm might produce.

FIXED AND VARIABLE COSTS

Recall from the discussion of production that the short run is a period during which a firm cannot vary the use of all factors of production. Usage of some factors of production is fixed with respect to the volume of output, whereas usage of other factors of production is variable with respect to the volume of output. The former are fixed factors of production or simply fixed inputs, and the latter are variable factors of production or simply variable inputs. In the short run during which operating decisions are made, a firm incurs some costs from use of these fixed factors, and these costs are called fixed costs. In addition, a firm incurs some costs from use of variable factors, and these costs are called variable costs.

---

45   See Susan F. Haka, "A Review of the Literature on Capital Budgeting and Investment Appraisal: Past, Present, and Future Musings," *Handbook of Management Accounting Research*, ed. Christopher S. Chapman, Anthony G. Hopwood, and Michael D. Shields (Oxford, UK: Elsevier, 2007), p. 712ff.

Fixed costs are fixed with respect to volume of output, and variable costs vary with respect to volume. Short-run cost functions are essentially operating cost functions that express the relationship between costs of production and output of product with fixed facilities, meaning that plant and equipment are given and fixed. To summarize, therefore, variable costs such as labor and materials increase as the volume of output increases. Fixed costs such as general and administrative expenses remain constant as the volume of output increases.

When making operating decisions about production with fixed facilities, some costs of production are fixed, and some costs of production are variable. Some costs also might be semi-fixed or semi-variable. These costs increase or decrease in a stepwise manner as output is increased or decreased. Semi-fixed or semi-variable costs are constant when the volume of output varies within a given range. They increase or decrease only when the volume of output moves outside this range.

The distinction between costs is determined strictly on the basis of whether a cost varies with the volume of output. In this sense, fixed costs are fixed with respect to the volume of output, and variable costs are variable with respect to the volume of output. Stated differently, fixed costs are all costs associated with use of factors of production that are fixed with respect to the volume of output, and variable costs are all costs associated with use of variable factors of production that are variable with respect to the volume of output.

In accounting practice, fixed costs broadly include expenses not included in cost of goods sold, and variable costs are expenses circumscribed by cost of goods sold. In other words, cost of goods sold comprises variable costs, whereas selling expenses, general administrative expenses, and depreciation comprise fixed costs. Fixed costs are also called overhead expenses or simply overhead. In effect, this accounting distinction recognizes expenses directly incurred in producing products and other expenses only indirectly involved.

TOTAL COST FUNCTIONS

A firm's total fixed costs (TFC) are its costs that do not depend on the volume of output produced by the firm. Examples of fixed costs include costs such as interest on borrowed funds, property taxes, fire insurance premiums, management salaries, and the cost of leased land or leased plant and equipment. A firm's fixed costs are incurred regardless of the volume of output and are incurred even if a firm shuts down and produces no output whatsoever. A firm's total variable costs (TVC) are its costs that depend on the volume of output produced by the firm. Variable costs typically include the costs of raw materials, energy, labor, and inputs of other factors of production that can be varied in the short run. A firm's total costs (TC) are the sum of total fixed costs and total variable costs. Therefore, the total cost function can be stated as

TC=TFC+TVC

Consider a small manufacturing firm. Suppose the business has annual fixed costs of $36,500. Therefore, fixed costs are $100 per day. For the purpose of estimating a daily total cost function, the daily fixed cost function can be expressed as

TFC=100

Fixed costs are $100 per day.

In addition, suppose that managers use volume and cost data to estimate variable costs with respect to volume. The relationship between volume and variable costs can be used to estimate variable costs per day. The daily total variable cost (TVC) function can be expressed as

$$TVC = 50Q - 12Q_2 + Q_3$$

Q is the volume of output. Clearly, total variable costs increase with increases in volume of output (Q).

Since total cost is the sum of total fixed cost and total variable cost, the daily total cost (TC) function is

$$TC = 100 + 50Q - 12Q_2 + Q_3$$

The total cost function reflects total costs per day of producing output with given facilities. In other words, a short-run total cost function specifies the costs required to produce any given volume of output with given facilities.

AVERAGE COST FUNCTIONS

Managers always want to know something about cost per unit of output. For a chemical plant producing diammonium phosphate, the plant manager will want to know the cost per ton of product. For a plant producing automobile tires, the plant manager will want to know the cost per tire. Cost per ton and cost per tire are examples of average cost. Each element in the cost structure can be stated in terms of an average. In other words, total fixed cost can be divided by volume of output to obtain average fixed cost, total variable costs divided by volume of output to obtain average variable cost, and total cost divided by volume of output to obtain average total cost. In business practice, average total cost usually is expressed as unit cost.

Average Fixed Cost (AFC): Fixed Cost per Unit

As stated previously, average fixed cost (AFC) is total fixed cost divided by volume (Q) of output. Therefore, the average fixed cost function is

$$AFC = TFC/Q$$

AFC expresses fixed cost per unit of output such as fixed cost per ton or fixed cost per tire. In the present case, the daily average fixed cost function is

$$AFC = 100/Q$$

AFC clearly declines continuously as the volume of output produced increases. Using the AFC function, average fixed cost at any volume can be determined by substitution. For example, average fixed cost at the volume of ten is

$$AFC = 100/10$$

$$AFC = 10$$

Average fixed cost is $10 at the volume of ten. Figure 4.1 shows average fixed cost of 100/Q, which continuously declines with respect to volume.

FIGURE 4.1
AVERAGE FIXED COST: FIXED COST PER UNIT

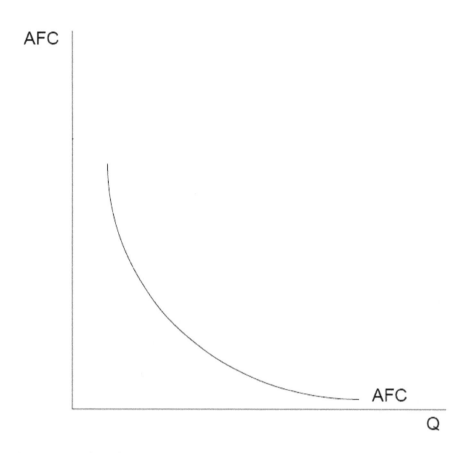

Average Variable Cost (AVC): Variable Cost per Unit

Earlier, average variable cost (AVC) was defined as total variable cost divided by volume (Q) of output. Therefore, the daily average variable cost function is

$AVC=TVC/Q$

The AVC function expresses variable cost per unit of output such as variable cost per ton or variable cost per tire. When production is undertaken with fixed facilities, average variable cost ordinarily falls over some range of output and then rises thereafter. In the present case, the daily average variable cost function is

$AVC=(50Q-12Q_2+Q_3)/Q$

Therefore, the AVC function is

$AVC=50-12Q+Q_2$

Using the function, average variable cost at any volume can be estimated by substitution. For example, average variable cost at the volume of ten is

$AVC=50-12(10)+(10^2)$

$AVC=50-120+100$

$AVC=30$

Average variable cost is $30 at the volume of ten. Figure 4.2 depicts average variable cost. When graphed, this daily average variable cost function is typical. It is U-shaped, meaning that AVC falls until a minimum of $14.00 is reached at the volume of 6, and then rises thereafter. Rising average variable cost reflects diminishing returns.

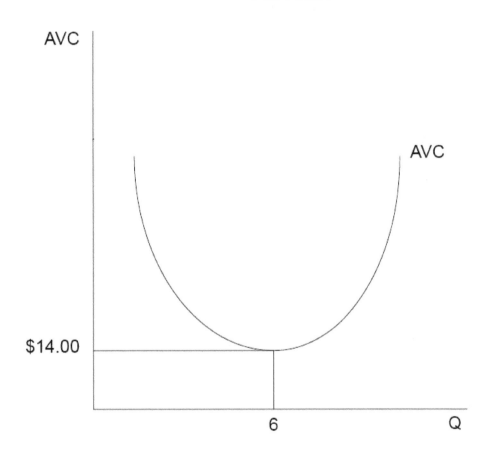

FIGURE 4.2
AVERAGE VARIABLE COST: VARIABLE COST
PER UNIT

Average Total Cost (ATC): Total Cost per Unit

As stated previously, average total cost (ATC) is total cost divided by volume (Q) of output. Therefore, the daily average total cost function is

$ATC=TC/Q$

The ATC function expresses total cost per unit of output such as total cost per ton or total cost per tire. In the present case, the daily average total cost function is

$$ATC=(100+50Q-12Q_2+Q_3)/Q$$

Therefore, the ATC function is

$$ATC=100/Q+50-12Q+Q_2$$

Using the function, average total cost can be determined for any volume of output by substitution. For example, average total cost at the volume of ten is

$$ATC=100/10+50-12(10)+(10^2)$$

$$ATC=10+50-120+100$$

$$ATC=40$$

Average total cost is \$40 at the volume of ten. Figure 4.3 shows average total cost. When graphed, this daily average total cost function is typical. As in the case of average variable cost, average total cost also is U-shaped, falling and then reaching a minimum of \$29.29 at a volume of 7, and then rising thereafter. Rising average total cost reflects diminishing returns.

FIGURE 4.3
AVERAGE TOTAL COST: TOTAL COST PER UNIT

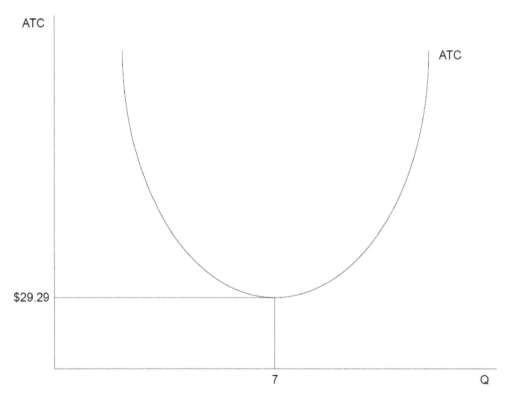

Average total cost is simply average fixed cost plus average variable cost. Average total cost and average variable cost are closer and closer as volume of output increases. The reason is that the difference between average total cost and average variable cost is average fixed cost, and average fixed cost is smaller and smaller as volume of output increases. Figure 4.4 shows average variable cost, and average total cost. Notice that the two are closer and closer as volume increases.

FIGURE 4.4
AVERAGE VARIABLE COST AND AVERAGE TOTAL COST

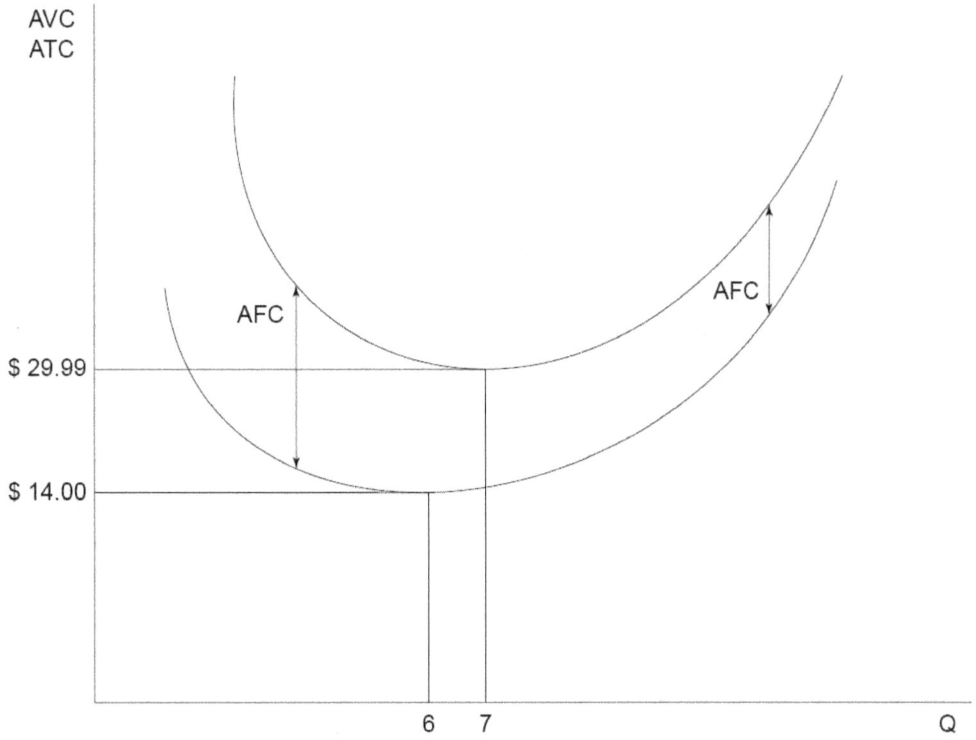

THE MARGINAL COST FUNCTION

When managers know the average total cost of production or the cost per unit of output, what they know deals with the past. In the case of diammonium phosphate, for example, the plant manager always wants to know the cost per ton of product. However, if the plant is producing a certain number of tons of product per day or week or month, cost per ton of product is the average total cost of producing the last so many tons. It may not tell the manager much about how much the next ton produced would cost, which would be the cost of adding one ton per day to volume. For the purpose of making decisions, how much the next ton of product is expected to cost is important and downright critical if the plant manager is motivated to make as much profit as possible from producing and selling product.

Strictly speaking, marginal cost refers to the rate of change in total cost with respect to volume of output. Practically speaking, marginal cost is the change in total cost due to a change in volume of output. In other words, marginal cost can be regarded as the incremental cost of adding one more unit to the volume of output. In the example of diammonium phosphate, marginal cost is the incremental cost of adding one more ton of product to the volume produced per day or per week or per month. It is the expected cost of the next ton of product. Therefore, the marginal cost (MC) function with respect to volume of output (Q) is MC=ΔTC/ΔQ. Since fixed costs are constant with respect to output, the only change in total cost when volume of output changes is the change in variable cost. Therefore, the marginal cost function can be restated as MC=ΔTVC/ΔQ.

Estimating Marginal Cost

Marginal cost can be estimated by linear interpolation or by calculus. Linear interpolation is estimating an unknown quantity between two known quantities. The noted physicist, Emanuel Derman, says in his famous book, *My Life as a Quant,* "Interpolation is calculating the 'middle' value of a mixture from known values of its ingredients at either end."[46] When estimated by linear interpolation, marginal cost usually is called incremental cost.

A marginal cost function is determined by calculus. Bear in mind, however, that calculus gives a precise measure of the rate of change in total cost, but the total cost function is only an estimate of the true but unknown relationship between cost and volume of output. Thus, even with the use of calculus, marginal cost is only an estimate of the rate at which cost is changing with volume.

The first derivative of the total cost function is the marginal cost function. Obtaining the first derivative is simple. Fixed cost does not change with volume. In the total cost function referenced above, fixed cost is $100. This fixed cost of $100 does not figure in marginal cost. However, any element of cost that does change with volume is indicated with Q. Therefore, for every instance in which a Q appears in the total cost function, multiply the exponent times the coefficient for Q, and then subtract one from the exponent. In the present case, recall that the daily total cost function is

$TC=100+50Q-12Q_2+Q_3$

Therefore, the marginal cost function is

$MC=50Q^0-24Q_1+3Q_2$

Since Q^0 is one and Q_1 is written as Q with the exponent of one implied,

$MC=50-24Q+3Q_2$

Once calculus has been used to determine the marginal cost function, marginal cost at any volume of output can be obtained by substitution. For example, when ten units of output are produced, marginal cost is

$MC(10)=50-24(10)+3(10^2)$

$MC(10)=50-240+300$

$MC(10)=110$

When ten units of output are produced, the total cost of production is changing at the rate of $110 per unit with respect to volume. This result can be interpreted as the expected cost of the next unit of output.

TOTAL, AVERAGE, AND MARGINAL COSTS

---

46   Emanuel Derman, *My Life as a Quant: Reflections on Physics and Finance* (New York: John Wiley & Sons, 2004), p. 214.

Total, average, and marginal cost functions can be used to develop a table in which entries illustrate important relationships between cost and output. In Table 4.4, the present case is used to drive entries for total fixed cost (TFC), total variable cost (TVC), total cost (TC), marginal cost (MC) estimated by calculus and by interpolation, average fixed cost (AFC), average variable cost (AVC), and average total cost (ATC).

Marginal cost estimated by linear interpolation shown in Table 4.4 is determined in the following way. Consider total cost at volumes of 7, 8, and 9 tons per day. At the volume of 7, total cost is $205, at the volume of 8, $244, and at the volume of 9, $307. Between the volume of 7 and 8, incremental total cost is $244–$205=$39. Between the volume of 8 and 9, incremental total cost is $307–$244=$63. To estimate the rate at which total cost is changing at the volume of 8, linear interpolation can be used. The middle value that lies between $39 and $63 is $39+$63=$102÷2=$51, which is an estimate of the rate at which total cost is changing at the volume of 8 tons per day. Between 8 and 9, incremental cost is $63, and between 9 and 10 is $400–$307=$93. To estimate the rate at which total cost is changing at the volume of 9, linear interpolation can be used. The middle value that lies between $63 and $93 is $63+$93=$156÷2=$78.

Table 4.4
Schedule of Total, Average, and Marginal Costs

Q	TFC	TVC	TC	MC Interpolation	MC Calculus	AFC	AVC	ATC
0	100	0	100					
1	100	39	139	30	29	100.00	39.00	139.00
2	100	60	160	15	14	50.00	30.00	80.00
3	100	69	169	6	5	33.33	23.00	56.33
4	100	72	172	3	2	25.00	18.00	43.00
5	100	75	175	6	5	20.00	15.00	35.00
6	100	84	184	15	14	16.67	14.00	30.67
7	100	105	205	30	29	14.29	15.00	29.29
8	100	144	244	51	50	12.50	18.00	30.50
9	100	207	307	78	77	11.11	23.00	34.11
10	100	300	400	111	110	10.00	30.00	40.00
11	100	429	529	150	149	9.09	39.00	48.09
12	100	600	700	195	194	8.33	50.00	58.33
13	100	819	919	246	245	7.69	63.00	70.69
14	100	1,092	1,192	303	302	7.14	78.00	85.14
15	100	1,425	1,525	366	365	6.67	95.00	101.67
16	100	1,824	1,924	435	434	6.65	114.00	120.25
17	100	2,295	2,395	510	509	5.88	135.00	140.88
18	100	2,844	2,944	591	590	5.56	158.00	163.56
19	100	3,477	3,577	678	677	5.26	183.00	188.26
20	100	4,200	4,300		770	5.00	210.00	215.00

RELATIONSHIPS AMONG AVERAGE AND MARGINAL COST FUNCTIONS

Managers often use known information about average cost, either average total cost or average variable cost, to estimate the unknown marginal cost of a change in output. However, average cost and marginal cost are generally different to some extent or another. Nevertheless, definite relationships are found among average cost functions and the marginal cost function. The relationships can be expressed succinctly in three statements.

First, when average cost is decreasing, marginal cost is less than average cost. When marginal cost is less than average cost, average cost is being pulled down by changes in cost that are less than the average. If average variable cost or average total cost is falling, marginal cost is less than the respective average cost. Second, when average cost is increasing, marginal cost is more than average cost. When marginal cost is more than average cost, average cost is being pulled up by changes in cost that are more than the average. If average variable cost or average total cost is rising, marginal cost is greater than the respective average cost. Third, when average cost neither increases nor decreases with respect to output, marginal cost is equal to average cost. When marginal cost is the same as average cost, the average does not change. If average variable cost or average total cost is neither falling nor rising, marginal cost is equal to the respective average cost.

These foregoing relationships follow from the mathematical properties of average cost and marginal cost, but they also are intuitive. If the average increases when one more thing is added, then the value of the most recently added thing must be greater than the average. Conversely, if the average falls, the value of the most recently added thing must be less than the average. Finally, if the average remains the same, the value of the most recently added thing must be the same as the average.

Think about a basketball player who averages twenty points per game over the first ten games of a season. If this player were to score thirty-one points in the 11th game, his or her average points per game would increase from twenty points per game to twenty-one points per game. Thirty-one points are added to total points, which is greater than average points per game. Thus, the average is pulled up. If this player were to score only nine points in the 11th game, his or her average points would decrease from twenty points per game to nineteen points per game. Nine points are added to total points, which is lower than average points per game. Thus, the average is pulled down. If this player were to score twenty points in the 11th game, his or her average remains the same. Twenty points are added to total points, which is the same as average points per game. Thus, the average is unchanged. What is true for marginal points and average points for the basketball player is nonetheless true for marginal costs and average costs and marginal costs for the business firm.

Look again at Table 4.4 for evidence of these relationships. At low volumes of output, marginal cost is less than average variable cost and average total cost, and both average variable cost and average total cost fall with volume of output. At greater volumes of output, marginal cost is greater than average variable cost and average total cost, and both average variable cost and average total cost rise with volume of output. With respect to integer volumes of output, average variable cost reaches its minimum ($14.00) at a volume of six units, for which marginal cost and average variable cost are equal. With respect to integer volumes of output, average total cost reaches its minimum ($29.29) at a volume of seven units. Figure 4.5 graphs the relationship between marginal cost, average variable cost, and average total cost. Notice that marginal cost intersects both average variable cost and average total cost at their minimum points.

FIGURE 4.5
RELATIONSHIP AMONG AVERAGE VARIABLE COST,
AVERAGE TOTAL COST, AND MARGINAL COST

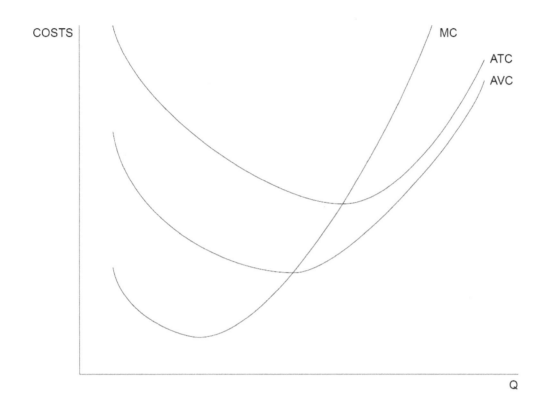

LONG-RUN COST FUNCTIONS

The long run is a production period during which inputs of all factors of production can be varied. Essentially, the long run is a planning horizon for making decisions about size of operations. In other words, the long run is a planning horizon for decisions dealing with facilities that are given and fixed in the short run during which operating decisions are made. When management makes long-run decisions, therefore, management makes decisions regarding the scale of physical plant and associated equipment as well as other matters concerning production.

Consider a firm that can operate a facility that can be built in five different sizes, ranging from small to large. Once management of the firm commits to a production facility of a particular size, it can vary volume of output only by varying inputs of factors other than plant size. The period of production in which management cannot adjust the size of its production facilities is the short run. For each plant size, there is an associated short-run average cost function. These average cost functions include the costs of all relevant variable inputs as well as the fixed cost of the plant itself. To illustrate this point, consider Figure 4.6. Short run cost functions are shown for each of five plant sizes from small to large. In this industry, firms that built small plants would have a cost disadvantage with respect to firms that build large plants.

FIGURE 4.6
SHORT RUN COST FUNCTIONS FOR FIVE PLANT SIZES

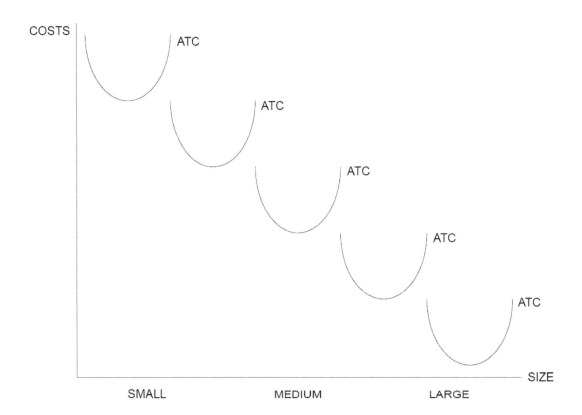

ECONOMIES OF SCALE

Recall from the discussion of production that returns to scale deal with the relationship between a proportionate change in all factors of production and the resulting change in output. Increasing returns to scale are evidenced when production relationships bring about increases in output proportionately greater than corresponding increases in scale. The cost equivalent of increasing returns to scale is lower average total cost with respect to scale. Economies of scale can be inferred from increasing returns to scale. Economies of scale may be defined as lower unit cost due to size of operations. Figure 4.7 shows economies of scale in an industry. Unit cost falls with increasing size of operations and then flattens. After economies of scale have been exhausted, there are no cost advantages to increased size.

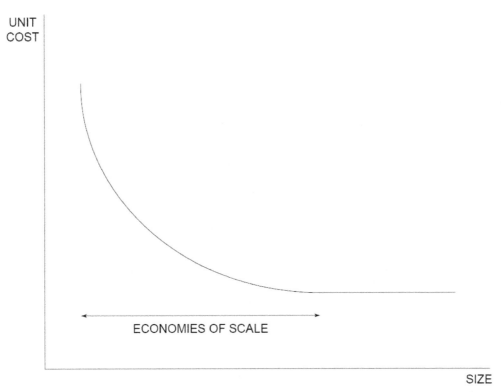

Economies of scale can arise from any business function, including operations, distribution, marketing, and finance. Economies might materialize in operations as specialized labor, machinery, and equipment are justified with larger scale. Economies can be actualized from pushing larger volume through distribution channels. Economies can be realized through spreading advertising and promotion outlays over a larger volume of output. Economies might arise through debt capital borrowed at lower interest rates than rates at which smaller firms borrow. Economies might be realized through buying materials, parts, or components in larger volume at a discount.

Diseconomies of Scale

Decreasing returns to scale are evidenced when increases in output are proportionately less than corresponding increases in scale. The cost equivalent of decreasing returns to scale is higher average total cost with respect to scale. Diseconomies of scale can be inferred from decreasing returns to scale. Diseconomies of scale may be defined as higher unit cost due to size of operations.

One source of scale diseconomies at the plant level is transportation costs. If a firm's customers were dispersed, then transportation costs of distributing output of product from one large plant would be more than transportation costs of distributing outputs from a number of strategically located smaller plants. Scale diseconomies also may result from problems associated with coordination of production flows and administrative control. The size of line and staff management and associated salary costs may increase more than proportionately as scale is increased. Losses may arise from delayed or flawed decisions attributable to a deeper hierarchy of management or to greater divergence separating individual performance and organizational performance.

Economies and Diseconomies

The notion of economies of scale fits well with experience. Industries in which the largest companies have lower costs by comparison to their smaller rivals seem ordinary. In the final analysis, when a business grows, there are forces that contribute to lower unit costs and other forces that contribute to higher unit costs. When economies of scale are observed, the former forces that lower unit costs with scale outweigh the latter forces that raise unit costs with scale. When economies of scale are realized, the factors that bring unit costs down are greater than factors that drive up unit costs.

John D. Rockefeller: Realizing the Potential for Economies of Scale

When John D. Rockefeller founded Standard Oil, the primary product was kerosene. Standard Oil consolidated numerous small plants into a few large refineries. Ninety percent of U.S. production was refined in these large refineries. Two-thirds of this production was exported to overseas markets. Standard Oil production represented twenty-five percent of world production. When petroleum was refined in small plants, typical refineries had costs of 2.5 cents per gallon of crude oil refined. After Standard Oil increased size of operations, average cost of kerosene was reduced from 2.5 cents per gallon to 0.452 cents per gallon, a whopping eighty-two percent decrease in cost per gallon in only five years! Rockefeller had the vision to see the potential for economies of scale, and the potential was realized through dramatic increases in size of operations.[47]

Minimum Efficient Scale

The shape of long-run average cost curves is important because of implications for plant scale decisions and effects on intensity of competition. In some industries, firms first encounter increasing returns to scale and thus economies of scale over some range of size. Afterwards, these firms face constant returns to scale over larger size of operations. In these cases, an L-shaped long-run average cost curve is observed. Figure 4.8 illustrates an L-shaped unit cost curve. Unit cost falls as size of operations is increased to a scale after which unit cost is constant with respect to scale. The plant size at which unit cost is lowest is the minimum efficient scale.

---

47   See Alfred D. Chandler, *Scale and Scope* (Cambridge, MA: Harvard University Press, 1990), pp. 24-25.

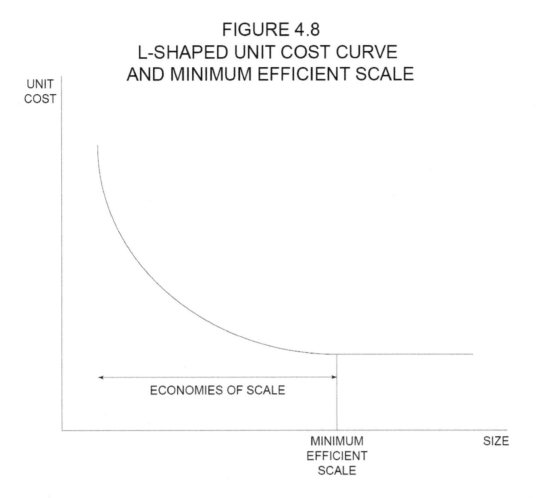

FIGURE 4.8
L-SHAPED UNIT COST CURVE
AND MINIMUM EFFICIENT SCALE

The size of operations and corresponding volume of output at which unit cost reaches a minimum vary from industry to industry. In a particular industry, minimum efficient scale (MES) is the smallest size of operations and corresponding volume of output at which unit cost is at a minimum. Minimum efficient scale infers that plant and equipment must be at least a certain size to have lowest unit costs. Therefore, minimum efficient scale refers to the size of plant at which further economies of scale cease to exist and beyond which unit costs are constant or rise.

Whether a market of given size is supplied by a large number of relatively small plants or by a small number of relatively large plants depends on minimum efficient scale. Competition tends to be more intense in industries where the minimum efficient scale is small relative to market demand. The number of competitors generally is large and competition is intense when MES is low relative to total market demand. This generalization follows from correspondingly low barriers to entry associated with low capital investment requirements. On the other hand, when minimum efficient scale is relatively large, capital investment and other requirements constitute a barrier to entry that tends to discourage and to limit the number of potential competitors. Market size always must be taken into account when considering the competitive impact of MES. Some markets are large enough to accommodate substantial numbers of very large competitors. Other markets are so small that only a few competitors can fit.

One reason why managers are so interested in knowing the minimum efficient scale of plant is that plants below this size operate at a competitive cost disadvantage. The cost disadvantage of plants that are 50% of minimum efficient scale can be significant in some industries. Consider Table 4.5, which presents somewhat dated but still illustrative information on eight industries. Plants that are 50% of minimum efficient scale have cost disadvantages ranging from as low as 1% for sulfuric acid to as high as 25% for bricks. When the cost disadvantage of operating plants that are sized below MES is relatively small, no serious competitive consequences are likely. The slightly higher unit costs of small producers can be overcome by factors such as superior customer service and regional location to cut transportation costs and delivery lags. In such instances, advantages of large-scale operations have little economic relevance. When the cost penalty of operating at half of MES is substantial, the cost disadvantage might lead to failure unless a firm expands scale.

Table 4.5 Cost Disadvantage of Plants 50% of Minimum Efficient Scale			
Industry	Cost Disadvantage (%)	Industry	Cost Disadvantage (%)
Flour Mills	3.0	Synthetic Rubber	15.0
Bread Making	7.5	Detergents	2.5
Paper Printing	9.0	Bricks	25.0
Sulfuric Acid	1.0	Machine Tools	5.0

Source: F.M. Scherer, Industrial Market Structure and Economic Performance, 2nd ed. (Chicago: Rand-McNally, 1980)

ECONOMIES OF SCOPE

Many firms produce a number of products. These firms might use inputs that are common to the production of several products. Economies of scope exist if a firm achieves cost savings as it increases the variety of goods it produces. Whereas economies of scale are defined in terms of declining average cost, economies of scope usually are defined in terms of the comparative total cost of producing a variety of goods together rather than separately. As a result, unit cost of producing each product is reduced. Thus, economies of scope might be regarded in terms of the comparative cost of producing related goods together in a plant versus separately in two or more plants. Economies of scope occur, therefore, when inputs such as labor and capital equipment can be shared in the production of different products and result in cost savings.

At the same time that Standard Oil was realizing economies of scale, Bayer, Hoechst, and BASF saw the potential for economies of scope. Larger plants could produce hundreds of dyes as well as many pharmaceuticals from the same raw materials and the same intermediate chemical compounds. Unit costs and prices could be reduced. Consequently, the three German firms were able to reduce the price of a new synthetic dye, red alizarin, from 270 marks per kilogram in 1869 to 9 marks in 1886. They were able to make comparable price reductions in their other dyes. The price reductions were the result of cost reductions.[48] Actually, realizing the potential for economies of scope was the outcome of scale and scope effects. In this historical case, dyes were made in larger plants and dyes were made together rather than separately. Generally, such cases are known as economies of scale and scope. More often than not, economies of scale and economies of scope are difficult to separate because the two are found together.

---

48   See Chandler, *ibid.*, pp. 25-26.

ECONOMIES OF EXPERIENCE

Economies of scale refer to cost advantages attributed to larger size of operations used to produce a larger volume of output. Moreover, as firms gain experience in the production of a product, their unit cost of production often declines. Greater cumulative total output over many time periods often provides manufacturing experience that enables firms to lower their unit cost of production. The effect is known as economies of experience, which is lower unit cost due to cumulative output of a particular product.

For many manufacturing processes, unit cost declines substantially as cumulative total output increases. As experience increases, management and workers alike become more and more knowledgeable about production techniques. Improvements in the use of production equipment and in production methods are important in this process, but reduced waste from defects also is important as workers become ever more proficient. The number of worker-hours necessary to produce a unit of output may decline for numerous reasons as more units of a product are produced. These reasons include increased familiarization with tasks, improvements in work methods and flow of work, and reductions in scrap and rework.

The Learning Curve

When knowledge gained from manufacturing experience is used to improve production methods so that output is produced with increasing efficiency, the resulting decline in unit cost is the effect of learning. The learning curve refers to cost advantages due to accumulating experience and know-how. The principle of the learning curve was noticed first in airplane manufacturing during the 1920s and made known in the 1930s. The learning curve is attributed to T.P. Wright. In 1925, Wright was commander of what later became Wright-Patterson Air Force Base in Dayton, Ohio. Wright noticed that in aircraft production, the average time needed to assemble each additional plane declined as more and more planes were produced. Through learning by doing, workers became better and faster at their jobs, and unit labor costs fell as a result. Furthermore, Wright observed that the rate of decline in cost per plane seemed to be about twenty percent when the number of assembled planes doubled. Wright wrote up his observation in a short article, published in 1936.[49]

The Progress Ratio

Over decades, the learning curve was developed more fully and applied more widely to many other assembly-type production processes. Forecasts of personnel, equipment, and raw material requirements and their associated costs based on the learning curve are now commonly used. Often, learning is characterized as a constant percentage decline in average labor costs as cumulative output increases. When characterized in this way, the result is called the learning rate. This percentage represents the proportion by which unit labor costs decline as cumulative output is doubled. Sometimes, the magnitude of learning and thus the learning rate is expressed in terms of a progress ratio. The progress ratio for a given production process is calculated by examining how much labor costs decline as cumulative output increases. The progress ratio, therefore, is

$$P = AC_2 / AC_1$$

49   See T.P. Wright, "Factors Affecting the Cost of Airplanes," *Journal of Aeronautical Science*, 3 (February 1936), pp. 122-128.

AC_1 is average labor cost of production when a firm has cumulative output of Q_1, and AC_2 is average labor cost of production when it has cumulative output of $Q_2=2Q_1$. Any progress ratio less than one suggests that learning is taking place. A progress ratio of one would indicate no learning whatsoever.

Progress ratios have been estimated for many industries and products. The median progress ratio for manufacturing appears to be about 0.8, meaning that for a typical firm, doubling cumulative output reduces unit labor costs by about twenty percent. Progress ratios vary from process to process, plant to plant, firm to firm, and industry to industry, however. While analysts may estimate that an industry has a progress ratio of 0.8, for example, the ratio does not imply that continual doubling of output in that industry inexorably leads to further and further labor cost reductions. Estimated progress ratios usually represent cost reductions over a range of output and do not indicate if and when learning economies might be exploited fully.

While the progress ratio concept has been applied mainly to cost measurement, it seems to apply as well to quality. For example, one finding is that more experienced medical providers result in significantly lower surgical mortality rates for a number of common surgical procedures. This finding has been used to argue for development of regional referral centers for provision of highly specialized medical care. These regional centers would perform many specific surgical procedures such as heart surgery, replacing local facilities with lower volumes and presumably higher mortality rates.[50]

The L-1011 Tristar

In the 1960s, American Airlines entered into discussions with Lockheed about interest in developing a new airliner capable of a large passenger load carried over long international distances. Lockheed had left the civil airliner industry in the late 1950s. Launched in 1957, Lockheed's Model L-188 Electra was the first large turboprop airliner produced in the United States. Tragically, wing vibration caused two crashes with fatalities. Even after costly modifications to fix the problem, no further orders were placed. Lockheed also blundered in designing and producing a military transport plane, the C-5A Galaxy. The U.S. Air Force discovered cracks in the wings, and Lockheed had to redesign the wing structure. Cost overruns burned cash and enervated Lockheed's interest in designing and producing a new wide-body civilian airliner.

In spite of business setbacks and other adverse circumstances, Lockheed soon had renewed interest in the civil airliner market. American Airlines appeared to be a timely opportunity, basically due to front-loading demand for a new generation of jumbo airliner. Lockheed's response to the conversation with American Airlines was the L-1011 Tristar, which had a passenger load of four hundred and a maximum airspeed of six hundred miles per hour. In summer 1971, Lockheed neared the end of almost four years of research, development, and testing. By then, a billion dollars had been sunk in the Tristar project.

Lockheed was desperate to put the L-1011 Tristar jumbo airliner into production, but the company did not have enough collateral to secure a loan. Lockheed was starved for cash and mired deeply in debt. Banks would not lend the company enough money to launch production. Worse, Tristar orders dwindled to nothingness. Lockheed booked 168 orders in 1968. However, orders had increased by only ten by

50   See Harold Luft, John Bunker, and Alain Enthoven, "Should Operations Be Regionalized? The Empirical Relation Between Surgical Volume and Mortality," *New England Journal of Medicine*, 301 (1979), pp. 1364-1369.

1971, and Lockheed had not received a single new order in more than a year. American Airlines betrayed Lockheed, instead choosing the McDonald-Douglas DC-10. Nevertheless, surrendering the Tristar was unthinkable because of the billion dollars of sunk cost. The threat of insolvency loomed. Do-or-die, a new line of credit in the amount of $250 million was imperative, but the company lacked the assets to pledge as collateral. The only recourse was a federal government loan guarantee. Lockheed needed a pledge that the U.S. Treasury would pay off the loan if the company defaulted.

Lockheed asked Congress for a federal loan guarantee of $250 million. The landscape of Congress was littered with a minefield of opposition. Although Lockheed was an important defense contractor, the Tristar was a commercial venture. Moreover, the Tristar was designed to use British engines made by Rolls Royce, a point that did not escape the attention of lawmakers who had special interests tied to General Electric and Pratt & Whitney. America had been in a recession ending only recently in November 1970, and 1972 was an election year. Weighing against the negative arguments was the matter of jobs. The claim amidst congressional testimony was that as many as sixty thousand jobs would be lost if the L-1011 failed to go forward. The Democratic Party controlled both the House and Senate. As the party of organized labor unions, affronting these labor unions was not good politics during a fragile recovery and going into an election year.

The bill was called the Emergency Loan Guarantee Act, legislation drafted specifically for the immediate advantage of Lockheed. During debate, questions arose dealing with whether the Tristar was economically sound. Specifically, many expert witnesses as well as members of Congress questioned whether the price of the Tristar would ever cover the costs of producing it. When the dust settled on the debate, the loan guarantee squeaked through the House by a margin of three votes. The bill then moved to the Senate, scheduled to recess for a month in August. Lockheed indicated that the company would be out of cash in September. Senate leadership brought the bill to a vote before the summer recess. When noses were counted before the vote, the bill was one vote short of passage and thus was expected to fail. The opposition of Senator Lee Metcalf of Montana was soft, however, and he realized that his vote was decisive. During the roll call vote, he changed his vote from nay to yea. Because of his change of heart or mind, the bill passed the Senate by a vote of 49-48.

In 1973, Uwe Reinhardt, a Princeton University professor, used the learning curve to deduce unit costs even before the first production model rolled off the assembly line.[51] Reinhardt found that the learning curve coefficient was 0.77, meaning that the variable cost per Tristar decreased 23 percent with each doubling of output. The first production model of the Tristar was known to cost around $100 million in variable costs. Based on a progress ratio of 0.77, the second production model would reduce variable cost per Tristar to around $77 million. The estimated variable cost per Tristar from the first through the 1,024th planes assembled is shown in Table 4.6.

---

51 U. E. Reinhardt, "A Breakeven Analysis for Lockheed's Tristar: An Application of Financial Theory," *Journal of Finance*, 28 (September 1973), pp. 821-838.

Table 4.6	
Learning Curve for the Lockheed L-1011 Tristar	
Cumulative Number of Tristars Produced	Average Variable Cost ($Million)
1	100
2	77
4	59
8	46
16	35
32	27
64	21
128	16
256	12
512	10
1,024	7

Notice that the average variable cost of a Tristar after 1,024 planes produced would be only one-fourteenth that of the first Tristar produced. Everyone involved with assembly would have become on average fourteen times more productive after years of doing the same work over and over, learning to be better and faster at the work. Of course, producing the second plane after the first one takes less time than producing the 1,024th Tristar after the 512th plane. The first cost reduction of twenty-three percent is experienced right away, perhaps in a month, but the tenth cost reduction of twenty-three percent materializes perhaps after a decade or more.

The original price for the Tristar was $14.7 million, but this price was driven down even before the first production model was sold due to fierce competition from Airbus and McDonnell-Douglas. Later, the price climbed a little, averaging around $15.5 million. Not taking into account the billion dollars of fixed costs associated with research and development, the variable cost per plane falls below the price of $15.5 only after 128 Tristars have been produced and sold. When approximately 144 Tristars have been produced and sold, variable cost per plane finally would be equal to price.

Now, consider both variable cost, reported in Table 4.6, and fixed cost, around one billion dollars already spent on research and development, to estimate total cost. This information is shown in Table 4.7.

Number of Planes	R&D Costs	Average Fixed Costs	Average Variable Costs	Average Total Costs
1	1,000	1,000	100	1,100
2	1,000	500	77	577
4	1,000	250	59	309
8	1,000	125	46	171
16	1,000	63	35	98
32	1,000	31	27	58
64	1,000	16	21	37
128	1,000	8	16	24
256	1,000	4	12	16
512	1,000	2	10	12
1,024	1,000	1	7	8

Table 4.7
Average Cost of L-1011 Tristars
($Million)

If each Tristar sells for $15.5 million, therefore, approximately 288 planes must be produced and sold to finally reach the volume at which fixed and variable costs per plane are equal to price. Approximately 144 planes must be produced and sold to cover only production costs, *i.e.*, variable costs. Based on the learning curve, the effect of this analysis was to question whether Congress should have approved a loan guarantee for a project that seemed so unlikely to succeed. Reinhardt argued that the Tristar would never be profitable. He was right. A volume of about 288 Tristars was needed to lower unit cost to price. Over thirteen years, 1972-1985, Lockheed produced and sold only 249, all produced and sold at a loss. Nevertheless, Lockheed paid off its federally guaranteed loan by 1977, and the company's dependency on the federal government ended. The dark side of the story is that over two decades, Lockheed bribed foreign government officials to win contracts for L-1011 deliveries. Lockheed almost foundered because of mounting losses on the Tristar and other aircraft projects. Lockheed righted itself only after redefining its core business as a major aerospace and defense producer at a time when the Reagan administration was expanding defense spending dramatically in the 1980s.[52]

Economies of Experience versus Economies of Scale

Distinguishing experience economies from scale economies is important. Economies of scale refer to lower unit cost when activities are undertaken on a larger scale. Economies of experience refer to reductions in unit cost due to accumulating experience with activities. Scale economies may be substantial even when experience economies are minimal. This situation is likely in capital-intensive activities such as manufacturing, petroleum refining, or chemical processing. Capital-intensive is descriptive of any production process requiring greater capital input than labor input in terms of cost. Experience economies may be substantial even when economies of scale are minimal. This situation is likely in labor-intensive

---

52   See Shlomo Maital, *Executive Economics* (N.Y.: Free Press, 1994), pp.142-150.

activities such as mining and agricultural industries. Labor-intensive is a reference to any production process that requires greater labor input than capital input in terms of cost.

Managers who do not distinguish carefully and correctly between economies of scale and economies of experience may draw incorrect inferences about the benefits of size. For example, if a large firm has lower unit costs because of economies of scale, then cutbacks in volume associated with scale would raise unit costs. If lower unit costs are the result of learning, the firm may be able to cut back volume without necessarily raising its unit costs. If a firm has a cost advantage due to a capital-intensive production process and resultant scale economies, then it may be unconcerned about labor turnover. On the other hand, a firm that has low unit costs due to learning may be highly concerned about labor turnover.

PRACTICE QUESTIONS

1. Distinguish between rigid mass production, flexible mass production, and continuous process production.

2. State the law of diminishing returns and distinguish it from decreasing returns to scale.

3. Both the law of diminishing returns and the concept of decreasing returns to scale infer that output per unit of additional input(s) eventually declines. The two are not equivalent, however. What is the most important difference between the two?

4. In a conversation, a manager comments, "When our plant capacity was doubled, we found we had to double every factor of production. What we found from day one was what we expected. We also doubled our output. Well, so much for the law of diminishing returns." Comment critically on this statement.

Answer each of the next THREE questions based on the following information. Suppose the total cost function for a product has been estimated as

$$TC = 10,000 + 5,000Q - 100Q_2 + 10Q_3$$

TC is the total cost per day of producing the product, and Q is the volume of production measured in tons per day.

5. What is the amount of fixed costs of production? How do you interpret these fixed costs of production?

6. What is the average cost per ton of the product when the volume of output is 8 tons per day?

7. What is the marginal cost of production when the volume of output is 8 tons per day?

Answer each of the next TWO questions based on the following information. Suppose the total cost function for a product has been estimated as:

$$TC = 1,000 + 500Q - 100Q_2 + 10Q_3$$

TC is the total cost per hour of producing the product, and Q is the volume of output of the product.

8. What is the total cost of production when 5 units per hour are produced? When 6 units per hour are produced? When 7 units per hour are produced? When 8 units per hour are produced?

9. What is marginal cost when 6 units per hour are produced? When 7 units per hour are produced?

Answer each of the next TWO questions based on the following information. Suppose management of a manufacturing firm has used company data and spreadsheet software to estimate the total cost function for one of its product. As estimated, the total cost function is

$$TC=100+25Q-5Q_2+Q_3$$

TC is the total cost per hour of producing the product, and Q is the volume of output of the product.

10. What is the total cost of producing five units of the product? What is the average total cost of producing five units of the product?

11. What is the marginal cost of producing five units of the product? Is the average total cost of production rising or falling when producing five units of the product?

12. Suppose management of a small manufacturing plant has estimated its cost function as

$$TC=10,000+1,000Q-100Q_2+2Q_3$$

TC is the total cost per hour of producing the product, and Q is the volume of output of the product.

Calculate the cost per unit of output expected at a volume of five units. Using interpolation or calculus, calculate the marginal cost of production expected at the volume of five units. Based on these calculations, is average cost of production rising or falling if five units are produced?

13. Distinguish carefully between economies and diseconomies of scale.

14. What is minimum efficient scale? How can minimum efficient scale explain the simple observation that some industries are characterized by a large number of small firms, whereas other industries are characterized by a small number of large firms?

15. Economies of scale and minimum efficient scale are related concepts. Write a clear statement of each concept, and express the relationship between the two concepts.

16. In a particular industry, suppose average total cost of production is lower for a small plant and equipment than for either a medium or large plant and equipment. What does this information suggest in terms of minimum efficient scale and the number and size of business firms in this industry?

17. Why do we observe a relatively large number of firms producing relatively low levels of output in some industries and a relatively small number of firms producing relatively high levels of output in other industries?

18. In one industry, diseconomies of scale are observed at the firm level when output is equivalent to five percent of industry output. In another industry, diseconomies of scale are found at the firm level when output is equivalent to thirty percent of industry output. What can be said about the minimum efficient scale in the two industries? What can be said about the number and relative size of firms in each of the two industries?

19. Suppose you are in an interview setting, and the company recruiter says he wants to conclude with a 60-second interview dealing with production concepts. Answer each of his inquiries:

a. Suppose facility planners for a chemical company know that, if a large plant with capacity of 600,000 tons per month is built and operated, cost per ton of product will be $85; if two medium plants each with capacity of 300,000 tons per month are built, cost per ton will be $87; and if three small plants each with capacity of 200,000 tons per month are built, cost per ton will be $91. From this information, can increasing, constant, or decreasing returns to scale be inferred? Why?

b. What is the law of diminishing returns?

20. Distinguish carefully between economies of scale and economies of experience. What is minimum efficient scale? Suppose a company builds a plant at 50% of minimum efficient scale. Would the plant operate at a cost advantage or cost disadvantage? Why?

21. Answer each of the following questions:

a. At an automobile assembly plant, managers use a progress ratio as the metric for learning. They have estimated the progress ratio to be 0.9. Currently, workers have assembled 1,000 vehicles of a particular model, and the cost per vehicle is $24,000. What is the expected cost per vehicle for the 2,000th vehicle?

b. In a chemical industry, cost per ton of product is known to be $75 for a plant built with capacity of 100 tons per day, $65 for a plant built with capacity of 200 tons per day, $60 for a plant built with capacity of 300 tons per day, and $58 for any larger plant. Does this information suggest increasing or decreasing returns to scale? What is the minimum efficient scale?

PRACTICE QUESTIONS (*AND ANSWERS*)

1. Distinguish between rigid mass production, flexible mass production, and continuous process production.

Rigid mass production involves output of a highly standardized product and also involves a high volume of output. Flexible mass production involves assembly from standardized and mass-produced components, but the result is a diversity of products to meet a diversity of customer tastes and preferences. Continuous process production is an integrated system of converting a continuous flow of raw materials into a continuous flow of output.

2. State the law of diminishing returns and distinguish it from decreasing returns to scale.

The law of diminishing returns to a variable factor states that, if technology and inputs of all factors of production except one are held constant, then successive, equal increments of a variable factor of production produce increments in output of product that eventually will diminish. Decreasing returns to scale are observed if all factors of production are increased and output increases by a smaller proportion.

3. Both the law of diminishing returns and the concept of decreasing returns to scale infer that output per unit of additional input(s) eventually declines. The two are not equivalent, however. What is the most important difference between the two?

The law of diminishing returns to a factor is a short-run concept. When inputs of one factor are increased while holding constant the inputs of at least one other factor, the marginal product from the variable input factor eventually declines. Decreasing returns to scale is a long-run concept. When inputs of all factors are increased in direct proportion, total product will increase less than proportionately.

4. In a conversation, a manager comments, "When our plant capacity was doubled, we found we had to double every factor of production. What we found from day one was what we expected. We also doubled our output. Well, so much for the law of diminishing returns." Comment critically on this statement.

The law of diminishing returns to a factor is a short-run concept, which means that it applies to operating decisions. When inputs of one factor are increased while holding constant the inputs of at least one other factor, the marginal product from the variable input factor eventually declines. Economies of scale is a long-run concept, which means that it deals with planning decisions. When inputs of all factors are increased in direct proportion and total product increases proportionately, this case is one of constant returns to scale. The law of diminishing returns does not apply to the case described by this person in conversation.

Answer each of the next THREE questions based on the following information. Suppose the total cost function for a product has been estimated as

$$TC=10,000+5,000Q-100Q_2+10Q_3$$

TC is the total cost per day of producing the product, and Q is the volume of production measured in tons per day.

5. What is the amount of fixed costs of production? How do you interpret these fixed costs of production?

Fixed costs are $10,000. This amount of cost is fixed with respect to the volume of output and does not vary when the volume of output varies.

6. What is the average cost per ton of the product when the volume of output is 8 tons per day?

Average total cost is

$$ATC=10,000/Q+5,000-100Q+10Q_2$$

By substitution,

$$ATC(8)=10,000/8+5,000-100(8)+10(8^2)$$

$$ATC(8)=1,250+5,000-800+640=\$6,090$$

ATC is $6,090 per day.

7. What is the marginal cost of production when the volume of output is 8 tons per day?

Using calculus,

$$MC=5,000-200Q+30Q_2$$

By substitution,

$$MC(8)=5,000-200(8)+30(8^2)=5,000-1,600+1,920=\$5,320$$

Marginal cost is $5,320 at a volume of 8 tons per day.

Answer each of the next TWO questions based on the following information. Suppose the total cost function for a product has been estimated as

$$TC=1,000+500Q-100Q_2+10Q_3$$

TC is the total cost per hour of producing the product, and Q is the volume of output of the product.

8. What is the total cost of production when 5 units per hour are produced? When 6 units per hour are produced? When 7 units per hour are produced? When 8 units per hour are produced?

By substitution,

$TC(5)=1,000+500(5)-100(5^2)+10(5^3)=1,000+2,500-2,500+1,250=\$2,250$

$TC(6)=1,000+500(6)-100(6^2)+10(6^3)=1,000+3,000-3,600+2,160=\$2,560$

$TC(7)=1,000+500(7)-100(7^2)+10(7^3)=1,000+3,500-4,900+3,430=\$3,030$

$TC(8)=1,000+500(8)-100(8^2)+10(8^3)=1,000+4,000-6,400+5,120=\$3,720$

9. What is marginal cost when 6 units per hour are produced? When 7 units per hour are produced?

Using calculus,

$MC=500-200Q+30Q_2$

$MC(6)=500-200(6)+30(6^2)=500-1,200+1,080=\$380$

$MC(7)=500-200(7)+30(7^2)=500-1,400+1,470=\$570$

Answer each of the next TWO questions based on the following information. Suppose management of a manufacturing firm has used company data and spreadsheet software to estimate the total cost (TC) function for one of its product. As estimated, the total cost function is

$TC=100+25Q-5Q_2+Q_3$

TC is the total cost per hour of producing the product, and Q is the volume of output of the product.

10. What is the total cost of producing five units of the product? What is the average total cost of producing five units of the product?

By substitution,

$TC(5)=100+25(5)-5(5^2)+53=100+125-125+125=\$225$

$ATC(5)=225/5=\$45$

ATC is $45 at the volume of five units per hour.

11. What is the marginal cost of producing five units of the product? Is the average total cost of production rising or falling when producing five units of the product?

Using calculus,

$MC=25-10Q+3Q_2$

By substitution,

$MC(5)=25-10(5)+3(5^2)=\$50$

Average total cost of production when producing five units is

$ATC(5)=\$45$

Since $MC(5)>ATC(5)$, ATC must be rising when five units are being produced.

12. Suppose management of a small manufacturing plant has estimated its cost function as

$$TC=10,000+1,000Q-100Q_2+2Q_3$$

TC is the total cost per hour of producing the product, and Q is the volume of output of the product.

Calculate the cost per unit of output expected at a volume of five units. Using interpolation or calculus, calculate the marginal cost of production expected at the volume of five units. Based on these calculations, is average cost of production rising or falling if five units are produced?

The average total cost function is

$$ATC=10,000/Q+1,000Q/Q-100Q_2/Q+2Q_3/Q=10,000/Q+1,000-100Q+2Q_2$$

By substitution,

$$ATC(5)=10,000/5+1,000-100(5)+2(5^2)=2,000+1,000-500+50=2,550$$

Using calculus,

$$MC=1,000-200Q+6Q_2$$

By substitution,

$$MC(5)=1,000-200(5)+6(5^2)=150$$

Since marginal cost at production of 5 units ($150) is less than average total cost at production of 5 units ($2,550), average total cost is falling.

13. Distinguish carefully between economies and diseconomies of scale.

Economies and diseconomies of scale deal with the relationship between scale and corresponding volume of output and costs of production. Suppose all factors of production are increased and thus costs of production are increased. If output is increased more than proportionately with respect to costs, economies of scale are experienced. If output is increased less than proportionately with respect to costs, diseconomies of scale are experienced. For example, if inputs of all factors of production are increased so that costs are doubled and output is more than doubled, economies of scale are experienced. If output is less than doubled, diseconomies of scale are experienced.

14. What is minimum efficient scale? How can minimum efficient scale explain the simple observation that some industries are characterized by a large number of small firms, whereas other industries are characterized by a small number of large firms?

Minimum efficient scale of production is the smallest size of operations and corresponding volume of output at which long-run average cost is at a minimum. In other words, minimum efficient scale is the scale of plant at which further economies of scale cease to exist and beyond which unit costs are constant or rise. Whether a market of a given size is supplied by a large number of relatively small firms or by a small number of relatively large firms depends on the technology of production in the industry, which is the primary factor in determining the minimum efficient scale. Competition tends to be more active in industries where the minimum efficient scale is small relative to market demand. When the minimum efficient scale is relatively large, the capital investment and other requirements constitute a barrier to entry that tends to discourage and to limit potential competitors.

15. Economies of scale and minimum efficient scale are related concepts. Write a clear statement of each concept, and express the relationship between the two concepts.

Economies of scale are evidenced by falling average cost with respect to scale, i.e., average cost falls with larger scale of production. Minimum efficient scale is the smallest scale at which average cost is at its minimum. The relationship between the two concepts is that, at any scale smaller than minimum efficient scale, economies of scale have not been realized, and average cost at this smaller scale is greater than average cost at minimum efficient scale, and that, once minimum efficient scale has been achieved, all economies of scale have been realized.

16. In a particular industry, suppose average total cost of production is lower for a small plant and equipment than for either a medium or large plant and equipment. What does this information suggest in terms of minimum efficient scale and the number and size of business firms in this industry?

The volume of output at which the potential for economies of scale is realized is relatively high in some industries and relatively low in others. In industries where the efficient scale is high relative to the overall market, we observe a few large firms supplying the market. In industries where the efficient scale is low relative to the overall market, we observe many small firms supplying the market.

17. Why do we observe a relatively large number of firms producing relatively low levels of output in some industries and a relatively small number of firms producing relatively high levels of output in other industries?

The volume of output at which the potential for economies of scale is realized is relatively high in some industries and relatively low in others. In industries where the efficient scale is high relative to the overall market, we observe a few large firms supplying the market. In industries where the efficient scale is low relative to the overall market, we observe many small firms supplying the market.

18. In one industry, diseconomies of scale are observed at the firm level when output is equivalent to five percent of industry output. In another industry, diseconomies of scale are found at the firm level when output is equivalent to thirty percent of industry output. What can be said about the minimum efficient scale in the two industries? What can be said about the number and relative size of firms in each of the two industries?

Diseconomies of scale suggest that average costs are rising with scale. In the former industry, the minimum efficient scale is reached at a relatively small scale of production compared to the market output, and average costs rise after this small scale of production is realized. Businesses involved in large-scale production will be at a cost disadvantage by comparison to those with small-scale production. In the latter industry, minimum efficient scale occurs at a relatively large scale so that businesses committed to small-scale production will be at a cost disadvantage. In the former industry, a large number of relatively small businesses would be expected, whereas in the latter, a few relatively large firms would be expected.

19. Suppose you are in an interview setting, and the company recruiter says he wants to conclude with a 60-second interview dealing with production concepts. Answer each of his inquiries:

a. Suppose facility planners for a chemical company know that, if a large plant with capacity of 600,000 tons per month is built and operated, cost per ton of product will be $85; if two medium plants each with capacity of 300,000 tons per month are built, cost per ton will be $87; and if three small plants each with capacity of 200,000 tons per month are built, cost per ton will be $91. From this information, can increasing, constant, or decreasing returns to scale be inferred? Why?

In this case, increasing scale (from 200,000 to 300,000 to 600,000) results in lower cost per unit of output, which indicates economies of scale. Increasing returns to scale can be inferred from economies of scale.

b. What is the law of diminishing returns?

The law of diminishing returns states that, if technology and inputs of all factors of production except one are held constant, then successive, equal increments of the variable factor of production yield increments in output of product that eventually will diminish. In other words, the law of diminishing returns states that increasing only the use of a variable factor of production while holding the use of all other factors of production constant eventually causes output to increase at a diminishing rate.

20. Distinguish carefully between economies of scale and economies of experience. What is minimum efficient scale? Suppose a company builds a plant at 50% of minimum efficient scale. Would the plant operate at a cost advantage or cost disadvantage? Why?

Economies involve lower cost per unit of output. Economies of scale involve a case in which cost per unit fall with size of operations and thus are attributable to scale of operations. Economies of experience involve a case in which cost per unit fall with cumulative volume of output produced. Minimum efficient scale is the smallest size of operations (and corresponding volume) at which cost per unit is at a minimum. If a plant is built only 50% of minimum efficient scale, then the plant will operate at a cost disadvantage with respect to other plants in the industry built at minimum efficient scale.

21. Answer each of the following questions.

a. At an automobile assembly plant, managers use a progress ratio as the metric for learning. They have estimated the progress ratio to be 0.9. Currently, workers have assembled 1,000 vehicles of a particular model, and the cost per vehicle is $24,000. What is the expected cost per vehicle for the 2,000th vehicle?

The progress ratio is

$P = AC_2/AC_1$

AC_1 *is average cost of production when a firm has cumulative output of* Q_1, *and* AC_2 *is average cost of production when it has cumulative output of* $Q_2=2Q_1$. *A progress ratio of 0.9 means that, with each doubling of output, cost per unit is reduced by ten percent. Therefore, the expected cost per vehicle for the 2,000th vehicle is $21,600, and the expected cost per vehicle for the 4,000th vehicle is $19,440.*

b. In a chemical industry, cost per ton of product is known to be $75 for a plant built with capacity of 100 tons per day, $65 for a plant built with capacity of 200 tons per day, $60 for a plant built with capacity of 300 tons per day, and $58 for any larger plant. Does this information suggest increasing or decreasing returns to scale? What is the minimum efficient scale?

This information suggests the presence of economies of scale, i.e., lower unit cost as scale is increased. If economies of scale are evident, then increasing returns to scale may be inferred. Minimum efficient scale, i.e., smallest size at which unit cost is lowest, is a plant built with capacity of more than 300 tons per day.

5. Profit Strategies And Market Valuations

PROFIT MAXIMIZATION

In its essential meaning, profit suggests advancement of interests. A firm's interests are advanced when revenue from sale of its product(s) is greater than the cost of producing its product(s). Comprehension and analysis of profit are central to managerial economics, managerial accounting, and managerial finance. At the heart of the matter is the principle of profit maximization. The emphasis on maximization leads to principles that show managers how to use revenue and cost information to maximize profits. This emphasis does not assert that all business decisions follow the principles of maximization at all times and in all situations. However, the principles of profit maximization are a lodestar to lead in the direction of greater profits.

To some, profit maximization is worrisome because maximization somehow seems farfetched, even unworkable in practical terms. For others, profit maximization sounds crass and attributes to business a maladroit insensitivity to social responsibilities. As though businesses have no financial interests whatsoever, corporate statements to the public unfailingly stress how companies have a social conscience, act on a social agenda, and comply with the dictates of social responsibility.

Apart from brooding about the practicality of maximization and pledging allegiance to social concerns, time and risk are two dimensions of profit maximization making it more complicated. The normal thinking is in terms of maximizing profits for the current period. However, decisions made for this period may have an effect on profits in subsequent periods. To think narrowly in terms of maximizing profits of the current period is to misrepresent business practice. In addition, business decisions are risk averse. Yet, returns are linked and geared to risk. Therefore, business decisions are tempered by the degree of risk that managers are willing to undertake.

The Ultimate Goal and the Primary Means

Not to put too fine a point on it, maximizing the value of a firm is taken for granted as the ultimate goal of the firm. For practical purposes, value of a firm can be viewed as the firm's market capitalization or "market cap." Market capitalization is the market value of a firm's outstanding shares of common stock, computed by multiplying common stock price by number of outstanding shares of common stock. In effect, maximizing the value of a firm is viewed as an end, and maximizing profit is seen as the primary means of maximizing the value of the firm. Formally, maximizing profits is a reference to maximizing the present value of an expected profit stream. In this light, decisions are fraught with uncertain outcomes. Risk is involved in almost all decisions. Risk aversion is an attitude that leads someone who is choosing among alternatives of equal value to select the alternative with the least degree of risk. Unfortunately, less risky projects tend to have lower expected profit rates, and more risky projects tend to have higher expected profit rates. Properly understood, therefore, profit maximization means maximization of expected present values of an expected profit stream subject to adjustment for risk.

MARGINAL PROFIT

Suppose plant management has estimated production and cost functions. Management also is fairly sure about the price at which plant output can be sold. Management is motivated to choose the volume at which the most profit is made. Accordingly, management could develop a table depicting profit expected at various volumes of output. Consider Table 5.1, which shows volume of output in tons per day; marginal profit ($\Delta\pi/\Delta Q$), change in profit with respect to change in volume; and average profit (π/Q), profit per ton of output. Average profit is calculated by dividing profit at any particular volume by volume itself. Marginal profit is estimated by linear interpolation, which is estimating a value midway between two known values. For example, total profit is $600 at a volume of 3 tons per day, $1,000 at a volume of 4 tons per day, and $1,350 at a volume of 5 tons per day. Between the volume of 3 and the volume of 4, total profit increases by $400. Between the volume of 4 and the volume of 5, total profit increases by a volume of $350. Linear interpolation estimates the rate of change in profit at the volume of 4 tons per day. So, marginal profit is the value at the midpoint of $350 and $400. Adding the two known values together and dividing by two to compute the midpoint, the answer is $375, an estimate of the rate at which profit is changing at a volume of 4.

Volume of Output Per Day	Total Profit	Marginal Profit (Interpolation)	Average Profit
0	0		
		100	
1	100	(125)	100
		150	
2	250	(250)	125
		350	
3	600	(375)	200
		400	
4	1,000	(375)	250
		350	
5	1,350	(250)	270
		150	
6	1,500	(100)	250
		50	
7	1,550	(0)	221
		−50	
8	1,500	(−75)	188
		−100	
9	1,400	(−150)	156
		−200	
10	1,200		120

Table 5.1
Relationship Between Output and Profit

Although contrived, Table 5.1 is helpful as an illustration. Since managers want to make the most profit from production and sale of their product, they should focus on marginal profit rather than average profit. Notice that the most profit that can be made is $1,550 per day at the volume seven tons. If managers were to choose the volume at which average profit is greatest, they would choose the volume of only five tons. At the volume of five tons, average profit is $270 but total profit is only $1,350 per day. If volume were increased to six tons, another $150 would be added to profit per day even though average profit actually falls to $250 per day. If volume were increased still further to seven tons, another $50 would be added to profit per day even though average profit falls still further to $221 per day. Also notice that marginal profit is $0 for the volume at which total profit per day is maximized. This particular observation leads to a general principle for profit maximization.

Marginal Revenue Equals Marginal Cost: Profit Maximization

Profit is a calculation involving revenues from sales and costs of production. In its simplest expression, total revenue from sales (TR) of a particular product is the price of a product (P) multiplied times the quantity of product produced and sold (Q), which is

$TR = PQ$

Interestingly, average revenue from sales (AR) is total revenue divided by the volume of the product produced and sold, which is

$TR/Q = PQ/Q = P$

Price is merely a special word used instead of average revenue from sales of a product. Marginal revenue (MR) from sales of a product is change in total revenue from sales with respect to change in the amount of a product produced and sold, which is

$MR = \Delta TR/\Delta Q$

On the other hand, marginal cost (MC) is change in total cost of production (TC) with respect to change in volume of output, which is

$MC = \Delta TC/\Delta Q$

In its simplest expression, therefore, profit (π) is the difference between total revenues from sales and total costs of production, which is

$\pi = TR - TC$

Marginal profit (Mπ) is change in profit with respect to change in volume of product produced and sold, which is

$\Delta \pi/\Delta Q = \Delta TR/\Delta Q - \Delta TC/\Delta Q$

Marginal profit can be restated as

$M\pi = MR - MC$

Thus, marginal profit is equal to marginal revenue minus marginal cost.

If MR>MC, marginal profit is positive. When MR>MC, producing and selling an additional unit of output adds more to revenues than to costs and thus adds to total profit. Total profit would be greater if volume were increased. If MR<MC, marginal profit is negative. When MR<MC, producing and selling an additional unit of output adds more to costs than to revenues and thus takes from total profit. Total profit would be greater if volume were decreased. If MR=MC, marginal profit is zero. When MR=MC, producing and selling an additional unit of output will not add to total profit. Total profit is maximized at the volume for which marginal revenue equals marginal cost. Technically, MR=MC is the necessary condition for profit maximization. Practically, it is a limit. As long as MR>MC, managers would want to increase the volume produced and sold. If they discover that MR<MC, managers know they are producing too much volume. Managers would want to produce no more than the volume at which MR=MC. In that sense, MR=MC is a limit.

PROFIT MAXIMIZATION: PRICE TAKERS

In highly competitive markets, the price of a product is determined in the overall market as the outcome of countless transactions between sellers and buyers. Once price is determined in the overall market based on the demand for and supply of the product, firms producing and selling this product in the market take this price as the price of their product. For commodities, the market price might be the spot price, the market price quoted for immediate payment and delivery. On the other hand, the forward price of a commodity is established in a futures contract that stipulates a price for payment and delivery at a specific future date. In the case of either a spot price or a forward price, the market price is determined. The difference is when delivery is designated to occur, immediately or at some specific date in the future. Price takers accept the spot price and the forward price, both of which are determined in commodity markets such as the Chicago Mercantile Exchange.

These conditions are common for a wide range of commodities, including food (corn, wheat, soybeans, live cattle, coffee, sugar), fibers (cotton), metals (gold, silver, platinum, copper, palladium), energy (light crude oil, heating oil, natural gas, unleaded gas), and other homogeneous, undifferentiated goods. Firms that produce commodities in these highly competitive markets are called price takers. When this price taker circumstance is evident, managers essentially are limited to deciding how much to produce and sell at the price determined in the overall market, which is taken as the price that can be charged for the product. Firms can sell all they want at the market price but none at a price even slightly higher than the market price. Of course, since firms can sell all they want at the market price, they have no incentive to reduce their own price below the market price.

Reconsider the necessary condition for profit maximization. In general, profit is maximized at the volume of production and sales at which marginal revenue equals marginal cost. For price takers, price is identical to marginal revenue since additional units of output can be sold at the market price. Therefore, the relationship between marginal revenue and marginal cost can be restated in terms of price and marginal cost. If P>MC, then total profit can be increased if more volume is produced and sold. If P<MC, then total profit can be increased if less volume is produced and sold. For price takers, the necessary condition for profit maximization is P=MC, which, in the practical sense of a limit, signals the most volume that management will want to produce and sell.

Loss Minimization

In a sense, P=MC tells management the best the firm can do. Management is charged with making operating decisions at the plant level. Presumably, management wants to make decisions that are best in terms of operating the plant. For example, management of a price taker firm would want to determine the volume at which the most profit is made, which is the volume at which P=MC. At times, however, there is no volume of output at which the plant or firm can make a profit. At such times, the best the plant can do is a loss at the volume for which P=MC. Since the firm cannot make a profit, any discussion of profit maximization is moot. Under these circumstances, management will want to minimize loss. Loss minimization is a corollary of profit maximization. When a loss is incurred at the volume for which P=MC, a fundamental decision must be made. Managers must decide whether to continue operations at a loss or to shut down operations. Shutting down should not be confused with going out of business or going bankrupt. Shutting down means curtailing production, as many manufacturers and chemical processors call it. Shutting down means laying off workers and ceasing production until price again is high enough to resume production. When price rises, management begins to consider calling back workers from their furlough and resuming production and sales. This decision is called the shutdown decision. The decision to shut down is not arbitrary. The shutdown decision is based on business principles.

Contribution Margin

An important but remarkably simple concept in business is known as contribution margin. Contribution margin is the difference between total revenue from sales and total variable costs, which is

CM=TR–TVC

The difference between a firm's total revenue and total variable costs is available to cover part or all of fixed costs. If all variable costs and all fixed costs are defrayed, remaining revenue is profit. For example, consider Table 5.2, which depicts a retailer's simplified income statement. The retailer had a contribution margin of $300,000, which was available to pay fixed costs of $160,000 and contribute $140,000 to profit. The retailer's contribution margin was thirty percent ($300,000/$1,000,000=0.3 or 30%). For every dollar of sales revenue, thirty cents was available to contribute toward covering fixed costs and contributing to profit.

Table 5.2 Income Statement: Contribution Margin Format	
Sales	$1,000,000
Less: Variable Costs	
Cost of Goods Sold	$500,000
Sales Commissions	$120,000
Delivery Charges	$80,000
Total Variable Costs	$700,000
Contribution Margin	$300,000
Less: Fixed Costs	
Advertising	$2,000
Depreciation	$12,000
Insurance	$6,000
Payroll Taxes	$13,000
Rent	$43,000
Utilities	$24,000
Salaries	$60,000
Total Fixed Costs	$160,000
Net Operating Profit	$140,000

The Shutdown Decision

Contribution margin also is used to analyze the situation when a loss would be incurred at any volume of output. Consider the volume at which operating loss is minimized, which is the volume at which MR=MC. At that volume, total revenue from sales (TR) is less than total costs (TC), which indicates an operating loss. The question is whether to operate at a loss or shut down. If total revenue from sales is greater than total variable costs (TVC), then the positive contribution margin (TR–TVC) is available to pay part but not all of fixed costs. The operating loss, therefore, would be part of fixed costs (TFC). On the other hand, if TR is less than TVC, then a business does not have enough sales revenue to pay all of its variable costs. If the business operates at a loss, it would lose all of its fixed costs and part of its variable costs. If the business shuts down, it would lose only its fixed costs. Clearly, shutting down is preferred to operating at a loss if TR is less than TVC, and operating at a loss is preferred to shutting down if TR is greater than TVC.

To visualize the shutdown decision for a plant, consider the bar charts in three panels of Figure 5.1. In 5.1(a), TR is greater than TC and thus greater than both TVC and TFC. The plant is operating at a profit. In 5.1(b), TR has fallen below TC but is still greater than TVC. The plant can operate at a loss, which would be part of its TFC. Shutting down would result in a loss of all of its TFC. A loss of part of its TFC is better than a loss of all of its TFC. Since TR is greater than TVC, the plant should be operated at a loss. In 5.1(c), TR has fallen below TVC. If the plant operates, it would lose all of TFC and part of TVC. Shutting down would result in a loss of all of its TFC. A loss of all of TFC is better than a loss of all of TFC plus part of TVC. Since TR is less than TVC, the plant should be shut down.

FIGURE 5.1
SHUTDOWN: TOTAL REVENUE LESS
THAN TOTAL VARIABLE COST

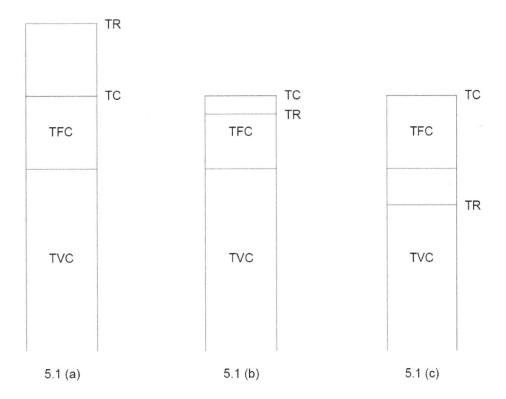

5.1 (a)   5.1 (b)   5.1 (c)

Contribution Margin Per Unit

At times, managers want to know a particular relationship between price and costs. The difference between total revenue from sales and total variable cost is total contribution margin. The difference between price (P) and average variable costs (AVC) is average contribution margin or contribution margin per unit. If price is greater than average variable cost, the margin above average variable cost is available as a contribution to payment of fixed costs and perhaps to profit. Therefore, contribution margin per unit is

$$CM_{UNIT} = P - AVC$$

Contribution margin per unit is the operational notion of contribution margin. Indeed, the usefulness of contribution per unit is so widespread in business practice that it is commonly called contribution margin even by people who know well the difference between contribution margin and contribution margin per unit.

The Shutdown Point: P=AVC

If price is above average total cost, price is high enough to cover all fixed costs and all variable costs as well as contribute to profit. If price is between average total cost and average variable cost, price is high enough to cover all variable costs and some but not all fixed costs. Although price is not high enough to contribute anything to profit, price is high enough to contribute to paying some of fixed costs. If management has decided on a volume of output that is best because it is the volume at which P=MC, the plant or firm would incur a loss. The loss is part of fixed costs. If the plant shuts down, it would lose all of its fixed costs. As long as price is greater than average variable cost, therefore, the best decision is to continue operations to minimize losses, losing some of fixed costs rather than all of fixed costs. The plant would incur a smaller loss if it continues operations. To state the same point differently, it would incur a larger loss if it shuts down. If price were below average variable cost, however, the plant would operate at a loss of all of its fixed costs and part of its variable costs. Management can shut down the plant or firm and limit its loss to fixed costs only. If price were below average variable cost, therefore, the plant would incur a smaller loss if it shuts down. Stated differently, it will incur a larger loss if the plant continues operations. For these reasons, P=AVC is the shutdown point.

To see the shutdown point for a plant, consider the three panels of Figure 5.2, each showing price (P), average total cost (ATC), average variable cost (AVC), and average fixed cost (AFC). In 5.2(a), P is greater than ATC and thus greater than both AVC and AFC. The plant is operating at a profit. In 5.1(b), P has fallen below ATC but is still greater than AVC. The plant can operate at a loss, which would be part of its AFC. Shutting down would result in a loss of all of its AFC. A loss of part of its AFC is better than a loss of all of its AFC. Since price is greater than AVC, the plant should be operated at a loss. In 5.1(c), P has fallen below TVC. If the plant operates, it would lose all of AFC and part of AVC. Shutting down would result in a loss of all of its AFC. A loss of all of AFC is better than a loss of all of AFC plus part of AVC. Since price is less than AVC, the plant should be shut down.

FIGURE 5.2
SHUTDOWN: PRICES LESS THAN
AVERAGE VARIABLE COST

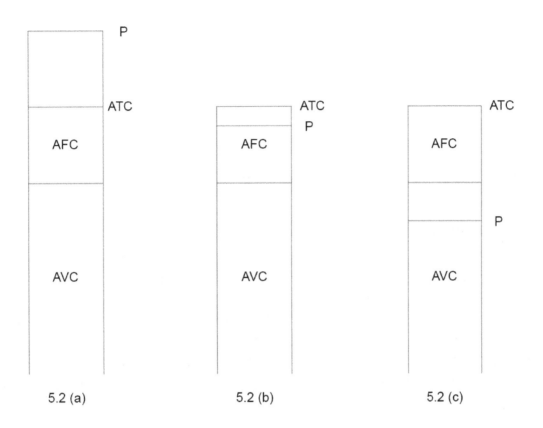

5.2 (a)　　　　　5.2 (b)　　　　　5.2 (c)

Wesson Enterprises

Wesson Enterprises is a business that specializes in production of a single product and operates one plant fully dedicated to production of the product. The undifferentiated product is produced by the ton. Management has estimated the plant's daily total cost (TC) function as

$$TC= 200-20Q+10Q_2$$

Q is volume of output per day. Management can sell as many tons as it chooses at a price of $180 per ton. Management wants to decide how much to produce at this price. Since Wesson Enterprises is a price taker, its marginal revenue is the same as price, $180. Every additional ton of product sold adds a constant $180 to total revenue. Using calculus, marginal cost is

$$MC=-20+20Q$$

To solve for the volume of output at which MR=MC, therefore,

$$180=-20+20Q$$

$$-20Q=-200$$

$$Q=10$$

Profit is maximized at the volume of 10 tons per day. Total profit is

$T\pi = TR - TC$

When volume is 10 tons per day, total revenue is

TR(10)=180(10)

TR(10)=1,800

Total revenue is $1,800 per day. When volume is 10 tons per day, total cost is

$TC(10) = 200-20(10)+10(10^2)$

TC(10)=200−200+1,000

TC(10)=1,000

Total cost is $1,000 per day. When volume is 10 tons per day, therefore, total profit is

$T\pi(10) = 1,800-1,000 = 800$

Total profit is $800 per day.

Average profit or profit per ton is P−ATC. When volume is 10 tons per day, average total cost is 1,000/10=100, which is $100 per ton. Average profit, therefore, is 180−100=$80 per ton. To see contribution margin per ton when volume is 10 tons per day, consider that average fixed cost is $20 per ton, and average variable cost is $80 per ton. Contribution margin per unit is 180−80=100, which is $100 per ton. This contribution margin per ton is above average variable cost and thus covers fixed cost, which is $20 per ton, and contributes $80 per ton to profit. Consider Table 5.3. Notice that marginal revenue ($180) and marginal cost ($180) are equal at a volume of 10 tons per day. Also notice that profit is greater at a volume of 10 tons per day than at any other volume.

Table 5.3 Wesson Enterprises Output, Revenue, Cost, and Profit					
Volume of Output	Total Cost	Marginal Cost (Calculus)	Total Revenue	Marginal Revenue (Calculus)	Total Profit
8	680	140	1,440	180	760
9	830	160	1,620	180	790
10	1,000	180	1,800	180	800
11	1,190	200	1,980	180	790
12	1,400	220	2,160	180	760

Table 5.3 shows profit and costs per day. When annualized, total fixed costs are 200(365)=73,000, which is $73,000. Total variable costs per day are −20(10)+10(102)=−200+1,000=800, which is $800. When annualized, total variable costs are 800(365)=292,000, which is $292,000. Therefore, annual total costs are $73,000+$292,000=$365,000. Total revenue per year is $1,800(365)=$657,000. Therefore, annual profit is $657,000−$365,000=$292,000.

Little Bahalia Specialists

Now, consider still another business, Little Bahalia Specialists. This business operates one plant and produces a single product, which is an undifferentiated commodity. The product price is determined by national market factors. This national market price is the price the company charges for its product. The current market price is $100 per ton, which has been stable for months and is not expected to change over the foreseeable future. Based on experience over the past five years, managers know how production costs respond to changes in volume of output. They predict production costs on the basis of a cost function, which is

$$TC = 1,000 - 20Q + 2Q_2$$

TC refers to daily total cost of production and Q to the daily volume of output. Managers hold themselves responsible for producing the volume at which the company makes the most profit or incurs the least loss.

Since the company is a price taker, marginal revenue is price, which is $100. Using calculus, marginal cost can be stated as

$$MC = -20 + 4Q$$

Setting marginal revenue equal to marginal cost to determine the profit-maximizing volume,

$$100 = -20 + 4Q$$

Solving for Q,

$$-4Q = -120$$

$$Q = 30$$

At this volume of 30 tons per day, total revenue from sales is

$$TR = 100(30) = 3,000$$

Total revenue is $3,000 per day. Total cost per day at this volume of 30 tons per day is

$$TC = 1,000 - 20(30) + 2(30^2)$$

$$TC = 1,000 - 600 + 1,800$$

$$TC = 2,200$$

Total cost is $2,200. At this volume of 30 tons per day, profit per day is

$$\pi = 3,000 - 2,200 = 800$$

Total profit is $800 per day.

However, suppose that the price of Little Bahalia's product falls from $100 per ton to $60 per ton. Management determines that a loss would be incurred at any volume of production. At the price of $60 per ton, management must decide whether to operate at a loss or shut down. Since the company is a price taker, marginal revenue is price, which now has fallen from $100 to $60. Marginal cost is unchanged and thus remains as $MC = -20 + 4Q$. Setting marginal revenue equal to marginal cost,

$$60 = -20 + 4Q$$

Solving for Q,

$$-4Q = -80$$

$$Q = 20$$

At this volume of 20 tons per day, total revenue from sales is

$$TR = 60(20) = 1,200$$

Total revenue is $1,200 per day. Total cost per day at this volume of 20 tons per day is

$$TC = 1,000 - 20(20) + 2(20^2)$$

$$TC = 1,000 - 400 + 800$$

$$TC = 1,400$$

Total cost is $1,400 per day. At this volume of 20 tons per day, profit per day is

$$\pi = 1,200 - 1,400 = -200$$

At the volume of 20 tons per day, a loss of $200 per day is incurred. This operating loss is less than daily fixed costs of $1,000, which is the daily loss that would be incurred if the plant were shut down.

In addition, consider that at the volume of 20 tons per day, total variable cost is $400 per day, and average variable cost is 400/20, which is $20. The price of $60 per ton is greater than average variable cost of $20. At the volume of 20 tons per day, therefore, there is a contribution margin per ton of $40 to pay fixed costs. The plant should be operated at a loss.

PROFIT MAXIMIZATION: PRICE SETTERS

Managers of firms that are price takers are not in a position to determine for themselves the price of their products. Managers essentially take the price determined in the market as the price of the product produced by their firms. Given that price, managers then decide how much to produce and sell. On the other hand, most firms have some control over the price of their products. Managers still decide how much to produce, but they also decide on the price of their product(s). In this sense, these firms are not price takers but rather are price setters, meaning that they can set their own prices. Still, they are governed by the same necessary condition for profit maximization, which is MR=MC. However, marginal revenue and price are not identical for price setters. A common mistake is setting price equal to marginal cost, which was appropriate for price takers. For price setters, marginal revenue must be determined and then set equal to marginal cost.

To sell more volume, price setters must reduce the price of their products. In effect, price setters choose the point on their demand curve at which profit is greatest. They choose a combination of price and volume at which profit is greatest. Selling more volume would require a lower price, whereas selling at a higher price would entail a lower volume. Unlike a price taker, a price setter cannot sell as much as it wants at a given price. Management is in a situation requiring choice of the best price and volume to maximize profit.

Beaver Dam Creek, Inc.

Beaver Dam Creek, Inc. is a firm that produces one product in one plant. It is a major competitor in its industry. Indeed, Beaver Dam Creek is able to command a premium price for its product. The demand for the product has been estimated in the form of an equation for the demand curve, which is

$P=580-2Q$

P is price, and Q is volume per day. The total revenue (TR) function, therefore, is

$TR=(580-2Q)Q$

$TR=580Q-2Q_2$

Using calculus, the marginal revenue (MR) function is

$MR=580-4Q$

Marginal revenue must be set equal to marginal cost for determination of the profit maximizing volume of production and sales. The total cost (TC) function has been estimated as

$TC=600-20Q+3Q^2$

Q is daily volume. Using calculus, the marginal cost (MC) function is

$MC=-20+6Q$

The volume of output per day at which MR=MC is

$580-4Q=-20+6Q$

$-10Q=-600$

$Q=60$

At the volume of 60 units per day, profit is maximized.

At the profit maximizing volume of 60 units per day, the profit-maximizing price of the product is found by substitution into the equation for the demand curve,

$P(60)=580-2(60)$

$P(60)=580-120$

$P(60)=460$

The profit-maximizing price is $460 per unit. The interpretation of this information is that the firm will maximize profit when it sets a price of $460 and produces a volume of 60 units.

When the firm maximizes profit at a volume of 60 units per day and a price of $460 per unit, its total revenue per day is

$TR=460(60)$

$TR=27,600$

Total revenue per day is $27,600. Total cost at a volume of 60 units per day is

TC(60)=600–20(60)+3(60²)

TC(60)=600–1,200+10,800

TC(60)=10,200

Total cost per day is $10,200. Profit, therefore, is $27,600–$10,200=$17,400 per day. When volume is 60 units per day, average total cost is 10,200/60=$170. Profit per unit, therefore, is P–ATC, which is $460–$170=$290.

Consider Table 5.4, which is an abridged schedule of output, revenue, cost, and profit of Beaver Dam Creek, Inc. Notice that marginal revenue ($340) and marginal cost ($340) are equal at the volume of 60 units per day, which also is the volume of output at which profit is maximized.

Table 5.4 Beaver Dam Creek, Inc. Output, Revenue, Cost, and Profit					
Volume of Output	Total Cost	Marginal Cost (Calculus)	Total Revenue	Marginal Revenue (Calculus)	Total Cost
58	9,532	328	26,912	348	17,380
59	9,863	334	27,258	344	17,395
60	10,200	340	27,600	340	17,400
61	10,543	346	27,938	336	17,395
62	10,892	352	28,272	332	17,380

The Profit-Maximizing Price

A well-known relationship permits managers to determine the profit-maximizing price directly if they know or at least can estimate marginal cost and can make a reasonable conjecture about price elasticity of demand. Although daunting to derive, the relationship is simple. In its final expression, the profit-maximizing price (P*) is

$P^* = MC/[1+(1/E_p)]$

MC is marginal cost, and E_p is price elasticity of demand.

While the equation looks rather obscure and esoteric, it is simply an algebraic manipulation of MR=MC. Indeed, it is identical to MR=MC. This particular formulation between price, marginal cost, and the price elasticity of demand is a useful concept. Notice that the profit-maximizing price varies inversely with unsigned price elasticity of demand. In other words, the more sensitive sales are to price, the lower the profit-maximizing price, other things being equal. The profit-maximizing price of a product depends on the marginal cost of producing the product and the price elasticity of demand for the product.

For example, suppose the marginal cost of a particular product is $10 and its price elasticity of demand is –2. By substitution,

$P^*=10/[1+(1/-2)]$

$P^*=10/[1+(-0.5)]$

$P^*=10/[1-0.5]$

$P^*=10/0.5$

$P^*=20$

The profit-maximizing price is $20.

Clearly, the profit-maximizing price depends on the price elasticity of demand. Given marginal cost, the profit-maximizing price is inversely related to the price elasticity of demand. Suppose the price elasticity of demand for the product had been –5 rather than –2. By substitution,

$P^*=10/[1+(1/-5)]$

$P^*=10/[1+(-0.2)]$

$P^*=10/[1-0.2]$

$P^*=10/0.8$

$P^*=12.5$

The profit-maximizing price is $12.50.

The clear implication is that the more sensitive sales are to price, the lower the profit-maximizing price, other things being equal. Another implication is that, the more sensitive sales are to price, the smaller the difference between the profit-maximizing price and marginal cost. As demand becomes more and more price elastic, the profit-maximizing price is closer and closer to marginal cost. This point means that markup over marginal cost is greater when demand is relatively price inelastic and thus sales are relatively insensitive to price.

For example, consider Table 5.5, which shows price elasticity of demand, marginal cost, and profit-maximizing price. As demand is more and more price elastic, the profit-maximizing price becomes smaller and smaller. In addition, as demand is more and more price elastic, the difference between the profit-maximizing price and given marginal cost becomes smaller and smaller. Given the importance of the price elasticity of demand in determining the profit-maximizing price of a product, it is not hard to see why managers are so intent on obtaining at least rough estimates of price elasticity product by product.

Table 5.5 Price Elasticity of Demand and Profit-Maximizing Price		
Price Elasticity of Demand	**Marginal Cost**	**Profit-Maximizing Price**
−1.25	10	50.00
−1.50	10	30.00
−2.00	10	20.00
−5.00	10	12.50

Markup and Price Elasticity of Demand: Grocery Items

The common sense of this analysis is that high markups over cost are expected for price inelastic items for which higher prices will not chase away business. Low markups over cost are expected for price elastic items. Consider markups for grocery items. Managers with years of grocery experience know that price sensitivity of items is the primary consideration in setting margins. Staple products such as coffee, ground beef, laundry detergent, milk, soft drinks, soup, and toilet tissue are price sensitive and thus command relatively low markups no more than ten percent, maybe fifteen percent at most. Products with high margins tend to be those for which demand is not particularly price sensitive. Brand name bread, cold cuts, cookies, delicatessen items, fresh fruit, fresh vegetables, nonprescription drugs, and spices are marked up thirty to sixty percent. A wide difference in margins is applied to related items. The markup on ground beef, for example, is typically no more than ten percent, but the markup on steak is as much as thirty-five percent. Ground beef is a relatively low-priced meat with wide appeal to large families, college students, and low-income groups whose price sensitivity is high. In contrast, relatively expensive sirloin, T-bone, porterhouse, and other cuts of steak appeal to higher-income groups with lower price sensitivity.

The point is that managers should base markups on a roughly inverse relationship with price elasticity of demand they discern for each of their products. In management practice, profit maximization is never complete, and solving for precise markups is probably going too far with the analysis. Cost estimates often are imprecise, and average cost or average variable cost often is an imperfect proxy for marginal cost. Available information on price elasticity is even more approximate. Furthermore, resources devoted to more exact information and its use may cost more than the extra profits they make possible. At least, however, the profit-maximizing price points the way.

Cost-Plus Pricing

The most common pricing practice used in business is cost-plus pricing, which is a form of markup pricing. Using cost-plus pricing, prices are set to cover all direct and indirect costs plus a percentage markup for profit contribution. In this way, cost-plus practices reflect differences in costs and price elasticity of demand. Most accounting systems can accommodate average costs, not marginal costs. Using average rather than marginal costs, cost-plus pricing constitutes a practical method for ensuring an approximation of MR=MC for each line of products sold.

Consider a retailing operation. Products are bought at wholesale prices for resale. Of course, the wholesale cost of products does not reflect indirect costs such as wages and salaries, utilities, and so forth. Generally, businesses use some sort of algorithm, called a fully allocated cost algorithm, to allot overhead costs to particular products. An algorithm is merely a step-by-step procedure. To approximate the total cost per unit of a product, the algorithm might be as simple as adding a fixed percentage to the direct cost. Next, a markup is added to the fully allocated cost. The retail price is cost plus a markup.

ECONOMIC VALUE ADDED (EVA)

In 1982, Joel M. Stern and G. Bennett Stewart founded Stern Stewart & Co. as a financial consulting firm. Together, they developed the concept of economic value added (EVA).[53] EVA is a registered trademark of the company. Stern Stewart developed a comprehensive approach to management and performance built around EVA, which is based on recognition of opportunity cost, particularly the opportunity cost of invested capital. As such, EVA is a measure of economic profit rather than accounting profit. To understand and appreciate the simple notion of EVA, consider the following digression on basic financial concepts used widely by managers.

The purpose of an income statement is to present a summary of operating and financial transactions that contributed to owner equity during an accounting period. Each entry in an income statement is a financial concept worthy of understanding. For example, consider the following depiction of selected items in an income statement:

Net Sales

−Cost of Goods Sold

=Gross Profit

−Selling Expenses

−General and Administrative Expenses

−Depreciation Expenses

=Operating Profit

±Extraordinary Items

=Earnings Before Interest and Taxes

−Net Interest Expenses

=Earnings Before Taxes

−Net Tax Expenses

=Net Earnings

Net sales represents gross dollar sales minus merchandise returns and allowances. Essentially, cost of goods sold (COGS) is cost of goods manufactured plus inventory at the beginning of an accounting period minus inventory at the end of the accounting period. Next, gross profit is net sales minus cost of goods sold. However, gross profit does not include indirect costs.

Selling expenses are incurred directly or indirectly in making sales, including items such as salaries of the sales force, commissions, and advertising outlays. General and administrative expenses are salaries, supplies, and other operating costs necessary to administration of the business. Selling and general administrative expenses (SG&As) are the sum of selling and general and administrative expenses. Sometimes, SG&As are called overhead expenses or simply overhead. Depreciation expenses account for reduced value of assets due to wear and tear, technical obsolescence, and other causes.

---

53   See G. Bennett Stewart, *The Quest for Value: A Guide for Senior Managers* (New York: Harper, 1991).

Operating profit is a measure of the firm's profit from operations that takes into account all of the firm's recorded expenses related to its operating activities. It takes account of COGS, SG&As, and depreciation. In other words, operating profit is net sales minus COGS, SG&As, and depreciation. Thus, operating profit measures a firm's recurrent business activities before interest expenses and taxes. Some events are not recurrent, however. Occurrences such as profit or loss from selling land or patents, destruction of assets resulting from fire or flood, or writing down inventory valuation are regarded as extraordinary items. Earnings before interest and taxes (EBIT) is operating profit less any extraordinary losses plus any extraordinary gains.

If there are no extraordinary losses or extraordinary gains, operating profit and EBIT are equivalent. Next, suppose taxes are subtracted from EBIT. The result is earnings after taxes and before interest. Stern Stewart gave this entry a name, Net Operating Profit After Taxes (NOPAT), which essentially is EBIT minus tax expenses. NOPAT lies at the heart of EVA.

The notion behind EVA is simple. A company adds value to the firm only if the return on its invested capital is greater than the cost of its invested capital. Economic Value Added (EVA) is the after-tax operating profit generated by a firm's capital minus the cost of the capital employed to generate the profit. At its simplest, therefore, economic value added for a particular year is a company's net operating profit after taxes minus a charge for the use of capital, which can be stated as

EVA=Net Operating Profit After Taxes–(Cost of Capital×Invested Capital)

EVA can be restated as

EVA=NOPAT–Capital Charge

In this formulation, net operating profit after taxes (NOPAT) is profit after subtracting cost of goods sold, SG&A expenses, depreciation expenses, and taxes. Capital is all the funds invested and thus tied up in fixed capital, mainly plant, equipment, and property, as well as working capital, mainly cash, inventories, and receivables.

EVA is a metric to measure how well a company has performed over a given reporting period, ordinarily a calendar year. For example, a firm's EVA for 2012 is a measure of how well the company performed in 2012. Therefore, economic value added is regarded as a performance measure.

Debt Capital and Equity Capital

A company's capital stems from debt and equity. Owners of a company have accumulated some capital as the result of borrowing, which is debt capital. Other capital is the result of investing, which is equity capital. The cost of debt capital is simple. It is simply interest charged by banks and bondholders. The cost of debt capital thus relates to servicing interest-bearing obligations, which is interest expenses reported on an income statement. This simplistic formulation does not include the tax savings of debt, which would be a significant adjustment for a company with a large proportion of debt capital.

On the other hand, the cost of equity capital is the return that owners forgo by investing in the company, which is the opportunity cost of equity capital. The cost of equity capital is what shareholders could earn by investing in another company having securities of equal risk. Opportunity costs are not captured in ordinary accounting systems and do not appear in ordinary financial statements. Stern Stewart utilizes the capital asset pricing model (CAPM) to determine the cost of equity capital. CAPM was developed originally by Harry Markowitz and later fine-tuned by William F. Sharpe. Along with Merton Miller, Markowitz and Sharpe were awarded the 1990 Nobel Prize in Economics. CAPM calculates a firm's cost of equity capital consisting of a risk-free rate of return for a stock market plus a risk premium that reflects how volatile its share price has been relative to that market.

When CAPM is not used, Stern Stewart suggests a rule of thumb to estimate the cost of equity capital. Shareholders earn about six percentage points more on stocks than on U.S. Treasury bonds. With the 30-year Treasury bond yield of, say, 2%, the cost of equity capital would be about 8% for a company in a business with average risk, more for a company in a business with above average risk, less for a company in a business with below average risk. In effect, this rule-of-thumb approach substitutes conjecture about risk for calculation of risk based on CAPM.

For a company that uses debt and equity capital, the appropriate cost of capital is the weighted average cost of capital (WACC). For example, suppose a company has a debt-to-equity ratio of 20% debt capital and 80% equity capital. If the cost of debt capital is 10% and the cost of equity capital is 20%, then the weighted cost of capital is calculated by assigning a 0.2 weight on the cost of debt capital and a 0.8 weight on the cost of equity capital,

$$WACC= 0.20(10)+0.80(20)=2.0+16=18$$

The weighted average cost of capital is 18%, which indicates the average cost of a dollar of debt and equity financing. This formulation is simplified, even oversimplified. A more precise WACC would take into account factors such as the tax deductibility of interest expenses.

A Restatement of EVA

The financial concept of EVA can be restated in a form that is highly useful for value creation. EVA can be rewritten as

$$EVA=NOPAT-(WACC \times Invested\ Capital)$$

Dividing both sides by Invested Capital,

$$EVA/Invested\ Capital=(NOPAT/Invested\ Capital)-WACC$$

NOPAT/Invested Capital is a firm's after-tax return on invested capital (ROIC). Therefore, EVA per dollar of Invested Capital is

$$EVA/Invested\ Capital=ROIC-WACC$$

Multiplying both sides by Invested Capital, EVA can be restated as

$$EVA=(ROIC-WACC) \times Invested\ Capital$$

The managerial meaning of this formulation of EVA is clear. If a firm's return on invested capital is greater than its weighted average cost of capital, the firm is creating or adding value. This generalization is true for the whole firm, and it is nonetheless true for each activity, each project, each segment, and each product line of the firm. This general concept also is helpful as a lodestar when considering new activities such as new products or new markets for extant products.

EVAluating South African Breweries

South African Breweries (SAB) is a company that owns hotels and shops in addition to being one of the world's biggest beer brewers. In 2002, SAB acquired Miller Brewing Company, which at the time elevated SAB from the fourth largest beer brewing company in the world to the second largest behind Anheuser-Busch. An abbreviated calculation of 1996 EVA for South African Breweries is shown in Table 5.6.

Table 5.6 EVAluating South African Breweries, 1996	
South African Breweries	**Rand (Million)**
1. Economic Capital	
Shareholder Equity	5,799
+Goodwill Written Off	1,521
+Capitalized Cumulative Unusual Loss	930
+Deferred Tax	405
+Minority Interests	2,352
+Total Debt	4,415
Total Equity and Debt Capital	15,422
2. Net Operating Profit After Tax (NOPAT)	
Operating Profit	3,406
+Interest Expense	689
−Unusual Gain	68
−Taxes	978
NOPAT	3,049
3. Weighted Average Cost of Capital (WACC)	
Cost of Equity Capital	20.4%
Cost of Debt Capital	10.7%
WACC	17.5%
4. EVA=NOPAT−(Capital×WACC)=3,049−(15,422×0.175)=3,049−2,699=350	350

Source: "Valuing Companies: A Star to Sail By?" The Economist (August 2nd-August 8th, 1997), p. 54.

First, SAB's economic capital is its equity and debt capital plus adjustments. Second, SAB's NOPAT is how much its assets earned after tax expenses. Third, SAB's cost of capital is calculated. The cost of SAB's debt capital is simply the average interest rate that the company pays. The CAPM is used to determine the cost of SAB's equity capital. Because SAB has more equity capital than debt capital, its weighted average cost of capital is 17.5%. Using elementary algebra, the debt-to-equity ratio was

20.4X+10.7(1–X)=17.5

20.4X+10.7–10.7X=17.5

9.7X=6.8

X=70.1

X–1=29.9

Therefore, the debt-to-equity ratio was 29.9/70.1. Fourth, the weighted average cost of capital is multiplied times SAB's capital employed. This capital charge is then deducted from SAB's NOP$_A$T. The result shows that SAB had a positive EVA of 350 million rand, approximately $80 million, in 1996. SAB's shareholders undoubtedly drank a beer or two to celebrate that good news.

Market Value, Market Value Added, and Economic Value Added

Stern Stewart kept track of EVA for thousands of companies. The company also tracked market value added (MVA), which is the market value of a company minus all debt and equity capital ever invested in the company. Accordingly, market value added is the value of a company over and above what has been invested in the company, calculated by

MV, which is price per share of common stock×number of shares outstanding

–Invested equity and debt capital over life of the company

=MVA, which is market value over and above what has been invested in the company

Therefore, MVA is the market capitalization of a company over and above the equity and debt capital that has been invested in the company. A positive MVA shows how much wealth has been created over the life of the company. For example, General Electric was formed in 1892. After 110 years, GE had a market cap of $322 billion. Over the 110 years, GE had invested $100 billion of debt and equity capital. Over the 110 years, therefore, GE added stockholder wealth of $222 billion. If MVA is negative, capital has been squandered and wasted so that wealth has been diminished. General Motors was formed in 1908. Almost a hundred years later, GM had a market cap of $105 billion. Over the years, GM had invested $119 billion. Over the same years, GM diminished stockholder wealth by $14 billion. EVA is a measure of annual performance, whereas MVA is a measure of wealth over the life of a company. Stern Stewart claims that wealth follows performance so that managerial decisions that result in high performance lead eventually to wealth creation, whereas managerial decisions that result in poor performance leads to wealth diminution.

A company with high operating profit but negative EVA has been compared to a basketball player who scores a lot of baskets only because he or she takes a lot of shots. The basketball team might win more games if the player passed the ball to other teammates who have a better shot. In the same way, a company with negative EVA would serve its stockholders better by returning funds to enable them to act on alternative investment opportunities that are greater than the company's own. For example, IBM had negative EVA of more than $1 billion in 1999. IBM shareholders could have earned more from investing retained earnings in securities of other companies with comparable risk.

Best and Worst Wealth Creators

In the 1990s, Stern Stewart compiled an annual listing of 1,000 companies ranked by MVA. Known as the Stern Stewart Performance 1000, the highest ranked companies were remarkably consistent from year to year. Almost always, General Electric was on top. Annually, General Motors was the cellar dweller. In the late 1990s and early 2000s, *Fortune* published the Stern Stewart Performance 1000 each year. Although dated, results illustrate the salient points of EVA and MVA. Results are shown for selected companies in Table 5.7. MVA rank is shown for 1999, 1998, and 1994. If the return on capital exceeds the cost of capital, then the company has used shareholder money advisedly, leading to positive EVA for the year.

Table 5.7
America's Greatest Wealth Creators, 1999

MVA Rank			Company	MVA ($Million)	EVA ($Million)	Return on Capital 1999 %	Cost of Capital 1999 %
1994	1998	1999					
13	3	1	Microsoft	328,257	3,776	56.2	12.6
1	1	2	General Electric	285,320	4,370	19.3	11.9
15	5	3	Intel	166,902	4,280	35.4	12.9
3	12	4	Wal-Mart	159,444	1,159	13.2	9.8
2	2	5	Coca-Cola	157,536	2,194	31.2	11.2
4	4	6	Merck	153,170	4,175	30.0	11.9
17	8	7	Pfizer	148,245	1,052	18.3	11.4
47	14	8	Cisco Systems	135,650	1,849	38.2	13.1
N/A	25	9	Lucent Technologies	127,265	1,514	17.5	11.6
10	10	10	Bristol-Myers-Squibb	119,350	2,273	26.8	11.2
1,000	16	11	IBM	116,572	−1,058	10.1	11.7
715	41	16	Dell	90,302	1,447	200.7	14.0
49	21	36	Hewlett-Packard	45,464	−593	10.6	12.8
991	290	43	Ford	38,509	2,545	13.8	9.5
226	80	56	Xerox	25,241	−680	6.8	9.1
53	65	59	Anheuser-Busch	24,598	517	14.1	9.0
16	71	83	Motorola	17,254	−2,830	−0.1	11.3
419	69	85	Monsanto	17,028	−229	6.8	8.1
60	66	87	H.J. Heinz	16,876	493	14.9	8.5
997	997	998	RJR Nabisco	−12,171	−1,449	3.4	7.5
995	1,000	1,000	General Motors	−17,943	−5,525	2.0	9.4

Source: "America's Greatest Wealth Creators," Fortune (November 10, 1997), pp. 265ff; "America's Greatest Wealth Creators," Fortune (November 9, 1998), pp. 193ff; and "America's Greatest Wealth Creators," Fortune (November 22, 1999), pp. 275ff.

Best and Worst Wealth Creators, 2000-2001

In its *Investor's Guide 2001*, *Fortune* again published an article based on the Stern Stewart Performance 1000. As a departure from past articles, however, rates of return and costs of capital were not published. In *Investor's Guide 2002*, the changed presentation was continued. Table 5.8 shows MVA rank for years 2001 and 2000 for selected companies. As usual, the top wealth creator was General Electric. In 2001, GE had created $312 billion in wealth, whereas AT&T stood last, having destroyed $94 billion.

Table 5.8 America's Best and Worst Wealth Creators, 2000-2001				
MVA Rank		**Company**	**MVA ($Million)**	**EVA ($Million) 2001**
2000	**2001**			
1	1	General Electric	312,092	5,943
3	2	Microsoft	296,810	5,919
4	3	Wal-Mart	198,482	1,596
16	4	IBM	142,625	1,236
9	5	Pfizer	141,764	942
8	6	Citigroup	140,426	4,646
15	7	Johnson & Johnson	137,424	2,440
5	8	Merck	135,561	4,836
11	9	Exxon Mobil	128,263	5,357
10	10	Intel	125,624	5,032
2	11	Cisco Systems	115,911	−365
6	15	Oracle	88,412	1,039
24	16	Philip Morris	78,107	6,085
21	19	Procter & Gamble	74,833	2,167
19	20	Home Depot	74,743	730
23	24	American Home Products	62,501	−2,154
56	42	Chevron-Texaco	27,238	4,046
50	45	McDonald's	24,597	269
90	203	Ford	4,275	1,991
994	987	Xerox	−6,712	−1,602
985	991	Bank One	−8,647	−2,851
998	998	General Motors	−34,456	−1,065
269	999	Lucent Technologies	−41,987	−6,469
1,000	1,000	AT&T	−94,270	−9,972

Source: Geoffrey Colvin, "America's Best & Worst Wealth Creators," Fortune (December 18, 2000), pp. 207ff.; David Stires, "America's Best & Worst Wealth Creators," Fortune (December 10, 2001), pp. 137ff.

MVPs of MVA

After 2001, *Fortune* did not publish the Stern Stewart Performance 1000. However, MVA rankings were published in the magazine, *CFO*, for 2002. In the rankings, MVA is reported along with Market Valuation (MV), Capital, EVA for 2002, and Sales for 2002. Table 5.9 shows MVA Rank, MVA, MV, Capital, and Sales for selected companies. Only 252 companies were ranked.

Table 5.9 MVPs of MVA, 2002						
MVA Rank 2002	Company	MVA ($Million)	MV ($Million) 2002	Capital ($Million)	EVA ($Million) 2002	Sales ($Million) 2002
1	General Electric	222,767	322,190	99,423	5,983	130,685
2	Microsoft	212,340	237,547	25,207	2,201	30,785
3	Wal-Mart	207,346	280,970	73,624	2,928	244,524
4	Johnson & Johnson	124,237	171,829	47,592	2,839	36,298
5	Merck	107,076	144,624	37,548	3,872	51,790
6	Procter & Gamble	92,231	133,248	41,017	2,315	42,606
7	IBM	90,422	193,955	103,533	−8,032	81,186
8	Exxon Mobil	85,108	273,634	188,526	−2,175	178,909
9	Coca-Cola	82,413	107,007	24,594	2,496	19,983
0	Intel	77,395	114,574	37,179	−3,736	26,764
15	Eli Lilly	57,366	74,761	17,395	1,096	11,078
20	Abbott Laboratories	49,181	71,352	22,171	1,562	17,685
29	DuPont	35,445	59,862	24,417	−96	24,134
30	Bristol-Myers-Squibb	33,872	58,015	24,142	777	18,119
46	Verizon	16,138	200,132	183,994	−5,612	67,625
69	Walt Disney	9,282	56,974	47,692	−2,072	25,779
95	Hewlett-Packard	5,476	63,243	57,767	−3,726	63,082
113	Ford	3,459	69,218	65,758	−4,826	162,586
117	Chevron-Texaco	3,135	93,457	90,322	−3,139	91,685
246	General Motors	−14,081	105,697	119,778	−5,065	184,214
249	AOL Time Warner	−27,148	103,550	130,697	−27,539	40,961
252	AT&T	−72,674	75,733	148,406	−27,116	49,931

Source: "MVPs of MVA," CFO (July 2003), pp. 59-66.

EVA Strategies: Growth, Improvement, and Reallocation

Companies that commit to management by EVA methods concentrate on three ways to improve their economic value added. First, invest capital where increased operating profit more than covers the charge for additional capital. This growth strategy includes introduction of new products, startup of new divisions, or expansion into new markets as long as expected operating profits are greater than the cost of any additional capital. Second, the improvement strategy looks to enhance operating profits without using additional capital or reduce capital while maintaining operating profits. Third, withdraw capital from operations that cannot generate operating profits greater than the cost of capital and reallocate it to activities that improve EVA. This reallocation strategy abandons any activity when it is not creating EVA and reallocates capital to activities that are creating EVA.

Consider a brief case study. CSX was created in November 1980 by a merger of the Chessie System and Seaboard Coast Line Industries, after which it became the largest U.S. railroad company. Headquartered in Richmond, Virginia, CSX is one of the components of the Dow Jones Transportation Average. CEO John W. Snow introduced the EVA concept in 1988. Snow appreciated the EVA concept based on what he learned while he earned the Ph.D. in economics at the University of Virginia in 1965. After serving as CEO of CSX, Snow was sworn in as Secretary of the Treasury on 3 February 2003. He announced his resignation on 30 May 2006.

CSX employed a lot of capital including a mammoth fleet of locomotives, railcars, and containers. When Snow became CEO, his stiffest challenge was the rapidly growing but low margin CSX Intermodal, which transported freight by rail to waiting trucks or ships. When capital costs were taken into account, CSX Intermodal had negative EVA of $70 million in 1988. Snow directed managers to improve EVA to at least break even within five years or CSX Intermodal would be sold.

In the next five years, freight volume rose by twenty-five percent, but the number of containers and trailers, which represented a lot of capital, was decreased from 18,000 to 14,000. Before, these containers and trailers would be grounded in terminals for weeks between runs. Once CSX managers recognized that these trailers and containers were idle capital, they figured out ways to return them to the rails in less than a week. The company also moved freight with a locomotive fleet of 100 instead of 150, which resulted in a reduction of $70 million in capital. Managers exceeded Snow's hurdle.

EVA Momentum

In 2006, Bennett Stewart left Stern Stewart to found evaDimensions. Once again, Stewart was instrumental in developing a new concept. Stewart originated EVA as a measure of economic profit rather than accounting profit. As CEO of evaDimensions, he originated a new ratio called EVA Momentum.[54] EVA Momentum is the change in EVA divided by prior period's sales, calculated simply as

EVA Momentum=(This Year's EVA−Last Year's EVA)÷Last Year's Sales

In this way, EVA Momentum is a measure of the rate at which a firm's economic profit is growing or shrinking scaled to a starting sales base. "It's the only percent metric where more is always better than less," Bennett says. "It always increases when managers do things that make economic sense."[55] In Table 5.10, EVA Momentum and EVA are shown for selected companies in the S&P 500. Data are based on trailing four quarters ended December 2010, January 2011, or February 2011.

---

54   Bennett Stewart, "EVA Momentum: The One Ratio that Tells the Whole Story," *Journal of Applied Corporate Finance*, 21 (Spring 2009), pp. 74-86.

55   Geoff Colvin, "A New Financial Checkup," *CNN Money* (January 11, 2010).

Table 5.10 EVA Momentum Ranking Selected S&P 500 Companies				
Rank	Company	Industry	EVA Momentum	EVA $Billion
1	Chesapeake Energy	Oil, Gas, Consumable Fuels	93.1%	$0.525
20	Applied Materials	Semiconductors, Semiconductor Equipment	23.3%	$0.602
30	Intel	Semiconductors, Semiconductor Equipment	14.9%	$7.079
33	Xerox	Electronics, Office Equipment	14.5%	$1.112
57	Google	Internet Software and Services	8.2%	$5.922
58	Apple	Computers and Peripherals	8.0%	$11.736
75	CSX	Freight Transportation	5.5%	$0.664
84	Microsoft	Software	5.1%	$16.007
95	Chevron	Oil, Gas, Consumable Fuels	4.8%	$12.101
100	DuPont	Chemicals	4.6%	$1.844
405	Verizon	Diversified Telecommunication Services	−0.3%	−$4.149
415	Kimberly Clark	Household and Personal Products	−0.4%	$1.771
417	Boeing	Aerospace and Defense	−0.5%	$1.187
428	Allstate	Insurance	−0.6%	−$0.304
443	General Mills	Food and Beverage	−1.3%	$0.977
446	Sara Lee	Food and Beverage	−1.4%	$0.304
473	Pfizer	Pharmaceuticals	−3.1%	$4.120
476	JPMorgan Chase	Diversified Financial Services	−3.5%	−$3.288
484	Monsanto	Chemicals	−4.8%	$0.354
490	Goldman Sachs	Capital Markets	−8.4%	$2.248

BREAKEVEN (COST-VOLUME-PROFIT) ANALYSIS

Many operating activities within a firm are based on anticipated volume of output. Analysis of interrelationships among a firm's unit sales, revenues, costs, and operating profit at various volumes of output is known as cost-volume-profit analysis or breakeven analysis. The term breakeven analysis comes from the prominent position of the breakeven point, the volume of output at which revenues and costs are expected to be exactly equal. The graphic form of this analysis is called a breakeven chart, which measures costs and revenues on the vertical axis and volume of output on the horizontal axis. In most breakeven charts, total cost (TC) and total revenue (TR) are assumed to be linear functions of the firm's volume of output. Profit or loss is the vertical difference between TR and TC at any particular volume. The breakeven point is the volume of output at which these two linear functions intersect, which is the volume at which TR=TC. In this case, total variable cost also is linear, rising from the origin and having the same slope as total cost. Figure 5.3 illustrates a breakeven chart, which depicts linear TR and

TC functions and indicates the breakeven point, designated as Q_{BE}. At volumes less than Q_{BE}, a loss is incurred. At volumes greater than Q_{BE}, a profit is made.

FIGURE 5.3
BREAKEVEN CHART

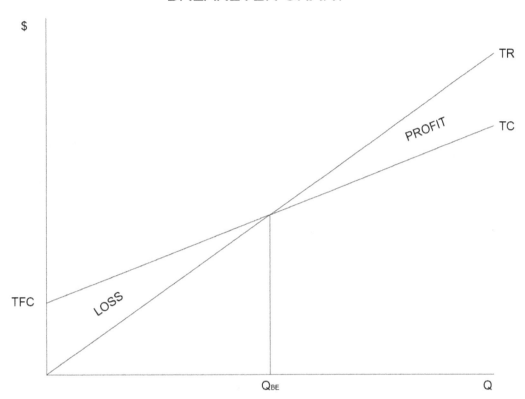

Ordinarily, a breakeven chart is drawn with total variable cost having its origin at total fixed cost so that a linear total cost function can be depicted. Linear total revenue implies that price is constant with respect to volume of output. In other words, breakeven analysis determines the breakeven volume of output based on a particular price. Notice that profits are implied to be greater as the volume of output increases. Below the breakeven volume, decreasing sales uniformly imply increasing losses.

The Breakeven Volume

Suppose the problems of cost and revenue estimation are solved satisfactorily. By definition, the breakeven point (Q_{BE}) occurs when total revenue (TR) equals total cost (TC), which is

TR=TC

By substitution,

PQ_{BE}=TFC+TVC

TVC at the breakeven volume is

$$TVC=(AVC{\times}Q_{BE})$$

Setting total revenue at the breakeven volume equal to total cost at the breakeven volume,

$$PQ_{BE}=TFC+(AVC{\times}Q_{BE})$$

Using a little algebra,

$$PQ_{BE}-AVCQ_{BE}=TFC$$

$$Q_{BE}(P-AVC)=TFC$$

$$Q_{BE}=TFC/(P-AVC)$$

Therefore, the breakeven volume of output is total fixed costs (TFC) divided by contribution margin per unit, which is P–AVC. The latter expression is extremely important in managerial decision making. The difference between selling price and variable cost per unit, which is contribution margin per unit, measures how much each unit of output contributes to meeting fixed costs and perhaps to making operating profits.

Consider a simple numerical example. Suppose management knows that total fixed costs of producing a product are $200,000, price is $100, and average variable cost is $80. To calculate the breakeven volume by substitution,

$$Q_{BE}=200,000/(100-80)$$

$$Q_{BE}=200,000/20$$

$$Q_{BE}=10,000$$

The breakeven volume is 10,000 units. Total revenue at the volume of 10,000 units is

$$TR=\$100{\times}10,000=\$1,000,000$$

Total cost at the volume of 10,000 units is

$$TC=\$200,000+(\$80{\times}10,000)=\$200,000+\$800,000=\$1,000,000$$

Therefore, TR=TC at the volume of 10,000 units.

Three Expressions of the Breakeven Volume

With use of the basic breakeven model, the breakeven volume can be expressed in one of three distinct ways: (1) number of units, (2) capacity utilization, or (3) dollar sales. To illustrate, consider a factory that can produce a maximum of 50,000 units of output per month. Units of output can be sold at a price of $100, variable costs are $50 per unit, and total fixed costs are $1,000,000.

Calculation of the number of units that must be produced and sold to break even is a direct application as before,

$$Q_{BE}=1,000,000/(100-50)$$

$$Q_{BE}=1,000,000/50$$

$$Q_{BE}=20,000$$

The breakeven volume is 20,000 units. To verify the breakeven volume, sales revenues and total costs can be calculated when 20,000 units are produced and sold. When 20,000 units are produced, total cost is

TC=1,000,000+50(20,000)

TC=1,000,000+1,000,000

TC=2,000,000

Total cost is $2,000,000 at the volume of 20,000 units. When 20,000 units are sold, total revenue is

TR=100(20,000)

TR=2,000,000

Total revenue at the volume of 20,000 units is $2,000,000. At a volume of 20,000 units, TR equals TC.

Capacity of the plant is 50,000 units. At the breakeven volume of 20,000 units, capacity utilization is 20,000/50,000, which is 40%. The breakeven point expressed in terms of output is likely to be meaningful to managers and others in operations. They understand that a volume of 20,000 per month must be produced at the plant to break even. The breakeven point expressed in terms of capacity utilization also is likely to be meaningful to managers and others in operations. Managers in operations understand that they must utilize 40% of plant capacity to break even.

The breakeven level of sales revenue is $2,000,000, which was determined above. This expression of the breakeven point is likely to be meaningful to managers and others in marketing and sales. Managers in marketing and sales understand that their sales must amount to $2,000,000 to break even.

Targeted Profit

Instead of focusing exclusively on the breakeven volume of output, suppose management wants an estimate of the volume (Q_{TP}) needed not only to cover all costs but also to make a targeted profit. The breakeven model can be modified as

$Q_{TP}=(TFC+\pi)/(P-AVC)$

Recall the previous example. Suppose management wants to make a targeted profit of $500,000.

Each of the three breakeven measures can be solved through direct substitution. First, the breakeven volume of output is

$Q_{TP}=(1,000,000+500,000)/(100-50)$

$Q_{TP}=(1,500,000)/50$

$Q_{TP}=30,000$

A volume of 30,000 units is required to cover all costs and make a profit of $500,000. Only 20,000 units are required to break even. To verify this finding, costs and revenues can be calculated for 30,000 units produced and sold. Total cost at the volume of 30,000 units is

TC=1,000,000+50(30,000)

TC=1,000,000+1,500,000

TC=2,500,000

Total cost at the volume of 30,000 units is $2,500,000. Total revenue at the volume of 30,000 units is

TR=100(30,000)

TR=3,000,000

Total revenue at the volume of 30,000 units is $3,000,000. The difference in revenues and costs is $500,000, which is the targeted profit objective. Sales revenue required to cover all costs and achieve this profit objective is $3,000,000, and required capacity utilization is 30,000/50,000, which is 60%.

DEGREE OF OPERATING LEVERAGE

Operating leverage refers to the ratio of a firm's total fixed costs (TFC) to its total variable costs (TVC), which is TFC/TVC. The higher this ratio of fixed to variable costs, the more leveraged the firm is said to be. As a firm becomes more automated, for example, the firm is substituting fixed costs for variable costs and thus is becoming more leveraged. The more leveraged the firm is, the more sensitive are the firm's profits to changes in the volume of output and sales.

The responsiveness or sensitivity of a firm's total profits to a change in its volume of sales can be measured by the degree of operating leverage (DOL), which is the percentage change in profit (π) divided by the percentage change in the volume of sales (Q). DOL is a measure of how sales growth translates into operating profit growth. Therefore, DOL can be expressed as

DOL=%$\Delta\pi$/%ΔQ

This expression of DOL can be restated as

DOL=$\Delta\pi$/π÷ΔQ/Q

DOL=($\Delta\pi$/ΔQ)(Q/π)

Now, consider that profit is

π=Q(P−AVC)−TFC

P is price. This expression is nothing more than total profit. Therefore, marginal profit is

$\Delta\pi$=ΔQ(P−AVC)

Substituting into DOL,

DOL=QΔQ(P−AVC)÷ΔQ/[Q/(P−AVC)−TFC]

This expression can be restated as

DOL=[Q(P−AVC)]/[Q(P−AVC)−TFC]

The numerator is the total contribution to fixed costs and to profits, whereas the denominator is total profit.

DOL for Three Systems of Production

Consider a case contrived to tease out the salient points and implications of DOL. Suppose managers must decide among three alternative systems of production. A highly automated system involves fixed costs of $100,000, which are much greater than the other two systems that are less automated. However, production using this highly automated system involves average variable costs of $2, which is much lower than the other two systems. Essentially, this system substitutes capital for labor, fixed cost for variable cost. A less automated system has total fixed costs of $60,000, and average variable costs are $3. A least automated system involves fixed costs of only $20,000, but average variable cost is $4. The price of the product is $5. In comparing these three systems, an important consideration is the degree of operating leverage.

Consider sales volume of 40,000 units. With fixed costs of $100,000, average variable costs of $2, and price of $5, DOL for the highly automated system is

DOL=[40,000(5–2)]/[40,000(5–2)–100,000]

DOL=[40,000(3)]/[40,000(3)–100,000]

DOL=120,000/[120,000–100,000]

DOL=120,000/20,000

DOL=6

At the volume of 40,000 units, operating profit would increase by six percent for every one percent increase in sales and would decrease by six percent for every one percent decrease in the volume of sales.

Again, consider sales volume of 40,000 units. With fixed costs of $60,000, average variable costs of $3, and price of $5, DOL for the less automated system is

DOL=[40,000(5–3)]/[40,000(5–3)–60,000]

DOL=[40,000(2)]/[40,000(2)–60,000]

DOL=80,000/[80,000–60,000]

DOL=80,000/20,000

DOL=4

At the volume of 40,000 units, operating profit would increase by four percent for every one percent increase in sales and would decrease by four percent for every one percent decrease in sales.

Once again, consider sales volume of 40,000 units. With fixed costs of $20,000, average variable costs of $4, and price of $5, DOL for the highly automated system is

DOL=[40,000(5–4)]/[40,000(5–4)–20,000]

DOL=[40,000(1)]/[40,000(1)–20,000]

DOL=40,000/[40,000–20,000]

DOL=40,000/20,000

DOL=2

At the volume of 40,000 units, operating profit would increase by two percent for every one percent increase in sales and would decrease by two percent for every one percent decrease in sales.

To reiterate, DOL is a measure of how sales growth translates into operating profit growth. Clearly, profit made from the highly automated system is more sensitive to changes in the volume of output and sales volume, meaning that profit accumulates faster with increases in volume. On the other hand, the higher the level of fixed costs, the higher the risk since these fixed costs must be met regardless of output. The degree of operating leverage is a measure that indicates such leverage and corresponding risk. The higher the DOL, the greater the operating leverage and corresponding risk. In addition, the breakeven point differs for the three systems. For the highly automated system, breakeven is at a volume of 33,333 units; for the less automated system, a volume of 30,000 units; and for the least automated system, a volume of 20,000 units.

PRACTICE QUESTIONS

1. Consider a business firm that produces two products, Iota and Pi. For the current level of production of each product, the direct labor costs, material costs, and other variable costs per unit of output are $100 for Iota and $200 for Pi. Prices charged for the two products are $150 for Iota and $250 for Pi. Calculate the contribution margin per unit for each product.

2. A high-tech business specializes in the production of a single product that no one firm among the many businesses in the industry ever has succeeded in differentiating. The market for this product is so competitive that no one firm has any control over price of the product. The price of the product as determined in the overall market is $500. This particular business knows its daily cost function, which has been estimated as

$$TC=6{,}000-300Q+10Q_2$$

TC refers to total cost of production and Q to the volume of production. If the goal of management is to make maximum profit (or to incur minimum loss) from production and sale of the product, how much of the product will the business produce, and how much total profit (loss) is made (incurred)?

3. Suppose a business produces a food product and because of successful differentiation has substantial control over price of the product. Management has good estimates of both the daily cost function and demand function for the product. The daily total cost function is

$$TC=100-10Q+Q_2$$

TC refers to total cost of production and Q to the volume of production. The demand curve is

$$P=50-2Q$$

P is price. If the goal of management is to make maximum profit (or to incur minimum loss) from production and sale of the product, how much of the product will the business produce, what price will the business charge, and how much total profit (loss) will the business make (incur)?

4. Suppose a company operates one plant and produces a single product, which is an undifferentiated commodity. The product price is determined by national market factors, *i.e.*, demand and supply. This national market price is taken by managers as the price the company charges for its product. The current market price is $155 per ton, which has been stable for months and is not expected to change over the foreseeable future. Based on experience over the past five years, managers know how costs behave with respect to volume of production. They predict daily production costs on the basis of a function, which is

$$TC=1{,}000-5Q+2Q_2$$

TC refers to total cost of production and Q to the volume of production. Managers hold themselves responsible for producing the volume at which the company makes the most profit or incurs the least loss. What volume should management choose to produce? How much profit will the company make or how much loss will the company incur? Should management operate or shut down?

5. Suppose a business produces a product that is highly differentiated. The product manager knows the production costs of the product from people in the engineering group and the demand for the product from people in his own brand group. The daily cost function estimated by the engineering group is

$$TC=500-10Q+Q_2$$

TC refers to total cost of production and Q to volume of production. The brand group estimates demand for the product from an equation for the demand curve, which is

$$P=150-9Q$$

Prefers to price of the product and Q refers to volume of sales. The product manager wants to price the product and sell a volume of product so that profit from production and sales can be maximized. What price should be charged, and how much of the product should be produced? How much profit will be made?

6. Suppose the operations manager of a chemical plant has the authority and responsibility to determine the best volume of output based on his knowledge of marginal cost and marginal revenue. The price of the product is constrained by intense competition in the industry, and the company therefore is a price taker. At present, the price of the chemical product produced at the plant is $75 per ton, and all output produced at the plant can be sold at this price. At the current operating volume of output, variable cost per ton of the product is $65, fixed cost per ton is $15, and thus total cost per ton is $80. Marginal cost has been estimated at $75 at the current volume and is rising with respect to any relevant volume greater than the current volume. Is the operations manager making the correct decision regarding volume of production, or should he choose to produce more or less volume? Why? Since a loss is incurred at the current volume, should the manager operate at a loss or shut down? Why?

7. Suppose a company operates one plant and produces a single product, which is an undifferentiated commodity. The product price is determined by national market factors, *i.e.*, demand and supply. This national market price is taken by managers as the price the company charges for its product. The current market price is $50 per ton, which has been stable for months and is not expected to change over the foreseeable future. Based on experience over the past five years, managers know how production costs respond to changes in volume of output. They predict production costs on the basis of a daily cost function, which is

$$TC=350-10Q+2Q_2$$

TC refers to total cost of production and Q to the volume of output. Managers hold themselves responsible for producing the volume at which the company makes the most profit or incurs the least loss. Answer each of the next questions based on this information.

a. What volume of output should management choose to produce?

b. How much profit will the company make, or how much loss will the company incur?

c. Suppose that the price of the commodity falls over time to $30. At that price of $30, should management operate at a loss or shut down. Why?

Consider the following information for a product, Madre, and answer each of the next *TWO* questions based on this information. Managers have estimated the price elasticity of demand for Madre to be –2.5. Variable cost per unit and marginal cost of producing Madre are constant at $120 over any relevant volume of output. Total fixed costs attributed to production of Madre are $20,000,000.

8. To maximize profit from the production and sale of Madre, what price should be charged? If the profit-maximizing price for Madre is charged, what is the breakeven volume of production?

9. If the profit-maximizing price for Madre is charged and the volume of output and sales is 500,000 units, what is the degree of operating leverage? Write a narrative interpretation of this calculation. If the volume of output were increased by 30%, *i.e.*, from 500,000 to 650,000, by what percentage would profit increase?

10. Suppose that a firm's average variable cost of production is constant at $10 and the price elasticity of demand for its product –2. What price would the firm charge to maximize its profit?

11. Typically, markups differ product by product in grocery stores. For example, the typical markup on spices is 50 percent, on coffee 10 percent, and on milk 5 percent. Using cost-plus pricing analysis, explain such differences.

12. Answer each of the following questions.

a. Consider a business that has 90% equity capital and 10% debt capital. The cost of equity capital is 20%, and the cost of debt capital is 10%. What is its weighted average cost of capital?

b. Consider a business that makes a net operating profit after taxes of $200,000,000 for 2009 while using debt and equity capital of $800,000,000. The weighted average cost of capital has been calculated to be 15%. Has the business added economic value in 2009? Why?

c. In 2002, Wal-Mart had sales of about $244 billion, net operating profit after taxes of about $10 billion, and employed about $73 billion in debt and equity capital. Wal-Mart's weighted cost of capital was 9.8%. What was Wal-Mart's EVA in 2002? [Round off calculations to nearest whole number.]

d. In 2002, IBM had MVA of about $90 billion, although it had negative EVA of about $8 billion. Interpret each calculation.

13. Suppose a business has an overall return on its invested capital of 12.5%, and its weighted cost of capital is 10.9%. At this time, the business produces and sells two products, Shane and Casablanca. The return on capital is 20.6% for Shane and 9.1% for Casablanca. In addition, management is considering the rollout of a third product, Rosebud, and is confident that the rate of return on capital will be 18.7% for this new product. If management adopts a growth strategy, what should it do with respect to these three products? If management adopts an improvement strategy, what should it do with respect to these three products? If management adopts a reallocation strategy, what should it do with respect to these three products?

14. Describe the concept of economic value added (EVA) carefully. Suppose a company made a profit of $650 million for 2009. The company's rate of return on invested capital for 2009 was 11.9%, and

its weighted average cost of capital was 12.6%. According to the concept of EVA, was value added to the company in 2009? Why?

15. Suppose a small business produces and sells a hat product, Kappa. The business has fixed costs of $7,200. The variable cost of producing Kappa is constant at $18 per unit. The business charges a price of $54 for Kappa. How much contribution margin is made per hat? How many hats would the business need to produce and sell to break even?

16. Suppose a business produces a food product, Eta. The business charges $28 for the product. The overhead of the business is $800,000 per year, and the direct costs of producing Eta are, per unit of output, $5 labor, $15 materials, and $5 other. Management has a profit objective of $130,000 for the year. To accomplish its objective on an annual basis, what is the breakeven volume of Eta?

17. Suppose a business is producing a woolen product, Lambda, at an annual rate of 480,000 units. Its total fixed costs are $6 million per year, and at its current rate of output, its total variable costs for the year will be $96 million. The price of the product is $250. What is the degree of operating leverage for Lambda? Suppose a new order is received, and, if filled, the rate of output will be increased by 10 percent. Calculate the percentage effect that this increase in output will have on the profit made from producing and selling Lambda.

18. A firm recently purchased a fleet of barges for transportation of coal. Annual fixed cost (TFC), tentative price per short haul (P), and the average variable cost (AVC) of each short haul are estimated as follows: TFC=$500,000, P=$13,000, and AVC=$3,000. Determine the number of short hauls that are needed each year for the barge company to break even. Determine the degree of operating leverage for short haul levels of 60, 80, and 100. Interpret the degrees of operating leverage.

PRACTICE QUESTIONS (AND ANSWERS)

1. Consider a business firm that produces two products, Iota and Pi. For the current level of production of each product, the direct labor costs, material costs, and other variable costs per unit of output are $100 for Iota and $200 for Pi. Prices charged for the two products are $150 for Iota and $250 for Pi. Calculate the contribution margin per unit for each product?

Contribution margin is price minus average variable cost. The profit contribution for Iota is $150–$100=$50 and for Pi $250–$200=$50.

2. A high-tech business specializes in the production of a single product that no one firm among the many businesses in the industry ever has succeeded in differentiating. The market for this product is so competitive that no one firm has any control over price of the product. The price of the product as determined in the overall market is $500. This particular business knows its daily cost function, which has been estimated as

TC=6,000–300Q+10Q²

TC refers to total cost of production and Q to the volume of production. If the goal of management is to make maximum profit (or to incur minimum loss) from production and sale of the product, how much of the product will the business produce, and how much total profit (loss) is made (incurred)?

The necessary condition for profit maximization is equality of marginal revenue (MR) and marginal cost (MC). In this case, marginal revenue is constant at $500, which is price. Marginal cost is, using calculus,

MC=−300+20Q

Profit maximization, therefore, is

−300+20Q=500

20Q=800

Q=40

To maximize profit, the amount produced is 40 units per day. Total cost (TC) when producing 40 units of the product per day is

TC(40)=6,000−300(40)+10(40²)=10,000

Total cost is $10,000 per day. Total revenue when selling 40 units of the product per day is

TR(40)=500(40)=20,000

Total revenue is $20,000. Total profit per day is $20,000−$10,000=$10,000.

3. Suppose a business produces a food product and because of successful differentiation has substantial control over price of the product. Management has good estimates of both the daily cost function and demand function for the product. The daily total cost function is

TC=100−10Q+Q_2

TC refers to total cost of production and Q to the volume of production. The demand curve is

P=50−2Q

P is price. If the goal of management is to make maximum profit (or to incur minimum loss) from production and sale of the product, how much of the product will the business produce, what price will the business charge, and how much total profit (loss) will the business make (incur)?

The necessary condition for profit maximization is equality of marginal revenue (MR) and marginal cost (MC). In this case, total revenue (TR) is

TR=PQ=(50−2Q)Q=50Q−2Q₂

Marginal revenue is

MR=50−4Q

Marginal cost is

MC=−10+2Q

The volume of output at which MR=MC is

50−4Q=−10+2Q

−6Q=−60

Q=10

The volume of output at which profit is maximized is 10 units per day. The price at which profit is maximized is

P=50−2(10)=30

The profit-maximizing price is $30. When 10 units of the product are produced per day and sold at $30 each, total revenue is $300. Total cost is

$TC(10)=100-10(10)+(10^2)=100$

Total cost is $100 per day. Total profit per day is $300-$100=$200.

4. Suppose a company operates one plant and produces a single product, which is an undifferentiated commodity. The product price is determined by national market factors, *i.e.*, demand and supply. This national market price is taken by managers as the price the company charges for its product. The current market price is $155 per ton, which has been stable for months and is not expected to change over the foreseeable future. Based on experience over the past five years, managers know how costs behave with respect to volume of production. They predict daily production costs on the basis of a function, which is

$TC=1,000-5Q+2Q_2$

TC refers to total cost of production and Q to the volume of production. Managers hold themselves responsible for producing the volume at which the company makes the most profit or incurs the least loss. What volume should management choose to produce? How much profit will the company make or how much loss will the company incur? Should management operate or shut down?

Since the company is a price taker, marginal revenue is equal to price, which is $155. Using calculus, marginal cost can be stated as MC=-5+4Q. Setting marginal revenue equal to marginal cost to determine the profit-maximizing volume,

155=-5+4Q

Solving for Q,

-4Q=-160

Q=40

At this volume per day, 40, total revenue from sales is

TR=155(40)=$6,200

Total cost at this volume per day, 40, is

TC=1,000-5(40)+2(40²)

TC=1,000-200+3,200

TC=$4,000

At this volume per day, 40, profit per day is

π=6,200-4,000=$2,200

5. Suppose a business produces a product that is highly differentiated. The product manager knows the production costs of the product from people in the engineering group and the demand for the product from people in his own brand group. The daily cost function estimated by the engineering group is

TC=500–10Q+Q$_2$

TC refers to total cost of production and Q to volume of production. The brand group estimates demand for the product from an equation for the demand curve, which is

P=150–9Q

Prefers to price of the product and Q refers to volume of sales. The product manager wants to price the product and sell a volume of product so that profit from production and sales can be maximized. What price should be charged, and how much of the product should be produced? How much profit will be made?

The total revenue function is

TR=150–9Q(Q)

TR=150Q–9Q$_2$

The marginal revenue function is

MR=150–18Q

The marginal cost function is

MC=–10+2Q

Setting marginal revenue equal to marginal cost to determine the profit-maximizing volume and solving for Q,

150–18Q=–10+2Q

–20Q=–160

Q=8

At this volume per day, 8, price will be

P=150–9(8)

P=150–72

P=$78

At this price, $78, and this volume per day, 8, total revenue from sales is

TR=78(8)

TR=$624

Total cost is

TC=500–10(8)+8^2

TC=500–80+64

TC=$484

Profit, therefore, is

$\pi=624-484$

$\pi=\$140$

Total profit is $140 per day.

6. Suppose the operations manager of a chemical plant has the authority and responsibility to determine the best volume of output based on his knowledge of marginal cost and marginal revenue. The price of the product is constrained by intense competition in the industry, and the company therefore is a price taker. At present, the price of the chemical product produced at the plant is $75 per ton, and all output produced at the plant can be sold at this price. At the current operating volume of output, variable cost per ton of the product is $65, fixed cost per ton is $15, and thus total cost per ton is $80. Marginal cost has been estimated at $75 at the current volume and is rising with respect to any relevant volume greater than the current volume. Is the operations manager making the correct decision regarding volume of production, or should he choose to produce more or less volume? Why? Since a loss is incurred at the current volume, should the manager operate at a loss or shut down? Why?

The correct volume is indicated by MR=MC. In this case, the chemical plant is a price taker, and MR=P. Price is $75 per ton, and marginal cost also is $75 per ton. Therefore, the manager is making the correct decision regarding volume, which is the volume at which profit is maximized or loss is minimized. However, the price of $75 per ton is less than total cost per ton, which is $80. Price is greater than variable cost per ton, which is $65. Consequently, the plant is able to cover all of its variable costs and part of its fixed costs. Its operating loss is part of its fixed costs. If the plant were shut down, the loss would be all of its fixed costs. The plant should be operated at a loss rather than shut down.

7. Suppose a company operates one plant and produces a single product, which is an undifferentiated commodity. The product price is determined by national market factors, *i.e.*, demand and supply. This national market price is taken by managers as the price the company charges for its product. The current market price is $50 per ton, which has been stable for months and is not expected to change over the foreseeable future. Based on experience over the past five years, managers know how production costs respond to changes in volume of output. They predict production costs on the basis of a daily cost function, which is

$TC=350-10Q+2Q_2$

TC refers to total cost of production and Q to the volume of output. Managers hold themselves responsible for producing the volume at which the company makes the most profit or incurs the least loss. Answer each of the next questions based on this information.

a. What volume of output should management choose to produce?

Since the company is a price taker, marginal revenue is equal to price, which is $50. Using calculus, marginal cost can be stated as MC=−10+4Q. Setting marginal revenue equal to marginal cost to determine the profit-maximizing volume,

50=−10+4Q

Solving for Q,

−4Q=−60

Q=15

b. How much profit will the company make, or how much loss will the company incur?

At this volume per day, 15, total revenue from sales is

TR=50(15)=$750

Total cost at this volume per day, 15, is

TC=350−10(15)+2(152)

TC=350−150+450

TC=$650

At this volume per day, 15, profit per day is

π=750−650=$100

c. Suppose that the price of the commodity falls over time to $30. At that price of $30, should management operate at a loss or shut down. Why?

Since the company is a price taker, marginal revenue is equal to price, which now has fallen to $30. Marginal cost is unchanged and thus remains as MC=−10+4Q. Setting marginal revenue equal to marginal cost to determine the profit-maximizing volume,

30=−10+4Q

Solving for Q,

−4Q=−40

Q=10

At this volume per day, 10, total revenue from sales is

TR=30(10)=$300

Total cost at this volume per day, 10, is

TC=350−10(10)+2(10²)

TC=350−100+200

TC=$450

At this volume per day, 10, profit per day is

π=300−450=−$150

At the volume of 10, a loss of $150 is incurred. This operating loss is less than fixed cost of $350, which is the loss that would be incurred if the plant were to shut down. In addition, consider that at the volume of 10, total variable cost is $100, and average variable cost is $10. Price, which is $30, is greater than *average variable cost, which is $10. At the volume of 10, therefore, there is a contribution margin of $20 to paying fixed costs. The plant should be operated at a loss.*

Consider the following information for a product, Madre, and answer each of the next *TWO* questions based on this information. Managers have estimated the price elasticity of demand for Madre to be –2.5. Variable cost per unit and marginal cost of producing Madre are constant at $120 over any relevant volume of output. Total fixed costs attributed to production of Madre are $20,000,000.

8. To maximize profit from the production and sale of Madre, what price should be charged? If the profit-maximizing price for Madre is charged, what is the breakeven volume of production?

The profit-maximizing price is

$P^* = [120/1 + (1/-2.5)]$

$P^* = [120/1 + (-0.4)]$

$P^* = 120/0.6$

$P^* = 200

At this price, $200, the breakeven volume is

$Q_{BE} = 20,000,000/(200-120)$

$Q_{BE} = 20,000,000/80$

$Q_{BE} = 250,000$

9. If the profit-maximizing price for Madre is charged and the volume of output and sales is 500,000 units, what is the degree of operating leverage? Write a narrative interpretation of this calculation. If the volume of output were increased by 30%, *i.e.*, from 500,000 to 650,000, by what percentage would profit increase?

The DOL is

$DOL = 500,000(200-120)/[500,000(200-120)-20,000,000]$

$DOL = 500,000(80)/[500,000(80)-20,000,000]$

$DOL = 40,000,000/[40,000,000-20,000,000]$

$DOL = 40,000,000/20,000,000$

$DOL = 2$

For every 1% change in volume and sales, there is a corresponding direct 2% change in profit. Therefore, if volume and sales are increased by 30%, then profit will be increased by 60%.

10. Suppose that a firm's average variable cost of production is constant at $10 and the price elasticity of demand for its product –2. What price would the firm charge to maximize its profit?

The profit-maximizing price is

$P^* = MC/[1 + (1/E_P)]$

If average variable cost (AVC) is constant, marginal cost is equal to AVC. By substitution, therefore,

$P^* = 10/[1 + (1/-2)] = 10/1 - 0.5 = 10/0.5 = 20

11. Typically, markups differ product by product in grocery stores. For example, the typical markup on spices is 50 percent, on coffee 10 percent, and on milk 5 percent. Using cost-plus pricing analysis, explain such differences.

> *Grocery managers know from experience that price sensitivity of items is the primary consideration in setting margins. Staple products such as bread, coffee, ground beef, milk, and soup are highly price sensitive and, because of their price elastic demand, convey relatively low margins. Products with high margins tend to be those for which demand is not as price sensitive.*

12. Answer each of the following questions.

a. Consider a business that has 90% equity capital and 10% debt capital. The cost of equity capital is 20%, and the cost of debt capital is 10%. What is its weighted average cost of capital?

> *$WACC = 0.9(20\%) + 0.1(10\%) = 18\% + 1\% = 19\%$*

b. Consider a business that makes a net operating profit after taxes of $200,000,000 for 2009 while using debt and equity capital of $800,000,000. The weighted average cost of capital has been calculated to be 15%. Has the business added economic value in 2009? Why?

> *The capital charge is $0.15 \times \$800,000,000 = \$120,000,000$. Therefore, the cost of capital employed in making the profit of $200,000,000 is less than the profit itself. Therefore, economic value of $80,000,000 has been added in 2009.*

c. In 2002, Wal-Mart had sales of about $244 billion, net operating profit after taxes of about $10 billion, and employed about $73 billion in debt and equity capital. Wal-Mart's weighted average cost of capital was 9.8%. What was Wal-Mart's EVA in 2002?

> *For 2002, Wal-Mart's EVA was*
>
> *$EVA = \$10 - (\$73 \times 0.098) = \$10 - \$7.2 = \$2.8$ billion.*

d. In 2002, IBM had MVA of about $90 billion, although it had negative EVA of about $8 billion. Interpret each calculation.

> *MVA is calculated over the life of a business, whereas EVA is calculated for a particular year. In 2002, IBM had negative EVA, meaning that its capital charge for 2002 was greater than its NOP_AT by the amount of $8 billion. The market value of IBM as of 2002 was the number of shares of IBM outstanding times the share price. MVA is the market value of IBM minus all equity and debt capital invested in IBM over the life of the business. Thus, the market value of IBM is $90 billion more than its owners have invested in IBM.*

13. Suppose a business has an overall return on its invested capital of 12.5%, and its weighted cost of capital is 10.9%. At this time, the business produces and sells two products, Shane and Casablanca. The return on capital is 20.6% for Shane and 9.1% for Casablanca. In addition, management is considering the rollout of a third product, Rosebud, and is confident that the rate of return on capital will be 18.7% for this new product. If management adopts a growth strategy, what should it do with respect to these three products? If management adopts an improvement strategy, what should it do with respect to these three products? If management adopts a reallocation strategy, what should it do with respect to these three products?

The growth strategy involves introduction of new products or penetration of new markets as long as expected operating profit more than covers the cost of any capital employed. In this case, the growth strategy suggests that Rosebud should be rolled out because the expected return on capital is greater than the cost of capital. The improvement strategy involves improvement of operating profit without using additional capital or maintaining operating profit while using less capital. In this case, the improvement strategy suggests that steps should be taken to improve the operating profit from Casablanca until the return on capital is greater than the cost of capital. The reallocation strategy involves withdrawal of capital from operations that cannot generate operating profit greater than the cost of capital and reallocate it to activities that improve EVA. In this case, the reallocation strategy suggests that capital should be withdrawn from Casablanca and reallocated to Shane (or Rosebud).

14. Describe the concept of economic value added (EVA) carefully. Suppose a company made a profit of $650 million for 2009. The company's rate of return on invested capital for 2009 was 11.9%, and its weighted average cost of capital was 12.6%. According to the concept of EVA, was value added to the company in 2009? Why?

Economic value added is net operating profit minus a capital charge, which is the weighted average cost of capital multiplied times capital employed in making the net operating profit. Economic value is added if the rate of return on invested capital is greater than the weighted average cost of capital. Although the company made a profit, its rate of return on invested capital is less than its weighted average cost of capital and thus added no value in 2009. Indeed, economic value added was negative in 2009.

15. Suppose a small business produces and sells a hat product, Kappa. The business has fixed costs of $7,200. The variable cost of producing Kappa is constant at $18 per unit. The business charges a price of $54 for Kappa. How much contribution margin is made per hat? How many hats would the business need to produce and sell to break even?

The contribution margin is price minus average variable cost. In this case, average variable cost is constant at $18. The breakeven level of output is

$$Q_{BE}=7,200/(54-18)=7,200/36=200$$

The breakeven point is 200 hats.

16. Suppose a business produces a food product, Eta. The business charges $28 for the product. The overhead of the business is $800,000 per year, and the direct costs of producing Eta are, per unit of output, $5 labor, $15 materials, and $5 other. Management has a profit objective of $130,000 for the year. To accomplish its objective on an annual basis, what is the breakeven volume of Eta?

Average variable cost is $5+$15+$5=$25. Contribution margin thus is $28−$25=$3. To achieve its profit objective, therefore, the level of breakeven volume of output required is

$$Q_{T}=(800,000+130,000)/3=930,000/3=310,000$$

The volume of 310,000 units of Eta is required to cover all costs and to achieve the targeted profit.

17. Suppose a business is producing a woolen product, Lambda, at an annual rate of 480,000 units. Its total fixed costs are $6 million per year, and at its current rate of output, its total variable costs for the year will be $96 million. The price of the product is $250. What is the degree of operating leverage for Lambda? Suppose a new order is received, and, if filled, the rate of output will be increased by 10 percent. Calculate the percentage effect that this increase in output will have on the profit made from producing and selling Lambda.

Contribution margin is expected to be 250–(96,000,000/480,000)=250–200, which is $50. The degree of operating leverage for Lambda is

DOL=[480,000(50)]/[480,000(50)–6,000,000]

DOL=24,000,000/(24,000,000–6,000,000)

DOL=24,000,000/18,000,000

DOL=1.33

If filled, a new order resulting in an increased output of 10 percent should increase profit by 10(1.33)=13.3 percent.

18. A firm recently purchased a fleet of barges for transportation of coal. Annual fixed cost (TFC), tentative price per short haul (P), and the average variable cost (AVC) of each short haul are estimated as follows: TFC=$500,000, P=$13,000, and AVC=$3,000. Determine the number of short hauls that are needed each year for the barge company to break even. Determine the degree of operating leverage for short haul levels of 60, 80, and 100. Interpret the degrees of operating leverage.

The breakeven number of short hauls is

Q_{BE}*=500,000/(13,000–3,000)=500,000/10,000=50*

Degrees of operating leverage are

DOL(60)=60(13,000–3,000)/[60(13,000–3,000)–500,000]=6

DOL(80)=80(13,000–3,000)/[80(13,000–3,000)–500,000]=2.67

DOL(100)=100(13,000–3,000)/[100(13,000–3,000)–500,000]=2

As the level of output and sales increases by 1%, the three degrees of operating leverage indicate that profit is expected to increase, respectively, by 6%, 2.67%, and 2%.

6. Six Sigma: Strategies For Improving Productivity, Cost, and Profit

THE QUALITY MOVEMENT

Consideration of productivity, cost, and profit in terms of quantity alone is a little like discussion of *Hamlet* without the Prince. As well as quantity, quality also must be considered. Nowadays, the most widely practiced methods to improve productivity, cost, and profit converge on quality. Indeed, most companies in the *Fortune* 500 practice the basic principles of Six Sigma to improve productivity, cost, and profit. Six Sigma is a name trademarked by Motorola in the 1980s, but Six Sigma is a child of quality parentage. The methods, techniques, and practices of Six Sigma originated in the quality movement and remain deep-rooted in concepts proceeding from the mid-1920s. Although first used in manufacturing, Six Sigma spread in recent decades to sectors such as chemical processing, automobile assembly, service provision, and even to nonprofit organizations.

As one of the first leaders of the quality movement, Dr. W. Edwards Deming said during his lifetime of advocating these concepts and methods, "Quality comes first." He meant that quality methods come first, and then improvements in productivity, cost, and profit follow. Most of the largest companies in America eventually became part of this quality movement. As its leader and spokesman, Deming was one of the most influential people of the Twentieth Century. Deming always acknowledged his friend and mentor, Dr. Walter A. Shewhart, as the true founder of the quality movement. Any profound understanding and deep appreciation of the quality movement begin with an appreciation of Shewhart and Deming, two truly remarkable people.

The quality movement was given many sobriquets by both its champions and its skeptics. A common name given to quality principles was total quality management (TQM). The acronym originated with Armand V. Feigenbaum in the 1950s without any assistance and certainly without any approval from Deming. To the contrary, Deming himself distained the epithet and acronym, and he disdained its use to denominate his philosophy and its corresponding principles and practices. In Japan, the practice of quality methods became known as companywide quality improvement, an appellative with which Deming was comfortable. Even in America, the concepts and methods of the quality movement were known variously as total quality leadership, continuous quality improvement, as well as proprietary names given it by specific companies. In the 1980s and afterwards, Motorola called its methodology Six Sigma, and the name stuck. Now, Six Sigma is a common term in business vocabulary. By whatever name it is known, countless companies, large and small, have achieved remarkable improvements in productivity, cost, and profit through quality commitments.

Quality is not limited to manufacturers and chemical processors. Businesses providing services also adopt the philosophy and practice the same principles and methods. Hotels such as Ritz-Carlton are examples. Quality is not limited to businesses. Cities such as Madison, Wisconsin, and counties such as Erie County, Pennsylvania, have practiced quality methods. Under the leadership of Admiral Frank B. Kelso, Chief of Naval Operations from 1990 to 1994, the U.S. Navy committed to the practice of these same quality methods in its Total Quality Leadership program. More recently, the U.S. Army Materiel Command committed to Lean Six Sigma, which combines elements of lean manufacturing and Six Sigma. Moreover, in 2007, the U.S. Army Armament Research, Development and Engineering Center (ARDEC) won the Malcolm Baldrige National Quality Award in the nonprofit category.

Adopting the nomenclature of martial arts, Six Sigma has spawned celebrated offspring known as Green Belts, Black Belts, and Master Black Belts. Green Belt certification is a nifty addition to anyone's résumé. Villanova University, for example, offers Green Belt certification online, a little pricey but carries three semester hour credits. The program consists of eight modules. Module 1 begins with "The History of Six Sigma" and "Prominent Figures in Six Sigma." The history of Six Sigma launches in the mid-1920s with the onset of the quality movement. Starring roles among prominent figures in Six Sigma belong to the two luminaries of the quality movement, Shewhart and Deming.

SEMINAL SIX SIGMA AT MOTOROLA

In the 1980s, Motorola formulated Six Sigma from elements of the quality movement. The stimulus for Six Sigma was survival. In the 1970s and beyond, Motorola was in an uncomfortable position. Year after year, the company found its performance surpassed by foreign competitors producing better products at lower cost. An experience of the 1970s was telling. A Japanese firm, Matsushita Electric, acquired a Motorola factory that manufactured Quasar branded television sets. The incoming Japanese managers immediately made radical changes in the way the factory operated. Under Matsushita management, the factory soon was producing television sets with only five percent of the defects under Motorola management. Yet, Japanese management used the same workforce, the same technology, and the same designs. The unmistakable conclusion was that the problem had been Motorola management. Matsushita managers reduced defects and elevated quality through means that had escaped the attention of Motorola managers. Japanese managers achieved quality improvement and cost improvement simultaneously.

Under Matsushita management, the previous Motorola focus on product attributes was shifted to focus on processes and systems.

Bob Galvin was named CEO of Motorola in 1958. He was the son of Paul Galvin, the founder of Motorola. In the early 1980s, Galvin realized that Motorola could not go on with business as usual. Bill Smith was a reliability engineer at Motorola, and he is credited with originating what became Six Sigma and selling the idea to Galvin. Smith recognized that Motorola defects were much higher than predicted from product tests. He concluded that a much higher level of internal quality was required, and Six Sigma methods were developed to meet the need. Given the backing of Galvin, Smith acted to institutionalize Six Sigma throughout Motorola. The outcome was a remarkable transformation of Motorola evidenced by higher quality and lower costs. In 1988, Motorola won the Malcolm Baldrige National Quality Award (MBNQ$_A$) in the manufacturing category. Receiving the MBNQ$_A$ requires a winning company to share its concepts and practices publicly. Motorola managers and engineers suddenly found themselves disclosing their methods to external colleagues and presenting results that demonstrated how far the company had advanced since implementing Six Sigma.

Six Sigma is a registered trademark of Motorola. By the 2000s and early 2010s, well over half of *Fortune* 500 companies had adopted Six Sigma initiatives to reduce costs and improve quality. Indeed, a list of Six Sigma companies is like a Who's Who of American business, including 3M, Advanced Micro Devices, Bank of America, Boing, Caterpillar, Corning, Dow, DuPont, General Electric, Heinz, Honeywell, Motorola, Northrop Grumman, PepsiCo, Samsung, Siemens, Textron, Toshiba, Xerox, and more. Six Sigma is disciplined implementation of quality principles and methods aimed at achieving virtually error-free business performance. If Six Sigma capability is achieved, the result is only 3.4 defects per million opportunities. What ultimately became Six Sigma in the 1980s began with quality control in the 1920s. Afterwards, the architecture of quality was grounded on a solid foundation of certain cornerstones that still provide the fundamental paradigm for Six Sigma.

WALTER A. SHEWHART

Development of the telephone spurred AT&T management to achieve high levels of reliable performance. In the early twentieth century, America was pioneering the widespread use of telephones. Handsets consisted of a few hundred parts. Switching equipment consisted of about 100,000 interdependent parts, many of them moving parts that embodied unimaginable complexity at the time. Failures of handsets, switching devices, or buried amplifiers could not be indulged if public expectations of reliable and instant communication at a distance were to be met.

Western Electric was the manufacturing division of AT&T. Western Electric endeavored to elevate the quality of its manufactured products. The pioneering reliability work was carried out by Western Electric's Engineering Department, first at its research laboratories in Lower Manhattan and later at research laboratories in the Hawthorne Works complex located in Chicago. The research investigated inspection and quality control. Inspection simply rejected defective product. Quality control sought to minimize if not eliminate sources of defective product. Inspection focused on the product, whereas quality control focused on processes and systems. In due course, management at Western Electric moved away from inspection and concentrated on quality control. Heading up this sea change to quality control was a physicist working as an engineer, Walter A. Shewhart.

In 1917, Walter A. Shewart earned a doctorate in physics from the University of California at Berkeley. However, Shewhart's career was mostly work as an engineer, first at Western Electric and then at Bell Telephone Laboratories. Shewhart believed that statistical theory could serve the needs of industry, particularly how statistics could be applied to production processes and systems. Before Shewhart, quality assurance was dependent on inspection. Shewhart championed quality assurance based on prevention rather than inspection. His vision concentrated on recognition that production is embedded in a system of related processes. He realized that statistics could discern what processes and systems are doing and then could be used to bring processes and systems under control and keep them under control. Once statistical control is established and maintained, the focus could turn to improvement of processes and systems. Shewhart's monumental book, *Economic Control of Quality of Manufactured Product*, was published in 1931, still regarded as a thorough exposition of the basic principles of quality control.[56]

In 1938, Dr. W. Edwards Deming invited Shewhart to lecture at the Graduate School of the U.S. Department of Agriculture where Deming was in charge of courses in advanced mathematics and statistics. Shewhart delivered four lectures. The lectures emphasized that statistics goes beyond measuring and predicting. The role of statistics extends to bringing about improvements in the things being measured. These lectures were published in 1939 as *Statistical Method from the Viewpoint of Quality Control*.[57] The book was edited by Deming and contained a Foreword written by Deming. The four chapters of the book mirrored Shewhart's four lectures: (1) Statistical Control, (2) How to Establish Limits of Variability, (3) The Presentation of the Results of Measurements, and (4) The Specification of Accuracy and Precision.

Shewhart also published numerous articles in professional journals, and many of his memoranda and reports were held internally at Bell Laboratories. One of these internal writings was a historic memorandum dated 16 May 1924. R.L. Jones had requested a recommendation for some type of report that could give pertinent information at a glance. Shewhart responded with his notable memorandum. Shewhart proposed a control chart to indicate whether or not variation in a process is predictable, under statistical control, and thus stable. In the one-page memorandum, one-third of which was his hand drawn control chart, Shewhart articulated the essential principles of quality control. As he pursued this work still further, Shewhart focused on the nexus between uniformity and quality. Uniformity was an objective, which led to the need to understand sources of variation and to find ways to minimize variation in processes. His emphasis was on prevention rather than correction of problems, errors, and defects. Shewhart developed the theory and methodology of statistical process control (SP_c), an assemblage of methods and practices to monitor, control, and improve processes.

W. EDWARDS DEMING

William Edwards Deming was born in Sioux City, Iowa, on 14 October 1900. His parents obtained forty acres of free land in Wyoming. In 1907, they moved the family to Camp Coulter, later named Powell. In 1917, Deming enrolled at the University of Wyoming and was graduated in 1921 with a degree in electrical engineering. He was graduated from the University of Colorado in 1924 with an M.S. in both mathematics and physics. In 1928, Deming was graduated from Yale with a Ph.D. in mathematical physics.

---

56   Walter A. Shewhart, *Economic Control of Quality of Manufactured Product* (New York: D. Van Nostrand Company, 1931).

57   See Walter A. Shewhart, *Statistical Method from the Viewpoint of Quality Control*, ed. W. Edwards Deming (Washington, D.C.: Graduate School of the U.S. Department of Agriculture, 1939).

Deming's first full-time job was in the Fixed Nitrogen Research Laboratory of the U.S. Department of Agriculture (USDA), where he worked as a mathematical physicist. From 1933, Deming was head of the Department of Mathematics and Statistics of the Graduate School of USDA. Beginning in 1939, Deming worked with the U.S. Census Bureau, where he was head mathematician and adviser in sampling. At the Census Bureau, Deming brought Shewhart's methods to clerical operations for the 1940 census, probably the first application of statistical quality control to a nonmanufacturing context. A pertinent annotation should be adjoined. Deming always referred to Shewhart as the Master. Those who knew Deming clearly understood his meaning. By his reference to Shewhart as the Master, Deming regarded himself as a mere disciple of the Master.

The Hawthorne Experiments

While studying for his doctorate, Deming worked summers at the Western Electric Hawthorne Works complex in Cicero, Illinois. This factory complex opened in 1905 and was operated until closure in 1983. A group of academicians and Western Electric managers made Hawthorne Works the location of one of the most famous industrial studies of the twentieth century. The studies began in 1924. The National Research Council of the National Academy of Sciences conducted illumination tests to determine if lighting was a significant factor in worker productivity. No consistent correlation was found. This outcome was surprising and suggested that other unknown factors were involved in worker productivity.

In 1927, a team from the Harvard Business School was invited to continue the studies. Elton Mayo and Fritz Roethlisberger led the studies. Mayo was a professor of industrial research, and Roethlisberger was his research assistant. Mayo stressed noneconomic factors involved in worker productivity and criticized business methods that took no account of human nature. From 1927 to 1932, Mayo and Roethlisberger undertook studies centered on the effects of working conditions on worker morale and productivity. Results of these studies indicated that output jumped when resources provided workers were improved, when trust and cooperation between workers and supervisors were fostered, when fear in the workplace was eliminated, and when monotony was reduced. The findings of the Hawthorne studies ran counter to so-called scientific industrial management developed by, *inter alia*, Frederick Winslow Taylor. The findings also challenged widely held assumptions about worker behavior. In particular, findings of the Hawthorne experiments indicated that workers were not motivated solely by narrow self-interest such as pay and benefits.

Organizations and individuals who were threatened by findings of the Hawthorne experiments sought ways to discredit the idea that workers were motivated by factors other than pay and benefits. Eventually, the intent to discredit led to invidious attacks on the methodology of the Hawthorne experiments. Years later, the hostile criticism was bestowed a measure of legitimacy when a new term entered the English language. In 1950, Henry Landsberger originated the term Hawthorne Effect. From the 1960s and beyond, Hawthorne Effect was a term meaning stimulation of output or accomplishment of any kind that ensues from the mere fact of being under observation. In other words, those who wrapped their arms around the Hawthorne Effect insisted that worker behavior is different if people know they are part of an experiment and thus are being observed. When people know they are part of an experiment and are being observed, therefore, results or findings of the experiment cannot be trusted because people will give their best efforts to accomplish whatever the experiment expects of them.

Despite decades of heated criticism, detraction, and other attempts to discredit results of the experiments, the Hawthorne findings survived in the quality movement and still stand. Indeed, the Hawthorne findings not only have survived, they have become the heartbeat of management and leadership in the quality movement. From the beginning of the quality movement, the focus has centered on providing workers with materials, tools, equipment, machinery, and training suitable for the job, thus facilitating their pride of workmanship; building trust and cooperation throughout an organization; eliminating fear in the workplace; and more that was motivated by the Hawthorne experiments and findings. Moreover, the Hawthorne experiments led to the onset of disciplines such as industrial sociology, industrial psychology, and to academic courses and programs in organizational behavior commonly offered in business schools. Indeed, organizational behavior is a curriculum standard required for business school accreditation by AACSB.

Deming insisted that he knew nothing about the studies during his work experience at Hawthorne Works. When the methodology of the Hawthorne experiments came under attack, however, Deming fiercely defended conclusions of the study. Indeed, Deming arrived at conclusions remarkably similar to those of the Hawthorne studies.

Stimulus of War

World War II began on 1 September 1939 when Hitler's forces stormed into Poland. America did not enter the war until more than two years later when Congress passed a declaration of war against Japan on 8 December 1941 followed by declarations of war against Germany and Italy on 11 December 1941. To date, these declarations of war are the last passed by the U.S. Congress. Even before entry, enormous demands were placed on U.S. industry to produce war materiel. To mobilize industry to meet the challenge, the U.S. War Department contacted Western Electric to infuse its quality control methods throughout America's rapidly expanding ordnance industry.

In 1942, Deming was retained as a consultant to the Secretary of War, Henry L. Stimson. Deming recommended a course to teach the basics of applied statistics to engineers. His idea was to teach Shewhart methods to engineers in America's key industries. Deming's recommendation was adopted, and the first course was held in the summer of 1942. The lead instructor was Deming, assisted by Eugene L. Grant of Stanford. During the war, more than 35,000 engineers were taught statistics and Shewhart methods. In 1946, Grant's book, *Statistical Quality Control*, was published.[58] It was the first comprehensive text on the subject.

When Japan surrendered aboard the USS Missouri on 2 September 1945, the occasion formally marked the end of military hostilities related to World War II. With General Douglas MacArthur's acceptance of Japan's surrender, the defeated people of Japan had to be enabled to support themselves. This need was daunting because occupation powers had removed more than one thousand top managers from Japanese industry. As a result, middle managers had to rebuild Japanese companies from their devastated condition. However, management training in Japan was nonexistent.

Homer M. Sarasohn was an engineer who had wartime service with MIT Radiation Labs and Raytheon. After the War, Sarasohn was tasked with establishing a radio receiver industry so that occupation powers could broadcast nationally to the Japanese people. At the time, General MacArthur was the Supreme

---

58   Eugene L. Grant, *Statistical Quality Control* (New York, NY: McGraw-Hill, 1946).

Commander of the Allied Powers (SCAP), the occupying government of Japan. General MacArthur supported a Sarasohn recommendation to set up a training program. The management training was based on the work of Shewhart. In this way, Sarasohn and another engineer, Charles W. Protzman, passed on what they had been taught during the war by the Western Electric training program.

In the meantime, Deming had left the Census Bureau in 1946 to establish a consulting practice in statistical studies. Because of his work at USDA and the Census Bureau as well as his expertise in statistics, the Economic and Scientific Section (ESS) of the War Department sent Deming to Japan in 1946. His original assignment was to study agricultural production and related problems. He was sent to Japan again in 1948 to conduct more studies for the occupation forces. During this engagement, Deming met Kenichi Koyanagi, one of the founding members of the Union of Japanese Scientists and Engineers (JUSE). Deming convinced Koyanagi that statistical methods were the key to rebuilding Japanese industry. Koyanagi proposed the idea to JUSE, which invited Deming to teach courses in statistical methods.

At the same time, Sarasohn and Protzman were teaching their management seminar. They wanted Walter Shewhart to teach statistical control. Shewhart was not available, and they turned to Deming. Under the auspices of the Supreme Commander of the Allied Powers, Deming arrived in Japan to lecture in June 1950. Deming taught Elementary Principles of the Statistical Control of Quality to 230 Japanese engineers and technicians. In July 1950, he met with twenty-one of Japan's leading industrialists to talk about quality. In this way, Deming successfully influenced a new group of managers who had risen to the top in Japanese business after the war. They were receptive.

In recognition of Deming's engagements in Japan, JUSE created the Deming Prize in December 1950. The first Deming Prize for Application was awarded in August 1951. A medal is awarded to Prize recipients. The silver medal is engraved with a quotation of Deming: "The right quality and uniformity are the foundations of commerce, prosperity, and peace." Nowadays, awards are made in three categories: the Deming Prize for Individuals; the Deming Distinguished Service Award for Dissemination and Promotion (Overseas); and the Deming Prize, formerly the Deming Application Prize. In recognition of the enormous impact that he had on Japanese industry in the postwar era, Deming received the honor of being one of the first Americans to receive the Second Order Medal of the Sacred Treasure, the highest award Japan confers on a foreigner. Emperor Hirohito bestowed the honor in May 1960.

Why Did Deming Go To Japan?

Among country people, there is a saying about a man who would rather tell a lie when the truth would make a better story. In the same vein, some would rather pass on a myth than to bother with veracity, which takes a little effort. The myth is that Deming went to Japan because his ideas were not accepted in America. In fact, Deming went to Japan because he was sent there by the War Department. His ideas were so acceptable that Sarasohn and Protzman chose him to teach statistical process control in their management seminar. His ideas were so acceptable that New York University appointed him to the faculty of its Graduate School of Business. As a consultant, Deming was unlikely to have chosen devastated, war-torn Japan as a venue for his consultancy. After all, consultants go where the money is. For this reason alone, Deming is unlikely to have thought of Japan. So, why did Deming go to Japan? His expertise, experience, and reputation led the War Department to send him there.

If Japan Can...Why Can't We?

When World War II ended and U.S. industrial capacity was redirected from a war to a peace footing, the environment of the marketplace shifted from national defense to seller paradise. Quantity was now the priority. Throughout the Great Depression of the 1930s, people wanted consumer goods but did not have the wherewithal to buy them. In the mid-1940s, people had money but consumer goods were not available because of World War II. In the late 1940s, people had money, and America's industrial capacity finally could produce vast quantities of consumer goods to satisfy pent-up demand. The discipline of quality dissipated. Producing and selling things, lots of things, became the preoccupation of industry.

During the same period of his work in Japan, Deming pursued a similar mission in the United States. However, managers in the United States took much longer to learn from his teachings. After all, business conditions in postwar America were totally different from those in Japan and, for that matter, Europe. In the United States, business was booming, and industry was unscathed from the war. Total attention could be focused on producing goods to sate the household appetite for things. Indeed, the U.S. economy was in expansion mode from June 1938 to July 1953 with only two brief contractions, one of eight months in 1945 and another of eleven months beginning in November 1948.

In 1946, Deming became a professor of statistics in the Graduate School of Business Administration at New York University. In the same year, he began the robust consulting practice that he maintained until his death in December 1993. From the time he left government service for consulting, Deming's letterhead and business card never changed. The letterhead and card always read, "Consultant in Statistical Studies." Deming developed an active consulting practice from the beginning. Over time, he was increasingly in greater demand as a consultant and lecturer. Yet, W. Edwards Deming was hardly a household name until much later.

Deming's familiarity in popular media and awareness in the general public can be dated to June 1980 when NBC aired a documentary, "If Japan Can...Why Can't We?" Deming's brusque style made good entertainment. The substance of his ideas was understated. In other words, the white paper was at times more concerned with the messenger than with the message. Those in corporate America and others who knew him well were disappointed that the program promulgated misconceptions about the man himself. Nevertheless, the documentary featured Deming and his role in Japan's economic transformation.

The NBC white paper brought Deming to the attention of senior executives who had not yet learned of his contribution to management and quality. Actually, a number of top executives had discovered the "man who invented quality" years earlier; although not yet CEO, Donald Petersen of Ford Motor Company was one such executive. At the time, Petersen headed the Taurus project that led to the "car that saved Ford." Petersen engaged Deming as a consultant, and Deming's work with Ford managers is the stuff of legend. The day after the NBC documentary was aired, Deming said his phone never stopped ringing.

Until his death on 20 December 1993, Deming had an active consulting practice. His schedule was booked years in advance. Each year, he gave as many as thirty four-day seminars to managers in the United States. Deming attracted an enormous following in the United States. Companies that learned from him and practiced his methods were deeply and completely won over by Deming's beliefs. Yet, the transformation in America was evolutionary. U.S. companies were slower at first in accepting Deming's agenda than their Japanese counterparts were. The reasons are understandable. Japan was rebuilding its industry from rock bottom. Deming's arrival at the behest of the U.S. War Department was serendipitous. Like the Phoenix of Egyptian mythology, Japanese managers resurrected Japanese industry from ashes on the wings of Deming's ideas. In the United States, industry merely was a matter of transforming military production to civilian production. There was not the same sense of urgency. By the time of his death in 1993, the philosophy and practice of quality had made their lasting impression on American business. Quality was no passing fad or flavor of the month. In the early 1980s, the practice of quality principles could give a company a competitive advantage. By the late 1990s and beyond, the practice of quality principles had become a competitive necessity.

As taught by Deming, quality and all of its pursuant ramifications developed into a kind of architecture erected on a sound foundation. No one cornerstone of the foundation supports the entire structure. In a holistic sense, all cornerstones taken together provide the bedrock foundation for quality improvement and quality leadership. The cornerstones then provide the foundation for improving productivity, cost, and profit.

PROPER UNDERSTANDING OF QUALITY

The first cornerstone is a proper understanding of quality. The American Society for Quality (ASQ) regards quality as "the totality of features and characteristics of a product that bear on its ability to satisfy a given need." This expression of quality is a bit wordy and perhaps more elegant than absolutely necessary, but it captures the proper understanding of quality. Quality concepts such as this one and other less lofty concepts are as applicable to services as to products. Deming often said in his seminars, "Quality is pride of workmanship in producing a product or service that exceeds the needs, requirements, or expectations of your customer." Essentially, quality is properly understood as products or services that meet or exceed customer needs, requirements, or expectations. Deming attributed his sense of quality to the master, Walter A. Shewhart.

If someone is asked what determines quality in a computer, characteristics such as speed, reliability, ease of use, memory storage, or some other attribute of quality is likely to be cited. Each is a characteristic or dimension of need, requirement, or expectation. A person somehow must weigh these dimensions to select a particular computer. Consider the purchase of an automobile. Perhaps someone thinks a quality car is a hybrid that operates with good gas mileage. Someone else thinks a quality car is a Corvette that accelerates from zero to sixty MPH in 3.4 seconds and a quarter mile in 11.5 seconds. Typical American drivers have changed their sense of needs, requirements, and expectations. With the run-up of gasoline prices, for example, Americans have shifted their preferences away from elephantine SUVs that guzzle gas. The computer company and the automobile company need to understand and anticipate customer needs, wants, and requirements. Depending on the product, the dimensions of quality include performance, timeliness, reliability, durability, aesthetics, interface, reputation, features, consistency, uniformity, accuracy, and more. For all of these various dimensions, the focus is on what the customer needs, wants, requires, or expects.

CENTRALITY OF THE CUSTOMER

External customers are people who purchase a product and thus financially support the business producing and offering it for sale. Obviously, a product that satisfies these people is important. Inside a plant or firm, on the other hand, employees typically pass on their work product to other employees, who are their internal customers. In a similar way, external suppliers are businesses or people outside a company who provide parts, components, materials, or services to a plant or firm. Inside the company, internal suppliers are employees who provide parts, components, materials, or services to other people in the business. Therefore, each worker in a plant, firm, or organization generally has a customer or customers, the people to whom the worker passes on his or her work product. In this sense, each worker is an internal supplier. In addition, each worker is an internal customer of preceding workers.

This particular cornerstone clearly deals with product coming off the line or service being provided in terms of how well the product or service meets the needs, requirements, and expectations of the external customer. However, this focus cannot be the only one. Focus also must be on the needs, requirements, and expectations of internal customers. Therefore, meeting or exceeding needs and requirements must be built into every process and every system in the organization. When quality is built into processes and systems, needs and requirements of internal customers are met.

American Customer Satisfaction Index

The American Customer Satisfaction Index (ACSI) was developed by the National Quality Research Center at the University of Michigan Business School. More than 50,000 people who recently purchased or used a product or service are surveyed by telephone interviews each year. Thus, customer evaluations of quality are based on actual experiences with particular goods and services. These goods and services are purchased in the United States and produced by both domestic and foreign firms. Based on survey results, the ACSI is an indicator of customer satisfaction. Customer satisfaction is measured for ten sectors, more than 230 firms, and more than 100 federal and local government services.

The ACSI uses an econometric model to produce four levels of indexed scores: a national customer satisfaction score, economic sector scores, specific industry scores, and scores for companies within these industries. Each score is based on a scale of 0 to 100 with 100 the highest possible score. The econometric model links customer satisfaction to customer expectations, perceived quality, and perceived value. Table 6.1 shows satisfaction measures for selected companies in five different industries for 2005-2013.

Table 6.1 American Customer Satisfaction Index 2005-2013 Selected Industries and Companies									
Industry and Company	**2005**	**2006**	**2007**	**2008**	**2009**	**2010**	**2011**	**2012**	**2013**
Food Manufacturing	82	83	81	83	83	81	81	83	81
H.J. Heinz	91	87	90	89	89	88	89	89	87
Kellogg	81	85	83	85	85	81	80	83	85
General Mills	82	84	83	84	83	83	83	83	87
Tyson Foods	79	78	78	80	82	77	79	81	80
Automobiles	80	81	82	82	84	82	83	84	83
Cadillac	86	84	86	85	89	86	87	86	85
Mercedes-Benz	80	82	83	82	86	86	86	85	88
Ford	75	77	80	80	83	82	84	83	83
Nissan	78	82	80	82	78	82	84	83	83
Airlines	66	65	63	62	64	66	65	67	69
Southwest	74	74	76	79	81	79	81	77	81
Delta	65	64	59	60	64	62	56	65	68
American	64	62	60	62	60	63	63	64	65
United	61	63	56	56	56	60	61	62	62
Limited Service Rest.	76	77	77	78	78	75	79	80	80
Domino's	71	75	75	75	77	77	77	77	81
Wendy's	75	76	78	73	76	77	77	78	79
McDonald's	62	63	64	69	70	67	72	73	73
KFC	69	70	71	70	69	75	75	75	81
Subscription TV Service	61	63	62	64	63	66	66	66	68
Direct TV	67	71	67	68	71	68	69	68	72
DISH Network	68	68	67	65	64	71	67	69	70
Cox	63	63	63	63	66	67	67	63	65
Charter	56	55	55	54	51	60	59	59	64

Satisfaction Not Guaranteed

In their eagerness to drive down costs, some companies lose track of the balance between costs and customer service. Smart companies such as Southwest Airlines and Costco have succeeded. Their well-trained employees bring about fewer complaints, which means "lower costs, a workforce free to make more sales, and happier customers willing to spend more money and tell their friends about it later."[59] Less smart companies experience a meltdown in customer satisfaction. In particular, Home Depot, Dell, and Northwest Airlines, acquired by Delta Air Lines in 2008, were clobbered when their zeal to cut costs

59   Brian Hindo, "Satisfaction Not Guaranteed," *Business Week* (June 19, 2006), pp. 32-36.

trimmed away customer satisfaction. In 2006, Home Depot was last among big retailers in terms of customer satisfaction, and Northwest Airlines was last among airlines. Other losers in customer dissatisfaction at that time were McDonald's, last in fast food, and Nextel, last in wireless phone service.[60] The latter, Nextel, was later acquired by Sprint.

Although making significant improvement in consumer satisfaction since 2006, Home Depot remains mired in the netherworld among specialty retailers. McDonald's also has improved its customer satisfaction, but the company still ranks below other fast food restaurants. Papa John's is ranked highest. Sprint Nextel now is above the industry average and ahead of Verizon. AT&T Mobility remains last in wireless telephone service. Dell still ranks far below Apple in personal computers.

FOCUS ON PROCESSES AND SYSTEMS

A process is a sequence of related tasks involved in accomplishing a particular outcome. In other words, a process is how work is done expressed as the sequential tasks involved in carrying out a particular kind of work. Thus, a process can be depicted by a sequence of all tasks directed at accomplishing the mission of a particular kind of work. A system consists of a sequence of related processes. Producing a product, for example, is ordinarily a system that involves a number of related and sequential processes.

Top management commitment to quality is directed at improving processes and systems. Joseph Juran, another early leader in the quality movement, emphasized what he called the 85/15 Rule, which recognizes that the potential for eliminating mistakes, errors, and defects lies mostly in improving processes, not in merely changing workers. At least eighty-five percent of problems can be corrected by improving processes and at most fifteen percent by changing workers with no changes in materials, methods, and machinery that people use in the process. When managers recognize that processes and systems create the majority of problems, they stop blaming individual workers.

Flowcharting

To understand particular processes and systems, a tool called flowcharting often is used. Flowcharting depicts the step-by-step process or system actually in use. More often than not, no one person understands an entire system. A worker might know his or her own process, but a flowchart unveils all processes in a system. Although the immediate purpose of flowcharting is to understand how a process or system is actually conducted, the ultimate intent of flowcharting is fundamental changes to eliminate and prevent waste in the form of delay, redundancy, scrap, or rework. Often, flowcharting unmasks such waste.

Flowcharting can be done simply with use of graphic symbols such as rectangles and diamonds. In flowcharting the step-by-step sequence of tasks that make up a process, a rectangle is used to depict an activity, which is an action or operation. A diamond is used to denote a decision leading to different pursuant activities. Each path emerging from the diamond results in a different activity. For example, consider the Naval Oceanographic Office (NAVO), which has a hydrography group that develops maps of the ocean floor known as smooth sheets used by submarine and surface fleets. NAVO research ships collect data and send the data back to the office at the Stennis Space Center in Mississippi. There, a man receives the data in a box. The hydrographic system begins in office with this process. The first action taken is to open the box. The second action is to look for the manifest, a kind of list of what is supposed

---

60   *Ibid.*, p. 33.

to be in the box. The third action is to check to see if what is supposed to be in the box is actually in the box. The next step depends on whether what is supposed to be in the box is in the box. A diamond with a yes path and a no path is used. If what is supposed to be in the box is in the box, the answer is yes, and a particular action follows. If something that is supposed to be in the box is not in the box, the answer is no, and a different action follows. This simple flowchart is shown in Figure 6.1.

FIGURE 6.1
NAVO HYDROGRAPHIC SYSTEM

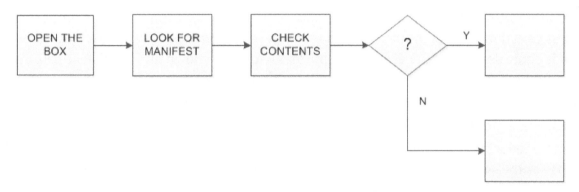

Fishbone Diagrams

Applied to processes and systems, the scientific method is a systematic way for teams to learn about processes and systems and to base changes on data rather than hunches, look for root causes of problems rather than react to symptoms, and seek lasting solutions rather than quick fixes. Fishbone diagrams are used routinely as the tool for root cause analysis. Fishbone diagrams channel analysis to the fundamental elements of a process, which are materials, machinery, methods, and people. To discern root causes, the usual practice is to keep asking the question "Is this problem a symptom of still another problem?" Ultimately, the answer is, "No." Only then is the analysis focused on the likely root cause of a problem.

Many times, the root causes of a problem are buried deep inside processes used to create a product or service. When the true source of a problem is unmasked, complexity can be revealed. Complexity is a general term for unnecessary work. In other words, complexity is anything that makes a process more complicated without adding any value. Seen in this way, complexity is steps or tasks in a process that add no value to a product or service. Complexity can take many forms, including defects, breakdowns, delays, redundancies, inaccuracies, inefficiencies, inaccuracies, and discrepancies. In a quality environment, project teams examine processes to identify non-value added activities and then work to track down the root causes of the problem.

When defects occur in products or when someone makes a mistake, work must be repeated and extra steps added to correct the error or dispose of the damage. Rework and scrap make the process more complex, resulting in waste. Many companies call this practice scraping burnt toast, a reference to steps taken to fix the final product rather than to prevent the problem. Joseph Sensenbrenner, former mayor of Madison, Wisconsin, once said that the government way to make toast is you burn, and I'll scrape.

Extra steps may seem normal so that everyone thinks inspection, rework, and scrap are the natural way to do things. Yet, the make, inspect, fix, and scrap sequence is a foolish succession that defies business sense. Rather than correcting problems downstream, the sensible priority should be bringing upstream processes under control so that downstream problems never occur.

STATISTICAL PROCESS CONTROL

Ordinarily, every product is the outcome of sequential processes. Each process can be understood as how a particular kind of work is done, the step-by-step sequence of tasks involved in completing the work. Together, interlinking sequential processes make up a system of production. If a process is operated consistently, then its performance can be predicted. Of course, no process is absolutely predictable, but the performance of any reasonably reliable process can be predicted within limits provided that nothing interferes arbitrarily with the process. The first issue, therefore, is the extent of these limits, which is the process variation. Greater process variation is equivalent to greater uncertainty, and lesser process variation is equivalent to greater certainty. A process with well-known and consistent performance is central to quality. Variation is the enemy of quality. Although all of the variation in a process cannot be eliminated, methods have been developed to measure, analyze, and reduce variation. In this ordered application of methods, the process can be made increasingly predictable and capable.

One means of reducing variation is standardization, which is simply ensuring that everyone involved in a process uses the same materials, machinery, equipment, tools, and methods. Standardization alone has significant potential to make the outcome of a process more uniform. Another means is to study a process, particularly to look for possible sources of variation, and then gather data. The ultimate purpose of study based on data is to make fundamental changes in the process that are expected to reduce variation and improve uniformity. Ultimately, therefore, the method is meant to uncover sources of variation that can be eliminated and to operate a process that is predictable within a narrow range. To reach this state of predictability, the difference between common causes and special causes of variation must be understood, and statistical process control must be comprehended.

Common and Special Causes of Variation

Variation is caused. Variation in outcomes of a process is likely to be caused by variation within the process. This intrinsic process variation is due to variation in people, variation in materials, variation in methods, variation in equipment, variation in working environment, and so forth. Consequently, stating precisely what might be the cause of any particular instance of variability might be difficult. To improve a process, however, the causes of variation must be understood.

In any process, many causes of small, chance variation combine to result in a predictable degree of variation. On occasion, however, there may be a significant, extraordinary cause of large, nonrandom variation that could not have been predicted. These extraordinary, unpredictable causes are not due to everyday, ordinary, inherent operation of the process, but they nonetheless cause significant shifts in process variation when they occur. For example, commuting over a twenty-four mile bridge involves countless chance causes of variation in commuting time, but the degree of variation is reasonably constant so that commuting time is predictably within a few minutes provided nothing extraordinary happens. A twenty-car pileup on the bridge would be extraordinary. Whereas variation of two or three minutes from average commuting time is ordinary from day to day, a two or three hour variation results from an extraordinary, unpredictable event such as a twenty-car accident.

Causes of variation fall into two basic categories: those common to the process or system and those unusual to the process or system. Causes of variation can be separated into two categories, common and special. In the 1920s, Walter Shewhart developed the idea of a control chart to determine when a process was stable, exhibiting only chance causes of variation, or when the process exhibited variation due to an assignable cause. Nowadays, special cause is used to refer to assignable causes and common cause to refer to chance causes. Knowing the difference between the two categories is critical because each requires a different reaction.

Common causes of variation are inherent in the process. Common cause variation is due to factors that are part of the process at all times, *viz.*, materials, machinery, methods, and people. Stated differently, common cause variation is due to a large number of sources of small variation characterized by a random pattern. For such reasons, common causes of variation mean no one cause can be determined. The sum of these small chance causes may result in a large degree of variation or a large number of defects, errors, or mistakes. Moreover, the sum of the common causes determines the limits of a process. Examples of common or causes include ordinary wear and tear of machines; variability in materials; computer response time; lapses from maintenance procedures; improper settings; critical differences in temperature, humidity, lighting, or cleanliness; and more.

Special causes of variation, on the other hand, are not part of the process all the time. Variation is due to special circumstances. Special causes of variation are due to factors or events that are outside the ordinary functioning of the process. They arise from unusual circumstances. For this reason, special causes often are called assignable causes, which mean these special causes can be identified. Special cause variation exhibits a nonrandom pattern because it is the result of special circumstances, a sudden malfunction, interruption, or glitch that is imposed on a process by something that happens outside the ordinary functioning of the process or system. Examples of special or assignable causes include such sudden, unexpected, unpredictable calamities as machine malfunctions, computer crashes, bad raw materials, power surges, and lightning strikes.

Standard Deviation

The lower-case letter sigma (σ) in the Greek alphabet is a symbol used universally in statistical notation to represent standard deviation. According to statistical lore, a Belgian astronomer named Quetelet is credited with popularizing standard deviation in the nineteenth century. He collected data on the height of soldiers and found that, when graphed, the measurements formed a symmetrical bell-shaped curve around average height. This bell curve eventually was widely observed in all kinds of natural phenomena.

Standard deviation indicates how tightly a set of values is clustered around the mean of the values. It is a measure of dispersal or variation in a group of numbers. When numbers are tightly bunched together around the mean, a graph would be a steep bell-shaped curve if the distribution were normal. When the numbers are spread widely apart, a graph would be a relatively flat bell-shaped curve if the distribution were normal. Standard deviation is a measure of dispersion or variation in a distribution of values. Consider the two panels of Figure 6.2, which show steep and flat normal distributions for a critical to quality attribute along with their means and ±3 standard deviations. Figure 6.2(a) shows a flat distribution with ±3 standard deviations far from the mean. Figure 6.2(b) shows a steep distribution with ±3 standard deviations close to the mean. Clearly, the flat distribution exhibits a lot of variation with wide dispersal from the mean, whereas the steep distribution shows little variation with values tightly bunched around the mean.

FIGURE 6.2
FLAT AND STEEP NORMAL DISTRIBUTIONS

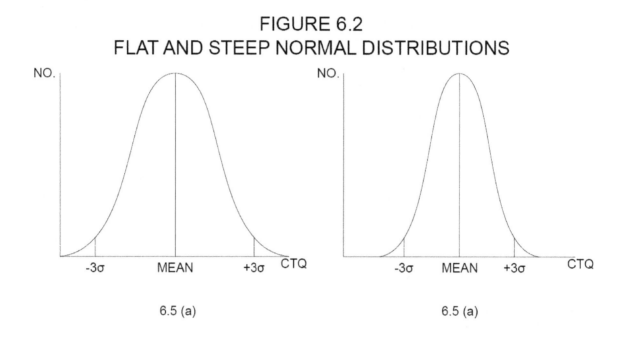

6.5 (a)   6.5 (a)

A step-by-step way to calculate standard deviation is simple. First, add the numbers in a population to calculate the mean. For each value, subtract each value from the average of all numbers and square the difference. Add up all squared values. Divide the sum of squared values by the number of values. Finally, find the square root of the number computed in the previous step. The result is the standard deviation from the mean of the data, actually one standard deviation from the mean.

For example, consider Table 6.2, which shows calculation of the standard deviation for closing prices of a common stock. The standard deviation from the mean is 6.7230. Actually, one standard deviation from the mean is 6.7230. Two standard deviations from the mean would be two times 6.7230, which is 13.4460. Three standard deviations from the mean would be three times 6.7230, which is 20.1690. When computed, ±1 s.d. includes 68.27% of all values in a population. Therefore, 68.27% of closing prices would fall between $104.73 and $118.17. When computed, ±2 s.d. includes 95.45% of all values in a population. In this case, 95.45% of closing prices would fall between $98.00 and $124.90. When computed, ±3 s.d. includes 99.73% of all values in a population. In this case, 99.73% of closing prices would fall between $91.28 and $131.62.

To illustrate this same point in still another way, consider that the average height of an adult American male is seventy inches. The standard deviation is approximately three inches. Therefore, 68.27% of adult American males fall within sixty-seven and seventy-three inches; 95.45% within sixty-four and seventy-six inches; and 99.73% within sixty-one and seventy-nine inches.

Table 6.2 Twenty-Day Standard Deviation for Closing Prices of a Common Stock				
Day	Close	20-Day Mean	Deviation	Deviation Squared
1	109	111.45	-2.45	6.0025
2	103	111.45	-8.45	71.4025
3	102	111.45	-9.45	89.3025
4	108	111.45	-3.45	11.9025
5	107	111.45	-4.45	19.8025
6	105	111.45	-6.45	41.6025
7	107	111.45	-4.45	19.8025
8	108	111.45	-3.45	11.9025
9	107	111.45	-4.45	19.8025
10	109	111.45	-2.45	6.0025
11	110	111.45	-1.45	2.1025
12	112	111.45	0.55	0.325
13	113	111.45	1.55	2.4025
14	114	111.45	2.55	6.5025
15	115	111.45	3.55	12.6025
16	121	111.45	9.55	91.2025
17	126	111.45	14.55	211.7055
18	122	111.45	10.55	111.3025
19	119	111.45	7.55	57.0025
20	122	111.45	10.55	111.3025
Sum	2,239			903.9755
Sum÷20	111.45			
Deviation^2÷20				45.1987
Standard Deviation				$\sqrt{45.1987} = 6.7230$

On a formula bar, STDEV might be displayed. STDEV is used when the group of numbers is only a partial sample of the whole population. The calculation for a sample drawn from a population is identical to the procedure shown above except the sum of squared values is divided by number of values in the sample minus one. On the other hand, STDEVP or STDEVPOP is used when the group of numbers is complete. The example shown in Table 6.2 is the entire population of closing stock prices, and thus the sum of squared values is divided by number of values in the population.

Statistical Control: Process Stability

Statistical control involves tracking down and eliminating special causes so that the only remaining variation in a process is due to common causes. Statistical control deals with process stability. A stable process is one in statistical control, meaning that the only variation is random and within the control limits of the process itself. These control limits are determined statistically from data and are depicted as two lines, the upper control limit (UCL) and the lower control limit (LCL) on a control chart. Recall that Walter Shewhart first depicted a control chart as a primary means of statistical process control.

Refer to the panels of Figure 6.3. Figure 6.3(a) shows a run chart that records periodic data taken on the diameter of a metal rod used in an electrical motor housing. In this case, diameter is critical to quality (CTQ). These data can be shown as a normal distribution, depicted in Figure 6.3(b). The mean is indicated along with ±3 standard deviations from the mean. In Figure 6.3(c), the normal distribution is rotated to the left. Again, the mean is indicated along with lines that depict +3 standard deviations from the mean and –3 standard deviations from the mean. The upper control limit (UCL) is +3 standard deviations. The lower control limit (LCL) is –3 standard deviations. Figure 6.3(c) is the control chart depicted by Shewhart.

FIGURE 6.3
CONTROL CHART FOR METAL RODS

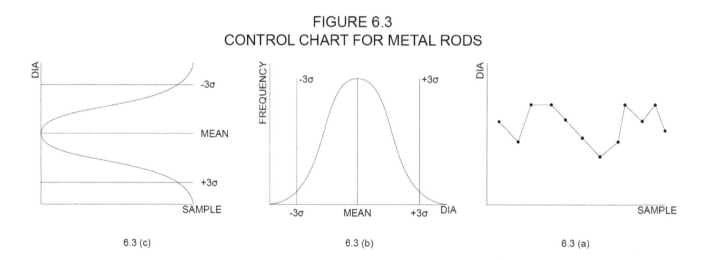

6.3 (c)   6.3 (b)   6.3 (a)

The two lines on a control chart, UCL and LCL, indicate limits to common cause variation inherent in the process. These control limits are calculated from data. They are not limits to what should be the performance of a process. Control limits are not specification limits, not tolerances. Control limits indicate the range of common cause variation actually expected in the process as operated currently. Any outcome outside the control limits would be unusual, the result of special circumstances. A control chart is depicted in Figure 6.4. Variation within the control limits is the result of common causes. Variation outside the control limits is due to a special cause.

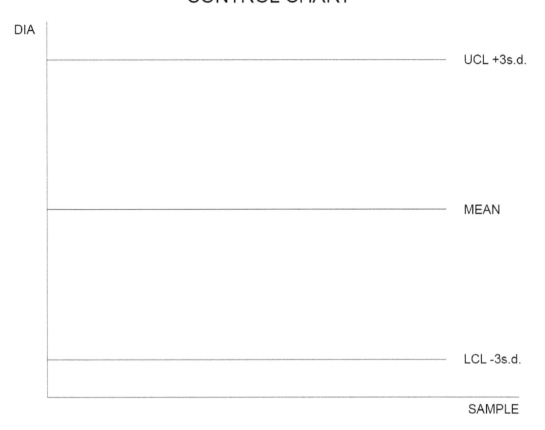

FIGURE 6.4
CONTROL CHART

Upper and Lower Control Limits: ±3 s.d.

Control charts are based on control limits that are ±3 s.d. The upper control limit (UCL) is +3 s.d., and the lower control limit (LCL) is –3 s.d. These control limits, ±3 s.d. include 99.73 percent of observed data. If an outcome falls outside these control limits, it would be an unusual occurrence, indeed. After all, only 0.27 percent of outcomes would fall outside ±3 s.d. These control limits thus provide a basis for immediate action when an unusual occurrence of variation occurs. Whenever an observation falls outside the ±3 standard deviations control limits, something highly unusual is indicated; this is a signal to search for a special cause. Workers and managers react to these signals by tracking down and eliminating the special cause. Once done, the process is brought into or back into statistical control, and the result is a stable process operating predictably within the control limits of ± 3 s.d.

Companies might use other indicators of special causes. Control charts can be separated into zones. Zone A is between two and three standard deviations above or below the mean. Zone B is between one and two standard deviations above or below the mean. Zone C is between the mean and one standard deviation above or below the mean. Based on zones, rules are followed to detect special causes of variation. Special causes are detected when (1) any outcome is beyond either control limit; (2) two of three consecutive outcomes are in Zone A, and all three outcomes are on the same side of the mean; (3) four of any five consecutive outcomes are in Zone B or Zone A, and all five are on the same side of the mean;

and (4) fifteen consecutive outcomes on either side of the mean are in Zone C. The zones are illustrated in Figure 6.5.

FIGURE 6.5
CONTROL CHART ZONES

Noise v. Signal

In devising a control chart, Walter Shewhart stipulated control limits of ±3 s.d. By using ±3 s.d. as control limits, Shewhart made a fundamental distinction. Some processes are predictable, whereas others are not. When a process is predictable, it displays variation due only to common causes or, to use Shewhart's own term, chance variation. The ability to distinguish between a predictable process and an unpredictable one depends upon the ability to distinguish between common cause variation and special cause variation. A predictable process can be perceived as the outcome of a large number of chance causes in which no one cause produces a predominating effect. When a cause does produce a predominating effect, it becomes an assignable cause.

The collective effects of many common causes can be likened to background noise. In physics, noise is a random and persistent disturbance that obscures or reduces the clarity of a signal. White noise is combined sounds of all frequencies taken together, which can be regarded as all tones humans can hear combined together. White noise comes from the idea that white light is all colors or frequencies of light combined. Picking out any one frequency among all frequencies would be difficult. It is so with common cause variation. Picking out any one cause among all common causes would be daunting. On the other hand, artillery fire could be heard against white noise. Artillery fire would be a signal that something unusual has happened. It is so with special cause variation. Separating the two types of variations is similar to separating a signal from noise in the process.

Specification Limits

So far, only process stability has been considered. Capability is the extent to which a stable process can meet needs and requirements of the customer, whether internal or external. Often, control limits are regarded as the voice of the process. Specification limits, on the other hand, are regarded as the voice of the customer. Control limits are calculated from data. Specification limits are prescribed by the customer based on their needs and requirements,. Specification limits are not calculated from data. Indeed, specification limits are not calculated at all but are stipulated by the customer, whether internal or external. Control limits appear on a control chart. Specification limits do not appear on a control chart. Specification limits might be shown on a histogram or some other graphic display that depicts the distribution of outcomes around a specification target. A control chart shows the arithmetic mean and distribution of outcomes around the mean. A graphical depiction of capability shows the target specified by the customer and distribution of outcomes around the specification target. Control charts and corresponding control limits show what the process is doing. Histograms or other graphic displays and corresponding specification limits show the extent to which the process is meeting needs and requirements. Figure 6.6 shows a histogram with the specification target centered on the mean along with specification limits specified by the customer. Specification limits are labeled as upper specification limit (USL) and lower specification limit (LSL). Items within the specification limits meet customer needs and requirements. Items outside the specification limits do not meet customer needs and requirements and must be reworked or scrapped.

FIGURE 6.6
SPECIFICATION TARGET, MEAN, AND SPECIFICATION LIMITS

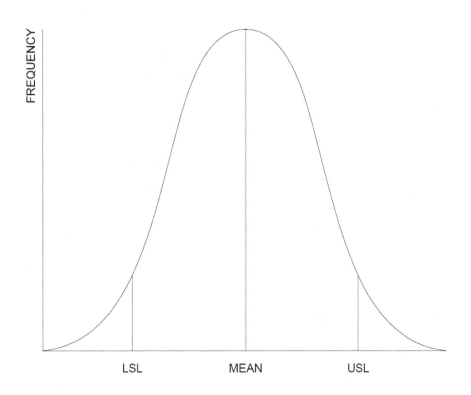

First Time Yield and Rolled Throughput Yield

In the simplest sense, a product characteristic either meets specifications or not. This all-or-nothing perspective is misleading. Reality shows that problems and corresponding costs increase as actual performance strays further from targeted performance. In this sense, the specification target is as important as the specification limits. Indeed, a Taguchi loss function, named for Dr. Genichi Taguchi, is used to show additional costs incurred as actual performance is further and further from the specification target but still within specification limits.

Capability once was considered in terms of simple yield, understood as proportion of defect-free items. For example, if a process resulted in 900 defect-free items and 100 scrapped items, the yield would be 900/1,000=0.9. The yield would be ninety percent. This traditional approach was discarded in favor of first time yield, which is the likelihood of items passing through a process without the need for scrap or rework. Of 1,000 items, suppose that 200 items had to be reworked and 100 items scrapped. The first time yield of defect-free product would be 700/1,000=0.7. The first-time yield would be only 70%. First-time yield measures the extent to which a process gets something right the first time.

Another concept is rolled throughput yield, which recognizes that processes are linked together in a sequence to form a system. Rolled throughput yield expresses the likelihood of an item passing through all processes in a system successfully the first time and thus requiring no rework or scrap. Perhaps five related processes make up a system. Suppose the first process has a first time yield of 0.91, the second 0.92, the third 0.93, the fourth 0.94, and the fifth 0.95. Rolled throughput yield would be 0.91×0.92×0.93×0.94×0.95=0.6953 or 69.53%. Only 69.53% of items pass through the five processes without being scrapped or reworked.

Defects per Million Opportunities

To ensure customer satisfaction, companies strive for defect-free performances. A defect is any instance, event, or opportunity in which the product fails to meet customer requirements. A defect-free performance, therefore, is a case in which a process succeeds in meeting customer requirements. A method of measuring performance must be established. Companies commonly use a metric known generally as total defects per unit (TDU). Total defects per unit usually are measured in terms of total defects per million, which is the standard metric for establishing how often defects are likely to occur. Performance is expressed in defects per million opportunities (DPMO). In other words, DPMO simply indicates how many defects can be expected if an activity were to be repeated a million times. By reducing DPMO, a company is able to produce more reliable products.

When manufacturing a product, there will always be some variation from specifications. For example, if metal rods specified to be one inch in diameter are being made, some naturally will be a little more than one inch and some slightly less than one inch. If diameter of all or a sample of these metal rods were measured and graphed, the distribution of these measurements would fall on a bell-shaped curve. On a histogram, the center of the curve represents the mean of the distribution, which may or may not be one inch. Keep in mind that as diameter measurements move farther from the mean, they also are more likely to be defective units, either too large or too small to meet requirements.

A final comment should be added; Six Sigma decouples the notions of defects and defectives. A defect is any characteristic of a product or service that does not conform to its specification, whereas a defective is any product or service that fails to meet the requirements of the customer. Presumably, defective product contains one or more defects. In the Six Sigma framework, defective products are still any observation outside the customer's specification limits, although such observations are extremely rare.

Sigma (Z) Score

The central tendency of a distribution is defined as its mean. In terms of stability, the centerline of a control chart is the mean. Control limits are ±3 s.d. In the case of capability, the focus on any graphical display such as a histogram is the target specified by the customer. For the sake of simplicity, suppose the target and mean coincide and thus are the same. The question of capability is how many standard deviations can be fit between the target or mean and the nearest specification limit. Z scores deal with this question. In statistics, a Z score indicates how many standard deviations an observation is above or below the mean. In Six Sigma, the Z score is used as the measure of capability. The Z score is calculated by obtaining the difference between the mean and the nearest specification limit, and then the difference is divided by the standard deviation. In Six Sigma, the Z score calculated in this way is called the sigma score. This sigma score is used to measure capability.

Suppose specification limits are symmetrical, meaning the USL and the LSL are equidistant from the specification target. Also suppose that the mean is centered on the specification target. The Z score or Sigma score can be calculated by the formula

$Z = [x - LSL] \div \sigma$

LSL is the lower specification limit, x is the mean, and σ is standard deviation from the mean. Since USL and LSL are symmetrical and equidistant from the specification target, the Z score or Sigma score also can be calculated by the formula

$Z = [USL - x] \div \sigma$

USL is upper specification limit, x is the mean, and σ is standard deviation from the mean.

For example, if the upper specification limit is 100, the mean is 80, and one standard deviation from the mean is 5, then the Z score is

$Z = [100 - 80] \div 5 = 4$

The interpretation is that four standard deviations can be fit between the mean and the upper specification limit. Another way of thinking about the Z score is that items within four standard deviations from the mean meet customer requirements. In other words, items as far as four standard deviations from the mean still meet customer requirements.

In Six Sigma, this Z score is the sigma score or just sigma, and it is used as a measure of capability. In the case calculated above, the process would be described as having four sigma capability. If variation in the process were reduced, then capability would be improved. Suppose that continual improvement methods are used successfully to reduce variation, and the standard deviation is reduced from 5 to 4. Consequently, with no change in the specification target, the Z score would be

$Z = [100 - 80] \div 4 = 5$

The interpretation is that five standard deviations can be fit between the mean and the upper specification limit. The process could be described as having five sigma capability, which can be interpreted as items within five standard deviations from the mean meet customer requirements. Another way of seeing the improved capability is that items as far as five standard deviations from the mean still meet customer requirements. If the standard deviation were lowered still further from 4 to 3.33, then the Z score would be

$$Z=[100-80]\div 3.33=6$$

The interpretation is that six standard deviations can be fit between the mean and the upper specification limit. The process could be described as having six sigma capability. All items that fall within six standard deviations from the mean meet customer requirements. Items as far as six standard deviations from the mean still meet customer requirements.

Technically, Z scores or Sigma scores are appropriate only if the distribution is normal, meaning that dispersion around the specification target is bell shaped. When the dispersion is skewed and thus not normal, the Z score or Sigma score breaks down.

Sigma Shift, Short-Term Sigma, and Long-Term Sigma

Six Sigma retained ±3 s.d. as control limits, +3 s.d. as the upper control limit (UCL) and −3 s.d. as the lower control limit (LCL) to determine stability, but Six Sigma relied on an upper specification limit (USL) and a lower specification limit (LSL) to measure capability. These specification limits express the extent to which departures from the specification target can still meet customer needs and requirements. From the beginning, however, Motorola engineers argued that a process can drift or shift ±1.5 s.d. in regular operation over time. In other words, shift happens (ugh!). This ±1.5 s.d. shift is a kind of entropy, an evolution from order to disorder in a closed system. In turn, this ±1.5 s.d. shift gave rise to the concepts of short-term sigma and long-term sigma. Short-term sigma refers to the capability designed into a process and typically achieved immediately after process launch. Long-term sigma refers to the expected capability of the process over time in which the ±1.5 s.d. shift materializes. The ±1.5 s.d. shift was based on empirical observation and experience rather than theoretical proof.

Reconsider the Z score. Now, it should be seen and interpreted as the short-term Z score, which can be restated as

$$Z_{ST}=[x-LSL]\div \sigma_{ST}$$

If specification limits are symmetrical, the short-term Z score also can be restated as

$$Z_{ST}=[USL-x]\div \sigma_{ST}$$

Z_{ST} is short-term Z score, x is the mean, LSL is the lower specification limit, USL is the upper specification limit, and σST is short-term standard deviation from the mean. Because of the sigma shift of 1.5 standard deviations, the long-term Z score is

$$Z_{LT}=Z_{ST}-1.5$$

Z_{LT} is the long-term Z score, and Z_{ST} is the short-term Z score.

Consider short-term capability of five sigma. Processes tend to increase in variability over time due to everyday deterioration of the conditions under which the processes are operated. As a result, process characteristics wander or drift from their original values by as much as 1.5 s.d. in one direction or the other. As the process wanders, this shift results in more defects. With the 1.5 s.d. shift, a process characteristic that had achieved short-term capability of five sigma slips back to long-term capability of 3.5 sigma. Suppose the mean and target coincide, and five standard deviations can be fit between the mean and the upper specification limit or lower specification limit. Now, suppose the mean shifts to the right so that only 3.5 standard deviations can be fit between the mean and the upper control limit. Without the shift, product falling within five standard deviations meets needs and requirements. With the shift, product falling within only 3.5 standard deviations meets needs and requirements.

To illustrate the sigma shift, think about the three panels of Figure 6.7. Panel 6.7(a) depicts coincidence of the specification target and the mean along with symmetrical specification limits. Suppose the upper specification limit (USL) is 100, the mean is 80, and the standard deviation is 4. Therefore, short-term capability is

$$Z_{ST}=[100-80]\div4=5$$

Capability is five sigma. Now, suppose the mean drifts or shifts to the right and settles at 86. This case is shown in Panel 6.7(b). The nearest specification limit is the USL. After the shift that occurs in the long term, capability is

$$Z_{LT}=[100-86]\div4=3.5$$

Now, capability is only 3.5 sigma. Before the shift, product within five standard deviations from the mean could meet customer requirements. After the shift, only product within 3.5 standard deviations from the mean meets customer requirements. On the other hand, suppose the lower specification limit is 60, the mean is 80, and standard deviation is 4. Therefore, short-term capability is

$$Z_{ST}=[80-60]\div4=5$$

Capability is five sigma. Now, suppose the mean drifts to the left and settles at 74. This case is shown in Panel 6.7(c). The nearest specification limit is the LSL. After the shift that occurs in the long term, capability is

$$Z_{LT}=[74-60]\div4=3.5$$

Now, capability is only 3.5 sigma. Before the shift, product within five standard deviations from the mean could meet customer requirements. After the shift, only product within 3.5 standard deviations from the mean meets customer requirements.

FIGURE 6.7
SIGMA SHIFT TO THE RIGHT OR TO THE LEFT

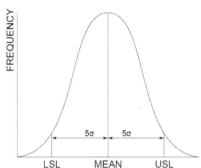 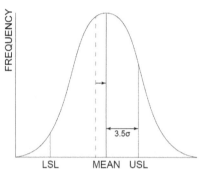 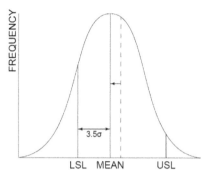

Motorola pushed these concepts to the extreme of targeting six sigma capability in the short term, which would achieve 4.5 sigma capability in the long term. The area outside ±4.5 s.d. is 0.0000068, which would be 6.8 defects per million, half on right tail of the distribution and half on the left tail of the distribution. The sigma shift cannot be both right and left at the same time. The sigma shift is either to the right or to the left. The area outside the right tail of +4.5 s.d. is 0.0000034, and the area outside the left tail of −4.5 s.d. is 0.0000034. Due to the sigma shift, therefore, six sigma capability results in 3.4 defects per million opportunities. In other words, six sigma capability is really 4.5 sigma capability, meaning 3.4 defects per million opportunities. Without the sigma shift, six sigma would translate into only two defects per billion. With the sigma shift, however, short-term capability of six sigma drops back to long-term capability of 4.5 sigma and 3.4 defects per million opportunities. Consider Table 6.3, which depicts defects per million opportunities without the sigma shift and defects per million opportunities with the sigma shift.

Table 6.3 Defects Per Million Opportunities Without Sigma Shift and With Sigma Shift		
Sigma Metric	**DP$_M$O Without Sigma Shift**	**DP$_M$O With Sigma Shift**
2.00	45,500	308,637
2.50	12,419	158,686
3.00	2,700	66,807
3.50	465	22,750
4.00	63	6,210
4.50	6.8	1,350
5.00	0.57	233
5.50	0.038	32
6.00	0.002	3.4

Process Capability Indices

Other measures also are used to ascertain the capability of a process to meet specifications. This set of process capability indices compares the voice of the process to the voice of the customer. These indices are particularly helpful when the mean is not centered on the target specification. The indices are the short-term capability index (C_p), adjusted short-term index (C_{PK}), long-term capability index (P_p), and adjusted long-term capability index (P_{PK}).

The simplest capability index is the short-term capability index (C_p). It compares the width of specifications, *i.e.*, USL minus LSL, to the short-term width of the process, *i.e.*, UCL minus LCL. To compare the width of the specification to the short-term width of the process, the formula for C_p is

$$C_p = (USL - LSL)/6\sigma_{ST}$$

USL–LSL is the voice of the customer and $6\sigma ST$ is the voice of the process. Thus, C_p is allowed variation divided by actual variation. In this way, voice of the customer divided by voice of the process. When calculated C_p is equal to one, the voice of the customer is equal to the voice of the process. When calculated C_p is less than one, the process is wider than the specification, resulting in defects falling in the space between control limits and specification limits. When calculated C_p is greater than one, the process width is less than the specification, resulting in few if any defects. Figure 6.8 illustrates each of these cases. Panel 6.8(a) shows C_p greater than one, meaning the width of specification limits is greater than the width of control limits; Panel 6.8(b) shows C_p equal to one, meaning the width of specification limits is equal to the width of control limits; and Panel 6.8(c) shows C_p less than one, meaning the width of specification limits is less than the width of control limits.

FIGURE 6.8
Cp, SPECIFICATION LIMITS, AND CONTROL LIMITS

Although simple, C_p is problematic. C_p compares only the widths of the process and the specification. The distribution of values may not be centered exactly between the specification limits. The distribution may be offset to the right so that the mean is closer to the USL than to the LSL or to the left so that it is closer to the LSL than to the USL. The calculated C_p would be the same whether the distribution is centered or not. The C_p calculation can be adjusted for the extent to which the distribution is offset. The result is the adjusted short-term capability index (C_{PK}), which compares the distance from the distribution mean (x) to each of the specification limits with the half-width of the short-term process variation. The adjusted short-term capability index is calculated with respect to the upper specification limit as

$$C_{PKU} = (USL - x)/3\sigma_{ST}$$

With respect to the lower specification limit, the adjusted short-term capability index is calculated as

$$C_{PKU} = (x - LSL)/3\sigma_{STp}$$

The smaller value of the two calculations is the adjusted short-term capability index. If the distribution is centered between specification limits, the calculated value for C_{PK} is equal to the calculated value for C_p. If the mean of the distribution is not centered, capability is diminished in proportion to how far it is offset. Table 6.4 shows the translation from C_{PK} to Sigma score without sigma shift. Generally, C_{PK} of 1.33 or more, *i.e.*, four sigma capability or more, indicates a process is capable in the short term. When C_{PK} is less than 1.33, variation is wide or variation is offset from the center of specification, perhaps a combination of both width and location.

	Table 6.4 Adjusted Short-Term Capability Index (C_{PK}), Sigma Score, Yield, and Defects per Million Opportunities		
Sigma	**C_{PK}**	**Yield (%)**	**DPMO**
1	0.33	68.27	317,310
1.5	0.50	86.64	133,614
2	0.67	95.45	45,500
2.5	0.83	98.7581	12,419
3	1.0	99.7300	2,670
3.5	1.17	99.9535	465
4	1.33	99.9937	63
4.5	1.5	99.99932	6.8
5	1.67	99.999943	0.57
5.5	1.83	99.999996	0.038
6	2.0	99.9999998	0.002

The same capability indices can be calculated for long-term variation. The long-term capability index (P_p) is

$P_p = (USL-LSL)/6\sigma LT$

In the same way, the adjusted long-term capability index (P_{PK}) is calculated with respect to the upper specification limit as

$P_{PK} = (USL-x)/6\sigma LT$

With respect to the lower specification limit, the adjusted long-term capability index is

$P_{PK} = (x-LSL)/6\sigma LT$

So, if $C_p=C_{PK}$ and $P_p=P_{PK}$, the process mean is centered between its specifications. Otherwise, the process mean is offset.

CONTINUAL IMPROVEMENT OF PROCESSES AND SYSTEMS

Statistical control basically means a process is within its limits of ±3 s.d. so that the only variation is due to common causes. Therefore, elimination of special causes is a critical first step. Once a process is in statistical control, an even harder job begins. Removing common causes requires profound knowledge of a process. Yet, improving a stable process is keyed on removing or mitigating common causes of variation. Consequently, the difficult problem of improving a process commences once statistical control is reached. Improving a process means finding ways to reduce variation from the mean, although improvement also may involve bettering the mean. Improvement of a stable process requires fundamental change in materials, methods, machinery, or people.

At the heart of the quality movement is the idea of continual improvement, also called *kaizen*, Japanese for continuous improvement or change for the better. A device central to continual improvement is the PDCA Cycle. The acronym stands for Plan, Do, Check, Act. Deming called it the Shewhart Cycle after the Master who originated it. Whatever it is called, the PDCA Cycle has been a staple of continual improvement, eventually laying the foundation on which the Six Sigma method of process improvement is built. Figure 6.9 illustrates the PDCA Cycle.

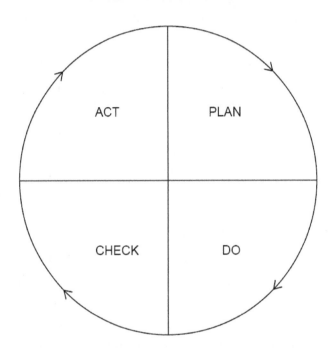

FIGURE 6.9
THE PDCA CYCLE

The first phase of PDCA is Plan. A process is examined to decide what fundamental change might improve it. Ordinarily, this step is implemented by organizing an appropriate team of workers who are closest to the process. The team uses devices such as a fishbone diagram to brainstorm about possible root causes of a problem. The endgame of this phase is to plan a fundamental change in the process meant to improve its outcomes.

The second phase of PDCA is Do, which does not mean to implement the planned change. Do means the fundamental change is tried on a small scale such as a pilot project, a test, or an experiment. This phase is meant to carry out exploratory procedures to develop data, information, or experience related to the fundamental change in the process.

The third phase of PDCA is Check. Observational evidence from the Do phase is analyzed and studied. The point is to check and study results to determine what has been learned from the fundamental change in the process. In particular, results are scrutinized critically to judge whether the process could be improved with implementation of the fundamental change.

The fourth phase of PDCA is Act. If the fundamental change has shown results that are promising when tried on a small scale, the change is implemented. Implementation takes the form of a redesigned process that integrates and incorporates the fundamental change.

PDCA is a cycle. Therefore, PDCA cycle does not end with the fourth phase, Act. The fifth phase is to repeat the Plan phase, except with new knowledge, which means planning still another fundamental change. The sixth phase is to repeat the Do phase, and ever onward.[61]

Late in his life, Deming changed Check to Study, and thus changed the PDCA Cycle to the PDSA Cycle. Evidently, he decided that Study was a more meaningful word. With only Check, something might be missed. In addition, he pointed out that Check could mean to block, rein in, or pull up short. Instead, Study the results to determine what has been learned, and then Act. Whether PDCA or PDSA, the Shewhart cycle is an adaptation of the scientific method applied to management planning and decision making. It represents a systematic way of increasing knowledge of processes and of implementing change.

Six Sigma Process Improvement, Process Design/Redesign, and Process Management

Management strategies based on Six Sigma commitment can be separated into process improvement, process design/redesign, and process management. Process improvement seeks to remove the root causes of problems while keeping intact the fundamental structure of the process. The emphasis is on finding solutions to the few vital problems that bedevil process capability. Process design/redesign arises from the frustration of the slow if not glacial pace of improvement that often resulted from the basic nature of the PDCA Cycle, which calls for making only one fundamental change during each cycle.

Near the end of his life, even Deming himself seemed to acknowledge that improvement by one change at a time was too slow. At one of his seminars, he once said, "You can't catch up with something that's going faster than you are." In the context, he seems to have meant that if a company has fallen behind competitors and is trying to catch up, grinding out one change at a time is not likely to close or overcome the gap. Incremental improvements alone, one change at a time, do not enable or empower a company to keep up with the rapid pace of change in technology, customer expectations, and competition. Six Sigma methods bring together process improvement and process design/redesign. Process design/redesign is effort not to improve but to replace a process or segment of a process with an altogether new one.

Process management goes beyond oversight and direction of business functions to understanding processes and flows of work. Processes are documented and managed end-to-end. Responsibility is assigned, which essentially designates process owners. Measures of inputs, outputs, and activities are thorough and meaningful. Process owners use their knowledge of the process to assess performance and take action as needed to address problems and opportunities. Process owners use process improvement and process design/redesign continually to raise levels of performance.[62]

---

61   W. Edwards Deming, *Out of the Crisis* (Cambridge, MA: Center for Advanced Engineering Study, Massachusetts Institute of Technology, 1986), p. 88. In addition, see Shewhart, *Statistical Method from the Viewpoint of Quality Control, op. cit.*, p. 45.

62   See Peter S. Pande, Robert P. Neuman, and Roland R. Cavanagh, *The Six Sigma Way: How GE, Motorola, and Other Top Companies are Honing Their Performance* (N.Y.: McGraw-Hill, 2000), pp. 35-36.

DMAIC

Ordinarily, Six Sigma utilizes a five-phase process improvement method. The phases are Define, Measure, Analyze, Improve, and Control. This method is known as DMAIC, pronounced "deh-MAY-ick." DMAIC did not displace PDCA. DMAIC is firmly grounded in Shewhart's PDCA cycle. Indeed, DMAIC is based on PDCA, building on the basic notions inherent in each phase of PDCA. The relationship between DMAIC and PDCA is reminiscent of a comment that Sir Isaac Newton wrote in a letter to a rival scientist, Robert Hooke, after publication of Newton's monumental and seminal *Principia* (1687). Newton said, "If I have seen further it is by standing on the shoulders of giants." Rather than humility, Newton evidently had a cruel sense of humor, having a laugh at the expense of another. Robert Hooke was a dwarf, a hunchbacked one at that, hardly a giant. The comment in his letter to Hooke was an insult rather than an expression of modesty. In this context, DMAIC has seen further by standing on the shoulders of PDCA.

The first phase of DMAIC is Define. A trained team is formed to work on the process improvement project. A team charter is articulated to state the problem, goals, and milestones. In this way, the charter circumscribes the overarching scope of the project. In effect, this charter is a mission statement, describing what is to be accomplished. Afterwards, one of the first tasks of the team is to identify customers as well as their needs and requirements. Critical-to-quality characteristics are identified and validated. The extant process is flowcharted.

The second phase of DMAIC is Measure. The focus turns to identifying key measures and then developing a plan for collecting data. A baseline for process performance is established to determine current capability.

The third phase of DMAIC is Analyze. Data are analyzed to determine gaps between current performance of the process and performance goals. Devices such as a fishbone diagram are used to determine possible sources of variation. A vital few root causes of variation are identified and verified.

The fourth phase of DMAIC is Improve. Possible solutions to the vital few causes are developed and tested. Best solutions are chosen based on small-scale studies or experiments and analysis of results. The process flowchart is edited so that the modification reflects the improvements. An implementation plan is developed.

In effect, the first four phases of DMAIC are replicative of the four phases of PDCA. The fifth phase of PDCA is Control. A plan to sustain improvements is developed. Knowledge and authority are transferred to the process owner who is then responsible for sustaining and auditing the redesigned process.

Each of the five phases is depicted in Table 6.5. The phases are shown as separate and distinct, but project teams often find that phases tend to overlap and interface in the course of their work.

	Table 6.5 Six Sigma Improvement Processes	
Phase	**Process Improvement**	**Process Design/Redesign**
1. Define	Identify the problem Define requirements Set goal	Identify specific or broad problems Define goal/change vision Clarify scope and customer requirements
2. Measure	Validate problem/process Refine problem/goal Measure key steps/inputs	Measure performance to requirements Gather process efficiency data
3. Analyze	Develop causal hypotheses Identify "vital few" root causes Validate hypothesis	Identify "best practices" Assess process design Value/non-value adding Bottlenecks/disconnects Alternate paths Refine requirements
4. Improve	Develop ideas to remove root causes Test solutions Standardize solution/measure results	Design new process Challenge assumptions Apply creativity Workflow principles Implement new process, structures, or systems
5. Control	Establish standard measures to maintain performance Correct problems as needed	Establish measures and reviews to maintain performance Correct problems as needed

Source: Peter S. Pande, Robert P. Neuman, and Roland R. Cavanagh, The Six Sigma Way: How GE, Motorola, and Other Top Companies are Honing Their Performance (N.Y.: McGraw-Hill, 2000), p. 39.

DMAICT and DMADV

DMAIC projects are mostly directed at improving existing processes, but they can be focused on process design/redesign efforts. In recent years, many companies have added T to DMAIC. The T refers to Transfer. Learning from one project may have applications that can be transferred elsewhere in the organization. The T results in DMAICT.

When developing altogether new processes, the DMADV methodology is more appropriate than DMAIC. For example, the gap between current performance and performance goals for a process might be so great that DMAIC methods fail. The DMADV methodology can be followed to replace a current process with a process designed from scratch. DMADV refers to Define, Measure, Analyze, Design, and Verify. The first three phases of DMADV are the same as in DMAIC. These three phases are followed by Design. The process is designed to meet customer requirements and specifications. The Verify phase involves confirmation and substantiation of process performance and its capability for meeting customer needs and specifications.

Six Sigma Infrastructure

Underlying Six Sigma is an organizational infrastructure to ensure that improvement initiatives have the necessary support and resources. Quality assurance once was largely left to management on the production floor and to statisticians in a quality department. On the other hand, Six Sigma depends on a small but critical infrastructure of people who institutionalize change. The infrastructure of Six Sigma begins with executive leadership by the CEO and other top managers. They empower downstream people in the infrastructure with freedom and resources to explore ideas for breakthrough improvements. Beginning with the CEO, therefore, Six Sigma is a top-down endeavor. After all, the CEO is responsible for performance of the overall organization.

The infrastructure of Six Sigma also engages champions and sponsors. Six Sigma champions are high-level managers who understand the details of Six Sigma and who are committed to its success. In large corporations, Six Sigma often has a full-time champion, perhaps an Executive Vice President. Champions also include leaders who apply Six Sigma in their day-to-day work and avow the Six Sigma gospel. Sponsors are process owners or system owners who initiate and coordinate Six Sigma improvement activities in their areas of authority and responsibility.

Belts of Many Colors

In 1990, Motorola engineers were engaged to assist Unisys in solving complex problems the company encountered with production of large-scale multilayer printed circuit boards for military applications. Motorola engineers trained and worked with a handful of Unisys engineers. Eventually, the problems were solved. Unisys managers wanted widespread practice of the statistical methods that Unisys engineers had learned. However, they were concerned about acceptance of these methods. One evening over dinner in Salt Lake City, Motorola engineers suggested denominating trained Unisys engineers with the appellation of Black Belts. The term used to ennoble trained and experienced engineers was meant to invoke the aura and mystique of martial arts discipline and skill that seemed to convey special powers. One Unisys manager proclaimed that he could sell the methods with that designation.

The evening meal birthed the use of Black Belt to designate someone who is a master of statistical problem solving. Later, the terms Green Belt and Master Black Belt were added to the Six Sigma vocabulary to designate people with degrees of expertise. Eventually, one of the most publicized aspects of Six Sigma was creation of a corps of experts known by nomenclature drawn from the martial arts and thus suggestive of heightened skill and discipline.

Master Black Belts are people with the highest level of technical proficiency. They understand the mathematical theory on which statistical methods are based. They can assist Black Belts in applying methods correctly. In this sense, they are internal consultants and coaches who devote their time to Black Belts and Green Belts. Black Belts operate under Master Black Belts to apply Six Sigma methods to specific projects. Black Belts focus on Six Sigma project execution. Generally, Black Belts are technically oriented people. They are expected to master a wide range of technical tools involving mathematics and statistics. Green Belts are Six Sigma project leaders capable of forming and facilitating Six Sigma teams and managing Six Sigma projects. Green Belt training involves classroom training often conducted in conjunction with a Six Sigma project. Green Belts link Six Sigma implementation with their other job responsibilities. They operate under the guidance of Black Belts. Therefore, different levels in the infrastructure hierarchy from Green Belt, to Black Belt, and then to Master Black Belt are based on the extent of training, expertise, and experience.

Jack Welch, CEO and Chairman of the Board of Directors of General Electric, retired in September 2001. While running GE, he was known as "the greatest manager on the planet Earth." While CEO and Chairman, Jack Welch told young managers to master the Six Sigma discipline that led to Black Belt designation if they wanted to move up at General Electric.[63] Indeed, Jack Welch told new hires that if they wanted to move up in the company, they must earn a Black Belt in Six Sigma.

EMPLOYEE INVOLVEMENT

The best ideas come from those closest to the work. An organization needs to enable people closest to the work to speak up when they have ideas and empower them to take action on their ideas. However, rarely does any one person have enough knowledge or experience to understand everything that goes on in a process, much less in a system. An old aphorism is "No one of us is as smart as all of us." For this reason, employee involvement often entails working together in teams. Some teams are natural work groups. Some are cross-functional teams. Others are cross-operational teams. Whatever the scope, teams synergistically pool the experiences, skills, and talents of their members. With proper training, teams often can tackle complex problems and come up with effective solutions.

When engaged as consultants and facilitators, strategic planners discovered a long time ago that top managers respond with "our people" when asked about an organization's strengths. These managers implied that one of the organization's greatest assets was its people. Upon further review, however, these consultants would find that the organization's people were treated more like liabilities than assets. Indeed, assets such as machinery and equipment were treated better than its people. Yet, employee involvement ultimately entails additional investment in people. At times, this investment is job training with a focus on skills and knowledge to do the job. Companies that commit to quality generally spend more than before on employee training. In addition, these companies not only spend more on employee training, they spend better on such training. At times, the investment is not in the form of training but instead on education, understood to be self-improvement with a focus on developing people themselves more fully. Whereas returns to investment in training might have its limits, investment in education could go on forever.

PARTNERSHIPS OF SUPPLIERS AND CUSTOMERS

Partnering is a common practice based on cooperative relationships among customers and suppliers. Partnering with external suppliers often involves movement towards single sourcing, which is the practice of using only one supplier or vendor as a sole source of certain materials, parts, components, or services. Single sourcing has been found to be most advantageous when fulfilling a given ongoing purchasing need. For example, if Ford decides to turn to LucasVarity for all of its antilock braking systems, then Ford is practicing single sourcing in its procurement of such systems.

---

63   See Hal Lancaster, "This Kind of Black Belt Can Help You Score Some Points at Work," *Wall Street Journal* (September 14, 1999), p. B1.

Single sourcing follows from the need to minimize variation. Even though two suppliers might deliver excellent materials, there will be differences. Sometimes, even lot-to-lot variation from any one supplier is enough to give fits to manufacturing. Variation between lots from two suppliers can stir up even more trouble. Consequently, companies have moved towards a single source for each material, component, part, or service. The underlying motivation is to lessen variation for each input and thus to improve overall quality and cost. The supplier has long-term customers and can commit investments while knowing the relationship is enduring. By investing in larger facilities with corresponding greater capacity, unit costs can be reduced. Greater cumulative output can reduce unit costs still further. Single source suppliers can work with their customers to understand requirements and to find out how inputs are being used, which allows the supplier to improve quality continually and lower unit costs for both buyer and supplier. Through mutual cooperation, they both gain. While the supplier makes more profit, a portion of the supplier's savings in cost to the company is passed to the buyer and ultimately to the customer.

Single sourcing generally establishes long-term relationships based on loyalty and trust. Of course, suppliers must be chosen with care. They should be chosen on the basis of their commitment to continual improvement of quality. Single sourcing is a practice carried out by largest and best firms that will never go back to the old way of spreading out purchases over seemingly countless vendors. Nevertheless, some argue that single sourcing sounds good in theory but will not work well in business practice. Critics argue that a second source serves as a kind of insurance. If a company's main supplier were to suffer a fire, flood, earthquake, tsunami, hurricane, tornado, or other calamity, the company would have a backup source. In rebuttal, defenders expostulate that refusing to single source when your competitor is single sourcing leaves a company at a competitive disadvantage. Defenders of single sourcing also point out that having two suppliers instead of one doubles the risk of calamity that might disrupt supplies. With two suppliers, there are twice as many plants, doubling the risk of fire, flood, earthquake, tsunami, hurricane, tornado, or other calamity.

ISO Certification

The acronym ISO is a reference to the International Organization for Standardization. ISO is a network of the national standards institutes of more than 160 countries with a Central Secretariat in Geneva, Switzerland. In the United States, the ISO organization is the American National Standards Institute (ANSI). In effect, ISO establishes standards for quality management systems. A company that has been audited independently and certified as compliant with ISO standards is ISO certified. ISO certification assures that quality methods are implemented. ISO does not certify products or services, and ISO does not itself certify organizations. Member countries have their own certification bodies that audit organizations applying for ISO certification. ISO certification must be renewed at regular intervals recommended by the certification body, usually three years.

ISO 9000 is a family of standards for quality management systems. ISO 9001 is one set of standards in the ISO 9000 family. Twenty requirements are embedded in ISO 9001. Among the ISO 9001 requirements are matters such as articulating a set of procedures that cover key processes, monitoring processes to ensure effectiveness, keeping appropriate records, checking product for defects with appropriate corrective action, reviewing processes periodically, examining quality systems for effectiveness, and facilitating continual improvement of processes and systems. Companies apply for and value ISO certification because of a number of reasons. Single sourcing alone is a powerful motivation. Most companies consider only suppliers that have ISO certification. Failure to achieve ISO certification is failure to be considered.

QUALITY COMES FIRST

Many sayings acquiesce in the inevitability of and acquiescence in errors and mistakes. To err is human. Everyone makes mistakes. Nobody's perfect. Nobody bats a thousand. Deming was not one to surrender to error and mistake and their aftermath. Ever the contrarian, Deming always said, "Quality comes first." He had in mind the sequence of quality, cost, productivity, and profit, followed by favorable effects on share price, as well as heightened security for workers, managers, and owners.[64] The point is that management cannot start after quality and produce the same beneficial effects that follow. For example, management cannot start with cost and move forward to productivity and profit. In and of itself, cost cutting alone does not deal with the cause of costs and does not attempt to make any fundamental change whatsoever and thus does not improve anything. When cost cutting takes the form of budget cutting, it can result in higher rather than lower costs. If the maintenance budget were cut by ten percent, planned and emergency maintenance would be attempted with a ten percent reduction in maintenance mechanics, maintenance materials, as well as maintenance tools and equipment. The result may be an increase in machinery failure in service and a corresponding increase in downtime, the cost of which easily can overwhelm any preceding cuts in the maintenance budget.

Suppose quality comes first, meaning that the cornerstones are practiced as methods and techniques to improve cost and productivity. To see the flow from improving cost and productivity to improving profit, consider the following case. Suppose a business produces a differentiated product that is sold by the ton. The product manager knows the production costs of the product from people in engineering and the demand for the product from people in marketing. The cost function estimated by the engineering group is

$$TC = 500 - 10Q + Q_2$$

TC refers to total cost of production per day and Q to volume of production per day. The marketing group estimates demand for the product from an equation for the demand curve, which is

$$P = 150 - 9Q$$

P refers to price of the product, and Q refers to volume of production and sales.

The product manager wants to price the product and sell a volume of product so that profit from production and sales can be maximized. The total revenue function is

$$TR = 150Q - 9Q(Q)$$

$$TR = 150Q - 9Q_2$$

Therefore, the marginal revenue function is

$$MR = 150 - 18Q$$

The marginal cost function is

$$MC = -10 + 2Q$$

---

64   *Ibid.*, p. 3.

Setting marginal revenue equal to marginal cost to determine the profit-maximizing volume and solving for Q,

$150-18Q=-10+2Q$

$-20Q=-160$

$Q=8$

At this volume, 8 tons per day, price per ton at which profit is maximized would be

$P=150-9(8)$

$P=150-72$

$P=78$

The price per ton is $78 per ton. At this price, $78 per ton, and this volume, 8 tons per day, total revenue per day from sales is

$TR=78(8)$

$TR=624$

Total revenue is $624 per day. Total cost per day is

$TC=500-10(8)+8^2$

$TC=500-80+64$

$TC=484$

Total cost is $484 per day. Therefore, profit per day is

$\pi=624-484$

$\pi=140$

Total profit is $140 per day.

Through cost improvement based on quality methods and techniques, suppose the total cost function is improved to

$TC=400-30Q+Q_2$

Some fixed costs have been eliminated, from $500 to $400. Factors that bring down variable costs improve from $-10Q$ to $-30Q$. The effects that cost improvement would have on price, volume, and profit can be calculated. The marginal cost function is now

$MC=-30+2Q$

Setting marginal revenue equal to marginal cost and solving for Q,

$150-18Q=-30+2Q$

$-20Q=-180$

$Q=9$

Volume is 9 tons per day. At this volume, 9 tons per day, price per ton would be

$$P=150-9(9)$$

$$P=150-81$$

$$P=69$$

Price is $69 per ton. At this price, $69 per ton, and this volume, 9 tons per day, total revenue per day from sales is

$$TR=69(9)$$

$$TR=621$$

Total revenue is $621 per day. Total cost per day is

$$TC=400-30(9)+9^2$$

$$TC=400-270+81$$

$$TC=211$$

Total cost is $211 per day. Therefore, profit per day is

$$\pi=621-211$$

$$\pi=410$$

Profit is $410 per day.

Everyone is better off as a result of the cost improvement. The seller makes more profit, and buyers can obtain more of the product at a lower price. As Deming said, "Quality comes first." What he meant was that improvement in productivity, cost, price, and profit follows the practice of quality principles.

When Quality Does Not Come First

Toyota has been more than a little fanatical about costs throughout its rise to global leadership in automobile manufacturing. In its unrelenting quest to bring about cost savings internally and to extract cost savings from its suppliers, Toyota historically was unwilling to compromise quality. However, by the mid-2000s, cost savings overrode and trumped quality. Once a leader in engineering, quality slipped noticeably. More than eight million Toyota vehicles were recalled due to mechanical failures, and U.S. regulators linked these mechanical failures to more than fifty deaths. Ignoring its earlier commitment to cost savings without compromising quality, the concentration on cost reduction went too far. Directives centered on cost savings overreached by half.

In 2005, Toyota President Katsuaki Watanabe crowed that the company had wrung more than ten billion dollars from global operating costs since 2000. Yet, the company pressed for more cuts. Suppliers were asked to design parts for the Toyota Camry. The goal was parts that were ten percent cheaper. One outcome of this strong-armed demand was a flaw in the Camry headliner, which is the fabric and composite lining that covers the inside roof. The headliner is made by compressing layers of materials while using heat to mold it. Toyota Boshoku, the lead Camry supplier, chose a carbon fiber material requiring so much heat that the headliner would catch on fire. A North American parts supplier did a teardown of a 2007 Camry, and its engineers were shocked by how much Toyota craftsmanship had been watered down.[65]

Recall British Petroleum (BP) and the 20 April 2010 explosion and sinking of the Deepwater Horizon Rig, leading to the loss of eleven lives and constituting the greatest environmental disaster in U.S. history. All seemed to agree that this atrocity was attributable to a focus on cost cutting. Over and over, BP made decisions that increased the risk of a blowout, and these decisions were driven by the goal of saving the company money. Well design, testing to ensure soundness of cementing, and more were based on cost considerations above all else. The result is well known, no pun intended.

DEMING'S FOURTEEN PRINCIPLES FOR TRANSFORMATION

Deming's book, *Out of the Crisis*, was published in 1986. The second chapter is "Principles for Transformation of Western Management."[66] In this chapter, Deming stated fourteen principles for this transformation, making the principles a philosophy to guide an organization from what it is to what it can be and ought to be. Deming realized that many people in western management were content to learn the statistical methods he taught to Americans during World War II and later to the Japanese. He believed that these statistical methods alone were not enough. After all, the statistical methods had evaporated from American industry during the postwar period. He pondered what might have caused such dissipation and how to avoid it in the future. He concluded that a philosophy of management was needed, principles consistent with statistical methods.

Deming was ready with principles to teach when he was sent to Japan by the War Department. Over time, he continued to refine and enlarge upon them. Eventually, some people designated the fourteen principles as the fourteen points. Deming himself said there were not always fourteen principles. When he first put them in writing in the late 1970s, there were ten or fewer. He encountered some problems found only in the United States, however. In America, he recognized matters such as fear, barriers, quotas, and slogans that needed to be addressed. These matters led to still other principles to make up the fourteen Principles for Transformation of Western Management.

1. CREATE CONSTANCY OF PURPOSE FOR IMPROVEMENT OF PRODUCT AND SERVICE

Deming began with a company's mission. He believed a company's basic mission is to stay in business and provide jobs. While maximizing the value of the firm might be the ultimate goal of a business, it is not the principal mission of the firm. Mission means what a person, firm, or organization is trying to accomplish. Mission implies a sense of purpose accompanied by determination and perseverance. Constancy in this first principle refers to unwavering steadfastness of purpose linked and geared to improving product and service to the customer. Many U.S. companies turned to Deming because they found that reducing or eliminating defects is not enough. These companies needed a commitment to enduring strategies and analytical methods. Even if they had long-term strategies, companies had allowed themselves to become sidetracked by short-term interests such as quarterly profits. Deming thought that

---

65   See Alan Ohnsman, Jeff Green, and Kae Inoue, "The Humbling of Toyota " *Bloomberg Business Week* (March 11, 2010).

66   Deming, *op. cit.*, pp. 18-96.

top management needed a passion for crafting and deploying improvement strategies to make certain that the company maintained its constancy of purpose.

Constancy of purpose calls on top leadership for a clear expression of the organization's vision, mission, and core values. This expression must be transparent and must communicate credibly why the organization is in business as well as its true aims, purposes, and character. Core values provide the spiritual basis for achieving the vision and accomplishing mission. A written document that communicates vision, mission, and core values is important, but it requires more than mere words. Meaningful action must transcend the words. The document must be embraced as a clarion call to action from top management down through the ranks. People in an organization work together better if they understand how their jobs are related to the aims, purposes, and culture of the organization. Their decisions are better when they understand where the organization is heading. The written document constitutes promises to employees and customers and provides a benchmark against which decisions and behaviors can be judged.

2. ADOPT THE NEW PHILOSOPHY

At times, Americans and others have been too tolerant of poor workmanship and sullen service. What was needed, Deming believed, was a kind of new belief system so that organizations no longer lived with commonly accepted mistakes, defective materials, sloppy workmanship, inexcusable delays, egregious errors, and so forth. What was needed was recognition and acceptance of the need for a changed attitude. Many companies realized that they must conduct their businesses differently from the past. "We cannot go on with business as usual," they said. Many companies, however, still did not grasp the enormity of the task. For example, some companies saw the need to adopt statistical process control (SP_c) in their manufacturing processes but left out marketing, sales, logistics, and other functions.

The message of the second Principle focused on the importance of everyone in the organization learning to assume his or her new responsibilities, beginning with learning what those responsibilities are. The Principle means that the philosophy of doing business must be changed. A new way of thinking is required. The late O. Dean Martin, a Methodist minister, once said, "It's easier to act yourself to a new way of thinking than to think yourself to a new way of acting." Actually doing it often leads to the new way of thinking. This new way of thinking must be centered on processes and ultimately quality of products and services. Deming recognized the mindset of some managers and even some customers was that mistakes, defective products, poor service, and breakdowns are inevitable. They foolishly thought that such problems were simply a cost of doing business, and they acquiesced in the notion that there are no alternatives. Other managers showed in dramatic fashion that this acquiescence in failure is not the way. A new way of thinking and acting is an opposing view.

3. CEASE DEPENDENCE ON MASS INSPECTION

At the time, many firms still inspected products as they came off the line or at major stages in the production process. Defective products were either scrapped or reworked. Of course, both scrap and rework were expensive. In effect, a company was paying some workers to make defects and then paying other workers to fix or dispose of the defects. Quality did not come from inspection but instead from improvement of processes. Deming knew that through training and empowerment, workers could be enlisted in this improvement. They are the ones directly involved from day to day with processes. Because they are engaged in the work, workers can identify problems. Workers who are valued for improving the process also have pride of ownership and workmanship.

Deming's message in this third Principle was to eliminate dependence on mass inspection. He thought that companies should rely instead on statistical means for controlling and improving processes. After all, the problem is in the process and the system, not in the product. Deming believed that depending on mass inspection is a little like treating a symptom while the disease is killing you. The disease is variation. Processes must be brought under statistical control, and sources of variation must be ascertained and effort directed toward reducing variation. Inspection merely finds and records failures.

Deming pleaded with management to stop depending on mass inspection. He said, "Routine 100 percent inspection to improve quality is equivalent to planning for defects, acknowledgment that the process has not the capability required for specifications."[67] Deming often referred to A.V. Feigenbaum, who estimated that fifteen to forty percent of manufacturing cost of a product is "waste embedded in it."[68] Of that cost, Deming said, handling damage alone can equal five to eight percent of the manufacturer's cost.[69]

Process improvement removes upstream deficiencies and thus prevents downstream problems, errors, defects, and failures. By spotting problems in a process early, defects can be nipped in the bud, as Barney Fife would say. Huge savings can be realized if it is not producing faulty products and thus not generating waste. Deming advocated working toward the virtual elimination of inspection in all but a few critical cases.

Deming made comments worth repeating about inspection. One, inspection does not improve quality, and it does not guarantee quality. Inspection is too late. By the time inspection occurs, good or bad quality is already in the product. As Harold Dodge said, "You cannot inspect quality into a product."[70] Two, with rare exceptions, mass inspection is unreliable, costly, and ineffective. Mass inspection does not make a clean separation of good items from bad items. Even with mass inspection, some bad products can end up in the hands of a customer. Even machines are fallible. Inspection by gauges does not guarantee quality. Adding more inspectors can be even worse. If several inspectors inspect a product or service, each inspector might be less vigilant, relying on the others to find the problems. Third, until their own work is brought into statistical control, inspectors themselves fail to agree with each other. Routine inspection becomes unreliable through boredom and fatigue.

Just for fun, become an inspector. The job is to inspect written materials for the letter F. So, read the following text carefully, and inspect it for the letter F.

FINISHED FILES ARE THE RESULT OF SCIENTIFIC STUDY
COMBINED WITH THE EXPERIENCE OF MANY YEARS.

This exercise is a case of visual inspection, the simplest inspection in practice. How many letters F are in the text? Most people count the wrong number, meaning that visual inspection has failed.

---

67 Deming, *op. cit.*, p. 28.

68 *Ibid.*, p. 12.

69 *Ibid.*

70 *Ibid.*, p. 29.

4. END THE PRACTICE OF AWARDING BUSINESS ON PRICE TAG ALONE

Purchasing departments often seek the low cost vendor item by item. Frequently, this practice leads to supplies of low quality. If a business accepts poor materials, parts, components, or services, output of product will be affected adversely. Poor materials, for example, lead to more rejects, more rework, or more delays, and thus drive up costs correspondingly. The decision to buy should be based on all costs instead of lowest procurement price. In the same way, contracts should be based on best value instead of lowest price. Deming said that purchasing departments should seek the best quality and achieve it with a single supplier in a long-term relationship.

Variation can creep into a process through materials or parts procured from suppliers. Continual improvement of a process or system can be accomplished only if suppliers deliver items of a predictable quality. Deming called on companies to "move toward a single supplier for any one item on a long-term relationship of loyalty and trust."[71] He acknowledged that use of a single supplier is not always practical. However, Deming insisted that a company should work closely with suppliers to convey its requirements and to help vendors to improve the quality of its products or services while reducing overall cost to the company.

When quality and consistency are the most important objectives, awarding supplier contracts to the lowest bidder is abandoned. As Deming said, "Price has no meaning without a measure of the quality being purchased."[72] Companies that practice just-in-time inventory control as a way to hold down inventory costs have no choice but to adopt this fourth Principle. A manufacturer must be able to rely on the supplier to deliver quality parts, components, or materials precisely on time. Indeed, the point of working closely with suppliers is to achieve low total cost rather than just low procurement price.

5. IMPROVE CONSTANTLY AND FOREVER THE SYSTEM OF PRODUCTION AND SERVICE

Deming emphasized that improvement in a process is not a one-time effort. Improvement is not a project that has a beginning and an end. Management, he believed, is obligated to look continually for ways to reduce waste, lower cost, and improve quality. One way to improve a process or system is to reduce variation that is part of all processes and systems. In fact, improving quality by reducing process variation is a cornerstone of the quality philosophy. For most of Deming's life, the PDCA Cycle was the method. From the 1980s, DMAIC has been the method for continual improvement.

Quality itself is a moving target. For example, military weaponry once considered effective is now obsolescent. Manual typewriters became dinosaurs when endangered by electric typewriters and desktop word processing. These meager examples underscore the need to pursue innovation to stay ahead of technology. Managers and leaders are responsible for processes and systems. Often, processes and systems are in place and thus are treated by management as though they are a kind of legacy, good or bad. However, managers remain responsible for process and system capability as well as appropriate action to improve. This fifth Principle means that managers and leaders must improve constantly and forever the processes and systems they oversee and direct.

---

71   William W. Scherkenbach, *The Deming Route to Quality and Productivity* (Rockville, MD: Mercury Press, 1986), p. 131.

72   Deming, *op. cit.*, p. 32.

6. INSTITUTE TRAINING

Often, workers have learned their job from another worker who was never trained properly. As often, workers merely follow instructions and directions, however unintelligent and empty-headed. Studies have shown that workers do not do their jobs properly because of three reasons. First, workers do not know what they are supposed to do. Second, workers do not know why they are supposed to do it. Third, workers do not how to do what they are supposed to do. No amount of fear, intimidation, humiliation, or ridicule will teach, show, demonstrate, explain, or provide practice leading to workers knowing what, why, and how to do what they are supposed to do. To be capable, workers should know what is expected, know how they are doing, know how to improve, and know they belong.

Overseeing, directing, or working in a process requires a profound understanding of how a process operates. For this reason alone, Deming emphasized the importance of training workers and managers alike to recognize when a process or system is in control and when it is out of control. In addition, workers and managers need to be trained to identify problems and to recognize improvement opportunities. Training is needed to distinguish between common causes and special causes of variation. Most companies have found that they also must train workers and managers alike to operate in cross-functional and even cross-operational teams. People who have worked for years in functional or operational silos, stovepipes, chimneys, or other such fiefdoms have a genuine need to learn team concepts and skills.

One reason why Deming focused so heavily on training is that reducing variation in employees is as important as reducing variation in items produced by machines or delivered by suppliers. As with everything else, workers should be brought into statistical control, meaning that their work is predictable. Once a work group is performing in a stable and thus a predictable manner, defects and problems that occur are not the fault of the workers but of the process and system. Once the performance of the workforce is under control, management and workers can begin to search for more efficient ways to perform a job.

In his book, *Out of the Crisis*, Deming stated that many industrial leaders believed that operational definitions are one of the most neglected requirements in business today.[73] He also said students in schools of business rarely learn about operational definitions. Operational definitions are meanings of terms and concepts stated so that they can be measured in specific contexts to obtain consistent results. This requirement implies that the operational definition of clean has a different meaning for a surgical operating room than for a cabinetry work floor or for a teenager's bedroom.

Deming said an operational definition "puts communicable meaning into a concept" by specifying how the concept is measured and applied within a particular set of circumstances.[74] Communicable meaning is not achieved until adjectives such as "good, reliable, uniform, round, tired, safe, unsafe, unemployed are expressed in measurable terms, meaning operational terms of sampling, test, and criterion."[75] To communicate effectively and avoid misinterpretations, customers and suppliers must use the same operational definitions for the same concepts. What is measured and how it is measured must be defined in

---

73   *Ibid.*, p. 276.

74   *Ibid.*

75   *Ibid.*, pp. 276-277.

operational terms. Training in operational definitions and metrics is critical because so much depends on measurement.

7. ADOPT AND INSTITUTE LEADERSHIP

The job of management, Deming argued, is not supervision but leadership. Deming said, "...the aim of leadership is not merely to find and record the failures of [people], but to remove the causes of failure; to help people to do a better job...."[76] Deming saw a difference between the supervisor who comes to work every day ready to direct everything versus the leader who comes to work every day ready to help people to do a better job. Clearly, people prefer to be led than managed and prefer to be empowered rather than controlled.

Deming said that a leader is "coach and counsel, not a judge. Judging people doesn't help them."[77] A successful leader develops knowledge so that people come to him or her for help and advice. The successful leader uses the power of his or her formal position sparingly. Leaders have power not by the authority of his or her position but rather by virtue of his or her character. Authority alone is hardly a virtue. By Deming's account, therefore, leadership involves transforming the role of manager from that of cop to coach. The job of a manager is not to catch people doing something wrong but to help people do something right. As a coach, a manager or supervisor teaches, shows, demonstrates, explains, shares experience, and provides practice. The coach is someone to whom people turn for the tools, equipment, machinery, materials, and methods to assure the job is done properly. His point was that no one is able to coach without knowledge of the work. Leaders must know the processes and the systems.

8. DRIVE OUT FEAR

Many employees are afraid to ask questions, speak up, or take a position even when they do not understand what the job is, how the job fits with jobs other people are doing, or how to do the job. In such cases, people continue to do things the wrong way or not do things at all. The economic loss from fear is appalling, Deming argued. To accomplish better quality and higher productivity, people must feel secure. He pointed out that secure means without fear. Secure workers are unafraid to express ideas and unafraid to ask questions.[78]

Lowe and McBean enumerated six "monsters of fear" and discussed their consequences.[79] Fear of reprisal and fear of failure are closely related. These fears result in a please-the-boss mentality as well as an aversion to taking risks or offering new ideas. Fear of providing information, which derives from fear of reprisal and fear of failure, leads to concealing information that could help to identify and solve problems. Another monster is fear of not knowing. In particular, this fear emerges in organizations where managers are expected to control everything in their fiefdoms. Managers in this environment involve themselves in even the most obscure details of work. Fear of giving up control lurks in organizations where management's job is viewed as controlling people rather than processes. Often, this fear results in

---

76   *Ibid.*, p. 248.

77   Quoted in Lloyd Dobyns and Clare Crawford-Mason, *Quality or Else: The Revolution in World Business* (New York: Houghton Mifflin, 1991), p. 165.

78   *Ibid.*, p. 59.

79   Theodore A. Lowe and Gerald M. McBean, "Honesty Without Fear," *Quality Progress* (November 1989).

attaining goals of one department or group at the expense of others. The final monster, fear of change, is an obvious impediment to process improvement.

A Japanese quality expert, Ichiro Miyauchi, said of his own country, "Our managers aren't interested in good news; they only want to know the bad news."[80] This one statement speaks volumes. Good news is not as likely to reveal opportunities for improvement. Managers must learn to appreciate opportunities that lie embedded in bad news. First, however, managers must change a business culture that is typically accustomed to killing the messenger of bad tidings.

The bottom line is that fear paralyzes a workforce that otherwise could be engaged actively in reducing variation. If an organization wants to improve continually, it needs continual information from its workforce. If the workforce is afraid, information will not reach leaders who can take appropriate action. What is needed is a "speak up" environment to displace a "shut up" culture. Every member of an organization has information that leaders could use to improve the organization. Lost opportunities for improvement mean the organization continues its faulty practices.

9. BREAK DOWN BARRIERS BETWEEN STAFF AREAS

Often, departments, functions, offices, directorates, sections, or other units of an organization compete against each other or have goals that conflict. These disparate areas do not work as a team so that they can foresee or solve problems. Worse, accomplishment of one area's goals could cause trouble for another. Ford's Donald Petersen referred to breaking down such barriers as dismantling chimneys. Tearing down such Berlin Walls involves mobilizing corporate domains to cooperate on common objectives as defined by customer needs and a company's improvement priorities. Breaking down barriers conjoins the efforts of teams, groups, and staff areas toward the aims and purposes of the organization. Teamwork at all levels in an organization is a major mechanism for implementing and sustaining quality improvement. An organization can operate effectively if departments talk with each other and try to help each other. In many companies, however, departments are concerned with protecting and filling their own rice bowls, thus pursuing their own interests instead of those of the organization.

Once people in one department start thinking of people in other departments as part of the larger team, it is easier to consider and set up cross-functional teams. Cross-functional teams include people from every department with an interest or a stake in solving problems that cut across departmental lines. In this way, cross-functional teams play a central role for organizations pursuing companywide quality. Cross-functional teams improve horizontal communication. When a team has members from different departments, more information flows between departments. A cross-functional team also promotes vertical communication. Decisions can be made better and quicker because needed information is more readily available. Teams of people working together promote cooperation within an organization. When one person, department, or team wins through competition, some other person, department, or team loses. When people cooperate, all parties can win.

10. ELIMINATE SLOGANS, EXHORTATIONS, AND TARGETS FOR THE WORKFORCE

Since workers alone can do little to change a process or system, the burden of responsibility for improvement rests with management. In and of themselves, slogans, exhortations, and targets never help anybody

---

80   Andrea Gabor, *The Man Who Discovered Quality* (New York: Times Books, 1990), p. 22.

to do a better job. Organizations often use posters or slogans that exhort employees to incarnate some ideal. Do it right the first time! Zero defects! Work smarter, not harder! What is wrong is using slogans, exhortations, and targets to call for increased levels of productivity but do not provide a method to achieve the new levels.

A business story begins with a manager calling a meeting of people under his supervision. He had a short, pointed message for them. The manager said, "By God, this year we're going to increase productivity by ten percent!" Then, he left the room. Immediately, one of the workers said, "I wonder why we didn't increase productivity by ten percent last year. We didn't have a plan last year, either." This story is undoubtedly apocryphal or an industrial myth equivalent to the urban myth of alligators in the sewer. Perhaps the story should begin with, "Once upon a time in a land far, far away." Fairy tale or not, it makes a point. Such slogans, exhortations, and targets are good examples of hoping without helping. Without methods and a plan, they are ineffective.

Slogans are not bad if they serve to encourage behavior within the control of the workforce. At Ford, "Quality is Job One" reflected the onset of an orientation to quality, and it was accompanied by training and new work practices. On the other hand, slogans can be demoralizing, especially when people perceive slogans as management's way of saying that workers are not putting forth their best efforts. In such cases, slogans are seen and heard as admonishments. Most people feel they are doing their best and trying their hardest, but flaws in the system are frustrating their efforts to do a better job. Management is responsible for the system that is frustrating workers, and targeting workers can aggravate their frustration. Deming suggested that posters and exhortations are aimed at the wrong people.[81] He suggested that it would be more appropriate for leaders to exhort themselves.

11a. ELIMINATE NUMERICAL QUOTAS FOR THE WORKFORCE

A numerical quota targets a number of items produced or actions taken. For example, a quota could be stated in terms of number of survey-miles logged by a research ship, regardless of usable data; number of claims processed by an insurance adjuster, regardless of errors; number of telephone calls handled by a customer service representative, regardless of follow up; or number of automobile tires made by a production worker, regardless of defects. Quotas take only quantity into account. Quotas can result in high cost. To hold a job, a worker will meet a quota without regard to quality. Deming argued that workers should not be subjected to a quota because they can work only as well as the process or system permits, assuming it is in control. As Deming said, "A quota is a fortress against improvement of quality and productivity. I have yet to see a quota that includes any trace of a system by which to help anyone to do a better job."[82] Instead, he said, management should provide training in the methods for improvement and institute these methods.

---

81   Deming, *op. cit.*, p. 66.

82   *Ibid.*, p. 71.

11b. ELIMINATE NUMERICAL GOALS FOR PEOPLE IN MANAGEMENT

Management by objectives (MBO) originated with Peter Drucker in his book, *The Practice of Management*.[83] When MBO is used for assessing managerial performance, people meet with their managers once or twice a year and are given objectives using numerical goals. The problem with MBO is that an organization usually can achieve almost any objective by paying a high enough price. MBO focuses on the end goal rather than the process or system. Without methods, numerical goals are crutches for hobbled leadership. In some cases, supervisors do not know how to do the jobs they supervise. Instead, they manage by the numbers. They count things. Numerical goals are substituted for leadership. In this way, supervisors can compare counts against quotas and evaluate people on the differences between the two.

Often, MBO is inconsistent with process improvement. Indeed, Point 11b is all about a leader's role in process improvement. After special cause variation has been removed from a process, leaders are responsible for improving the process itself by reducing common cause variation. Working under an MBO system, leaders pay most of their attention to meeting objectives instead of improving processes. After all, they are rewarded for meeting or surpassing short-term goals, not for improving processes. Even worse, one manager's objective may conflict with another manager's objective. For example, a production manager might be given an objective dealing with increased production, whereas a supply manager's objective is to reduce inventory. In such cases, MBO does not foster teamwork but often fosters internal competition that works against cooperation.

Deming had a view altogether different from that of Drucker. He said, "The job of management is to replace work standards by knowledgeable and intelligent leadership."[84] Deming was so persuasively critical of MBO that Drucker finally capitulated in the 1990s. Drucker himself downplayed the significance of MBO. "It's just another tool," he said. "It is not the great cure for management inefficiency.... Management by Objectives works if you know the objectives, 90% of the time you don't." Something that works only ten percent of the time is not likely to survive in the market for ideas.

12. REMOVE BARRIERS THAT ROB PEOPLE OF PRIDE OF WORKMANSHIP

People generally are eager to do a good job and distressed when they cannot. Too often, misguided supervisors, faulty equipment, inadequate tools, or shoddy materials stand in the way of doing a good job. Deming said everyone, leader and worker alike, has "a birthright, the right to be proud of his [or her] work, the right to do a good job."[85] Anything that stands in the way of this right is a barrier to pride of workmanship. Pride of workmanship means being able to do quality work.

One major barrier to pride of workmanship is annual ratings of performance. Deming pointed out that workers perform their work in a system, and their performance often is determined by that system, rarely the other way around. If Joseph Juran is correct in concluding that eighty-five percent of problems in an organization are the responsibility of its leaders rather than workers in the system, it makes no sense to blame workers for problems they cannot control. After all, the purpose of an annual performance

---

83   Peter F. Drucker, *The Practice of Management* (NY: Harper&Row, 1954).

84   Deming, *op. cit.*, p. 75.

85   *Ibid.*, p. 77.

rating presumably is to manage or control performance. In this sense, the rating is a poor surrogate for leadership.

An annual rating may be perceived as a form of inspection. After each rating, management uses the rating to sort out the good from the bad. Deming believed that managers are unable to make such judgments with any precision, particularly over the span of a single year. Another serious problem with an annual rating system is that it undermines teamwork. If one person does something to help another, the other person might be given a higher rating than the helping person. There is little if any incentive to cooperate. In fact, there are good reasons not to cooperate. Rating systems foster a culture in which people work toward personal interests instead of organizational interests.

Deming believed that rating systems are unfair and counterproductive. Without question, this belief is the most controversial and intriguing of his Fourteen Principles. It must be understood in the context of the theory of variation. Deming contended that the time-honored practice of performance appraisals, bonuses, and other rewards that brand a few employees winners and encourage constant competition in the ranks is fundamentally unfair and ultimately harmful to the interests of both company and employee. If the system in which people work is predictable and if management has done its job well in selecting employees, then most employees will perform at about the same level over time and only a few will perform exceptionally well or poorly. In addition, the influence of variation is such that it is virtually impossible to measure accurately the overall performance of individuals within a variable process or system.[86]

13. ENCOURAGE EDUCATION AND SELF IMPROVEMENT FOR EVERYONE

Managers and workers alike must be trained in the new methods, including teamwork and statistical tools. Deming's views on training stemmed from his understanding of variation and his conviction that training is linked directly to a company's ability to maintain and improve processes. His ideas about education and self-improvement seemed to follow directly from his ideas on training for skills, but they represented a personal view of the nature of work and motivation.

Often, Deming quoted Ecclesiastes 3:22, "Wherefore I perceive that there be nothing better than that a man should rejoice in his own work." A devout Episcopalian, Deming believed that this rejoicing comes from self-improvement and that it is a company obligation to offer opportunities for continuous education. Clearly, Deming believed that there is something inherently good about education. For its own sake, education is good for people and eventually will add something positive to an organization and society. "What an organization needs is not just good people," Deming said, "it needs people that are improving with education."[87] Ishikawa evidently agreed, saying, "Quality control begins with education and ends with education."[88] Everyone in an organization needs to be encouraged to pursue knowledge. Each of them needs to think of ways to apply new knowledge to their work. Continual improvement applies to people as well as processes. Education is not necessarily job related. When people learn about anything, it stimulates thinking. Learning helps people make new connections between even familiar

---

86   *Ibid.*, pp. 101-120.

87   *Ibid.*, p. 86.

88   K. Ishikawa, *What Is Total Quality Control? The Japanese Way*, trans. D.J. Lu (Englewood Cliffs, NJ: Prentice-Hall, 1985), p. 37.

ideas. This sort of stimulation can produce creative ideas about products, services, and processes, all of which can benefit organizations.

Learning is addressed in two of Deming's Fourteen Principles. The sixth Principle refers to the foundations of training for leaders and for employees. The thirteenth Principle refers to continual education and improvement of everyone on the job. In other words, the sixth Principle refers to training, especially job training and learning the skills needed to do a job. The thirteenth Principle deals with education, continual education, and continual self-improvement. In this light, Principle Six deals with job improvement, and Principle Thirteen concerns self-improvement.

14. TAKE ACTION TO ACCOMPLISH THE TRANSFORMATION

Principle Fourteen means taking action on the other thirteen Principles. It is a call for action. The transformation will not happen by merely issuing orders passed down through the ranks. The transformation requires study, discussion, patience, perseverance, and constant work by everyone in the organization. Leaders must develop and implement a plan for quality improvement. Top leaders cannot do it alone. One of the goals of an organization is to identify, organize, and educate a critical mass of individuals. Critical mass refers to people who have the power, knowledge, and leadership to begin and sustain the transformation. The critical mass must be identified and targeted early by top management. Consequently, members of the critical mass can be trained and subsequently develop an understanding of their new responsibilities.

To achieve the full potential of the quality mission, everyone in the organization will need to participate. A sense of community must be developed so that everyone understands and believes, "We are all in this together." The transformation is everyone's job. Open communication is an important key. Leaders provide planning, periodic updates, and reaffirmations of their intentions. Managers maintain close communications with leaders, with each other, and with people on their teams. All workers talk openly with each other and with their supervisors on many matters, including processes, problems, and improvements.

SIX SIGMA THEMES

Deming had Fourteen Principles for guiding and leading transformation from what an organization is to what an organization can be and ought to be. Likewise, Six Sigma has six themes that constitute its leadership system. When supported by Six Sigma methods, these Six Sigma themes make Six Sigma work to improve productivity and cost.[89]

1. Customer Focus

While adopting Deming's philosophy, countless companies vowed to meet or exceed customer needs, requirements, and expectations. However, gathering data and information on customers often was a one-time endeavor that overlooked the dynamic nature of customers and their needs, requirements, and expectations. In true Six Sigma commitment, Six Sigma improvements are regarded in terms of their ultimate impact on customer satisfaction. In Six Sigma, customer needs, requirements, and expectations are defined, and performance against these needs, requirements, and expectations is measured.

---

89   The following section is based on Pande, Neuman, and Cavanagh, *op. cit.*, pp. 15-18.

2. Data Management

Six Sigma methods are management by fact. Despite movement towards measurement, many businesses remained captive to opinions and assumptions. The methodology of Six Sigma clarifies the measures that are key to gauging business performance and then applies data and analysis to understand key variables and to optimize results. At a practical level, Six Sigma helps managers to know what the data needed and how the data are used.

3. Process Improvement

In Six Sigma, processes are where the action is, where the rubber meets the road. Whether designing products or services, measuring performance, or improving efficiency and customer satisfaction, Six Sigma focuses on processes as the key variable. Mastering processes is not merely a necessary evil but actually a way to build competitive advantage in delivering value to customers.

4. Proactive Management

In the military context, strategy is positioning one's own forces advantageously in advance of actual contact with the enemy. In the military or business context, the emphasis is on being proactive, acting in advance of events. Of course, the opposite is reactive, acting after being overtaken by events. Proactive management involves defining ambitious goals and reviewing them frequently; setting clear priorities; focusing on problem prevention instead of firefighting; and questioning how we do things here instead of passively acquiescing in how things are done here. Being truly proactive is actually a starting point for creativity and effective change. Six Sigma methods and practices replace reactive habits with a dynamic, responsive, proactive style of management.

5. Boundaryless Collaboration

"Boundarylessness" was one of Jack Welch's mantras for business success. Years before Six Sigma and especially afterwards, GE's famed CEO and Chairman of the Board of Directors was working to break down barriers and improve teamwork that crossed organizational lines. The Six Sigma methodology expands collaboration as people learn how their roles fit into the big picture and recognize the interdependence of activities. Boundaryless collaboration in Six Sigma requires an understanding of the needs of end users and of the flow of work through a process, system, or supply chain. Boundaryless collaboration also demands an attitude that is committed to using customer and process knowledge to benefit all parties. In this way, Six Sigma creates an environment and management structures that support true teamwork.

6. Tolerance for Failure

Driving for perfection and tolerating failure are complementary. No company can practice Six Sigma without new ideas and approaches, which always involve some risk. If people who see a possible path to better service, lower costs, or new capabilities fear the consequences of failure, they will not try. Six Sigma methods involve improving performance coupled with risk management. The message is clear. If you fail, make it a safe failure. The bottom line is to push continually to achieve perfection while being willing to accept and manage occasional setbacks.

THE LEAN MACHINE

Lean manufacturing or lean production emerged in the late 1980s and early 1990s. The lean philosophy is based on the idea that resource use for any goal other than creation of value for the customer is wasteful and thus subject to elimination. Essentially, therefore, lean production focuses on creating more value with less cost.

As a term, lean first entered business language in 1988 with publication of an article by John F. Krafcik, "Triumph of the Lean Production System."[90] The article was based on his M.S. thesis presented to the MIT Sloan School of Management. His thesis, *Comparative Analysis of Performance Indicators at World Auto Assembly Plants*, was a study of thirty-seven assembly plants. He realized the Toyota Production System (TP$_S$) made a critical difference. After graduation from MIT, Krafcik was the first American engineer hired by the New United Motor Manufacturing, Inc. (NUMMI), a joint venture of Toyota and General Motors. In 1990, he joined Ford and worked there for fourteen years. He rose to chief engineer for vehicle developments such as the Ford Expedition and Lincoln Navigator. In 2004, he left Ford for Hyundai Motor America as Vice President, Corporate Planning Division. Nowadays, Krafcik is President and CEO of Hyundai.

Krafcik's research agenda was continued by the MIT International Motor Vehicle Program and culminated in publication of the venerable best seller, *The Machine That Changed the World*.[91] Admission of lean production and lean manufacturing to the lexicon of business was immortalized. Beyond mere words and language, the outcome was lean production methods to identify and eliminate waste, thus leading to improvements in quality while at the same time reducing production costs and production time.

Lean thinking focuses on people who add value to a product. The idea is to transfer as much responsibility as possible to workers who actually produce the product. Lean thinking also analyzes the entire system of producing a product with the intention of eliminating activities that involve cost without adding anything to the value of the product. Lean thinking relies on loosely connected principles that are meant to eliminate waste and reduce cost. These principles include pull processing, which is producing a product only when customers want the product. This thinking emphasizes the difference between a push system and a pull system. A push system moves product through the manufacturing process and then tries to sell the products to customers. A pull system, on the other hand, produces products because a customer order has called for them. The goal is to be able to make a product so fast it can be made to order, thus eliminating the need to build up inventory in anticipation of customer demand. Other principles include perfect first-time quality, continuous improvement, and long-term relationships with suppliers.

Many Six Sigma organizations integrate lean thinking into their process improvement framework. For these organizations, the Six Sigma emphasis on process quality is conjoined with the lean production emphasis on waste elimination. Six Sigma and lean production are not competing methodologies. Lean thinking can be assimilated into Six Sigma. Whereas Six Sigma emphasizes process control and process capability, lean production focuses on process flow. Lean production seeks to reduce or eliminate delay in each activity of a process. Lean production also emphasizes separation of value-added and non-value added activities, and then eliminating root causes of non-value added activities and their costs. In a

---

90   John F. Krafcik, "Triumph of the Lean Production System," *Sloan Management Review*, 30 (Fall 1988), pp. 41-52.

91   James Womack, Daniel Jones, and Daniel Roos, *The Machine That Changed the World: The Story of Lean Production* (New York: HarperCollins, 1991).

sense, Six Sigma has a single-mindedness set on improving capability, hence quality. Lean production, on the other hand, has a likewise single-mindedness centered on waste, hence cost.

THE BLAME GAME

The focus of Six Sigma was credited as a main contributor to phenomenal growth in the U.S. economy throughout the 1990s forward to the mid-2000s. Then, the National Bureau of Economic Research announced that the U.S. economy slumped into a recession beginning in December 2007. Real Gross National Product declined during five of six quarters including four consecutive quarters, 3Q 2008 through 2Q 2009. Although seedlings of recovery sprouted in the third quarter of 2009, economists expected a jobless recovery. One reason cited for a jobless recovery was Six Sigma! To quote *Business Week*, "In an attempt to boost earnings without putting more people on the payroll, companies are embracing the controversial data-driven system that aims to radically reduce production defects and improve processes in everything from marketing to manufacturing."[92] In this one sentence, Six Sigma became controversial!

At the onset of the recession, companies not already on board increasingly turned to Six Sigma. *Business Week* cited companies as varied as Capital One, Merck, Pfizer, Cadbury, and Dunkin' Brands. According to *Business Week*,

Capital One says it has launched a Six Sigma initiative to "drive continuous improvement" in its operations, while Pfizer this year embarked on 85 Six Sigma projects to lower the cost of delivering medicines to patients in its pharmaceutical sciences division. "We're applying Lean Six Sigma across the whole R&D process," says Senior Vice-President Annette Doherty.... Even the Chicago law firm Seyfarth Shaw has become a Six Sigma devotee....[93]

However, the renewed interest in Six Sigma was not based on the cultural change ordinarily associated with Six Sigma initiatives. Instead, these newer initiates were looking for techniques that could produce results quickly. A Six Sigma consultant said that clients told him, "What I really want is results, and I want them in 90 days."[94] This obsession with quick results recalls Deming's criticism of managers who hope for instant pudding. Six Sigma initiatives can take months if not years to produce results. As one observer pointed out during the recession, "If you're thinking about it being useful for the current economic downturn, it may be a little late to start a lot of Six Sigma work."[95]

MALCOLM BALDRIGE NATIONAL QUALITY AWARD

Almost forty years after the Deming Prize was established in Japan, America finally established its own prize for quality. On 20 August 1987, President Ronald Reagan signed the Malcolm Baldrige National Quality Improvement Act of 1987. The Malcolm Baldrige National Quality Award (MBNQ$_A$) program makes annual awards for quality. The MBNQA is named for Malcolm Baldrige, Secretary of Commerce from 1981 until his death in a tragic rodeo accident in July 1987. Baldrige was a ardent proponent of quality management. He took a personal interest in the National Quality Improvement Act and helped draft one of the early versions. In recognition of his contributions, Congress named the award in his honor and memory.

---

92   "The Six Sigma Black Belts Are Back," *Business Week* (September 21, 2009), p. 064.

93   *Ibid.*

94   *Ibid.*

95   *Ibid.*, 065.

The MBNQA was envisioned as a standard that would elevate U.S. companies to world-class quality. U.S. companies are recognized for their achievements in quality and business performance, and MBNQA recipients raise awareness of quality as a competitive edge. Originally, three categories were created: manufacturing, service, and small business. Beginning in 1999, education and healthcare categories were authorized. In 2004, President Bush signed legislation that authorized still another category for nonprofit and government organizations. Three awards may be made annually in each of the categories.

The Winners Circle

MBNQA criteria are a framework that any organization can use to improve overall performance. Seven classes of criteria make up the award. In addition to use by MBNQA applicants, the criteria are used by organizations for self-assessment and development of performance and business processes. The 2011-2012 criteria are (1) Leadership; (2) Strategic Planning; (3) Customer Focus; (4) Measurement, Analysis, and Knowledge Management; (5) Workforce Focus; (6) Operations Focus; and (7) Results. Starting in 2012, MBNQA applicants must meet one of several criteria: previously won the MBNQA but not within the past five years; received the top award between 2007 and 2011 from a member of the Alliance for Performance Excellence; applied for the MBNQA between 2007 and 2011 and earned a high score in both organizational processes and results but did not receive a site visit; applied for the MBNQA between 2007 and 2011 and received a site visit; has more than twenty-five percent of its workforce outside its home state; or does not have an available Alliance for Performance Excellence program. The Alliance for Performance Excellence is a body of state, local, regional, and sector specific Baldrige-based programs.

An independent Board of Examiners appraises the applications. Examiners are private sector experts in quality. In 2013, the Board had about five hundred examiners. A team of examiners visits companies that pass an initial review. The site visit verifies information in the application and clarifies questions that come up during the review. Each applicant can count on as much as one thousand hours of review. Regardless of outcome, each applicant receives a written summary of strengths and areas for improvement in each area addressed by the criteria.

In 2012, thirty-nine organizations applied for an MBNQA, including one manufacturer, three service companies, two small businesses, three educational organizations, twenty-five healthcare organizations, and five nonprofit or governmental organizations. Winners were Lockheed Martin Missles and Fire Control (manufacturing), MESA Products, Inc. (small business), North Mississippi Health Services (health care), and City of Irving (nonprofit). In 2013, twenty-two applications were submitted. No awards were given in any business category. Winners were Pewaukee School District (Pewaukee, WI, education), Baylor Regional Medical Center at Plano (Plano, TX, health care), and Sutter Davis Hospital (Davis, CA, health care).

For the first time in 2012, organizations were recognized for best practices in one or more of the MBNQ$_A$ categories of criteria. Judges chose and honored Maury Regional Medical Center, Columbia, Tennessee, for strategic planning and workforce focus; Northwest Vista College, San Antonio, Texas, for leadership and customer focus; and PricewaterhouseCoopers Public Sector Practice, McLean, Virginia, for leadership and workforce focus. In 2013, Duke University Hospital (Durham, NC) and Hill County Memorial (Fredricksburg, TX) were recognized for their best practices in leadership.

The MBNQA was awarded first in 1988 and has been awarded each year afterwards. Table 6.6 shows winners in manufacturing, service, and small business year by year, 1988 to 2012. Table 6.7 shows winners in education and healthcare, 2001-2013. Table 6.8 shows winners in the new category of nonprofit organizations, 2007-2013.

Table 6.6 Malcolm Baldrige National Quality Award Winners: Manufacturing, Service, and Small Business, 1988-2012			
Year	Manufacturing	Service	Small Business
1988	Motorola Inc. (Schaumburg, Illinois) Westinghouse Electric Corp. Commercial Nuclear Fuel Division (Pittsburgh, PA)		Globe Metallurgical Inc. (Beverly, OH)
1989	Milliken & Company (Spartanburg, SC) Xerox Corp. Business Products and Systems (Rochester, NY)		
1990	Cadillac Motor Car Division (Detroit, MI) IBM Rochester (Rochester, MN)	Federal Express Corp. (Memphis, TN)	Wallace Co. Inc. (Houston, TX)
1991	Solectron Corp. (Milpitas, CA) Zytec Corp. (Eden Prairie, MN)		Marlow Industries Inc. (Dallas, TX)
1992	AT&T Network Systems Group/ Transmission Systems Business Unit (Morristown, NJ) Texas Instruments Inc. Defense Systems & Electronics Group (Dallas, TX)	AT&T Universal Card Services (Jacksonville, FL) The Ritz-Carlton Hotel Co. (Atlanta, GA)	Granite Rock Co. (Watsonville, CA)
1993	Eastman Chemical Co. (Kingsport, TN)		Ames Rubber Corp. (Hamburg, NJ)

1994		AT&T Consumer Communications Services (Basking Ridge, NJ) GTE Directories Corp. (Dallas/Fort Worth, TX)	Wainwright Industries Inc. (St. Peters, MO)
1995	Armstrong World Industries Inc. (Lancaster, PA) Corning Inc. Telecommunications Products Division (Corning, NY)		
1996	ADAC Laboratories (Milpitas, CA)	Dana CommercialCredit Corporation (Toledo, OH)	Custom Research Inc. (Minneapolis, MN) Trident Precision Manufacturing Inc. (Webster, NY)
1997	3M Dental Products Division (St. Paul, MN) Soletron Corp. (Milpitas, CA)	Merrill Lynch Credit Corp. (Jacksonville, FL) Xerox Business Services (Rochester, NY)	
1998	Boeing Airlift and Tanker Programs (Long Beach, CA) Solar Turbines, Inc. (San Diego, CA)		Texas Nameplate Co., Inc. (Dallas, TX)
1999	STMicroelectronics, Inc.-Region Americas (Carrollton, TX)	BI Performance Services (Minneapolis, MN) The Ritz-Carlton Hotel Company, L.L.C. (Atlanta, GA)	Sunny Fresh Foods (Monticello, MN)
2000	Dana Corporation-Spicer Driveshaft Division (Toledo, OH) KARLEE Company, Inc. (Garland, TX)	Operations Management International, Inc. (Minneapolis, MN)	Los Alamos National Bank (Los Alamos, NM)
2001	Clarke American Checks, Inc. (San Antonio, TX)		Pal's Sudden Service (Kingsport, TN)

2002	Motorola, Inc. Commercial, Governmental and Industrial Solutions Sector (Schaumburg, IL)		Branch-Smith Printing Division (Fort Worth, TX)
2003	Medrad, Inc. (Idianola, PA)	Boeing Aerospace Support (St. Louis, MO) Caterpillar Financial Services Corp. (Nashville, TN)	Stoner, Inc. (Quarryville, PA)
2004	The Bama Companies (Tulsa, OK)		Texas Nameplate Co. (Dallas, TX)
2005	Sunny Fresh Foods, Inc. (Monticello, MN)	DynMcDermott Petroleum Operations (New Orleans, LA)	Park Place Lexus (Plano, TX)
2006		Premier, Inc. (San Diego, CA)	MESA Products, Inc. (Tulsa, OK)
2007			PRO-TEC Coating Co. (Leipsic, OH)
2008	Cargill Corn Milling North America (Wayzata, MN)		
2009	Honeywell Federal Manufacturing & Technologies (Kansas City, MO)		MidwayUSA (Columbia, MO)
2010	Medrad (Warrendale, PA) Nestlé Purina Petcare Co. (St. Louis, MO)		Freese and Nichols, Inc. (Ft. Worth, TX) K&N Management (Austin, TX) Studer Group (Gulf Breeze, FL)
2011			
2012	Lockheed Martin Missles and Fire Control (Grand Prairie, TX)		MESA Products, Inc. (Tulsa, OK)

Year	Education	Healthcare
Table 6.7 **Malcolm Baldrige National Quality Award Winners:** **Education and Healthcare, 2001-2013**		
2001	Chugach School District (Anchorage, AK) Pearl River School District (Pearl River, NY) University of Wisconsin-Stout (Menomonie, WI)	
2002		SSM Health Care (St. Louis, MO)
2003	Community Consolidated School District 15 (Palatine, IL)	Baptist Hospital (Pensacola, FL) Saint Luke's Hospital (Kansas City, MO)
2004	Kenneth W. Monfort College of Business (Greeley, CO)	Robert Wood Johnson University Hospital (Hamilton, NJ)
2005	Richland College (Dallas, TX) Jenks Public Schools (Jenks, OK)	Bronson Methodist Hospital (Kalamazoo, MI)
2006		North Mississippi Medical Center (Tupelo, MS)
2007		Mercy Health Systems (Janesville, WI) Sharp HealthCare (San Diego, CA)
2008	Iredell-Statesville Schools (Statesville, NC)	Poudre Valley Health System (Fort Collins, CO)
2009		AtlantiCare (Egg Harbor Township, NJ) Heartland Health (St. Joseph, MO)
2010	Montgomery County Public Schools (Rockwille, MD)	Advocate Good Samaritan Hospital (Downers Grove, IL)

Year		
2011		Henry Ford Health System (Detroit, MI) Schneck Medical Center (Seymour, IN) Southcentral Foundation (Anchorage, AK)
2012		North Mississippi Health Services (Tupelo, MS)
2013	Pewaukee School District (Pewaukee, WI)	Baylor Regional Medical Center at Plano (Plano, TX) Sutter Davis Hospital (Davis, CA)

Table 6.8 **Malcolm Baldrige National Quality Award Winners:** **Nonprofit Organizations, 2007-2012**	
Year	**Nonprofit**
2007	City of Coral Springs (Coral Springs, FL) U.S. Army Armament Research, Development and Engineering Center (ARDEC) (Picatinny Arsenal, NJ)
2008	
2009	VA Cooperative Studies Program Clinical Research Pharmacy Coordinating Center (Albuquerque, NM)
2010	
2011	Concordia Publishing House (St. Louis, MO)
2012	City of Irving (Irving, TX)

PRACTICE QUESTIONS

1. Leaders of organizations often commit to the quality movement in the belief that improving quality can improve cost. How can cost be lowered through improving quality?

2. The quality movement is based on a proper understanding of quality as well as a focus on customers, processes, and continuous improvement. Briefly explain each cornerstone and develop a sense of how these elements are mutually related.

3. In the quality movement, what is regarded as complexity? What are some basic types of complexity?

4. One tool commonly used in the quality movement is flowcharting processes and systems. How is flowcharting used and how is it used to reduce and eliminate "complexity?"

5. Distinguish carefully between common causes and special causes of variation. Using this distinction, describe stable processes and capable processes.

6. Statistical control deals with process stability and process capability. Describe a stable process. Describe a capable process.

7. What is the PDCA Cycle, and how is it used in continual improvement?

8. Suppose a process is stable. Managers and workers have a goal of improving capability and use the Six Sigma method of process improvement. Briefly describe each of the five phases in this method of continuous improvement.

9. Consider a particular process in manufacturing a product. Distinguish carefully between common causes and special causes of variation within this process. Using this distinction, describe the conditions for stability in this process.

10. Suppose a process is stable, and process capability is five sigma. Write a careful interpretation of stability for this process and of the calculated capability of this process, *i.e.*, five sigma.

11. Answer each of the next questions regarding quality.

a. Suppose 100,000 items of a product are produced. However, 5,000 of the items had to be scrapped.

b. Another 5,000 of the items had to be reworked to meet specifications. Calculate the first-time yield, and write a narrative interpretation of the calculated first-time yield.

c. Suppose the first time yield is 0.93 for one process in a system, 0.94 for a second process, and 0.95 for a third process. Calculate the rolled throughput yield, and write a narrative interpretation of the rolled throughput yield.

d. Suppose the upper specification limit for a process is 1,000, the mean is 880, and the standard deviation is 25. Calculate the short-term Z Score. Write a narrative interpretation of the Z Score.

e. Suppose the upper specification limit for a process is 1,000, the target is 880, and the standard deviation is reduced from 25 to 24. Does this reduction result in more or less process capability? How do you know?

f. Suppose the upper specification limit for a process is 1,000, the target is 880, and the standard deviation is 24. Calculate the long-term Z score. Write a narrative interpretation of the long-term Z score.

Questions for Contemplation, Discussion, and Argument

12. Suppose you are one of the direct reports to a CEO who has heard of the quality movement and who wants to know more about it. In a monthly meeting with his direct reports, he talks momentarily about wanting to learn more about this quality movement. Next, he suddenly turns to you and says, "I've heard of this man they call Dr. Deming, but I don't know a whole lot about him. What can you tell me about him?" What would you say?

13. Dr. Deming articulated Fourteen Principles for Transformation, known in the vernacular of the quality movement as the 14 Points. Which of the 14 Points are directed toward reducing variation?

PRACTICE QUESTIONS *(AND ANSWERS)*

1. Leaders of organizations often commit to the quality movement in the belief that improving quality can improve cost. How can cost be lowered through improving quality?

They accept what Dr. W. Edwards Deming always said: "Quality comes first." Dr. Deming meant that management's responsibility is to make fundamental changes in the production system so that cost and productivity can be improved. In addition, he meant that exhortations to improve cost and productivity will not work unless there is a plan. Cutting cost by cutting budgets, for example, will not work. Indeed, both cost and productivity may worsen. Productivity and cost improve with quality. The fundamental reason is less scrap, less rework, fewer defects. Defects cost as much to produce as perfectly good items. Rework is a cost, meaning that even more cost is being embedded in the product. Scrap is a cost that cannot be recovered through sale of the product. Improvements in the system come first, and then improvements in cost, productivity, and profit will follow along with higher share price and greater security for managers, workers, and owners.

2. The quality movement is based on a proper understanding of quality as well as a focus on customers, processes, and continuous improvement. Briefly explain each cornerstone and develop a sense of how these elements are mutually related.

Properly understood, quality is producing a product or providing a service that meets or exceeds customer needs, requirements, or expectations. This focus on customers includes external customers who purchase the product as well as internal customers, who are the people inside the organization to whom workers pass on their work product. A process is a sequence of related tasks involved in carrying out a particular kind of work. In this way, a process is how this particular work is done. The focus on processes is intended to discover ways in which the process can be redesigned to eliminate waste in meeting or exceeding the needs or requirements of internal and, ultimately, external customers. Continuous improvement of processes refers to the ongoing, never-ending method involved.

3. In the quality movement, what is regarded as complexity? What are some basic types of complexity?

Often, root causes of a problem arise inside processes used to create a product or service. Even when sources of a problem are masked, however, complexity can be detected. Complexity is a general term for unnecessary work, i.e., anything that makes a process more complicated without adding value to a product or service. Types of complexity include (1) mistakes and defects, (2) breakdowns and delays, (3) inefficiencies, and (4) variation. In a quality environment, project teams examine processes to identify problems that fall into one or more of these categories, then work to track down the root causes with the mission of eliminating and preventing them through redesign. When defects occur in products or services or when someone makes a mistake, work must be repeated and extra steps added to correct the error or dispose of the damage. Sometimes, supply or production systems break down, and real work is put on hold and displaced because of repair or delay. Sometimes, more material, time, and movement are used than absolutely necessary.

4. One tool commonly used in the quality movement is flowcharting processes and systems. How is flowcharting used and how is it used to reduce and eliminate complexity?

Top management commitment to quality is directed at improving processes and systems. The potential for eliminating mistakes and errors lies mostly in improving processes, mainly changing materials, methods, and machinery that people use in processes. Once supervisors and managers recognize that processes create the majority of problems, they will stop blaming individual workers. Instead, they will identify the process that needs improvement, and they will be more likely to seek out and find the true source of a problem. To understand particular processes and systems inside an organization, a tool called flowcharting often is used. The intent of flowcharting is, first, to obtain from those closest to the work the step-by-step process or system actually in use. More often than not, no one person has a deep understanding of an entire process or system. Ultimately, the intent of flowcharting is to redesign processes and systems to prevent and eliminate waste in the form of scrap or rework. Often, flowcharting unmasks waste in the form of no customer for some activity or work product, redundancy of work, rework required because internal needs are not met, and delay designed into processes and systems.

5. Distinguish carefully between common causes and special causes of variation. Using this distinction, describe stable processes and capable processes.

Causes of variation can be separated into two categories, common and special. Common causes of variation are inherent in a process over time and thus affect everyone working in the process and affect all outcomes of the process. In other words, common cause variation is attributable to factors that are part of the process all of the time. Since common cause variation is a part of the process itself, the variation itself is characterized by a random pattern. Stated still differently, common-cause variation is due to a large number of sources of small variation. The sum of these small causes may result in a high level of variation or a large number of defects, errors, or mistakes. In addition, the sum of the common causes determines the limits of a process and its capability as currently operated. On the other hand, special causes of variation are not part of the process all the time. They arise from unusual and thus special circumstances. For this reason, special causes often are called assignable causes. Special cause variation exhibits a nonrandom pattern because it is the product of special circumstances, a temporary glitch in the process or system such as the malfunctioning of a single piece of machinery or the use of unusual materials.

6. Statistical control deals with process stability and process capability. Describe a stable process. Describe a capable process.

Statistical control involves tracking down and eliminating special causes so that the only remaining variation in a process or system is due to common causes. In other words, statistical control deals with process stability and process capability. A stable process is one in statistical control, meaning that the only variation is random and within the control limits of the process itself. These control limits are determined statistically and are depicted as two lines, the upper control limit and the lower control limit, on a control chart. These two lines indicate limits to common cause variation inherent in the process as it operates currently. These control limits are calculated from measurements actually taken on the process. Control limits are not specification limits. Control limits simply indicate how much variation to expect in the process. Process capability deals with the extent to which the product or service meets customer needs or requirements. Upper and lower specification limits that designate customer requirements are used to determine capability.

7. What is the PDCA Cycle, and how is it used in continual improvement?

The PDCA Cycle is the staple of continual improvement. The acronym stands for Plan, Do, Check, Act. The PDCA Cycle has four steps. Step One is to examine a process and decide what change might improve it. This step is implemented by organizing an appropriate team of workers who are closest to the process. The point of the Step One is to plan a change in whatever you are trying to improve. Step Two is to carry out the plan, preferably on a small scale. This step is the do step in which you search for data on hand that could answer the question raised in Step One, carry out the tests, or implement the change on a small scale. Step Three is to observe the results. This step is the check phase of the cycle. Step Four is to study results and decide what you have learned from the change. In other words, you identify and act on what is learned. The PDCA Cycle is a cycle. Therefore, it does not end with Step Four. Step Five is to repeat Step One, except with new knowledge. Step Six is to repeat Step Two and onward. The activities central to each of the four phases can be restated. In the plan phase, (1) identify what is to be improved, (2) plan changes that might lead to improvements, (3) decide on data that are needed, and (4) determine how, when, and by whom data will be collected. In the do phase, (1) gather data to determine a baseline, (2) make planned changes, and (3) gather data to determine what happened after the changes. In the check phase, (1) compare results of changes with what was planned, and (2) determine whether changes led to improvement. Finally, in the act phase, (1) determine the changes that should be implemented, (2) institutionalize the changes, (3) educate the workforce to the changes, (4) assess application to other parts of the organization, (5) monitor the process, and (6) repeat the PDCA Cycle. The PDCA Cycle is an adaptation of the scientific method applied to management planning and decision making. It represents a systematic way of increasing our knowledge of processes and of implementing change to assess whether improvements resulted.

8. Suppose a process is stable. Managers and workers have a goal of improving capability and use the Six Sigma method of process improvement. Briefly describe each of the five phases in this method of continuous improvement.

Ordinarily, Six Sigma utilizes a five-phase improvement cycle: Define, Measure, Analyze, Improve, and Control. Like other improvement models, DMAIC is grounded in Shewhart's PDCA cycle. So, DMAIC begins with (D) define the problem(s), (M) measure key steps or inputs into the process, (A) analyze the process to determine root causes of problems, (I) improve the process by developing changes that remove root causes, and (C) control the process to maintain the improved performance.

9. Consider a particular process in manufacturing a product. Distinguish carefully between common causes and special causes of variation within this process. Using this distinction, describe the conditions for stability in this process.

Common causes of variation are attributable to factors—methods, materials, machinery, and people—that are inherent and fundamental aspects of a process. Common cause variation is an accumulation of countless sources of small variation. When taken together, these numerous sources of variation form a random pattern. On the other hand, special causes of variation in a process are due to factors that are not fundamental elements of the process, which means these factors are not part of the process all of the time. The variation due to unusual, special causes is characterized by a nonrandom event that occurs because of uncommon circumstances. Stability in a process indicates predictability, and a stable process is one in which all variation is due to common causes and thus is random. In other words, stability means that all variation in a process falls within ±3 s.d. of the mean.

10. Suppose a process is stable, and process capability is five sigma. Write a careful interpretation of stability for this process and of the calculated capability of this process, *i.e.*, five sigma.

Capability in a process refers to how well the outcome of the process meets customer needs or requirements. Sigma is the metric used to measure capability. If a process is stable, all outcomes fall within ±3 s.d. Capability is measured by a Z score, which determines how many standard deviations can be fit between the specification target and the nearest specification limit. Five sigma capability means that five standard deviations can be fit between the target and the nearest specification limit. In other words, outcomes within five standard deviations of the specification limits meet customer needs and requirements.

11. Answer each of the next questions regarding quality.

a. Suppose 100,000 items of a product are produced. However, 5,000 of the items had to be scrapped.

Another 5,000 of the items had to be reworked to meet specifications. Calculate the first-time yield, and write a narrative interpretation of the calculated first-time yield.

First-time yield is 9,000/1,000=0.9, which indicates that 90% of items do not require either scrap or rework.

b. Suppose the first time yield is 0.93 for one process in a system, 0.94 for a second process, and 0.95 for a third process. Calculate the rolled throughput yield, and write a narrative interpretation of the rolled throughput yield.

The rolled throughput yield is (0.93)(0.94)(0.95)=0.831 or 83.1%, which indicates the likelihood that an item will emerge from the three processes without being scrapped or requiring rework.

c. Suppose the upper specification limit for a process is 1,000, the mean is 880, and the standard deviation is 25. Calculate the short-term Z Score. Write a narrative interpretation of the Z Score.

The Sigma (Z) score is

Z=(1,000−880)÷25=4.8

The Z score means that 4.8 standard deviations can be fit between the mean of 880 and the specification limit of 1,000, i.e., outcomes as far as 4.8 standard deviations from the mean still meet customer specifications.

d. Suppose the upper specification limit for a process is 1,000, the target is 880, and the standard deviation is reduced from 25 to 24. Does this reduction result in more or less process capability? How do you know?

When the standard deviation is reduced from 25 to 24, the Sigma (Z) Score is now

$Z=(1{,}000-880)\div 24=5$

The Z score means that five standard deviations can be fit between the mean of 880 and the specification limit of 1,000. Variation has been reduced, and capability has been increased, evidenced by the larger Z score.

e. Suppose the upper specification limit for a process is 1,000, the target is 880, and the standard deviation is 24. Calculate the long-term Z score. Write a narrative interpretation of the long-term Z score.

Long-term Sigma (Z) Score is Short-term Sigma (Z) Score minus 1.5 standard deviations to account for Six Sigma Shift. Therefore, short-term capability is

$Z_{ST}=(1{,}000-880)\div 24=5$

Long-term capability is

$Z_{LT}=5.0-1.5=3.5$

Due to the Sigma Shift, only 3.5 standard deviations can be fit between the mean and the upper specification limit, i.e., only outcomes as far as 3.5 standard deviations from the mean meet customer specifications.

7. Pricing Strategies

PRICING IN THE MARKETING MIX

Marketing mix is a term in wide usage to indicate variables that a firm integrates to sell its product(s). Since 1960, marketing mix has been distilled down to a catchy if not cutesy four Ps, *viz.*, product, price, promotion, and place (location). The importance of price in the marketing mix has been questioned from time to time. Through the mid-1970s, non-price factors such as product and promotion steadily grew in importance while disparaging the relevance of price. By the end of this period, more than half of managers responding to a survey did not identify price as one of the five most important policies in their own firm's marketing success.[96] More recently, however, price again has been elevated to a prominent position. After the product itself, pricing now is viewed as the most important factor in the marketing mix, place and promotion trailing badly. Indeed, value marketing is based on a strategic merger of product and price.

Price is the only element in the marketing mix that produces revenue. All other elements result in cost. Moreover, price is the most flexible element. Unlike product design or distribution channels, price can be changed readily. At the same time, however, price is troublesome. For most firms, pricing decisions have many different dimensions that devolve into a number of complex, intricate issues that must be addressed. How prices should be set relative to costs is one issue, price relationships among different products are another. Still another issue is whether the same price should be set for all customers at all times and in all places, not to mention whether price is the main competitive factor and whether price is constrained by intense competition. Responsive pricing decisions ultimately shape pricing strategy. In a sense, pricing strategies are practical means of applying the principles of profit maximization. The underlying principle is marginal revenue equals marginal cost. In business practice, pricing strategies are meant as surrogates for the profit maximizing principle.

---

96   See Robert A. Robicheaux, "How Important Is Pricing in Competitive Strategy?" *Proceedings: Southern Marketing Association*, ed. Henry W. Nash and Donald P. Robin (January 1976), pp. 55-57. Also see "Pricing in an Inflation Economy," *Business Week* (April 6, 1974), pp. 43-49.

COST-PLUS PRICING

In the past fifty years or more, a number of surveys dealing with pricing practices have been conducted. Results consistently have indicated that cost-plus pricing is the most common pricing practice in America and other parts of the developed world. In effect, cost-plus pricing is a rule-of-thumb or short cut method of pricing products meant to maximize profit. The usual method is first to estimate the average variable cost (AVC) for a normal volume of output. Next, the firm adds to AVC an average overhead charge meant to reflect fixed costs, usually expressed as a percentage of AVC so that an estimated fully allocated average total cost (ATC) is obtained. In retailing, for example, AVC is the wholesale price of an item. If the retailer knows that fixed costs are ten percent of variable costs (TFC/TVC=10%), then ten percent of AVC is added to each item to obtain a rough estimate of ATC for each item. Finally, a markup over estimated ATC is added to this fully allocated average total cost to arrive at a final price. The markup can vary from item to item depending on how sensitive unit sales are to price, a low markup for items that are relatively sensitive and a high markup for items that are relatively insensitive to price.

To make things even simpler, some retailers just ignore fixed costs and use the wholesale price paid to suppliers as the cost term. Indirectly, they incorporate coverage of fixed costs into the markup. Sometimes, a fixed amount is applied instead of a percentage. In the case of retail chains or franchises, the fixed amount might be determined by the central office to make price determination easy for store managers or franchisees. This practice is known as turnkey pricing. A more complicated variation of cost-plus pricing is activity-based pricing. Instead of using a fixed cost percentage across the board to allocate overhead, every activity is linked to resources it uses. For example, a product requiring refrigeration or freezer storage would be allocated a larger percentage than a product requiring only ordinary shelf storage.

Cost Plus a Markup Dependent on Price Elasticity of Demand

Through the markup, cost-plus pricing is influenced by the price elasticity of demand. Recall that the profit-maximizing price is equivalent to the principle of profit maximization, which is marginal revenue equals marginal cost. The profit-maximizing price was developed in terms of its relationship to marginal cost. Even when describing the practice of cost-plus pricing in terms of fully allocated cost, markup depends on the price elasticity of demand. In general, the profit-maximizing markup is lower when the unsigned price elasticity of demand for the product is greater, indicating greater sensitivity of unit sales to price.

Previously, the profit-maximizing price was stated with marginal cost in the numerator. As a practical approximation, the profit-maximizing price (P*) can be restated as

$$P^*=ATC/[1+(1/E_p)]$$

ATC is average total cost, and EP is price elasticity of demand. For example, suppose fully allocated average cost is $40 and the estimated price elasticity of demand is –2. The profit-maximizing price is

$$P^*=40/[1/1+(1/-2)]$$

$$P^*=40/[1/1+(-0.5)]$$

$$P^*=40/0.5$$

$$P^*=80$$

The profit-maximizing price is \$80. The profit-maximizing markup, therefore, is \$40, which is a markup of 100 percent over fully allocated average cost.

Now, suppose the fully allocated average cost is \$40 for another product, and its estimated price elasticity of demand is –5. The profit-maximizing price is

$P^*=40/[1+(1/-5)]$

$P^*=40/[1+[-0.2]$

$P^*=40/0.8$

$P^*=50$

The profit-maximizing price is \$50. The profit-maximizing markup, therefore, is \$10, which is a markup of 25 percent over fully allocated average cost. In the light of these two examples, the profit-maximizing markup is seen to vary inversely with unsigned price elasticity of demand. When the price elasticity of demand is –2, the optimal markup is 100 percent, but when it is –5, the optimal markup is only 25 percent.

Companies make costly attempts to estimate demand elasticity. To estimate relationships, some companies use statistics to analyze existing data on past prices, amounts sold, competitor prices, advertising outlays, and other factors. Data can be either longitudinal over time or cross-sectional over different locations at the same time. Proper statistical techniques require quantitative skill. Some companies use price experiments. Prices are systematically varied, and results are observed. Still other companies maintain consumer laboratories in which buyer behavior can be observed directly, particularly the relationship between price and amounts purchased. Still other companies conduct market experiments. Two different markets that are similar in terms of population, age distribution, ethnicity, income, and so forth provide the opportunity to set different prices for the same product in the two markers and collect data. Whether one method or another is used to develop information regarding the sensitivity of unit sales to price, firms apply a higher markup to products with unit sales that are less sensitive to price than to products with unit sales more sensitive to price. This observation makes sense. The more sensitive unit sales of a product are to its price, the smaller the markup. A large percentage markup would drive away a lot of business if unit sales are highly sensitive to price.

Grocery stores and other retailers commonly use some form of cost-plus pricing. Supermarkets illustrate cost-plus pricing. Generally, markups and profit margins on staples such as bread, milk, flour, rice, and soap are lower than on other items. To increase overall store profitability, many supermarkets have added delicatessen, bakery, and floral departments to the mix of products they sell. Items in these departments sell at higher profit margins. To accommodate the needs of such high profit margin activities, existing shelf space is reallocated from lower profit margin items, and overall store size is expanded. To the extent that unsigned price elasticity of demand is lower for products such as proprietary drugs and fresh vegetables than for products such as coffee or breakfast cereal, this system of pricing comes close to maximizing profits. In general, it seems likely that store managers attach high markups to products for which customers are not affected much by price and thus the unsigned price elasticity of demand is low. On the other hand, products for which customers are highly price conscious and thus for which unsigned price elasticity of demand is correspondingly high, store managers realize they must keep markups low. To do otherwise would be foolish since customers simply would go elsewhere.

TARGET RETURN ON INVESTMENT

Certain conditions are often found only in big business or market leaders with substantial control over price. Under such conditions, the markup can be set to achieve a target return on investment, a first cousin of cost-plus pricing. Under target return on investment pricing, management adopts and adheres to a rate of return on investment. This delimitated return is prorated for the number of units scheduled for production over the planning horizon. In equation form, target return on investment may be expressed variously. A usual form states that price is determined by variable costs per unit, fixed costs per unit, and a target return on capital, which can be expressed as

$$P = AVC_L + AVC_M + AVC_{MKT} + TFC/Q + \pi K/Q$$

P is price, AVC_L is labor cost per unit, AVC_M is material cost per unit, AVC_{MKT} is marketing cost per unit, TFC is total fixed or indirect costs, Q is scheduled volume, K is total gross operating assets, and π is targeted rate of return on investment. Target pricing is particularly suited for use in an industry where price leadership is prevalent. As costs increase, for example, the price leader in an industry might increase its price, which then is followed by other firms in the industry.

Twenty Large Industrial Companies

Pricing decisions and strategies are tied closely to the objectives of a business firm. In other words, pricing practices are driven to some extent by pricing objectives. Studies of pricing practices and objectives in U.S. industry have been conducted and reported, but the most widely read study on pricing objectives of major corporations was a survey conducted by Robert F. Lanzillotti. Although more than fifty years old, the study still has value. However, some of these large companies have merged or have been acquired by other companies, and some of these large companies no longer have the control over price that they had fifty years ago.

Lanzillotti based his study on interviews with executive officers of twenty large companies. The interviews were designed to determine each firm's principal and collateral pricing objectives. The survey disclosed four dominant pricing objectives: pricing to achieve a target return on investment, pricing to achieve a target share of the market, pricing to stabilize prices, and pricing to meet competition. The most common pricing objective found in the survey was pricing to achieve a target rate of return on investment, which was stated as a primary goal of ten companies and a collateral goal of another three. The range of target rates of return after taxes was from eight to twenty percent. Firms that stated a target return on investment as their primary objective were market share leaders in their respective industries and thus had market power to achieve targeted returns. Achieving a target rate of return is clearly a long-range objective since firms were concerned with the average rate of return. The actual return may exceed the target in some years and fall short in others. A summary of responses is given below in Table 7.1.

Table 7.1 Pricing Goals of Twenty Large Industrial Companies		
Company	**Principal Pricing Goal**	**Collateral Pricing Goals**
Alcoa	20% on investment (before taxes); higher on new products (about 10% effective rate after taxes)	"Promotive" policy on new products; and price stabilization
American Can	Maintenance of market share	"Meeting competition" (using cost of substitute product to determine price); and price stabilization
A&P	Increasing market share	Generally "promotive" (low-margin) policy
duPont	Target return on investment, no specific figure given	Charging what traffic will bear over long run; and maximum return for new products, "life-cycle" pricing
Esso (Standard Oil of N.J.)	"Fair-return" target, no specific figure given	Maintaining market share; and price stabilization
General Electric	20% on investment (after taxes); 7% on sales (after taxes)	Promotive policy on new products; and price stabilization on nationally advertised products
General Foods	33□% gross margin ("□ to make, □ to sell, and □ for profit"); expectation of realizing target only on new products	Full line of food products and novelties; and maintaining market share
General Motors	20% on investment (after taxes)	Maintaining market share
Goodyear	"Meeting competitors"	Maintain "position;" and price stabilization
Gulf	Follow price of most important marketer in each area	Maintain market share; and price stabilization
International Harvester	10% on investment (after taxes)	Market share: ceiling of "less than a dominant share of any market"
Johns-Manville	Return on investment greater than last 15-year average (about 15% after taxes; higher target for new products	Market share not greater than 20%; and price stabilization
Kennecott	Stabilization of prices	
Kroger	Maintaining market share	Target return of 20% on investment before taxes
National Steel	Matching the market, price follower	Increase market share
Sears, Roebuck	Increasing market share (8-10% regarded as satisfactory share)	Realization of traditional return on investment of 10-15% (after taxes); and generally promotive (low-margin) policy
Standard Oil (of Indiana)	Maintain market share	Stabilize prices; and target return on investment (none specified)
Swift	Maintenance of market share in livestock buying and meat packing	

Union Carbide	Target return on investment	Promotive policy on new products; "life cycle" pricing on chemicals generally
U.S. Steel	8% on investment (after taxes)	Target market share of 30%; stable price; and stable margin

Source: Robert F. Lanzillotti, "Pricing Objectives in Large Companies," American Economic Review, 48 (December 1958), pp. 924-927.

OTHER PRICING STRATEGIES

Usually, pricing strategies are driven by strategic objectives. Common strategic objectives begin with maximizing profit, which has been emphasized previously. However, profit is like a magnet in a market economy, attracting entrants and stimulating capacity expansion. Maximized profit thus is a carrier of risk. Some businesses measure performance in terms of overall revenues. In effect, their strategic objective is to achieve targeted business receipts, which is a surrogate for market share and profitability. Some businesses explicitly establish the strategic objective of maintaining or enhancing market share, which generally is linked in turn to profitability. An aggressive market share strategy generally involves attaining increased market share by lowering prices in the short term, leading to increased sales, which in the longer term leads to lower costs through economies of scale and experience and ultimately to greater profits due to increased volume and market share. Finally, some companies are content to meet competition. Prices are set reflect the typical industry price, perhaps with small occasional adjustments made to account for differentiated features of a company's specific product(s). Companies that adopt this strategic objective usually work backwards from price to cost rather than from cost to price so that target profit margins can be realized.

Several pricing strategies are used under certain circumstances. For example, pricing a new product is a circumstance that may lead to price strategies different from those applied to developed products. Even for product introductions, circumstances may differ. A new product may have no substitutes in the market, or it may have a number of substitutes. Pricing strategies may differ as markedly as circumstances. A number of circumstances and corresponding price strategies are considered below.

PENETRATION PRICING

When introducing a new product or entering a maturated product into a new geographic market, a firm might set a price for its product below the prevailing market price for incumbent competitive products. The relatively low price is intended to establish initial sales of a product and to seize a market share larger than could be expected from pricing at the market. This strategy is called penetration pricing, its name derived from market penetration.

Two conditions particularly favor penetration pricing as a pricing strategy. One, demand for the product is relatively price elastic. Thus, a relatively large number of customers can be attracted by a price slightly lower than the prevailing price. If successful, penetration pricing leads to large sales volume and perhaps lower unit cost. Therefore, the second condition is that a large sales volume is needed to realize the potential for economies of scale and learning so that lower unit cost per unit can be achieved. Once a firm's market penetration objective is achieved, strategies can be refocused on improving profitability, including plans to raise the price gradually over time. Penetration pricing often sacrifices short-run profitability for long-run profitability.

The most serious risk of deploying a penetration pricing strategy is that competing incumbent firms will follow suit by reducing their prices. If competitors reduce their prices correspondingly, this reaction nullifies any advantage sought through penetration pricing. If prices themselves are widely dispersed, the impact of this risk may be mitigated. Another risk is that the penetration price may negatively impact image, particularly if buyers associate quality with price. In other words, potential customers might take for granted that the product is low in quality because it is low in price.

Loss Leader Pricing

A variation on penetration pricing and also a common practice is loss leader pricing, which involves selling a particular product below cost. Retailers frequently single out a product that shoppers would be likely to purchase and then price it below cost to attract a large number of customers to their stores. Once in the store, customers also will purchase other products for which a hefty profit margin is realized. The point of loss leader pricing is to stimulate store traffic. Indeed, retailers often place a loss leader at the back of a store so that customers must walk past racks or shelves of other displayed items that have high profit margins. In this sense, a successful loss leader is actually a profit leader. After all, a retailer is concerned with the total profit from operations rather than the margin of profit or loss on any one product. When a retailer prices a product below cost, the expectation is that sales of all products and total profit will be increased.

Manufacturers typically fight against their brands being used as loss leaders because the practice can dilute brand image and give rise to complaints from other retailers who charge list price. Manufacturers have tried to restrain such intermediaries from loss leader pricing through retail or resale price maintenance, which sets a minimum price or price floor for their products. Retail price maintenance is the case of a manufacturer specifying a minimum price or downright setting a retail price for a product. The practice can be interpreted as a form of price fixing. Indeed, it often is called vertical price fixing. Under antitrust laws, resale price maintenance can be illegal where the effect is to lessen competition substantially or tend to create a monopoly. A way around such price floors is to offer customers a discount on any item sold. For example, Bed Bath & Beyond periodically mails customers a coupon for a twenty percent discount on any one item sold in its stores.

Perhaps more than a little apocryphal, whisper on the streets is that movie theaters make little if any profit on ticket sales alone. For the most part, ticket revenues are passed along to distributors, leaving theaters only a little to cover costs and make a profit. The larger part of their profit comes from sales of popcorn, candy, drinks, and other comestibles. Of course, popcorn is a highly effective vehicle for delivery of salt, which in turn produces a prodigious thirst that can be quenched at the venue only by theater drinks. In effect, this case is the equivalent of loss leader pricing. Theaters entice customers through a low price for tickets only to charge them a high price for their consumables.

PRICE SKIMMING

When a new product is introduced, pricing the product is both difficult and critical, especially if the product is a durable good with a relatively long useful life and thus purchased infrequently. The difficulty of pricing a new product arises from the paucity of sure and confident knowledge about demand for the product. If the price were set too low, some customers would be able to buy the product at a price below what they would have been willing to pay. Lost revenues and profits would be gone forever. Under such circumstances, many firms have adopted a strategy of price skimming, a reference to skimming the cream off the top. By analogy, price skimming is setting a high price when a product is introduced and gradually lowering the price subsequently. Often, price skimming is called riding down the demand curve since it involves selling as much as the seller can at a high price, then lowering price and selling as much as the seller can at that price, and so forth. The practice of price skimming, therefore, involves charging a relatively high price for a short time when an innovative or greatly improved product is launched into a market. The objective is to skim off customers who are willing to pay more to have the product sooner. Price is lowered later when sales to early adopters fizzle.

Over the years, DuPont has been a conspicuous practitioner of price skimming. With each of its innovations such as cellophane, nylon, Teflon, Kevlar, Freon, and so on, Du Pont estimates the highest price it can charge given comparative benefits of its new product. In particular, DuPont sets a high price that makes the new material barely worthwhile for some segments of the market to adopt. When sales of the new material slow, DuPont lowers price to reel in the next price-sensitive layer of buyers. In this way, DuPont skims a maximum amount of revenue from various market segments.

Consider the book market for fiction. When a James Patterson, Mary Higgins Clark, or W.E.B. Griffin novel first appears in hardback, the price is high, about $35 or so. The physical cost of paper, printing, and binding might be as much as $3 or so. The remaining $32 or so is royalty to the author, overhead expense for the staff of editors, proofreaders, publicists, and so forth, and profit for the publisher. A year afterwards when hardback sales have slowed, the novel is published in paperback selling at a price of $8 or $9. The cost of paper, printing, and binding is a little lower because cheaper paper is used and binding is glue rather than stitching. Fixed costs have been covered when the hardback book was printed and sold. Readers who cannot wait buy the hardback at $35. These readers who cannot wait are the equivalent of early adopters. When sales wane after one year in hardback, the novel is published in paperback and purchased by other price-sensitive readers who are enticed by the lower price of $8 or $9. Book publishing is a classic example of price skimming.

There are several advantages of price skimming. When highly innovative products are rolled out, research and development costs are likely to be high. In addition, the costs of introducing products through advertising and promotion are likely to be high. In such cases, the practice of price skimming allows a return on the setup costs. By charging a high price initially, a company can build an image of high quality for the product. Charging a high price initially also allows a company the option of reducing the price when the threat of competition arises. By contrast, a lower initial price would be difficult to increase without the risk of losing sales volume.

Certain conditions temper the zeal for market skimming. First, the innovativeness, quality, or image of the product must support the higher price, and enough buyers must want the product at that price to make the strategy worthwhile. Second, the unit cost of producing a relatively small volume must not be so high that it more than cancels the advantage of charging a higher price. Finally, competitors must not be able to enter the market immediately and undercut the higher price.

PRESTIGE PRICING

Some products are priced to enhance the perception of quality and exclusivity. In other words, high prices are set to attract customers seeking prestige from ownership, use, or display of a product. Prestige pricing is the practice of charging a high price with the deliberate intent to limit the number of potential buyers. Unlike price skimming, prestige pricing involves a high price for a product during its entire sales cycle. The point of prestige pricing is to set such a high price that only a few buyers can afford the product, and then ownership, use, or display of the product conveys an aloof sense of exclusivity. This practice has been the strategy of Rolex. Other watches made from similar high quality materials are priced well below Rolex. Mercedes and BMW are high-priced automobiles and certainly have succeeded in attracting a loyal, prestige-oriented clientele. Driving either model makes a statement, and owning or leasing either model carries with it a sense of exclusivity. Other companies based on prestige pricing and thus offer prestige brands are Cartier, Ferragamo, Gucci, Hermes, Lalique, Louis Vuitton, Mont-Blanc, Patek Philippe, Tiffany, and Versace. Showing off any genuine products with such prestige branding is an ostentatious exhibit of elitism meant to convey a sense of separation from ordinary, average, common, run-of-the-mill people as well as to imply an entitlement to be viewed and treated as superior.

PRICE LINING

Ordinarily, firms set prices hoping to maximize profits from sales of their products. The product itself and particular quality characteristics of the product already are determined and established. The process goes from product design to price. In some circumstances, this process is reversed. A price point may be specified, and the firm then attempts to design and produce a product with quality characteristics that will allow it to be competitive with other products in the same price range. Given a price constraint within a certain range, the firm attempts to develop a product with a set of quality characteristics that will lead to a competitive product at that price point.

This practice is called price lining, which technically refers to setting a price point and then developing a product that is competitive and can be sold profitably at that price. Instead of deciding first on the type of product to produce and then on the price to charge, the order is reversed. Price lining is not inconsistent with the notion of profit maximization based on cost-plus pricing. Price lining simply stands cost-plus pricing on its head. For example, reconsider target return on investment. Instead of price as the end result of design, production, and marketing, price is the starting point with design, production, and marketing afterwards.

The automobile industry has product lines and corresponding price points that have been established over time. In the case of Ford, for example, the Ford brand itself is meant to be the basic car with broad appeal. The Lincoln brand is aimed at the wealthiest or most prestige-conscious group of customers. Within the Ford and Lincoln brands are a number of lines. Within the Ford brand, for example, the economy line is the Focus, which competes with economy lines of other U.S. and foreign automakers. The mid-price product line includes the Fusion and Taurus. The sporty line is the Mustang. In each of these lines, Ford competes with similar cars made by General Motors and Chrysler as well as foreign manufacturers. Each line in the Ford model group is priced closely with the price of similar-sized GM and Chrysler vehicles. The objective of each automaker is to create a vehicle in that price and model range. If price must be increased significantly above competitive makes, the product will not sell well.

Until acquired by R.J. Reynolds in 1982, Heublein was the American producer and distributor of Smirnoff, the best selling vodka by far. In the 1960s, Smirnoff was the target of another brand, Wolfschmidt. Smirnoff and Wolfschmidt were dominant brands at the time. The price of Wolfschmidt was reduced to twelve dollars per case, one dollar per bottle. Sales of Wolfschmidt soared. Heublein managers considered strategies to counter and thwart the marketing gambit by Wolfschmidt. Hublein could lower the price of Smirnoff to match the price of Wolfschmidt and thus protect market share. Hublein could keep the price of Smirnoff unchanged and increase advertising and promotion outlays. Hublein could keep the price of Smirnoff and advertising outlays unchanged and lose market share. Any one of the three strategies would lead to lower profits. Instead, Heublein turned to still another strategy. Heublein raised the price of Smirnoff! The company then introduced a new brand, Relska, to compete directly with Wolfschmidt. Furthermore, Heublein introduced another brand, Popov, priced lower than Wolfschmidt. The scheme bracketed Wolfschmidt and protected Hublein's flanks, good strategy in business and in war. Smirnoff remained the leader in vodka sales. Wolfschmidt never recovered.

Essentially, this overall strategy was price lining. The price-lining strategy positioned Smirnoff as Hublein's premium brand of vodka and thus commanded a premium price. Not only that, Heublein introduced Relska to compete at the prevailing price point in the middle market and Popov to compete at the prevailing price point in the economy market. This clever strategy led to a large increase in overall profits. The irony is that Heublein's three brands were close in taste and manufacturing costs. Managers at Heublein knew that the price of a product often signals its quality. Using price as a signal, Heublein sold roughly the same product at three different quality positions and associated price points. In other words, the company sold practically the same product at three different price points.

PRICE DISCRIMINATION

Pricing and markup decisions are more complex when a firm sells products in a number of different markets. In dealing with multiple markets or several classes of customers, there is the potential for enhancing profits by applying different markups and charging different prices in each market or to each class of customer. Such market segmentation is common. Since such practices are so widespread, a deep understanding of these pricing practices is an important aspect of understanding business. The generic term for these pricing practices and the various forms in which they are found is price discrimination. Taken literally, price discrimination is the practice of setting different prices for the same product, whether good or service. Price discrimination is practiced whenever different classes of customers are charged different prices for the same product. Although discrimination of any kind carries a certain negative connotation, price discrimination is merely a technical term meaning price differentiation. By whatever name, price discrimination is evident whenever customers are charged different prices or when price differences are not proportional to cost differences.

To elaborate still further, price discrimination refers to charging different prices for different quantities of a product, different prices at different times, different prices to different customer groups, or different prices in different markets, when these price differences are not grounded on cost differences. The incentive is that a firm can increase its profits for a given volume of sales by practicing price discrimination. Examples of price discrimination are power companies that charge lower prices per kilowatt hour of electricity to industrial users than to residential users; domestic companies that charge lower or higher prices abroad than at home for various products and services, ranging from books to medicines and leaded crystal; entertainment venues that charge lower prices for afternoons than for evening performances of movies and theatrical plays; hotels that charge lower room rates for conventioneers; and various businesses that charge lower prices for senior citizens through discounts for prescription medications, hotel reservations, and restaurant meals. These examples are merely illustrative of the pervasiveness of price discrimination in the U.S. economy. However, price differences based on cost differences in supplying a product or service in different quantities, at different times, to different customer groups, or in different markets are not forms of price discrimination. The practice of price discrimination involves price differences without any underlying cost differences.

Price discrimination is not a *per se* violation of any U.S. law, including antitrust laws. Almost all price discrimination is legal. Illegal cases of price discrimination are instances "where the effect of such discrimination may be to substantially lessen competition or tend to create a monopoly in any line of commerce." This language is quoted from the Clayton Act of 1914. The Robinson-Patman Act, enacted in 1936, amended the Clayton Act. Robinson-Patman added language, "or to injure, destroy, or prevent competition." Technically, Robinson-Patman dealt with price differences rather than price discrimination. Nevertheless, Robinson-Patman was aimed at practices that allowed large chain stores to purchase items at lower cost than smaller retailers. Since the 1960s, the Federal Trade Commission and Department of Justice have not enforced Robinson-Patman. Injured businesses can bring private lawsuits, but such litigation is costly, thus making such lawsuits unlikely.

Feasibility and Profitability Conditions for Price Discrimination

A seller who sets discriminatory price differences as a matter of pricing policy is discriminating systematically. To do so, a firm must have enough market power to establish and maintain price differences. The purpose of systematic discrimination is to increase profits from what the seller otherwise would make if all of its product were sold at one price. Systematic price discrimination means that some customers will pay higher prices than others. Consequently, any kind of systematic price discrimination has one important prerequisite. Customers must be prevented from dealing with one another. Otherwise, there will be arbitrage, meaning that buyers who pay the higher price would buy the product from a buyer who paid the lower price.

Ordinarily, three conditions are met for a firm to practice price discrimination. Two conditions deal with the feasibility of price discrimination. However, these feasibility conditions are satisfied in the case of many businesses, but these businesses still do not discriminate systematically even though systematic price discrimination is feasible. When price discrimination is feasible but not practiced, the reason usually is that price discrimination is no more profitable than charging the same price to all customers, at all times, for all quantities, and in all markets. The third condition deals with profitability.

For price discrimination to be feasible, two conditions must be satisfied. First, the firm must have some control over price of the product. Some firms have no control over the price of the product they sell and thus are price takers. Therefore, these price taker firms cannot practice price discrimination because they have no control over price. Therefore, the seller must be a price setter. Second, the firm must be able to separate buyers into two or more market segments without any significant problem of resale of the product between market segments. In other words, the market for a product must be separable into two or more submarkets or market segments with no problem of resale from the low price segment to the high price segment.

A market segment is a fragment of the overall market. Quantities of the product, times when the product is used, or customer classes for the product must be separable. If the market is truly segmented along any of these lines, arbitrage must be unlikely. Otherwise, individuals or firms will purchase the product where or when it is priced low and resell it where or when the product is priced high, thereby undermining a firm's effort to charge different prices for the same product. It almost goes without saying that the cost of separating and policing market segments must not exceed extra revenue derived from price discrimination. In addition, the practice must not breed customer resentment and ill will.

The boundary that is established to keep segments separate is called the rate fence. In the case of electricity, natural gas, and water consumption, industrial, commercial, and residential premises keep the markets separate. Transportation costs and trade restrictions keep domestic and foreign markets separate. In the case of services, markets are separated naturally by the fact that most services cannot be transferred or resold to other people easily if at all. Movie entertainment enjoyed by a child cannot be resold and used by an adult. Prescriptions filled for senior citizens cannot be resold legally or used legally by junior citizens. However, if jewelers deeply discounted diamonds to senior citizens, these elderly people could buy diamonds at the discounted price charged by jewelers and then resell the diamonds below the price charged by jewelers to other buyers. Put differently, if jewelers deeply discounted diamonds to senior citizens, every young man in love would ask his grandmother to go to the jewelry store to buy an engagement ring. If resale of a product cannot be prevented, the seller of the product is not likely to be able to charge a higher price to certain buyers.

When a seller has some degree of power over price of a product and the market for the product can be segmented without the problem of resale, price discrimination is feasible. A third condition must be satisfied. Price discrimination must be more profitable than a uniform price across all customers. The profitability condition is that the price elasticity of demand must differ for groups of buyers separated into submarkets or market segments. To elaborate, the price elasticity of demand for the product must differ for different quantities of the product, for different times, for different customer classes, or for different geographic markets. If the price elasticity of demand is the same for different quantities, times, customers, and market segments, the firm would not be able to increase its profits by practicing price discrimination.

Once again, recall the profit-maximizing price. This price can be expressed in terms of marginal cost or average total cost in the numerator. To simplify, consider the profit-maximizing price (P^*) with marginal cost in the numerator, which is

$$P^*=[MC/1+(1/E_p)]$$

MC is marginal cost, and E_p is price elasticity of demand. Suppose that marginal cost is \$40 and that, for one age group or for one geographic market, the price elasticity of demand is –2. By substitution, the profit-maximizing price is

P*=[40/1+1/−2)]

P*=[40/1−0.5]

P*=40/0.5

P*=80

The profit-maximizing price is $80. The markup ($40) over marginal cost is 100%. On the other hand, suppose that, for another age group or geographic market, the price elasticity of demand is −5. By substitution, the profit-maximizing price is

P*=[40/1+1/−5)]

P*=[40/1−0.2]

P*=40/0.8

P*=50

The profit-maximizing price is $50. The markup ($10) over marginal cost is 25%.

This outcome is the general case. When price discrimination is feasible and profitable, a higher price will be charged in market segments in which demand is less price elastic, and a lower price will be charged in market segments for which demand is more price elastic. For example, senior citizens are known to be far more price sensitive than younger cohorts. Consequently, where or when feasible, senior citizens pay a lower price, and younger cohorts pay a higher price.

Airlines take price discrimination to an extreme. Airlines charge different fares to passengers on the same flight depending on seating class, time, day, season, passenger's company, passenger's past business, passenger's status, and more. This systematic price discrimination is called yield management, a practice meant to realize as much revenue as possible in filling plane seats. Yield management also is practiced by other businesses such as hotels.

Coupons can be used for this purpose. Producers of consumer goods such as food and household products often distribute coupons through mail, print media, and on-line sites. These coupons enable the bearer to buy the firm's product at a discount. Coupon users tend to have less brand loyalty than other buyers. Evidence indicates that coupon users also are more sensitive to price than nonusers. In the case of cake mix, for example, the price elasticity of demand has been reported to be about −0.43 for coupon users but only about −0.21 for nonusers. For cat food, the price elasticity of demand has been estimated at about −1.13 for coupon users but only about −0.49 for nonusers.[97] In general, these studies show that coupon users are about twice as price sensitive than nonusers. By issuing coupons, firms selling these and other products divide their customers into two groups, those who bother to use coupons and those who do not. Coupon users are charged a lower price than coupon nonusers.

Financial aid policies of colleges and universities have changed the character of tuition practices. Private schools in particular have made an art if not a science of price discrimination. Schools post a list price called tuition, which is set far above what most people can or will pay and then offer varying discounts called financial aid so that each customer is charged what the traffic will bear. This practice explains why financial aid recipients often come from families most Americans hardly regard as needy and sometimes

---

97   See C. Narasimhan, "A Price Discrimination Theory of Coupons," *Marketing Science* (Spring 1984).

come from families most Americans regard as affluent. Academic institutions engage in this price discrimination as an accepted norm.

In addition to the kind of financial aid that is simply a paper discount called a scholarship, some financial aid involves money in the form of federal government grants and student loans. Unfortunately, these federal government programs almost certainly guarantee that tuition will rise to unaffordable levels. At the center of federal government aid formulas is an expected family contribution. Consequently, even a small college such as St. Olaf College in Northfield, Minnesota, could lose millions of dollars annually in federal aid if it kept tuition affordable. Federal subsidies and virtual exemption from antitrust laws have resulted in skyrocketing tuition, collusion, and price discrimination.[98]

TRANSFER PRICING

Large firms typically are organized into semiautonomous operating divisions. Each division has both responsibility and authority for making operating decisions. A transfer price is the administrative price charged by one part of a company for products it provides to another part of the same company. In this way, each division's contribution to profit or loss can be determined. This divisional contribution to profit or loss can be used to evaluate divisions and division managers based on performance. Since these transfer prices are set within an organization, they are administratively controlled rather than determined by any market mechanism.

Despite obvious internal business advantages, transfer pricing has the potential to create problems. The price at which each intermediate product is transferred from the selling to the buying division affects the imputed revenues of the selling division and the imputed costs of the buying division. A tension can develop between selling divisions and buying divisions. The selling division wants a high transfer price, whereas the buying division wants a low transfer price. Some method must be established to resolve disputes and to relax this tension. Another problem arises due to tax considerations. When different company operations are taxed at different rates because of different tax jurisdictions, the transfer price may book income in a less heavily taxed jurisdiction. Again, some method must be established to determine transfer prices so that legal requirements regarding taxation are satisfied.

To summarize, a company often is organized into divisions that produce and then transfer products to other divisions. An automobile manufacturer often assigns production of an engine to one division, which the division supplies to an assembly division of the same company. Crude oil is passed from the production operations of an integrated oil company to its refining operations. In turn, its refining operations may deal with a marketing division, and both may buy and sell refined products outside the company. A phosphate mining division transfers its product to a fertilizer division. In all of these cases, a transfer price is the internally controlled price at which one company division transfers its products to another division for further handling or processing and eventual sale. Some method must be established to determine these transfer prices, and the method must satisfy both business objectives and legal requirements.

Some transfer pricing methods are fairly common. However, the methods implemented to determine transfer prices vary with business conditions and business circumstances. In some circumstances, the product of a division can be priced by reference to the market price for a comparable product. The comparable uncontrolled price method can be used to determine the transfer price based on the market

---

98   See Gary Putka, "Ivy League Discussions on Finances Extended to Tuition and Salaries," *Wall Street Journal* (May 8, 1992), pp. A$_1$, A4.

price for a similar, perhaps equivalent product. For example, a sulfur mining company might sell some of its product on the open market and transfer some of its product to a company-owned fertilizer division. The open market price is a comparable uncontrolled price. The cost-plus method commonly used to price finished products is also a transfer price method. An appropriate markup on cost incurred by the selling division is used to determine the transfer price. The markup could be based on a comparable uncontrolled price or based on the markup of the final finished product. Variations of this approach include cost plus a fixed fee, cost plus a fixed percentage of cost, full cost plus a markup, or even limiting the transfer price to variable cost or marginal cost. If an external market for the intermediate product is available, then the market price can be used as the transfer price.

Transfer Pricing by Transnational Corporations

Transfer prices have become a daunting challenge in dealing with multinational companies that make parts, components, or materials in one country and assemble those parts, components, or materials in another country. In this context, transfer price is reference to a price charged for goods or services transported between subsidiaries of a multinational corporation, which can be a tempting enticement to set transfer prices to minimize taxes paid to different jurisdictions. By artificially overpricing intermediate products shipped to a semiautonomous division of the firm in a high-tax nation, a multinational corporation can minimize its tax bill and increase its profits. In the same way, underpricing products shipped from the division in the high-tax nation, a multinational corporation can minimize its tax bill and increase its profits.

Most countries regulate transfer prices and enforce tax laws based on the arm's length principle defined in the OECD (Organization for Economic Cooperation and Development) Transfer Pricing Guidelines for Multinational Enterprises and Tax Administration. In the United States, transactions between related or affiliated parties that are reported for tax purposes are governed by the Internal Revenue Service Code. For tax purposes in the United States and in other developed countries of the world, an arm's length test is applied. An arm's-length transaction is an exchange between two unrelated parties not in collusion with each other. In the specific case of transfer pricing by transnational corporations, arm's-length is the price an unrelated party would pay for the products under the same circumstances. For transnational corporations, therefore, an arm's length transaction is a transaction that is conducted as if the divisions or subsidiaries are unrelated.

The arm's length test provides general guidance only and is consequently vague. As a result, transnational corporations have leeway in setting transfer prices to minimize their overall taxes and maximize their profits. However, the leeway involves risk that transfer prices do not meet legal requirements. Consequently, most companies enter into an Advance Pricing Agreement (APA) with tax authorities. An APA is an agreement between a company and the appropriate tax authority that future transactions will be conducted at the agreement price, which is accepted as the arm's length price for a designated time. A retroactive APA can be used to reduce tax exposure in past years, but an APA is used primarily to avoid any future risk of income adjustments that could result in large tax liabilities. The intent of an APA is to avoid transfer price disputes. Such disputes continue nonetheless.[99]

---

99 See "I.R.S. Investigating Foreign Companies for Tax Cheating," *New York Times* (February 10, 1990), p. 1; "Big Japan Concern Reaches an Accord on Paying U.S. Tax," *New York Times* (November 11, 1992), p. 1; and "Why Do Foreign Companies Report such Low Profits on Their U.S. Operations?" *Wall Street Journal* (November 2, 1994), p. A$_1$.

The U.S. Internal Revenue Service has investigated many U.S. subsidiaries of foreign firms on suspicions that they have underpaid U.S. corporate income taxes. For example, the IRS charged Toyota with systematically overcharging its U.S. subsidiary for most of the vehicles and parts sold in the United States. The effect of these actions was to transfer profits that would have been booked and taxed in the United States rather than in Japan. Of course, Toyota denied any wrongdoing. However, Toyota agreed to pay the IRS about $1 billion in settlement of these claims. The U.S. subsidiary of Yamaha paid only $5,272 in taxes in the early 1980s, whereas IRS accountants claim that proper accounting of transfer prices would have resulted in $127 million in taxes.[100] More recently GlaxcoSmithKline announced on 11 September 2006 that the company had settled a transfer price dispute with the I.R.S., agreeing to pay more than $3 billion in taxes related to an assessed income adjustment due to improper transfer pricing.

On the dark side of the global recession beginning in the late 2000s, international tax authorities in previously tax-friendly countries such as China and India looked to extract more revenues from U.S. transnational corporations. Their probes targeted transfer pricing of items between subsidiaries and subsequent allocation of taxable income among various countries. Larry Harding, CEO of High Street Partners, says transfer pricing is "the lowest-hanging fruit, because it's very subjective and most companies don't have adequate documentation to back up their assertions."[101] Garry Stone, global transfer pricing leader for PricewaterhouseCoopers, underscored the breadth and depth of the issue when he said, "There's an explosion of transfer-pricing controversies out there."[102]

The Internal Revenue Service continues to be aggressive in pursuing transfer price cases. The IRS went to court to force Xilinx, a semiconductor company, to allocate stock option expenses to its Irish subsidiary. The result boosted the company's U.S. tax bill by about $40 million. Other high tech companies such as Apple, Cisco Systems, and Cadence Design Systems followed suit and coughed up additional taxes. One metric of IRS aggression is number of employees on its international staff. The IRS added twelve hundred people to its international staff in 2009, and the 2010 budget called for another eight hundred.[103]

Transfer pricing continues to be one of the most critical issues facing transnational companies. Clearly, the Internal Revenue Service and other equivalent tax authorities worldwide are intensifying their scrutiny of how corporations allocate income and expenses among related entities abroad because of the potential to shift income inappropriately to lower tax reductions. As transfer pricing examinations increase, tax authorities are increasingly prone to impose adjustments and penalties.

Ernst & Young's *Global Transfer Pricing Survey 2007-2008* showed that transfer pricing continues to be the greatest international tax issue to transnational companies. The report covered 850 transnational enterprises in twenty-four countries. Key findings of the report showed that forty percent of respondents identified transfer pricing as their most important tax issue; fifty-two percent of respondents had undergone a transfer pricing review since 2003, with twenty-seven percent resulting in adjustments by tax authorities; eighty-seven percent of respondents considered transfer pricing a risk issue in relation to managing financial statement risk; and sixty-five percent of respondents from parent transnational

---

100   See L. Martz, "The Corporate Shell Game," *Newsweek*, (April 15, 1991), pp. 48-49.

101   Alix Stuart, "Transfer Pricing: A World of Pain," *CFO* (September 2009), p. 20.

102   *Ibid.*

103   *Ibid.*

enterprises believed transfer pricing documentation is more important today than two years ago, but only one-third of multinational enterprises prepared transfer pricing documentation on a concurrent globally coordinated basis.

Amid such international scrutiny, companies sense urgency to minimize their audit exposure. To mitigate such exposure, transnational enterprises are turning to transfer pricing specialists to manage the development of strategies for transfer pricing method, compliance, and audit defense. Consequently, demand is escalating for expertise in international taxation, particularly international transfer pricing and advance pricing agreements. Nowadays, a transfer price specialist can look forward to a rewarding career.

PRACTICE QUESTIONS

1. Suppose management of a business uses cost-plus pricing for its only product. Over the normal or standard volume of output, fully allocated average cost is practically the same, $120. The price elasticity of demand for the product has been estimated to be –2. What price should be charged if profit is to be maximized?

2. Suppose management of a business uses cost-plus pricing for its only product. Fully allocated cost is $30. The price elasticity of demand for the product has been estimated as –1.5. To maximize profit, what should the percentage markup be? What if the price elasticity of demand for the product is estimated as –3?

3. A survey by Robert F. Lanzillotti indicated four dominant pricing objectives among twenty large corporations. What was the most common pricing objective? How can this most common pricing objective be reconciled with pricing to maximize profit?

4. Briefly explain each of the following pricing practices: (1) cost-plus pricing, (2) penetration pricing, (3) loss leader pricing, (4) predatory pricing, and (5) limit pricing.

5. 5. Certain conditions favor penetration pricing. What are these conditions and how do they foster the practice of penetration pricing?

6. What are the two conditions necessary to make price discrimination feasible? Even if feasible, a business may not practice price discrimination. Why not?

7. What are the two feasibility conditions for price discrimination? Suppose management of a business determine that these feasibility conditions are met with respect to its basic product. In addition, management has estimated the price elasticity of demand for its basic product in two widely separated market segments. In one market segment in the Southeast, the price elasticity of demand is –2.4, and for another market segment in the Northwest, it is –4.8. If management wants to make the most profit from production and sale of its basic product, should management practice price discrimination by charging a higher price in one market segment and a lower price in the other market segment? If so, in which market segment should the higher price be charged?

8. Explain the need for transfer prices in a multidivisional firm and the tensions that can develop among division managers.

9. Why does transfer pricing policy give rise to the need for application of an "arm's length test" to multinational corporations?

PRACTICE QUESTIONS *(AND ANSWERS)*

1. Suppose management of a business uses cost-plus pricing for its only product. Over the normal or standard volume of output, fully allocated average cost is practically the same, $120. The price elasticity of demand for the product has been estimated to be –2. What price should be charged if profit is to be maximized?

The profit-maximizing price is

$P^* = ATC/[1+(1/E_p)]$

By substitution

$P^* = 120/[1+(1/{-}2)]$

$P^* = 120/[1{-}0.5]$

$P^* = 120/0.5$

$P^* = 240$

The profit-maximizing price is $240.

2. Suppose management of a business uses cost-plus pricing for its only product. Fully allocated cost is $30. The price elasticity of demand for the product has been estimated as –1.5. To maximize profit, what should the percentage markup be? What if the price elasticity of demand for the product is estimated as –3?

The profit-maximizing price is

$P^* = ATC/[1+(1/EP)]$

If fully allocated cost is $30 and $E_p = {-}1.5$,

$P^* = 30/[1+(1/{-}1.5)]$

$P^* = 30/[1+({-}0.67)]$

$P^* = 30/0.33$

$P^* = 90$

The profit-maximizing price is $90, and the markup is 200% over cost. If EP=–3,

$P^* = 30/[1+(1/{-}3)]$

$P^* = 30/[1+({-}0.33)]$

$P^* = 30/0.67$

$P^* = 45$

The profit-maximizing price is $45, and the markup is 50%.

3. A survey by Robert F. Lanzillotti indicated four dominant pricing objectives among twenty large corporations. What was the most common pricing objective? How can this most common pricing objective be reconciled with pricing to maximize profit?

The most common pricing objective was pricing to achieve a target rate of return on invested capital. The four dominant pricing objectives, including the most common one, are not inconsistent with profit maximization. The pricing objectives are basically intended to promote progress toward achieving the ultimate objective of maximum profit.

4. Briefly explain each of the following pricing practices: (1) cost-plus pricing, (2) penetration pricing, (3) loss leader pricing, (4) predatory pricing, and (5) limit pricing.

(1) Cost-plus pricing refers to setting the price of a product equal to the average variable cost (or fully allocated average total cost) of its production plus a markup. (2) Penetration pricing refers to setting the price of a product below the price(s) charged by rival firms that sell the same or a similar product, with the intent of establishing or increasing market share. (3) Loss leader pricing refers to setting the price of one product below its cost to attract customers who not only purchase the product on sale but also other products at their regular price. (4) Predatory pricing refers to the practice of a financially strong firm setting a price that is so low that it drives financially weaker firms out of business. (5) Limit pricing refers to setting price below the minimum average variable cost of a new firm that considers entry to an industry, with the intent of discouraging these new firms from entering the industry.

5. Certain conditions favor penetration pricing. What are these conditions and how do they foster the practice of penetration pricing?

Two conditions particularly favor penetration pricing as a pricing strategy. One, demand is relatively price elastic, and thus a relatively large number of customers can be attracted by a lower price. Two, an increase in sales volume is needed to realize the potential for economies of scale and learning so that lower costs per unit of output can be achieved.

6. What are the two conditions necessary to make price discrimination feasible? Even if feasible, a business may not practice price discrimination. Why not?

Two conditions are necessary for successful price discrimination (1) some degree of control over price and (2) market segmentation with no possibility of resale between segmented markets. Even if these two conditions are met, practicing price discrimination may not be any more profitable than not practicing price discrimination. To be more profitable, the price elasticity of demand in the market segments must be different.

7. What are the two feasibility conditions for price discrimination? Suppose management of a business determine that these feasibility conditions are met with respect to its basic product. In addition, management has estimated the price elasticity of demand for its basic product in two widely separated market segments. In one market segment in the Southeast, the price elasticity of demand is –2.4, and for another market segment in the Northwest, it is –4.8. If management wants to make the most profit from production and sale of its basic product, should management practice price discrimination by charging a higher price in one market segment and a lower price in the other market segment? If so, in which market segment should the higher price be charged?

Two conditions are necessary for successful price discrimination (1) some degree of control over price and (2) market segmentation with no possibility of resale between segmented markets. The profitability condition is that the price elasticity of demand must be different for segmented markets. This condition is met, and price discrimination is more profitable than price uniformity. The higher price should be charged in the market segment in which unsigned price elasticity of demand is lower, which is the Southeast, and the lower price should be charged in the market segment in which unsigned price elasticity of demand is higher, which is the Northwest.

8. Explain the need for transfer prices in a multidivisional firm and the tensions that can develop among division managers.

Often, a company is organized into divisions that sell products to each other. Prices are required or implied in all transactions between divisions. A transfer price is the price at which one operating division transfers its product(s) to another division for further handling or processing and eventual sale. Transfer prices are important when decisions are decentralized and division managers are encouraged to maximize divisional profits. One division can increase its profits at the expense of another division by increasing the transfer price at which it sells or forcing down the transfer price at which it buys. In other words, the price at which each intermediate product is transferred from the selling to the buying division affects the revenues of the selling division and the costs of the buying division. Understandably, determination of the transfer price can be contentious between the selling and buying divisions, and an ongoing tension between them is ordinary.

9. Why does transfer pricing policy give rise to the need for application of an "arm's length test" to multinational corporations?

When an enterprise operates across national borders, additional profit opportunities arise because of different rates of corporate taxes in different countries. By artificially overpricing intermediate products shipped to a division of the firm in a higher-tax nation and underpricing products shipped from the division in the high-tax nation, a multinational corporation can minimize its tax bill and increase its profits. Governments of high-tax countries seek to minimize the loss of tax and customs revenues resulting from transfer pricing by applying an "arm's length" test. Arm's-length is the price an unrelated party would pay for the products under the same circumstances. This test provides general guidance only and is vague on many issues. As a result, multinational corporations have great leeway in setting transfer prices to minimize their overall taxes and maximize profits.

8. Integration and Outsourcing

BUSINESS BOUNDARIES

In conversational usage, the term "strategy" is broad, generally meaning something roughly equivalent to plan. In this sense, strategy is just a method or scheme worked out beforehand to accomplish an objective. Even in this ordinary usage, strategy has two important elements. Strategy presumes an objective, and strategy is something worked out beforehand. In military usage, strategy has the same meaning. Strategy means positioning one's own forces advantageously prior to actual engagement with the enemy. In a looser military sense, strategy and tactics are relative terms referring, respectively, to large-scale and small-scale military operations. Strategy is the general scheme for conduct of a war, tactics the planning and execution of means to achieve strategic objectives.

In business, strategy is concerned with big issues. One big issue is the boundaries of a business. In any context, boundaries indicate limits, and business firms must deal strategically with the fundamental issue of what its limits are. An offshore sulfur mining operation that has four hundred men and women on site at any given time must decide whether to use employees to provide food service or engage a company such as Aramark to provide food service. A large company must decide whether to use employees to provide custodial services for its corporate headquarters or contract with a company such as ServiceMaster to provide these custodial services. An automobile manufacturer must decide whether to make its own antilock braking systems or buy antilock braking systems from a company such as LucasVarity. All of these decisions deal with the fundamental issue of what a firm itself chooses to do and what a firm decides not to do. In turn, all of these decisions deal with limits, which is to say boundaries.

A firm's boundaries demarcate what the firm does itself and, for that matter, what the firm does not do. In business, boundaries are delineated by horizontal and vertical limits. A firm's horizontal boundaries deal with the scope and volume of products produced and sold. No firm produces or sells everything or produces or sells anything in infinite amount. Every firm has its limits regarding what it produces and the amounts produced. A firm's vertical boundaries draw a line that separates business activities and business functions a firm itself performs from activities and functions the firm depends on external market specialty firms to perform for it. In the latter case, a firm purchases parts, components, materials, products, or services from these specialist firms. For example, the Ford Motor Company can make all of the parts and components needed for each of its models. On the other hand, Ford can buy some of these parts and components from Bosch, LucasVarity, or CTS, merely three of numerous manufacturers that specialize in production of automobile parts, components, and materials. Incidentally, CTS was the manufacturer of the faulty accelerator assembly that resulted in the 2009 Toyota recall of vehicles subject to sudden unintended acceleration. General Motors makes its own antilock braking systems, whereas Ford buys antilock braking systems. This make-or-buy decision is one of the important strategic decisions taken by businesses.

THE VERTICAL CHAIN

Production of any good or provision of any service is a process usually requiring a wide and deep range and sequence of activities. The process can be imagined as beginning with acquisition of resources such as raw materials and then continuing with a sequence of activities such as making or buying parts, assembly, warehousing, marketing, and eventually distribution and sale of finished products. From the starting line to the finish line, this successive sequence of any number of activities or functions is known as the vertical chain. In this business language, chain is contemplated in the context of series. In general, series means a number of objects or events arranged or coming one after the other in succession. Seen in the light of this context, chain suggests a series of things closely linked or connected such as the chain of command or the chain of evidence.

One of the fundamental issues and central decisions in business strategy is how to organize the vertical chain. A firm might decide strategically to extend its limits along the vertical chain to encompass almost every activity and function. On the other hand, a firm might decide to impose limits that circumscribe only a few activities or functions along the vertical chain and thus use the market to do everything else. In any event, vertical boundaries can be viewed as limits to what a firm itself does along the vertical chain. The decision to limit itself to doing some but not all activities along the vertical chain is a decision to rely on other businesses to do those activities or functions on the vertical chain not performed by the firm itself.

Consider Figure 8.1, which illustrates a vertical chain. The vertical chain depicts a sequence of functions and activities that begins with raw materials and continues with inbound logistics, warehousing, intermediate processing, transportation, warehousing, final assembly, outbound logistics, warehousing, delivery, and sales. The overall vertical chain is supported by services such as accounting, finance, human resource management, marketing, sales, and other support services. Some of these support services might be performed by the firm itself and thus would fall within limits of the firm. Other support services might be performed through outsourcing to specialty firms and thus would fall outside limits of the firm.

In the nineteenth century, the vertical chain typically was organized through intermediaries such as factors, agents, and brokers. In this way, the typical firm was extremely limited in terms of its vertical boundaries. In manufacturing, for example, firms were demarcated by their own operations, relying on outsiders to do everything else in the vertical chain. Such firms did not use employees to acquire raw materials or to deliver and sell their product. By the early twentieth century, however, large firms were vertically integrated, meaning that large hierarchical firms performed many if not most of the links in the vertical chain themselves. For such large firms, the fundamental choice along the vertical chain was integration or outsourcing, meaning do it yourself or engage someone else to do it for you.

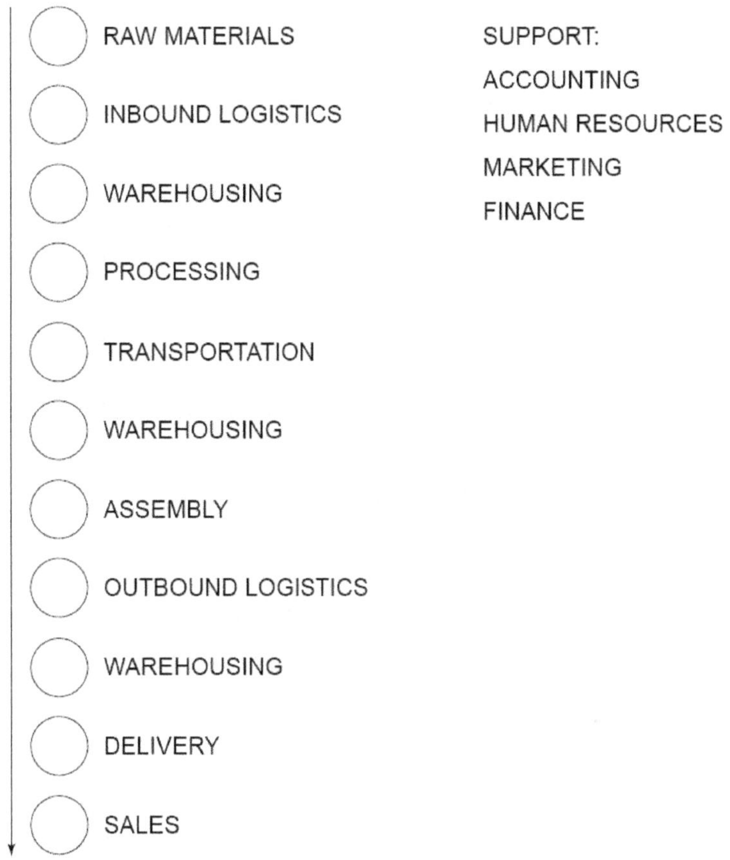

Nowadays, many firms are vertically integrated to one degree or another. For example, International Paper is the world's largest paper company. International Paper owns land, grows trees, cuts timber, mills timber, makes paper products, and distributes these paper products to markets where paper products are sold. Many other firms are not vertically integrated. One might be tempted to say these firms are vertically disintegrated, although this term would

FIGURE 8.1
THE VERTICAL CHAIN

RAW MATERIALS

INBOUND LOGISTICS

WAREHOUSING

PROCESSING

TRANSPORTATION

WAREHOUSING

ASSEMBLY

OUTBOUND LOGISTICS

WAREHOUSING

DELIVERY

SALES

SUPPORT:
ACCOUNTING
HUMAN RESOURCES
MARKETING
FINANCE

be misleading. More properly, many firms are vertically integrated, whereas many other firms are not vertically integrated. For example, Nike and Benetton perform only a few activities or functions in their vertical chain. Nike is a typical fabless firm, meaning that the firm does no fabricating. A fabless firm is a business that does not have its own manufacturing facilities. Nike controls the design and promotion of their products, but Nike relies on external manufacturers known as "fabs" for actual fabrication. Apart from design and promotion, all other activities and functions are contracted out and performed by specialist firms. The final word is simple. The vertical boundaries of a firm clearly define activities or functions a firm performs itself opposed to those the firm purchases from independent specialty firms, whether services, materials, parts, or components. Vertical boundaries are a matter of strategy.

VERTICAL INTEGRATION

When a firm provides an activity or function on its vertical chain, it is vertically integrated in that particular activity or function, meaning the part, component, material, or service is within the vertical limits of the firm. Exxon Mobil, Royal Dutch Shell, and British Petroleum are described routinely as fully integrated oil companies, meaning that these companies do everything from exploration through refining. Integration infers a choice and strategy to provide the part, component, material, or service within the limits of the firm. Once, for example, Kimberly-Clark was highly integrated. In the late 1990s, however, Kimberly-Clark disposed of its pulp operations. Business media reported that the divestiture reduced vertical integration from eighty percent to thirty percent.

Consider multinational oil companies again. Exxon Mobil, Royal Dutch Shell, and British Petroleum are active along the vertical chain from crude oil exploration to refined product sale. Their own geologists search for a reservoir of crude oil. Once found, company employees drill a well. Often, crude oil is transported in tankers owned by the company and operated by its shipping division. Crude oil is processed in a company refinery where a range of oil products is made. These products can be sold as commodities or marketed to customers. When marketing gasoline, for example, the product is sold to distributors or independent operators. Retailing through company owned gasoline stations is rare, however. For example, Exxon Mobil has left the retail market altogether, leaving it to distributors and independent operators. Nevertheless, multinational oil companies are classic cases of vertical integration, handling most of the activities and functions along the vertical chain from beginning to end or almost to the end.

Sometimes, strategic movements away from vertical integration are called downsizing or rightsizing. In 1993, for example, the CEO of Hewlett-Packard, John Young, described downsizing in his company during the early 1990s. Young said, "We used to bend all the sheet metal, mold every plastic part that went into our products. We don't do those things anymore, but somebody else is doing it for us."[104] This comment is a reference to true outsourcing, where activities once handled or administered in-house are transferred to an external source. In this way, a firm becomes less integrated.

When industrial firms such as Hewlett-Packard increasingly use the market for activities or functions on their vertical chains and use the market to provide parts, components, materials, and services, they pull back their own vertical boundaries. In other words, they become less vertically integrated. The vertical boundaries of a firm may shrink even as its industry and its own production and sales are growing. As Exxon Mobil left the retail market altogether, the company phased out its company-owned stores. This strategic decision made Exxon Mobil less vertically integrated. The company continued to sell gasoline and other products to branded distributors who pay Exxon Mobil for use of its company name. Indeed, oil companies in general are leaving the retail market. Less than five percent of U.S. gasoline stations are company owned. Increasingly, oil companies are content with wholesaling rather than retailing.

Forward and Backward Integration

In business, one firm's relationship to another firm often is described in terms of being upstream or downstream. The terms must be recognized as relative. A given firm may be upstream from some firms but downstream from others. For example, the Ford Motor Company is downstream from U.S. Steel, but Ford Motor Company is upstream from regional distributors such as Quality Ford. Along a given firm's vertical chain, the flow is from raw materials and component parts to assembly or manufacturing and then through to distribution and sale. The earlier links in the vertical chain are upstream in the production process, the later downstream. For example, lumber flows from upstream timber forests to downstream lumber mills. However, any activity in the vertical chain is upstream from later activities

104   *Chicago Tribune* (February 21, 1993), Section 1, p. 15.

in the sequence but downstream from earlier activities in the sequence. The vertical chain is a series of upstream and downstream activities and functions. A firm is vertically integrated to the extent that these upstream and downstream activities and functions are within its limits.

Forward integration is extending limits to include a downstream part, component, material, product, or service. Raw materials suppliers can integrate forward into production. In the 1920s, for example, Alcoa integrated forward to manufacturing aluminum foil. Until recently, Levi Strauss was a manufacturer. Since 2002, Levi's integrated forward to retailing by opening Original Levi's Stores and Dockers Shops. Many other apparel manufacturers also now operate company stores. For example, Ralph Laurent and Liz Claiborne operate company stores in shopping malls where independent retailers such as Macy's, Dillard's, and Nordstrom also sell their products.

Backward integration is extending limits to include an upstream part, component, material, product, or service. Retailers can integrate backward into distribution. For example, Wal-Mart developed a sophisticated warehouse and distribution network in the 1960s. Aluminum refiners have acquired bauxite companies, thus extending their limits to embrace bauxite mining. In 2012, Delta Airlines announced that a subsidiary, Monroe Energy, was acquiring an oil refinery. The Trainer refinery near Philadelphia produces jet fuel as well as other petroleum products. The acquisition was reported as backward integration.

ORGANIZATION OF THE VERTICAL CHAIN

Organization of the vertical chain is a matter of choice, presumably based on strategy. Firms can organize around transactions with market specialists or they can organize internally through vertical integration. The strategic choice is between integration and using the market. Vertical integration decisions are much broader and deeper than calculating the benefits and costs or judging the advantages and risks of using the market. Various aspects of integration decisions are difficult to quantify and thus difficult to factor into any calculus of benefits and costs or advantages and risks. In any event, vertical integration is chosen strategically for a number of different reasons.[105]

At times, vertical integration is motivated by the intent to foreclose competitors from entering a market. In other words, vertical integration is a strategic barrier to entry. For example, an established incumbent firm may integrate backward to lock up the supply of an essential input. Even if the firm does not control all of the input market, vertical integration may nonetheless foreclose entry. If only a few residual suppliers make the key input available, entrant firms may be deterred and incumbent competitors unable to expand without significantly driving up the price of the input. If entrant or incumbent firms anticipate foreclosure, they may try to lock up their own sources of supply. Foreclosure or fear of foreclosure also might motivate forward integration. If barriers to entry restrict sales into wholesale and retail markets, a manufacturer might integrate forward into wholesale and retail distribution to secure market access or prevent foreclosure by incumbent firms already integrated forward.

Vertical integration also might be motivated to acquire information. This motivation holds for both backward and forward integration. Consider backward integration. In some cases, having suppliers inside the firm and outside the firm can enlarge on information available to a firm. Consider a firm that is negotiating a contract with an outside supplier that is one of only a few such vendors. To negotiate effectively, information about the supplier's production costs would be helpful. Maintaining a small

---

105   Michael E. Porter, *Competitive Strategy* (New York: Free Press, 1980), p. 301.

division internally provides limited but relevant information about costs. Even modest integration improves the firm's ability to bargain with its suppliers. In the same way, forward integration also provides valuable information.

MAKE OR BUY

As the scale of enterprises grew from the late nineteenth century into the twentieth century, larger manufacturing firms began to perform more and more functions and activities themselves. These increasingly integrated firms accommodated and coordinated the flow of production through their own vertical chain. Integration was essential to support large volumes of output required to justify large capital investments in mass production facilities. Nowadays, many manufacturing firms are well known and widely recognized for their capabilities in activities related and even unrelated directly to production. Capabilities are activities a firm does better than other firms. Capabilities are embedded in business functions. Manufacturers turn to specialty firms to provide parts, components, materials, and services, particularly when these specialty firms have capabilities that these manufacturers do not have. Whether based on capabilities or other considerations, the decision comes down to either make or buy. The make-or-buy decision is a fundamental choice between producing something in-house and purchasing it from an outside supplier. Turning to an independent outside supplier is called using the market.

Many business firms have succeeded by providing most of their own activities and functions. Many other firms have succeeded by relying heavily on independent specialty providers for such activities and functions. When a firm turns to these specialty providers, the firm is using the market. Many firms, for example, use the market to support their production, distribution, and sales. Firms specializing in activities or functions often are recognized leaders that perform these activities better and often at lower cost than firms could provide such activities to themselves. Well known specialists include Leo Burnett, which provides market research and creates advertisements for large businesses; ServiceMaster, which supervises janitorial personnel for hospitals, schools, and businesses; Bosch, which makes automobile parts; and FedEx, which distributes products to customers of many manufacturers and retailers. Accordingly, a manufacturer can obtain a superior marketing program, improve the effectiveness of housekeeping, procure high quality and low cost automobile parts, and secure fast low-cost distribution without having to perform any of these activities itself.

These days, many companies and their managers have been influenced greatly by the concept of core competencies. *Core competencies* are skills and capabilities that cannot be imitated easily by a competitor.[106] Core competencies constitute a company's expertise, which gives the company a competitive edge. The point of core competencies, however, centers more on what a firm decides not to do rather than what it does. Building a business around core competencies correspondingly means excluding itself from other parts of the vertical chain. A fabless firm is a business that does no manufacturing, instead turning to foundries that manufacture to order. In the semiconductor industry, for example, Cirrus Logic limits itself to design and sale of hardware devices. Cirrus Logic turns to a semiconductor foundry such as Taiwan Semiconductor Manufacturing Corporation, which will manufacture to order.

Nothing is sacred where using the market is concerned. Even small companies use the market so that they too can concentrate on their core competencies. Of forty-two companies visited by Rosabeth Moss

---

106   See Gary Hamel and C.K. Prahalad, *Competing for the Future* (Cambridge, MA: Harvard Business School Press, 1994).

Kanter, she found the most likely activities to be outsourced were food, payroll, cleaning, building maintenance, mail, security, local transportation, travel arrangements, public relations, child care, training, technical writing, and printing. Manufacturing companies were outsourcing activities such as metal fabrication, painting, die cutting, and even assembling.[107]

Technically, using the market and outsourcing are different. Outsourcing is transferring the performance of functions once handled or administered in-house to an external source. Offshoring refers to the practice of outsourcing by turning to foreign providers of goods and services. Most of the media attention to offshoring has dealt with turning to countries such as India for information services.

BENEFITS AND COSTS OF USING THE MARKET

To mold make-or-buy decisions thoughtfully and thus to define boundaries carefully, management must weigh the benefits and costs or the advantages and risks of using the market. If costs or risks of using the market are believed to exceed the benefits or advantages, management has an interest in finding a way to establish, maintain, or develop more fully its own capability and capacity. If benefits or advantages are believed to be greater than the costs or risks, management should use the market. Of course, firms sometimes have little choice. They lack the capacity or capability to undertake an activity and use the market as a matter of necessity rather than for strategic or operational reasons.

The benefits and costs of using the market can be summarized and stated briefly. Benefits may be considered to be advantages. Costs may be considered to be disadvantages or risks. Mainly, there are two advantages of using the market. First, specialist firms might be able to achieve economies of scale and experience that in-house provision cannot achieve while producing only enough volume to meet a firm's own needs. Second, specialist firms are subject to market pressures to be efficient and innovative. On the other hand, overall corporate success may hide inefficiencies and lack of innovativeness that are associated with in-house provision. There are three main disadvantages of using the market, which essentially are the consequences of risks that could materialize. One, coordination of production flows might be compromised if a firm relies on activities and functions provided by independent specialists. Two, private information of value to a firm may be leaked when an activity or function is performed by an independent specialty firm. Three, using specialty firms may involve contract costs that can be avoided by performing the activity in-house.

ADVANTAGE OF USING THE MARKET: ECONOMIES OF SCALE AND EXPERIENCE

Consider automobile production. An automobile manufacturer requires a vast variety of upstream inputs, including steel, aluminum, glass, upholstery, floor mats, tires, antilock braking systems, stereo sound systems, fan belts, batteries, cigarette lighters, jacks, mufflers, shock absorbers, computer chips, windshield wipers, radiators, and so forth. An automobile manufacturer such as Ford could integrate upstream and produce components such as antilock braking systems itself, or Ford can obtain them from an independent manufacturer such as LucasVarity or Bosch. When economies of scale or economies of experience are realized, firms having a larger size of operations can produce greater volume at lower unit cost. Independent specialty firms concentrate on provision of a particular product or service utilized by other businesses. In this way, specialist firms can operate at greater scale and volume, thus

---

107   See Rosabeth Moss Kanter, *World Class: Thriving Locally in the Global Economy* (New York: Simon & Schuster, 1995).

achieving lower unit costs. The reason is that a specialty firm can aggregate the demands of many buyers, whereas a vertically integrated firm produces only enough to meet its own needs. Integration ordinarily is small-scale production by comparison to a specialty firm's large-scale production.

Recall that the minimum efficient scale of production is the smallest size of operations and corresponding volume of output at which unit cost is lowest. If Ford produces antilock brakes to meet its own needs, unit cost would be relatively high because the production scale is likely to be less than minimum efficient scale. If Ford expanded the scale of production and volume of output to minimum efficient scale, Ford would need to find buyers beyond its own needs. However, other car makers such as General Motors and Chrysler would be reluctant to buy antilock braking systems from Ford. As competitors, GM and Chrysler would fear that Ford would use its power to put them at a disadvantage by charging them higher prices, a tactic called vertical price squeeze. They also might fear that Ford would withhold or delay product delivery during periods of peak demand.

Ford itself might be reluctant to undertake a major expansion into antilock brake manufacturing, which would be a distraction from its core business. Firms are reluctant to diversify in this manner. Instead, Ford could purchase antilock brakes from LucasVarity, which can produce and sell antilock braking systems to Ford as well as other car makers. In this way, LucasVarity expands scale and volume well beyond minimum efficient scale. Some of cost savings can be passed along to Ford and other carmakers. Consequently, Ford can buy antilock braking systems from LucasVarity at a price that is lower than the cost to produce these systems in-house. The same point is true for countless other automobile parts, components, and materials.

ADVANTAGE OF USING THE MARKET: MARKET PRESSURE

A second advantage that buying has over making is that a specialty firm typically has stronger incentives to hold down costs and to innovate by comparison to a division performing the same activity within a vertically integrated firm. If a specialty firm fails to produce efficiently or to innovate, it loses business. A division within a vertically integrated firm does not face equivalent pressure. The division has a somewhat captive market. In addition, when common overhead or joint costs are allocated across divisions, measuring any one division's contribution to overall corporate profitability becomes difficult and may mask inefficiency and complacency.

Without comparable market competition, knowledge and awareness of internal performance is clouded. To the extent that divisional performance is difficult to discern, shirking on the job might be administratively unobservable and thus have no administrative consequences. Moreover, the situation can lead division managers to behavior that is inconsistent with corporate interests. For example, they might carry out operations in the easiest way and thus cut corners on product quality or cost control. The bottom line is that administrative pressures within a company are not regarded as equivalent to the market pressures facing market specialty firms.

RISK OF USING THE MARKET: THREATS TO COORDINATION OF PRODUCTION FLOWS

A key factor in realizing the potential for economies of scale is coordination of production flows from raw materials through to delivery and sale of finished goods. A number of people make decisions that depend in part on decisions of others. For example, suppliers must plan and fulfill orders for parts and materials of the right design and quality. Without coordination of operational and logistical activities, bottlenecks may develop that hinder if not obstruct the production system from successful completion of all subsequent activities. Failure of one supplier to deliver materials, parts, or components on schedule or of the right design and quality can shut down an entire factory, which is a dire consequence of coordination failure. Coordination requires a good fit into critical-to-quality characteristics such as timing fit, size fit, color fit, sequence fit, and so forth. Without proper coordination, any of the many materials, parts, or components can arrive too late or in forms and dimensions that do not meet requirements. In such cases, bottlenecks that hinder or even block further production can ensue.

Coordination is especially important and the risks especially great in processes with design attributes, which are qualities or characteristics that need to relate or interface in a precise manner.[108] When such attributes do not mesh appropriately, the product itself loses a significant portion if not all of its value. When design attributes are critical to quality, a downstream firm normally understands how various inputs relate to each other. However, various upstream suppliers may not coordinate with each other although their materials, parts, or components must interface precisely if the downstream final product is defect-free. Failure to achieve the right relationship or interface can be very costly. As a result, it often makes sense to integrate critical upstream and downstream activities and rely on administrative control to achieve appropriate coordination rather than rely on independent firms and hope that coordination emerges automatically through the market mechanism.

Firms often rely on contracts to assure coordination. Such contracts may specify delivery dates, design tolerances, or other performance criteria that are critical to an uninterrupted production flow. Failure to meet specified contractual terms might result in paying a hefty penalty, financial or otherwise. On the other hand, suppliers might receive a substantial bonus for exceeding certain specified contractual expectations. Of course, coordination problems also can arise between internal divisions of vertically integrated firms. However, coordination problems frequently are more daunting and potentially more serious when dealing with independent specialty firms under contract. The potential for control problems is exacerbated when a firm deals with numerous independent firms in the production flow. Contracts with a number of specialty firms cannot match the administrative control within the firm itself.

In some cases, firms even use the market to assure coordination! These firms rely on independent firms that specialize in coordination. These specialty firms are generally known as supplier coordinators. They provide all aspects of coordination services. Supplier coordinators conduct supplier reviews, develop supplier contract terms, engage in price negotiations, make orders, manage inventories, and then monitor, control, and otherwise implement supplier relations. In effect, these independent specialty firms are supply chain coordinators.

RISK OF USING THE MARKET: LEAKING PRIVATE INFORMATION

A firm's private information is knowhow, methods, or whatever that the firm does not want to be known to anyone else, particularly rivals, competitors, or entrants. Private information often gives a firm its competitive advantage. The information may relate to production technique, product design, customer information, or some other valued knowledge or capability. When firms use the market to obtain materials, parts, and components or bring on board highly specialized services, they risk disclosure of crucial

---

108   See Paul Milgrom and John Roberts, *Economics, Organization and Management* (Englewood Cliffs, NJ: Prentice-Hall, 1992).

private information to outsiders. Leakage of vital private information can result in a blunder of historic proportion and literally change the course of a company and its strategic direction.

The disastrous consequences of information leakage can be seen in IBM's experience with developing a personal computer based on a new operating system that would feature the operational convenience of Macintosh. Indeed, Bill Gates reportedly exclaimed in 1981, "I want Mac on a P_c!" Whether true or just another apocryphal story, his outcry materialized through product development of Windows. Version 1.0 emulated the Macintosh environment but merely extended MS-DOS. Rather than develop its new operating system itself, IBM nevertheless decided to engage Gates' obscure company, Microsoft.

Armed with information that IBM planned to introduce a product that could make its Windows product obsolete, Microsoft redoubled efforts to improve and upgrade Windows. Windows 2.0 was released in 1987 but proved only slightly more popular than Windows 1.0. Microsoft finally achieved serious success with Windows 3.0 released in 1990. Windows 3.0 finally made the IBM P_c a serious competitor to the Apple Macintosh. Windows 3.0 was wildly successful, selling about ten million copies in two years before the release of version 3.1. Serious tensions developed in the Microsoft/IBM relationship, and the relationship was terminated. Windows had become so widely used and so popular that few personal computer users ever switched to the IBM operating system.

RISK OF USING THE MARKET: TRANSACTION COSTS

The concept of transaction costs was recognized first by Ronald H. Coase, who won the Nobel Prize in Economics in 1991. In a famous paper, Coase asked an interesting question.[109] Given the known efficiencies of competitive markets, why does so much economic activity take place within firms where market transactions are replaced by centralized directions? Coase concluded there must be costs to using the market that can be avoided through internalization. These costs have come to be known as transaction costs.

Transaction costs include the time and expense required to negotiate, write, and enforce contracts. In this sense, transaction costs are contract costs. These costs arise when parties to a transaction have a chance to act opportunistically to act on their own narrow gain at the expense of the broader relationship. Transaction costs include actual adverse consequences of opportunistic behavior as well as costs of trying to prevent such self-serving behavior. Contract costs are certainly one component of transaction costs. After all, a key purpose of contracts is to protect each party's interests in an exchange relationship. However, transaction costs can take more subtle forms.

Production of aluminum requires several stages.[110] First is mining bauxite ore, composed mainly of hydrous aluminum oxides and aluminum hydroxides. Second is refining the bauxite ore into alumina, which is aluminum oxide (Al_2O_3). Third, alumina is electrochemically reduced to aluminum in reduction cells or pots. Next, the molten aluminum is cast into ingots or bars; rolled into sheets, plates, or foil; or drawn into rods. Then, these intermediate shapes are shipped to processing plants where the aluminum is forged into customer products.

Mineralogical properties of bauxite vary considerably across deposits. Bauxite consists of forty-five to sixty percent aluminum oxide, twelve to thirty percent water, and various other impurities. The aluminum

---

109   Ronald Coase, "The Nature of the Firm," *Economica*, 4 (1937), pp. 386-405.

110   See John Stuckey, *Vertical Integration and Joint Ventures in the Aluminum Industry* (Cambridge, MA: Harvard University Press, 1983).

refinery for a particular bauxite deposit cannot accept ore from another bauxite deposit without incurring substantial expense to reengineer the plant. As a result, a bauxite supplier and an alumina refiner are strongly dependent on each other. Less than one percent of aluminum in the United States comes from domestic bauxite. Major bauxite producers include Australia, Brazil, Guinea, Jamaica, and republics of the former U.S.S.R.

Suppose a bauxite mining company and an aluminum refining company agree to a contract that specifies the price the refiner will pay the miner for delivered bauxite. This dependency can create problems. For example, both parties can be surprised by an unexpected surge in demand for finished aluminum. The refiner would like to process more bauxite to make additional profits. The bauxite miner recognizes the additional profits that the refiner stands to make and tries to force the refiner to pay more than the contract price for bauxite in exchange for accelerated and heightened delivery of bauxite ore. The two sides hire lawyers, and subsequent negotiations consume the time of top management on both sides. Eventually, production of both bauxite and alumina is increased only after costly delays and legal expenses. One consequence of delay is lost profit from producing more alumina at the sudden spike in price.

At the heart of this example from the aluminum business is absence of a contract that ensures performance. No contract is ever complete in the sense that it covers every conceivable occurrence of events in the life of the contract. In this case, the bauxite miner and alumina refiner failed to anticipate a sharp and sustained increase in the demand for aluminum and a corresponding increase in the price of aluminum. Given their complete reliance on each other, they end up in a costly battle over how to divide resulting profits. Eventually, the firms might do what nearly all alumina refiners and bauxite miners have done, which is to merge into a single firm.

Specific Assets and the Holdup Problem

A specific asset is an investment made to support a particular transaction. A wholly specific asset cannot be redeployed to another transaction without sacrifice in the value of the asset or cost in adapting the asset to the new transaction. Reconsider the case of the alumina refiner and the bauxite miner. An alumina refiner makes a specific investment when a refinery is built to accommodate a particular grade of bauxite ore. After it is set up, the refinery cannot be reconfigured to handle other grades of bauxite without incurring significant expenditures to redesign the facility. The bauxite miner may have no other potential customer because no other refinery is built to process its particular grade of bauxite. In this particular case, neither party to the transaction can switch trading partners without incurring significant costs. The reason is that assets involved must be reconfigured to be valuable in a new relationship, or investments must be made all over again in the new relationship. To one degree or another, this situation implies that investments in specific assets lock in one party or both parties to the relationship.

In each case of asset specificity, a business makes an expensive, specialized investment and at the same time finds itself in a tenuous bargaining position. Once the specialized investment is made, possibilities for a holdup are created. The buyer might attempt to exploit a seller who has made specific investments and thus is dependent on the buyer. Indeed, the buyer may threaten a unilateral termination of the relationship if the seller does not agree to terms highly favorable to the buyer. This sort of opportunistic behavior is known as the holdup problem, which arises when one party in a contractual relationship exploits the other party's vulnerability due to investment in specific assets. Once specialized investment is made, the possibility of holdup can make a particular transaction unattractive unless some way is devised to guard against holdup. Some form of vertical integration provides this insurance. For example, bauxite mining and alumina refining can be brought under unified ownership through merger or acquisition. Still another possibility is setting up a joint venture, which is a company owned jointly by the buyer and seller with the limited intent to share in the specific investment required to support the transaction.

A SUMMARY: MAKE-OR-BUY DECISIONS

The make-or-buy decision involves a calculated balancing of benefits and costs or advantages and risks of using the market. Managers can find themselves bogged down in the mire of complexity riddled through the decision-making process. A manager first must assess whether the market provides an alternative to vertical integration. If the market cannot provide a particular material, part, component, or service, then the firm must take on the task itself or find a supplier that is willing to form a joint venture or strategic alliance to take on the task. If the market offers an alternative to vertical integration, then the manager must determine whether using the market would be impeded by information, coordination, or holdup problems. If such problems are unlikely or are inconsequential, then the firm should use the market. If such problems are likely or are consequential, the manager must determine whether these problems can be prevented either through a contract favoring use of the market or through internal governance favoring integration.

TAPERED INTEGRATION: MAKE AND BUY

Mazda has an interesting history. The company can be traced back to 1920 when it was a machine tools manufacturer and turned to vehicle manufacturing in 1931. Although its automobiles always bore the name Mazda, the company itself was not named Mazda until 1984. The founder of the company was Jujiro Matsuda, who was a Zoroastrian. Mazda Is a reference to Ahura Mazda, a divinity exalted as the source of wisdom, intelligence, and harmony by the ancient Iranian prophet Zoroaster.

In the early 1970s, Ford entered a relationship with Mazda. Ford imported the Mazda pickup truck rebranded as the Courier. From 1972 to 1983, the Courier was part of the Ford line. In 1984, Ford decided to design, produce, and sell its own small pickup truck, which was the Ranger. However, the close relationship between the two companies did not end. Mazda was amidst a decline that resulted in financial turmoil. In 1979, Ford Motor Company provided badly needed cash when the company acquired a financial stake in Mazda that amounted to seven percent. During the 1980s, Ford's financial stake in Mazda grew to twenty-seven percent. In 1997, Ford's financial stake was increased to 33.4 percent, giving Ford controlling interest in Mazda.

In part, Ford's investment in Mazda was motivated by an interest in globalizing Ford's interests more fully, but the acquisition also was a way for Ford to acquire information about Mazda methods in manufacturing. Only a year after Ford made its original investment in Mazda, Ford opened a 1.8 million square feet plant in Batavia, Ohio. The facility was opened to produce automatic transmissions and other parts and components. In the mid-1980s, Ford did not have the capacity to fulfill all its needs for transmissions at Ford Batavia. Ford contracted with Mazda to make some of these same transmissions for automobiles Ford was selling in the United States. Ford and Mazda manufacturing sites made transmissions to the same set of blueprints and thus the same product specifications. The transmissions made at Ford Batavia and Mazda were installed only on American automobiles.

After a certain number of the automobiles had been sold and placed in service by their owners, Ford found that the transmissions it made were costing more in terms of warranty and also were generating more customer complaints about noise. Ford took the unusual step of breaking down a few transmissions from both Ford and Mazda facilities and then measuring parts and components. In particular, the focus was on valves, valve bores, and valve springs, the control valve components that make a transmission shift automatically. Gauging these components and others in transmissions made by Mazda showed little or no variations from product specifications. Closer investigation revealed that Ford's manufacturing was based on mere conformance to specifications, whereas Mazda's manufacturing was based on continuously reducing variability around target values rooted in product specifications. Batavia transmissions exhibited a much higher level of variation than the Mazda transmissions. In a product as complex as an automatic transmission, the interaction of parts caused more failures in the Ford Batavia product. In fact, Mazda was using only twenty-seven percent of tolerance, whereas Ford was using seventy percent.[111]

Some final ironies should be recorded to end this story. In 1997, Mazda faced serious financial difficulties. Ford bailed out Mazda, infusing badly needed cash by increasing Ford's share of ownership of Mazda to an interest of 33.4 percent. On 18 November 2008, however, Ford announced it was selling twenty percent of its holdings in Mazda, thus reducing its ownership stake to only 13.4 percent. In this way, Ford surrendered its controlling interest, but the sale provided about $540 million of needed cash to Ford and thus strengthened its balance sheet. Even with its 13.4 percent interest in Mazda, Ford remains Mazda's largest shareholder and keeps its seat on the Mazda Board of Directors. Ford and Mazda continue their ongoing joint ventures. On 23 January 2006, Ford announced that the Batavia transmission plant would be closed in 2008. On Friday, 13 June 2008, Ford closed the Batavia transmission plant. Friday the 13th was indeed an unlucky day for nearly 800 workers who lost their jobs.

In the Ford and Mazda case, Ford made some of its transmissions and bought some transmissions made by Mazda for its Ford vehicles. The make and buy decision was a classic case of tapered integration, which is a composite of vertical integration and market transactions. In the case of tapered integration, a manufacturer produces some amount of an input and purchases the remaining portion from independent firms. Tapered integration also is found when a firm sells some of its product through an internal sales force and relies on an independent firm to sell the rest.

Tapered integration has several benefits. First, tapered integration enlarges a firm's input or output channels without requiring substantial capital outlays, which is particularly helpful to fledgling firms experiencing growth. Second, a firm can use information about the cost and profitability of its internal channels as an aid in negotiating contracts with independent channels. Third, a firm also can use threats to use the market more extensively as a means of motivating performance of its own internal channels. Fourth, a firm can develop internal input supply capabilities as protection against holdup by independent input suppliers. In other words, tapered integration is a threat to manufacture items with expanded capacity rather than buy from specialty firms.

---

111   See L.A. Ealey, *Quality by Design: Taguchi Methods and U.S. Industry* (Dearborn, MI: ASI Press, 1988).

STRATEGIC ALLIANCES AND JOINT VENTURES

An alternative to integration is strategic alliances or joint ventures. Firms turn to strategic alliances as a way to organize complex business transactions without sacrificing autonomy. In a strategic alliance, two or more firms agree to collaborate on a project, share information, or share productive resources. A horizontal strategic alliance involves collaboration between firms in the same industry. A vertical strategic alliance involves collaboration between firms that have supplier and buyer relationships. Alliances also may involve firms that are neither in the same industry nor related through the vertical chain. Cisco Systems is an example of a company that has entered into countless strategic alliances, including formal collaborations with IBM, Intel, Hewlett-Packard, Microsoft, Motorola, Nokia, Oracle, Fujitsu, EMC^2, SAP, EDS, and more.

A joint venture is a particular type of strategic alliance in which two or more firms create and jointly own a new independent enterprise. In October 2007, for example, Molson Coors and SABMiller announced that the two companies were forming a joint venture called MillerCoors to merge their North American operations. At the time, Miller Brewing was the second largest U.S. brewer with market share of about twenty percent, and Coors Brewing the third largest with market share of about eleven percent. Anheuser-Busch controlled nearly half the U.S. beer market. Therefore, Anheuser-Busch and MillerCoors would control more than eighty percent of the U.S. beer market. On 5 June 2008, the Department of Justice announced approval of the MillerCoors joint venture, saying that MillerCoors was not likely to lessen competition substantially. Indeed, the joint venture was expected to bring down prices. Meanwhile, the Belgium brewing company, InBev, announced that it had completed the acquisition of Anheuser-Busch.

PRACTICE QUESTIONS

1. Describe the vertical chain. What is meant by the vertical boundaries of a firm? What is a vertically integrated firm? What is a vertical merger?

2. Describe the vertical chain and explain the meaning of upstream and downstream activities.

3. What is meant by the make-or-buy decision? Why would one firm decide to be vertically integrated and another firm decide not to be vertically integrated?

4. The make-or-buy decision has been described as resolving the tension between two main benefits and three main costs of using the market. Briefly describe the benefits and costs of using the market, and explain the resolution.

5. What is tapered integration? What are the benefits?

Questions for Contemplation, Discussion, and Argument

6. Historically, product markets have been dominated by large firms and service markets by small firms. This historical trend may be reversing. What factors might be involved?

7. Trade barriers between European nations continue to fall. Many experts believe that this phenomenon will allow businesses in different parts of Europe to merge. What effect, if any, will this phenomenon have on competition with U.S. and Japanese firms in Europe and elsewhere? Does the answer depend on the industry under consideration?

PRACTICE QUESTIONS (AND ANSWERS)

1. Describe the vertical chain. What is meant by the vertical boundaries of a firm? What is a vertically integrated firm? What is a vertical merger?

Production is a process usually requiring a wide range of activities. The process begins with acquisition of raw materials and ends with distribution and sale of finished goods. Ordered from the first activity to the last, this sequence of activities is known as the vertical chain. One of the fundamental issues and central decisions in business strategy is how to organize the vertical chain. The vertical boundaries of a firm define activities a firm performs itself as opposed to those the firm purchases from independent firms in the market. A vertically integrated firm is a hierarchical organization in which many if not most or even all of the steps in the vertical chain are performed by the firm itself. A vertical merger involves a union of businesses coming together from different parts of the vertical chain.

2. Describe the vertical chain and explain the meaning of upstream and downstream activities.

Production usually requires a fairly wide range of activities. The process that begins with acquisition of raw materials and ends with distribution and sale of finished goods is known as the vertical chain, a reference to various links in the production chain. In general, products flow along the vertical chain from raw materials and component parts to manufacturing, through distribution and retailing. Early steps in the vertical chain are upstream in the production process, and later steps are downstream. A vertically integrated firm thus is one that performs many if not all of the steps in the vertical chain itself.

3. What is meant by the make-or-buy decision? Why would one firm decide to be vertically integrated and another firm decide not to be vertically disintegrated?

Essentially, any business confronts a fundamental decision with respect to every activity in the vertical chain, viz., whether the business itself should provide the activity or use the market. When deciding in favor of the former, the decision is to "make." When deciding in favor of the latter, the decision is to "buy." When firms use the market to obtain activities and inputs, they choose to pull back their own vertical boundaries, i.e., become less vertically integrated. Using the market is not always the preference, however. A firm must address certain issues before it can determine for itself the best way to organize. To make associated make-or-buy decisions thoughtfully and define boundaries carefully, management of a firm must compare the benefits and costs of using the market. Sometimes, firms must use the market because they lack the capacity or capability to perform a task in-house. In the long run, if costs of using the market exceed the benefits, the firm must find a way to establish, maintain, and develop more fully its own in-house capabilities. Otherwise, the firm must bear the ongoing burden of inefficient use of independent firms. Mainly, there are two benefits of using the market. First, market firms might be able to achieve economies of scale that in-house provision cannot while producing only enough volume for a firm's own needs. Second, market firms are subject to the discipline of the market and must be efficient and innovative to survive. On the other hand, overall corporate success may hide inefficiencies and lack of innovativeness of in-house provision. There are three main costs of using the market. One, coordination of production flows through the vertical chain may be compromised when an activity is purchased from an independent market firm rather than performed in-house. Two, private information may be leaked when an activity is performed by an independent market firm. Three, transacting with independent market firms may involve costs that can be avoided by performing the activity in-house.

4. The make-or-buy decision has been described as resolving the tension between two main benefits and three main costs of using the market. Briefly describe the benefits and costs of using the market, and explain the resolution.

The decision of a firm to perform an upstream, downstream, or professional supporting activity itself or purchase it from an independent firm is called a make-or-buy decision. The make decision involves performing an activity within the firm itself. The buy decision, on the other hand, involves using the market, i.e., turning to specialized providers outside the firm for provision or performance. In general, the two main benefits of using the market are that market firms can achieve economies of scale and are disciplined by the market itself. The main costs associated with using the market are costs associated with coordination required between steps in the vertical chain, appropriation of information, and transactions. The decision to make or buy is centered on conjecture about the magnitude of benefits and costs associated with using the market. If the benefits of using the market are regarded as greater than costs of doing so, the tension is resolved in favor of using the market. If the costs are regarded as greater than the benefits, the activity in question is provided or performed internally.

5. What is tapered integration? What are the benefits?

Tapered integration represents a mixture of vertical integration and market exchange. A manufacturer might produce some amount of an input itself and purchase the remaining portion from independent firms. It might sell some of its product through an in-house sales force and rely on an independent manufacturers' representative to sell the rest. Tapered integration has several benefits. First, it expands a firm's input and/or output channels without requiring substantial capital outlays, which is helpful to growing firms such as fledgling retail chains. Second, a firm can use information about the cost and profitability of its internal channels to help negotiate contracts with independent channels. A firm also can use threats to use the market further to motivate performance of its own internal channels. Third, a firm can develop internal input supply capabilities to protect itself against holdup by independent input suppliers.

9. Competitive Analysis and Market Structures

MICHAEL E. PORTER

Michael E. Porter is a professor in the Harvard Business School. His course at Harvard is *Microeconomics of Competitiveness*. The course is taught in partnership with more than sixty other universities around the world, using curriculum, video content, and instructor support developed by the Institute. He also created and chairs Harvard's program for newly appointed CEOs of corporations with revenues of two billion dollars or more. The New CEO Workshop is given twice annually, and it is focused on the challenges facing new CEOs in assuming leadership, setting their agendas, and addressing issues such as strategy, board governance, communication, and values.

In the 1970s, Michael E. Porter wrote a series of articles culminating in publication of two highly influential books, *Competitive Strategy* in 1980 and *Competitive Advantage* in 1985.[112] The two books are regarded as companions, meaning they should be read together in sequence. In 1990, he had still another book published, *Competitive Advantage of Nations*, which completed a kind of trilogy.[113] More recently, Porter had an updated and revised book published. Published in 2008, *On Competition: Updated and Expanded Edition* consists of twelve articles on strategy and competition.[114] Included are his original articles, "What is Strategy?" and "The Five Competitive Forces that Shape Strategy."

Beginning with *Competitive Strategy*, Porter and his books were influential because he wrote for the management practitioner, especially the experienced manager. In the introduction to *Competitive Strategy*, Porter indicated the primary readership he had in mind. "This book is written for *practitioners*, that is, managers seeking to improve the performance of their businesses...."[115] At the time the book was pub-

---

112   Michael E. Porter, *Competitive Strategy: Techniques for Analyzing Industries and Competitors* (New York: Free Press, 1980); and Michael E. Porter, *Competitive Advantage: Creating and Sustaining Superior Performance* (New York: Free Press, 1985).

113   Michael E. Porter, *Competitive Advantage of Nations* (New York: Free Press, 1990).

114   Michael E. Porter, *On Competition, Updated and Expanded Edition* (Cambridge, MA: Harvard Business Press Books, 2008).

115   Porter, *Competitive Advantage*, p. xv.

lished, these experienced management practitioners were a neglected lot. They were nonetheless open to and downright hungry for penetrating insights leading to profound knowledge of their industries and competitive strategies to accomplish operating objectives. What they needed was a fundamental structure to support a system of ideas and organizing principles. With a structure, industries and firms could be analyzed and corresponding competitive strategies could be developed and implemented. Moreover, both analysis and related strategies would be grounded in business experience and based on business information from functional areas such as accounting and marketing. In particular, these experienced managers needed a framework to organize information about an industry that then could be shaped and crafted into strategies.

In *Competitive Strategy*, Porter developed and presented a framework that accommodated and facilitated exploration of competitive factors affecting the profits of an industry and thus a typical firm in the industry. A framework is a fundamental structure to organize thinking and analysis. Porter said five competitive forces help to understand the overall profitability expected in a given industry. These five forces serve as a framework to explain, *inter alia*, why one industry is profitable while another is not and why one industry is more profitable than another industry. Porter suggested that such industry differences are attributed to the effects on profitability of these five competitive forces, which are the nature and intensity of competition constituting internal rivalry, the threat of entry, the threat of substitute products, the bargaining power of buyers, and the bargaining power of suppliers.

This framework of five competitive forces was structured to be a vehicle for developing competitive strategy that fits the interests of a company to the business environment in which it competes. A key aspect of a firm's environment is the industry or industries in which it competes. In any industry, the nature and intensity of competition are not a matter of coincidence or luck, good or bad. The state of competition depends on basic competitive forces. The collective strength of these forces determines the ultimate profit potential in the industry. Simply put, industries do not have the same profit potential. As the collective strength of these forces differ, industries and thus typical firms in these industries differ fundamentally in their ultimate profit potential.[116]

THE FIVE FORCES

Five forces analysis systematically and comprehensively applies economic tools to analyze an industry in depth. In Porter's framework, the five forces affecting profitability of an industry are nature and intensity of internal rivalry among incumbent competitors, threat of entry by new competitors, pressure from substitute products external to the industry, bargaining power of suppliers to firms in the industry, and bargaining power of buyers from firms in the industry. Figure 9.1 illustrates the five forces framework. Internal rivalry is in the center of this framework because the nature and intensity of competition may be affected by each of the other four forces. In other words, internal rivalry is the hub, and the other four forces are like spokes.

---

116   *Ibid.*, pp. 3-4.

FIGURE 9.1
THE FIVE FORCES

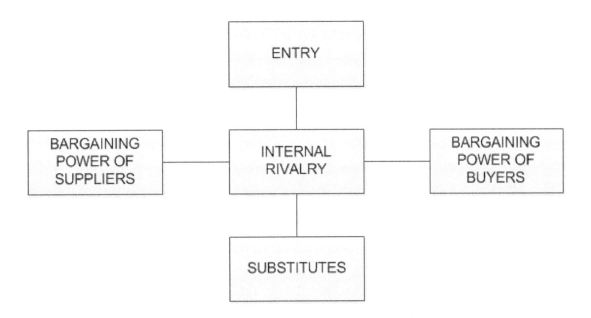

For a company in an industry, the goal of competitive strategy is to maneuver for a favorable position so that the company can defend itself against the threats of these competitive forces or can influence them in its favor. The key to developing competitive strategy is to delve beneath the surface to identify, analyze, and understand each of the five forces and how they affect an incumbent company. As Porter says, "Knowledge of these underlying sources of competitive pressure highlights the critical strengths and weaknesses of the company, animates its positioning in its industry, clarifies the areas where strategic changes may yield the greatest payoff, and highlights the areas where industry trends promise to hold the greatest significance as either opportunities or threats."[117]

As a framework, therefore, Porter meant five forces analysis as the fundamental structure and method for examining an industry in terms of effects on profits. Each force is analyzed to determine the degree that conditions and factors constituting this force are great enough to threaten industry profits. The framework is meant to be comprehensive, and working through each of the five forces requires systematic consideration of all significant economic factors affecting an industry. As the case with any other model, however, the five forces framework has limitations. Mainly, five forces analysis is focused on competitive forces. This focus alone limits any direct account of government regulation and policy. Moreover, five forces analysis is focused on industries and effects on a typical firm must be inferred. Finally, five forces analysis does not provide quantitative metrics to measure threats or opportunities.

---

117   *Ibid.*, p. 4.

INTERNAL RIVALRY

Internal rivalry refers to maneuvering by firms for favorable position in terms of market share, profit margin, or some other measure of performance within an industry. Porter himself described internal rivalry as "jockeying for position–using tactics like price competition, advertising battles, product introductions, and increased customer service or warranties."[118] In maneuvering for position and advantage, therefore, firms may compete on a number of price and non-price dimensions. Price competition erodes profits by driving down price-cost margins. Non-price competition erodes profits by driving up fixed costs such as new product development and marginal costs such as improvements in product quality.

Intense rivalry among firms in an industry threatens and reduces profitability. As the intensity of competition ramps up, profit margins are driven down. Profits in an industry are greater when incumbent firms avoid costly price wars. Simple observation reveals that firms in industries with a history of facilitating practices such as price leadership are likely to fare better than firms in industries with a history of repeated episodes of ruthless, cutthroat price warfare. When firms somehow find a way to avoid intense competition and thus escape its consequences, substantial profits can be realized through such cooperation. However, in an industry in which cooperation results in extraordinary profits, incentives that threaten the common purpose arise. Any given firm must consider and weigh the temptation to whittle its price below the common level with the intent to increase its market share and increase its own profits. The lure and menace of these treacherous enticements loom over firms in the industry, creating a relentless tension. Cooperation is good for industry profits, but cheating is good for a firm in the industry as long as other firms do not cheat at the same time. Certain conditions tend to heat up the intensity of price competition.

Prices and profit margins tend to be lower when many firms operate and compete in a market or industry. A large number of firms generally riles up rivalry because of the simple reason that more firms compete for the same customers. Competition is intensified with a larger number of firms.

In an industry that is stagnant and characterized by slow or even declining market growth, firms cannot grow without drawing customers away from competitors, which is called sheep stealing. In effect, sheep stealing is building up one's own flock by stealing sheep from another's flock. Wooing away customers and sales from competitors generally elicits a competitive response that tends to intensify competition.

Firms with excess capacity may be motivated to boost sales. Such firms can increase volume of output quickly to draw customers from rivals. In addition, the only cost of utilizing excess capacity is variable cost because fixed cost of the capacity already has been incurred. Trying to sell larger volumes of product generally leads to a fight for market share and results in intensified rivalry.

When costs differ significantly among firms in an industry, low-cost producers may conclude that high-cost competitors might be forced to leave the industry if the prevailing industry price can be driven lower. Therefore, low-cost firms might cut their prices as a predatory act to drive out high-cost incumbent firms. Price cutting also might discourage entrant firms.

When customers can switch easily from one seller to another or from one firm's product to another firm's product, the struggle to maintain or capture customers is greater than otherwise. Thus, firms are inclined to undercut prevailing prices to fuel substantial increases in market share.

---

118 Porter, *op. cit.*, p. 17.

THE THREAT OF ENTRY

In business, entry is a simple concept. Entry is the onset of production and sales of a product by a new firm in a market. In other words, entry is introduction of a new product into a market. Acquisition into the market is not considered entry because a new product is not introduced in the market. Entry may involve a start-up firm or a diversifying firm. The distinction is important when costs of entry and strategic responses to entry are assessed.

Firms new to a market are called entrants. They threaten the sales and profits of firms already in the market, called incumbents. Entrants take market share away from incumbents. This effect reduces share of the profit pie. When entrants introduce new products, reduce prices, or deploy other strategies to establish and solidify their market position, they also intensify competition. This effect reduces size of the profit pie.

Profits made by incumbent firms are like a magnet and tend to attract entrant firms. Entrants to an industry or market bring with them new capacity coupled with a passion to grab market share. Newcomer firms pull some business from incumbent firms, essentially dividing up market demand among more sellers. In this way, entrant firms intensify internal rivalry and diminish profit margins. Before deciding to enter a market, an entrant firm must assess post-entry competition, which represents the likely response of incumbent firms if entry occurs. If post-entry competition is expected to intensify because incumbents are likely to slash prices in an attempt to keep the newcomer from taking away sales, then the promise of healthy post-entry profits made by entrants is diminished. Indeed, losses might be incurred.

To assess what post-entry competition may be like, a firm considering entry may use different types of information about incumbents, including information regarding historical pricing practices, costs, and capacity. Even when a firm considering entry believes post-entry competition will be moderated, it still might not enter if there are significant barriers to entry. After all, incumbent firms devise and implement strategies to reduce the threat of entry. In other words, incumbent firms try to erect strategic barriers to entry.

Barriers to Entry

The threat of entry into an industry depends on barriers to entry and reaction the entrant firm can expect from incumbent firms. If entry barriers are high and/or the entrant firm can expect retaliatory reactions from incumbent competitors, the actual threat of entry is low. Entry barriers may be structural or strategic. *Structural barriers to entry* are conditions of entry such as technology, cost, and demand. Economies of scale and experience may endow significant cost advantages to incumbent firms. Capital requirements may compel large financial investment, perhaps involving risky and unrecoverable upfront costs of research and development. If such circumstances stand in the way of entry, industry conditions favor incumbents over entrants. Particularly in Europe, structural barriers are regarded as economic or innocent barriers. *Strategic barriers to entry* refer to actions concocted by incumbent firms to deter entry. These barriers are deliberate actions taken by incumbent firms to reinforce their positions against the threat of entry. Therefore, strategic barriers are not inherent conditions of an industry that naturally favor incumbents. Strategic barriers are erected through actions deliberately taken with the intent to prevent or deter entry. In Europe, strategic barriers are considered to be behavioral.[119]

---

119 Porter, *op. cit.*, pp. 7-17.

A number of strategic barriers to entry are practiced. These strategies include aggressive price reductions intended to realize significant economies of experience, giving an incumbent a cost advantage that entrants could not match even if they entered at the same scale. Of course, aggressive price reductions can be undertaken for other reasons. An incumbent might practice limit pricing, which is a credible threat to set its price below what would be an entrant's average variable cost. An incumbent also might use aggressive price reductions to drive other incumbents from the market, which also serves to discourage entrants. If an incumbent firm were to reduce price below its own average variable cost, however, the incumbent would be likely to face antitrust trouble. The likelihood of antitrust attention is heightened still further if the incumbent raises prices after other incumbents are driven from the market. An incumbent might use aggressive price reductions to earn a reputation for toughness. Another way to establish and maintain a credible reputation for toughness is through convincing announcements to do whatever it takes to maintain and secure dominant market shares. Black and Decker and McCormick Spices have succeeded in signaling entrants that they will do whatever is necessary to secure their share of the market, even engage in sustained price wars. Other strategies also are undertaken to prevent or at least deter entry. For example, intensive advertising might be designed to create strong brand loyalty, giving an incumbent a marketing advantage that would be costly for entrants to overcome.

When feasible, an incumbent might acquire patents for all conceivable variants of a product, thus foreclosing entrants from the market. For example, Nestle registered 1,700 patents to protect its single-serve coffee capsules for use in its Nespresso machines. Obviously, almost all of these patents were mere variants of the capsule that Nestle actually produced. Nestle never planned to produce the patented variants, which were sleeping patents. However, Sara Lee somehow wove its way through this labyrinth and introduced its own lower priced coffee capsules for use in Nestle's machine. Previously, only the pricier Nestle capsules could be used. In June 2010, Nestle sued Sara Lee for patent infringement. In April 2012, Nestle won its case before the European Patent Office.

Sleeping patents are not limited to the United States. In 2005, the European Commission estimated that one-third of European patents are not used for any industrial or commercial purpose. Patent laws in many countries require compulsory licensing of an invention at reasonable terms if the patentee does not use the invention within a specified time. These laws are seldom used, however. In the United States, some companies buy up patents but do not utilize them, a practice known as patent trolling. Intellectual Ventures, for example, is a patent hoarding company that held more than 30,000 patents in 2010 without using any one of them. One motive for holding these patents is the opportunity to file lawsuits for patent infringement, which in effect monetizes the sleeping patents.

Finally, incumbents may choose to hold excess capacity for strategic reasons. By holding excess capacity, incumbents affect how entrants view post-entry competition. Holding excess capacity can be perceived as a signal of incumbent willingness to flood the market with product and slash prices if entry occurs. After all, only variable cost would be incurred. Excess capacity serves as a credible threat that incumbents will utilize the capacity should entry occur.

Deployment of Strategic Barriers

Considerable attention has been devoted to entry deterrence, but evidence regarding the extent to which these strategies are practiced has been meager. Limited evidence came from antitrust cases. Apart from antitrust cases, knowledge of entry deterrence was scant. Understandably, firms were reluctant to report that they strategically deter entry. Disclosure would lay bare sensitive competitive information, and it might denude violations of state or federal antitrust statutes. Despite concerns, Robert Smiley nonetheless convinced major consumer product makers to disclose their actual use of entry-deterring strategies.[120]

Smiley surveyed product managers at nearly 300 firms. To assure frankness, he promised them complete anonymity. These product managers disclosed their frequent or at least occasional use of several strategies, including aggressive price reductions to move down the learning curve, resulting in a cost advantage that later entrants could match only by investing in learning themselves; intensive advertising to create brand loyalty; acquiring patents for all conceivable variants of a product; enhancing reputation for toughness if not predation through announcements or some other instrument; limit pricing; and holding excess capacity. The first three strategies create high entry costs. The last three strategies change entrant expectations regarding post-entry competition.

Table 9.1 presented below gives the percentage of product managers who reported that their firms frequently or occasionally use each of the six strategies for new products and existing products. In the case of exploiting the learning curve, these product managers reported on new products only.

Table 9.1 Reported Use of Strategic Barriers to Entry (Percent)						
	Learning Curve	Advertising	R&D/Patents	Reputation	Limit Pricing	Excess Capacity
New Products						
Frequently	26	62	56	27	8	22
Occasionally	29	16	15	27	19	20
Existing Products						
Frequently		52	31	27	21	21
Occasionally		26	16	22	21	17

Over half of all product managers reported frequent use of at least one strategic barrier to entry, and virtually all reported occasional use of one or more such strategies. Product managers reported that they rely much more on strategies that increase entry costs than strategies that affect an entrant's perception about the nature of post-entry competition. Perhaps managers do not think much about post-entry competition. Perhaps they believe potential entrants already have strongly held beliefs about the nature of post-entry competition and that these beliefs cannot be swayed. Managers also reported they are more likely to pursue entry-deterring strategies for new products than for existing products, especially strategies affecting entry costs. Smiley reported that product managers often felt that competition among existing products was so intense that no entry-deterring strategies were needed. In other words, entry was blockaded. As in the case of internal rivalry, certain conditions affect the threat of entry into an industry. When these conditions materialize in an industry, the threat of entry is either heightened or lowered.

If economies of scale characterize an industry and minimum efficient scale (MES) is large relative to the size of the market, an entrant must achieve a substantial market share associated with minimum efficient scale. If the entrant does not, the entrant would compete at a significant cost disadvantage. Therefore, industries with large MES deter entry. If a steep learning curve due to experience characterizes an industry, unit costs drop quickly with cumulative output. If this condition characterizes an industry, an entrant firm would face a significant cost disadvantage upon entry. Industries with significant economies of experience deter entry.

If consumers are highly involved with products and thus are brand loyal, entrants must invest heavily to establish brand awareness and to build up reputation. Diversifying entrants using a brand umbrella may be more successful than startup entrants. Regardless, overcoming loyalty to incumbent brands would require substantial financial commitments and thus will deter entry.

If incumbent firms have locked up technologies, sources of raw materials, distribution channels, or advantageous locations, limited access to critical factors of production also means limited entry. Moreover, when an industry requires specialized technology or plant and equipment, potential entrants are reluctant to invest in specialized assets that cannot be sold or converted into other uses if the venture fails. In addition, when firms already hold specialized assets, they fiercely resist efforts by other firms to take their market share. Therefore, entrants can anticipate aggressive post-entry rivalry.

THE THREAT OF SUBSTITUTES

In a broad sense, firms in an industry compete with each other and with firms in other industries producing substitute products. After all, bagels are substitutes for ready-to-eat breakfast cereal, apple juice for orange juice, vodka for gin, desktop printers for photocopiers, and electric razors for safety razors. The availability of substitute products limit the potential returns of an industry by placing a constraint on prices that firms in the industry can charge. Substitute products erode profits in the same way and as surely as entrant firms by pulling business from incumbent firms and intensifying internal rivalry. New substitutes frequently have costs likely to decline over time due to experience and scale economies. Consequently, new substitutes may pose large threats to established products and incumbent firms even if at first they seem feckless and harmless.

Substitute products outside an industry presumably perform the same *raison d'etre* as the product of the industry. For example, sugar producers in America were confronted with large-scale commercialization of high fructose corn syrup, a sugar substitute. Many people have found little use for wristwatches since cell phones provide time as well if not better. The big four breakfast cereal companies were faced with a growing appetite for bagels. Gin martinis gave way to vodka martinis. Gin companies lost sales and profits, and vodka companies gained sales and profits. Producers of fiberglass insulation found their ability to raise prices tempered by the large number of insulation substitutes, including cellulose, rock wool, and polystyrene plastic.[121] Although five forces analysis does not consider demand directly, it does consider important substitutes and complements, both of which are factors that significantly affect demand. Substitutes erode profit in the same way as entrants by drawing away business and intensifying internal rivalry. Complements boost the demand for the product under consideration, which then enhances profit opportunities for the industry.

---

121   Porter, *op. cit.*, pp. 23-24.

In assessing the threat of substitutes, product performance characteristics must be considered when identifying substitutes. The threat of substitutes is greatest when close substitutes are available to meet the same need, requirement, taste, or some other important characteristic. Value is a factor when considering the threat of substitutes. Seemingly close substitutes may represent little threat if they are priced too high. New products may be weak substitutes at first, but they gain in importance as manufacturers ride down the learning curve and prices fall correspondingly. Price elasticity of industry demand also is a factor. When unsigned industry price elasticity is high, buyers are price sensitive. Rising industry prices would motivate consumers to purchase substitute products.

BARGAINING POWER OF SUPPLIERS TO THE INDUSTRY

Someone once said, "You don't negotiate from strength. You dictate from strength." The degree of bargaining power of suppliers is the extent to which they have the strength to negotiate, demand, dictate, or otherwise insist on transaction terms that are favorable to suppliers and thus unfavorable to firms in the industry. Supplier bargaining power is the ability of suppliers to demand higher prices for their materials, parts, components, or services. Suppliers can exert pressure and thus exercise bargaining power over firms in an industry by threatening to raise prices or reduce the quality of purchased goods and services. Powerful suppliers thereby can squeeze profits from an industry unable to recover cost increases through increases in its own prices. Therefore, supplier power generally refers to the ability of suppliers to negotiate or dictate prices that are so favorable to suppliers that profits are extracted from the firms that are their customers.

Several factors determine the bargaining power of suppliers.[122] As the number of suppliers grows, for example, their bargaining power weakens. The extreme case occurs when the supply industry is so highly competitive that suppliers are price takers, meaning that prices are determined by the interaction of supply and demand in the overall market. If suppliers are price takers, they have no bargaining power whatsoever.

Suppliers can erode industry profits if suppliers are concentrated or if incumbent firms are locked into relationships with suppliers because of relationship-specific investments. A supplier with pricing power can raise prices when the industrial market is faring well, thereby extracting a share of the industry's profits. On the other hand, the same supplier may lower prices when the industrial market is not doing well. This pricing strategy permits the supplier to extract profits over time without driving the market to ruin. In a similar manner, a supplier with a relationship-specific investment made by firms in an industry can squeeze profits in the good times for the industrial market and ease up during the bad times. In some industries, suppliers are dominated by a few companies and are more concentrated than firms in the industry to which they sell. Dominant suppliers selling to an industry of small powerless firms are able to exert influence on price and other terms.

When supplier products are differentiated or characterized by high switching costs, the ability of buyers to play one supplier against the other is limited. Differentiation and high switching costs strengthen the hand of suppliers. In some industries, suppliers pose a credible threat of forward integration into the industry. If suppliers could enter the industry to which they provide parts, components, materials,

---

122 *See* Porter, *op. cit.*, pp. 27-28.

or services, this threat of entry is a check against industry ability to improve terms on which incumbent firms make purchases.

BARGAINING POWER OF BUYERS FROM THE INDUSTRY

The bargaining power of buyers is the ability of buyers to demand transaction terms favorable to buyers and thus unfavorable to firms in the industry. In effect, buyers of an industry's product force down prices, bargain for higher quality or more services, or play competitors against each other, all at the expense of industry profitability. Buyer power is analogous to supplier power. It refers to the ability of particular customers to negotiate prices so favorable that buyers succeed in extracting profits from firms in an industry.

Buyer power is related to internal rivalry, but the two competitive forces are distinctly different concepts. In many markets, particular buyers have little power to negotiate with sellers, but the markets are nevertheless intensely price competitive. This case is evident in many retail markets and spot markets for commodities. Profit margins are low in these markets because sellers compete for the business of price-sensitive buyers. The inclination of buyers to shop for the best price is a source of internal rivalry, not buyer power.

The conditions making buyers powerful tend to mirror those making suppliers powerful. A buyer or buyer group is powerful if one or more critical conditions are met.[123] For example, buyer power is heightened in industries where buyers are concentrated or they purchase large volumes relative to sales of firms in the industry. If a buyer makes purchases in large volume, this concentration of sales raises the importance of the buyer's business. Large-volume buyers are particularly strong if the industry is characterized by high fixed costs, which raises the stakes to keep capacity fully utilized.

In some cases, the products that buyers purchase are a significant portion of the buyer's costs, purchases, incomes, or budgets. In this case, buyers are more likely to shop for a favorable price and purchase selectively. In other cases, the products that buyers purchase from the industry are standardized or undifferentiated. When buyers are sure they can find alternative products, they can play one company against another. This opportunity is greatest when buyers face few switching costs. On the other hand, when switching costs are significant, they lock in a buyer to particular sellers.

In some industries, buyers are businesses that make low profits. Low profits create significant incentives to lower their costs through purchases at lower prices. Generally, highly profitable buyers are not as price sensitive. In other industries, buyers pose a credible threat of backward integration. If buyers already are partially integrated or pose a credible threat of backward integration, they are in a position to insist on concessions. Many companies, especially major automobile makers, are well known for using the threat of self-manufacture as bargaining leverage. Indeed, some of them have engaged in the practice of tapered integration. In these cases, not only is the threat of further integration particularly credible, partial integration gives these companies detailed knowledge of costs that is a great aid in negotiation.

---

123 *Ibid.*, pp. 24-26.

STRATEGIES FOR COPING WITH THE FIVE FORCES

Five forces analysis identifies threats to industry profits. All firms in the industry must cope with these threats. In coping, firms may pursue several strategies. Firms may position themselves to outperform their rivals by developing a cost or differentiation advantage that somewhat insulates them from the five forces. Firms may limit itself to an industry segment in which the five forces are less severe. A firm may try to redefine or delimit the five forces. For example, firms may try to reduce internal rivalry by creating switching costs. A manufacturer might require customers to use its parts to keep a warranty in effect. This practice would create a switching cost in the form of a voided warranty and thus discourage customers from purchasing parts from another supplier. In addition, firms may reduce the threat of entry by pursuing entry-deterring strategies or try to reduce buyer or supplier power by tapered integration.

MARKET STRUCTURE

The structure of a market refers to the number of firms and characteristics of firms in a market. Some market structures consist of a few large firms, whereas others are composed of many small firms. In national markets, the number of firms in a market usually corresponds inversely to size. Some industries are populated with large firms, whereas other industries consist of small firms. In some industries, the largest firm in the industry is relatively large, whereas in other industries, the largest firm is relatively small. Thus, some markets or industries are structured with a large number of small firms, whereas others are structured with a small number of large firms.

Each year in May, *Fortune* publishes its special *Fortune* 500 issue. The *Fortune* 500 ranks U.S. firms by revenues. In Table 9.2, revenues of the largest firm in selected U.S. industries are shown for 2012. America's largest company was Wal-Mart, which nosed out Exxon Mobil. In the General Merchandisers industry, Wal-Mart was the largest firm and had revenues of $469.162 billion in 2012. In the Petroleum Refining industry, Exxon Mobil had revenues of $449.886 billion in 2012. In these two industries, the largest firm is indeed large, very large. On the other hand, the largest firm in the Publishing, Printing industry was R.R. Donnelley & Sons, which had revenues of only $10.222 billion in 2012. In the Hotels, Casinos, Resorts industry, the largest firm was Marriott International, which had revenues of $11.814 billion in 2012. In these two industries, the largest firm is relatively small, very small.

Table 9.2 Largest Firms in Selected U.S. Industries, 2012		
Industry (No. of Companies in Fortune 500)	**Largest Company (Revenues Rank)**	**Revenues ($Billion)**
Aerospace and Defense (12)	Boeing (30)	81.698
Airlines (6)	United Continental Holdings (79)	37.152
Apparel (4)	Nike (126)	24.128
Beverages (3)	Coca-Cola (57)	48.017
Chemicals (15)	Dow Chemical (52)	56.786
Commercial Banks (18)	J.P. Morgan Chase (18)	108.184
Computer Software (4)	Microsoft (35)	73.723
Computers, Office Equipment (5)	Apple (6)	156.508
Construction and Farm Equipment (6)	Caterpillar (42)	65.875
Diversified Outsourcing Services (2)	Aramark (205)	13.505
Engineering, Construction (10)	Fluor (110)	27.577
Entertainment (7)	Walt Disney (66)	42.278
Food and Drug Stores (8)	CVS Caremark (13)	123.133
Food Consumer Products (15)	Pepsico (43)	65.492
Food Services (4)	McDonald's (111)	27.567
Forest and Paper Products (3)	International Paper (107)	27.833
General Merchandisers (10)	Wal-Mart Stores (1)	469.162
Hotels, Casinos, Resorts (6)	Marriott International (230)	11.814
Household and Personal Products (6)	Procter & Gamble (28)	85.120
Information Technology Services (7)	IBM (20)	104.507
Internet Services and Retailing (7)	Amazon.com (49)	61.093
Mail, Package, and Freight Delivery (2)	United Parcel Service (53)	54.127
Metals (8)	ALCOA (128)	23.700
Mining, Crude Oil Production (14)	ConocoPhillips (45)	63.373
Motor Vehicles and Parts (15)	General Motors (7)	152.256
Oil and Gas Equipment, Services (6)	Halliburton (106)	28.503
Petroleum Refining (11)	Exxon Mobil (2)	449.886
Pharmaceuticals (13)	Johnson & Johnson (41)	67.224
Publishing, Printing (3)	R.R. Donnelley & Sons (264)	10.222
Railroads (3)	Union Pacific (136)	20.926
Specialty Retailers: Apparel (5)	TJX (115)	25.878
Specialty Retailers: Other (22)	Costco (22)	99.137
Telecommunications (17)	AT&T (11)	127.434
Tobacco (3)	Philip Morris International (99)	31.377

Source: Fortune (May 20, 2013), pp. F-33ff.

To reiterate, the largest firm is indeed large in some of these industries. In other industries, even the largest firm is relatively small. Size clearly differs from one industry to another. However, size is not the only characteristic to consider in market structure. Another characteristic is homogeneity of product. In industries such as metals and chemicals, products are homogeneous, and various sellers can meet product requirements equally well. In other markets such as automobiles, soft drinks, and apparel, products are differentiated rather than homogeneous. As a result, different customers tend to have preferences for one product rather than another. Still another characteristic is concentration. In some industries, sales are concentrated in a few large firms, whereas in other industries sales are dispersed among a lot of small firms. Concentration is an important characteristic of market structure.

DEFINING INDUSTRIES USING SIC AND NAICS CODES

To restate the point, market structure refers to the number and characteristics of firms making up a market. A given firm may compete in several product markets at the same time. It may face differing degrees of competition in each of these product markets because market structures may be different for each product. The process leading to identification of the market or markets in which a firm competes is known as market definition, which in turn is used to define a relevant market. Closely related to market definition is industry definition. A simple and common approach is to define industries according to an industrial classification system. In the United States, industries were defined since the 1930s through use of the Standard Industrial Classification (SIC) system.

In the 1930s, the need for an industrial classification system was recognized. In 1934, an Interdepartmental Conference on Industrial Classification recommended development of an industrial classification of statistical data. In 1937, the Central Statistical Board established an Interdepartmental Committee on Industrial Classification to develop a classification plan for use by the federal government. A Technical Committee was established to prepare the proposed standard classification of industries. The result was the Standard Industrial Classification (SIC) System. The SIC is a system of codes used to group companies by industry. Basically, SIC provided a framework for collection, tabulation, presentation, and analysis of data. In 1997, however, the North American Industry Classification System (NAICS) replaced SIC as a response to the North American Free Trade Agreement (NAFTA). The NAICS was developed jointly by the United States, Canada, and Mexico to provide commonality and comparability in statistics about business activity across North America.

Under auspices of the Department of Commerce and the Census Bureau, the economic census is a major source of facts about the structure of the nation's economy. In particular, the economic census provides a comprehensive statistical profile of large segments of the U.S. economy. The Census Bureau takes an economic census every five years, covering years ending in 2 and 7, *e.g.*, 1992, 1997, 2002, 2007, 2012, 2017, 2022, and so on. Each economic census is published by the U.S. government four years or so after the census is taken. The economic census is a primary source of data concerning changes in the number and size distribution of competitors, output, and employment in various industries.

Table 9.3 is based on the SIC system and shows sectors described by two-digit classifications. Below the two-digit major group or sector level, the SIC system proceeds to levels of ever narrowly defined activity. The SIC system proceeds from general two-digit industry groups to four-digit product groups. To illustrate, consider Table 9.4, which shows the narrowing that occurs when moving from the two-digit food and kindred products industry group to the eventual four-digit industry categories.

Table 9.3 Standard Industrial Classifications of Economic Activity	
Sector	**Two Digit SIC Codes**
Agriculture, Forestry, and Fisheries	01-09
Mining	10-14
Contract Construction	15-17
Manufacturing	20-39
Transportation; Communication; Electric, Gas, and Sanitary Services	40-49
Wholesale and Retail Trade	50-59
Finance, Insurance, and Real Estate	60-67
Services	70-89
Public Administration	91-97
Nonclassifable Establishments	99

Table 9.4 Census Classification from Two-Digit to Four-Digit Codes		
Digit Level	**SIC Code**	**Description**
Two	20	Food and Kindred Products
Three	202	Dairy Products
Four	2021	Creamery Butter
Four	2022	Natural, Processed, and Imitation Cheese
Four	2023	Condensed and Evaporated Milk
Four	2024	Ice Cream and Frozen Desserts
Four	2025	Fluid Milk

Industry Definition: 4-Digit SIC Codes

When SIC was used before NAICS, economists and business analysts generally agreed that four-digit SIC codes usually corresponded closely with the definition of an industry. In other words, establishments grouped at the four-digit level usually indicated an industry within which products are competitive. Caution was necessary, however, in relying exclusively on SIC codes to define industries. Although products with the same SIC code often shared the same product performance characteristics and in fact were competing products, this conclusion was not always the case. For example, pharmaceuticals shared the same four-digit SIC code (2834), but not all pharmacy drugs are substitutes for each other. In this particular case, the four-digit SIC was too aggregated for any meaningful identification of competitors. In other cases, firms that competed with each had different SIC codes. An example is variety stores (5331), department stores (5311), and general merchandise stores (5399). These SIC codes were too narrow for a meaningful identification of competitors.

NAICS

On 8 December 1993, President Clinton signed into law the North American Free Trade Agreement (Tradado de Libre Comercio de América del Norte). NAFTA became effective on 1 January 1994. The United States, Canada, and Mexico used incompatible statistical systems for industrial classification. A new industrial classification system was needed even before NAFTA was signed into law. SIC codes used by the United States had been designed when manufacturing rather than services dominated the U.S. economy. This transformation alone had rendered SIC somewhat obsolete. NAFTA merely exacerbated problems with SIC as an industrial classification system. As a replacement for SIC codes, the North American Industrial Classification System (NAICS) was adopted in 1997. NAICS was developed in conjunction with the U.S. Economic Classification Policy Committee, Statistics Canada, and Mexico's Instituto Nacional de Estadistica, Geografia e Informatica. NAICS modernized the U.S. industrial classification system and provided comparability in business statistics among the three North American countries.

NAICS uses a six-digit numbering system. The first two digits designate a sector. For example, 31, 32, or 33 would indicate the manufacturing sector. The third digit designates a subsector. The code beginning with 331 would indicate the primary metal manufacturing subsector. The fourth digit designates an industry group. The code of 3315 would indicate the foundries industry group. The fifth digit designates an NAICS industry. The code of 33152 would indicate the nonferrous metal foundries NAICS industry. The sixth digit designates a U.S. national industry. The code of 331521 would indicate aluminum die-casting foundries as a U.S national industry.

Beginning with the 1997 Economic Census, data are published on the basis of the North American Industry Classification System (NAICS). Most 1997 census reports cover one of twenty NAICS sectors shown in Table 9.5. These twenty NAICS sectors are subdivided into ninety-six subsectors (three-digit codes), 313 industry groups (four-digit codes), and as implemented in the United States, 1,170 industries (five- and six- digit codes). While many of the individual NAICS industries correspond directly to industries as defined under the SIC system, most groupings at higher levels do not. Particular care must be taken in comparing data for retail trade, wholesale trade, and manufacturing, which are sector titles used in both NAICS and SIC but cover somewhat different groups of industries.

Table 9.5 NAICS Sectors and Codes	
Sector	**NAICS Two-Digit Code**
Agriculture, Forestry, Fishing, and Hunting	11
Mining	21
Utilities	22
Construction	23
Manufacturing	31-33
Wholesale Trade	42
Retail Trade	44-45
Transportation and Warehousing	48-49
Information	51
Finance and Insurance	52
Real Estate and Rental and Leasing	53
Professional, Scientific, and Technical Services	54
Management of Companies and Enterprises	55
Administrative and Support and Waste Management and Remediation Services	56
Educational Services	61
Health Care and Social Assistance	62
Arts, Entertainment, and Recreation	71
Accommodation and Food Services	72
Other Services (except Public Administration)	81
Public Administration	92

Industry Definition: 6-Digit NAICS Codes

Reconsider Food and Kindred Products, shown in Table 9.4. In the NAICS system, this classification is Food Manufacturing, and it includes Dairy Product Manufacturing, Ice Cream and Frozen Desert Manufacturing, as well as other subdivisions. For purposes of comparison, the NAICS codes are shown in Table 9.6. Whereas industries are defined as a rule of thumb by four-digit SIC codes, industries are commonly defined by six-digit NAICS codes.

Table 9.6 NAICS System for Food Manufacturing	
Classification	**NAICS Code**
Sector: Manufacturing	31-33
Subsector: Food Manufacturing	311
Industry Group: Dairy Product Manufacturing	3115
NAICS Industry: Dairy Product (except Frozen) Manufacturing	31151
U.S. National Industry: Fluid Milk Manufacturing	311511
U.S. National Industry: Creamery Butter Manufacturing	311512
U.S. National Industry: Cheese Manuracturing	311513
U.S. National Industry: Dry, Condensed, and Evaporated Dairy Product Manufacturing	311514

CONCENTRATION RATIOS

Often, industries or relevant product markets are described as being concentrated or unconcentrated. In the case of concentrated industries or product markets, modifiers such as moderately concentrated and highly concentrated are used. The meaning is simple. If an industry or product market is concentrated, sales are centered on just a few sellers, whereas if an industry or product market is unconcentrated, sales are spread over a large number of sellers. Characterizations such as highly concentrated, moderately concentrated, and unconcentrated provide a quick assessment of the likely nature of competition in an industry or product market. These characterizations are aided by metrics, meaning measures of market concentration.

A common measure of product market or industry structure is a concentration ratio. Two common concentration ratios are the 4-firm concentration ratio and the 8-firm concentration ratio. A 4-firm concentration ratio is the combined market share of the four largest firms in an industry, and the 8-firm concentration ratio is the combined market share of the eight largest firms in an industry. In 2007, for example, the 4-firm concentration ratio for breakfast cereal manufacturing was 80.4, which indicates that the combined market share of the four largest breakfast cereal manufacturers was 80.4 percent. The 8-firm concentration ratio was 91.9, which means the eight largest breakfast cereal manufacturers had 91.9 percent of total sales.

When calculating market share, sales revenue usually is used, although concentration ratios based on measures such as value of shipments also are used. The numbers four in four-firm concentration ratios and eight in eight-firm concentration ratios are somewhat arbitrary and a matter of convenience and tradition. For most industries, the Census Bureau publishes concentration ratios for the largest four, eight, twenty, and fifty manufacturing firms.

HERFINDAHL-HIRSCHMAN INDEX (HHI)

Another common measure of concentration is known as the Herfindahl-Hirschman Index (HHI). The HHI is named primarily for Orris C. Herfindahl, the economist once credited with using it first to measure and analyze industry concentration. Herfindahl developed the index while writing a Ph.D. dissertation at Columbia University on concentration in the steel industry. Upon further review, however, Albert O.

Hirschman was found to have used the same index much earlier. Therefore, the concentration measure is called the Herfindahl-Hirschman Index.[124]

Conceptually, HHI equals the sum of squared market shares of all firms in a market. By squaring market shares, HHI places more weight on firms with large market shares. The higher the HHI, the more concentrated sales are in an industry or market. HHI is regarded as a more reliable measure of market concentration than a four-firm or an eight-firm concentration ratio. For example, suppose five firms in an industry have the following market shares: 30%, 20%, 20%, 20%, and 10%. The four-firm concentration ratio is 90, meaning the four largest firms have ninety percent of total sales. By squaring market share for each of the five firms, *i.e.*, $30^2+20^2+20^2+20^2+10^2$, HHI would be 2,200. On the other hand, suppose in another industry the largest firm has sixty percent of sales, and the other four have only ten percent of sales each. Again, the four-firm concentration ratio is 90, meaning that the four largest firms have ninety percent of total sales. However, by squaring the market share of each firm, *i.e.*, $60^2+10^2+10^2+10^2+10^2$, HHI would be 4,000, indicating a much greater market concentration.

Minimum Value of HHI

HHI can range from approximately zero if each firm in an industry has an infinitesimal market share to 10,000 if one firm supplies an entire market so that it has a 100 percent market share. The larger the HHI measure, the more highly concentrated the market. Usually, however, HHI for any industry is truncated to include only the largest fifty firms. This convention is practiced by the federal government in its reporting of HHI by industry. After all, the HHI is constructed to emphasize the market shares of the largest sellers in an industry, which allows exclusion of firms so small that their influence on competition can be ignored. When calculating HHI, it also is usual and common to restrict calculation to firms with market shares of one percent or larger since the squared shares of smaller firms are too small to affect the overall HHI by enough to matter. If calculation of HHI is truncated, the result is called the minimum value of HHI, meaning HHI is at least as large as the value calculated.

As a matter of language and more, an industry or product market is regarded as unconcentrated if the HHI is less than 1,500. An industry or product market is regarded as moderately concentrated if HHI is between 1,500 and 2,500. An industry or product market is regarded as highly concentrated if HHI is more than 2,500. This language is used by the Antitrust Division of the Department of Justice and by the Federal Trade Commission. These categories shape antitrust enforcement.

Table 9.7 shows market shares and concentration in the world tire industry for 1990. The 4-firm concentration ratio is 64, meaning that the four largest firms had 64 percent of the market. The 8-firm concentration ratio is 82.5 percent, meaning that the eight largest firms had 82.5 percent of the market. HHI is at least 1,242, which is the minimum value of HHI. Evidently, the tenth largest firm had less than one percent of sales. In the language of business and public policy, the world tire industry was unconcentrated because the HHI is less than 1,500.

---

124   For an interesting historical note, see O. Hirschman, "The Paternity of an Index," *American Economic Review*, 54 (September 1964), pp. 761-762.

Table 9.7 Market Shares and Concentration in the World Tire Industry, 1990		
Company	Market Share (Per Cent)	Market Share Squared
Michelin	21.5	462
Goodyear	19.0	361
Bridgestone/Firestone	16.5	272
Continental	7.0	49
4-Firm Concentration Ratio	64.0	
Pirelli	6.0	36
Sumitomo	6.0	36
Yokohama	4.5	20
Toyo	2.0	4
8-Firm Concentration Ratio	82.5	
Cooper	1.5	2
Sum of Tabulated Market Shares	84.0	
Minimum Value of HHI		1,242

Source: The Economist (June 8-14, 1991)

CONCENTRATION STATISTICS FOR MANUFACTURING

Concentration ratios and the HHI are reported in the *Census of Manufactures* as a special publication of the U.S. Census Bureau called *Concentration Ratios in Manufacturing*. Four-firm, eight-firm, twenty-firm, and fifty-firm concentration ratios are reported along with HHI. Table 9.8 shows concentration statistics for U.S. manufacturing by SIC code for selected industries. Industries are shown by 4-digit SIC code along with 4-firm concentration ratio, 8-firm concentration ratio, 20-firm concentration ratio, and HHI. These concentration statistics are based on data from the 1992 Census of Manufactures, but not published until 1996.

Table 9.8 Concentration Statistics for Selected U.S. Manufacturing Industries, 1992						
SIC Code	Industry	Number of Firms	4-Firm CR	8-Firm CR	20-Firm CR	HHI
2024	Ice cream and frozen desserts	411	24	40	68	293
2033	Canned fruits and vegetables	502	27	42	64	301
2037	Frozen fruits and vegetables	182	28	42	65	313
2041	Flour and other grain mill products	230	56	68	83	972
2043	Cereal breakfast foods	42	85	98	99+	2,253
2047	Dog and cat food	102	58	77	92	1,229
2085	Distilled and blended liquors	43	62	82	97	1,123
2273	Carpets and rugs	383	40	53	76	854
2448	Wood pallets and skids	1,902	5	7	13	14
2731	Book publishing	2,504	23	38	62	251
2771	Greeting cards	157	84	88	95	2,922
2841	Soap and other detergents	635	63	77	85	1,584
2911	Petroleum refining	131	30	49	78	414
3221	Glass containers	16	84	93	100	2,162
3334	Primary aluminum	30	59	82	99+	1,456
3411	Metal cans	132	56	74	91	1,042
3511	Turbines and turbine generators	64	79	92	98	2,549
3562	Ball and roller bearings	123	51	65	89	852
3565	Packaging machinery	590	16	25	44	154
3571	Electronic computers	803	45	59	82	680
3581	Automatic vending machines	105	52	73	91	844
3635	Household vacuum cleaners	35	59	86	99+	1,174
3711	Motor vehicles and car bodies	398	84	91	99	2,676
3823	Process control instruments	822	27	38	52	256
3931	Musical instruments	437	25	41	68	304
3995	Burial caskets	195	64	72	82	2,149

Source: "Concentration Ratios in Manufacturing," 1992 Census of Manufactures, (Washington, D.C.: U.S. Department of Commerce, Economics and Statistics Administration, Bureau of the Census, 1996).

Beginning with the 1997 Economic Census, concentration ratios in manufacturing were based on NAICS codes. Concentration data for the 2007 Economic Census are shown in Table 9.9.

	Table 9.9					
	Concentration Statistics for Selected U.S. Manufacturing Industries, 2007					
NAICS Code	Industry	Number of Firms	4-Firm CR	8-Firm CR	20-Firm CR	HHI
311111	Dog and cat food mfg	199	71.0	83.5	92.6	2,315
311211	Flour milling	172	54.5	87.7	82.9	831
311230	Breakfast cereal mfg	35	80.4	91.9	99.6	2,425
311411	Frozen fruit, juice, and vegetable mfg	148	41.1	55.6	74.6	587
311421	Fruit and vegetable canning	537	24.4	36.5	57.4	255
311520	Ice cream and frozen dessert mfg	347	52.7	66.3	84.0	954
312140	Distilleries	80	69.5	87.1	98.6	1,519
314110	Carpet and rug mills	276	63.6	74.5	87.5	1,650
315111	Sheer Hosiery mills	45	69.4	85.1	97.5	1,584
316991	Luggage mfg	191	32.2	49.7	70.6	400
321920	Wood container and pallet mfg	2,646	11.3	14.2	20.6	51
324110	Petroleum refineries	98	47.5	73.1	92.4	806
325611	Soap and other detergent mfg	659	67.1	78.6	84.6	2,025
326211	Tire mfg (except retreading)	90	77.6	93.4	98.2	1,735
331111	Iron and steel mills	235	52.1	67.0	84.3	786
332431	Metal can mfg	68	76.5	94.6	98.8	1,786
332911	Industrial valve mfg	387	27.1	40.1	61.6	304
332991	Ball and roller bearing mfg	116	58.9	72.7	91.0	1,834
333311	Automatic vending machine mfg	86	45.4	71.3	90.9	734
333993	Packaging machinery mfg	558	24.0	32.8	49.0	208
334112	Computer storage device mfg	116	75.6	87.8	95.8	2,982
335212	Household vacuum cleaner mfg	30	70.7	96.3	99.6	1,519
336111	Automobile mfg	174	67.6	91.3	99.2	1,449
339911	Jewel (except costume) mfg	1,652	28.5	38.4	55.2	347
339992	Musical instrument mfg	580	32.2	49.4	62.3	405

Source: "Concentration Ratios in Manufacturing," 2007 Census of Manufactures, (Washington, D.C.: U.S. Department of Commerce, Economics and Statistics Administration, Bureau of the Census), issued May 2011.

RESEARCH AND DEVELOPMENT, ADVERTISING, AND PROFITS

Firms and industries differ with respect to underlying technologies used to produce goods and services. Technological advantage often is gained through engaging in research and development (R&D) and obtaining patents for resulting inventions. A common metric is R&D spending as a percentage of sales. Table 9.10 provides this metric for selected firms. In 1993, the average firm spent 3.8 percent of its sales on R&D activity. However, R&D spending varies significantly across industries. In the healthcare industry, for example, American Home Products used eight percent of its sale revenue for R&D. In the food industry, on the other hand, Kellogg invested less than one percent of its sales revenue in R&D. Clearly, the amount spent on R&D depends on characteristics of the industry in which a firm operates.

Table 9.11 also shows considerable variation across firms in outlays on advertising. Firms such as Kellogg in the food industry spent about ten percent of their sales revenue on advertising. Firms such as General Motors in the automobile industry spent only about one to two percent of their sales revenue on advertising. Clearly, advertising intensities vary across firms in different industries. Finally, Table 9.10 points out variations in profit across firms operating in different industries. General Motors generated more sales revenue than any other firm but, as a percentage of sales revenue, GM's profits were low. Profit as a percentage of sales revenue is a common measure of firm performance.

Table 9.10 R&D, Advertising, and Profits as a Percentage of Sales for Selected Firms				
Company	Industry	R&D (% of Sales)	Advertising (% of Sales)	Profits (% of Sales)
American Home Products	Healthcare	8.0	6.0	24.0
AT&T	Telecommunications	5.1	1.2	9.3
Boeing	Aerospace	6.5	NA	7.2
Eastman Kodak	Leisure Products	8.0	3.1	5.2
General Motors	Automotive	4.4	1.2	1.9
Kellogg	Food	0.6	10.0	1.6
Microsoft	Softward	12.5	NA	37.3
Pepsico	Consumer Products	0.5	4.2	9.7
Procter & Gamble	Personal Care	3.1	7.9	1.1

Source: Advertising Age (September 28, 1994, pp. 3-11; Business Week (June 27,1994), pp. 81-10.

MARKET STRUCTURES BY TYPE

Market structures have different characteristics regarding the number of firms, size of firms, nature of product, power over price, ease of entry, and other dimensions. Based on such different characterizations, different terms are used to characterize and distinguish market structures. Market structures have been grouped into four basic categories, which are perfect competition, monopolistic competition, oligopoly, and monopoly. In business practice, perfect competition and monopolistic competition are terms rarely if ever spoken or heard. On the other hand, the terms are common in academics and have their uses in pure economic theory. Oligopoly and monopoly are familiar terms in business practice.

PERFECT COMPETITION

Technically, perfect competition is a market structure with countless buyers and sellers of a homogeneous product, no one of which has any control over price; no barriers to entry or exit; and buyers have perfect and costless information regarding availability, price, and quality of the product. Under such strict conditions, a single market price is determined by the interaction of all sellers and all buyers, and this price is beyond the control of any buyer or seller. When the price is determined in the overall market in which sellers and buyers interact and transact, firms in the market become price takers, meaning they take the price determined in the market as their own price. If a firm charges so much as one penny more than this market price, it can sell none of the product. If it charges so much as one penny less than this market price, the firm needlessly gives up sales revenues because the firm can sell as much as it wants at the market price. The only decision made by each firm is how much output to produce and sell at the market price.

No market satisfies the strictest conditions for perfect competition. In this sense, perfect competition is a little like the unicorn. Everybody knows what a unicorn looks like, but no one has ever seen a unicorn. Likewise, everybody knows what perfect competition is, but no one has ever seen an exacting example. Even so, many markets are close to perfect competition. Consider hog farming in the United States. Traditionally, the U.S. pork industry has consisted of thousands of relatively small hog farms. These family hog farms have been important to the economy of states such as Iowa, and commercial herds are found in locations nationwide, Florida to Hawaii, Texas to Minnesota. Hog farmers typically sell live hogs to processors, usually at livestock auctions. Hog farmers have little if any control whatsoever over the price of their product. These hog farmers face similar costs for their inputs and use similar methods of production. Packing plants are willing to purchase as many hogs as an individual farmer wants to sell at the market price so that no one farmer has an incentive to lower the selling price below the market price. Basically, the only distinction between herds is whether or not they have been certified as free of brucellosis, a bacteria-caused disease that infects people as well as livestock.

At any given time, the primary determinant of pork prices is supply. High feed prices can lead hog farmers to take more of their animals to auction, and large herds brought to market can cause hog prices to plummet. In an attempt to protect their income, some farmers attempt to limit their exposure to the price they receive by selling on the futures market or by withholding their animals from the market. Once processed, pork is delivered to supermarkets where butchers cut the meat into familiar products such as pork chops, pork loins, and pork ribs. Once at the store, pork competes with other meats such as beef and poultry as well as seafood.

The processing stage of the pork industry is more concentrated than hog farming. The top five pork processors are Smithfield, IBP, Conagra, Cargill, and Farmland. These large companies control about two-thirds of pork processing. Smithfield has the world's largest pork processing plant located in Tar Heel, North Carolina, where about 5,000 people are employed. A single packing plant typically slaughters and processes many thousands of hogs a day, originating from herds raised and kept in ten or more states. Hog farmers receive about twenty-five percent of the retail dollar spent on pork, whereas packers such as Smithfield receive about sixteen percent.

MONOPOLISTIC COMPETITION

In 1933, Edward Chamberlain introduced the term monopolistic competition to characterize markets with two main features.[125] First, many sellers as well as ease of entry and exit characterize the market. Second, each seller offers a product differentiated from the rest. Hence, monopolistic competition means a market with similar products but differentiated in some way, perhaps by brand. Bayer Aspirin and

---

125   Edward Chamberlain, *The Theory of Monopolistic Competition* (Cambridge, MA: Harvard University Press, 1933).

Walgreens Aspirin are both acetylsalicylic acid and thus are competitive, but Bayer has a monopoly on Bayer Aspirin since Bayer is the only producer and seller of Bayer Aspirin. The notion of product differentiation is that buyers make choices among competing products on the basis of factors such as price, taste, scent, location, convenience, or some other real or imagined difference. Monopolistic competition is evident in markets such as retail banking, dry cleaning and laundry services, restaurants, convenience stores, as well as products such as grade A dark amber maple syrup, AA batteries, and 100 watt light bulbs. Although individual firms engaged in monopolistic competition are able to maintain some control over price, their pricing discretion is limited severely by competition from firms offering close if not identical substitutes.

Distinctions are made between vertical differentiation and horizontal differentiation. Vertical differentiation refers generally to making a product better than the products of competitors. Horizontal differentiation indicates making the product no better or worse than competitors but distinctive or different from those of competitors, which may involve making it appealing to one class of potential customers but unappealing to other potential customers. For example, the producer of a cleaning product engages in vertical differentiation when the producer enhances the cleaning effectiveness of its product, thus making it better than products offered by other firms. This differentiation makes the product more attractive to all potential customers. The producer engages in horizontal differentiation when it adds a pine scent to the cleaner. This differentiation makes the cleaning product more appealing to consumers who associate pine aroma with a clean house but perhaps less appealing to other consumers who are adversely sensitive to the aroma of a pine forest in their homes or who associate other scents such as a lemon scent with cleanliness.

Sellers of vertically differentiated products may charge higher prices since at least some customers may be more willing than others to pay for additional quality. If these sellers charge the same price and the product is truly more effective, buyers generally will prefer the product to other products of lesser quality and will buy the better product. On the other hand, if sellers of horizontally differentiated products charge the same price, consumers will disagree about which product is preferred, and each seller will capture a share of the market. In either vertical differentiation or horizontal differentiation, sales of a product do not fall to zero when its price is raised above that of other products, which makes monopolistic competition unlike perfect competition.

An important source of differentiation is geography, mainly because consumers prefer stores offering convenient access. In a metropolitan market for dry cleaning, for example, dry cleaning stores are horizontally differentiated because their locations differ. The idea that differentiated products can be represented by distinct locations can be applied to various settings, including location on a straight line continuum representing characteristics such as sportiness of automobiles, sweetness of colas, or cut of business suits. Individuals with strong preferences for conservative suits would be located at one end of the continuum, whereas individuals who prefer stylishly hip suits would be at the other end.

If preferences are highly idiosyncratic, tastes differ markedly from one person to the next, and buyers might be reluctant to switch from seller to seller just to act on a lower price. In this case, different sellers could keep loyal followings even if they raise prices. For example, someone who is salt sensitive and limits sodium intake because of high blood pressure might eat Spoon Size Shredded Wheat, which has zero sodium content. If the price of another wheat cereal loaded with sodium were lowered, the salt sensitive buyer would not switch to the other brand. Post, the maker of Spoon Size Shredded Wheat, could raise price without losing the loyalty of the salt sensitive buyer.

OLIGOPOLY

In a market with many if not countless sellers, no one seller believes that pricing or production decisions will affect the overall market price or volume of production. Such beliefs make sense in a market with many sellers. In a market with only a few sellers, however, it seems reasonable to expect that pricing and production decisions of any one firm will affect overall industry price and production volumes. A market in which actions of a few firms materially affect the industry price is called an oligopoly. In the United States, aluminum, cigarettes, electrical equipment, glass, breakfast cereals, greeting cards, and burial caskets are produced and sold under oligopolistic conditions. In each of these industries, a small number of firms produce a dominant percentage of industry output. Correspondingly, sales are concentrated on a small number of firms.

All oligopolies are not alike. Oligopolies differ by the nature of product produced. In some oligopolistic industries, products are homogeneous. Examples are industries such as aluminum, nickel, copper, gold, sulfur, and steel. In other oligopolies, products are differentiated. Examples include automobiles, home appliances, breakfast cereals, and cigarettes. The type of product produced, homogeneous or differentiated, affects strategic behavior. Broadly speaking, economists and business analysts refer to two patterns of such behavior, cooperative or non-cooperative. Cooperative oligopolists tend to follow any change made by rival firms. For example, if a rival raises price, a cooperative oligopolist would go along with the move and raise its price correspondingly. Non-cooperative oligopolists, on the other hand, do not accommodate such changes. If a rival firm were to raise price, other firms would keep their prices low to attract sales away from the higher price producer.

However, oligopolists have other ways to compete. Some oligopolistic markets are characterized by intensive price competition. In other oligopolistic markets, firms do not compete extensively on the basis of price but in other ways such as advertising, product quality, service, and related marketing strategies. Cooperative oligopolists producing identical products tend to behave in unison much like a monopoly. Cooperative oligopolistic firms tend to act as one. Differentiated products make cooperation more difficult, and competition is more difficult to contain. Many models have been developed to understand how firms should behave and explain how firms actually do behave in oligopolistic markets. A central element of most models is the careful consideration of how firms respond to each other and to opportunities in the market.

MONOPOLY

Taken literally, monopoly is the case of one seller supplying an entire market or one producer comprising an entire industry. Less restrictively, monopoly power deals with unrestrained control over price. Frank Fisher, a noted antitrust economist, described monopoly power as "the ability to act in an unconstrained way."[126] Examples of unconstrained actions include increasing prices or reducing product quality without losing customers to other firms. A firm can take such actions if its customers cannot take their business elsewhere easily. Competition comes from fringe firms, small firms collectively accounting for a small

---

126   Frank Fisher, *Industrial Organization, Antitrust, and the Law* (Cambridge, MA: MIT Press, 1991).

market share. A monopolist usually ignores fringe firms when setting its own price since it does not believe that decisions made by fringe firms can affect its profitability materially.

The common belief is that a monopolist's extraordinary profits come at the expense of consumers. Concern over detrimental effects of monopoly pricing on consumer welfare lies at the heart of antitrust policies in the United States and the European Union. In both jurisdictions, antitrust laws and policies are aimed at deterring creation and exercise of monopoly power. This point of view is not universally embraced, however. Another economist, Harold Demsetz, noted that high prices and correspondingly large profits do not necessarily justify government efforts to bust up monopolies and prevent new ones from forming.[127] Demsetz argued that most monopolies arise when a firm discovers a more efficient way to manufacture a product or creates a new product to fulfill unmet consumer needs. Consumers benefit from such innovations, but innovation is risky. Firms continue to innovate only if they expect large profits when successful. If Demsetz is correct, then restrictions on monopolies actually may hurt consumers in the long run by choking off innovation.

Many firms have built substantial market power and make large profits through innovation. Wal-Mart dominates retailing in many markets, but it achieved this status through efficiencies resulting in low costs. Wal-Mart gained market dominance by giving a stake in its efficiencies to consumers in the form of lower prices. Another example is Xerox, which innovated the eponymous technique known as xerography and once dominated the plain paper copier market. Most countries recognize that benefits offset the downside of monopoly at the front end of innovation and routinely award patents to protect innovators from competition. While the patentee receives large profits, consumers realize the benefits of the innovative new product. Without patents, firms might be unwilling to make investments necessary to innovate for fear others would steal their products without making similar investments themselves.

PRACTICE QUESTIONS

1. Michael E. Porter organized analysis of industries into five forces, and the analysis is known as "Five Forces Analysis." Describe the overall framework and its purpose.

2. Consider the following information regarding a particular industry. Calculate the 4-firm concentration ratio, 8-firm concentration ratio, and the HHI for this industry.

12 Firms Ranked by Market Share (%), Highest to Lowest											
Market Share	20	15	13	12	10	9	6	5	4	3	2	1

---

127   Harold Demsetz, "Two Systems of Belief About Monopoly," *Industrial Concentration: The New Learning*, eds. H. Goldschmidt, *et al.* (Boston: Little Brown, 1974).

3. The following table presents market share data on the top five beer brewers in the United States for 1968 and 1979. Assume that the residual market share is spread equally over twenty other brewers. Answer each question below based on this information.

Year	Anheuser-Busch	Miller	Schlitz	Pabst	Coors	All Others
1968	16.5	4.3	10.4	10.0	4.8	54.0
1979	25.9	20.0	9.9	8.6	7.4	28.2

a. What is the four-firm concentration ratio (C_4) for the brewing industry for 1968? What is the eight-firm ratio (C_8) for 1979?

b. What is the Herfindahl-Hirshman Index (HHI) for 1968? What is the HHI for 1979?

c. Based on the HHI, was the trend in the brewing industry for 1968-1979 toward more concentration or less concentration? Explain.

4. Answer the next question based on information shown in the table below, which reports market shares (%) for the largest twenty financial institutions in the New Orleans area as of June 30, 2003.

Institution	Market Share (%)	Institution	Market Share (%)
Hibernia	27.2	Fifth District S&L	1.6
Bank One	18.9	Parish National	1.4
4Whitney	17.3	Iberia	1.4
Regions	7.1	Crescent Bank & Trust	1.3
Fidelity Homestead	3.2	Liberty Bank & Trust	1.25
First Bank & Trust	2.2	Metairie Bank & Trust	1.2
Amsouth	2.2	Bank of N.O.	0.8
First American	1.8	Guaranty Saving	0.7
Gulf Coast Bank & Trust	1.7	First National	0.6
Omni	1.7	Central Progressive	0.6

a. Calculate the 4-firm concentration ratio. Interpret this calculation.

b. Calculate the 8-firm concentration ratio. Interpret this calculation.

c. Calculate the minimum value of HHI.

5. Answer the next question based on the following information. In 1996, more than 5 million computer notebooks were sold. The following market shares (%) were widely reported in magazines such as P_c Magazine (August 1997, p. 106). The market shares for sixteen companies with a market share of 1% or more are shown below.

Vendor	Market Share	Vendor	Market Share
Toshiba	23	WinBook	3
IBM	11	AST	2
Compaq	9	Gateway	2
Dell	5	ZDS	2
NEC	5	Digital	2
HP	4	Acer	2
Apple	4	Fujitsu	1
TI	3	Micron	1

a. What is the 4-firm concentration ratio? Interpret this calculation.

b. What is the 8-firm concentration ratio? Interpret this calculation.

c. What is the minimum value of HHI?

6. Why are markets for various commodities such as agricultural products and metals regarded as close to perfect competition?

7. Many markets are described as being monopolistically competitive. What is monopolistic competition? What role is played by differentiation?

Questions for Contemplation, Discussion, and Argument

8. In any metropolitan area such as the Greater New Orleans area, the dry cleaning market is regarded as a case of monopolistic competition. Why?

9. During the week of March 9, 1997, the Federal Trade Commission (FTC) voted to block a merger between office supply companies Staples and Office Depot despite claims by the companies that the merger would result in "greater efficiencies." Why would the FTC move to block such a merger?

10. Consider two industries with comparable consumer demands. In one industry, production involves substantial fixed costs. In the other industry, production involves minimal fixed costs. Which one of the two industries is more likely to evidence price rivalry during its growth? How would price rivalry in each industry change if demand declines unexpectedly?

11. A firm in one geographic market has achieved minimum efficient scale is highly profitable. Another firm in the same product market but a different geographic market also has achieved minimum efficient scale is not profitable at all. Provide an explanation for these observations.

PRACTICE QUESTIONS *(AND ANSWERS)*

1. Michael E. Porter organized analysis of industries into five forces, and the analysis is known as "Five Forces Analysis." Describe the overall framework and its purpose.

Porter developed a framework that accommodates exploration of economic factors affecting the profits of an industry. This framework was structured to formulate competitive strategy, which is relating a company to its environment. The key aspect of a firm's environment is the industry or industries in which it competes. In any industry, the state of competition depends on basic competitive forces. The collective strength of these forces determines the ultimate profit potential in the industry, where profit potential is understood to be long-run return on invested capital. Industries do not have the same profit potential. As the collective strength of these forces differ, industries differ fundamentally in their ultimate profit potential. Porter organized these economic factors into five major forces. Five forces analysis systematically and comprehensively applies economic tools to analyze an industry in depth. In Porter's framework, the five forces are (1) internal rivalry, (2) entry, (3) substitute products, (4) supplier power, and (5) buyer power. Internal rivalry is in the center of this framework because it may be affected by each of the other four forces. For a business unit in an industry, the goal of competitive strategy is to find a position in the industry where the company can defend itself best against these competitive forces or can influence them in its favor. As a framework, therefore, Porter meant five forces analysis as the fundamental structure and method for examining an industry in terms of effects on profits. Each force is assessed by asking the same basic question, viz., to what degree are conditions and factors constituting this force great enough to threaten reduction or even elimination of industry profits?

2. Consider the following information regarding a particular industry. Calculate the 4-firm concentration ratio, 8-firm concentration ratio, and the HHI for this industry.

12 Firms Ranked by Market Share (%), Highest to Lowest											
Market Share	20	15	13	12	10	9	6	5	4	3	2	1

The four-firm concentration ratio is

$C_4 = 20+15+13+12=60,$

The four largest firms have 60% of the market. The eight-firm concentration ratio is

$C_8 = 20+15+13+12+10+9+6+5=90$

The eight largest firms have 90% of the market. The HHI is

$HHI = 20^2+15^2+13^2+12^2+10^2+9^2+6^2+5^2+4^2+3^2+2^2+1^2$

$HHI = 400+225+169+144+100+81+36+25+16+9+4+1=1,210$

3. The following table presents market share data on the top five beer brewers in the United States for 1968 and 1979. Assume that the residual market share is spread equally over twenty other brewers. Answer each question below based on this information.

Year	Anheuser-Busch	Miller	Schlitz	Pabst	Coors	All Others
1968	16.5	4.3	10.4	10.0	4.8	54.0
1979	25.9	20.0	9.9	8.6	7.4	28.2

a. What is the four-firm concentration ratio (C_4) for the brewing industry for 1968? What is the eight-firm ratio (C_8) for 1979?

$C_4(1968)=16.5+10.4+10.0+4.8=41.7$

The four largest brewers had 41.7% of sales in 1968. In 1979, twenty other brewers equally share the market share of 28.2%. Therefore, 28.2%÷20=1.41%.

$C_8(1979)=25.9+20.0+9.9+8.6+7.4+1.41+1.41+1.41=76.03$

The eight largest brewers had 76.03% of sales in 1979.

b. What is the Herfindahl-Hirshman Index (HHI) for 1968? What is the HHI for 1979?

$HHI(1968)=16.5^2+4.3^2+10.4^2+10.0^2+4.8^2+20(2.7^2)$

$HHI(1968)=272.25+18.49+108.16+100.00+23.04+145.80=668$

$HHI(1979)=25.9^2+20.0^2+9.9^2+8.6^2+7.4^2+20(1.41^2)$

$HHI(1979)=670.81+400.00+98.01+73.96+54.76+39.76=1,337$

c. Based on the HHI, was the trend in the brewing industry for 1968-1979 toward more concentration or less competition? Explain.

The trend was toward more concentration as indicated by the increase in the HHI from 668 in 1968 to 1,337 in 1979.

4. Answer the next question based on information shown in the table below, which reports market shares (%) for the largest twenty financial institutions in the New Orleans area as of June 30, 2003.

Institution	Market Share (%)	Institution	Market Share (%)
Hibernia	27.2	Fifth District S&L	1.6
Bank One	18.9	Parish National	1.4
4Whitney	17.3	Iberia	1.4
Regions	7.1	Crescent Bank & Trust	1.3
Fidelity Homestead	3.2	Liberty Bank & Trust	1.25
First Bank & Trust	2.2	Metairie Bank & Trust	1.2
Amsouth	2.2	Bank of N.O.	0.8
First American	1.8	Guaranty Saving	0.7
Gulf Coast Bank & Trust	1.7	First National	0.6
Omni	1.7	Central Progressive	0.6

a. Calculate the 4-firm concentration ratio. Interpret this calculation.

The 4-firm concentration ratio is

C_4 =27.2+18.9+17.3+7.1=70.5

The four largest banks had 70.5% of the market.

b. Calculate the 8-firm concentration ratio. Interpret this calculation.

The 8-firm concentration ratio is

C_8 =27.2+18.9+17.3+7.1+3.2+2.2+2.2+1.8=79.9

The eight largest banks had 79.9% of the market.

c. Calculate the minimum value of HHI.

The minimum value of HHI is

$HHI=27.2^2+18.9^2+17.3^2+7.1^2+3.2^2+2(2.2^2)+1.8^2 +2(1.7^2)+1.6^2+2(1.4^2)+1.3^2+1.25^2+1.2^2$

$HHI=739.84+357.21+299.29+50.41+10.24+9.68+3.60+5.78+2.56+3.92+1.69+1.56+1.44=1,487$

5. Answer the next question based on the following information. In 1996, more than 5 million computer notebooks were sold. The following market shares (%) were widely reported in magazines such as P_c *Magazine* (August 1997, p. 106). The market shares for sixteen companies with a market share of 1% or more are shown below.

Vendor	Market Share	Vendor	Market Share
Toshiba	23	WinBook	3
IBM	11	AST	2
Compaq	9	Gateway	2
Dell	5	ZDS	2
NEC	5	Digital	2
HP	4	Acer	2
Apple	4	Fujitsu	1
TI	3	Micron	1

a. What is the 4-firm concentration ratio? Interpret this calculation.

The 4-firm concentration ratio is 23+11+9+5=48, meaning that, in 1996, 48% of sales of computer notebooks were concentrated in the four largest firms.

b. What is the 8-firm concentration ratio? Interpret this calculation.

The 8-firm concentration ratio is 23+11+9+5+5+4+4+3=64, meaning that, in 1996, 64% of sales of computer notebooks were concentrated in the eight largest firms.

c. What is the minimum value of HHI?

Minimum HHI=$23^2+11^2+9^2+2(5^2)+2(4^2)+2(3^2)+5(2^2)+2(1^2)$=529+121+81+50+32+16+20+2=851

6. Why are markets for various commodities such as agricultural products and metals regarded as close to perfect competition?

A perfectly competitive market is a benchmark against which actual markets are compared. As a standard for comparison, a perfectly competitive market is one in which products are identical, barriers to entry are absent, and sellers are so numerous that no one seller has any control over price so that all sellers are price takers. In the case of commodities such as agricultural products and metals, these conditions are evident to a degree.

7. Many markets are described as being monopolistically competitive. What is monopolistic competition? What role is played by differentiation?

Monopolistic competition characterizes markets with two main features. First, there are many sellers. When there are many sellers, no one seller can take an action that will materially affect other sellers. Second, each seller is slightly differentiated from the rest. When products are homogeneous, buyers willingly switch from one seller to another to obtain even a small price saving. Not all buyers will switch readily however, if they do not agree on which product is best. The notion of product differentiation is that buyers make choices among competing products on the basis of factors other than just price. Distinctions are made between vertical differentiation and horizontal differentiation. The distinction corresponds roughly to the distinction between making a product better than the products of competitors (vertical differentiation) versus making the product distinctive from those of competitors (horizontal differentiation), which may involve making it better, more attractive, or more suitable for one class of potential customers, but making it worse, less attractive, or less suitable for other potential customers. Vigorous monopolistic competition is evident in industries such as banking, container and packaging, discount and fashion retail, electronics, food manufacturing, office equipment, paper and forest products, and most personal and professional services. Although individual firms are able to maintain some control over pricing policy, their pricing discretion is limited severely by competition from firms offering close substitutes.

10. Competitive Advantage

VALUE CREATION

Profitability varies across industries depending on competitive conditions. Profitability also varies among firms within an industry. Some firms make profits that exceed the industry average and that exceed profits made by their chief competitors. Firms with superior returns evidently have positioned themselves favorably with some sort of competitive advantage. A framework for analyzing firms in an industry in terms of their competitive performance is known as the value creation framework, a device once again attributed to Michael E. Porter.[128] The value creation framework provides a structure to organize thinking about a firm's position in an industry and strategically guiding a firm in its pursuit of a competitive advantage. What five forces analysis provides for understanding industry conditions, the value creation framework provides for understanding a firm's competitive performance within its industry. When a firm outperforms its industry and its chief rivals, the firm achieves a competitive advantage. The metric of performance is profitability. When a firm or business unit within a firm has profitability greater than the rate of profit of other firms competing in the same industry or market, the firm has a competitive advantage. The competitive advantage can be based on either cost or differentiation. Thus, a firm in a particular industry might outperform its competitors because it has a cost advantage, or a firm might outperform its competitors because it has a differentiation advantage.

CONSUMER SURPLUS IN THE VALUE CREATION FRAMEWORK

A basic way of viewing business reality suggests that a firm's profitability and thus its performance depend not only on industry conditions but also on the value that a firm embeds in its product(s) relative to its competitors. Consequently, a firm can achieve a competitive advantage only if the firm develops capabilities that allow it to create and offer more product value than its competitors. A firm that creates and offers more value than its competitors can make greater profits and deliver greater benefits to

---

consumers than its competitors. The value a firm creates and offers depends on both its cost position and its differentiation position relative to competitors.

Value creation deals with the concept of perceived benefit and price. Imagine the perceived benefit of a product as the worth of a unit of the product to a consumer. This seemingly abstract concept can be reified a little more concretely as the most a consumer would be willing to pay for a product. Perceived benefit depends on attributes such as performance, reliability, durability, accuracy, aesthetics, image, or some other characteristic. Therefore, perceived benefit, B, is a dollar measure of what one unit of a product is worth to a particular customer and understood as the most a particular customer would be willing to pay for a unit of the product.

Consumer surplus is the difference between the perceived benefit per unit of the product, B, and the purchase price of a product, P. Therefore, consumer surplus is a measure of how much better off a buyer expects to be if a transaction is consummated. Consumer surplus is perceived benefit minus price, B–P, the difference between what a consumer would be willing to pay and what the consumer actually pays. In effect, consumer surplus implies that some gross perceived benefit, B, is priced away, leaving only net perceived benefit, B–P. Figure 10.1 is a simple bar chart showing consumer surplus. The height of the bar is perceived benefit, B. Price is designated as P on the bar chart. The difference on the bar chart, B–P, is consumer surplus.

A simple model of consumer behavior is that a consumer will purchase a product only if consumer surplus is positive. Given a choice between competing products, a consumer will purchase the product for which consumer surplus is believed to be greatest. Competition among firms in a market can be imagined as an ongoing process in which firms submit consumer surplus offers to consumers who then choose the product that offers the greatest consumer surplus.

VALUE MAPS AND INDIFFERENCE CURVES

To compete successfully, a seller must deliver consumer surplus. Sometimes, a value map is used to illustrate the competitive implications of consumer surplus. The horizontal axis of a value map represents the level of a key attribute or conglomeration of attributes, which for simplicity can be called quality. From left to right indicates greater quality. The vertical axis depicts the price of the product. From bottom to top indicates higher price. An upward-sloping indifference curve shows that any price-quality combination along the indifference curve yields the same consumer surplus. In this way, the indifference curve depicts the tradeoff between quality and price, which is how much more consumers would be willing to pay for more quality. Figure 10.2 shows a typical value map and indifference curve.

FIGURE 10.1
CONSUMER SURPLUS

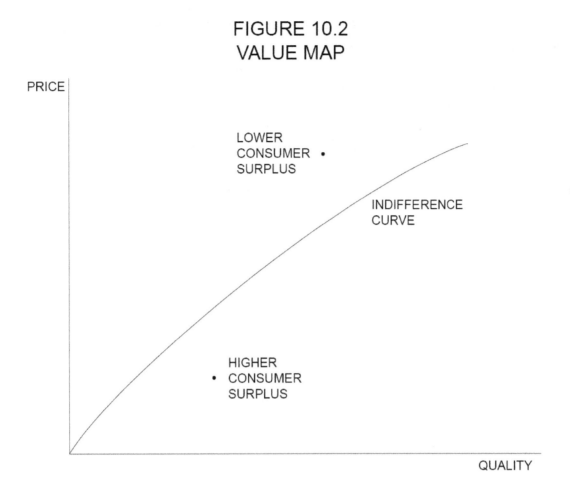

FIGURE 10.2
VALUE MAP

Presumably, consumers choosing among products located along the indifference curve would be indifferent regarding their choice from the offerings because consumer surplus is the same along the indifference curve. Products offering price-quality combinations located below a given indifference curve yield consumer surplus higher than that yielded by products along the indifference curve. From the consumer's perspective, such products provide greater value since these products offer the same quality as products on the indifference curve but at a lower price. Products offering price-quality combinations located above a given indifference curve yield consumer surplus lower than that yielded by products along the indifference curve. From the consumer's perspective, such products provide inferior value since these products offer the same quality as products on the indifference curve but at a higher price.

Take for granted that consumers will choose products that offer the best values. A firm offering consumers less value than its rivals will lose the fight for their business. A firm offering consumers more value will win the battle. When differences in value offered by firms in an industry are evident, market shares are not stable. Firms offering product with greater value will increase their market share, whereas firms offering product with lesser value will lose market share. When quality-price positions are lined up along the same indifference curve, firms offer consumers the same consumer surplus or value. The firms have achieved consumer surplus parity. If firms achieve consumer surplus parity in a market in which consumers have the same preferences, no consumer within that market has an incentive to switch from one seller to another. Market shares will be stable.

The steepness of an indifference curve indicates the tradeoff between price and quality. A steeply upward-sloping indifference curve indicates that consumers are willing to pay considerably more to obtain additional quality, whereas a somewhat flat indifference curve indicates that extra quality is not worth much to customers. Firms overestimating the willingness of consumers to trade off price for quality risk overpricing their products and either losing market share to competitors or never becoming a viable competitor in the first place. The two panels of Figure 10.3 illustrate quite different indifference curves. Panel 10.3(a) shows a steep indifference curve indicating that consumers are willing to pay much more for even a little more quality. Panel 10.3(b) shows a relatively flat indifference curve indicating that consumers are not willing to pay much more for a lot more quality.

FIGURE 10.3
STEEP AND FLAT INDIFFERENCE CURVES

10.3(a)   10.3(b)

VALUE CREATION AND COMPETITIVE ADVANTAGE

As goods move along the vertical chain, value is created. Indeed, Porter gave a name to this rendition of the vertical chain, calling it the value chain. Perceived benefit represents value that consumers ultimately derive from the finished good. Cost represents value sacrificed when converting inputs into outputs of finished products. Value created is the difference between value embedded in the finished good, perceived benefit B, and value sacrificed to produce the finished good, cost, C. Figure 10.4 is a bar chart that illustrates value created. Once again, the height of the bar is perceived benefit, B. Price is designated as P on the bar. Unit cost is designated as C on the bar. Value created is perceived benefit minus unit cost, B–C.

Value created, perceived benefit minus unit cost, is divided between consumers and producers. Consumer surplus is perceived benefit minus price, B–P, which represents value created that is appropriated by the consumer. The seller uses part of the price to pay the labor, capital, and material costs incurred in making the finished product and retains the remainder. Producer surplus, therefore, is price minus average total cost, P–C, which represents value created that the producer retains as a residual. In this way, value created is divided between consumers and producers. Seeing value created as the sum of consumer surplus and producer surplus provides an important perspective and insight,

Value Created=Consumer Surplus+Producer Surplus

This perspective can be restated as

Value Created=(B–P)+(P–C)

B is perceived benefit per unit, P is price, and C is average total cost. Since P cancels,

Value Created=B–C

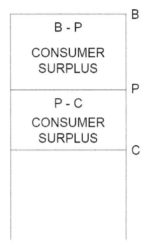

FIGURE 10.4
VALUE CREATED

This perspective shows how much value ensues to buyers as consumer surplus and to sellers as producer surplus.

No business can exist for long without creating value. To achieve a competitive advantage by outperforming competitors in terms of profitability, a business must create value and create more value than its competitors, which is to say generate greater B–C. A firm that creates more value than its competitors will be able to match or exceed the consumer surplus offers of its competitors and end up with higher profit. In a market situation where all firms have attained consumer surplus parity, the firm that creates more value will be more profitable than its rivals. Understanding value creation is a first step in assessing a firm's potential for achieving a competitive advantage.

Competitive advantage cannot be reduced to a bare formula or a simple algorithm. Nevertheless, amidst the different ways that firms position themselves to compete, broad commonalities can be discerned. Such discernment suggests two broad approaches to achieving competitive advantage, one based on cost, the other on differentiation. Recall the value creation framework. Essentially, value created can be distilled down to a simple formulation, which is

Value Created=B–C

This simple conceptualization suggests that competitive advantage could be based on either B or C. The objective of competitive advantage could be pursued through the means of a cost advantage or a differentiation advantage.

Pursuing a cost advantage essentially is seeking to attain lower C while maintaining B equal or at least comparable to competitors. This cost advantage might be exploited by offering a product of the same quality but at a lower price, thus offering consumers greater consumer surplus and value. Pursuing a differentiation advantage basically is seeking to offer higher *B* while maintaining C equal to or at least comparable to competitors. This differentiation advantage might be exploited by offering a product of higher quality but at the same price, thus offering consumers greater consumer surplus and value.

COST ADVANTAGE

A firm with a cost advantage creates more value than its competitors by offering products that have a lower cost with the same or perhaps lower perceived benefit. This cost advantage can materialize in different ways. The firm can achieve benefit parity by offering the same B as its rivals. On the other hand, the firm might achieve only benefit proximity, which involves offering B not much less than competitors. With benefit proximity, a firm must underprice its rivals by more than enough to offset the lower B. Underpricing can be more profitable if a firm's cost advantage is bigger than the price differential between the firm and its competitors. If so, the firm can increase consumer surplus and its own profit simultaneously.

The two panels of Figure 10.5 illustrate benefit parity and benefit proximity. Panel 10.5(a) illustrates benefit parity. Bar charts for two competitors are shown. Both offer the same quality, but one firm has a cost advantage and thus outperforms the other firm. Outperformance is shown as a greater profit margin, P–C. Panel 10.5(b) shows benefit proximity. Again, bar charts are shown for two competitors. One competitor offers quality close but not equal to the quality of the other competitor. However, this competitor has a cost advantage greater than the difference in quality. Even though the competitor has not been able to achieve benefit parity, it can outperform the other competitor. Outperformance is shown as a greater profit margin, P–C.

FIGURE 10.5
BENEFIT PARITY AND BENEFIT PROXIMITY

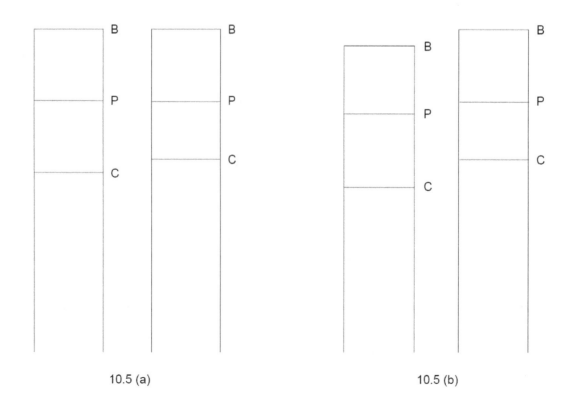

10.5 (a)   10.5 (b)

When a product is of lower quality and cost than competing products, it can compete advantageously with those other products if the cost differential exceeds the quality differential. This point is thought to explain why many people continue to use the U.S. Postal Service rather than private delivery services such as Federal Express or United Parcel Service. According to the American Consumer Satisfaction Index, Federal Express is the leader in express delivery. The U.S. Postal Service express and priority mail is close behind. Evidently, the cost savings from use of USP_S are worth the slightly lower quality.

Building competitive advantage on the basis of cost is likely to be undertaken under certain conditions. One circumstance is that economies of scale and experience are potentially significant, but no firm in the market is exploiting them. Strategies aimed at increasing market share and accumulating experience will give the firm a cost advantage that smaller, less experienced rivals cannot match. If the market itself is growing, however, other firms also may gain the scale and experience necessary to achieve the same cost position.

Opportunities to lift perceived benefit are limited by the nature of the product itself. This condition is found in commodity products such as chemicals, metals, and basic foodstuffs. If so, opportunities for creating additional value may come more from lowering C than from increasing B. However, differentiation is not limited to physical attributes of a product. Opportunities for differentiation might be found through better service, superior location, or more timely delivery than competitors offer.

For some products, consumers are relatively price sensitive and thus are unwilling to pay much more for better product quality. This circumstance occurs when consumers are more sensitive to price than to quality. Indeed, the product might be a search good rather than an experience good. A search good is a product with objective attributes the typical buyer can discern and assess easily at the time of purchase. Examples include 100W light bulbs, AAA batteries, 2% fat milk, and grade A dark amber maple syrup. For products with search good characteristics, the best opportunity to sustain a lasting competitive advantage comes in keeping costs lower than competitors, while taking care to match any initiative to enlarge on any dimension of product quality.

An experience good, on the other hand, is a product with quality attributes that can be assessed only after the buyer has used it for a while. Examples include technologically complex products such as digital cameras, automobiles, cellular phones, and high definition television sets. For experience goods, the potential for differentiation lies largely in upgrading features. If buyers can discern among different offerings, so can competitors, which raises the risk that any upgrade will be matched.

DIFFERENTIATION ADVANTAGE

A firm that creates a competitive advantage based on differentiation creates more value than its competitors by offering a product with higher perceived benefit, B, for the same or perhaps slightly higher cost, C. The differentiating firm can exploit its advantage by setting a price that allows it to offer higher consumer surplus than its rivals while also achieving a higher profit margin. As with cost advantage, parity and proximity are important in differentiation. A successful differentiating firm might achieve cost parity, meaning the same C. Instead, a successful differentiating firm might achieve cost proximity, meaning that C is not much higher than competitors.

The two panels of Figure 10.6 illustrate cost parity and cost proximity. Panel 10.6(a) shows bar charts for two competitors. One offers more quality but has the same cost. In other words, this competitor has achieved cost parity. A premium price can be charged because quality is greater. Clearly, this competitor outperforms the other competitor because of a greater profit margin, P–C. Panel 10.6(b) again shows bar charts for two competitors. One offers more quality but has slightly higher cost. This competitor has achieved cost proximity. The higher premium price is greater than the higher cost. Once again, this competitor outperforms the other competitor since it has a greater profit margin, P–C.

FIGURE 10.6
COST PARITY AND COST PROXIMITY

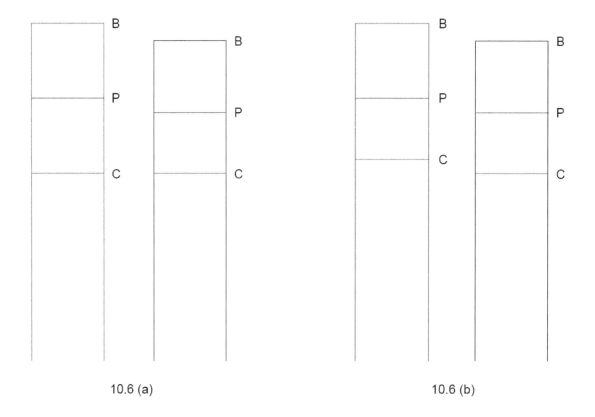

10.6 (a)   10.6 (b)

Building a competitive advantage based on differentiation is likely to be undertaken in particular circumstances. For example, the product might be an experience good rather than a search good. In this case, differentiation can be based on attributes as illusory as image, reputation, or credibility, which are more difficult to imitate or neutralize than objective product features or performance characteristics.

In any event, differentiation is favored if typical consumers are willing to pay a significant price premium for additional quality attributes. In this case, a firm that can offer even a few additional features may be able to command a significant price premium. Another circumstance is that economies of scale or experience might be significant, but existing firms already are exploiting them. In this case, opportunities for achieving a cost advantage are limited, and the best route toward value creation lies in offering a product especially tailored to a particular niche of the market.

MARGIN AND SHARE STRATEGIES

Consider a firm that has a cost advantage. If the firm offers a product that is relatively price inelastic, customers are not particularly price sensitive. Even deep price cuts by the firm will not increase its sales or market share significantly. Under such conditions, a firm might seek to exploit its cost advantage through a margin strategy. The firm can match prices set by its competitors and outperform its competitors through a higher price-cost margin. On the other hand, if the firm offers a product that is relatively price elastic, customers are price sensitive. In this case, a modest price cut by the firm can bring about significant increases in its sales and market share. When this condition is evident, the firm can exploit its cost advantage through a share strategy. The firm underprices its competitors to gain sales and grow market share.

Now, consider a firm that has a differentiation advantage. If the firm offers a product that is relatively price inelastic, customers are not very price sensitive. Even large price hikes will not diminish market share significantly. A firm can follow a margin strategy, charging a premium price by comparison to its competitors. Although the margin strategy sacrifices some market share, it exploits the firm's differentiation advantage through higher profit margins. On the other hand, if the firm offers a product that is relatively price elastic, customers are price sensitive. In this case, a modest price hike by the firm could offset its differentiation advantage. The firm might exploit its differentiation advantage through a share strategy, charging the same price as other firms and thus capturing greater market share.

These points relating price elasticity of demand and strategy are depicted in Table 11.1. Bear in mind, however, that factors other than price elasticity of demand are in play when forming strategy. Notably, firms consider the likely reactions of competing firms to changes in price. For example, when customers are price sensitive, a share strategy based on cutting price to exploit a cost advantage would be undermined if competitors quickly matched any price cut. The result would be a thinner profit margin and little if any gain in market share.

Table 11.1 Competitive Advantage and Price Elasticity of Demand		
Demand	**Cost Advantage (Lower C than Competitors)**	**Differentiation Advantage (Higher B than Competitors)**
Relatively Price Elastic	Modest price cuts gain significant market share Exploit cost advantage through higher market share than competitors Share strategy: Underprice competitors to gain market share	Modest price hikes lose significant market share Exploit differentiation advantage through higher market share than competitors Share strategy: Maintain price parity with competitors, letting differentiation drive market share increases
Relatively Price Inelastic	Even large price cuts gain little market share Exploit cost advantage through higher profit margins Margin strategy: Maintain price parity with competitors, letting lower costs drive higher profit margins	Even large price hikes lose little market share Exploit differentiation advantage through higher profit margins Margin strategy: Charge price premium relative to competitor prices

STUCK IN THE MIDDLE

Commonalities across industries can be discerned in the different ways that firms position themselves to compete. In the language of strategic management, these commonalities can be described as generic strategies, a concept introduced by Michael Porter. A firm's generic strategy describes in general terms how the firm positions itself to compete in the market it serves. If a company has cost leadership in its market or industry, the company can produce products at lower cost per unit than it competitors. A cost leader company can undercut competitor prices and sell more than they do, or it can match competitor prices and attain higher price-cost margins than they can. If a company has benefit leadership in its market or industry, company products are capable of commanding a price premium relative to competitor prices. A benefit leader company can match competitor prices and sell more than they do, or it can charge a price premium and attain higher price-cost margins.

Porter introduced the term "stuck in the middle" to describe the uncomfortable position of a firm that has neither a cost advantage nor a benefit advantage. A firm stuck in the middle is beat on cost by one competitor and beat on quality by another competitor. Firms that are stuck in the middle are typically less profitable than competitors that have staked out clear positions of cost leadership or benefit leadership. Often, firms find themselves stuck in the middle because they simply fail to make decisions about how to position themselves.

Strategic positions typically require tradeoffs. A firm positioned to deliver superior customer benefits typically incurs higher costs to do so. In the same way, a firm that pursues a low-cost position typically compromises its ability to deliver customer benefits. Porter said that the pursuit of differentiation advantage is usually incompatible with the pursuit of cost advantage. Firms that attempt to pursue both strategies simultaneously, he argued, often end up stuck in the middle, providing less perceived benefit than firms focused on differentiation and incurring a higher unit cost than firms focused on cost. Porter's argument is based on a simple economic tradeoff. Higher quality products usually cost more to produce. Higher advertising and promotion expenditures may be required to inform or persuade consumers that a product is special.

Porter also argued that firms actually succeeding at both cost and differentiation often create separate business units for each strategy. One unit focuses on cost advantage, the other on differentiation advantage. Perhaps one unit produces a no-frill product at a low cost, whereas the other unit produces an up-scale product. Separating strategies into different units having a different focus, a business is less likely to be stuck in the middle. Even if separate units are not created, a fighting brand might be developed. A fighting brand is a lower priced, lower quality version of the main brand. The fighting brand protects the reputation of the main brand. Under the banner of the fighting brand, the company competes against firms that offer products with inferior quality and low prices.

Lessons can be learned from the notion of stuck in the middle. If consumer tastes run to extremes so that they tend to be either extremely cost sensitive or extremely benefit conscious, then products positioned in the middle will struggle. In trying to accomplish both cost and benefit objectives simultaneously, a firm may fail to invest in developing capabilities necessary to succeed in either dimension. In these ways, Porter's admonition against getting stuck in the middle may have merit. Beyond that, however, the conditions under which the pursuit of a differentiation advantage may be consistent with achieving a superior cost position arise frequently enough that it would be incorrect to conclude that differentiation and cost advantages are generally incompatible.

In business practice, a firm's advantage is rarely based entirely on cost or differentiation. By comparison to competitors, a number of companies seem to deliver a higher B at a lower C. The tradeoff between differentiation and cost may not be as strong as arguments suggest. Several factors might weaken the tradeoff between differentiation and cost positions in an industry. A firm that offers high-quality products might increase its market share, which then reduces average cost because of economies of scale or experience. In addition, the rate at which accumulated experience reduces costs seems to be greater for higher quality products than for lower quality products. The reason is that production workers must exercise more care to produce a higher quality product, which often leads to the discovery of bugs and defects that might be overlooked when producing lower quality products.

Stuck in the Middle: Philips Ending Production of TVs for U.S. Market

Royal Philips Electronics is a consumer electronics mammoth. Yet, in April 2008, Philips announced that the company was withdrawing from manufacturing television sets for sale in the United States or Canada. The Philips brand for television sets was sold to Funai Electric, which already made and sold lower-priced television sets branded as Emerson, Sylvania, and Symphonic in the North American market. At the time, prices for flat panel television sets were falling. Philips found itself in a difficult position. While the Philips name and brand were well known, the company itself admitted its television sets had not occupied the premium brand position of Sony and Samsung and yet could not compete on the low end with commodity brands such as Vizio and Westinghouse. Philips was stuck in the middle, unable to compete at the high end occupied by Sony and Samsung or at the low end occupied by Vizio and Westinghouse.

PRACTICE QUESTIONS

1. Explain the basic concept of value creation, including an explanation of each element in the formulation. What are the implications for competitive advantage?

2. Explain the basic concept of value creation. In this context, discuss cost advantage and differentiation advantage.

3. In some cases, firms try to establish a cost advantage. What are the conditions that favor a cost advantage?

4. In some cases, firms try to establish a differentiation advantage. What are the conditions that favor a differentiation advantage?

5. In *Competitive Advantage*, Michael Porter argued that cost and differentiation advantages are incompatible. Porter said that firms trying to achieve both are likely to be stuck in the middle. What did he mean?

6. A large company outperforms its competitors, and management has concluded that the company offers more consumer surplus than its competitors even though it has not achieved benefit parity.

   a. Explain this conclusion in terms of the value creation framework.

   b. Has the company based its competitive advantage on cost or differentiation? Why?

Question for Contemplation, Discussion, and Argument

7. In a recent interview on CNBC, a CEO said, "I am in an industry in which incumbent producers have a huge cost advantage because of economies of scale and scope." Why would incumbent firms have a cost advantage attributable to scale and scope by comparison to entrant firms?

PRACTICE QUESTIONS *(AND ANSWERS)*

1. Explain the basic concept of value creation, including an explanation of each element in the formulation. What are the implications for competitive advantage?

Value creation deals with perceived benefits and consumer surplus. Perceived benefit is what a unit of the product is worth to a consumer. Consumer surplus is the difference between perceived benefit and price, and thus is a measure of how well off a buyer expects to be if the transaction is consummated. A simple model of consumer behavior is that a consumer will purchase a product only if consumer surplus is positive, and given a choice between competing products, the consumer will purchase the one for which consumer surplus is greatest. To compete successfully, a seller must deliver consumer surplus. Sometimes, a value map is used to illustrate the competitive implications of consumer surplus. The horizontal axis represents the level of a key attribute, which for simplicity can be called quality. The vertical axis shows the price of the product. An upward-sloping indifference curve shows that, for a given customer, any price-quality combination along the indifference curve yields the same consumer surplus. In other words, a consumer choosing among products located along the indifference curve would be indifferent among the offerings. Products offering price-quality combinations located below a given indifference curve yield a consumer surplus higher than that yielded by products along the indifference curve. From the consumer's perspective, such products provide superior value. Products offering price-quality combinations located above a given indifference curve yield a consumer surplus lower than that yielded by products along the indifference curve. From the consumer's perspective, such products provide inferior value. A firm offering a consumer less surplus than its rivals will lose the fight for that consumer's business. When price-quality positions are lined up along the same indifference curve, i.e., when firms offer a consumer the same amount of consumer surplus, we say that the firms have achieved consumer surplus parity. If firms achieve consumer surplus parity in a market in which consumers have identical preferences, i.e., the same indifference curves, no consumer within that market has an incentive to switch from one seller to another, and market shares will be stable. If all firms in a market offer the same quality, then consumer surplus parity reduces to the simple condition that each firm charge the same price. When a firm loses consumer surplus parity, its sales will slip, and its market share will fall correspondingly. The steepness, i.e., the slope, of an indifference curve, indicates the tradeoff between price and quality. A steeply sloped indifference curve indicates that consumers are willing to pay considerably more to obtain additional quality, while a somewhat flat indifference curve indicates that extra quality is not worth much to customers. Firms overestimating the willingness of consumers to trade off price for quality risk overpricing their products and either losing market share to competitors or never becoming a viable competitor in the first place.

2. Explain the basic concept of value creation. In this context, discuss cost advantage and differentiation advantage.

Value created is the difference between value embedded in a finished product and value sacrificed to produce the finished product. Total value created is divided between consumers and producers. Consumer surplus is perceived benefit minus price, and it represents the portion of value created ultimately captured by the consumer. The seller keeps a portion of price and uses the rest to pay for the labor, capital, and materials used to convert unfinished components into finished products. The producer's profit margin, which is price minus average total cost, represents the portion of value created the producer captures. Adding together consumer surplus and the producer's profit,

Value Created=Consumer Surplus+Producer Profit

This perspective can be restated as

Value Created=(B−P)+(P−C)=B−C

B is perceived benefit, P is price, and C is average total cost. This simple formulation suggests that competitive advantage could be built on either B or C, either a differentiation advantage or cost advantage. A differentiation advantage is offering a higher B while maintaining a C comparable to competitors. A cost advantage attains a lower C while maintaining a B comparable to competitors. The pursuit of differentiation advantage is usually incompatible with the pursuit of cost advantage.

3. In some cases, firms try to establish a cost advantage. What are the conditions that favor a cost advantage?

Building competitive advantage on the basis of cost position is likely to be undertaken only under certain conditions. First, economies of scale and learning are potentially significant, but no firm in the market is exploiting them. Strategies aimed at increasing market share and accumulating experience will give the firm a cost advantage that smaller, less experienced rivals cannot match. If the market itself is growing, however, other firms may gain the scale and experience necessary to achieve the same cost position. Second, opportunities for enhancing perceived benefit are limited by the nature of the product itself, which might pertain to "commodity" products such as chemicals and metals. If so, opportunities for creating additional value may come more from lowering C than from increasing B. Still, drivers of differentiation include far more than just the physical attributes of the product. Opportunities may exist for differentiation through better post-sale service, superior location, or more rapid delivery than competitors offer. Third, consumers are relatively price sensitive and are unwilling to pay much of a premium for enhanced product quality, performance, or image, which would occur when consumers are more price sensitive than quality sensitive. Opportunities for additional value creation are much more likely to arise through cost reductions than through benefit enhancements. Fourth, the product is a search good rather than an experience good. A search good is a product with objective quality attributes the typical buyer can access easily at the time of purchase. An experience good is a product with quality that can be assessed only after the consumer has used it for a while. With search goods, the potential for differentiation lies largely in enhancing the product's observable features. If buyers can discern among different offerings, so can competitors, which raises the risk that enhancements will be imitated. When this case is evident, the best opportunity for a firm to create a lasting competitive advantage will come in keeping its costs lower than competitors, while taking care to match their initiatives in product enhancement.

4. In some cases, firms try to establish a differentiation advantage. What are the conditions that favor a differentiation advantage?

Building a competitive advantage based on differentiation is likely to be undertaken in certain circumstances. First, the typical consumer is willing to pay a significant price premium for attributes that enhance perceived benefit. In this case, a firm that can differentiate its product by offering even a few additional features may be able to command a significant price premium. Second, economies of scale or learning are significant, and because of their size or cumulative experience, existing firms already are exploiting them. In this case, opportunities for achieving a cost advantage over these larger firms are limited, and the best route toward value creation lies through horizontal differentiation, i.e., offering a product especially well tailored to a particular niche of the market. Third, the product is an experience good rather than a search good. In this case, differentiation can be based on image, reputation, or credibility, which are more difficult to imitate or neutralize than objective product features or performance characteristics.

5. In *Competitive Advantage*, Michael Porter argued that cost and differentiation advantages are incompatible. Porter said that firms trying to achieve both are likely to be stuck in the middle. What did he mean?

The pursuit of differentiation advantage is usually incompatible with the pursuit of cost advantage. Firms that attempt to pursue both strategies simultaneously often become "stuck in the middle," providing less perceived benefit, B, than firms that have focused on pursuing a differentiation advantage and incurring a higher per unit cost, C, than firms that have focused on seeking cost advantage. Higher quality or better performing products often cost more to produce. Producing a higher quality product may involve more upfront design work, more expensive components, and more highly skilled labor. To the extent that differentiation is based on meeting various customer needs, it also may require more custom building and thus a less standardized production process. Higher advertising and promotion expenditures may be needed to shape consumer perceptions that the product is special, and greater spending on a sales force may be required if differentiation is created through superior customer service.

6. A large company outperforms its competitors, and management has concluded that the company offers more consumer surplus than its competitors even though it has not achieved benefit parity.

a. Explain this conclusion in terms of the value creation framework.

The company evidently has achieved benefit proximity, which involves offering a B not much less than its competitors. Since the company outperforms its competitors even though the company has not achieved benefit parity, the company must be underpricing its rivals by more than enough to offset the lower B, thereby offering more consumer surplus.

b. Has the company based its competitive advantage on cost or differentiation? Why?

The company must have a substantial cost advantage. Underpricing is profitable because the company has a cost advantage that is bigger than the price differential between the company and its competitors.

11. Antitrust, Mergers, and Acquisitions

THE BUSINESS CLIMATE FOR ANTITRUST LAW

Recall the mid-1800s. For the most part, the character of the U.S. economy was comprised of small firms that sold products in local markets. The face of business was reshaped by invention and innovation that led to mass production, branding, as well as national and even international distribution channels. Large firms arose to produce and sell products in local, regional, national, and even international markets. With size came market power, and this unprecedented power fostered fierce, ruthless competition. Big business often drove smaller firms from markets and industries. These big, powerful firms acquired small firms on terms decidedly favorable to the former. In this ruthless business climate, the trust form of enterprise emerged and flourished. Under a trust arrangement, shareholders of otherwise competitive firms agreed to turn over stock in their companies in exchange for trust certificates that entitled them to a share of the trust's common profits. A group of trustees then operated the trust as a monopoly that controlled the volume of overall output, which enabled higher prices and profits.

The general public and officials elected to represent the public recognized that something was wrong with this picture. It did not pass the smell test. Among other consequences, city life was changing for the worse. Working people in cities and factory towns faced a grim life characterized by child labor, long hours of work, meager wages, and crowded housing in slums that were breeding grounds for disease. Someone or something had to be blamed. Big business was blamed. Something had to be done. The something done was legislation, the Sherman Antitrust Act of 1890. From that time onward, America's antimonopoly laws and policies have been known as antitrust laws and policies. The reason is simple. Trust was the form of monopoly first attacked. The Standard Oil Trust was the poster child of monopoly.

THE STANDARD OIL TRUST

John D. Rockefeller was a high school dropout, a self-made man starting his working life as an assistant bookkeeper at the age of sixteen. He quickly rose above such humble beginnings. Standard Oil had its roots in 1867 as an Ohio partnership led by twenty-eight year old John D. Rockefeller, his brother William Rockefeller, Henry Flagler, Samuel Andrews, and a silent partner, Steven V. Harkness. The partnership was known as Rockefeller, Andrews & Flagler. In 1870, John D. Rockefeller and his partners incorporated Standard Oil of Ohio. The one-time bookkeeper was the largest shareholder in the company, initially holding thirty percent of the stock.

Not content with a limited role in the industry, Standard Oil bought out small independent refiners on terms that generally were favorable to the sellers. Refiners who refused to sell could not compete at a cost disadvantage and left the industry. In less than two months in 1872, Standard Oil had the Cleveland refining business to itself. Next, the focus switched to dominating the refining business nationally. Standard Oil companies spread over several states, literally coast to coast. By 1879, Standard Oil had about ninety percent of the oil refining business in America, and about seventy percent of production was exported overseas.

At the time, refining was primitive, essentially cooking the oil and purifying it. The main product refined from petroleum was kerosene, but other petroleum-based products were produced, including gasoline. No market could be found for the sale of gasoline. It was an unwanted byproduct. Refiners dumped gasoline surreptitiously and illegally into the Cuyahoga River at night, and the Cuyahoga often caught fire. Standard Oil was able to reduce its cost per gallon of kerosene from 2.5 cents to less than 0.5 cents, more than an eighty percent decrease. The price per gallon of kerosene was reduced from fifty-eight cents to twenty-six cents, a fifty-five percent reduction.

Standard Oil authority was centralized in the company's main headquarters in Cleveland. Decisions were made in a cooperative manner so that there was no competition among the various companies waving the Standard Oil flag. Ohio state law was enacted with the aim of limiting the size of companies. Ohio state law also prohibited corporations from owning stock in other corporations. Rockefeller's behemoth found itself in noncompliance. Looking for a way to get around such law, Rockefeller's attorney, Samuel Dodd, proposed formation of a trust controlled by nine trustees.

The basic idea of a trust was simple. Corporations would assign their stock to the board of trustees, and the trustees would issue trust certificates to the stockholders. Instead of controlling disparate companies directly, Rockefeller would control these companies through the trust. By consolidating all or most companies in an industry under the governance of one controlling board, the industry was essentially monopolized. Through this legal technicality, Rockefeller could expand and control the oil industry. On 2 January 1882, the Standard Oil Trust became a reality. In this way, Rockefeller combined numerous companies spread across dozens of states under a single group of trustees. Other giant enterprises followed suit. Trusts were organized in as many as two hundred industries, including railroads, coal, steel, tobacco, sugar, and meatpacking.

Nevertheless, the state of Ohio took Standard Oil to court, and the company was ordered to dissolve the trust in 1892. In effect, however, only Standard Oil of Ohio was separated from the trust without giving up control of that company. Meanwhile, New Jersey changed its incorporation laws to permit a company to hold shares in companies incorporated in other states. In 1899, the Standard Oil Trust was given new life as a holding company known as Standard Oil Company of New Jersey, which held stock in forty-one other companies, which in turn controlled still other companies, which in turn controlled yet other companies. From the public point of view, Standard Oil was pervasive in industry, controlled by a select group of directors accountable to no one other than Standard Oil itself. Deep-seated antipathy for Standard Oil and trusts of any kind was widespread throughout the general public.

In 1901, President Theodore Roosevelt declared war on monopolies. He was not as concerned about breaking up trusts as he was about redressing abuses. In 1903, President Roosevelt asked Congress to create a Department of Commerce and Labor and a Bureau of Corporations to investigate business combinations and throttle practices harmful to the public. In 1906, the Bureau of Corporations filed a report on Standard Oil's operations in Kansas, which led to a federal antitrust suit against Standard Oil. Three years later, the U.S. Circuit Court for the Eastern District of Missouri ruled against Standard Oil.

In 1911, the U.S. Supreme Court upheld the lower court judgment. Standard Oil of New Jersey was ordered to dissolve into thirty-four separate, independent, and competitive companies, each with its own distinct shareholders and board of directors. When the dust settled on this massive dissolution, the resulting companies formed the core of the U.S. oil industry, including Exxon (once Standard Oil of New Jersey) and Mobil (once Standard Oil of New York), now Exxon Mobil; ConocoPhillips, (Conoco was once Standard Oil's company in the Rocky Mountain states); Chevron (once Standard Oil of California); Amoco (once Standard Oil of Indiana) and Sohio (once Standard Oil of Ohio), now BP of North America; Atlantic Richfield (once Standard Oil's company in the Atlantic states), now also part of BP of North America; Marathon (once Standard Oil's company in western Ohio and other parts of Ohio not covered by Sohio); and other smaller companies.

The breakup of Standard Oil had an ironic aftermath. By 1911, John D. Rockefeller had retired from any management role in Standard Oil, but he owned a fourth of all shares of the companies. Not long after the dissolution, share prices doubled. He emerged from the dissolution wealthier than ever. Thanks to the breakup ordered by the U.S. Supreme Court, he was now the richest man in the world!

THE SHERMAN ANTITRUST ACT

Although public sentiment strongly favored reform, general belief in private enterprise also was strongly held. Several states passed laws dealing with the problem of trusts, but these laws were limited to intrastate business. The U.S. Congress has the power to regulate interstate commerce. Article 1, Section 8, Clause 3 of the U.S. Constitution is known as the Commerce Clause, which gives Congress the exclusive authority to regulate commerce between and among states, foreign nations, and Indian tribes. In 1890, the federal government response to widely held sentiments and beliefs culminated in passage of the Sherman Antitrust Act, named for an Ohio Republican, Senator John Sherman. Senator Sherman was the brother of William Techumseh Sherman, famed Union General who carried out the scorched earth policy of President Lincoln's unlimited war against civilians as well as their property in Southern states. General Sherman's march to the sea included burning Atlanta to the ground, the centerpiece of *Gone With the Wind*.

The Sherman Act passed 51-1 in the U.S. Senate and 242-0 in the U.S. House of Representatives. On 2 July 1890, President Benjamin Harrison signed the Sherman Antitrust Act into law. The Sherman Act applied to domestic companies and foreign companies doing business in the United States, enabling the Attorney General to prosecute trusts and dissolve them. With penalties as amended by the Antitrust Criminal Penalty Enhancement and Reform Act of 2004, the substance of the Sherman Act is found in two short sections:

Section 1. Every contract, combination in the form of trust or otherwise, or conspiracy, in restraint of trade or commerce among the several States, or with foreign nations, is declared to be illegal. Every person who shall make any contract or engage in any combination or conspiracy hereby declared to be illegal shall be deemed guilty of a felony, and, on conviction thereof, shall be punished by fine not exceeding $100,000,000 if a corporation, or, if any other person, $1,000,000, or by imprisonment not exceeding ten years, or by both said punishments, in the discretion of the court.

Section 2. Every person who shall monopolize, or attempt to monopolize, or combine or conspire with any other person or persons, to monopolize any part of the trade or commerce among the several States, or with foreign nations, shall be deemed guilty of a felony, and, on conviction thereof, shall be punished by fine not exceeding $100,000,000 if a corporation, or, if any other person, $1,000,000, or by imprisonment not exceeding ten years, or by both said punishments, in the discretion of the court.

In this way, therefore, restraint of trade and monopolization of trade were made illegal. The biggest problem with the Sherman Antitrust Act was rooted in interpretation. Its simple common law language did not disclose whether structure or conduct was at issue. Section 1 language, "combination in the form of trust or otherwise," seemed to aim at monopolistic structure. Pursuant language, "conspiracy, in restraint of trade or commerce," appeared to focus on certain kinds of monopolistic conduct. Its language also left unclear exactly what conduct was considered to be restraints of trade. When a legislative act is unclear, courts are expected to provide clarification. To some extent, however, courts added to the confusion in the early years of interpretation and enforcement.

THE RULE OF REASON

In 1911, two major antitrust cases were heard before the U.S. Supreme Court. The cases involved Standard Oil and American Tobacco. Both seemed to be the epitome of monopoly. Standard Oil and American Tobacco appeared to evidence both the structure and the conduct made illegal by the Sherman Antitrust Act. At the time, Standard Oil controlled about ninety percent of oil refining, and American Tobacco controlled perhaps as much as ninety percent of tobacco products. In addition, both companies had deployed questionable tactics to gobble up competition or drive competition out of business. In decisions announced on the same day, the U.S. Supreme Court found both Standard Oil and American Tobacco guilty of violating the Sherman Act and ordered dissolution of both companies.

In its decisions, the U.S. Supreme Court declared that the Sherman Antitrust Act did not make illegal every business practice that seemed to restrain trade. Only unreasonable practices were made illegal. Combinations and conduct unreasonably restraining trade were subject to legal action under antitrust law. Size, structure, and pursuant monopoly power alone were not illegal without unreasonable conduct. This doctrine departed from previous case law, which interpreted the Sherman Antitrust Act to hold that all combinations and conduct restraining trade were illegal. This declaration became known and is still known as the rule of reason. The Court seemed to say that structure alone was not a criterion for unreasonableness. Presumably, a business that achieved monopoly status would not violate the Sherman Antitrust Act if it achieved that status while using reasonable tactics. Pursuant court cases confirmed that a business violated the Sherman Antitrust Act only if it had evidenced unreasonable conduct. For example, antitrust cases were brought against Eastman Kodak, International Harvester, and U.S. Steel. The three companies controlled commanding shares of their respective markets. All three cases were found in favor of the companies. The cases were dismissed on grounds that the companies had not evidenced unreasonable conduct.

The ALCOA Case

An odd challenge to the rule of reason was the Aluminum Company of America (ALCOA) case. Prosecution began in 1937 when the Justice Department charged ALCOA with illegal monopolization and demanded dissolution of the company. In 1942, the trial judge dismissed the case. The Justice Department appealed to the U.S. Supreme Court. However, some Supreme Court Justices were ALCOA shareholders and recused themselves. In 1944, the U.S. Supreme Court announced it could not assemble a quorum to hear the case and referred the matter to the U.S. Court of Appeals, Second Circuit. In 1945, Judge Learned Hand wrote the opinion for the Second Circuit. ALCOA was found to be an illegal monopoly even though the company had engaged in no overt illegal acts.

In his majority opinion, Judge Learned Hand actually praised ALCOA for its technological efficiency and innovation. ALCOA had deterred entry by adding capacity in advance of demand and maintaining a low profit margin. Judge Hand nevertheless found ALCOA guilty of monopolizing the aluminum industry. The intent to monopolize was inferred not from unreasonable tactics to establish and maintain a monopoly. The intent to monopolize was inferred from ALCOA's efficiency! Entry was not profitable because ALCOA was so efficient that it made aluminum available at a relatively low price. Judge Hand's decision stated that efficiency was no defense against the Sherman Antitrust Act and that size alone was sufficient proof of violation. ALCOA controlled ninety percent of the market as defined by the Court. Judge Hand's ALCOA decision suggested that mere size of market domination was unlawful even if the defendant had done everything possible to avoid becoming dominant. The ALCOA decision appeared to inveigh against the rule of reason. Irrespective of conduct or actions, the mere structure of ALCOA made the company a monopoly. In other words, the ALCOA decision made monopoly in and of itself illegal rather than acts or conduct meant to monopolize. ALCOA's offense was bigness.

The ALCOA case had an even odder denouement. Judge Hand remanded the matter back to the trial court. Meantime, the U.S. government wanted to dispose of aluminum refining assets accumulated during World War II. ALCOA agreed the company would not bid on these assets, which were then acquired by Reynolds and Kaiser. In 1947, ALCOA argued in the trial court that two new entrants were operating in the aluminum industry. The problem had solved itself. The district court judge ruled against divestiture in 1950. The odd saga of the ALCOA case came to an anticlimactic end.

THE *PER SE* RULE

The history of antitrust law also has been marked by conduct that courts have declared *per se* (in and of itself) violations. This precedent is known as the *per se* rule. Actually, the *per se* rule predates the rule of reason. The *per se* rule traces its origins to a U.S. Supreme Court case, Drystone Pipe & Steel Co. v. U.S., decided in 1899. In general, *per se* means intrinsically or inherently illegal without requiring extrinsic proof of any surrounding circumstances such as lack of knowledge, negligence, or intention. A *per se* violation involves conduct that violates the Sherman Antitrust Act whether the intention or result is reasonable or not. Indeed, *per se* conduct is regarded as presumption of unreasonableness. *Per se* violations are illegal whether or not the conduct is shown to harm competition.

In effect, the *per se* rule deals with collusion among persons who conspire through unlawful agreements to deceive and deprive others. Thus, this conspiracy is seen as fraud or unfair advantage. Collusion is generally illegal in the United States, European Union, and other countries. However, conscious parallelism is a form of tacit collusion that often circumvents prosecution because it produces no smoking gun of evidence. Conscious parallelism occurs without any actual spoken or written agreement. For example, a competitor might take the lead in raising prices, and other competitors follow the lead by raising their prices correspondingly. Clearly, this anticompetitive practice of price leadership is harmful to consumers, but it is difficult to prosecute. Essentially, the *per se* rule is aimed at price fixing, bid rigging, and market allocation.

Price Fixing

Price fixing is a collusive agreement and thus a conspiracy among business competitors to sell their products or services at the same price, presumably higher than the competitive price. The competitors are involved in a conspiracy that allows them to avoid price competition, to raise prices above what would be the competitive level, and thus to realize profits above what would be made under competitive conditions. In 1926, the U.S. Supreme Court held that price fixing violates the Sherman Antitrust Act whether the resulting price is reasonable or not. This finding made price fixing a *per se* violation.

Price fixing can be found in unusual circumstances. For years, Coors sold its lager beer products in only eleven states (Arizona, California, Colorado, Idaho, Kansas, Nevada, New Mexico, Oklahoma, Utah, Wyoming, and some counties in Texas). Coors maintained that distribution was limited because its product was not pasteurized and thus deteriorated in taste if not refrigerated. Distributors were prohibited from selling Coors beer outside their territory, and Coors terminated distributor agreements when the prohibition was violated. Outside those eleven states, therefore, availability of Coors was dependent on personal distribution. President Gerald Ford, for example, had cases of Coors flown to Washington every Thursday for Mexican food night at the White House. When Coors was bought in one of the eleven states and then personally transported to a location outside these states and sold, a case of Coors was priced at $15 or more in the early 1970s, the equivalent of about $87 or so in 2013 currency. Company policy and antitrust law collided. In 1970, Coors was charged by the Federal Trade Commission for its use of exclusive territories and maximum resale price maintenance at the wholesale level and minimum resale price maintenance at the retail level. In 1975, the U.S. Supreme Court found the company's distribution policy was tantamount to price fixing and unreasonable restraint of trade.

A long-standing question has been whether or not resale price maintenance is tantamount to price fixing and thus a *per se* violation. Resale price maintenance is an agreement between manufacturer and distributors to sell a product at a certain price (resale price maintenance), at or above a minimum floor (minimum resale price maintenance), or at or below a price ceiling (maximum resale price maintenance). These agreements limit resellers from competing on the basis of price. Historically, resale price maintenance was regarded as vertical price fixing. On 28 June 2007, however, the U.S. Supreme Court decided that such price constraints are not *per se* unlawful. They must be judged under the rule of reason.

Bid Rigging

At times, contracts are awarded after a call for competitive bids. If a bidder meets conditions of the call, the low competitive bidder wins the contract. Bid rigging is a collusive agreement among competitors that is considered a form of fraud. In effect, bid rigging occurs in situations meant to be competitive bidding for a contract. The competitive nature of the process is compromised if a conspiracy assures that one particular bidder wins the bid. Bid rigging is a *per se* violation.

Bid rigging can take many forms. Bid suppression involves conspirators who agree not to submit a bid so that another conspirator can succeed in winning the contract. Cover bidding, also known as courtesy bidding or complementary bidding, involves conspirators who bid high or who stipulate terms known to be contractually unacceptable. Subcontract bid rigging involves conspirators who do not submit bids or submit cover bids meant to be unsuccessful. In exchange, these conspirators are given subcontracts for parts of the successful bidder's contract. Bid rotation involves conspirators who take turns being the successful bidder. Still another form is a conspiracy to write bid specifications that only one bidder can qualify.

Market Allocation

Market allocation refers to an agreement between competitors to divide markets, thus avoiding competition in these markets. By collusive agreement, each competitor sells exclusively in its allocated market. Other competitors will not enter such allocated markets. In effect, competing firms divide up customers so that only one competitor is allowed under the conspiratorial agreement to sell to, buy from, or bid on contracts let by those customers. Market allocation is a *per se* violation.

Punishments for *Per Se* Violations

Price fixing, bid rigging, and market allocation are now treated as violations of Section 1 of the Sherman Antitrust Act and generally are prosecuted criminally by the Antitrust Division of the U.S. Department of Justice. Agreement, unreasonable restraint of trade, and interstate commerce are the essence of a Section 1 violation. Attempts alone are not violations. However, mail and wire fraud statutes are used to prosecute attempts to fix prices, rig bids, or allocate markets when U.S. mail or interstate phone lines are used in the attempt.

Price fixing, bid rigging, and market allocation by companies and individuals are felonies punishable by a fine of up to $10 million for corporations and a fine of up to $350,000 or three years imprisonment (or both) for individuals involving offenses committed before 22 June 2004. The Antitrust Criminal Penalty Enhancement and Reform Act raised maximum Sherman Antitrust Act penalties to $100 million dollars for corporations and $1 million dollars and ten years imprisonment for individuals. There is an alternative to these statutory caps. The alternative subjects offenders to a fine of "twice the gross gain or twice the gross loss" resulting from a violation. To date, the largest fine imposed for a price-fixing conspiracy is $500 million. In 1999, F. Hoffman-La Roche, a Swiss company, was fined $500 million for leading a worldwide conspiracy to raise and fix prices for vitamins. In March 2012, Japanese automobile supplier Yazaki was fined $470 million for price fixing, the second largest fine for a corporation at the time. Four Yazaki executives, all Japanese, were sentenced to two years in prison. In September 2012, AU Optronics (AU) was held guilty of price fixing. AU is a Taiwanese manufacturer of thin-film transistor liquid crystal display panels. The fine was $500 million, and two senior executives were sentenced to three years in prison. In January 2009, a former shipping executive with Sea Star Line, Peter Baci, was sentenced to a four-year prison sentence for his role in a six-year conspiracy to allocate customers, rig bids, and fix prices for water freight shipping between the coastal United States and Puerto Rico. The four-year sentence is the longest imposed in the United States for a single antitrust violation.

Criminal prosecution, imprisonment, and fines are not the only deterrents to antitrust crimes. When the U.S. government or its agencies are the victims of antitrust violations, the Department of Justice may seek treble damages and civil penalties up to treble damages. In addition, private parties, including state and local governments, can recover three times the damages they incur as a result of an antitrust violation. They can refer to successful federal prosecution of collusion as *prima facie* evidence against a defendant.

Section 2 of the Sherman Antitrust Act prohibits monopolization as well as attempts and conspiracies to monopolize. Violations of Section 2 are not prosecuted criminally except for special circumstances. Criminal prosecution is pursued in circumstances in which violence is used or threatened as a means of discouraging or eliminating competition. These circumstances usually involve organized crime. Tony Soprano, beware!

THE CLAYTON ACT, 1914

What constituted unreasonable conduct remained a vexing enigma that eluded understanding and baffled many people within business and legal communities. Original supporters of the Sherman Antitrust Act were discombobulated about what they regarded as a failure to enforce its provisions. Businesses were likewise upset because they could not discern the rules of the antitrust game. The situation and timing were right for Congress to go back to the drawing board to draft legislation that would clarify by statute what constituted unlawful acts. The result was the Clayton Act of 1914.

The Clayton Act was passed mainly to clarify the rule of reason. President Woodrow Wilson signed it into law on 15 October 1914. Henry De Lamar Clayton, a congressman from Alabama, drafted the language of the Act. Basically, the Clayton Act made unlawful a number of specific business practices. Indeed, the intent of the Clayton Act was to be more precise and to strengthen antitrust prosecutors by allowing them to strike at potentially anticompetitive practices "in their incipiency." In addition, the Clayton Act identified certain practices as unlawful "where the effect may be to substantially lessen competition or tend to create a monopoly." Whereas the Sherman Antitrust Act was a short piece of legislation of only eight sections, the Clayton Act was lengthy, containing twenty-six sections. Five sections are most important.

Section 2: Price Discrimination

Section 2 of the Clayton Act was a lengthy, wordy provision. Essentially, Section 2 made price discrimination unlawful under certain circumstances or conditions. As amended by the Robinson-Patman Act of 1936, the language used is, "It shall be unlawful for any person engaged in commerce...to discriminate in price between different purchasers of commodities of like grade and quality...where the effect of such discrimination may be to substantially lessen competition or tend to create a monopoly in any line of commerce, or to injure, destroy, or prevent competition...."

Section 2 was meant to protect smaller firms from larger companies that slashed prices on particular goods in particular markets for the purpose of driving smaller firms out of those markets. The language stated explicitly that nothing in the Clayton Act prevented price discrimination based on "differences in grade, quality, or quantity of the commodity sold" or "difference in the cost of selling or transportation." Section 2 also did not prevent "discrimination in price in the same or different communities made in good faith to meet competition." Basically, therefore, Section 2 limited the practice of price discrimination. Nowadays, price discrimination is hardly ever regarded as anticompetitive.

Section 3: Exclusive Contracts, Requirements Contracts, and Tying Contracts

Section 3 of the Clayton Act stated that "it shall be unlawful for any person...to lease or make a sale or contract for sale of...goods...on the condition...that the lessee or purchaser thereof shall not use or deal in the...goods...of a competitor or competitors of the lessor or seller, where the effect of such lease, sale, or contract...may be to substantially lessen competition or tend to create a monopoly in any line of commerce."

The excessively wordy Section 3 basically prohibited exclusive contracts in which a seller offered to sell or lease a product to a firm only if the firm agreed not to buy or lease any products from the seller's competitors. Also prohibited were requirements contracts in which buyers agreed to purchase all of their requirements from a given seller. Finally, tying contracts were prohibited. These contracts require a buyer to purchase another product in addition to purchasing quantities of the product the buyer really wants. In other words, the buyer of one product must agree to purchase still other presumably unwanted products from the same seller. Under tying contracts, a firm with a patent on a vital process could use licensing or other arrangements to restrict competition. Nowadays, most economists believe that exclusive dealing is rarely anticompetitive and rarely unlawful. As elsewhere in the Clayton Act, the test is whether the effect of exclusive, requirements, or tying contracts lessens competition substantially or tends to create a monopoly.

Section 6: Collective Bargaining

Section 6 of the Clayton Act begins by asserting, "That the labor of a human being is not a commodity or article of commerce." This language reads more like philosophy than legislation. Section 6 specifically exempted collective bargaining by organized labor unions from antitrust prosecution. Language stated that nothing in the Clayton Act forbade the existence and operation of labor organizations and that labor organizations could not be held or construed to be unlawful combinations or conspiracies in restraint of trade. Before 1914, the Sherman Act had been used to stifle union activity. For example, union strikers were found in violation of Section 2 as attempts to monopolize. The Clayton Act provided safe harbor.

Section 7: Acquisitions of Stock and Interlocking Stockholdings

Section 7 of the Clayton Act prohibited any corporation from acquiring all or any part of the stock of another corporation where the effect was to lessen competition substantially or tend to create a monopoly. Acquiring all of the stock of another corporation involves control through stock ownership, and the Clayton Act provides a basis for enjoining such stock acquisitions where such activity has substantial anticompetitive effects. Acquiring part of the stock of another corporation involves interlocking stockholding. In the 1950s, for example, DuPont and Christiana Securities, both controlled by the du Pont family, were forced to sell their huge chunk of GM stock. DuPont had bought about twenty-five percent of GM stock in 1919. Over the next four decades, GM bought most its seat cover fabrics, paints, and glues from DuPont. In 1957, the Supreme Court found that other firms had been unfairly excluded from selling fabrics, paints, and glues to GM and ordered DuPont to sell its GM stock.

Section 8: Interlocking Directorates

Section 8 of the Clayton Act forbade competing corporations from having interlocking directorates, arrangements under which competing corporations had common members on their boards of directors. In such cases, neither corporation is likely to act independently of the other, which can be anticompetitive. Serving on several boards of directors is commonplace and widespread and is unlawful only if conflicts of interest bring about substantial lessening of competition or tendency to create a monopoly, which is rare.

FEDERAL TRADE COMMISSION ACT, 1914

A month before the Clayton Act was signed into law, Congress passed legislation to create the Federal Trade Commission (FTC). President Woodrow Wilson signed The Federal Trade Commission Act into law on 26 September 1914. The language of the Federal Trade Commission Act was intentionally vague. Section 5 simply stated that "unfair methods of competition in commerce are hereby declared unlawful" and then empowered and directed the FTC to prevent and redress unfair methods. In effect, Section 5 granted the FTC broad powers to define business practices that constituted unfair competition. With these broad powers, the FTC began operation on 15 March 1915. The intent was to make the newly created independent agency the federal government's chief trustbuster. The Federal Trade Commission is composed of five members appointed by the President and confirmed by the Senate for staggered terms of seven years.

The U.S. Department of Justice can institute civil proceedings and criminal proceedings. However, civil proceedings ordinarily are the purview of the FTC. Because the Clayton Act did not create any criminal offenses, the Department of Justice does not bring charges under the Clayton Act unless Sherman Antitrust Act violations also are at issue. In most instances, therefore, the FTC enforces compliance with the Clayton Act. Since the FTC is an administrative agency of the executive branch, it has no criminal jurisdiction. The FTC holds hearings if law violations are suspected. If the FTC determines that a company has engaged in illegal activities, it either negotiates an agreement in which the company consents to stop the practice or it initiates adjudicative proceedings that may result in an order to cease and desist the practice. Cease and desist orders brought under the Clayton Act are subject to review by appellate courts. The FTC also can order that a company charged with a violation of the law make some sort of restitution to consumers harmed by its unlawful actions.

THE ROBINSON-PATMAN ACT, 1936

The Sherman Antitrust Act, the Clayton Act, and the Federal Trade Commission Act have been amended several times. One amendment dealt with Section 2, which limited the practice of price discrimination. The Robinson-Patman Act was passed in 1936. The intent was to protect small independent wholesalers and retailers from large chain stores or mail-order houses. Small businesses argued that the bargaining strength of mass distributors enabled chain stores and mail-order houses to pay lower prices unjustified by cost differences and then to undercut the smaller independent competitors who had to pay higher prices. The intention of the amendment, therefore, was to make charging different prices to different buyers unlawful unless the price differences were justified by cost differences, with the burden of proof on the seller. Technically, Robinson-Patman dealt with price differences rather than price discrimination.

The language of the Clayton Act was repeated in the Robinson-Patman Act. Price differences as defined in the Robinson-Patman Act were made unlawful only where the effect may be to substantially lessen competition or tend to create a monopoly or injure, destroy, or prevent competition. In general, therefore, Robinson-Patman prohibits sales involving differences in price to equally situated distributors where the effect of the sales is to harm competition. The harm to competition criterion is the make-or-break legal point. The vague, poorly written legislation led the Department of Justice to abandon enforcement decades ago. For all practical purposes, the FTC also has brought Robinson-Patman cases to a grinding halt. Nowadays, Robinson-Patman claims are limited to lawsuits between private parties.

THE WHEELER-LEA ACT, 1938

The authority of the FTC was increased in 1938 with passage of the Wheeler-Lea Act, which amended the original Federal Trade Commission Act. The Act amended Section 5, which proscribed unfair methods of competition. Section 5 empowered the FTC to restrict practices that were unfair to competitors. Consumers were not protected under provisions of Section 5. Wheeler-Lea added a clause to Section 5 that stated, "unfair or deceptive acts or practices in commerce are hereby declared unlawful." This language was meant to protect consumers as well as competitors. In particular, Wheeler-Lea empowered the FTC to protect consumers from false advertising.

THE CELLER-KEFAUVER ACT, 1950

The Celler-Kefauver Act was passed in 1950. It amended Section 7 of the Clayton Act. Taking control of another firm by purchasing its stock was made unlawful by Section 7 if the effect was to lessen competition substantially or tended to create a monopoly. Section 7 neglected taking control of another firm by purchasing its plant and equipment even when the adverse effect on competition was substantial. Although the Clayton Act dealt with trust-type combinations of competitors, it neglected merger-type combinations of competitors. This loophole was closed with passage of the Celler-Kefauver Act. Section 7 was amended to apply the same provisions to asset acquisitions as had applied previously only to stock acquisitions. In effect, the amended Section 7 stated that a merger is unlawful when the effect of such acquisition lessens competition substantially or tends to create a monopoly.

THE HART-SCOTT-RODINO ANTITRUST IMPROVEMENT ACT, 1976

The Hart-Scott-Rodino Antitrust Improvement Act of 1976 amended both the Sherman Antitrust Act and the Clayton Act by making mergers somewhat easier to attack. It required companies to notify the FTC and the Antitrust Division of the Department of Justice of an intention to merge if certain asset or sales hurdles are exceeded. Consequently, before certain mergers, tender offers, or other acquisitions can close, parties must file a *Notification and Report Form* with the FTC and the Department of Justice. A thirty-day waiting period ensues during which additional information may be requested to assess whether the transaction violates antitrust law. Regulators may request time beyond the thirty days to review additional information. Certain complicated mergers such as Exxon and Mobil were under review for almost a year before settlement. Closing is unlawful during the waiting period.

MERGERS AND ACQUISITIONS

Sometimes, a firm grows by combining with another enterprise. This kind of immediate growth is described as merger and acquisition (M&A). Essentially, acquisition is a takeover in which a dominant firm acquires a subordinate enterprise in exchange for consideration given by the dominant firm. Conventionally, a larger firm takes over a smaller firm. When this convention is not the case and a smaller firm takes over a larger firm, it is called a reverse takeover. On the other hand, merger is a consolidation in which two companies form a new company, and the old companies are dissolved. Nowadays, the distinction between mergers and acquisitions is somewhat blurred. There are three major types of mergers and acquisitions.

Horizontal merger or lateral integration is the case in which the firms involved are in the same industry or market and regarded as competitors. Examples would include mergers of two grocery store chains, two commercial banks, two automobile manufacturers, or two ready-mix concrete companies. Vertical merger or vertical integration is the case in which the firms involved have a supplier and customer relationship in the vertical chain. Examples would include mergers of a bauxite mining company and an aluminum refining company, an automobile manufacturer and an automobile parts manufacturer, or a textile company and an apparel manufacturer. Conglomerate merger is a form of diversification in which the firms involved are unrelated. Examples would include mergers of an insurance company and a book publisher, a cosmetics company and an automobile rental company, or a fast food restaurant chain and an eyeglasses retailing chain. Often, this type of transaction is regarded as the corporate equivalent of portfolio diversification such that, when one activity is facing financial difficulties, perhaps other activities are doing much better so that overall performance is favorable.

MERGER GUIDELINES

Antitrust agencies of the federal government may challenge horizontal mergers. In most cases, courts have supported government challenges. Antitrust agencies have either blocked mergers or demanded remedies to remove anticompetitive effects as a condition of approval. During the 1960s and 1970s, the U.S. government was frequently successful in challenging vertical and conglomerate mergers if they involved large firms. Afterwards, the government has shown little interest in vertical and conglomerate mergers. At present, vertical and conglomerate mergers are unlikely to be challenged unless such mergers would somehow increase horizontal market power substantially.

More than eighty countries around the world have antitrust laws, and about forty-five of these countries provide some sort of merger review. Merger guidelines in the United States and Europe are similar. In Japan, merger guidelines are more lax. In the United States, *Merger Guidelines* are internal rules used by the Department of Justice (DOJ) and the Federal Trade Commission (FTC) for use in scrutinizing and perhaps challenging a potential merger or acquisition on grounds of market concentration or harm to competition within a relevant industry or market. The first *Merger Guidelines* were developed by the DOJ in 1968 and remained in use until 1982 when they were revised. The 1982 *Merger Guidelines* relied heavily on HHI and recognized efficiency of production and economies of scale. *Merger Guidelines* were revised again in 1984, replaced altogether in 1992, and once again revised in 1997. On 19 August 2010, DOJ and FTC released the latest version of *Merger Guidelines*. From the 1980s, the DOJ and the FTC have depended heavily on HHI in deciding whether or not to seek an injunction to block a particular horizontal merger.

Relevant Product and Geographic Markets

A perplexing, yet necessary problem in competition law is determining relevant markets. A relevant market defines the market in which two or more products compete. In general, the relevant product market identifies the products or services that compete with each other, and the relevant geographic market identifies the geographic area within which competition in the relevant product market takes place. Using language from European Union commercial law, a relevant product market comprises all products or services regarded as interchangeable or substitutable by consumers by reason of product or service characteristics, their prices, and their intended use. Moreover, a relevant geographic market comprises the area in which concerned firms are involved in the supply of products or services and in which the conditions of competition are sufficiently homogeneous.

The FTC and DOJ have lost some merger challenges in court largely because of problems arising from defining markets. The 2010 *Guidelines* dilute the emphasis on market definition and accentuate other economic tests that indicate whether a merger would result in antitrust concerns. For example, the 2010 *Guidelines* introduced the concept of "upward pricing pressure" resulting from a horizontal merger.

SSNIP Analysis

Since publication of the 1982 Merger Guidelines, the U.S. Department of Justice has used a conceptual guideline to identify competitors in both relevant product markets and relevant geographic markets. The concept is known as SSNIP, and it is one approach to define a relevant product market. SSNIP analysis attempts to determine if a merger of firms would facilitate a small but significant and non-transitory increase in price, known as the SSNIP criterion. To use the convoluted language of the *Merger Guidelines*, a relevant market is "a product or group of products and a geographic area in which it is sold such that a hypothetical, profit-maximizing firm, not subject to price regulation, that was the only present and future seller of those products in that area would impose a 'small but significant and non-transitory' increase in price above prevailing or likely future levels." The SSNIP criterion also is used in the European Union (EU), recognized officially in "Commission's Notice for the Definition of the Relevant Market."

In effect, SSNIP analysis identifies the smallest grouping of products for which a hypothetical monopolist could raise prices by five percent. Essentially, the SSNIP test asks whether a monopolist or its equivalent could sustain a price increase of five percent for at least one year. The range of products and the geographic area identified by SSNIP analysis constitutes the relevant market. The United States uses a five percent test, but some other countries such as the United Kingdom and the European Union use a five to ten percent test. The basic issue is whether a price increase of five percent would be profitable. Profitability hinges on how sensitive unit sales are to price, which is to say the price elasticity of demand.

Although a torturous concept, SSNIP analysis is sensible but also problematic. Often, SSNIP analysis is not practical. Cutting through the fog of legalese, the SSNIP criterion implies that two firms are competitive if a price increase by one causes many of its customers to do business with the other. This implication is nothing more than the concept of substitutes. Cross elasticity, for example, can accomplish the same objective.

HHI: The Metric for Concentration

The DOJ and the FTC regard industries or markets with an HHI of more than 2,500 to be highly concentrated, an HHI between 1,500 and 2,500 to be moderately concentrated, and an HHI below 1,500 to be unconcentrated. Mergers involving an increase in HHI of less than 100 are unlikely to have adverse competitive effects and ordinarily require no scrutiny. These mergers are not likely to be challenged. Mergers resulting in a post-merger HHI of less than 1,500 also are unlikely to have adverse competitive effects and ordinarily require no scrutiny. These mergers resulting in unconcentrated markets are not likely to be challenged. Mergers resulting in moderately concentrated markets that involve an increase in HHI of more than 100 raise significant competitive concerns and warrant scrutiny. If the post-merger HHI is between 1,500 and 2,500, therefore, competitive concerns are heightened and scrutiny might result in the merger being challenged. Mergers resulting in highly concentrated markets that involve an increase in HHI between 100 and 200 raise significant competitive concerns and warrant scrutiny. Mergers resulting in highly concentrated markets that involve an increase in HHI of more than 200 are presumed likely to enhance market power. Therefore, if the post-merger HHI is more than 2,500, competitive concerns are heightened still further and scrutiny will be more intense. Mergers are likely to be challenged.

Although market concentration is measured by HHI, DOJ and FTC also consider other factors in deciding whether to challenge a horizontal merger. Other factors include ease of entry, financial condition, foreign competition, and efficiency. In addition, the Department of Justice and Federal Trade Commission can rely on merger remedies. The most common remedy is divestiture of assets. The fundamental goal of a divestiture is to preserve the competition that existed prior to the proposed merger or acquisition. Both agencies focus on ensuring that appropriate assets are divested.

FTC MERGER REMEDIES

The Federal Trade Commission has policies and practices meant to restore the pre-merger competitive environment, which is the ultimate goal of divestiture. The FTC places the burden on merging companies to demonstrate that divestiture of assets will enable the buyer of the assets to compete effectively and eliminate anticompetitive effects of the transaction. When settled, a consent order is issued. A consent order is an agreement between the merging companies and the FTC. Increasingly, the FTC has required the merging companies to find an up-front buyer of the assets they propose to divest and execute an acceptable agreement with the buyer before the FTC accepts a consent order. These up-front buyers are more likely to be required when there is concern about the viability of the proposed assets or the existence of acceptable buyers.

The FTC may insist on a crown jewel provision, which requires the divestiture of additional assets in the event that the merging companies fail to divest the original assets by the time stipulated in the consent order. The FTC might insist on a crown jewel provision even when an up-front buyer exists. For example, when Chevron and Texaco merged, the consent order required the companies to divest Texaco's entire U.S. general aviation fuel marketing business in the event that the parties did not divest Texaco's general aviation fuel marketing business in fourteen states to Avfuel, the up-front buyer. The intent of a crown jewel provision is to mitigate risk in the event that the sale to the up-front buyer falls through.

Exxon Mobil: Largest Divestiture in FTC History

Market-by-market scrutiny was focused on the 1999 merger of Exxon and Mobil. More accurately, Exxon acquired Mobil in an $81 billion deal. The acquisition was approved in a 4-0 vote by the Federal Trade Commission roughly a year after Exxon announced its plan to buy Mobil, the second largest oil company in the industry. The eleven-month review of the deal was one of the longest by the FTC. Oddly, the Exxon Mobil merger brought back together two pieces of the former Standard Oil Company, which was split apart in 1911 due to a Supreme Court decision.

In many markets, the market share as measured by HHI held by Exxon and Mobil service stations led to required divestiture of some properties. Such divestiture was a condition for approval. On 30 November 1999, the Federal Trade Commission announced that it had accepted a proposed settlement of charges that Exxon's acquisition of Mobil would violate antitrust laws. The settlement required the largest retail divestiture in FTC history, involving the sale of 2,431 Exxon and Mobil gas stations in Northeastern states and Atlantic states (1,740), California (360), Texas (319), and Guam (12). In addition, an Exxon refinery in Benicia, California, terminals, a pipeline, jet turbine oil business, and other assets were sold. The FTC commented that the proposed merger posed competitive problems in moderately concentrated markets and in highly concentrated markets. After the dust settled, Exxon Mobil was left atop the three super majors. The other two are Royal Dutch/Shell and BP Amoco, which at the time awaited regulatory approval for its purchase of Atlantic Richfield.

MERGER REMEDIES: THE ANTITRUST DIVISION

Policies and practices of the Antitrust Division of the Department of Justice are similar to those of the FTC. The most significant distinction between the two federal agencies relates to the requirement of an up-front buyer. The Department of Justice has not adopted a similar policy. On the other hand, the Department of Justice uses an analogue of the FTC's up-front requirement known as the fix-it-first policy. Under a fix-it-first remedy, the parties agree to a structural change designed to eliminate anticompetitive concerns prior to the consummation of the merger.

In the fix-it-first approach to proposed mergers and acquisitions, measures are usually calculated market by market. The HHI is calculated market by market to measure concentration, and such calculations then are used to guide divestiture. For example, when Bank One acquired First National Bank of Commerce (FCOM) in 1998, the Department of Justice examined bank deposits in each market where these two banks operated in Louisiana. Some branches had to be divested because HHI otherwise would have been too high in certain markets.

In a memorandum, "Divestiture Questions & Answers," which was circulated for internal use by FCOM employees, the following questions were addressed.

What is a Divestiture? Why does FCOM have to divest branches? The Department of Justice does not allow any financial institution to control more than 35% of all bank deposits in its market. The combined FCOM/Bank One would exceed that market share and would be in violation of antitrust laws if some branches were not divested (*i.e.*, spun off or sold to another financial institution)....

How do the regulators come up with that 35% figure? The Federal Reserve uses a statistical measure called the Herfindahl-Hirschman Index (HHI) to determine a bank's share of a particular market, both pre- and post-merger. The Department of Justice conducts its own antitrust review of a particular merger. Both agencies review other aspects of the two banks as well, such as Community Reinvestment Act performances, small business lending, and middle market-sized business loans for both organizations.

Where are the divestitures taking place? FCOM anticipates divesting eight branches in Lake Charles, eight in Monroe, two in Ruston, and seven in Lafayette. It is important to note, however, that even after the divestiture occurs, between them FCOM and Bank One will have twenty branches in the Lake Charles market, eighteen in the Monroe market, seven in the Ruston market, and twenty-nine in the Lafayette market....

Banc One Corporation of Columbus, Ohio, branded its banks as Bank One. In 1998, Banc One and First Chicago also merged, essentially a Banc One acquisition. In 2004, Banc One itself was acquired in a merger with J.P. Morgan Chase. Branches, credit cards, and so forth have been rebranded with the Chase nameplate.

THE TRUSTBUSTER'S NEW TOOLS

At times, determination of a relevant market is difficult to accept with a straight face. Particularly when firms occupy smaller market niches, the putative line of business can be downright comical. The focus on market definition and market share has proved embarrassing at times to the FTC and DOJ in their attempts to block mergers. For example, in June 2007, the FTC argued in federal court that the proposed merger of Whole Foods and Wild Oats should be enjoined. At the time, Whole Foods and Wild Oats had only three hundred stores, a tiny fraction of the thirty-four thousand supermarkets in the United States. Undaunted, the FTC argued that the relevant market was "premium, natural and organic supermarkets." The court decided the definition was too narrow. After all, national supermarket chains such as Safeway, regional supermarkets such as Publix, and local supermarkets such as Rouses also sell premium, natural, and organic products. The court found against the government. A settlement was reached. The Wild Oats brand was sold. Twelve Wild Oats and one Whole Foods store were sold. Leases and assets of nineteen stores were sold.

Frustration with HHI has led economists, lawyers, and others to explore new paths. Analysis seems to be shifting from an obsession with market share to a focus on the constraint each firm has on the other's prices. Instead of calculating market shares, they seek to gauge if a merger or acquisition will drive prices higher then they would be otherwise. In particular, economists now are attempting to model behavior and then predict what will happen if the merger or acquisition is permitted.

In 1995, for example, Interstate Bakeries proposed to acquire rival Continental Baking. Economists from the Department of Justice obtained scanner data from a commercial information company, which provides weekly details about average prices and sales volumes for dozens of different breads in various cities. They concluded that each company's brand was the main restraint on the other's price. The Department of Justice turned to a fix-it-first remedy. Interstate agreed to sell some of its brands and bakeries. The empirical analysis went still further in the case of the proposed 1996 merger of Staples and Office Depot, two chains of office supply superstores. By traditional measures such as the HHI, the merger posed no problems mainly because thousands of retailers sell office supplies. However, prices and quantities for every item sold by each chain were examined, and this careful scrutiny unmasked a pattern. Staples prices were lower in cities where Office Depot also had a store than in cities where Office Depot did not have a store. This pattern was taken as strong evidence that the merger would allow Staples to raise prices. In 1997, a federal court judge granted the FTC motion for an injunction, which blocked the merger.

When scanner data or similar information sources are available, some practitioners, including some within the Department of Justice, suggest that defining a market no longer is needed as part of antitrust analysis. To date, courts have not accepted that view. However, this econometric approach clearly has influenced all parties involved. Economists, lawyers, and judges can use such data to predict whether a merger will raise prices.[129]

PRACTICE QUESTIONS

1. What is the rule of reason, and what major court cases was the doctrine first stated?

2. What is the *per se* rule?

3. The following table presents market share data on the top five beer brewers in the United States for 1968 and 1979. Assume that the residual market share is spread equally over twenty other brewers. Answer each question below based on this information.

Year	Anheuser-Busch	Miller	Schlitz	Pabst	Coors	All Others
1968	16.5%	4.3%	10.4%	10.0%	4.8%	54.0%
1979	25.9%	20.0%	9.9%	8.6%	7.4%	28.2%

a. Suppose that, in 1979, Miller proposed a merger with Schlitz. If the U.S. Department of Justice (DOJ) *Merger Guidelines* had been respected at that time, would DOJ have blocked the merger? Why?

b. Suppose that, in 1979, Miller proposed a merger with one of the other twenty brewers who shared the remaining market equally. If the DOJ *Merger Guidelines* had been respected, would DOJ have blocked the merger? Why?

4. Consider two competing retail store chains that have announced a merger. Based on SIC and NAICS codes, the HHI for this industry is 1,118, and, if consummated, the merger will increase the HHI to 1,170. In market-by-market analysis, however, the HHI is 1,900 in several local markets, and the merger will increase the HHI to more than 2,100 in these particular markets. What is the Department of Justice likely to do?

5. What is the crown jewels provision that the FTC uses as a merger remedy?

PRACTICE QUESTIONS *(AND ANSWERS)*

1. What is the rule of reason, and what major court cases was the doctrine first stated?

In its decisions in the Standard Oil and American Tobacco cases of 1911, the U.S. Supreme Court declared that the Sherman Antitrust Act did not make illegal every action that seemed to restrain trade, only those actions that were "unreasonable." This declaration became known and is still known as the "rule of reason." The Court implied that structure alone was not a criterion for unreasonableness. Presumably, a

---

129   See "The Economics of Antitrust," *The Economist* (May 2nd-May 8th, 1998), pp. 62-64.

business that achieved near monopoly status would not violate the Sherman Antitrust Act if it achieved that status while using "reasonable" tactics. Pursuant court cases confirmed that a business violated the Sherman Antitrust Act only if it had evidenced unreasonable conduct.

2. What is the *per se* rule?

In general, per se means inherently illegal without requiring any extrinsic proof of any surrounding circumstances. A per se violation involves conduct that violates antitrust law whether the result is reasonable or not. Indeed, per se conduct is regarded as presumption of unreasonableness. Examples of per se violations are price fixing, bid rigging, and market allocation.

3. The following table presents market share data on the top five beer brewers in the United States for 1968 and 1979. Assume that the residual market share is spread equally over twenty other brewers. Answer each question below based on this information.

Year	Anheuser-Busch	Miller	Schlitz	Pabst	Coors
1968	16.5%	4.3%	10.4%	10.0%	4.8%
1979	25.9%	20.0%	9.9%	8.6%	7.4%

a. Suppose that, in 1979, Miller proposed a merger with Schlitz. If the U.S. Department of Justice (DOJ) *Merger Guidelines* had been respected at that time, would DOJ have blocked the merger? Why?

If DOJ followed its Merger Guidelines, it probably would have blocked the merger because the merger would have increased the HHI by more than 100, from 1,337 to 1,733, which is an increase of 396.

b. Suppose that, in 1979, Miller proposed a merger with one of the other twenty brewers who shared the remaining market equally. If the DOJ *Merger Guidelines* had been respected, would DOJ have blocked the merger? Why?

If DOJ followed its Merger Guidelines, it probably would not have blocked the merger because the merger would have increased the HHI by less than 100, from 1,337 to 1,393, which is an increase of 56.

4. Consider two competing retail store chains that have announced a merger. Based on SIC and NAICS codes, the HHI for this industry is 1,118, and, if consummated, the merger will increase the HHI to 1,170. In market-by-market analysis, however, the HHI is 1,900 in several local markets, and the merger will increase the HHI to more than 2,100 in these particular markets. What is the Department of Justice likely to do?

The industry is unconcentrated. The increase in HHI would be only 52, which is within Merger Guidelines. The problem is in local markets where the HHI is 1,900 and will be increased by more than 200 if the merger is not blocked. The Department of Justice could apply the fix-it-first" policy and thus require the two competing chains to divest assets.

5. What is the crown jewels provision that the FTC uses as a merger remedy?

Often, the FTC requires that merger parties find an acceptable buyer for assets it proposes to divest and execute an acceptable agreement with the buyer before the FTC accepts the proposed consent order. These up-front buyers are more likely to be required when there is concern about the adequacy of the proposed asset package, the existence of an acceptable buyer, or the viability of the asset package

----

pending the divestiture. The FTC may insist on a crown jewel provision, which requires the divestiture of an expanded package of assets compared to the original asset package in the event that the acquiring company fails to divest the original asset package in the time proscribed by the consent decree. The FTC may insist on a crown jewel provision even when an up-front buyer exists. For example, in the proposed merger of Chevron and Texaco, the consent order required the parties to divest Texaco's entire U.S. general aviation fuel marketing business in the event that the parties did not divest Texaco's general aviation fuel marketing business in fourteen states to Avfuel, the up-front buyer. The justification for a crown jewel provision when there is an up-front buyer in hand is to mitigate risk in the event that the sale to the up-front buyer falls through.

12. Macroeconomics for Executives

MICROECONOMICS AND MACROECONOMICS

As a prefix, micro is derived from a Greek root, *mikros*, meaning small. The prefix macro comes from *makros*, meaning large. Both micro and macro are used widely as prefixes. In the English language, the prefixes are affixed to microscope, microbiology, microbrewery, microcosm, and so forth, as well as macrobiotic, macrocosmic, macroclimatic, macrophage, and so forth. In economics and business practice, distinctions are made between microeconomics and macroeconomics. In the former case, microeconomics deals with parts, segments, or sectors of the overall economy. Microeconomics scrutinizes such matters as the operations of a firm, characteristics of an industry, or components of a sector, which are constituent parts of all firms, all industries, and all sectors. On the other hand, macroeconomics deals with the structure and performance of an entire economy. In this way, overall aspects and workings of an economy can be viewed with emphasis on aggregates such as national employment, national income, national output, as well as relationships among sectors of the national economy.

NATIONAL INCOME AND PRODUCT ACCOUNTS

One of the most fundamental concepts and metrics in macroeconomics is gross domestic product (GDP), which is the total market value of all final goods and services produced within a country during a particular time period such as a calendar year. GDP measures the value of goods and services produced. During any year, some goods and services are produced but not sold. Unsold production is considered as additions to inventory. Moreover, some goods and services were produced in previous years, *e.g.*, vintage automobiles such as the 1954 Corvette or the 1964 Mustang, houses built in the Victorian era, and the iPhone introduced in 2007. To reiterate, GDP is a macroeconomic measure of the market value of goods and services currently produced domestically.

Some goods and services are not exchanged in markets, however, and thus have no prices to determine their market value. For example, government services provided by public school teachers, firemen and policewomen, military personnel such as soldiers and sailors, and other government employees such as governors and Central Intelligence Agency case officers are not sold in markets. The value of such services is entered at cost in GDP computation as though such government services have market value equal to cost.

GDP can be viewed as a measure of total income or total expenditure. The reason is that every transaction involves two parties, a buyer and a seller. Every dollar of spending by a buyer is a dollar of income for the seller. Therefore, GDP can be computed by adding up total expenditure in the economy or by adding up total income in the economy. Along with other measures such as National Income, GDP is one of several metrics in the National Income and Product Accounts. These accounts are kept and reported periodically by the Bureau of Economic Analysis, an agency of the Department of Commerce.

The National Income and Product Accounts (NIPA) report measures in addition to GDP. By adding income receipts from the rest of the world and subtracting income payments to the rest of the world, the result is gross national product (GNP). By subtracting "consumption of fixed capital" to account for depreciation, the result is net national product (NNP). After adjusting for "statistical discrepancy," the result is national income (NI). After a number of other adjustments such as subtracting corporate profits, contributions for social security, net interest, and government enterprise surplus, the result is personal income (PI). Subtracting personal taxes from personal income, the result is disposable personal income (DPI). Disposable personal income is available to spend or save. Table 12.1 shows each of the measures for the second quarter of 2013.

Table 12.1 NIPA Measures, 2Q 2013 ($Billion)	
Gross Domestic Product	16,661.0
Plus: Income receipts from the rest of the world	817.0
Less: Income payments to the rest of the world	570.1
Equals: Gross National Product	16,907.9
Less: Consumption of fixed capital	2,631.9
Equals: Net National Product	14,276.0
Less: Statistical discrepancy	162.5
Equals: National Income	14,438.5
Less: Corporate profits with inventory valuation and capital consumption adjustments	2,087.4
Less: Taxes on production and imports less subsidies	1,079.9
Less: Contributions for government social insurance, domestic	1,100.3
Less: Net interest and miscellaneous payments on assets	444.0
Less: Business current transfer payments (net)	125.8
Less: Current surplus of government enterprises	−39.0
Plus: Personal income receipts on assets	1,944.0
Plus: Personal current transfer receipts	2,430.9
Equals: Personal Income	14,065.0
Less: Personal current taxes	1,664.8
Equals: Disposable Personal Income	12,400.1
Less: Personal outlays	11,837.0
Equals: Personal Saving	563.2
Personal Saving as a percentage of Disposable Personal Income	4.5

Source: Bureau of Economic Analysis, National Income and Product Accounts, Table 1.7.5 and Table 2.1

Exclusions and Imputations

GDP is meant to be comprehensive. Although GDP implies measurement of all goods and services produced, however, it is not totally comprehensive. GDP excludes illegal or illicit products and services. For example, transactions involving cocaine, heroin, and marijuana are excluded except in the states where marijuana has been legalized. Where illegal, gambling and prostitution are excluded. GDP also excludes items that are produced and consumed at home. For example, vegetables grown in a home garden for home consumption rather than sale are excluded. Services such as lawn mowing, house cleaning, and babysitting provided at home also are excluded from GDP. If the same services were provided by a business, the value of the services would be included in GDP.

GDP deals with market values and thus uses market prices to add up the value of goods and services. In a limited number of cases, however, market value is imputed. For example, GDP includes the market value of housing services. For rental housing, this value is a straightforward measurement based on rent. However, GDP imputes the rental value of owner-occupied housing, which is based on the notion that owners pay rent to themselves. Therefore, the rental value of owner-occupied housing is imputed and included in GDP.

Final Goods and Services

Another important aspect deals with GDP as a measure of final goods and services. International Paper makes paper stock. Hallmark uses this paper stock to make greeting cards. The paper stock is an intermediate good. The Hallmark card is a final good. GDP includes the value of final products such as Hallmark cards. The reason is that the value of intermediate goods is included in the value of the final good. Adding the value of paper stock to the value of the Hallmark card would be double counting the value of the paper stock. On the other hand, when an intermediate good is produced and added to inventory to be used or sold in a different calendar year, the intermediate good is considered to be inventory investment and included in GDP. When the inventory of the intermediate good is sold later, the firm's inventory investment is negative and the GDP for the later period is reduced accordingly.

Goods and Services Currently Produced

Still another important aspect of GDP deals with inclusion of goods and services currently produced. GDP does not include transactions involving items produced in the past. When Ford produces and sells a new car to an authorized Ford distributor or to a rental company in 2013, the value of the car is included in 2013 GDP. When a used 2008 Ford is sold in 2013, the value of the used car is not included in 2013 GDP. However, if a used car salesman is compensated with a commission in 2013, the commission value of his or her services is included in 2013 GDP.

Goods and Services Produced Domestically

A final important aspect of GDP is that it measures the value of production within the geographic boundaries of a country. When an American company such as Freeport-McMoRan operates a mining facility in Irian Jaya that produces copper and gold ore in Indonesia, the value of the copper and gold is included in Indonesian GDP rather than American GDP. When a German company such as Daimler AG operates a Mercedes-Benz assembly plant in Alabama, the production and income that result from the assembly operation appear in American GDP and American National Income rather than German GDP and German National Income. Items are included in a nation's GDP if the items are produced domestically regardless of the nationality or corporate headquarters of the producer.

COMPONENTS OF GDP

In any economy, spending takes many forms. Basically, gross domestic product (GDP) is disaggregated into four components of spending: consumption (C), investment (I), government purchases of goods and services (G), and net exports (NX), which can be expressed as an identity,

GDP=C+I+G+NX

In this formulation, C is personal consumption expenditures, which consists of household spending on durable and nondurable goods and services.

I is gross private domestic investment, which consists of capital equipment, software, inventories, and structures. Investment also includes expenditure on new residential housing.

G is government consumption expenditures and gross investment, which includes federal, state, and local government spending on goods and services. The category of government spending includes only purchases of goods and services and does not include transfer payments such as social security, temporary assistance for needy families (welfare), Medicaid, food stamps, and unemployment compensation. No product or service is provided in exchange for such payments. In other words, a transfer payment is not made in exchange for a currently produced good or service. However, when social security recipients receive their monthly checks and purchase goods and services with the income, these goods and services are counted as any other.

NX is net exports of goods and services, which consists of domestically produced goods and services purchased by buyers in other countries (exports=X) minus domestic purchases of goods produced in other countries (imports=M). Many products are assembled domestically with materials, parts, and components produced in foreign countries. Ford automobiles, for example, typically consist of parts manufactured in Japan, Mexico, Thailand, Spain, and Germany, but final assembly might take place in Kansas City. Rather than sort out foreign from domestic parts, the U.S. Commerce Department simply subtracts the value of all imports from the value of total spending. Exports are added to total spending, and imports are subtracted from total spending. Nonetheless, a Boeing aircraft produced in Washington and sold to British Airways increases net exports, but a Mercedes-Benz produced in Germany and sold to a distributor in America decreases net exports.

REAL GDP

GDP is a measure of total spending on goods and services. If GDP increases from one year to the next, one of two events or a combination of the two must have occurred: (1) a larger volume of output of goods and services was produced, which is regarded as a real change in GDP because real goods and services are involved, or (2) the same volume of goods and services were produced but sold at higher prices. These two effects are quite different and should be separated appropriately. In particular, a measure of goods and services produced and not affected by changes in prices of those goods and services is a better measure of overall performance. To do so, a measure of real GDP is used.

Real GDP is a measure of the value of goods and services after adjustment for changes in prices of those goods and services. In other words, real GDP is a measure of the value of goods and services at constant prices. In practical terms, real GDP is calculated with use of prices during a base year. In effect, prices in the base year provide the basis for comparing quantities and values of goods and services in subsequent years. Therefore, nominal GDP uses current prices to place a value on goods and services produced, whereas real GDP uses constant base-year prices to place a value on goods and services produced. Because real GDP is not affected by changes in prices, changes in real GDP reflect only changes in the value of goods and services due to changes in amounts of goods and services produced. In this way, real GDP is regarded as a better gauge of how the economy is performing.

A useful statistic for real GDP is the implicit price deflator for GDP. The GDP deflator is a measure of the current level of prices relative to the level of prices in the base year, which is 2009. Actually, the U.S. Department of Commerce does not freeze prices at year 2009 levels. From 1996, Commerce has used chain-weighted price indices. A chain-weighted price index uses a moving average of price levels in consecutive years as an inflation adjustment. Nonetheless, the GDP deflator indicates the rise in nominal GDP attributable to a rise in prices rather than a rise in quantities of goods and services produced.

The GDP deflator is used to calculate real GDP from nominal GDP. In 2Q 2013, for example, the GDP deflator was 106.165. Therefore, real GDP is nominal GDP is divided by 1.06165. Because of the moving average involved in chained dollars, the result will not be precise. Actually, different implicit price deflators are used for different components of GDP. This practice recognizes that prices rise at different rates for different components. In 2Q 2013, for example, the deflator for personal consumption expenditures was 106.878; for gross private domestic investment, 103.206; for exports, 112.034; for imports, 113.411; and for government consumption expenditures and gross investment, 107.485. Not all categories have experienced price increases since 2009. Within personal consumption expenditures, for example, durable goods had a deflator of only 95.016, indicating lower prices now than in 2009. The deflator for equipment and software is 100.500, indicating prices virtually the same as in 2009. Also notice that the deflators for imports and exports indicate that prices received for exports have risen less than prices paid for exports. For more detail, see Table 12.2.

Table 12.2 Price Indexes for Gross Domestic Product, 2Q 2013 Index Numbers, 2009=100 Seasonally Adjusted	
Gross Domestic Product	106.165
Personal Consumption Expenditures	106.878
Goods	105.740
Durable Goods	95.016
Nondurable Goods	111.126
Services	107.477
Gross Private Domestic Investment	103.206
Fixed Investment	103.478
Nonresidential	103.008
Structures	106.521
Equipment	100.500
Intellectual Property Properties	104.071
Residential	105.396
Change in Private Inventories	—.—
Net Exports of Goods and Services	—.—
Exports	112.034
Goods	112.771
Services	110.451
Imports	113.411
Goods	115.028
Services	106.165
Government Consumption Expenditures and Gross Investment	107.485
Federal	107.229
National Defense	107.512
Nondefense	106.760
State and Local	107.676

Source: Bureau of Economic Analysis, National Income and Product Accounts, Table 1.1.4

Table 12.3 shows nominal and real GDP as well as components of GDP for the second quarter, 2013. Real GDP is based on chained 2009 dollars, which means that a price index based on year 2009 prices is used to adjust nominal GDP. Consumption spending constituted about sixty-eight percent of real GDP, investment spending about sixteen percent, and government purchases of goods and services about eighteen percent. Net exports were negative, representing less than minus three percent of real GDP.

Table 12.3 Gross Domestic Product, Nominal and Real, 3Q 2012 Seasonally Adjusted at Annual Rates ($Billion)		
Measure	**Nominal GDP**	**Real GDP**
Gross Domestic Product	16,661.0	15,679.7
Personal Consumption Expenditures	11,427.1	10,691.9
Goods	3,848.5	3,639.6
Durable goods	1,257.5	1,323.2
Nondurable goods	2,591.0	2,331.7
Services	7,578.6	7,051.5
Gross Private Domestic Investment	2,621.0	2,524.9
Fixed investment	2,543.8	2,458.4
Nonresidential	2,030.6	1,971.3
Structures	452.6	424.8
Equipment	934.6	929.9
Intellectual Property Products	643.5	618.3
Residential	513.2	487.1
Change in private inventories	77.2	56.6
Net Exports of Goods and Services	−509.0	−424.4
Exports	2,238.9	1,998.4
Goods	1,548.8	1,373.4
Services	690.2	624.9
Imports	2,747.9	2,422.9
Goods	2,288.7	1,989.6
Services	459.3	432.6
Government Consumption Expenditures and Gross Investment	3,121.9	2,904.5
Federal	1,252.6	1,168.2
National defense	776.3	722.0
Nondefense	476.3	446.2
State and local	1,869.3	1,736.0

Source: *Bureau of Economic Analysis, National Income and Product Accounts, Table 1.1.5 and Table 1.1.6*

Recession

The National Bureau of Economic Research (NBER) fixes a date for the beginning and end of expansions and contractions in the economy. Popular media mistakenly but knowingly report that the onset of a recession is two consecutive quarters of negative growth in real GDP. NBER explicitly denies this misguided notion. To quote the organization itself, "The NBER does not define a recession in terms of two consecutive quarters of decline in real GDP." According to NBER, "Rather, a recession is a significant decline in economic activity spread across the economy, lasting more than a few months, normally visible in real GDP, real income, employment, industrial production, and wholesale-retail sales."

On 11 December 2008, NBER announced that the U.S. economy was amidst a recession that began in December 2007. The NBER Business Cycle Dating Committee reached this conclusion even though real GDP had not declined in a single quarter of 2007! When the U.S. Bureau of Economic Analysis reported final estimates of negative real GDP for 1Q 2008, 3Q 2008, 4Q 2008, 1Q 2009, and 2Q 2009, the recession announced by NBER was affirmed. However, NBER did not date the recession from 3Q 2008, but rather dated it back to the end of the fourth quarter of 2007. On 20 September 2010, NBER announced the recession ended in June 2009. The recession lasted only eighteen months.

CONSUMER PRICE INDEX

The GDP deflator is one measure to infer changes in prices over time. Other measures are the consumer price index (C_pI) and the producer price index (PPI). The consumer price index is a measure of the overall prices of goods and services bought by consumers. Each month, the Bureau of Labor Statistics (BLS), an agency of the U.S. Department of Labor, computes and reports the C_pI. Actually, BLS reports two indices, C_pI-U and C_pI-W. The former, C_pI-U, is a consumer price index for urban consumers, which constitutes about eighty-seven percent of the U.S. population. The latter, C_pI-W, is a price index for urban wage earners and clerical workers, which constitutes only thirty-two percent of the population. C_pI-W is of interest only for historical purposes as a continuation of the consumer price index prior to development of the C_pI-U in 1978. In addition to the consumer price index for the overall economy, BLS also calculates several other price indices. For example, BLS reports the consumer price index for regions such as Boston, New York, and Los Angeles, and for some categories of goods and services such as food, clothing, and energy. It also calculates the producer price index, which measures the cost of a basket of goods and services bought by firms rather than consumers.

Each month, BLS data economic assistants visit or call thousands of retail stores, service establishments, rental properties, doctor offices, and so forth. They obtain price data on about 80,000 items to measure price changes in the C_pI, both C_pI-U and C_pI-W. Price data are sent to BLS headquarters in Washington, D.C. Commodity specialists who have detailed knowledge about particular goods and services review the data. These commodity specialists check the data for accuracy and consistency. They also make appropriate adjustments due to considerations such as changes in size or quantity of a packaged item and value of features or quality.

BLS relies on a base that is the benchmark against which other years are compared. Currently, the base is 1982-1984. To calculate the index, the price of a basket of goods and services in each year is divided by the price of the basket in the base of 1982-1984 and then multiplied by 100 to state the consumer price index. In this way, the consumer price index can be used to calculate the inflation rate, which is the percentage change in the price index from the preceding period. Table 12.4 shows the annual average C_pI-U for 2000-2012 along with percentage change in C_pI-U.

Year	Annual Average C_pI-U Based on 1982-1984=100	Percentage Change
2000	172.2	3.4
2001	177.1	2.8
2002	179.9	1.6
2003	184.0	2.3
2004	188.9	2.7
2005	195.3	3.4
2006	201.6	3.2
2007	207.3	2.8
2008	215.3	3.8
2009	214.5	−0.4
2010	218.1	1.6
2011	224.9	3.2
2012	229.6	2.1

Table 12.4
C_pI-U, 2000-2012

Source: Bureau of Labor Statistics, History of C_pI-U U.S. All Items Indexes and Annual Percent Changes From 1913 to Present

Market Basket Weights

The C_pI-U and the C_pI-W make use of a market basket developed from detailed expenditure information provided by families and individuals regarding what they actually bought. This information is collected from the Consumer Expenditure Survey every two years. In each of those two years, about 10,000 families from around the country provided information on their spending habits in a series of quarterly interviews. To collect information on frequently purchased items such as food and beverages, another 7,500 families in each of the two years kept diaries listing everything they bought during a two-week period.

Altogether, more than 30,000 families and individuals provide spending information for use in determining the relative importance of the more than two hundred categories in the C_pI index structure. The categories are arranged into eight major groups: Housing, such as rent of primary residence, fuel oil, and furniture; Food and Beverages, such as breakfast cereal, chicken, milk, and beer; Transportation, such as new vehicles, air fares, gasoline, and automobile insurance; Medical Care, such as prescription drugs, physician services, hospital services, and eyeglasses; Apparel, such as shirts, dresses, shoes, and jewelry; Recreation, such as television sets, pets and pet supplies, sports equipment, and admission tickets; Education and Communication, such as tuition, postage, telephone services, and computer software; and Other Goods and Services, such as tobacco products, personal services, and funeral expenses. Each of these eight major groups and categories within groups is weighted. Products on which consumers spend the most are given the most weight. BLS sets these weights on the basis of survey results, thus defining the market basket of goods and services that consumers buy. Table 12.5 depicts the weights by group and selected subgroups reported by BLS for December 2012.

Table 12.5 C_pI-U Market Basket Weights by Group and Selected Subgroup U.S. City Average, December 2012		
Group, Subgroup	**Subgroup Weight in C_pI**	**Group Weight in C_pI**
HOUSING		41.021%
Shelter	31.681%	
Fuels and Utilities	5.300%	
Household Furnishings and Operations	4.040%	
FOOD AND BEVERAGES		15.261%
Food	14.312%	
Food Away From Home	5.713%	
Alcoholic Beverages	0.949%	
TRANSPORTATION		16.846%
Private transportation	15.657%	
New and Used Motor Vehicles	5.551%	
Motor Fuel	5.462%	
Public Transportation	1.189%	
MEDICAL CARE		7.163%
Medical Care Commodities	1.714%	
Medical Care Services	5.448%	
APPAREL		3.564%
Men's and Boys' Apparel	0.858%	
Women's and Girls' Apparel	1.495%	
RECREATION		5.990%
Video and Audio	1.897%	
Pets, Pet Products and Services	1.099%	
Sporting Goods	0.461%	
Photography	0.109%	
EDUCATION AND COMMUNICATION		6.779%
Education	3.281%	
Communication	3.499%	
OTHER GOODS AND SERVICES		3.376%
Tobacco and Smoking Products	0.805%	
Personal Care	2.571%	

Source: Bureau of Labor Statistics, Relative Importance of Components in Consumer Price Indexes

GDP Deflator and the CPI

The GDP deflator and consumer price index are different. The GDP deflator reflects the prices of all goods and services produced domestically, whereas the consumer price index reflects only the prices of goods and services bought by consumers. For example, if the price of an F/A-18E/F Super Hornet rises, the plane is part of GDP, but it is not part of the basket of goods and services bought by consumers. Therefore, the higher price would be reflected in the GDP deflator but not in the C_pI.

ECONOMIC GROWTH AND PRODUCTIVITY

Inferences about standard of living are drawn from GDP per capita, especially real GDP per capita. In 2011, GDP per capita in America was about $48,300, which was twice that of Saudi Arabia, three times that of Malaysia, four times that of Costa Rica, five times that of Thailand, six times that of China, seven times that of Egypt, eight times that of Libya, nine times that of Armenia, ten times that of Bolivia, twenty times that of Kyrgyzstan, thirty times that of Zambia, forty times that of Haiti, fifty times that of Afghanistan, sixty times that of Niger, seventy times that of Eritrea, eighty times that of Somalia, ninety times that of Zimbabwe, and more than one hundred times that of Congo. Clearly, the U.S. standard of living is greater than that of any of these countries, in some cases by a large multiple.

Real GDP per employed person in the United States was $106,541 in 2011. It is easy to understand why there is such a close nexus between productivity and standard of living. The more workers can produce, the more goods and services are available and thus the higher standard of living. Table 12.6 depicts real GDP per capita and real GDP per employed person for twenty developed countries.

Table 12.6 Real GDP per Capita, Real GDP per Employed Person 2011				
Country	Real GDP per Capita	Rank	Real GDP per Employed Person	Rank
United States	48,282	3	106,541	2
Canada	40,489	10	80,357	13
Australia	41,340	7	80,330	14
Japan	34,294	16	68,537	18
Republic of Korea	30,254	19	62,119	19
Singapore	60,742	2	99,415	4
Austria	42,066	5	85,816	6
Belgium	38,767	12	93,317	5
Czech Republic	26,169	20	54,226	20
Denmark	40,930	9	82,378	10
Finland	37,636	13	80,779	12
France	35,133	15	85,152	8
Germany	39,186	11	77,978	16
Ireland	41,537	6	102,983	3
Italy	32,100	18	78,813	15
Netherlands	42,824	4	85,437	7
Norway	61,869	1	116,251	1
Spain	32,501	17	81,417	11
Sweden	41,316	8	84,816	9
United Kingdom	35,688	14	76,638	17

Source: U.S. Department of Labor, Bureau of Labor Statistics, Division of International Labor Comparisons, International Comparisons of GDP per Capita and per Hour, 1960-2011 (November 7, 2012), Table 1a and Table 2a.

DETERMINANTS OF PRODUCTIVITY

Explaining the large variation in real GDP and living standards around the world is not difficult. The explanation can be condensed down to productivity. Productivity refers to a measure of the value of goods and services that a worker produces. However, such simplicity is seductive but perplexing because it dodges the question of what determines productivity. In the sense of GDP per worker, productivity is determined by certain known factors.

First, workers are more productive when they have tools, equipment, machinery, and plant with which to work. The stock of structures, tools, equipment, and machinery used to produce goods and services is physical capital. Furniture makers who have saws, lathes, planers, and drill presses can work more quickly and accurately than those without such specialized woodworking equipment. An important feature of capital is that it is a produced factor of production. Capital is a factor in the production process that in some previous time period was an output from the production process. A lathe used to make the leg of a table was itself once the output of a firm that manufactures lathes. Capital is a factor of production used to produce all kinds of goods and services, including more capital. However, physical capital is not the sole determinate of productivity. Human capital, natural resources, and technology also contribute to productivity.

Another determinant of productivity is human capital, which is knowledge and skills that workers acquire through education, training, and experience. Although less tangible than lathes, bulldozers, and buildings, human capital is like physical capital in many ways. Human capital raises the ability to produce goods and services, and human capital requires inputs in the form of teachers, trainers, libraries, laboratories, and student time.

Still another determinant is natural resources, which are inputs provided by nature such as land, rivers, and mineral deposits. Natural resources can be either renewable or nonrenewable. A timber forest is renewable, whereas extractable resources such as coal and crude oil are not. Differences in natural resources are responsible for at least some of the differences in standards of living around the world. Although important, natural resources are not absolutely necessary for a high standard of living. Japan, for example, is one of the richest countries in the world despite having little in the way of natural resources. International trade has made Japan's success possible. Japan imports natural resources it needs and then exports manufactured goods. On the other hand, natural resources are no guarantee of prosperity. Nigeria, for example, is blessed with natural resources, but this blessing has led to conflict rather than prosperity. Despite its rich natural resources, Nigeria remains a poor, corrupt, and unstable country.

Another determinant of productivity is technological knowledge, which is an understanding of the best ways to produce goods and services and the technical skills to act on this understanding. Technological knowledge takes many forms. Some technology is common knowledge that once used by one person or firm is available to others. Other technology is proprietary, known only by the company that discovers it. Even so, most technology is proprietary only for a short time.

SAVING AND INVESTMENT

Because capital is a produced factor of production, a society can change the amount of capital it has available for production of goods and services. If a large quantity of new capital goods is produced, then a larger stock of physical capital will be available in the future to produce more of all types of goods and services. Therefore, one way to raise future productivity is to invest more current resources in the production of capital. However, devoting more resources to producing capital requires devoting fewer resources to producing goods and services for current consumption. To invest more in capital, a society must consume less and save more of its current income. The growth in productivity and income that arises from capital accumulation requires a society to give up current consumption of goods and services to gain more consumption of goods and services in the future. Saving and investment in capital thus are important factors in the determination of productivity and standard of living.

FINANCIAL INSTITUTIONS

In the most general sense, a financial system links savers and borrowers. Savers supply funds to the financial system with the expectation that they will receive the funds back with interest or some other return at a later date. Borrowers demand funds from the financial system with the knowledge that they will be required to pay the funds back with interest or some other return in the future. The financial system is comprised of various financial institutions that help to orchestrate the nexus linking savers and borrowers. Financial institutions can be grouped into two important categories: financial markets and financial intermediaries. Financial markets are institutions through which those who save can supply funds directly to those who want to invest. The two most important financial markets in the U.S. economy are the bond market(s) and the stock market(s). Financial intermediaries are financial institutions through which savers can provide funds indirectly to investors or borrowers. The term intermediary reflects the role of these institutions in standing between savers and borrowers. The two most important types of financial intermediaries are banks and mutual funds.

Financial Markets

When a large corporation needs to borrow funds to finance construction of a new factory, the company can borrow directly from the public by selling corporate bonds that specify the obligations of the company to bond holders. Each bond stipulates the date on which the loan will be repaid, called the date of maturity, and the rate of interest to be paid periodically until the loan matures. The buyer can hold the bond until maturity or sell the bond to someone else before maturity. Another way for a corporation to raise funds to build a new factory is to sell stock in the company. Stock represents ownership in a firm and therefore is a proportionate claim on any profits the firm makes. For example, if a corporation were to sell a million shares of stock, then each share would represent ownership of one millionth of the business. Moreover, each share of stock would entitle the stockholder to one millionth of any profits the firm makes. The sale of stock to raise funds is called equity finance, whereas the sale of bonds is called debt finance. The owner of shares of a corporation's stock is a part owner, whereas the owner of a corporation's bond is a creditor of the corporation.

Secondary Markets

After a corporation issues stock by selling shares to the public, these shares are traded on organized stock exchanges. A corporation itself receives no funds when shares of its stock change hands. The most important U.S. stock exchanges are the New York Stock Exchange and NASDAQ (National Association of Securities Dealers Automated Quotation). Most of the world's countries have their own stock exchanges. The prices at which shares trade on stock exchanges are determined by the demand for and supply of listed stocks.

Various stock averages and indices measure the performance of selected stock prices. A stock average is computed as the average share price for a particular group of stocks. The most familiar stock average is the Dow Jones Industrial Average (DJIA), which has been computed regularly since 1896. The DJIA is based on the stock prices of thirty major companies. Effective 23 September 2013, the thirty companies comprising the DJIA are 3M, American Express, AT&T, Boeing, Caterpillar, Chevron, Cisco Systems, Coca-Cola, DuPont, Exxon Mobil, General Electric, Goldman Sachs, Home Depot, Intel, IBM, Johnson & Johnson, JP$_M$organ Chase, McDonald's, Merck, Microsoft, NIKE, Pfizer, Procter & Gamble, Travelers,

United Technologies, UnitedHealth, Verizon, Visa, and Wal-Mart. Editors of the *Wall Street Journal* chose these thirty companies.

The DJIA is computed using a price-weighted system. Simply put, the prices of all thirty stocks are added together and then divided by a number called the DJIA divisor. The DJIA divisor is adjusted over time to account for the effect on the average resulting from stock splits and structural changes such as constituent substitutions. For example, consider the problem created when stocks split from time to time. Suppose three stocks are trading at $15, $20, and $25. The average of the three is $20. If the company with the $20 stock has a 2-for-1 split, its shares suddenly are priced at half of their previous level. The $20 stock now sells for $10. The average falls to $16.66. The divisor must be changed from 3.0 to 2.5 to keep the average at $20. Since 23 September 2013, the DJIA Divisor has been 0.15571590501117. Therefore, the stock prices of the thirty companies making up the DJIA are added and then divided by 0.15571590501117. A $1 change in the share price of any one of the thirty stocks in the DJIA affects the price-weighted average equally. For example, for a $1 increase in the common stock price of any of the thirty industrials will change the DJIA by 6.42 points [1/0.15571590501117=6.42].

The NASDAQ Composite Index and S&P 500 Index are weighted by market value rather than price. Each stock affects the index in proportion to its market value. A stock index takes into account the total market capitalization of the companies it tracks, not just their share prices. A company with twice the market capitalization than another has twice the effect on the stock index. Standard & Poor's (S&P) 500 Index is based on 500 major companies, and the NASDAQ Composite is based on about 2,700 companies.

Financial Intermediaries

If the owner of a local store wants to finance an expansion of his or her business, the owner takes a route quite different from a large corporation. Unlike large corporations, a small storeowner is unlikely to raise funds in bond or stock markets. The local storeowner is likely to finance his or her business expansion with a loan from a local bank. Banks are the financial intermediaries with which people are most familiar. One of the primary roles of banks is to accept deposits and use these deposits to make loans. Thus, a commercial bank is the intermediary between depositors and borrowers.

Another financial intermediary of great importance in the U.S. economy is the mutual fund. A mutual fund is an institution that sells shares to the public and uses the proceeds to buy a portfolio of various stocks, bonds, or both stocks and bonds. If the value of the portfolio rises, the shareholder benefits. If the value of the portfolio falls, the shareholder incurs the loss. The primary advantage of mutual funds is that they allow people with small amounts of money to diversify. People who hold a diverse portfolio of stocks and bonds face less risk. Mutual funds also give people access to the information and skills of professional money managers.

THE MONEY STOCK

The amount of money in the economy at any time is called the money stock or the money supply, which has a powerful effect on many economic variables. How much is the stock of money? How much is the supply of money? As President Clinton said under oath, "It depends on what the meaning of 'is' is." The answer to such questions depends on how money is defined.

The basic money stock includes currency, consisting of paper bills and coins in the hands of the public. Actually, so-called paper money is made of 75% cotton and 25% linen, hardly paper in an ordinary sense. However, the basic money stock is not limited to currency. The money stock also includes demand deposits, which are bank accounts that can be accessed simply by writing a check. Checks are almost as widely accepted as currency. In addition to demand deposits, which essentially are balances in checking accounts, other accounts can be transferred readily to demand deposits. For example, balances held in a savings account can be transferred easily to a checking account. In addition, depositors who hold balances in money market mutual funds can write checks against their balances. Therefore, balances held in these other accounts also are part of the basic U.S. money stock.

Several measures of the money stock are in current use. One measure is M1, which includes currency, traveler's checks, demand deposits, and other checkable deposits. Another measure is M2, which includes everything in M1 plus savings deposits, small denomination time deposits less than $100,000, and money market mutual funds. Still another measure is called M3. The Board of Governors of the Federal Reserve System decided that, effective 23 March 2006, M3 no longer will be published. This decision was based on the notion that the M3 measure "does not appear to convey any additional information about economic activity that is not already embodied in M2 and has not played a role in the monetary policy process for many years."

Table 12.7 shows M1 and M2 components for the week ending 7 October 2013. The M1 stock of money was $2,551.9 billion, and the M2 stock of money was $10,904.6 billion. Recall that nominal GDP was $16,661.0 billion at the end of 2Q 2013. Therefore, M1 money turned over about six-and-a-half times. This turnover of money is called the velocity of circulation.

Table 12.7 M1 and M2 Money Stock Measures Seasonally Adjusted Week Ending 7 October 2013	
Money Stock Components	**$Billion**
Currency[1]	1,147.5
Travelers checks[2]	3.6
Demand deposits[3]	934.8
Other checkable accounts[4]	466.0
Equals M1	2,551.9
Savings deposits[5]	7,141.1
Small-denomination time deposits[6]	553.5
Retail money funds[7]	658.1
Equals M2	10,904.6

Source: Federal Reserve, Money Stock Measures, H.6 (508) Table 3 and Table 4.

[1]Currency outside U.S. Treasury, Federal Reserve Banks and vaults of depository institutions.

[2]Outstanding amount of U.S. dollar-denominated of traveler's checks of nonbank issuers. Traveler's checks issued by depository institutions are included in demand deposits.

[3]Demand deposits at domestically commercial banks, U.S. branches and agencies of foreign banks, and-Edge Act corporations (excluding amounts held by depository institutions, U.S. government, foreign banks and official institutions) less cash items in the process of collection and Federal Reserve float.

[4]NOW and ATS balances at domestically chartered commercial banks, U.S. branches and agencies of foreign banks, and Edge Act corporations; NOW and ATS balances at thrift institutions, credit union share draft balances, and demand deposits at thrift institutions.

[5]Savings deposits include money market deposit accounts.

[6]Small-denomination time deposits are those issued in amounts of less than $100,000. All IRA and Keogh account balances at commercial banks and thrift institutions are subtracted from small time deposits.

[7]IRA and Keogh account balances at money market mutual funds are subtracted from retail money funds.

Show Me the Money!

By the way, intraday on 18 October 2013, the Census Bureau estimated the U.S. population at 316,903,200. The amount of U.S. currency in circulation at the week ending 7 October 2013 was $1,147,500,000,000. On average, therefore, each American, whether man, woman, or child, has $3,620.98 of U.S. currency in his or her wallet or piggybank! Where is this U.S. currency? Some of it is held abroad where people, commercial banks, and central banks hold U.S. currency because of its relative stability and acceptability. Undoubtedly, some currency is held by drug dealers, tax evaders, and other criminals who find it incriminating to hold their wealth in bank balances. Intraday on 18 October 2013, the U.S. Census Bureau estimated the world's population at 7,118,563,800. On average, therefore, every person in the world holds an average of $161.20 of U.S. currency. In fact, of course, no one knows for sure exactly who holds all this currency or where this currency is located.

THE QUANTITY THEORY OF MONEY

Some economists regard themselves as monetarists. A monetarist is an economist who strongly believes the performance of the economy is determined by changes in the money supply. Led by Nobel Laureate Milton Friedman, monetarists emphasized a relationship between the quantity of money and nominal GDP. Thus, monetarists embrace the quantity theory of money. The quantity theory is wrapped around the equation of exchange, which is

MV=PT

M is the money supply, say M1; V is the velocity of circulation, the turnover of the money supply; P is the price level; and T is volume of transactions of goods and services. In effect, PT is nominal GDP.

Therefore, using latest releases regarding M1 and GDP,

$2,551.9×6.5289=$16,661.0

If velocity is relatively constant, then the supply of money clearly determines nominal GDP! For example, if velocity is relatively stable, an increase in the money supply will cause either an increase in the general price level or an increase in real goods and services. The former is inflation, the latter real growth in the economy.

Friedman, the Federal Reserve, and the Great Depression

Milton Friedman (31 July 1912-16 November 2006) was well known for his articulate support of a political philosophy based largely on limited government intrusion in personal lives and equally limited government intervention in markets. This classically liberal philosophy was most evident in *Capitalism and Freedom*[130] and *Free to Choose,*[131] the latter written with his wife, Rose, also an economist. *Free to Choose* was developed into a ten-part television series, *Free to Choose*, aired in 1980 on P$_B$S. *Free to Choose* was the best selling nonfiction book of 1980. In 1976, Friedman was awarded the Nobel Prize "for his achievements in the fields of consumption analysis, monetary theory and history and for his demonstration of the complexity of stabilization policy."

In 1963, a book written by Milton Friedman and Anna J. Schwartz was published.[132] They corralled massive historical data and provided astute analysis to show that monetary policy matters profoundly in management of an economy. They also provided persuasive evidence regarding the cause of the Great Depression. The root cause of the economic collapse of 1929-1933 was the Federal Reserve!

When the Great Depression was first underway, the Federal Reserve was only fifteen years from its establishment in 1914. In the spring of 1928, the Federal Reserve tightened monetary policy, and the tightening continued until the stock market crash in October 1929. Another tightening occurred in September 1931. Such tightening and the ongoing collapse of commercial banks resulted in a precipitous drop in the money supply. Further tightening occurred in late 1932 and early 1933 when the Federal Reserve once

---

130   Milton Friedman, *Capitalism and Freedom* (Chicago, IL: University of Chicago Press, 1962).

131   Milton Friedman and Rose D. Friedman, *Free to Choose* (New York, NY: Harcourt Brace Jovanovitch, 1980).

132   Milton Friedman and Anna J. Schwartz, *A Monetary History of the United States, 1863-1960* (Princeton, NJ: Princeton University Press, 1963).

again reduced the stock of money. As a result, the economy took its deepest plunge between November 1932 and March 1933. From 1929 to 1933, the money supply fell by twenty-seven percent and GDP was twenty-nine percent lower. The unemployment rate hit twenty-five percent in 1933. Consequently, Friedman and Schwartz referred to the 1929-1933 period as the Great Contraction. The Great Contraction, they said,

> "is in fact a tragic testimonial to the importance of monetary forces."[133] Worldwide, the years 1929-1933 were direful. In 1929, more than twenty-five thousand banks operated in the United States. In 1933, only twelve thousand still operated.

On 8 November 2002, Ben S. Bernanke was invited to speak at a conference to honor Milton Friedman on the occasion of his ninetieth birthday. At the time, Bernanke was a member of the Board of Governors. On 1 February 2006, he was sworn in as Chairman of the Board of Governors, a position he still holds in 2013. At the conclusion of his speech, Bernanke said,

Let me end my talk by abusing slightly my status as an official representative of the Federal Reserve. I would like to say to Milton and Anna: Regarding the Great Depression. You're right, we did it. We're very sorry. But thanks to you, we won't do it again.

At the time, Ben Bernanke had no idea that, six years later, he would be Chairman of the Board of Governors midst a severe contraction of the U.S. economy. In particular, he had no idea that his promise to Friedman, "we won't do it again," would be tested in 2008 and beyond.

THE FEDERAL RESERVE

Some agency must be responsible for regulating the U.S. monetary system. In America, that regulatory agency is the Federal Reserve, informally called the Fed. The Fed is an example of a central bank, an institution designed to oversee a banking system and regulate the amount of money in an economy. Other central banks around the world include the Bank of England, Bank of Japan, Bank of Israel, Central Bank of Jordan, Bangladesh Bank, Banco Central de Honduras, Banco de México, Bank of Canada, Banco Central do Brasil, Banca d'Italia, Banque de France, Deutsche Bundesbank, Banco Central de Chile, Reserve Bank of Australia, People's Bank of China, Central Bank of Iraq, Central Bank of the Russian Federation, State Bank of Vietnam, and Bank of Jamaica, each of which is the country's equivalent of the Federal Reserve System.

The first institution with responsibilities of a U.S. central bank was the First Bank of the United States, chartered in 1791. Its twenty-year charter was not renewed in 1811. After a lapse of five years, the Second Bank of the United States was chartered in 1816. Again, its twenty-year charter was not renewed in 1836. The years 1836-1862 are known as the Free Banking Era, during which state-chartered banks issued their own bank notes backed by specie, either gold or silver coins. The National Banking Act of 1863 created a system of national banks. The Comptroller of the Currency was created to supervise national banks. One outcome was a uniform national currency, which was national bank notes. However, bank panics in 1873, 1893, and 1907 fomented support for a centralized banking system. In 1913, legislation to establish a central bank was sponsored by Congressman Carter Glass of Virginia and Senator Robert L. Owen of Oklahoma. After months of grueling hearings, debates, and amendments, the Federal Reserve Act

---

133   *Ibid.*, p. 300.

finally was passed and signed into law by President Woodrow Wilson. Regional banks of the Federal Reserve System began operations in 1914.

The Federal Reserve System is comprised of the Federal Reserve Board with headquarters in Washington, D.C., and twelve regional Federal Reserve banks located in Atlanta, Boston, Chicago, Cleveland, Dallas, Kansas City, Minneapolis, New York, Philadelphia, Richmond, San Francisco, and St. Louis. Each regional bank has a Board of Directors consisting of members drawn from local banking and business communities. Each Board elects a president of the regional bank. The Fed is directed by the Board of Governors, which consists of seven members appointed by the President and confirmed by the Senate. Governors have 14-year terms to give them independence from political pressures when they formulate monetary policy. The most important member of the Board is the Chairman, currently Ben S. Bernanke, who replaced Alan Greenspan in 2006. The Chairman directs the Fed staff, presides over Board meetings, and testifies regularly about Fed policy before Congressional committees. The President appoints the Chairman to a four-year term. Bernanke was appointed by President Bush and reappointed by President Obama.

The Fed has two related jobs. Its first responsibility is to regulate commercial banks and ensure the safety and soundness of the commercial banking system. Monitoring the financial condition of commercial banks is largely the responsibility of regional Federal Reserve banks. The Fed's other responsibility is to control the money supply. Decisions by policymakers concerning the money supply constitute monetary policy. At the Fed, the Federal Open Market Committee directs monetary policy. An important aspect of the Federal Reserve must be emphasized. The Federal Reserve is independent, meaning the Fed is independent of the President and independent of Congress. Thus, the Federal Reserve is an independent central bank. Neither the President nor Congress can tell the Fed what to do or what not to do. Fed decisions do not require ratification by Congress or approval of the President.

The Federal Open Market Committee

The Federal Open Market Committee (FOMC) was created with passage of the Banking Act of 1935. The FOMC is comprised of the seven members of the Board of Governors and five of the twelve regional bank presidents. All twelve regional presidents attend each FOMC meeting, but only five vote. The five with voting rights rotate among the twelve regional presidents over time. The president of the New York Fed always has a vote, however, because Fed purchases and sales of U.S. Treasury bills are conducted at the New York Fed's trading desk. Indeed, the New York Fed president is vice chairman of the Board of Governors. The FOMC meets about every six weeks in Washington, D.C., to discuss the condition of the economy and consider changes in monetary policy, mainly changes in the federal funds rate.

The Fed's main monetary tool is open market operations, which are the purchase and sale of U.S. Treasury bills. If the FOMC decides to increase the money supply, the Fed purchases U.S. Treasury bills from primary dealers. After the purchase of these T-bills, reserves are added to the banking system and eventually the money supply is increased. In business language, liquidity is added to the economy, meaning that money is more liquid than T-bills. In this way, open market purchases of T-bills increases the money supply. If the FOMC decides to decrease the money supply, the Fed sells U.S. Treasury bills to primary dealers. After the sale, the money that the Fed receives for the T-bills is removed from the banking system. In business language, liquidity has been mopped up. In this way, an open market sale of T-bills decreases reserves and eventually decreases the money supply.

Ordinarily, the Fed carries out monetary policy through three basic tools: reserve requirements, open market operations, and the discount rate. Mid-2007 through late 2008 was not ordinary, however. In addition to the ordinary instruments of monetary policy, the Fed developed new extraordinary facilities for addressing liquidity and credit shortfalls in the financial system. By late 2010, most of these facilities had expired. The Fed also engaged in quantitative easing, which is building its own balance sheet. Quantitative easing involved purchases of U.S. Treasury bonds and mortgage-backed securities. The U.S. Treasury also developed extraordinary programs to prop up bank safety and soundness through purchases of toxic assets, mainly illiquid mortgages, as well as injections of capital through purchase of stock in selected commercial banks.

RESERVE REQUIREMENTS

The Fed specifies reserve requirements that regulate the minimum amount of reserves that banks must hold against their deposits. Actually, reserve requirements deal with net transactions accounts, which specify in detail what is included in deposits. In effect, reserve requirements apply only to transactions accounts, which are components of M1. Reserve requirements influence how much money the banking system can create with each dollar of reserves. An increase in reserve requirements would mean that banks must hold more reserves and, therefore, can loan less of dollars that are deposited. In this way, the money supply is decreased. Conversely, a decrease in reserve requirements would increase the money supply.

The Fed rarely changes reserve requirements because frequent changes would disrupt the business of banking. When the Fed increases reserve requirements, for example, banks would find themselves short of reserves even though they have seen no change in deposits. As a result, they would curtail lending until reserves are built to the new required level. Effective 27 December 2012, reserve requirements are 0% for the first $12.4 million of deposits, 3% for deposits between $12.4 million and $79.5 million, and 10% on deposits greater than $79.5 million. For all practical purposes, therefore, the reserve requirement is ten percent. A bank's reserves are determined on the basis of daily average deposits over a 14-day reserve maintenance period that begins on a Thursday and ends on a Wednesday fourteen days later. A bank's average reserves over the two-week maintenance period must equal or exceed the required percentage of its average deposits in the two-week period. Banks receive credit in one two-week period for small amounts of excess reserves they held in the previous period, and a small deficiency in one period may be made up with excess reserves in the following period. However, banks that fail to meet their reserve requirements are subject to financial penalties. Required reserves must be held as vault cash or a deposit maintained with one of the twelve regional Federal Reserve banks.

Deposit Expansion Multiplier

In a fractional reserve system, banks are required to hold only a fraction of deposits as reserves. In the U.S. banking system, the fraction is basically ten percent. A new deposit in the banking system can increase the money supply as much as ten times the deposit. This effect is called the deposit expansion multiplier. Consider what happens when the Federal Reserve buys $100,000,000 of U.S. Treasury bills from a primary dealer. When the Fed writes a check for $100,000,000, this check constitutes a new deposit into the banking system and a potential increase of $1,000,000,000 in the money supply. This expansion is shown in Table 12.8. On the other hand, suppose the Fed sells $100,000,000 of U.S.

Treasury bills to a primary dealer. When the primary dealer writes a check to the Fed for $100,000,000, this check constitutes a withdrawal from the banking system and a potential decrease of $1,000,000,000 in the money supply.

Table 12.8 Deposit Expansion Multiplier			
Bank	Deposits	Reserves	Loans
1	$100,000,000	$10,000,000	$90,000,000
2	90,000,000	9,000,000	81,000,000
3	81,000,000	8,100,000	72,900,000
4	72,900,000	7,290,000	65,610,000
5	65,610,000	6,561,000	59,049,000
6	59,049,000	5,904,900	53,144,100
7	53,144,100	5,314,410	47,829,690
8	47,829,690	4,782,969	43,046,721
...	...	...	...
Total	$1,000,000,000	$100,000,000	900,000,000

The connection between reserve requirements and money creation or money destruction is not as strong as implied from the deposit expansion multiplier. Depository institutions do not always make loans to the brink of their limits. In other words, banks do not always reduce their reserves to the absolute requirement. Moreover, the total amount of loans is not always deposited. Some portion of loans is kept as currency. Thus, the deposit expansion multiplier must be seen as the limit of effects on the money supply. In the example depicted in Table 12.8, the most effect of the $100,000,000 purchase of T-bills on the money supply is $1,000,000,000. In practice, the effect is much less.

OPEN MARKET OPERATIONS

The Fed conducts open market operations when it buys or sells U.S. Treasury bills, from primary government securities dealers, which are banks and securities broker-dealers approved for trade in government securities with the Federal Reserve Bank of New York. Twenty-one primary dealers are on the Fed's list. These twenty-one primary dealers are Bank of Nova Scotia, New York Agency; BMO Capital Markets Corp.; BNP Paribas Securities Corp.; Barclays Capital Inc.; Cantor Fitzgerald & Co.; Citigroup Global Markets Inc.; Credit Suisse Securities (USA) LLC; Daiwa Capital Markets America Inc.; Deutsche Bank Securities Inc.; Goldman, Sachs & Co.; HSBC Securities (USA) Inc.; Jefferies LLC; J. P. Morgan Securities LLC; Merrill Lynch, Pierce, Fenner & Smith Incorporated; Mizuho Securities USA Inc.; Morgan Stanley & Co. LLC; Nomura Securities International, Inc.; RBC Capital Markets, LLC; RBS Securities Inc.; SG Americas, LLC; and UBS Securities LLC.

On behalf of the Federal Reserve System, the New York Fed's Open Market Desk engages in trades to implement monetary policy. Purchases of government securities add reserves to the banking system, whereas the sale of government securities drains reserves from the banking system. Treasury bills or T-bills are issued in maturities of 28 days, 91 days, 182 days, and 364 days. To increase reserves and thus the money supply, the Fed instructs its traders at the New York Fed to buy T-bills from primary dealers. The Trading Desk of the New York Fed pays for the T-bills by sending funds to a primary dealer's account, and the New York Fed takes delivery of the T-bills. This action adds reserves to the banking system. Therefore, buying T-bills increases reserves in the banking system and thus increases the money supply. To reduce reserves and thus the money supply, the Fed does the opposite. The Trading Desk of the New York Fed sells T-bills to primary dealers. The Trading Desk of the New York Fed delivers T-bills to the primary dealer, and the account of the primary dealer is debited. This action takes reserves from the banking system. Therefore, selling T-bills reduces reserves in the banking system and thus decreases the money supply.

The Federal Funds Rate

Open market operations are fairly easy to conduct. The Fed can use open market operations to change the money supply by a small or large amount on any day without major changes in laws or bank regulations. Consequently, open market operations are the tool of monetary policy that the Fed uses most often. Open market operations are under the control of the Federal Open Market Committee (FOMC). The main concern is the federal funds rate, the interest rate charged by commercial banks for overnight loans to other commercial banks. Some commercial banks have excess reserves, whereas other commercial banks are short of required reserves. The latter can borrow reserves from the former at the federal funds rate. The federal funds rate is not under the direct control of the Fed. The FOMC sets a target federal funds rate and conducts open market operations to achieve its target. The Fed calls its target the intended federal funds rate.

Beginning in the fourth quarter of 2007, the intended federal funds rate was reduced dramatically to stimulate a sluggish economy. At its meeting on 31 October 2007, the FOMC lowered the federal funds rate from 4.75% to 4.50%; on 11 December 2007, from 4.50% to 4.25%; on 22 January 2008, from 4.25% to 3.50%; on 30 January 2008, from 3.50% to 3.00%; on 18 March 2008, from 3.00% to 2.25%; on 30 April 2008, from 2.25% to 2.00%; and on 8 October 2008, from 2.00% to 1.50%. This latter reduction of fifty basis points was coordinated with five other central banks that also reduced their rates by fifty basis points. These central banks were the European Central Bank, the Bank of England, the Swedish Riksbank, the Bank of Canada, and the Swiss National Bank. On 29 October 2008, the FOMC acted once again, lowering the federal funds rate another fifty basis points to 1.00%. Finally, on 16 December 2008, the FOMC took unprecedented action. For the first time in its history, the FOMC set a range, 0.00% to 0.25%. At each of its pursuant meetings, the range of 0.00%-0.25% has been left unchanged.

To restate a point, the FOMC sets a target or intended federal funds rate. Ordinarily, U.S. Treasury bills are bought and sold with the intent to maintain the intended rate. However, the financial and commercial crisis of September 2008 resulted in remarkable departure from the intended rate of 2.00% although no official action was taken to change the intended rate. Whether intentional or unintentional, the FOMC had difficulty in achieving its intended rate of 2.00%. During the last two weeks of September 2008, the actual overnight rate varied from a rate approaching 0.00% to 10.00%. The daily effective federal funds rate, which is the volume-weighted average of rates on trades arranged by major brokers, eroded to 1.08% on 26 September 2008. Four business days later, on 2 October 2008, the daily effective rate closed at 0.67%. For a depiction of daily effective federal funds rate and the range of low and high rates for September 2008, see Table 12.9. Clearly, the Fed experienced difficulty in controlling the daily effective federal funds rate.

Table 12.9 Federal Funds Rate, September 2008					
Date	Daily Effective Rate	Range		Standard Deviation	Target Rate
		Intraday Low	Intraday High		
30	2.03	0.00	10.00	1.95	2.00
29	1.56	0.01	3.00	0.93	2.00
26	1.08	0.00	3.00	0.69	2.00
25	1.23	0.00	3.00	0.66	2.00
24*	1.19	0.01	3.25	0.66	2.00
23	1.46	0.06	3.00	0.69	2.00
22	1.51	0.00	3.50	0.92	2.00
19	1.48	0.00	3.50	1.01	2.00
18	2.16	0.00	6.00	1.13	2.00
17	2.80	0.25	6.00	0.78	2.00
16	1.98	0.01	6.00	1.10	2.00
15	2.64	0.01	7.00	1.72	2.00
12	2.10	1.75	2.94	0.10	2.00
11	2.00	1.00	2.50	0.19	2.00
10*	2.12	1.50	2.63	0.18	2.00
09	1.96	1.63	2.19	0.07	2.00
08	1.92	1.00	2.50	0.22	2.00
05	1.97	1.00	2.25	0.10	2.00
04	1.99	1.00	2.50	0.13	2.00
03	2.01	1.50	2.50	0.09	2.00
02	1.96	0.13	2.38	0.31	2.00

Source: Federal Reserve Bank of New York, Federal Funds Data Historical Search

*Indicates the last day of a maintenance period

Interest on Required and Excess Reserves

The Emergency Economic Stabilization Act of 2008 was passed by Congress and signed into law on 3 October 2008. The Act was meant to revive credit markets. The Act also gave the Fed more power over short-term interest rates. For the first time in its history, the Fed was authorized to pay interest on required and excess reserves held at the Federal Reserve. Initially, the interest rate on required reserves was set at ten basis points below the intended federal funds rate. With an intended federal funds rate of 1.50% at the time, the interest rate on required reserves would be 1.40%. The interest rate on excess reserves was set at seventy-five basis points below the intended federal funds rate. With an intended federal funds rate of 1.50% at the time, the interest rate on excess reserves would be 0.75%. The effective date for paying interest on required and excess reserves was 9 October 2008.

On 22 October 2008, the Fed announced a change in the formula used to determine the interest rate paid on excess reserves. Under the new formula, the interest rate on excess reserves would be only thirty-five basis points below the intended federal funds rate. After the federal funds rate was lowered to 1.00%, the interest rate on excess reserves was 0.65%, and the interest rate on required reserves was 0.90%. The effective date of the new formula was 23 October 2008. The Fed believed that a narrower spread between the intended federal funds rate and the interest rate on excess reserves would result in effective rates closer to the intended rate. In effect, this action built a kind of floor at thirty-five basis points below the intended federal funds rate. The dust eventually settled on formula tweaking, and the interest rate for both required and excess reserves was set at 0.25%.

This seemingly simple authority encourages commercial banks to deposit excess reserves with the Fed rather than dumping them into money markets and distorting the overnight federal funds rate. In this way, paying interest on excess reserves allows the Fed to provide liquidity during times of distress without affecting the federal funds rate. Thus, payment of interest on reserves enables the Fed to direct credit policy separate and independent from monetary policy. In other words, the Fed is able to expand or grow its balance sheet as necessary to provide the liquidity necessary to support financial stability while at the same time implementing monetary policy that is appropriate for the economy. Before this simple authority, Fed actions taken to address liquidity and credit problems in the economy worked against its monetary policy evidenced by lack of control over the federal funds rate.

The Fed's traditional approach to realizing the intended federal funds rate has been buying and selling U.S. Treasury bills in the open market. Once the Fed began to pay interest on required and excess reserves, the Fed indirectly encouraged commercial banks to keep reserves at the Fed. Banks should be unwilling to lend reserves at a rate lower than they can receive from the Fed. In principle, the Fed can maintain a lower bound on the federal funds rate. In practice, however, the federal funds rate settled somewhat below the interest rate on reserves largely because of the high volume of excess reserves. As excess reserves decline and financial conditions stabilize, the interest rate paid on reserves is expected to be an effective tool for controlling the federal funds rate. Indeed, interest paid on reserves has evidenced greater control over the intended federal funds rate. Consider Table 12.10, which shows daily effective rates for September 2013, as well as intraday low rates, intraday high rates, and the standard deviation. By comparison to federal funds data for September 2008, shown in Table 12.9, greater control over the federal funds rate is clear.

Table 12.10 Federal Funds Rate, September 2013					
Date	Daily Effective Rate	Range		Standard Deviation	Target Rate
		Intraday Low	Intraday High		
30	0.06	0.00	0.3125	0.08	0.00-0.25
27	0.08	0.03	0.3125	0.06	0.00-0.25
26	0.08	0.04	0.3125	0.06	0.00-0.25
25	0.08	0.04	0.3125	0.06	0.00-0.25
24	0.09	0.04	0.3750	0.06	0.00-0.25
23	0.09	0.04	0.3750	0.06	0.00-0.25
20	0.08	0.04	0.3750	0.06	0.00-0.25
19	0.09	0.04	0.3125	0.06	0.00-0.25
18*	0.08	0.04	0.3125	0.06	0.00-0.25
17	0.08	0.04	0.3125	0.06	0.00-0.25
16	0.08	0.04	0.3125	0.06	0.00-0.25
13	0.08	0.04	0.3125	0.06	0.00-0.25
12	0.08	0.03	0.3125	0.06	0.00-0.25
11	0.08	0.04	0.3125	0.05	0.00-0.25
10	0.08	0.04	0.3125	0.05	0.00-0.25
09	0.08	0.04	0.3125	0.05	0.00-0.25
06	0.08	0.04	0.3750	0.06	0.00-0.25
05	0.08	0.03	0.3750	0.06	0.00-0.25
04*	0.08	0.04	0.3750	0.04	0.00-0.25
03	0.09	0.04	0.3125	0.06	0.00-0.25

Source: *Federal Reserve Bank of New York, Federal Funds Data Historical Search*

Indicates the last day of a maintenance period

DISCOUNT RATE

The last monetary tool is the discount rate, which is the interest rate on loans that the Fed makes to commercial banks through their regional Federal Reserve Bank. Regional banks lend funds at the discount window. A discount window loan is secured by collateral that exceeds the loan amount. Depository institutions that maintain transactions accounts or non-personal time deposits subject to reserve requirements are entitled to borrow at the discount window. Such depository institutions include commercial banks, thrifts, credit unions, industrial loan companies (LLCs), and U.S. branches and agencies of foreign banks. Prior to passage of the Depository Institutions Deregulation and Monetary Control Act of 1980, borrowing at the discount window had been restricted to commercial banks that were members of the Federal Reserve System.

Historically, the discount window was rarely used. Until 2003, the discount rate was normally below the federal funds rate. To discourage banks from borrowing at the discount window and then lending at the federal funds rate, the Fed required a bank to prove it had exhausted all other sources of funds. Consequently, discount window loans were seen as the last resort of a bank in distress. Borrowing at the discount window was regarded as an admission of weakness. In 2003, the Fed changed this perception. The discount rate would be set above the federal funds rate, hoping to pacify banking uneasiness that borrowing at the discount rate is a sign of weakness. In spite of the change, borrowing at the discount window remained insignificant until September 2008 during the liquidity and credit crises.

Nowadays, the Fed actually offers three discount window programs: primary credit, secondary credit, and seasonal credit, each with its own interest rate. Primary credit loans are usually overnight. Secondary credit is meant to meet short-term liquidity needs or to resolve severe financial difficulties. Seasonal credit is meant for relatively small depository institutions that have recurring intra-year fluctuations in their funding needs, mostly banks in agricultural communities and seasonal resort communities.

For all practical purposes, the Fed uses the term discount rate to mean the primary credit rate. On 18 March 2008, the Board of Governors lowered the primary credit discount rate to 2.50% and the secondary credit discount rate to 3.00%. On 30 April 2008, the primary rate was lowered to 2.25% and the secondary rate 2.75%. On 8 October 2008, the Fed reduced the primary rate to 1.75% and the secondary rate to 2.25%. On 29 October 2008, the primary discount rate was lowered to 1.25% and the secondary discount rate to 1.75%. Most recently, on 16 December 2008, the primary discount rate was reduced to 0.50% and the secondary rate to 1.00%. At its meeting on 19 February 2010, the Fed raised the primary discount rate to 0.75% and the secondary discount rate to 1.25%.

The Fed can alter the money supply by changing the discount rate. A higher discount rate discourages banks from borrowing reserves from the Fed. Thus, an increase in the discount rate reduces the money supply. Conversely, a lower discount rate encourages bank borrowing from the Fed, increases reserves, and increases the money supply.

THE SUBPRIME CRISIS

Historically, banks lent money to homeowners for their mortgage and accepted the risk of default. The originator assumed the credit risk. Over the years, financial innovations swerved from this traditional practice. Nowadays, banks can sell their rights to mortgage payments and thus transfer the associated credit risk to investors through a process called securitization. Securities purchased by these investors are mortgage-backed securities and collateralized debt obligations. This practice is based on originate to distribute, meaning credit risk assumed with origination of a mortgage is spread broadly to investors. When homeowners default, cash flowing into mortgage-backed securities declines. Simply put, when mortgage delinquencies occur, securities backed with mortgages lose value. If mortgage delinquencies or defaults are widespread, mortgage-backed securities lose most of their value.

Subprime lending is the practice of making loans to borrowers who do not qualify at market interest rates. Such borrowers typically have weak credit histories. They also might have insufficient incomes and thus foretell inadequate repayment capacity. Clearly, such loans entail higher risks of default than loans to prime borrowers. Subprime borrowers were teased into mortgages through loan incentives such as easy initial terms. They also were seduced by a trend of rising housing prices that seemed to promise they would be able to refinance later at favorable terms. Adjustable rate mortgages (ARMs) with highly favorable initial terms were particularly popular with subprime lenders and borrowers. Indeed, more than three-fourths of subprime mortgages were adjustable rate mortgages.

Throughout 2006-2007, mortgage interest rates rose. During the same time, housing prices peaked and then dropped. Subprime borrowers found refinancing more and more difficult. Defaults and foreclosures rose as low ARM rates were reset higher. The subprime mortgage bubble burst. By summer 2007, the collapsed bubble constituted a subprime crisis that had international scope. The worldwide scramble for corrective responses ensued, particularly in the United States and Europe. Beginning in late 2007 and continuing throughout 2008 and beyond, the responses were sweeping in scope and breathtaking in magnitude.

MARK-TO-MARKET

At its simplest, mark-to-market is the accounting practice of recording the value of an asset in terms of its current market value rather than its book value. Problems arise when the current market basis does not accurately reflect the true value of an asset. This situation can materialize when a company is mandated to calculate value of an asset during unfavorable or volatile times such as a financial crisis. If liquidity is tight or if investors are fearful about business conditions, for example, the current value of a bank's assets could be much lower than the actual value. This case popped up during the financial crisis of 2008 and 2009 when many securities held on bank balance sheets could not be valued appropriately because markets for these securities stalled and then came to a screeching halt. After the onset of the subprime crisis, mortgage-backed securities marked to market lost most of their value even though most of such securities still had strong cash flows.

Most of the general public has never heard of the Financial Accounting Standards Board (FASB), even fewer of FASB Statement 157. FASB (pronounced FA$_Z$-bee) 157 requires publicly traded companies to classify their assets according to the certainty with which fair values can be calculated. Level One assets have market prices and thus are easy to determine a fair value. Level Two assets do not have available market prices and thus are marked at fair value based on prices of similar securities. Level Three assets do not have market prices and do not have comparable market prices of similar securities, thus requiring assumptions about values.

FASB 157 was intended to inform investors and regulators about the accuracy of a company's asset estimates. Many companies, particularly banks, had to write down billions of dollars in Level Three assets following the subprime meltdown and correlated credit crisis. Although not regarded as a cause of the financial crisis, mark-to-market exacerbated the severity of worsening financial conditions. Responding to jawboning by Capitol Hill, the Financial Accounting Standards Board voted unanimously on 2 April 2009 to give auditors more flexibility in valuing illiquid mortgage assets that may have long-term value. By easing FASB 157, the new guidelines allowed valuation based on a price that would be received in an orderly market rather than a forced liquidation. Banks and their auditors were allowed to use significant judgment when valuing illiquid assets.

CREDIT DEFAULT SWAPS

In 2008 Lehman Brothers was forced into bankruptcy. At the heart of the Lehman Brothers bankruptcy was a vast, opaque credit derivative called credit default swaps, which are little known and even less understood. Warren Buffet once called them "weapons of financial mass destruction." A credit default swap (CDS) is a contract between two counterparties, one the buyer and the other the seller. The buyer of a CDS makes periodic payments to the seller of the CDS in exchange for a payoff in the event of default or other credit event involving a third party known as the reference entity. If the reference entity defaults, the buyer of the CDS delivers the defaulted asset to the seller of the CDS for payment of the par value, which is known as physical settlement, or the seller pays the buyer the difference between the par value and the market price of the specific debt instrument, which is known as cash settlement. On the one hand, a CDS is insurance against the default of financial instruments such as bonds. On the other hand, a CDS is like a trip to the casino. Buying and selling credit default swaps are essentially bets placed on bond defaults. Indeed, the buyer of a CDS does not need to own a bond to buy the CDS that insures it! When the buyer does not hold the bond and thus has no insurable interest, the buyer has a naked CDS.

CDS contracts are bought and sold over-the-counter. Essentially, CDS contracts are not regulated. Consequently, little is known about the exposures of specific institutions to specific credit defaults. Of course, financial institutions know their own exposures, but disclosure is not mandatory. Moreover, financial institutions have little if any incentive to disclose their exposure voluntarily. The CDS market is not liquid because CDS contracts have not been regularized like stock options traded on an exchange. CDS contracts are merely two-party negotiations that often have terms peculiar to the specific transaction. Credit default swaps are vast in total, mind-boggling in scope. The Comptroller of the Currency reported that, at the end of 2011, the total amount of outstanding credit derivatives from reporting U.S. banks was $14.8 trillion, a little below the peak of $16.4 trillion at the end of 1Q 2008. Another aspect of the CDS market is that such sums are far bigger than the underlying securities that the CDS market insures. Consequently, deep and wide adverse credit events can significantly stress national and global financial systems.

Lehman Brothers was a global financial services firm. Lehman Brothers also was on the Federal Reserve's list of primary government securities dealers. In 2008, Lehman Brothers faced immense losses due to mortgage-backed securities. The losses forced Lehman Brothers to consider a distress sale of the company. Talks with Barclays, Bank of America, and the Korea Development Bank were fruitless. Without U.S. government involvement in the sale of Lehman Brothers, the possibilities of a rescue were nil. Two days later, Lehman Brothers filed for Chapter 11 bankruptcy. Only five days later, Judge James Peck approved a bankruptcy plan to sell off Lehman Brothers assets.

Lehman Brothers had hundreds of billions of dollars of outstanding debt. When the company was forced into bankruptcy, sellers of CDS contracts were obligated to pay buyers of CDS contracts a cash settlement to make the buyers whole. When Lehman Brothers debt was auctioned, the final auction price was $8.625, meaning that the debt was worth only $8.625 for every $100 of initial face value. Sellers of Lehman Brothers CDS contracts were obligated to pay the insured counterparties a cash settlement of the remaining $91.375 for every $100 of Lehman Brothers face value. At the same time, American International Group (AIG) also had vast exposure to the CDS market. U.S. authorities thought AIG was too big to fail. The U.S. government made an initial $85 billion loan to AIG, followed by another $37.8 billion loan. With more than $120 billion in U.S. government loans, AIG survived.

The Lehman Brothers bankruptcy and the AIG bailout clearly showed the danger of exposure to the CDS market for major sellers of CDS contracts. Movement is underway by the U.S. Security Exchange Commission to standardize and regulate the CDS market, providing disclosure and transparency. Such movement is likely to end with control through a formal exchange such as the Chicago Board Options Exchange.

BAILOUTS, ACQUISITIONS, AND BANKRUPTCIES

To stimulate the heartbeat of the U.S. economy, monetary and fiscal responses were undertaken. Between September 2007 and October 2008, for example, the federal funds rate was lowered from 5.25% to 1.00% through eight separate actions. The primary discount rate was lowered from 5.75% to 1.25% through the same eight actions. On 13 February 2008, the Economic Stimulus Act of 2008 was signed into law. The stimulus package was $168 billion, mainly in the form of income tax rebates to invigorate the economy. Unfortunately, the rebate checks coincided with higher gasoline prices and higher food prices. The rebates consequently did not have the expected effect on purchases of manufactured goods. The Housing and Economic Recovery Act of 2008 included six separate major sections meant to restore confidence in the U.S. mortgage market. Then, the bailouts began in earnest, not to mention the acquisitions and bankruptcies.

From its founding in 1923, Bear Stearns grew into one of the largest global investment banks as well as a securities trading and brokerage firm. Bear Stearns pioneered securitization and asset-backed securities. As losses accumulated in those markets during 2007 and 2008, Bear Stearns actually increased its exposure to mortgage-backed securities. The financial viability of Bear Stearns suffered fatal wounds from losses. By early 2008, Bear Stearns faced collapse, leading to a distress sale. On 16 March 2008, JP$_M$organ Chase acquired Bear Stearns for the bargain basement price of two dollars per share, totaling $236 million. The acquisition was conditioned on a nonrecourse Federal Reserve loan of $29 billion to Bear Stearns. A nonrecourse loan is a loan secured by a pledge of collateral. If the borrower defaults, the lender can seize the collateral, but the lender's seizure is limited to the collateral. Usually, assets provide collateralization value over and above the loan amount. The Federal Reserve accepted less liquid assets of Bear Stearns as collateral. The effect was that the Federal Reserve would absorb any loss if the value of Bear Stearns assets fell below their collateralized value.

In September 2008, the bailout environment escalated from a trickle to a deluge. Fannie Mae (Federal National Mortgage Association) is a stockholder-owned corporation chartered by the U.S. Congress. Fannie Mae participates in the secondary mortgage market by purchasing and thus securitizing mortgages, which provides liquidity to the primary mortgage market. Freddie Mac (Federal Home Loan Mortgage Corporation) is also a government-sponsored enterprise. Freddie Mac was authorized to make loans and loan guarantees. Basically, Freddie Mac bought mortgages, consolidated them into a pool, and then sold the pool as mortgage-backed securities. On 7 September 2008, the Federal Housing Finance Agency (FHFA) placed both Fannie Mae and Freddie Mac into conservatorship. As conservator, FHFA took control of Fannie Mae and Freddie Mac operations. The U.S. Treasury agreed to ensure that both Fannie Mae and Freddie Mac continued to meet obligations to holders of bonds issued or guaranteed by these two government-sponsored enterprises. In this way, U.S. taxpayers stood behind about five trillion dollars of Fannie Mae and Freddie Mac debt.

Also in September 2008, the Bank of America acquired Merrill Lynch for $50 billion, and Lehman Brothers declared bankruptcy. Next, the Federal Reserve provided an emergency loan of $85 billion to AIG. This intervention gave the U.S. government an eighty percent equity stake in AIG. In just three weeks, AIG had drawn down more than $70 billion of the $85 billion and announced that the company would take an additional $37.8 billion in secured funding from the Federal Reserve. Still in September 2008, Washington Mutual (WaMu) declared bankruptcy, making it the largest bank failure in U.S. history. The U.S. Office of Thrift Supervision seized WaMu and announced it would sell most of its functional assets to JPMorgan Chase.

By the end of September 2008, the subprime crisis had broadened and deepened to a generalized liquidity and credit crisis. The urgent response was the Emergency Economic Stabilization Act of 2008, signed into law on 3 October 2008. The Act created the Troubled Assets Relief Program, which authorized $700 billion to purchase illiquid, risky mortgage-backed securities from financial institutions. Soon, Secretary of the Treasury Henry Paulson expanded the authorization to accommodate capital injections into banks. The intent of the Act was to purchase bad assets, reduce uncertainty surrounding the value of assets, and restore confidence in U.S. credit markets.

U.S. TREASURY TROUBLED ASSET RELIEF PROGRAM

The Emergency Economic Stabilization Act of 2008 authorized the U.S. Treasury to establish the Troubled Asset Relief Program (TARP), managed by a newly created Office of Financial Stability. TARP gave the U.S. Treasury authority to use $250 billion immediately, another $100 billion that required Presidential certification of need, and still another $350 subject to Congressional approval. The U.S. Treasury was authorized "to buy residential and commercial mortgage loans, credit card securitizations, auto loans and other financial assets for which there is no current market."

Only six days later on 9 October 2008, Secretary of the U.S. Treasury Henry Paulson announced that the Treasury Department was considering equity stakes in banks. Although this maneuver was not monetary policy as such, the maneuver was a bearer of monetary effects. Capital ratios are required as a measure of financial soundness. Capital requirements declined significantly as a result of the growing liquidity and credit crisis. Banks began to hold cash idle to make sure they would not be caught in a capital squeeze. Hoarding cash exacerbated a worsening cutoff of credit needed by businesses and consumers. As morphed by Paulson, TARP was not limited to purchases of toxic assets but rather extended to injections of capital in exchange for preferred, nonvoting stock. Consequently, the U.S. government suddenly had an equity stake in private commercial banks.

On 14 October 2008, Paulson announced the U.S. Treasury would use the immediate $250 billion of TARP authority to buy equity stakes in nine large American banks and in a number of smaller banks. The nine banks were Goldman Sachs, Morgan Stanley, JP$_M$organ Chase, Bank of America, Merrill Lynch, Citigroup, Wells Fargo, Bank of New York Mellon, and State Street. The Bank of New York Mellon was chosen as the custodian overseeing the fund. A total of $125 billion was used to buy preferred stock in these nine large banks. In exchange for its capital investment, the U.S. Treasury would receive annual dividends of five percent for five years and nine percent afterwards. The escalation from five to nine percent provided an incentive for banks to buy out the preferred stock held by the U.S. Treasury. Another $125 billion was used to buy preferred stock in smaller banks that needed capital. The remaining $100 billion of Treasury authority would be used to buy bad debts from financial institutions. These bad debts were mainly non-performing mortgages and other toxic assets.

AMERICAN RECOVERY AND REINVESTMENT ACT: THE STIMULUS PACKAGE

Days after the inauguration of President Barack Obama, a bill was introduced in the House of Representatives. Although it was dubbed the stimulus package and worse, the official name was the American Recovery and Reinvestment Act of 2009. On 17 February 2009, President Obama signed the bill into law. The so-called stimulus package totaled $789 billion. About thirty-seven percent, $288 billion, was in the form of tax relief; about eighteen percent, $144 billion, for state and local government relief, mainly to prevent cuts in health and education programs and to ward off state and local tax increases; and the remaining forty-five percent, $357 billion, for federal social programs and federal spending programs, including $111 billion for infrastructure and science, $81 billion for protecting the vulnerable, $59 billion for healthcare, $53 billion for education and training, $43 billion for energy, and $8 billion for other. The stimulus package was basically a Christmas tree ornamented with earmarks for a number of special interest projects.

EXPANSIONS AND CONTRACTIONS (RECESSIONS)

Economic activity fluctuates from time to time. In most years, the production of goods and services rises. These good times are regarded as an expansion of the economy. In some years, however, this usual growth does not occur. Firms find themselves unable to sell all of the goods and services they have to offer, and they cut back on production. Workers are laid off, unemployment rises, and factory capacity is left idle. With the economy producing fewer goods and services, real GDP and measures of income fall. Such a period of falling incomes and rising unemployment is called a contraction, but the more familiar term is a recession.

The National Bureau of Economic Research (NBER) determines dates for peaks and troughs in the U.S. economy. NBER defines a recession as a significant decline in economic activity spread across the economy, lasting more than a few months, normally visible in real Gross Domestic Product (GDP), real income, employment, industrial production, and wholesale-retail sales. In determining whether a recession has begun, NBER places substantial weight on real GDP. The Bureau of Economic Analysis (BEA) provides quarterly estimates of real GDP. Consequently, NBER turns to monthly estimates of real GDP provided by sources such as Macroeconomic Advisers. NBER also relies on monthly indicators such as personal income less transfer payments and employment. In addition, NBER refers to monthly indicators of industrial production and volume of sales in manufacturing and wholesale-retail sectors.

Print and broadcast media often assert that a recession is onset by two consecutive quarters of declining real GDP. Although most recessions identified by NBER involve two or more quarters of declining real GDP, some do not. NBER does not rely on any rule of thumb such as two consecutive quarters and does not use real GDP data exclusively. NBER explicitly says, "The NBER does not define a recession in terms of two consecutive quarters of decline in real GDP."

Recessions start at the peak of economic activity and end at the trough of economic activity. NBER normally waits until a recession is no longer in doubt and an accurate date can be assigned. Typically, the beginning of a recession is not declared by NBER until six to eighteen months afterwards. The most recent recession began in December 2007 and ended in June 2009, making it an eighteen-month recession. Yet, NBER did not announce the recession until December 2008, a year after the recession started. Expansions start at the trough of economic activity and end at the peak of economic activity. The beginning of an expansion also is declared six to eighteen months afterwards. The expansion that began in June 2009 was not announced until September 2010, some fifteen months later.

Expansions and contractions from 1854 to the present are shown in Table 12.11. The Great Depression is usually dated from the stock market crash on 24 October 1929 to the U.S. entry into World War II in December 1941. Nevertheless, a rather lengthy fifty-month expansion occurred from March 1933 to May 1937. Another lengthy expansion, lasting eighty months, began in June 1938, more than three years before the United States entered World War II. From August 1929 to October 1945, the U.S. economy expanded during 130 months and contracted only 64 months. By the way, the October 1873 to December 1879 contraction was known as the Long Depression.

Table 12.11		
Expansions and Contractions, 1854-Present		
Expansions: Trough to Peak	Contractions (Recessions): Peak to Trough	Duration (Months)
December 1854-June 1857		30
	June 1857-December 1858	18
December 1858-October 1860		22
	October 1860-June 1861	8
June 1861-April 1865		46
	April 1865-December 1867	32
December 1867-June 1869		18
	June 1869-December 1870	18
December 1870-October 1873		34
	October 1873-March 1879	65
March 1879-March 1882		36
	March 1882-May 1885	38
May 1885-March 1887		22
	March 1887-April 1888	13
April 1888-July 1890		27
	July 1890-May 1891	10
May 1891-January 1893		20
	January 1893-June 1894	17
June 1894-December 1895		18
	December 1895-June 1897	18
June 1897-June 1899		24
	June 1899-December 1900	18
December 1900-September 1902		21
	September 1902-August 1904	23
August 1904-May 1907		33
	May 1907-June 1908	13
June 1908-January 1910		19
	January 1910-January 1912	24
January 1912-January 1913		12
	January 1913-December 1914	23
December 1914-August 1918		44
	August 1918-March 1919	7
March 1919-January 1920		10

	January 1920-July 1921	14
July 1921-May 1923		22
	May 1923-July 1924	14
July 1924-October 1926		27
	October 1926-November 1927	13
November 1927-August 1929		21
	August 1929-March 1933	43
March 1933-May 1937		50
	May 1937-June 1938	13
June 1938-February 1945		80
	February 1945-October 1945	8
October 1945-November 1948		37
	November 1948-October 1949	11
October 1949-July 1953		45
	July 1953-May 1954	10
May 1954-August 1957		39
	August 1957-April 1958	8
April 1958-April 1960		24
	April 1960-February 1961	10
February 1961-December 1969		106
	December 1969-November 1970	11
November 1970-November 1973		36
	November 1973-March 1975	16
March 1975-January 1980		58
	January 1980-July 1980	6
July 1980-July 1981		12
	July 1981-November 1982	16
November 1982-July 1990		92
	July 1990-March 1991	8
March 1991-March 2001		120
	March 2001-November 2001	8
November 2001-December 2007		73
	December 2007-June 2009	18
June 2009-		

Source: National Bureau of Economic Research, U.S. Business Cycle Expansions and Contractions

UNEMPLOYMENT

The most human dimension of a recession is unemployment. In 1980 when the unemployment rate averaged only four percent, jobs were abundant. Nearly anyone who wanted a job could find one. Unemployed people mainly consisted of workers between jobs. Employers joked about what they called the mirror test. If a person's breath could fog a mirror, the person could be hired. On the other hand, the unemployment rate in late 2009 exceeded ten percent. As late as April 2010, the unemployment rate was 9.9 percent before settling in the range of 9.6 percent. In mid-2012 and beyond, the unemployment rate settled at a little over or under eight percent. Many highly qualified workers lost their jobs and had difficulty in finding new ones. This case is not workers between jobs, meaning someone leaves one job and takes another available job within a few weeks or months.

To make sense of unemployment data, the way in which unemployment is measured must be understood. Each month, the Census Bureau surveys a sample of about sixty thousand households. This survey is called the *Current Population Survey*. People are asked questions to determine whether persons age sixteen and older are employed or unemployed. To be unemployed, a person must be looking for work but unable to find a job. To be counted as employed, a person must have a job outside the home or a paid job inside the home. The labor force consists of all people age sixteen and over who are either employed or unemployed. People who work at home without pay and people who are not looking for a paid job are not part of the labor force. On the other hand, some people look for a job for months or years without success and give up looking. These discouraged workers also are not part of the labor force. Part-time workers are considered employed. A part-time worker is a person who works between one and thirty-four hours weekly. The unemployment rate is the number of unemployed persons divided by the number of workers in the labor force.

In August 2013, the civilian noninstitutional population was 245.959 million. The civilian labor force was 155.486 million, which was a labor force participation rate of 63.2 percent. The total of employed workers was 144.170 million. The number of unemployed workers was 11.316 million, which was 7.3 percent of the labor force. The number of persons not in the labor force was 90.473 million.[134] Table 12.12 shows the annual average unemployment rates for 2000-2012 and monthly unemployment rates for January 2013-August 2013.

---

134 Bureau of Labor Statistics, Employment Status of the Civilian Population by Sex and Age, Table A-1.

Table 12.12 Annual Unemployment Rate, 2000-2012, Monthly Unemployment Rate, January 2013-August 2013	
Year and Month	**Unemployment Rate**
2000	4.0
2001	4.7
2002	5.8
2003	6.0
2004	5.5
2005	5.1
2006	4.6
2007	4.6
2008	5.8
2009	9.3
2010	9.6
2011	8.9
2012	8.1
January 2013	7.9
February 2013	7.7
March 2013	7.6
April 2013	7.5
May 2013	7.6
June 2013	7.6
July 2013	7.4
August 2013	7.3

Source: Bureau of Labor Statistics, Employment Status of the Civilian Noninstitutional Population 16 Years and Over, 1978 to Date, Table A-1

Unemployment differs significantly by gender and ethnicity. Consider seasonally adjusted data from August 2013 for people age sixteen and over. For men, the unemployment rate was 7.7 percent, whereas for women, the unemployment rate was 6.8 percent. For white men twenty years and over, the unemployment rate was 6.2 percent, and for white women, 5.5 percent. For white men and women age 16-19, the unemployment rate was 20.5 percent. For black or African American men twenty years and over, the unemployment rate was 13.5 percent, and for black or African American women, 10.6 percent. The unemployment rate for black or African American men and women age 16-19 was 38.2 percent. Overall, the unemployment rate for white men and women was 6.4 percent, for black or African American men and women, 13.0 percent, and for Hispanic or Latino men and women, 9.3 percent.[135]

Some believe that the most enduring damage of unemployment is inflicted on young people age 16-24 years. For this cohort of high school graduates through newly graduated college students, the damage might be deep and enduring, creating disillusionment that characterizes a "lost generation."[136] In August 2013, the unemployment rate for white men and women age 16-24 was 11.3 percent and age 20-24, 7.8 percent; for black or African American men and women age 16-24, 18.5 percent and age 20-24, 10.4 percent; for Asian men and women age 16-24, 9.0 percent and age 20-24, 4.9 percent; and for Hispanic or Latino men and women age 16-24, 17.5 percent and age 20-24, 12.6.[137]

Extended joblessness of such magnitude can depress lifetime income significantly. Those who recognize that joblessness hits young people disproportionately hard also believe that government action must be taken before the damage worsens. Many favor subsidizing education and training as well as lowering the minimum wage for young people and trainees. Cutting the minimum wage is a remedy based in part on recognition that government has contributed mightily to the problem and ought to conduce correspondingly to amelioration of the problem. The federal minimum wage recently has been hiked by forty percent, making young workers far less appealing to hire. Some European countries already have responded by enacting subminimum wages for young people and people engaged in apprenticeships.

LEADING ECONOMIC INDICATORS AND CONSUMER CONFIDENCE

The Conference Board is a worldwide nonprofit organization. The Conference Board conducts business research, holds conferences, convenes executives, and networks more than sixteen hundred corporations in almost sixty countries. Its worldwide conferences bring together more than twelve thousand senior executives annually. More than one hundred CEOs address Conference Board events each year. The Conference Board is best known for two of its products, the Leading Economic Indicators and the Consumer Confidence Index.

The Index of Leading Economic Indicators (LEI) is intended to foresee if not foretell future economic activity. Until 1995, the U.S. Department of Commerce compiled the LEI. Afterwards, the Conference Board has compiled the LEI. The LEI is based on values for ten key variables while using 2004 as a base (2004=100). Historically, these variables have turned downward before a recession and turned upward before an expansion. The ten components of the LEI are listed below:

1. Average number of initial applications for unemployment insurance, *i.e.*, initial jobless claims

2. Number of manufacturers' new orders for consumer goods and materials, *i.e.*, factory order sreport

3. Speed of delivery of new merchandise to vendors from suppliers, *i.e.*, purchasing managers index report

4. Amount of new orders for capital goods unrelated to defense, *i.e.*, factory orders report

---

135 Bureau of Labor Statistics, Employment Status of the Civilian Noninstitutional Population by Sex and Age, Table A-3; Employment Status of the Civilian Population by Race, Sex, and Age, Table A-2; and Employment Status of the Civilian Noninstitutional Population by Race, Hispanic or Latino Ethnicity, Sex and Age, Seasonally Adjusted, Table A-4.

136 Peter Coy, "The Lost Generation," *Business Week* (October 19, 2009), pp. 033-035.

137 Bureau of Labor Statistics, Employment Status of the Civilian Noninstitutional Population 16 to 24 Years of Age by School Enrollment, Age, Sex, Race, and Hispanic or Latino Ethnicity, and Educational Attainment, Table A-16.

5. Amount of new building permits for residential buildings, *i.e.*, housing starts report

6. Level of the S&P 500 stock index

7. Inflation-adjusted money supply (M2)

8. Spread between long-term (10-year Treasury note) and short-term (federal funds rate) interest rates (yield curve)

9. Consumer sentiment, *i.e.*, expectations portion of the University of Michigan's Consumer Sentiment Index Average weekly hours worked by manufacturing workers, *i.e.*, the employment report.

10. The LEI is reported around the middle of each month. Generally, three consecutive months of decline in the LEI signals a recession. However, the LEI is not foolproof or failsafe. The time lag between the signal of a recession and an actual recession has varied significantly. In addition, the LEI sometimes turned downward, thus signaling a recession, but no recession occurred. In other words, the LEI sounded a few false alarms. One cannot help but recall a comment attributed to Nobel Laureate Paul Samuelson, "Economists have correctly predicted nine of the last five recessions."

The Consumer Confidence Index (CCI) is meant to measure how consumers feel about the state of the economy. The CCI was started in 1967 and uses 1985 as a base so that 1985=100. The CCI is calculated each month on the basis of a survey of five thousand households to gauge consumer opinion of current conditions and future expectations. The monthly survey is conducted by TNS, the world's largest custom research company. Household opinions dealing with current conditions make up forty percent of the CCI. The remaining sixty percent deals with their expectations of future conditions. In this way, the CCI is a monthly report detailing consumer attitudes and buying intentions. The survey itself consists of five questions that ask household opinion of the following:

1. Current business conditions

2. Business conditions for the next six months

3. Current employment conditions for the next six months

4. Employment conditions for the next six months

5. Total family income for the next six months

Survey respondents are asked to answer each question as positive, neutral, or negative. Once data have been collected, a relative value is calculated for each question separately. Positive responses for each question are divided by the sum of positive and negative responses. The relative value for each question is compared against each relative value for 1985. This procedure results in an index value for each question. The index values for all five questions are averaged to form the CCI. The index values for questions one and three form the Present Situation Index, and the average of index values for questions two, four, and five constitute the Expectations Index.

The University of Michigan Consumer Research Center has a similar index known as the Index of Consumer Sentiment (ICS). The Center telephones about five hundred consumers for an interview. These consumers are asked five questions concerning their household financial conditions and their expectations for one year, their expectations for business conditions in one year as well as expectations for five years, and their buying plans. The ICS is intended to determine how consumers view prospects for their own financial situation as well as for the economy over the near term and the long term.

AGGREGATE DEMAND

Describing patterns that economies experience as they fluctuate over time is easy. Explaining what causes these fluctuations is more difficult. An accessible model of short run economic fluctuations focuses on aggregate demand. Without technical adornments, aggregate demand is simply the total amount of goods and services that households, businesses, and governments are willing to purchase. At times, overall production of goods and services (real GDP) may not be great enough to satisfy anyone's sense of full employment. A high rate of unemployment along with sagging incomes may characterize the economy. The underlying cause may be as simple as insufficient spending and thus insufficient aggregate demand in the private sector. If so, the solution to this problem may be as simple as government action to stimulate aggregate demand. The two basic means for such stimulation are monetary policy and fiscal policy, either one of which can affect aggregate demand. Monetary and fiscal policies are meant to stimulate aggregate demand during times of slumping production, employment, and incomes and to dampen aggregate demand during times of robust production, employment, and incomes that threaten to accelerate inflation.

Monetary Policy

The Fed affects aggregate demand when it changes monetary policy. Suppose the Fed increases the money supply by buying Treasury bills in open market operations. Next, suppose the price level does not respond in the short run to this monetary injection. An increase in the money supply shifts the money supply curve to the right. If the money demand curve has not changed, interest rates fall to balance money supply and money demand. The lower interest rate reduces the cost of borrowing and the return to saving. Households buy more and larger houses, stimulating the demand for residential investment. Firms spend more on new factories and new equipment, stimulating business investment. Households save less and spend more on consumption goods. For all of these reasons, the quantity of goods and services demanded at the given price level rises. For any given price level, a higher money supply leads to lower interest rates, which in turn increases the quantity of goods and services demanded. Thus, monetary injection increases aggregate demand.

Discussion of Fed policy could focus on the interest rate rather than the money supply as the Fed's policy instrument. Indeed, the Fed conducts monetary policy by setting a target for the federal funds rate. The FOMC sets a target for the federal funds rate rather than for the money supply. The Fed's decision to target an interest rate does not fundamentally alter analysis of monetary policy. When the FOMC sets a range for the federal funds rate, the Fed's traders are told to conduct open market operations to ensure that the daily effective federal funds rate stays within the intended range. That is, when the Fed sets an intended federal funds rate, the Fed commits itself to maneuvering the money supply to ensure that the effective rate coincides with the intended rate.

Therefore, monetary policy can be viewed as setting an intended federal funds rate or a targeted money supply. When the FOMC lowers the intended federal funds rate, the Fed's traders buy T-bills, and this purchase increases the money supply and lowers interest rates. When the FOMC raises the intended federal funds rate, the Fed's traders sell T-bills, and this sale decreases the money supply and raises interest rates. Thus, monetary policy to expand aggregate demand can be described either as increasing the money supply or as lowering interest rates. Monetary policy to contract aggregate demand can be described either as decreasing the money supply or as raising interest rates.

Fiscal Policy

The federal government can influence the behavior of the economy with fiscal policy. Like the word realtor, the word fiscal is a two-syllable word that many people inevitably pronounce as though it is a three-syllable word. Fiscal is pronounced FIS-cal. Pronouncing fiscal policy incorrectly as though fiscal is a three-syllable word comes out as though it is physical policy. What physical policy might be is left to imagination regarding imbroglios of President Clinton in the Oval Office of the White House.

When the federal government changes its own purchases of goods and services, it affects aggregate demand. Suppose the U.S. Navy places a $10 billion order for two hundred F/A-18E/F fighter/attack Super Hornets. This order raises the demand for output produced by Boeing, which induces the company to hire more workers and increase production. The increase in demand for Boeing planes is reflected in an increase in the aggregate demand for goods and services. The increase in aggregate demand could be larger than $10 billion.

When the federal government buys $10 billion of goods from Boeing, the purchase has expansive effects. The immediate impact of the higher demand is to raise employment and incomes. As workers earn higher incomes, they increase spending on consumer goods. As a result, the government purchase raises the demand for the products of many other firms in the economy as well. Because each dollar spent by the government can raise the aggregate demand for goods and services by more than a dollar, government purchases are said to have a multiplier effect on aggregate demand. The multiplier effect continues even after this first round. When consumer spending rises, the firms that product these consumer goods hire more people. Consumer spending is stimulated once again. Thus, greater demand leads to higher income, which in turn leads to even greater demand. Once all these effects are added together, the total impact on the quantity of goods and services demanded can be much larger than the initial impulse from higher government spending. This multiplier effect arising from consumer spending can be strengthened by the response of investment to higher levels of demand. For instance, Boeing might respond to the greater demand for military planes by deciding to buy more equipment or build another plant. In this case, government demand spurs greater demand for investment goods. This positive feedback from demand to investment is called the investment accelerator.

Although the multiplier effect suggests that the effect on aggregate demand can be larger than an increase in government purchases, another effect that works in the opposite direction. While an increase in government purchases stimulates the demand for goods and services, it also could cause interest rates to rise. Higher interest rates choke off the demand for goods and services. Again, consider what happens when the U.S. Navy buys $10 billion of planes from Boeing. This increase in demand raises the incomes of the Boeing workers and workers of other firms because of the multiplier effect. As incomes rise, households generally choose to hold more money for transactions. The increase in income increases the demand for money. Suppose the Fed does not change the money supply. When the higher level of income shifts the money demand curve to the right, the interest rate rises to balance money supply and money demand. The increase in the interest rate in turn reduces the quantity of goods and services demanded.

In particular, because borrowing is more expensive, the demand for residential and business investment goods declines. The increase in government purchases increases the demand for goods and services, but it also may diminish private investment. This crowding out effect partially offsets the impact of government purchases on aggregate demand. The initial impact of the increase in government purchases is to shift the aggregate demand curve, but once crowding out takes place, the aggregate demand curve drops back. Of course, the Fed could accommodate fiscal policy with an increase in the money supply that would neutralize the crowding out effect.

The other important instrument of fiscal policy is taxation. When the federal government cuts tax rates, it increases household take-home pay. Households will save some of this additional income, but they will also spend some of it on consumer goods. Because it increases consumer spending, the cut in tax rates increases aggregate demand. Similarly, a tax rate increase depresses consumer spending and decreases aggregate demand. The size of the shift in aggregate demand resulting from a change in tax rates is also affected by the multiplier and crowding out effects. When government cuts tax rates and stimulates consumer spending, disposable incomes rise, which further stimulates consumer spending. This is the multiplier effect. At the same time, higher income leads to higher money demand, which tends to raise interest rates. Higher interest rates would make borrowing more costly, which reduces investment spending. This outcome is the crowding out effect. To reiterate, the Fed could accommodate fiscal policy with an increase in the money supply that would neutralize the crowding out effect.

BUDGET DEFICITS AND THE NATIONAL DEBT

In simple language, a budget deficit occurs when the federal government spends more than its revenues. In more perfumed language, a budget deficit means that outlays exceed receipts. A budget surplus occurs when the federal government spends less than it takes in so that receipts exceed outlays. A deficit or surplus is a flow, meaning that a deficit or surplus is measured per year. During any year that a budget deficit occurs, the deficit is covered by issuance of debt in the form of U.S. Treasury short-term bills and notes or long-term bonds. Treasury bills or T-bills are sold at a weekly auction, and they are sold at a discount from their face value. T-bills are issued in maturities of 28 days, 91 days, 182 days, and 364 days. Treasury notes or T-notes are issued in maturities of two, three, five, seven, and ten years, and earn a fixed interest rate every six months until maturity. Treasury bonds or T-bonds are issued in a term of thirty years and, like T-notes, earn a fixed interest rate every six months until maturity. When a surplus occurs, Treasury bills, notes, and bonds can be retired. The Bureau of Public Debt, an agency of the U.S. Treasury manages the national debt. Any year in which a deficit occurs, the deficit adds to national debt, often called public debt.

Consider Table 12.13, which shows receipts, outlays, surplus or deficit, and debt by fiscal year since 1990. Off-budget items are not subject to the budget process. The main off-budget items are the Social Security Trust Funds and the U.S. Postal Service. However, some appropriations such as the Iraq war have been supplemental appropriations and thus off-budget. The late 1990s and early 2000s were times of on-budget surplus. Beginning in 2002, large unprecedented on-budget deficits were passed by Congress. As a result of these deficits, the national debt ballooned to more than sixteen trillion dollars.

Year	On-Budget Receipts	On-Budget Outlays	On-Budget Surplus or Deficit	Off-Budget Surplus or Deficit	Federal Debt	Federal Debt/GDP %
2000	1,544.6	1,458.2	86.4	149.8	5,628.7	57.3
2001	1,483.6	1,516.0	−32.4	160.7	5,769.9	56.4
2002	1,337.8	1,655.2	−317.4	159.7	6,198.4	58.8
2003	1,258.5	1,796.0	−538.4	160.8	6,760.0	61.5
2004	1,346.4	1,913.3	−568.0	155.2	7,354.7	63.0
2005	1,576.1	2,069.7	−318.3	175.3	7,905.3	63.6
2006	1,798.5	2,233.0	−493.6	186.3	8,451.4	64.0
2007	1,932.9	2,275.0	−434.5	181.5	8,950.7	64.6
2008	1,865.9	2,507.8	−641.8	184.3	9,986.1	69.7
2009	1,451.0	3,000.7	−1,549.7	137.0	11,875.9	85.2
2010	1,531.0	2,901.5	−1,370.5	77.0	13,528.8	94.2
2011	1,737.7	3,104.5	−1,366.8	67.2	14,764.2	98.7
2012	1,896.5	3,290.4	−1,393.9	67.0	16,350.9	104.8

Table 12.13
Federal Receipts, Outlays, Surplus or Deficit, Debt, and Debt/GDP, 2000-2011 ($Billion)

Source: Office of Management and Budget, Table 1.1, Summary of Receipts, Outlays, Surpluses, and Deficits: 1789-2017; Table 7.1, Federal Debt at the End of Year: 1940-2017

At the end of 2012, about sixty-seven percent of the national debt was marketable, consisting of T-bills, T-notes, T-bonds, and TIP$_S$ (Treasury Inflation Protected Securities). Marketable securities amounted to $11,053.2 billion. Of total marketable Treasury securities, about fifteen percent was T-bills, about sixty-six percent was T-notes, about eleven percent was T-bonds, and eight percent was TIP$_S$. The remainder of the national debt was nonmarketable, consisting of U.S. savings securities, foreign series, government account series, and other. Nonmarketable securities are held by government agencies such as the Highway Trust Fund, Federal Housing Administration, Federal Supplementary Medical Insurance Trust Fund, Deposit Insurance Fund, Unemployment Trust Fund, Federal Disability Insurance Trust Fund, Federal Employees Retirement Fund, and Federal Old-Age and Survivors Insurance Trust Fund.

Once, the national debt was dismissed on grounds that "we owe it to ourselves." This adage now seems hollow as a drum. Treasury securities are owned by individuals, depository institutions such as banks and thrifts, pension funds, insurance companies, mutual funds, state and local governments, and foreign governments. U.S. national debt held by foreigners and thus owed to foreigners is approaching fifty percent! At the end of July 2013, the ten major foreign holders of Treasury securities were headed by China ($1,277.3 billion) followed by Japan ($1,135.4 billion); Caribbean Banking Centers, including Bahamas, Bermuda, Cayman Islands, Netherlands Antilles, and Panama ($287.7 billion); Oil Exporters, including Ecuador, Venezuela, Indonesia, Bahrain, Iran, Iraq, Kuwait, Oman, Qatar, Saudi Arabia,

United Arab Emirates, Algeria, Gabon, Libya, and Nigeria ($257.7 billion); Brazil ($256.4 billion); Taiwan ($185.8 billion); Switzerland ($178.2 billion); Belgium ($167.7 billion); United Kingdom ($156.9 billion); Luxembourg ($146.8 billion); and Russia ($131.6 billion). The grand total of holdings of marketable and nonmarketable Treasury securities by foreigners was $5,590.1 billion, about one-third of total Treasury securities outstanding.

PRACTICE QUESTIONS

1. What is Gross Domestic Product (GDP)?

2. Would the following items be included or excluded from GDP for the United States in 2012:

a. A home built and sold for $214,000 in 1995 and sold for $250,000 in 2012

b. A home built and sold in 1995 for $214,000 and rented in 2012 for $2,000 per month

c. Rental value of $24,000 of an owner-occupied residential home built and purchased in 1995

d. Interest of $12,000 paid in 2012 on a home mortgage originated in 1995

e. Market value of $18 million of shoes made in Brazil for Nine West, a U.S. company

f. Market value of $18 million of cowboy boots made in Texas and sold in Mexico

g. Market value of $18 million of CDs recorded and produced in Los Angeles and sold in Europe

3. Distinguish between government purchases and government transfer payments.

4. What is real GDP?

5. Distinguish between M1 and M2 definitions of money.

6. Describe the Federal Open Market Committee (FOMC). What are open market operations? How do the purchase and sale of government bonds affect interest rates?

7. What is the federal funds rate? Suppose the Fed sets a target of 2% for the federal funds rate. How does the Fed maintain that target rate?

8. What is the primary discount rate? How does the primary discount rate differ from the federal funds rate?

PRACTICE QUESTIONS *(AND ANSWERS)*

1. What is Gross Domestic Product (GDP)?

GDP is the total market value of all final goods and services produced within a country during a particular time period such as a calendar year.

2. Would the following items be included or excluded from GDP for the United States in 2012:

a. A home built and sold for $214,000 in 1995 and sold for $250,000 in 2012

The sale price of the home would not be included in GDP for 2012.

b. A home built and sold in 1995 for $214,000 and rented in 2012 for $2,000 per month

The rental income of $24,000 would be included in GDP for 2012.

c. Rental value of $24,000 of an owner-occupied residential home built and purchased in 1995

The imputed rental income of $24,000 would be included in GDP for 2012.

d. Interest of $12,000 paid in 2012 on a home mortgage originated in 1995

The interest of $12,000 would be included in GDP for 2012.

e. Market value of $18 million of shoes made in Brazil for Nine West, a U.S. company

The $18 million of shoes would not be included in GDP for 2012 for the United States but would be included in GDP for Brazil.

f. Market value of $18 million of cowboy boots made in Texas and sold in Mexico

The $18 million of cowboy boots would be included in U.S. GDP.

g. Market value of $18 million of CDs recorded and produced in Los Angeles and sold in Europe

The $18 million of CDs would be included in U.S. GDP.

3. Distinguish between government purchases and government transfer payments.

Government purchases include spending on goods and services by local, state, and federal levels of government. Government purchases do not include transfer payments such as social security or aid to families with dependent children since no good or service is provided in return. Transfer payments merely redistribute income from one group to another.

4. What is real GDP?

Real GDP measures the value of goods and services over time after correcting for changes in prices of those goods and services. In other words, real GDP is a measure of the value of goods and services at constant prices. In practical terms, real GDP is calculated with use of a price index determined for a base year. In effect, prices in the base year provide the basis for comparing quantities and values of goods and services in different years.

5. Distinguish between M1 and M2 definitions of money.

M1 includes currency, traveler's checks, demand deposits, and other checkable deposits. M2 includes everything in M1 plus savings deposits, small time deposits, money market mutual funds, and a few other minor categories.

6. Describe the Federal Open Market Committee (FOMC). What are open market operations? How do the purchase and sale of government bonds affect the supply of money and ultimately interest rates?

The FOMC is comprised of the seven members of the Board of Governors and five of the twelve regional bank presidents. The five with voting rights rotate among the twelve regional presidents over time. The president of the New York Fed always gets a vote. The FOMC meets about every six weeks in Washington, D.C., to discuss the condition of the economy and consider changes in monetary policy such as changes in interest rates. Through decisions of the FOMC, the Fed has the power to increase or decrease the amount of money in the economy. The Fed's primary tool is open market operations, which are the purchase and sale of T-bills. If the FOMC decides to increase the money supply, the Fed creates money and uses the money to purchase T-bills from the public in secondary bond markets. After the purchase of these T-bills, more money is in the hands of the public. In this way, an open market purchase of T-bills by the Fed increases the money supply. Conversely, if the FOMC decides to decrease the money supply, the

Fed sells T-bills to the public. After the sale, the money that the Fed receives for the T-bills is out of the hands of the public. In this way, an open market sale of T-bills by the Fed decreases the money supply. Through its effects on the supply of money, the Fed can influence interest rates.

7. What is the federal funds rate? Suppose the Fed sets a target of 2% for the federal funds rate. How does the Fed maintain that target rate?

In recent years, the Fed has conducted monetary policy by setting a target for the federal funds rate, which is the interest rate that banks charge one another for short-term loans. When the FOMC sets a target for the federal funds rate of, say, two percent, the Fed's traders are told to conduct open market operations to ensure that the effective rate equals two percent. That is, when the Fed sets a target for the interest rate, it commits itself to adjusting the money supply to make the effective federal funds rate coincide with the intended rate. When the FOMC lowers the intended federal funds rate, the Fed's traders buy T-bills, and this purchase increases the money supply and lowers the federal funds rate. When the FOMC raises the target, the traders sell Y-bills, and this sale decreases the money supply and raises the federal funds rate.

8. What is the primary discount rate? How does the primary discount rate differ from the federal funds rate?

Federal Reserve banks are authorized to lend funds to depository institutions at the discount window. All depository institutions that maintain transactions accounts or non-personal time deposits subject to reserve requirements are entitled to borrow at the discount window. The discount rate is the interest rate charged to commercial banks on loans they receive from their regional Federal Reserve Bank. The primary discount rate differs from the federal funds rate. The former is a rate set by the Federal Reserve System as the interest rate charged when a commercial bank borrows from a regional Federal Reserve Bank. The latter is an intended or target interest rate for cases in which one commercial bank borrows from another commercial bank.

485

13. International Trade and International Finance for Executives

INTERNATIONAL TRADE

International trade deals with exports and imports of goods and services. Most U.S. exports represent the physical movement of merchandise from the United States to foreign countries. These exports are goods that are grown, produced, or manufactured in the United States, as well as items of foreign origin that have been enhanced in value or improved in condition by further processing or manufacturing in the United States. U.S. exports also include services such as travel and tourism; entertainment; education and training; professional business services such as accounting, advertising, consulting, and legal services; banking, financial, and insurance services; architectural, construction, and engineering services; transportation services; and information services. Indeed, the United States leads the world as exporter of services. Thus, exports are goods and services originating in one country and sold in other countries. On the other hand, imports are the inflow of goods and services.

Sometimes, reference is made to America's trading partners. These trading partners are countries with which the United States trades. Trading partners can be measured and ranked by adding imports and exports together. Table 13.1 depicts the top ten countries with which the United States trades. These countries represent 67.26 percent of U.S. imports and 60.74 percent of U.S. exports.

Table 13.1 Top Ten Countries with which the United States Trades April 2013 and Year to Date $Billion		
Country	Total Imports and Exports April 2013	Total Imports and Exports Year to Date
Canada	54.75	208.98
Mexico	44.24	164.53
China	42.09	167.43
Japan	17.04	67.11
Germany	13.62	51.55
Korea, South	8.79	34.23
United Kingdom	7.81	32.58
France	6.75	24.20
Switzerland	6.32	19.55
India	5.73	20.56

Source: U.S. Census Bureau

U.S. Trade Deficits and Trade Surpluses

Balance of trade is a component of the balance of payments. Deficit or surplus results from comparing a country's expenditures on imports of goods and services with receipts for exports of goods and services. When reference is made to the U.S. trade deficit, the meaning is that the value of imported goods and services exceeding the value of exported goods and services. A trade surplus means the value of exported goods and services exceeds the value of imported goods and services. The last year that the United States had a trade surplus was 1975 when the trade surplus was a little more than twelve billion dollars. As recent as the early 1980s, the U.S. trade deficit was modest, ranging between sixteen and fifty-seven billion dollars annually. Beginning in the late 1990s, annual trade deficits exploded, topping $700 billion. The trade deficit was more than $708 billion in 2005 and more than $753 billion in 2006. The trade deficit remained in the area of $700 billion for both 2007 and 2008. The U.S. trade deficit was $559.9 billion for 2011, down from the heights of 2005-2008 but still hefty. In 2012, the U.S. trade deficit was down modestly to $540.4 billion.

If silver lines this cloud hovering over America, the trade deficit largely reflects the international reach of U.S. companies. Approximately one-third of the trade deficit is the outcome of trade with U.S. owned subsidiaries abroad, *e.g.*, an automaker that imports cars assembled in Mexico or a bank that uses call centers in India. Trade between foreign affiliates such as offshore subsidiaries can increase or decrease the trade deficit. Table 13.2 depicts the top ten countries with which the United States has a trade deficit and the top ten countries with which the United States has a trade surplus.

Country	Deficit April 2013	Deficit Year to Date	Surplus April 2013	Surplus Year to Date
Table 13.2 Top Ten Countries with which the United States has a Trade Deficit or a Trade Surplus April 2013 and Year to Date ($Billion)				
China	−24.110	−93.196		
Japan	−6.942	−25.520		
Germany	−6.094	−19.936		
Mexico	−4.432	−17.551		
Saudi Arabia	−2.563	−8.341		
Canada	−2.432	−12.193		
India	−2.420	−6.917		
Ireland	−2.399	−8.623		
Korea, South	−2.380	−6.982		
Italy	−2.029	−6.862		
Hong Kong			2.447	11.624
United Arab Emirates			1.992	8.711
Netherlands			1.648	5.633
Switzerland			1.432	1.554
Belgium			1.326	4.183
Brazil			1.188	5.467
Australia			1.076	5.083
Panama			0.775	3.510
Singapore			0.757	3.852
Argentina			0.595	1.679

Source: U.S. Census Bureau

U.S. Trade Deficit with China

The United States began trading with China only in the mid-1970s after President Nixon's historic trip to open up relations with the country. U.S. exporters had high hopes that the world's most populous country eventually would become the world's largest consumer market for American products. Although U.S. exports to China grew, U.S. imports from China are now about four times U.S. exports to China. In 2008, the U.S. trade deficit with China was $268 billion, the largest ever recorded with any country. In 2011, a new record was set when the U.S. trade deficit with China topped $295 billion. The 2012 goods trade deficit was a whopping $315 billion. However, closer inspection of these numbers unmasks some grounds for overstatement. "Made in China" often means that multinational companies in Japan, South Korea, Taiwan, and even the United States are using China as the assembly point in their far-flung global operations. China imports components of television sets, automobiles, refrigerators, microwave ovens, and consumer electronics. When these products are assembled and shipped out as final products, China's exports appear to be much greater than they actually are. Consequently, China's trade surplus with the United States is somewhat exaggerated, to some extent more apparent than real. Nevertheless, America imports so much from China because U.S. retailers such as Wal-Mart and other giant retailers find the least costly goods in China. The good news is that U.S. consumers have benefitted from the availability of low-cost goods "Made in China."

The United States lost almost six million manufacturing jobs during the 2000s, a decline of almost thirty-three percent. The United States is not alone. Over the same period, Japan witnessed manufacturing job losses of more than fifteen percent. Other developed countries experienced similar manufacturing job losses. In a world of finger pointing, the blame for losses in manufacturing jobs was pointed at offshoring. In particular, rounding up the usual suspects corralled one culprit, "Made in China." Some of these job losses may be attributed to China, but even China lost manufacturing jobs! Indeed, China probably lost more manufacturing jobs than the United States. What lies behind manufacturing job losses is automation, which results in significant gains in labor productivity. Fewer workers are required due to advances in labor productivity.

TRADE BARRIERS

One traditional way to limit imports is the use of tariffs. A tariff is a duty or tax on imported goods, making foreign goods more expensive and less attractive to consumers. Tariffs raise the prices of imported goods, thereby making them less competitive within markets of the importing country. In some cases, a tariff is merely another means used by government to raise revenue. For example, the United States has a tariff on coffee, which is not produced commercially in the domestic economy. The U.S. tariff schedule is lengthy, constituting thousands of items, everything from "live asses other than purebred breeding asses" to "tailor dummies and other mannequins; automatons and other animated displays used for shop window dressing."

Most tariffs are ad valorem, meaning the duty is a certain percentage of the value of the good. For example, imported automobiles are subject to a 2.5 percent ad valorem tariff. If a $100,000 automobile is imported from Germany, the importer must pay the U.S. government $2,500 as a duty. Some tariffs are specific, meaning a flat tax on the quantity imported. Examples of a specific tariff include 3.9 cents per kilogram levied on condensed milk, sweetened, in airtight containers; 3 cents per liter of rice wine or sake; and 15 cents per kilogram of turkeys, not cut in pieces, fresh or chilled. For some products, a combined ad valorem and specific duty, called a two-part tariff, is imposed. Examples include wrist watches with cases of or clad with precious metal, not electrically operated, with automatic winding with 17 jewels or less in movement, which are subject to a specific tariff of $1.61 each plus a 4.4 percent tariff on the case and strap, band or bracelet.

As tariffs have been lowered worldwide, nontariff barriers to international trade have burgeoned. Nontariff barriers include government laws, regulations, policies, or practices meant to protect domestic industries or domestic products from foreign competition. These nontariff barriers can take many forms such as import quotas; standards, testing, labeling, and certification requirements; antidumping measures; and more. For example, authorities at the U.S. Food and Drug Administration do not allow transit of drugs untested in the United States even though foreign governments claim they have been tested and declared safe. The FDA regards restriction as necessary to protect the American public, whereas foreign governments view the policy as simply another trade restriction. Such restriction is a matter of dispute. Of course, some standards have a legitimate purpose such as safety or compatibility with other products. At times, however, quality and performance standards are nothing more than barriers to trade. For example, in a dispute settled in 1992, Canada did not accept U.S. testing standards for plywood, contending that U.S. standards were inadequate in areas such as allowable size of knotholes. The effect was clear. U.S. plywood was barred from entering Canadian markets. In recent years, nontariff barriers have proliferated.

A common nontariff device to curb imports is the use of import quotas, which are established to control the amount or volume of commodities that can be imported into the United States during a specified period of time. Countries can set these limits on imports unilaterally. An absolute quota limits the quantity of goods that may enter the commerce of the United States in a specific period, usually a year. When an absolute quota is filled, further imports are debarred for the remainder of the quota period. Some absolute quotas are worldwide, whereas others are allocated to specific foreign countries. Examples of absolute quotas include textiles, raw cotton, syrups, peanuts, and certain wheat products. A tariff rate quota permits a specified quantity of imported goods to enter the United States at a reduced rate of custom duties during the quota period. Quantities in excess of the quota quantity are charged a higher duty rate. Examples of tariff rate quotas include anchovies, olives, tuna, brooms, and wool apparel.

Consider the U.S. sugar quota of 1.3 million metric tons. About eighty-five percent of sugar consumed by U.S. consumer is grown domestically. The remaining fifteen percent is imported from about forty countries under a quota-allocating system and Mexico, which is not limited by the quota under terms of the North American Free Trade Agreement. Jamaica and Haiti have not exercised their quota in recent years, using their sugar production internally. Consequently, imported sugar has amounted to only about 1.2 million metric tons, some 180,000 metric tons below the quota. The domestic price of sugar is inflated by import restrictions designed to protect U.S. sugar growers. Recently, the difference between the global price of sugar and the U.S. price of sugar widened to an unprecedented gap. In late March 2010, the domestic price of sugar was 35.02 cents per pound, whereas the world price was 19.67 cents per pound, a price gap of 15.35 cents per pound.

Sugar is the poster child for a tariff rate quota. If any country reaches its allocated quota, it can export sugar over the quota by paying a tariff of 15.36 cents per metric ton. Thus, on 12 March 2010, a country would have found exporting over and above the quota at the razor's edge of being economically feasible since the gap between the U.S. price of sugar and the global price of sugar was 15.35 cents per pound. Of course, the gap would need to be greater than 15.36 cents per pound to be economically feasible because of freight costs.[138]

Dumping and Antidumping Duties

Under U.S. law, merchandise exported to the United States and sold at less than fair value is illegal when such sales materially injure or threaten to materially injure U.S. producers of like merchandise. Determination that sales are made at less than fair value involves a comparison to normal value. The

---

138   See Carolyn Cui, "Price Gap Puts Spice in Sugar-Quota Fight," *wsj.com*, 15 March 2010.

price at which the merchandise is sold within the exporting country or to other countries is compared to the price at which the merchandise is sold in the United States. A cost-of-production provision requires that a determination of dumping disregard sales in the home market of the exporting country or in third-country markets that are made below cost. In simple language, therefore, dumping is the international term meaning a firm sells products in another country at prices below the price set in the home country or below average cost. Antidumping duties are tariffs levied on foreign firms as a penalty for dumping. In the United States, domestic companies can file an antidumping petition under regulations of the Department of Commerce (DOC). The DOC calculates the extent to which the U.S. price is less than fair value, and the International Trade Commission (ITC) determines injury. If the domestic industry establishes that it is injured significantly by dumping, antidumping duties are imposed of the imported products at a percentage rate calculated to counteract the dumping margin. Dumping margin is the difference between the fair price and the export price.

WORLD TRADE ORGANIZATION

Article 1, Section 8, Clause 3 of the U.S. Constitution gives Congress the power "to regulate commerce with foreign nations." Since the beginning, Congress has used the Commerce Clause actively and frequently to erect trade barriers, particularly tariffs. During the Great Depression of the 1930s, the United States and many other industrial countries raised tariffs with the intent of aiding domestic producers. The Great Depression was onset by an unprecedented contraction in the money supply but was exacerbated by the Smoot-Hawley Tariff Act of 1930, which raised tariffs to historically high levels. Other countries retaliated with higher tariffs, and the result was decimation of international trade.

Questioning the wisdom of tariff policies led to passage of The Reciprocal Trade Agreements Act (RTAA). RTAA gave the president authority to negotiate tariff reductions with foreign nations. Bilateral reductions in tariffs and other trade restrictions led twenty-three countries to meet in 1947 and assent to the General Agreement on Tariffs and Trade (GATT). GATT was meant to prevent any lapse back into the benighted protectionist practices of the Depression years. As a multinational consortium, GATT reduced tariffs and other restrictions on trade. However, GATT failed to create an oversight body to rule on claims that nations had violated terms of the treaty.

The World Trade Organization (WTO) was the successor to GATT. WTO commenced on 1 January 1995. The goals of WTO are to provide a forum for trade negotiations, foster respect for trade agreements, and monitor trade policies of its members. In late 2012, WTO consisted of 157 member countries accounting for about ninety-five percent of international trade. Another twenty-seven governments had observer status, and most sought admission to full membership. WTO headquarters are located in Geneva, Switzerland.

At the heart of WTO is conflict resolution. Essentially, WTO is concerned with broken promises to comply with provisions of the WTO agreement. Since 10 January 1995, more than 450 trade disputes have arisen, including twenty-six during 2012. About two-thirds of trade disputes are settled out of court, meaning that the complainant country settles its dispute with the respondent country. If the dispute is not resolved through consultation or mediation within sixty days, the complainant country can request formation of a Dispute Panel. Dispute Panels are similar to tribunals, but panelists usually are chosen in consultation with the countries in dispute. If the two sides cannot agree on the panelists, the WTO Director-General appoints them.

Once the Dispute Panel has been formed, it normally has six months to read written briefs from both sides, conduct hearings, consider written rebuttals, and take expert testimony before submitting an interim report. After review by the two countries and perhaps further hearings, the final report is submitted to the two countries and distributed to all WTO members. If the Dispute Panel finds that the disputed trade practice violates WTO agreements or obligations, it recommends that the practice cease and the respondent country be brought back into conformity with WTO rules. Either side can appeal a Dispute Panel's ruling, but appeals must be based on points of law. In some cases, both sides appeal. Any appeal is subject to a hearing before three members of the standing body of a seven member Appellate Body. Members of the Appellate Body have four-year terms, and they have acknowledged standing in the field of law and international trade. They are not affiliated with any government. The Appellate Body can uphold, modify, or reverse the Dispute Panel's findings and conclusions. Appeals are concluded within ninety days.

Within WTO, the Dispute Settlement Body (DSB) is the governing system that adjudicates trade disputes between specific governments. The DSB is a convened session of the General Council of WTO, comprised of representatives of all WTO member governments. The DSB makes decisions regarding trade disputes based on recommendations of a Dispute Panel or perhaps a report from the Appellate Body, which might have revised the Dispute Panel recommendations if a party to the trade dispute chose to appeal them. Only the DSB can make decisions. A Dispute Panel and the Appellate Body can make recommendations only. Oddly, DSB uses a process called reverse consensus. Dispute Panel recommendations, perhaps as revised by the Appellate Body, are adopted unless a consensus of members vote against adoption. Consensus to reject means any country wanting to block a ruling has to persuade all other WTO members, including its adversary in the case, to share its view. This odd procedure would mean that the winning country would have to vote with the losing country to reject the ruling. Of course, this outcome never has materialized. Consequently, the reverse consensus process is tantamount to a guarantee that recommendations of the Dispute Panel or the Appellate Body will be accepted by DSB. The entire process from consultation to final action by the DSB is completed within one year without appeal and one year and three months with appeal.

Once DSB has decided on a trade dispute, DSB can direct the offending government to take action to bring its laws, regulations, or policies into compliance with WTO agreements. This direction is the only outcome that WTO can specify. WTO has no enforcement authority. It cannot impose fines, levy sanctions, modify tariffs, or override the laws of any country. In the United States, for example, the U.S. President and the U.S. Congress decide whether to implement a DSB decision. They can revise U.S. law, compensate a harmed WTO member country through reductions in tariffs or other trade barriers, or take no action and thus accept the risk that the harmed WTO country may retaliate by raising tariffs or other barriers to U.S. exports. DSB gives governments a reasonable time to redress grievances and to restore compliance with trade agreements. Almost all WTO members voluntarily implement DSB decisions within the reasonable time.

U.S. Trade Disputes

Both as plaintiff and defendant, the United States has been involved in a large number of trade disputes. Most of these disputes receive little notice. Other trade disputes have had higher profile, usually because of political intrigue. In March 2002, for example, the U.S. government imposed thirty percent tariffs on a range of imported steel products. This hefty tariff was based on the claim that an unexpected surge of imported steel had entered the U.S. market and materially damaged U.S. steelmakers. The claim was bolstered by still another claim that the imported steel was priced below the cost of production. The expressed intent of the tariff was to give U.S. steelmakers time to rebuild their industry and make it competitive with foreign steelmakers. The European Union and eight other steel producing countries complained to WTO, which ruled decisively that the U.S. steel tariffs were noncompliant under world trade rules.

WTO found no surge of steel imports and no evidence of dumping. Under WTO rules, the European Union and other countries were entitled to impose retaliatory tariffs equal to the amount of damage the U.S. tariffs caused to their industries. The tariffs could have been applied to any combination of U.S. exports to the European Union. The EU planned duties of eight percent to thirty percent applied to various U.S. goods with a total value of more than two billion dollars. Their list was chosen to cause maximum political damage to President Bush, including items such as Florida citrus fruits, clothing and shoes, tobacco, rice, paper and cardboard, and pleasure boats. All of these items were produced in Southern states, which were particularly loyal to President Bush. Other items on the list were steel products, watches, eyeglasses, and hand tools. The U.S. steel tariffs were dropped.

U.S. v. China Trade Skirmish

For a number of years, Big Labor and its Democratic allies have blamed China for the loss of manufacturing jobs. In 2001, China joined the World Trade Organization and committed to the rules of the WTO. For the most part, however, the Bush White House gave China a pass. After all, Big Labor had not supported President Bush financially or otherwise. On the other hand, Big Labor contributed more than fifty million dollars to the Obama campaign in 2008. Big Labor had bought and paid for President Obama's ear, as formidable as his ears are. During the first year of his presidency, President Obama fired a shot across the bow of China. He slapped a thirty-five percent tariff on Chinese tire imports. This get-tough policy on China reverberated against the United States. U.S. tire manufacturers such as Goodyear and Cooper have Chinese factories that make tires sold in the United States. Overall, Chinese tires amounted to seventeen percent of tires sold in the United States. Most of the tires coming from China are sold under private label names and discount brands. The tires are sold through large retailers and national auto chains. Although China mainly exports tires at the low end of the market, China exports tires at all price points. Low-end tires are priced in the range of $50 to $60, whereas premium tires sell at $200 to $250.

The Tire Industry Association, which represents U.S. tire retailers, said the tariff was ill advised and would lead to higher prices for struggling consumers. Jim Mayfield, president of Del-Nat Tire Corp., a large importer and distributor of Chinese tires estimated that prices for low-end tires would rise by twenty percent to thirty percent.[139] The Tire Industry Association also claimed that the tariff would hurt tire retailers, and predicted that it would cost more jobs than it saves and would not bring back jobs that organized labor claims have been lost. C. Fred Bergsten, Director of the Peterson Institute for International Economics, agreed. He said, "It was folly and will probably cost jobs here."[140]

The Obama tariff stirred up a hornet's nest at home, and it moved China to retaliate. Immediately, China's Ministry of Commerce said the country was starting internal antidumping procedures against

139   Timothy Aeppel, "Tariff on Tires to Cost Consumers," *Wall Street Journal* (September 14, 2009), p. A3.

140   Nina Easton, "Why Obama Fired a Shot," *Fortune* (October 26, 2009), p. 96.

U.S. exporters of chicken and auto products. This particular retaliation was not likely to harm U.S. producers significantly. China already blocked U.S. exports of poultry products in retaliation for a similar U.S. block of Chinese poultry. In addition, China already had raised tariffs on imported auto parts.[141] Denying that the United States and China were in a trade war, chief White House economist Lawrence Summers conceded that it was merely a "contained skirmish."[142]

WTO Opposition

WTO opponents believe the organization is a kind of international bully if not an evil empire. In November 1999, a group of anti-globalization activists gathered in Seattle with the express intent to disrupt a WTO meeting. WTO already had become a lightning rod. Participants in these violent protests wanted to spark a downright revolution against entrenched global economic interests. Grassroots organizers from around the world opposed WTO because they contended that it supports the interests of large corporations over the interests of people and nature. Protests against WTO have continued. In 2003, a protest in Miami involved 10,000 demonstrators opposed to WTO and a proposed Free Trade Area of the Americas (FTAA) that would promote trade among nations in North America and South America. FTAA would eliminate government policies designed to limit trade between such nations. In fact, WTO has far less power than its critics attribute to it. Its small staff and correspondingly small budget reflect its limited mandate. WTO does not make policy and does not dictate rules of behavior. Its Director-General cannot comment on the policies of member nations. WTO has little authority to deal with the needs and difficulties of developing countries and of formerly communist countries making the transition to market-based economies.

PERMANENT NORMAL TRADE RELATIONS

When the United States joined GATT, most favored nation (MFN) status was granted to all other GATT countries, even extending to some countries that were not members of GATT. From the beginning, MFN was a status granted by one nation to another nation in international trade. A country granted MFN status would be given trade advantages such as low tariffs that any other nation also received. In effect, MFN was a nondiscriminatory guarantee that assured that a country would not be treated any worse than any other country with MFN status. In 1951, the U.S. Congress directed President Harry Truman to revoke MFN status to the Soviet Union and other communist states. Yugoslavia was spared this revocation. Throughout the Cold War, most communist states were denied MFN or were required to meet certain conditions to be granted MFN status. In 1998, the United States changed the nomenclature of most favored nation to normal trade relations (PNTR). All but a handful of countries had most favored nation status, making the term somewhat of a misnomer. In part, however, the changed nomenclature was motivated by pique and disgruntlement. Many people objected that some totalitarian governments around the world were blessed with most favored nation status, an implication that did not seem warranted.

The World Trade Organization requires members to grant one another most favored nation status. As a member of the WTO, the United States respects this requirement. The WTO allows preferential treatment of developing countries, regional free trade areas such as NAFTA and EU, and customs unions, which are free trade areas with a common external tariff. In the United States, however, PNTR is the term used for most favored nation status. Granting PNTR or MFN status also has domestic advantages.

---

141   Ian Johnson, "China Strikes Back on Trade," *Wall Street Journal* (September 14, 2009), pp. A$_1$, A3.

142   Easton, *loc. cit.*

Having one schedule of tariffs for all countries simplifies the tariff system and opens up the tariff system to transparent scrutiny. PNTR or MFN also imposes restraint on domestic special interests that seek protectionist measures.

For many years, the People's Republic of China required an annual waiver to maintain the trade status of PNTR or MFN. The waiver was in effect since 1980. Each year to 1999, congressional legislation was introduced to disapprove the president's waiver. The legislation was meant to condition PNTR or MFN status on meeting certain human rights requirements that went beyond freedom of emigration. Every year, this legislation failed to pass. With China's attempt to join the WTO, congressional action was required to grant PNTR to China. In late 1999, the required legislation was passed. The following year, China was allowed to join the WTO. In a related matter, Vietnam was given temporary PNTR status in 2001 on the basis of a year-to-year waiver. Vietnam has had PNTR status since December 2006.

Sanctions

Sanctions are unilateral or multilateral coercive measures adopted against nations or persons based on legal, political, or social motives. The Office of Foreign Assets Control (OFAC) of the Department of the Treasury administers and enforces financial, economic, and trade sanctions based on U.S. foreign policy. OFAC also enforces national security sanctions against targeted foreign countries, terrorists, international narcotics traffickers, and arms traffickers. Thus, sanctions are directed mainly towards countries and specially designated nationals (SDNs). If a country is on the sanctioned list, OFAC has the authority to prohibit a U.S. citizen or business from engaging in financial transactions with the government on the list without a license from the U.S. government.

In addition to sanctions that are specific to countries, non-country specific sanctions also are imposed. For example, the United States and more than seventy other countries have agreed to abide by the Kimberley Process Certification Scheme (KP_cS) for rough diamonds. These countries agreed to prohibit the importation of rough diamonds from and the exportation of rough diamonds to non-participants. Shipments of rough diamonds from or to a participant are controlled through the KP_cS. KP_cS was meant to stop the trade of diamonds to fund violent civil conflicts in many African countries.

On 7 February 1962, the United States imposed an embargo against Cuba, known in Cuba as *el bloqueo*, the blockade. The trade embargo was unilaterally imposed after the Castro government expropriated properties of U.S. citizens and corporations. The embargo was codified into law in 1992 with passage of the Cuban Democracy Act, which stated the explicit purpose of "bringing democracy to the Cuban people." In 1996, Congress passed the Cuban Liberty and Democracy Solidarity Act, which further restricted U.S. citizens from doing business in Cuba or with Cuba. This Act also mandated restrictions on providing public or private assistance to any regime in Cuba unless and until claims against the Cuban government were settled. In 1999, President Clinton modified the trade embargo by requiring that foreign subsidiaries of U.S. companies cease and desist trading with Cuba. A year later, however, he authorized the sale of certain humanitarian products to Cuba. The Cuban embargo is still in effect, and it continues to seriously restrict U.S. businesses from conducting trade with Cuban interests. However, notwithstanding the embargo, the United States is the fifth largest exporter to Cuba, representing six percent of Cuba's imports.

INTERNATIONAL MONETARY FUND

The International Monetary Fund (IMF) is an international organization apart from the World Trade Organization. The IMF was created in July 1944. Representatives of forty-five governments met in Bretton Woods, New Hampshire, and they agreed on a basic framework for international economic cooperation. On 27 December 1945, the IMF was formally organized when twenty-nine countries signed its Articles of Agreement. The IMF now has more than 180 members with headquarters in Washington, D.C. The IMF has oversight over the global financial system, concentrating on macroeconomic policies of its member countries. Particular attention is focused on policies that have repercussions on exchange rates and the balance of payments. In addition, the IMF offers financial and technical assistance to its members. Indeed, the IMF is a kind of international lender of last resort.

As lender to financially distressed regimes, IMF is positioned to demand conditions for such loans. Often, IMF demands were heavy handed and meddlesome. Governments developed a deep loathing and enmity for the IMF. The detestation was due to conditions tied to loans. In some cases, these conditions forced countries to free up their markets, adopt freely fluctuating exchange rates, curtail state spending, and other stern, harsh, disagreeable demands. Some countries chose to pay off IMF loans ahead of schedule rather than comply with what they regarded as demands originating with an overbearing agent of the United States.

In the early 2000s, the IMF dwindled in relevancy as a lender. As late as 2007, IMF lending was less than $2 billion. In late 2008, however, the IMF seemed to rebound as sovereign debt mounted in many countries. Loans were extended to Iceland ($2 billion), Ukraine ($16 billion), and Hungary ($25.1 billion). The most visible loan was approved for Greece in conjunction with the EU. The three-year IMF loan was for €10 billion, including €5.5 billion made available immediately. Performance criteria focused on reducing fiscal deficits and placing national debt-to-GDP on a downward trajectory. Greece also was implored to enhance competitiveness with pro-growth policies and reforms to modernize the economy.

Exacerbating this problem of mounting debt was the problem of plummeting currencies of emerging-market countries. Countries such as Pakistan, Belarus, Turkey, Serbia, and the Baltic republics were prominent candidates for loans. The IMF seemingly repositioned itself to move away from the harsh austerity measures demanded in the 1990s. Emergency procedures were developed to disburse loans faster and with fewer conditions. Nevertheless, the IMF is still seen in emerging-market countries as a puppet of the United States.[143]

WORLD BANK

The World Bank is an internationally supported bank that provides financial and technical assistance to developing countries for programs meant to alleviate poverty. The World Bank was established on 27 December 1945, the same day as the International Monetary Fund. At first, the World Bank focused on rebuilding Europe after World War II. Next, it began to rebuild the infrastructure of Europe's former colonies. Since the late 1960s, the World Bank focus has centered on reducing poverty, managing state debt, and making structural changes. The World Bank headquarters are located in Washington, D.C.

---

143   See Steve LeVine, "The IMF is Back, Kinder and Gentler," *Business Week* (November 10, 2008), pp. 30ff.

The World Bank's recent programmatic focus is on achieving Millennium Development Goals, which call for the eliminating poverty and fostering sustainable economic development. The International Bank for Reconstruction and Development (IBRD) is a World Bank agency that makes loans primarily to middle-income countries at interest rates a little over its own AAA-rated borrowings from capital markets. The International Development Association (IDA) is another World Bank agency. The IDA provides low interest or interest-free loans and grants to low-income countries that have no access whatsoever to international credit markets. The IDA is funded by periodic grants from highly developed countries.

THE G8 AND THE G20

The idea of a forum for the world's major industrialized democracies emerged after the 1973 oil crisis. In 1975, French President Valéry Gistard d'Estaing invited the heads of government from West Germany, Italy, Japan, United Kingdom, and United States to a summit in Rambouillet. The six leaders agreed to an annual meeting. The result was the Group of Six, more commonly known as G6. In 1976, Canada joined the group, and it morphed into the Group of Seven. In 1997, Russia was admitted to the group, making it the Group of Eight, or simply G8. The President of the European Commission has attended all annual meetings since 1977 but cannot host or preside. The Council President of the European Commission also regularly attends the annual summit.

Since the beginning, the G8 was meant to be an informal forum. It does not have an administrative structure. The annual G8 summit was not a venue to develop details or to settle any vexing controversy. However, the annual three-day event was a setting that brought eight of the world's most powerful leaders to talk and think about topics of global scope such as terrorism and mutual interests such as international finance and foreign affairs. The member country hosting the G8 summit is responsible for organizing the annual summit. The presiding G8 head of state sets the agenda. G8 summits have rotated in the order of France, United States, United Kingdom, Russia, Germany, Japan, Italy, and Canada. In 2004, President George W. Bush hosted the 30th G8 summit in Sea Island, Georgia. In 2012, President Barack Obama hosted the 38th G8 summit in Chicago.

The G20 is a group of twenty finance ministers and central bank governors from nineteen countries plus the European Union. The nineteen member countries are Argentina, Australia, Brazil, Canada, China, France, Germany, India, Indonesia, Italy, Japan, Mexico, Russia, Saudi Arabia, South Africa, South Korea, Turkey, United Kingdom, and the United States. These countries represent more than eighty percent of world trade. The G20 is a forum for deliberation on matters dealing with international finance. In this way, the G20 deals with issues beyond the limited responsibilities of any one government. G20 heads of state also convene periodically.

REGIONAL TRADE AGREEMENTS

In recent years, the global economy has been gravitating to a middle ground. Nations have formed regional agreements. Countries of geographic proximity agree to trade freely among themselves but retain trade barriers against other countries. The best known and most important regional trade agreements are the North American Free Trade Agreement (NAFTA) and the European Union (EU).

North American Free Trade Agreement

The North American Free Trade Agreement originated with Canadian Prime Minister Brian Mulroney, U.S. President George H.W. Bush, and Mexican President Carlos Salinas de Gortari. The three leaders signed NAFTA in December 1992, but ratification required legislative approval in the three countries. Significant opposition arose in all three countries. In the United States, President Bill Clinton made approval of NAFTA one of his major legislative priorities. After passage in Congress, President Clinton signed NAFTA into law on 8 December 1993. Initial provisions of NAFTA became effective on 1 January 1994, and final provisions were implemented on 1 January 2008. NAFTA created a free trade area that eliminated trade barriers among the three countries. Each country remained free to pursue its own trade policies regarding other countries. NAFTA granted Mexico greater access to Canadian and U.S. markets. Canadian and U.S. trade with Mexico expanded, and Mexico diverted trade with other partners. Prices of exports to Mexico fell precipitously. Canada and the United States already had a bilateral trade agreement, and NAFTA did not materially affect trade between the two countries.

NAFTA has had only marginal effects on the U.S. economy. Indeed, NAFTA can be seen as mere pittance, a tiny part of the overall U.S. economy. Furthermore, NAFTA has had an insignificant effect on U.S. jobs. Politicians bent on making NAFTA the bane of all that ails the economy claim that NAFTA has destroyed a million U.S. jobs. Even if this unsubstantiated claim were true, the loss of one million jobs must be seen against the backdrop of some twenty million jobs created over the life of NAFTA. More than 150 million people have jobs in the United States, and NAFTA seems to have cost relatively few American workers their jobs. Even so, the United States had a trade deficit with Canada and Mexico of about $99 billion in 2011, which is about one-half of one percent of the U.S. economy.

In her failed candidacy for the Democratic nomination for President, Senator Hillary Clinton tried to distance herself from her husband's NAFTA legacy. She proposed to "fix" NAFTA to make trade "work for working families," whatever that means. In his successful candidacy, Senator Barack Obama intoned woeful jeremiads, claiming that "entire cities...have been devastated as a consequence of trade agreements that were not adequately structured to make sure that U.S. workers had a fair deal." He also proposed to "fix" NAFTA. After his election as the 44th President of the United States on 4 November 2008, President Obama softened his rhetoric and moderated his stance towards NAFTA. Indeed, President Obama treated NAFTA with benign neglect. To date, he has yet to pinpoint on any map where entire cities have been devastated by NAFTA. "Fixing" NAFTA would not be easy. Any changes whatsoever would require renegotiation with Canada and Mexico. Canadian Prime Minister Stephen Harper was quoted as saying, "Of course, if any American government ever chose to make the mistake of opening [NAFTA], we would have some things we would want to talk about as well." This threat evokes the imagery of Pandora's box.[144]

European Union

The European Union began modestly in 1951 with the Treaty of Paris. Six somewhat battered industrial countries pooled their coal and steel interests and removed protective tariffs on them. France, Germany, Italy, Belgium, Luxembourg, and the Netherlands formed the European Coal and Steel Community (ECSC). Soon afterwards, these countries eliminated all shared tariff barriers and facilitated the free movement of workers and money among themselves. In 1957, ECSC morphed into the European Economic Community

---

144   See Philip Legrain, "5 Myths About NAFTA," *Washington Post* (April 6, 2008), p. B03.

(ECC), nicknamed the Common Market. The stage was set for a grand drama that would embrace a union of countries from the Atlantic to the Aegean. From its humble origin involving six countries and two products, the European Union was birthed.

The European Union (EU) was created with the Treaty of Maastricht, signed on 7 February 1992. The Treaty became effective on 1 November 1993. The EU now has twenty-eight members. EU countries (and year of entry) are Austria (1995), Belgium (1958), Bulgaria (2007), Croatia (2013), Cyprus (2004), Czech Republic (2004), Denmark (1973), Estonia (2004), Finland (1995), France (1958), Germany (1958), Greece (1981), Hungary (2004), Ireland (1973), Italy (1958), Latvia (2004), Lithuania (2004), Luxembourg (1958), Malta (2004), Netherlands (1958), Poland (2004), Portugal (1986), Romania (2007), Slovakia (2004), Slovenia (2004), Spain (1986), Sweden (1995), and United Kingdom (1973). Official candidates for EU membership are Iceland, Macedonia, Montenegro, Serbia, and Turkey, all waiting in the wings for admission. Potential candidates for EU membership are Albania, Bosnia and Herzegovina, and Kosovo. Other European countries have not expressed interest in candidacy. These uninterested countries include Norway, Russia, and Switzerland.

Like NAFTA, the European Union (EU) is a free trade area. Unlike NAFTA, the EU is also an economic union. As an economic union, EU coordinates some external and internal economic policies, including trade agreements with nations outside the union. Barriers to international migration are lowered so that a citizen of one EU country is free to live and work in any other member nation. In 1993, the EU further solidified by agreeing to adopt the Euro as a common currency. Seventeen countries in the EU have adopted the Euro as a replacement for their former currencies. In these countries, the Euro is their common currency and sole legal tender.

The Eurozone, which technically is the Euro Area, consists of seventeen countries of the European Union that have adopted the euro as their sole currency. The seventeen states are Austria, Belgium, Cyprus, Estonia, Finland, France, Germany, Greece, Ireland, Italy, Luxembourg, Malta, Netherlands, Portugal, Slovakia, Slovenia, and Spain. Other EU member countries have retained their own currencies, although the euro is accepted as legal tender. Monetary policy of the Eurozone is the responsibility of the European Central Bank. Fiscal policy is crafted in the Broad Economic Policy Guidelines, which are meant to provide policy coordination among the Eurozone countries. To assure the stability of the euro, Eurozone countries must commit to respect the Stability and Growth Pact, which sets limits on budget deficits and national debt along with fines and sanctions for exceeding the limits. Originally, the Pact set a limit of three percent of GDP for a yearly budget deficit. After Portugal, Germany, and France exceeded the limit in 2005, reforms were adopted to allow flexibility.

In early 2010, fears of sovereign debt default materialized in the EU. The debt crisis concerned the Eurozone countries of Greece, Ireland, Portugal, and Spain. The debt crisis led to a euro crisis, and the euro exchange rate plummeted. The crisis was fed by abuses in Greece. Successive Greek governments ran large deficits. Debt-to-GDP soared well above one hundred percent. To give the appearance of complying with the Eurozone Guidelines, Greece willfully and wantonly misreported its official economic statistics. Indeed, over many years, Greece paid Goldman Sachs and others to arrange transactions that hid the country's actual borrowing. These deceptive deals enabled Greece to spend beyond its means while hiding actual deficits and debt from the EU.

In 2009, Greece finally came clean. The deficit was revised from about six percent to almost thirteen percent of GDP. In 2010, the Greek budget deficit was estimated at almost fourteen percent of GDP, making the Greek deficit one of the highest in the world relative to GDP. Debt-to-GDP was estimated at about 120 percent. To head off the likelihood of sovereign debt default and slow the free fall of the euro, Eurozone countries and the International Monetary Fund took action. On 2 May 2010, Eurozone countries and the IMF agreed to a €110 billion loan for Greece conditioned on implementation of harsh austerity measures to reduce deficits and debt. A week later, Europe's finance ministers approved a comprehensive bailout package of almost a trillion dollars meant to ensure financial stability in Europe.

INTERNATIONAL FINANCE

International trade deals with the exchange of goods and services across borders. Such international exchanges of goods and services are accommodated by the use of money. However, money used to facilitate international trade brings up the complication of different currencies. Indeed, the use of many different currencies around the world has created a currency Tower of Babel. Incidentally, Babel is not pronounced as though it is babble. There is no babble in Babel. The correct pronunciation of Babel is BAY-bul. Exporting a product from the United States to France originates a need for dollars to make payment to the U.S. seller. Importing a product to the United States from France originates a need for euros to make payment to the French seller. Such international exchanges of goods and services give rise to currency markets, also called foreign exchange markets.

The market in which currencies are bought and sold is known as a currency market, sometimes called a foreign exchange market. Currency is a commodity no different from wheat or copper. Currency markets operate as any other market in which the price of a commodity is determined. Buyers who are in currency markets to purchase a particular currency such as dollars represent the demand side of these markets. Presumably, these buyers of dollars want to use dollars to buy U.S. goods or services. Others who are in currency markets to sell a currency such as dollars represent the supply side of these markets. Presumably, these sellers of dollars want to acquire some other currency to buy goods or services from the country using that currency.

The demand for and supply of a currency establish a currency market equilibrium price of that currency. The currency market equilibrium price of dollars, for example, is called the exchange rate because it is the rate at which people must give up currency such as euros to get another currency such as dollars. In late-August 2008, for example, the exchange rate of dollars for euros was 0.6763. This exchange rate meant that $100 could buy a little more than 67 euros. The reciprocal of the dollars to euros exchange rate was 1/0.6723. The exchange rate of euros for dollars was 1.4874, meaning that 100 euros could buy $148.74. Only two months later, in late-October, the exchange rate of dollars for euros fell to 0.7632, meaning $100 could buy a little more than 76 euros. The exchange rate of euros for dollars was 1.3102, which meant that 100 euros could buy only $131.02. Clearly, the dollar had strengthened significantly against the euro over this two-month period. In mid-April 2009, the exchange rate of euros for dollars remained at about the same level, 1.3026. However, by early November 2009, the euro had strengthened to 1.486. Throughout early 2010, the euro weakened significantly, falling by eighteen percent at one point. On 2 June 2010, the euro stood at only 1.2206 with most currency traders predicting the euro would fall below 1.2000, which it did before rebounding, and a few expecting parity with the dollar by year end. The few were wrong. By November 2010, the euro was back in the neighborhood of 1.40, signifying that the dollar had weakened and the euro strengthened. In late 2013, the euro hovered in the range of 1.30 to 1.35.

If U.S. demand for European goods and services were to increase, then more euros would be required to consummate this demand with actual purchases. This increase in demand for European goods and services correspondingly increases the demand for euros, depicted as a shift of the demand curve for euros to the right. Excess demand for euros would arise at the present exchange rate. The currency market equilibrium price of euros would increase. The same outcome can be depicted in terms of dollars. If U.S. demand for European goods and services were to increase, then the supply curve for dollars would shift to the right to reflect people making more dollars available in exchange for euros. Excess supply of dollars would arise at the present exchange rate. The currency market equilibrium price of dollars would decrease.

When the currency market equilibrium price of the dollar rises, the dollar appreciates or becomes stronger. Basically, the dollar is more valuable relative to another currency, meaning that the dollar now can buy more goods or services produced in the country using that currency. When the currency market equilibrium price of the dollar falls, the dollar depreciates or becomes weaker. In this case, the dollar is less valuable relative to another currency, meaning that the dollar now can buy fewer goods or services produced in the country using that currency. Many people equate a strong currency with a strong economy. Actually a strong currency benefits some households and businesses and hurts others. A strong dollar means that Americans can buy a lot of foreign currency and thus a lot of foreign-made goods and services with relatively few dollars. On the other hand, a strong dollar means more foreign currency is required to buy U.S. goods and services, thereby discouraging foreign purchases of American products.

BALANCE OF PAYMENTS

When someone buys a smartphone, a flat panel television set, or an opera ticket, he or she must make payment to a business. The business receives the payment. The outflow of money from the buyer in this transaction is equal to the inflow of money to the seller. The same is true of international transactions. The outflow of money from a buyer in one country is equal to the inflow of money to a seller in another country. The equality between the inflow of funds and the outflow of funds is called the balance of payments. Theoretically, therefore, the balance of payments should be zero, meaning that the inflow of funds and outflow of funds should balance. This theoretical balance is rare. For example, freely fluctuating exchange rates can give rise to discrepancies.

U.S. payments to other countries take one of four forms: (1) payments associated with purchases of imports by households, businesses, or governments, including merchandise and services such as engineering, consulting, and accounting; (2) returns on assets owned by foreign investors such as rent paid by U.S. tenants to foreign owners of real estate, stock dividends paid by U.S. corporations to foreign owners of their stock, and interest on debt held by foreigners; (3) transfers by U.S. households, businesses, and governments to other countries such as funds a U.S. immigrant sends back home to family and aid the U.S. government provides to the government of another country; and (4) purchases of physical or financial capital in other countries by U.S. households, businesses, or governments such as when U.S. investors buy real estate in another country or purchase bonds issued by a corporation in another country. A country's total payments abroad, therefore, is the sum of these four factors, which is

Purchases of imports

+Returns on assets owned by foreigners

+Transfers abroad

+Purchases of foreign capital

=Total payments to other countries

A country's receipts are the opposite of the four forms of payments. These receipts can take one of four forms: (1) receipts associated with sale of exports; (2) return on foreign assets owned by U.S. investors; (3) transfers received in the United States from foreign households, businesses, and governments; and (4) purchases of physical or financial capital in the United States by foreign households, businesses, or governments. A country's total receipts from abroad, therefore, is the sum of these four factors, which is

Sale of exports

+Returns on domestically owned foreign assets

+Transfers received from foreigners

+Purchases of domestic capital by foreigners

=Total receipts from other countries

CURRENT ACCOUNT, CAPITAL ACCOUNT, AND FINANCIAL ACCOUNT

Current, capital, and financial accounts allow study of the nature of payments a country makes and its receipts. The Bureau of Economic Analysis (BEA) reports all three accounts quarterly and annually. The current account embraces net exports, net return on investments, and net transfers. When the United States buys more goods and services than it sells and thus has a current account deficit, it must finance the deficit by borrowing or by selling more capital assets than it buys. Therefore, a country with a persistent current account deficit is exchanging capital assets for goods and services. In the balance of payments, this selling of America appears as an inflow of foreign capital.

The category of net purchases of domestic capital is disaggregated into a capital account and a financial account. The capital account is a record of capital transfers between U.S. residents and foreign residents. As such, the capital account includes an admixture ranging from debt forgiveness to sales and purchases of intangible assets such as patents, copyrights, trademarks, franchises, and leases. The financial account is a record of transactions between U.S. residents and foreign residents resulting in changes in the level of international claims and liabilities. In other words, the financial account records transactions in assets such as bonds, stocks, and real estate.

U.S. BALANCE OF PAYMENTS

The net flow of payments into and out of the United States is obtained by subtracting payments from receipts, which results in net exports, net return on assets, net transfers, and net purchase of capital. The sum of net exports, net return on assets, and net transfers is the current account. The sum can be positive or negative, meaning the current account can be positive or negative. In recent years, the sum has been decidedly negative for the United States, and thus the U.S. current account has been chronically negative. More funds are flowing out of the United States in these categories than flowing in. When more current account funds are flowing out, funds in other categories must be flowing in. Otherwise, the balance of payments would not balance.

In recent years, funds associated with net purchase of capital have flowed into the United States. This category constitutes the capital and financial accounts. When the United States runs a current account deficit, the consequence is a surplus in the capital and financial accounts that is equal to the deficit in the current account. In other words, the United States must sell more financial or physical assets to other countries than it buys from them. The U.S. current account was in deficit by $475 billion in 2012, an increase from $466 billion in 2011. In Table 13.5, the U.S. balance of payments is shown for 2Q 2013. The current account was in deficit by $98.9 billion.

Table 13.3 U.S. Balance of Payments, 2Q 2013 ($Billion)	
Category	**2Q 2013**
Net exports	−117.8
Net return on assets	53.1
Net transfers	−34.2
Current Account balance	−98.9
Capital Account balance*	
Financial Account balance	73.1
Statistical Discrepancy[1]	25.8
Net Balance	0.0

Source: Bureau of Economic Analysis, U.S. International Transactions Accounts Data

*Not available for the second quarter because source data were not yet available. Net payments were near zero, $0.1 billion, in the first quarter, 2013.

[1] Includes statistical discrepancies, accounting conventions, and exchange rate movements that change the recorded value of transactions.

CHINA BUYS THE WORLD

China's large trade surplus has resulted in a vast jackpot of foreign currency reserves totaling more than $2 trillion that can be used for direct foreign investment to obtain productive assets in other countries. Indeed, China has been on a spending spree. In the 2000s, China focused on natural resources to fuel its economy, acquiring a financial stake in oil in Nigeria, Congo, Brazil, and Kazakhstan; natural gas in Iran; and iron ore in Australia. Buying stakes in foreign companies or buying foreign companies outright is a process that the Chinese call its "going out" strategy to balance its economy. As Bill Powell says, "China's corporate sector does not need to invest in and run factories that sell sneakers for Nike or toys for Mattel or auto parts for Magna. Chinese companies need to *become* Nike, Mattel, and Magna. They need, in consultant speak, to move up the value chain."[145]

145   Bill Powell, "It's China's World (We Just Live In It)," *Fortune* (October 26, 2009), pp. 90.

As China's state-owned companies increase their foreign investments, some countries have begun to react with limits on Chinese acquisitions. For example, Australia's foreign investment review board recommended that no foreign company should be allowed more than a fifteen percent stake in any of Australia's natural resource companies. This recommendation was directed at China after the country's state-owned aluminum company failed in its effort to acquire about twenty percent of Rio Tinto, a giant Australian mining company.

WHAT, ME WORRY?

With apologies to Alfred E. Neuman, *Mad*'s iconic character, "What, me worry?" Specifically, why should we worry about the current account deficit? Countries that hold dollars as foreign exchange and U.S. government securities can reach a tipping point beyond which they do not want or need more dollars or U.S. Treasury securities. As the United States continues to sell physical and financial assets to foreigners, a limit can be reached. America still has a choice. The value of exports and imports can be brought back into balance or the consequences of doing nothing can be put off until years from now. If recent history is any guide to future expectations, the deficit in the current account will continue to be treated with benign neglect. In other words, the United States will keep drifting and dreaming until it is too late. Two of the saddest words in the English language are too late.

PRACTICE QUESTIONS

1. What is a trade deficit?

2. What is dumping?

3. What is the World Trade Organization?

4. How does the World Trade Organization settle trade disputes?

5. What is the meaning of permanent normal trade relations?

6. Describe the balance of payments.

7. If the current account is negative, what is the consequence on the financial account?

PRACTICE QUESTIONS *(AND ANSWERS)*

1. What is a trade deficit?

When a country has a trade deficit, the value of imported goods and services exceed the value of exported goods and services.

2. What is dumping?

Dumping deals with sales of merchandise exported to the United States at "less than fair value," which is illegal when such sales materially injure or threaten to materially injure U.S. producers of like merchandise. Fair value involves a comparison to "normal value." The price at which merchandise is sold within the exporting country or to third countries is compared to the price at which merchandise is sold in the United States. A statutory cost-of-production provision requires that dumping determination ignore sales in the home market of the exporting country or in third-country markets that are made below cost, i.e., at prices that are too low to cover all costs within a reasonable period of time in the normal course of business. In simple language, therefore, dumping is the international term meaning a firm sells products in another country at prices below the price set in the home country or below average cost. Antidumping duties are tariffs levied on foreign firms as a penalty for dumping.

3. What is the World Trade Organization?

To extend bilateral reductions in tariffs and other trade restrictions to a broad group of nations led twenty-three countries to meet in 1947 and join in the first General Agreement on Tariffs and Trade (GATT). As a multinational consortium, GATT reduced tariffs and other restrictions on trade. The World Trade Organization (WTO) was formed after GATT negotiations in 1995. The WTO provides a forum for trade negotiations, fosters respect for trade agreements, and monitors trade policies of its members, and provides a mechanism to resolve trade disputes. WTO headquarters are located in Geneva, Switzerland.

4. How does the World Trade Organization settle trade disputes?

Within WTO, the Dispute Settlement Body (DSB) is the governing system that adjudicates trade disputes between specific governments. DSB makes decisions regarding trade disputes based on recommendations of a Dispute Panel and perhaps a report from the Appellate Body of WTO. Only the DSB can make decisions. A Dispute Panel and the Appellate Body can make recommendations only. The reverse consensus process used by the WTO almost guarantees that Dispute Panel recommendations, perhaps as amended by the Appellate Body, will be accepted by DSB. Once DSB has decided on a trade dispute, DSB can direct the offending government to take action to bring its laws, regulations, or policies into compliance with WTO agreements. This direction is the only outcome that WTO can specify. WTO has no enforcement authority. It cannot impose fines, levy sanctions, modify tariffs, or override the laws of any country.

5. What is the meaning of permanent normal trade relations?

When the United States joined the General Agreement on Tariffs and Trade (GATT) in 1948, the United States agreed to grant most favored nation (MFN) status to all other countries, even extending to some countries that were not members of GATT. From the beginning, MFN was a status granted by one nation to another nation in international trade. MFN meant that a country granted MFN status would be given all trade advantages such as low tariffs that any other nation also received. In 1998, the United States changed the nomenclature "most favored nation" to "permanent normal trade relations."

6. Describe the balance of payments.

The balance of payments recognizes the truism that total payments to other countries are equal to total receipts from other countries. The equality between the inflow of funds from other countries and the outflow of funds to other countries is called the balance of payments.

7. If the current account is negative, what is the consequence on the financial account?

The current account reflects payments for goods and services as well as transfers made between countries. The current account can be positive or negative. For example, in recent years, the United States has had a current account deficit. When the United States runs a current account deficit, it has a surplus in the capital and financial account equal to the deficit in the current account. In other words, the United States must sell more financial or physical assets to other countries than it buys from them.

Company Index

Name Index

Subject Index

CPSIA information can be obtained
at www.ICGtesting.com
Printed in the USA
JSHW021016131219
2861JS00002BA/5

9 780988 919358